DICTIONARY OF
CHRISTIAN
LORE AND LEGEND

An example of the complex symbolism of early-medieval Christian art: marble columns (the Earth) support an arch (the Heavens) at the apex of which is the figure of God the Father. Within this portico is a cross with the *Agnus Dei,* Christ the sacrificial lamb. Birds, possibly peacocks, symbols of immortality, cling to the pendant sacred letters A-ω, again signifying Christ. At the base of each column are deer, recalling the words of the Psalmist, 'As the hart panteth after the water brooks, so panteth my soul after thee, O God.' (*Sacramentarium Gelasianum,* northern Gaul, *c.* 750.)

J CJ METFORD

DICTIONARY OF
CHRISTIAN
LORE AND LEGEND

283 ILLUSTRATIONS

THAMES AND HUDSON

EDITHAE
coniugi coniunx dilectissimae
consorti studiorum
laborum gaudiorum

© *1983 Thames and Hudson Ltd, London*

Contents

Foreword

6

Abbreviations

10

Notes

11

Sources of the illustrations

11

THE DICTIONARY

12

Foreword

For almost two thousand years Christian themes have inspired artists, musicians and writers. A visit to an art gallery, an evening at an opera or concert performance, contemplation of the sculptural ornamentation of a church or cathedral, all confirm how essential to full appreciation is some knowledge of Christian culture. Poems, essays, novels, even colloquial speech, contain Christian references. Therefore the purpose of this dictionary is to provide, in convenient and concise form, a guide to the essentials of this Christian tradition in the arts, music and literature. It is intended for the non-specialist.

An explanation of the words 'lore' and 'legend' as used in the title of this Dictionary may be helpful to the reader. By 'lore' is meant the learning and background knowledge associated with Christian culture. 'Legend' is used in its original sense of 'something to be read', a narrative which may be historical, traditional, or symbolic, without pre-judgment as to its veracity.

Items have been selected for inclusion in accordance with the following principles:

1 As the church building is the centre of worship and the principal focus of artistic endeavour, brief definitions are given of its architectural features and furnishings.

2 The liturgy, whether referred to as Mass, Eucharist or Holy Communion is the central rite. Its ceremonial, vestments worn, sacred vessels and parts set to music are described. Eucharistic devotions and the Hours of the Divine Office are included. Reference is also made to each of the Seven Sacraments.

3 Seasons of the Christian year, their origin, and the customs associated with them are mentioned.

4 Especially in the Middle Ages, it was believed that the visible, temporal universe contained symbols which, if properly interpreted, would reveal the divine truths of the invisible, eternal world. Fruits, flowers, colours, numbers, precious stones and many other material objects are therefore listed and their symbolism explained. So also is animal symbolism, derived from misinformation about the strange habits of real or mythical creatures and the moral implications of their behaviour.

5 Although the Old and New Testaments were the ultimate source of Christian culture, they were used selectively. Subjects from the Old Testament were chosen because they foreshadowed persons or incidents in the New dispensation. The present work is not therefore a dictionary of the Bible. Only those biblical events and characters, typologically associated, which appear most frequently as subjects in art, music and literature are treated.

6 Comparison of a biblical source with its artistic expression will reveal many deviations and additions, derived from apocryphal writings, theological commentaries, allegorical interpretations of texts, and the visions of mystics. These are explained.

7 Saints present a problem for a work of this size and scope. There are at least four thousand of them on record. The principle adopted is to select those most frequently depicted, even if their existence is now shown to have been doubtful, and despite their having been demoted or excluded from the revised Roman Catholic Calendar of 1969. Art has paid little regard to hagiographical niceties. Legends associated with saints are what matter, not verifiable historical careers.

8 Although Western Christian art since the late Middle Ages has been mainly Catholic in inspiration, the Byzantine heritage is important and is not overlooked. The words 'West' and 'East' have been used as convenient shorthand for the Latin tradition of Rome and the Greek tradition of Constantinople, together with other Oriental Churches.

9 Since the Second Vatican Council (1962-5) many changes have taken place in the Roman Catholic Church. There have also been reforms in the Anglican communion of churches. These have been noted where appropriate, but it must be emphasized that this work is intended to be a concise introduction to traditional Christian culture.

10 Tales have improved in the telling and the sources of many have been difficult or impossible to determine. It has therefore been judged wiser in most cases to leave origins unspecified. Some traditional stories have been recapitulated in Jacobus de Voragine's so-called *Golden Legend (Legenda Aurea)* which was 'Englished' by William Caxton (*c.* 1421-91), reprinted with introduction by F. S. Ellis, London, 1922 (7 vols), and translated by Granger Ryan and Helmut Ripperger, New York, 1941. For apocryphal narratives, Montague Rhodes James, *The Apocryphal New Testament*, Oxford, 1924 (or later reprints), is useful. A more detailed study is E. Hennecke, *New Testament Apocrypha* (2 vols), London, 1963-5. F. L. Cross and E. A. Livingstone, *The Oxford Dictionary of the Christian Church,* London, 1974, is a mine of accurate information on the historical and theological aspects of Christianity, as is *The Catholic Encyclopedia* (15 vols) and index, 1907-14. Standard Works of reference on the iconography of Christian art are: Louis Réau, *Iconographie de L'Art Chrétien* (6 vols), Paris, 1955-9; Engelbert Kirschbaum, ed. *Lexikon der christlichen Ikonographie* (8 vols), Freiburg, 1968-76; and Gertrud Schiller, *Ikonographie der christlichen Kunst*, 1966 (2nd ed. 1969-), the first two volumes of which have been translated by Janet Seligman, London, 1971-2.

It is hoped that this Dictionary will provide hours of informative browsing as well as being a welcome work of reference.

The visual arts

The destruction and plunder of churches and monasteries by generations of entrepreneurs and collectors have made it comparatively rare to find a work of art in the context for which it was intended. The few surviving west fronts, tympana, portals and windows of great cathedrals provide compendia of

Christian subjects visually represented in sculpture and stained glass. Most mosaics and fresco paintings, however, must be sought in public collections, and even then it is unusual to see the complete design. Large modern canvasses are the exception. In earlier periods altar-pieces were dismembered and panels distributed. Sacred vessels, ivories and tapestries were similarly dispersed.

Many of these fine works have been preserved from decay in great national collections. So numerous are they that it is impossible to make a selection even of the most outstanding examples. It is hoped that the reader will seek them out and be guided to their fuller appreciation by this book. A key word in the title, e.g. *Assumption, *Deposition, *Salome, St *Vincent, will provide the initial reference.

Literature

Just as the Bible lies at the very heart of Christianity, so literature continues to reflect the deepest influences of the religion. In the Middle Ages drama was used by the Church to instruct the faithful, even if secular elements intruded. In England, the miracle plays given at York, Chester, Coventry and Wakefield paved the way for Milton's Samson Agonistes (1671), and, in far more recent times, for Oscar Wilde's Salome (richly illustrated by Aubrey Beardsley, 1893), and George Bernard Shaw's Androcles and the Lion (1912).

The *Psalms and the Book of *Job in the Bible have served as models for poetry that is full of references – both direct and more arcane – to Christian sources: Dante's Divine Comedy (early 14th century), and Milton's *Paradise Lost (1667) and Paradise Regained (1671) are among the greatest; but the poems of John Donne, Gerard Manley Hopkins and T. S. Eliot, on a smaller scale, are as powerful. William Blake employs Christian terms and concepts to construct a cosmic system of his own in verse epics.

Among prose writers on Christian themes are Leo Tolstoy, who explores the *Sermon on the Mount in essays (1883-95) and in his War and Peace (1863-9), Gustave Flaubert (Three Tales, 1877), Nikos Kazantzakis (Christ Recrucified, 1954), Thomas Mann (*Joseph and his Brothers, 1933-43), Joris-Karl Huysmans (Là-bas, 1891, La cathédrale, 1898), D. H. Lawrence (The Rainbow, 1915, *Aaron's Rod, 1922) and James Joyce (Portrait of the Artist as a Young Man, 1914-15), all of whom have invested new meaning in Christian symbols and themes.

Music

Music and devotion have been associated from the days of the Early Christian Church. Most *Psalms and other parts of the *Office were originally sung in *plainchant, a single, non-metrical melodic line. With the development of polyphony (two or more melodies in combination) the rich potential for musical settings of the liturgy began to be thoroughly exploited, and by the time of Josquin Desprez (second half of the 15th century) the *Mass and the motet had become established as the chief genres of vocal music. Since then the Mass has been set to music by composers as diverse as Byrd, Beethoven and Bernstein. Beethoven's Missa Solemnis (1822), like Bach's towering masterpiece the Mass in B Minor, was conceived on too large a scale to be used liturgically, while the monumental *Passions of Bach and Handel already have the dramatic element that was to make many subsequent compositions more suitable for the concert hall than the church. Among these may be mentioned the *Requiems of Berlioz and Verdi, the *Stabat Maters by Rossini and Penderecki, and the *Te Deum and *Psalm 150* (1892) by Bruckner.

Operas based on biblical subjects were not common until the 19th century. The most popular included Rossini's *Mosè in Egitto* (*Moses in Egypt, 1818), Verdi's treatment of *Nebuchadnezzar's oppression of the Israelites in *Nabucco* (1842), and Saint-Saëns' *Samson et Dalila* (Samson and *Delilah, 1877). Although centred on the theme of the *Holy Grail, it is doubtful whether Wagner's music drama *Parsifal* (1882) is by intent a Christian opera, despite its *Good Friday music. A masterpiece of decadence is Strauss' *Salome* (1905). Lives of saints are potentially good material for opera: Verdi and Tchaikovsky each based one on the story of *Joan of Arc, while Massenet's *Thaïs* (1894) concerns the courtesan who become a saint.

A popular genre midway between the liturgical and the operatic is the oratorio. Handel wrote many celebrated works in this form, of which the best known is *Messiah* (1741-2), while Haydn's *Creation* (1798) has proved equally durable, and certainly more so than Beethoven's *Christ on the Mount of Olives* (1803), on the theme of the *Agony in the Garden. In the 19th century, especially in Britain with its tradition of provincial choirs, oratorio came into its own, those of Mendelssohn, notably *Elijah* (1846) and St *Paul* (1836), achieving considerable fame. Edward Elgar produced two masterpieces of English festival oratorio in The *Apostles* (1903) and *The Kingdom* (1906), the latter on the story of the *Pentecost. Honegger's *King *David* (1921) and Walton's *Belshazzar's Feast* (1931) are among the many other treatments of biblical themes by composers of the present century.

Abbreviations

1 Books of the Bible (canonical and deutero-canonical) in alphabetical order of the abbreviations used.

(= indicates an alternative title or variant in the *Vulgate).

Ac	Acts	Jude		Jude
Am	Amos	1 Kg		1 Kings
Bar	Baruch			= 3 Kings
Bel	Bel and the Dragon	2 Kg		2 Kings
1 Chr	1 Chronicles			= 4 Kings
	= 1 Paralipomenon	Lam		Lamentations
2 Chr	2 Chronicles	Lev		Leviticus
	= 2 Paralipomenon	Lk		Luke
Col	Colossians	1 Mac		1 Maccabees
1 Cor	1 Corinthians	2 Mac		2 Maccabees
2 Cor	2 Corinthians	Mal		Malachi
Dan	Daniel			= Malachias
Dt	Deuteronomy	Mic		Micah
Ec	Ecclesiastes			= Micheas
Eccl	Ecclesiasticus	Mk		Mark
	= Sirach	Mt		Matthew
Eph	Ephesians	Nah		Nahum
1 Esd	1 Esdras	Neh		Nehemiah
2 Esd	2 Esdras			= Nehemias or 2 Esdras
Est	Esther	Num		Numbers
Ex	Exodus	Ob		Obadiah
Ez	Ezekiel			= Abdias
	= Ezechiel	1 Pet		1 Peter
Ezr	Ezra	2 Pet		2 Peter
	= 1 Esdras	Prov		Proverbs
Gal	Galatians			= Wisdom
Gen	Genesis	Ps		Psalms
Hab	Habakkuk	Rev		Revelation
	= Habacuc			= Apocalypse
Hag	Haggai	Rom		Romans
	= Aggeus	Rt		Ruth
Heb	Hebrews	1 Sam		1 Samuel
Hos	Hosea			= 1 Kings
	= Osee	2 Sam		2 Samuel
Is	Isaiah			= 2 Kings
	= Isaias	Sg		Song of Songs
Jam	James			= Canticles of Canticles
Jb	Job	1 Th		1 Thessalonians
Jdt	Judith	2 Th		2 Thessalonians
Jer	Jeremiah	1 Tim		1 Timothy
Jg	Judges	2 Tim		2 Timothy
Jl	Joel	Tit		Titus
Jn	John	Tob		Tobit
1 Jn	1 John	Wis		Wisdom
2 Jn	2 John	Zech		Zechariah
3 Jn	3 John			= Zacharias
Jonah	Jonah	Zeph		Zephaniah
	= Jonas			= Sophonias
Jos	Joshua			
	= Joshue			

Biblical references are given as: Mk (= Mark) 1 (= Chapter 1) : 2 (verse 2). The numbering of the Psalms often differs in the Authorized and Vulgate versions. The Vulgate number is given in brackets: Ps 60 (61).

2 Other abbreviations

AV *Authorized Version (King James' Bible)   *b.* born   *c. circa* (about)   *cd.* canonized   *d.* died
NT New Testament   OT Old Testament   St Saint   SS Saints   Vg *Vulgate version   An asterisk (*) indicates a cross-reference. Essential references only are indicated.

Notes

1 Biblical quotations in English are from the Authorized Version of the Bible. Those in Latin are in the Vulgate version.
2 The dates given for kings and queens are their life-span; e.g. Henry VIII (1491-1547) came to the throne of England only in 1509.
3 The dates given for Popes represent the period of their papal reign.
4 For ease of reference an asterisked word may refer to the singular or plural form of the head-word entry.
5 Where a head-word has an alternative form, it is given in brackets, e.g. St Anne (Anna), baldacchino (baldachino). The Vulgate form is also given in brackets, e.g. Haggai (Aggeus).
6 Dates are AD unless specified as BC.

Sources of illustrations

Photographic credits precede illustration page numbers; locations follow them in brackets. (a – above, b – below, c – centre)

Accademia, Venice: 217a; ACL, Brussels: 43a, 93a, 155b (Koninklijke Museum voor Schone Kunsten, Antwerp), 15a, 71b, 91b, 265a (St Pierre, Louvain), 107a, 157b (St Bavon, Ghent), 99a (Musées Royaux des Beaux-Arts, Brussels), 101b (Liège), 121a (Museum of the Cathedral of St-Sauveur, Bruges), 143b (Communal Museum, Bruges), 251a (Memling Museum, Bruges); Alinari, Florence: 21a (S Cecilia, Rome), 39a (Museo di Arte Antica, Lisbon), 35b, 73a, 113a, 247a (Uffizi, Florence), 79b (Galleria dell' Accademia, Florence), 85a, 129b (Museo Nazionale, Florence), 87b (S Apollinare in Classe, Ravenna), 97a (Brancacci Chapel, Sta Maria del Carmine, Florence), 107 (S Maria Formosa, Venice), 145a Lateran Museum, Rome), 149b (Arena Chapel, Padua), 169a (Basilica di S Marco, Venice), 177a (Basilica di S Pietro in Vincoli, Rome), 193b (Basilica Vaticana, Rome), 195a, 203a (Vaticano, Rome), 199a (St Peter's, Rome), 243b (Camposanto, Pisa); Alte Pinakothek, Munich: 43b, 151; Anderson, Rome: 53a (Museo di Capodimonte, Naples), 101a, 139b (Arena Chapel, Padua), 163b (St Peter's, Rome), 241a (S Maria della Vittoria, Rome), 249a (S Francesco, Arezzo), 269a, 271a (Sistine Chapel, Rome); Archives Photographiques, Paris: 67a (Moulins Cathedral), 105a (Louvre, Paris), 219b (St-André-le-Bas, Vienne), 249b (St-Julien-de-Jonzy); Archivio Fotografico, Galleria Vaticani, Rome: 267a (Grotto of St Peter's, Rome); Ashmolean Museum, Oxford: 199b; Lala Aufsberg: 215b (S Rufino, Assisi); Bandieri: 263a (Galleria Estense, Modena); Roloff Beny: 191b (Roccamandolfi, Italy); I. Bessi: 35a, 89a (Cathedral, Pisa), 145b (Baptistery, Pisa), 153a (Palazzo Rosso, Genoa), 207a (S Andrea, Pistoia); Bibliothèque Royale, Brussels: 105b; Bibliothèque de la Ville, Epernay: 173a; Bildarchiv d. Ost. Nationalbibliothek, Vienna: 21b (Franciscan Church, Salzburg); Bodleian Library, Oxford: 49b; Bristol Art Gallery: 83a; British Library, London: 75a; British Museum, London: 25b, 31b, 47b, 51b, 57a, 119b, 125a, 135a, 137b, 145c, 185a; Brogi: 119a (Baptistery, Siena); Bulloz: 27b (Louvre, Paris), 111b (Tours Museum), 259b (Private Collection); Cambridge University Library: 201b; Lucca Chmel: 97b (St Stephen's, Vienna, choir-stall, now destroyed); J. Ciganovic-Omcikus: 67b (Tempio Malatestiano, Rimini); City Art Gallery, Manchester: 161b; City of Birmingham Museum and Art Gallery: 121c; Cleveland Museum of Art: 159b, 257a; Cliché des Musées Nationaux: 211c (Louvre, Paris); Courtauld Institute of Art, London: 15b (Abbey of St Denis), 39b (Cluniac Church, Payerne), 49a (Parish Church, Fontaines les Dijon), 241b (Chartres Cathedral); F. H. Crossley: 175b (Wells Cathedral); El Escordial, Madrid: 173b, 229b; Fitzwilliam Museum, Cambridge: 141a; Frick Collection, New York: 239b; Giraudon, Paris: 13a (Musée des Beaux-Arts, Alais), 19a (Musée Fabre, Montpellier), 79a (Palais des Beaux-Arts, Lille), 81b (Louvre, Paris), 121b (Musée Condé, Chantilly), 131a (St Sulpice, Paris), 171a (Private Collection), 261a (Bibliothèque Nationale, Paris), 272 (Amiens Cathedral); Glasgow Art Gallery and Museum: 135c (Burrell Collection); Grassi:

123a (Opera del Duomo, Siena); Abraham Guillen: 117b (Church of La Merced, Peru); Gundermann: 37a (Parish Church, Creglingen); Hermitage, Leningrad: 15a; Hessische Landesbibliothek, Wiesbaden: 55b; Hirmer: 163a (National Museum, Ravenna), 183a (Lateran Museum, Rome), 187b (San Colombano, Bobbio), 221a (San Vitale, Ravenna), 221c (Sant'Ambrogio, Milan), 225a (Archaeological Museum, Istanbul); Hürlimann: 61b; Icon Museum, Recklinghausen: 103b; Israel Government Press Office: 17a; Israel Museum, Jerusalem: 135b; Property of the Italian Government: 63b; Jewish Museum, London: 223b; A. F. Kersting: 33b (Malmesbury Abbey, Wiltshire); Statens Konstmusee, Stockholm: 231a, 239a (Palacio de Livia, Madrid); Samuel H. Kress Collection, Allentown Art Museum, Pennsylvania: 69a; Kunsthalle, Hamburg: 95a, 179b; Kunsthistorisches Museum, Vienna: 13c, 85b, 115a, 165a, 235b; Kunstmuseum, Düsseldorf: 269b; Lady Lever Art Gallery, Port Sunlight: 223a; Louvre, Paris: 133b; Marburg: 59a, 117b (Hildesheim Cathedral), 81a (Strasbourg Cathedral), 149a (Rheims Cathedral), 211b (Aachen Cathedral), 221b (Städelsches Kunstinstitut, Frankfurt); Mas: 127a (Museo Provincial, Seville), 51a, 127b, 129a, 211a (Prado, Madrid), 259a (San Nicolas, Valencia), 261b (Museo de Arte Catalûna, Barcelona); Leonard von Matt: 159a (S Apollinare in Classe, Ravenna); Metropolitan Museum of Art: 147; Ministero della Pubblica Istruzione, Rome: 117a, 189b, 195b, 201a (Museo dell' Opera del Duomo, Siena); Ann Munchow: 13b (Suermondt Ludwig Museum, Aachen); Musée de Cluny, Paris: 165b; Musée Ochier, Cluny: 115b; Museo di Castelvecchio, Verona: 251b; Museo Civico Archeologico, Bologna: 207b; Museo dell' Istituto Ellenico, Venice: 143a; Museum of Art, R.I. School of Design, Providence: 197a; Museum Boymans-van Beuningen, Rotterdam: 41a; Museum of Fine Arts, Boston: 209b; Museum of London: 23b; National Gallery of Art, Washington: 133a, 203b, 253b; National Gallery of Ireland, Dublin: 37b, 73b, 83b, 181b, 251a; National Gallery, London: 19b, 27a, 47a, 69b, 87a, 93b, 109b, 155a, 167b, 169b, 171b, 197b, 209a, 233, 235a, 243a, 245a, 247b, 253a; National Gallery, Stuttgart: 43a; National Museum of Ireland, Dublin: 193a; New Museum, Damascus: 249c; Antonello Perissinotto: 231b; Pierpont Morgan Library, New York: 243c; Pontificia Commissione di archeologia sacra: 99b (catacombs of Priscilla, Rome); J. Powell: 141b, 191a (Monastery Church, Daphni); Private Collection: 77b, 161a; Rheinisches Bildarchiv, Cologne: 123b; Rheinisches Landesmuseum, Bonn: 29a, 219a; Rijksmuseum, Amsterdam: 205b; Jean Roubier: 23a (Pilgrimage Church, Conques); San Francesco Upper Church, Assisi: 71a; Scala, Florence: 125b (Benaki Museum, Athens), 245b (S Marco, Florence); R. W. Schlegelmilch: 65b (Domschatz, Aachen); Edwin Smith: 271b (S Zeno, Verona); Henk Snoek: 175a (Coventry Cathedral); Sotheby's: 95b; Staatliche Kunsthalle, Karlsruhe: 77a; Staatliche Museen, Gemäldegalerie Dahlem, Berlin: 53b, 103a, 197c, 227a, 229a; Tate Gallery, London: 29b, 55a, 213b, 265b; Universiteitsbibliotheek, Amsterdam: 237b; Victoria and Albert Museum, London: 33a, 47c, 63a, 137a, 153b, 213a, 255a, 255b; Westminster Abbey, London (National Monuments Records): 53c.

A The *Greek letter alpha, a symbol of the *Trinity because it is made with three strokes of the pen.

A – M – Ω The initial letters of the words *Alpha Mu Omega*, the *Greek names of the first, middle and last letters of the Greek alphabet, a sacred *monogram signifying that *Jesus is eternal, 'the same yesterday, today, and forever' (Heb 13 : 8).

A – Ω (or ω) A sacred *monogram, composed of the initial letters of the words *Alpha and *Omega, the *Greek names of the first and last letters of the Greek alphabet, symbolizing *God, who is 'the beginning and the end' (Rev 22 : 13). The letters are frequently attached to the transverse beam of a *cross, a letter on either side, or combined with the *Chi-Rho monogram. *Christ as *Pantocrator is sometimes shown holding an open book on which these letters are inscribed.

Aaron Elder brother of *Moses and his spokesman because Moses was 'slow of speech, and of a slow tongue' (Ex 4 : 10). He was the traditional founder of the hereditary Jewish priesthood and an OT *type of *Christ. When crowned with a *tiara he represents the *Pope; and when wearing a *mitre, the Christian priesthood. The elaborate OT description of his vestments (Ex 28 : 4-39) included a turban or mitre; a breastplate set with twelve gems, one for each of the *Twelve Tribes of Israel, with the *Urim and the Thummim in it (Lev 8 : 8); and a gorgeous robe adorned with bells. This influenced his representation in art. One of his *attributes is a *censer, because he alone could offer incense in the *Holy of Holies.

Aaron was closely associated with Moses in events connected with the *Exodus from Egypt; angered his brother when he fashioned a *Golden Calf for the Israelites to worship; and was divinely assisted to overcome the revolt of *Korah.

The miraculous flowering of Aaron's *rod or *wand (his other attribute) was the divine indication of the exclusive right of his tribe to the privileges of priesthood. Aaron and the head of each of the other tribes of Israel laid their staffs in the *Ark of the Covenant. Aaron's rod blossomed and produced ripe *almonds, a sign that the tribe of Levi, of which he was the leader, had been divinely chosen for the office (Num 17 : 1-11).

Aaron, like his brother Moses, was not allowed to enter the *Promised Land. He died on the Mountain of Hor when he was 123 years old (Num 20 : 12; 24-9). He was the ancestor of St *Elizabeth, mother of St *John the Baptist (Lk 1 : 5).

Abaddon A Hebrew word meaning 'destruction' or 'perdition'. It signifies 'death'; *Sheol, the abode of the dead; or the lowest part of Sheol where sinners are punished. St *John the Divine used the word as a proper noun, the equivalent of the Greek *Apollyon, 'the destroyer', the Angel of the *Bottomless Pit, equated with *Satan (Rev 9 : 11).

Abbé Originally the French title of an *abbot, but from the 16th century onwards applied to anyone wearing secular ecclesiastical *dress, and to *clerics, not necessarily in *Holy Orders, who were either tutors or engaged in similar educational occupations.

Abbess The head, or *superior, of an *abbey or a community of *nuns, especially those who follow the *Rule of St Benedict. The title is sometimes extended to superiors of houses of the Second *Franciscan Order, popularly called *Poor Clares, and to certain colleges of *canonesses. In medieval times, abbesses enjoyed extensive temporal and spiritual powers (including the wearing of a *mitre), but these were restricted by the *Council of Trent. As the female equivalent of *abbots they hold office for life, except among the Poor Clares. They must be at least forty years old and to have been professed nuns for ten years. They are elected by their sister nuns in secret ballot.

An abbess in art wears a *ring and holds a *pastoral staff, or *crosier, and may often be shown crowned or with a *crown at her feet. Notable in art were the saintly abbesses SS *Bridget of Sweden, *Clare of Assisi, *Teresa of Ávila, *Walburga, *Werburg and *Winifred.

Abbey A *monastery occupied by no fewer than twelve *monks or *nuns, and under the control of an *abbot or *abbess, who, if founders, may be depicted with a replica of their abbey. After the *Reformation, many British abbeys either became churches or were secularized.

Abbot The head, or *superior, of an *abbey, a religious community of at least twelve *monks, usually *Benedictines, *Cistercians or certain *Orders of *Canons Regular. The title is derived from the Aramaic *abba*, 'father', implying, according to the *Rule of St Benedict, that the abbot, elected for life by his house and possessing extensive powers, is the father of his monks. His female equivalent is an *abbess.

In art an abbot wears a *ring and a *mitre and carries a *pastoral staff or *crosier. Among notable saints who were abbots were *Antony of Egypt, *Bernardino of Siena and *Bernard of Clairvaux.

Abdias The Vg form of AV *Obadiah, one of the *prophets.

Abdon and Sennen, SS Persians, said to have been noblemen, and to have lived in Córdoba where they were imprisoned because they refused to sacrifice to idols. They were taken to Rome during one of the *persecutions of Christians *c*.303 and thrown to the lions who refused to touch them. They were then beheaded. Their remains were placed in the *catacombs of Ponziano where a fresco of the 6th or 7th century showed them dressed as Persians, in fur cloaks, receiving crowns of martyrdom from *Christ who descends in a cloud. In the 10th century, *Cluniac monks from Arles-sur-Tech hid their relics in two barrels of wine and took them to their *monastery in the

Notes

1 Biblical quotations in English are from the Authorized Version of the Bible. Those in Latin are in the Vulgate version.

2 The dates given for kings and queens are their life-span; e.g. Henry VIII (1491-1547) came to the throne of England only in 1509.

3 The dates given for Popes represent the period of their papal reign.

4 For ease of reference an asterisked word may refer to the singular or plural form of the head-word entry.

5 Where a head-word has an alternative form, it is given in brackets, e.g. St Anne (Anna), baldacchino (baldachino). The Vulgate form is also given in brackets, e.g. Haggai (Aggeus).

6 Dates are AD unless specified as BC.

Sources of illustrations

Photographic credits precede illustration page numbers; locations follow them in brackets. (a – above, b – below, c – centre)

Accademia, Venice: 217a; ACL, Brussels: 43a, 93a, 155b (Koninklijke Museum voor Schone Kunsten, Antwerp), 15a, 71b, 91b, 265a (St Pierre, Louvain), 107a, 157b (St Bavon, Ghent), 99a (Musées Royaux des Beaux-Arts, Brussels), 101b (Liège), 121a (Museum of the Cathedral of St-Sauveur, Bruges), 143b (Communal Museum, Bruges), 251a (Memling Museum, Bruges); Alinari, Florence: 21a (S Cecilia, Rome), 39a (Museo di Arte Antica, Lisbon), 35b, 73a, 113a, 247a (Uffizi, Florence), 79b (Galleria dell' Accademia, Florence), 85a, 129b (Museo Nazionale, Florence), 87b (S Apollinare in Classe, Ravenna), 97a (Brancacci Chapel, Sta Maria del Carmine, Florence), 107 (S Maria Formosa, Venice), 145a Lateran Museum, Rome), 149b (Arena Chapel, Padua), 169a (Basilica di S Marco, Venice), 177a (Basilica di S Pietro in Vincoli, Rome), 193b (Basilica Vaticana, Rome), 195a, 203a (Vaticano, Rome), 199a (St Peter's, Rome), 243b (Camposanto, Pisa); Alte Pinakothek, Munich: 43b, 151; Anderson, Rome: 53a (Museo di Capodimonte, Naples), 101a, 139b (Arena Chapel, Padua), 163b (St Peter's, Rome), 241a (S Maria della Vittoria, Rome), 249a (S Francesco, Arezzo), 269a, 271a (Sistine Chapel, Rome); Archives Photographiques, Paris: 67a (Moulins Cathedral), 105a (Louvre, Paris), 219b (St-André-le-Bas, Vienne), 249b (St-Julien-de-Jonzy); Archivio Fotografico, Galleria Vaticani, Rome: 267a (Grotto of St Peter's, Rome); Ashmolean Museum, Oxford: 199b; Lala Aufsberg: 215b (S Rufino, Assisi); Bandieri: 263a (Galleria Estense, Modena); Roloff Beny: 191b (Roccamandolfi, Italy); I. Bessi: 35a, 89a (Cathedral, Pisa), 145b (Baptistery, Pisa), 153a (Palazzo Rosso, Genoa), 207a (S Andrea, Pistoia); Bibliothèque Royale, Brussels: 105b; Bibliothèque de la Ville, Epernay: 173a; Bildarchiv d. Öst. Nationalbibliothek, Vienna: 21b (Franciscan Church, Salzburg); Bodleian Library, Oxford: 49b; Bristol Art Gallery: 83a; British Library, London: 75a; British Museum, London: 25b, 31b, 47b, 51b, 57a, 119b, 125a, 135a, 137b, 145c, 185a; Brogi: 119a (Baptistery, Siena); Bulloz: 27b (Louvre, Paris), 111b (Tours Museum), 259b (Private Collection); Cambridge University Library: 201b; Lucca Chmel: 97b (St Stephen's, choir-stall, now destroyed); J. Ciganovic-Omcikus: 67b (Tempio Malatestiano, Rimini); City Art Gallery, Manchester: 161b; City of Birmingham Museum and Art Gallery: 121c; Cleveland Museum of Art: 159b, 257a; Cliché des Musées Nationaux: 211c (Louvre, Paris); Courtauld Institute of Art, London: 15b (Abbey of St Denis), 39b (Cluniac Church, Payerne), 49a (Parish Church, Fontaines les Dijon), 241b (Chartres Cathedral); F. H. Crossley: 175b (Wells Cathedral); El Escorial, Madrid: 173b, 229b; Fitzwilliam Museum, Cambridge: 141a; Frick Collection, New York: 239b; Giraudon, Paris: 13a (Musée des Beaux-Arts, Alais), 19a (Musée Fabre, Montpellier), 79a (Palais des Beaux-Arts, Lille), 81b (Louvre, Paris), 121b (Musée Condé, Chantilly), 131a (St Sulpice, Paris), 171a (Private Collection), 261a (Bibliothèque Nationale, Paris), 272 (Amiens Cathedral); Glasgow Art Gallery and Museum: 135c (Burrell Collection); Grassi:

123a (Opera del Duomo, Siena); Abraham Guillen: 117b (Church of La Merced, Peru); Gundermann: 37a (Parish Church, Creglingen); Hermitage, Leningrad: 15a; Hessische Landesbibliothek, Wiesbaden: 55b; Hirmer: 163a (National Museum, Ravenna), 183a (Lateran Museum, Rome), 187b (San Colombano, Bobbio), 221a (San Vitale, Ravenna), 221c (Sant'Ambrogio, Milan), 225a (Archaeological Museum, Istanbul); Hürlimann: 61b; Icon Museum, Recklinghausen: 103b; Israel Government Press Office: 17a; Israel Museum, Jerusalem: 135b; Property of the Italian Government: 63b; Jewish Museum, London: 223b; A. F. Kersting: 33b (Malmesbury Abbey, Wiltshire); Statens Konstmusee, Stockholm: 231a, 239a (Palacio de Livia, Madrid); Samuel H. Kress Collection, Allentown Art Museum, Pennsylvania: 69a; Kunsthalle, Hamburg: 95a, 179b; Kunsthistorisches Museum, Vienna: 13c, 85b, 115a, 165a, 235b; Kunstmuseum, Düsseldorf: 269b; Lady Lever Art Gallery, Port Sunlight: 223a; Louvre, Paris: 133b; Marburg: 59a, 117b (Hildesheim Cathedral), 81a (Strasbourg Cathedral), 149a (Rheims Cathedral), 211b (Aachen Cathedral), 221b (Städelsches Kunstinstitut, Frankfurt); Mas: 127a (Museo Provincial, Seville), 51a, 127b, 129a, 211a (Prado, Madrid), 259a (San Nicolas, Valencia), 261b (Museo de Arte Cataluña, Barcelona); Leonard von Matt: 159a (S Apollinare in Classe, Ravenna); Metropolitan Museum of Art: 147; Ministero della Pubblica Istruzione, Rome: 117a, 189b, 195b, 201a (Museo dell' Opera del Duomo, Siena); Ann Munchow: 13b (Suermondt Ludwig Museum, Aachen); Musée de Cluny, Paris: 165b; Musée Ochier, Cluny: 115b; Museo di Castelvecchio, Verona: 251b; Museo Civico Archeologico, Bologna: 207b; Museo dell' Istituto Ellenico, Venice: 143a; Museum of Art, R.I. School of Design, Providence: 197a; Museum Boymans-van Beuningen, Rotterdam: 41a; Museum of Fine Arts, Boston: 209b; Museum of London: 23b; National Gallery of Art, Washington: 133a, 203b, 253b; National Gallery of Ireland, Dublin: 37b, 73b, 83b, 181b, 251a; National Gallery, London: 19b, 27a, 47a, 69b, 87a, 93b, 109b, 155a, 167b, 169b, 171b, 197b, 209a, 233, 235a, 243a, 245a, 247b, 253a; National Gallery, Stuttgart: 43a; National Museum of Ireland, Dublin: 193a; New Museum, Damascus: 249c; Antonello Perissinotto: 231b; Pierpont Morgan Library, New York: 243c; Pontificia Commissione di archeologia sacra: 99b (catacombs of Priscilla, Rome); J. Powell: 141b, 191a (Monastery Church, Daphni); Private Collection: 77b, 161a; Rheinisches Bildarchiv, Cologne: 123b; Rheinisches Landesmuseum, Bonn: 29a, 219a; Rijksmuseum, Amsterdam: 205b; Jean Roubier: 23a (Pilgrimage Church, Conques); San Francesco Upper Church, Assisi: 71a; Scala, Florence: 125b (Benaki Museum, Athens); 245b (S Marco, Florence); R. W. Schlegelmilch: 65b (Domschatz, Aachen); Edwin Smith: 271b (S Zeno, Verona); Henk Snoek: 175a (Coventry Cathedral); Sotheby's: 95b; Staatliche Kunsthalle, Karlsruhe: 77a; Staatliche Museen, Gemäldegalerie Dahlem, Berlin: 53b, 103a, 197c, 227a, 229a; Tate Gallery, London: 29b, 55a, 213b, 265b; Universiteitsbibliotheek, Amsterdam: 237b; Victoria and Albert Museum, London: 33a, 47c, 63a, 137a, 153b, 213a, 255a, 255b; Westminster Abbey, London (National Monuments Records): 53c.

A The *Greek letter alpha, a symbol of the *Trinity because it is made with three strokes of the pen.

A – M – Ω The initial letters of the words *Alpha Mu Omega*, the *Greek names of the first, middle and last letters of the Greek alphabet, a sacred *monogram signifying that *Jesus is eternal, 'the same yesterday, today, and forever' (Heb 13 : 8).

A – Ω (or ω) A sacred *monogram, composed of the initial letters of the words *Alpha and *Omega, the *Greek names of the first and last letters of the Greek alphabet, symbolizing *God, who is 'the beginning and the end' (Rev 22 : 13). The letters are frequently attached to the transverse beam of a *cross, a letter on either side, or combined with the *Chi-Rho monogram. *Christ as *Pantocrator is sometimes shown holding an open book on which these letters are inscribed.

Aaron Elder brother of *Moses and his spokesman because Moses was 'slow of speech, and of a slow tongue' (Ex 4 : 10). He was the traditional founder of the hereditary Jewish priesthood and an OT *type of *Christ. When crowned with a *tiara he represents the *Pope; and when wearing a *mitre, the Christian priesthood. The elaborate OT description of his vestments (Ex 28 : 4-39) included a turban or mitre; a breastplate set with twelve gems, one for each of the *Twelve Tribes of Israel, with the *Urim and the Thummim in it (Lev 8 : 8); and a gorgeous robe adorned with bells. This influenced his representation in art. One of his *attributes is a *censer, because he alone could offer incense in the *Holy of Holies.

Aaron was closely associated with Moses in events connected with the *Exodus from Egypt; angered his brother when he fashioned a *Golden Calf for the Israelites to worship; and was divinely assisted to overcome the revolt of *Korah.

The miraculous flowering of Aaron's *rod or *wand (his other attribute) was the divine indication of the exclusive right of his tribe to the privileges of priesthood. Aaron and the head of each of the other tribes of Israel laid their staffs in the *Ark of the Covenant. Aaron's rod blossomed and produced ripe *almonds, a sign that the tribe of Levi, of which he was the leader, had been divinely chosen for the office (Num 17 : 1-11).

Aaron, like his brother Moses, was not allowed to enter the *Promised Land. He died on the Mountain of Hor when he was 123 years old (Num 20 : 12; 24-9). He was the ancestor of St *Elizabeth, mother of St *John the Baptist (Lk 1 : 5).

Abaddon A Hebrew word meaning 'destruction' or 'perdition'. It signifies 'death'; *Sheol, the abode of the dead; or the lowest part of Sheol where sinners are punished. St *John the Divine used the word as a proper noun, the equivalent of the Greek *Apollyon, 'the destroyer', the Angel of the *Bottomless Pit, equated with *Satan (Rev 9 : 11).

Abbé Originally the French title of an *abbot, but from the 16th century onwards applied to anyone wearing secular ecclesiastical *dress, and to *clerics, not necessarily in *Holy Orders, who were either tutors or engaged in similar educational occupations.

Abbess The head, or *superior, of an *abbey or a community of *nuns, especially those who follow the *Rule of St Benedict. The title is sometimes extended to superiors of houses of the Second *Franciscan Order, popularly called *Poor Clares, and to certain colleges of *canonesses. In medieval times, abbesses enjoyed extensive temporal and spiritual powers (including the wearing of a *mitre), but these were restricted by the *Council of Trent. As the female equivalent of *abbots they hold office for life, except among the Poor Clares. They must be at least forty years old and to have been professed nuns for ten years. They are elected by their sister nuns in secret ballot.

An abbess in art wears a *ring and holds a *pastoral staff, or *crosier, and may often be shown crowned or with a *crown at her feet. Notable in art were the saintly abbesses SS *Bridget of Sweden, *Clare of Assisi, *Teresa of Ávila, *Walburga, *Werburg and *Winifred.

Abbey A *monastery occupied by no fewer than twelve *monks or *nuns, and under the control of an *abbot or *abbess, who, if founders, may be depicted with a replica of their abbey. After the *Reformation, many British abbeys either became churches or were secularized.

Abbot The head, or *superior, of an *abbey, a religious community of at least twelve *monks, usually *Benedictines, *Cistercians or certain *Orders of *Canons Regular. The title is derived from the Aramaic *abba*, 'father', implying, according to the *Rule of St Benedict, that the abbot, elected for life by his house and possessing extensive powers, is the father of his monks. His female equivalent is an *abbess.

In art an abbot wears a *ring and a *mitre and carries a *pastoral staff or *crosier. Among notable saints who were abbots were *Antony of Egypt, *Bernardino of Siena and *Bernard of Clairvaux.

Abdias The Vg form of AV *Obadiah, one of the *prophets.

Abdon and Sennen, SS Persians, said to have been noblemen, and to have lived in Córdoba where they were imprisoned because they refused to sacrifice to idols. They were taken to Rome during one of the *persecutions of Christians *c.*303 and thrown to the lions who refused to touch them. They were then beheaded. Their remains were placed in the *catacombs of Ponziano where a fresco of the 6th or 7th century showed them dressed as Persians, in fur cloaks, receiving crowns of martyrdom from *Christ who descends in a cloud. In the 10th century, *Cluniac monks from Arles-sur-Tech hid their relics in two barrels of wine and took them to their *monastery in the

Pyrenees where the saints became the centre of a cult. Their special virtue was to put to flight *wild men who ate babies.

Abednego The name given to Azariah, companion to *Daniel in exile, who refused to bow to a graven image and was cast into the *Fiery Furnace (Dan 1 : 7; 3 : 13; 3 : 30). His fellow-Hebrews were *Mesach and *Shadrach.

Abel The second son of *Adam and *Eve. He was a shepherd whose sacrifice of the firstborn of his lambs was acceptable to God, whereas the corn (or other 'fruit of the earth') offered by his elder brother *Cain, a tiller of the soil, was rejected. Overcome by jealousy, Cain enticed Abel into the open country and murdered him, according to tradition with the jawbone of an ass (Gen 4 : 1-8). Adam and Eve are shown lamenting his death. They were comforted when their third son *Seth was born.

Abel is an OT *type of *Christ, *Shepherd of mankind. His violent death foreshadows the *Crucifixion. Jesus placed Abel first in the line of OT *martyrs (Mt 23 : 35). He was one of the *Just released from Limbo by Christ at the time of the *Descent into Hell.

Abélard, Peter One of the great medieval theologians and philosophers (1079-1142). The story of his ill-fated love for his pupil is recounted under the entry *Héloïse and Abélard. After the terrible revenge taken on him by Héloïse' uncle, Canon Fulbert of Notre-Dame, he fled from Paris in 1118 and became a *monk of St Denis. In 1121, despite his vigorous defence, his *Summi Boni*, a treatise on the *Trinity, was condemned to be burned. He then established near Troyes an *oratory dedicated to the *Paraclete, became *abbot of St Gildas in Brittany, and returned to lecture in Paris in 1136. Accused of heresy by St *Bernard of Clairvaux, he suffered the indignity of having his writings publicly burned. His spirit broken, he retired to *Cluny where he died in 1142.

Abgar's letter to Jesus In the archives of Edessa, now Urfa, in Syria, *Eusebius, the 4th-century Christian historian, was shown an exchange of letters between *Jesus and Abgar V Ukkama, 'the Black' (9-46). The toparch, or king, had heard of the miraculous cures which Jesus was performing without drugs or herbs and had realized that he must be either *God himself or the Son of God. By the hand of his courier Ananias ('Hannan' in Syriac), he sent Jesus a letter in which he begged him to come to Edessa, 'a city small indeed, but noble', to cure him of an affliction. Jesus replied commending Abgar's faith in him but saying that he had to remain in *Jerusalem because the time was approaching when he would fulfil there the things for which he was sent. He promised that after his *Ascension he would send one of his disciples to cure the king and give life to his people.

Eusebius translated the letters from Syriac into Greek and incorporated them in his *Ecclesiastical*

The three persons of the Trinity: the Father as Ancient of days, wearing a tiara, the Son indicating the wound in his side, and the Holy Spirit as a dove, displaying a book bearing the symbolic **A- ω** (late 15th century).

A 5th-century bronze cross, based on the monogram Chi-Rho, with pendant **A- ω.**

Aaron as High Priest, with a jewelled breastplate, holding a censer and an incense boat, with a sacrificial lamb at his feet (Netherlands, late 17th century).

History (I : 13). He also included the translation of a note which said that St *Thomas the Apostle sent Thaddaeus (Addai), one of the seventy *disciples, to Edessa where he lodged in the house of Tobias the Jew. Abgar, hearing of his power to cure, suspected that he was the disciple promised by Jesus. A vision assured him that it was so, and he sent for him. Thaddaeus healed him in the name of the Lord and was commanded to preach the *Gospel to Abgar's subjects.

A more detailed account of these events, giving rise to the story of the image of Jesus, 'not made by hand' (Greek *acheiropoitos*), the Holy *Mandeylion, appeared in *The Doctrine of Addai the Apostle*, a Syriac work of the late 4th century. (There were later elaborations.) Hannan gave Jesus Abgar's message at the house of *Gamaliel. As he was an artist, he painted Jesus' picture to take back to his master. Alternatively, because Jesus could not go to Edessa in person, he wiped his face in a napkin and left the imprint of his features on it so that Abgar should see his image. (As this legend resembled the story of St *Veronica, it was later explained that she was a princess of Edessa.)

On his way back to Edessa, Ananias lodged outside the city of Hierapolis and hid the portrait (or the napkin) for safety under a pile of newly made bricks. At midnight the inhabitants saw that the heap was surrounded by what they thought was fire, but which was actually light from the image. Next day the holy features were found to be imprinted on one of the bricks.

Another version of the legend is that Jesus gave the napkin to St *Thomas the Apostle, telling him that he should send Thaddaeus with it to Edessa. When the disciple entered Abgar's chamber, he showed him the portrait and the king sprang from his bed, cured of his leprosy and his lameness.

Eusebius' account, accepted as genuine by the *Orthodox Churches but rejected in the *Gelasian Decree* as *apocryphal, may have originated in an attempt by 4th-century Syrian Christians to prove the apostolic foundation of their Church. Although some writers held that Jesus had sent his reply to Abgar by word of mouth, copies of his letter were worn as *amulets for protection against sickness and peril. Etheria, a nun, probably from Spain, who made a *pilgrimage to the *Holy Land *c.*388, was shown Abgar's statue in Edessa, given copies of the correspondence and told that when the original of Jesus' letter was read at the city gates during a siege the enemy fled in terror.

Abigail Beautiful wife of Nabal the Carmelite. When *David and his followers took refuge in the wilderness to escape the anger of King *Saul, Nabal refused his assistance. Abigail feared David's vengeance and secretly conveyed a large quantity of provisions to the exiles. When she returned home, she found Nabal carousing and drunk and so could not tell him what she had done. He later died of a seizure on hearing what had happened. David, impressed by her beauty, married Abigail (1 Sam 25 : 2-42).

Abigail personifies feminine prudence and, when depicted kneeling before David to plead for her husband, is an OT *type of St *Mary the Virgin interceding for mankind. As she styled herself David's 'handmaid', her name was used in literature as synonymous with 'servant'.

Abishag (Abisag) the Shunammite When King *David was very old he could not keep warm in bed, although his servants piled coverlets on him. They sought out a most beautiful girl, Abishag of Shunem, to cherish him and to lie on his breast to warm him, but David remained cold and impotent (1 Kg 1 : 1-4). Abishag was relegated to the royal harem. *Solomon, to protect his right to the throne, had his brother Adonijah killed because he sought to marry her (1 Kg 2 : 13-25).

Abishag was thought to be the Shulamite maid of the *Song of Songs* (Sg 6 : 13). Her unconsummated association with David prefigured the chaste marital relationship of St *Joseph and St *Mary the Virgin.

Ablutions The ceremonial washing with wine, or with water and wine, or water only, of the *chalice and *paten, used for the consecrated elements of the *Mass, and of the thumbs and index fingers of the *celebrant after distribution of the bread and wine, or after touching the *Host. At first this took place in the *sacristy at the conclusion of the service. By the 10th century it had become customary to wash the priest's hands immediately after the act of Holy *Communion, the water being poured down the *piscina. Today's practice was later regularized whereby the chalice and fingers were cleansed with wine and water which was then drunk by the celebrant.

Abner Cousin of King *Saul and commander-in-chief of his army. After Saul's death he tried to maintain the dynasty, but was opposed by *David and his general *Joab. A trial of strength between twelve picked men from either side failed to resolve the issue and in the ensuing battle Abner was reluctantly obliged to kill Asahel, Joab's brother. Later, when Abner came to David's camp to make peace, Joab, pretending to speak to him in private, 'smote him there under the fifth rib' (2 Sam 3 : 27). This is the origin of the metaphorical phrase, 'a stab in the back' Joab's action foreshadowed the treachery of *Judas when he betrayed Jesus in the Garden of *Gethsemane.

Abomination of Desolation The AV phrase (Mk 13 : 14; Mt 24 : 15) echoing 'the abomination that maketh desolate' (Dan 11 : 31), the idol and altar set up in the *Temple of Jerusalem by Antiochus Epiphanes in 168 BC. It was variously understood as a cryptic apocalyptic reference to *Antichrist; to the destruction of the Temple by Titus in the year 70; and to the murder of St *James the Less, 'the Lord's brother'. The insignia which the Roman conquerors placed in the Temple may also have been intended. St *Jerome was of the opinion that the words indicated the statue of *Caesar which *Pilate was said to have erected in the sacred precincts.

Abraham The first of the OT *Patriarchs was born Abram, son of *Terah, of Ur of the Chaldees, and was given the name Abraham, meaning 'father of many nations', when God made a covenant with him, promising that his descendants should inherit Canaan, the *Promised Land. The token of the covenant was that every male child should be circumcised (Gen 17 : 1-14).

According to a legend in the *c.*2nd-century *Midrash Rabbah*, Abraham was told to sell figurines made by his father, but smashed them as a sign that he would no longer be associated with idolatry. Obeying God's command, he later left Haran, where Terah and his family had settled, taking with him his wife *Sarah, his nephew *Lot and other members of his family to Canaan. He remained there until famine forced him to seek food in Egypt (Gen 12 : 1-10). On his return to the Holy Land he separated from Lot because there was not sufficient pasture for their flocks, but was later obliged to rescue his nephew from the ruler of Elam and his allies. After the battle he was blessed by *Melchizedek, (Gen 14 : 1-12).

Sarah was barren, so gave Abraham her Egyptian maid *Hagar as a concubine. She bore him a son, *Ishmael. Three *angels (symbols of the *Trinity) later visited Abraham's tent and announced that Sarah would bear a son, *Isaac. To test Abraham's faith, God ordered him to sacrifice Isaac, but when he saw that Abraham was prepared to go even to that length to obey him, he substituted a ram and renewed his covenant with him. Abraham circumcised Isaac to seal the bargain with God (Gen 22 : 1-20).

Abraham is depicted as an old man with white hair and a flowing beard, indicating not only his venerable status, but also recalling the tradition that he was the first man whose hair turned white. His *attribute is a *knife, recalling the sacrifice of Isaac. In Romanesque art he may be dressed as a warrior when he is blessed by Melchizedek and offered bread and wine. An apocryphal *Apocalypse of Abraham*, possibly of the 1st century AD, recounts Abraham's visions of the *Fall of mankind and the destruction of the *Temple in Jerusalem, and concludes with a reiteration of God's promise to free his nation from foreign oppression. *Testament of Abraham*, possibly of the 2nd century, tells how the Archangel St *Michael gave Abraham a vision showing two roads, one leading to *Hell, which most people choose, and the other to *Paradise, where Abraham himself finally finds rest and receives souls. He was one of the *Just whom Christ released from Limbo on his Descent into Hell.

Abraham's bosom In the parable of *Dives and Lazarus (Lk 16 : 19-33) the rich man is condemned to the flames of *Hell, but the beggar reposes in the 'bosom' (obsolete AV for 'lap') of *Abraham, who holds the souls of the righteous in *Paradise where they live in eternal bliss. The Vg phrase is *in sinu ejus*, where *sinus* means either 'lap', 'curve', or the pocket of a Roman toga. Souls are therefore sometimes shown reposing in a napkin held in Abraham's hands.

Abraham being blessed by Melchizedek (Dieric Bouts, 1464-7).

Saved souls repose in **Abraham's bosom** (St Denis abbey, late 12th-early 13th century).

Absalom Third son of King *David, renowned for his beauty — 'from the sole of his foot even to the crown of his head there was no blemish in him' (2 Sam 14 : 25) — and for his long, flowing hair, which was to prove his downfall. When his half-brother *Amnon raped his sister *Tamar, and King David refused to punish the seducer, he took her under his protection. For two years he bided his time to avenge the outrage. Then he invited David's sons to his farm for a sheep-shearing feast, made Amnon drunk and ordered his servants to kill him (2 Sam 13 : 1-29). Absalom sought refuge in Geshur with his grandfather, King Talmai, but after five years David forgave him, raising him up and kissing him fondly when he knelt before him, an action regarded as symbolic of divine forgiveness (2 Sam 14 : 33). Later, wishing to supplant his father, Absalom curried favour with the Israelites, so that 'he stole the hearts of the men of Israel' (2 Sam 15 : 6). He then secretly gathered an army together at his birthplace, Hebron, and marched on Jerusalem. David fled, but counter-attacked and defeated the rebels in the wooded country near Ephraim. Hoping to escape, Absalom rode away on a mule, but his long hair caught in the branches of an oak. His mount ran away and he was left dangling in the air. *Joab, David's commander, killed him with three lance-thrusts (2 Sam 18 : 1-17). When the king heard of the death of his beloved son, he cried out in his grief, 'O my son Absalom, my son, my son Absalom! Would God I had died for thee, O Absalom, my son, my son!' (2 Sam 18 : 33). He then secretly promised *Bathsheba that *Solomon should be his heir (1 Kg 1 : 6). Absalom's fatal revolt against his father and his untimely death symbolize the punishment of sinners who rebel against God.

Absolution The forgiveness by *Christ of those who have confessed their *sins either privately or in public and are truly penitent. *Catholic doctrine holds that this *grace may be conveyed through a formal act by a *bishop or a *priest, who address individuals in what is called the indicative method: 'I absolve thee . . . in the name of the Father and of the Son and of the Holy Spirit'. The *Protestant position denies that an ordained minister has the power to absolve, and limits him to the precatory method (also used in Catholic and *Orthodox traditions) whereby, after public confession by the congregation, he prays to God to absolve them. He may also use the declaratory method, stating that God does forgive those who truly and earnestly repent of their sins and intend to lead a new life (See *Confessor; *Confessional; *Penance).

Abstinence A penitential act, usually not eating meat on *Fridays and certain other days, such as the Saturdays in *Lent, *Ash Wednesday and the *vigils of the feasts of *Christmas, *Pentecost and the *Assumption.

Abyss The Greek word *abyssos*, the equivalent of the *Bottomless Pit, in the midst of which was a lake of fire where the enemies of God, rebel

*angels, *dragons and sinners were condemned to eternal damnation. It is thus synonymous with *Hell.

Acacia A bush with leaves resembling tongues of flame; said to be the *burning bush in which the *angel of God appeared to *Moses (Ex 3 : 2), thus a symbol of the immortality of the soul, because the fire did not consume the bush.

Acacius, St One of the *Fourteen Holy Helpers, said to have been martyred with 10,000 other Christians on Mount *Ararat. He was invoked against headaches because he was depicted with a *crown of thorns.

Acanthus A plant with scalloped leaves used as an ornamental carving on *capitals or columns, symbolizing *Paradise because it was thought to grow there.

Accidie A Latin word, derived from the Greek for 'indifference', the name for one of the *Seven Deadly Sins. In a secular sense it generally signifies *sloth, but for *monks and *hermits, who are particularly prone to this sin, it denotes a spiritual barrenness and a disinclination either to work or to pray.

Aceldama (Akeldama) The Potter's Field, according to one text (Mt 27 : 3-10), was purchased by the chief priests and elders for the burial of strangers or (possibly) criminals. They paid for it with the thirty pieces of silver which they had paid *Judas for the *Betrayal of Jesus, and which he returned to them before he hanged himself. Another version (Ac 1 : 16-19) states that Judas himself bought the field with the 'blood-money', but fell headlong there 'and all his bowels gushed out', so that the place was given the name Aceldama, meaning 'the field of blood'. It was believed that the soil from this place caused bodies to be consumed quickly. Empress *Helena took some to Rome and a quantity was brought back by Crusaders in 1218 for the Campo Santo, the cemetery in Pisa.

Acolyte In the *Roman Catholic Church, the highest of the original four Minor Ecclesiastical *Orders. An acolyte is subject to the *deacon. His duties include lighting and extinguishing altar *candles, preparing wine and water for *Mass, and carrying a torch or candle in processions. Acolytes were first recorded in Rome in 251. In *Anglican churches a *server performs functions similar to those of a Roman acolyte. The word is derived from the Greek *acolouthos*, 'attendant'.

Acorn Symbol of latent strength because it grows into a stout oak.

Actor In Early Christian times an execrated profession, but it was rehabilitated by St *Genesius who became the patron saint of actors, and by St Porphyrius (*d.362) who stood on the stage in front

of *Julian the Apostate and declared himself a
Christian.

Adam The name of the first man and possibly a
pun, because according to the second account of
the *Creation of the World he was made out of 'the
dust of the ground' (Hebrew *adamah*) and God
'breathed into his nostrils the breath of life; and
man became a living soul' (Gen 2 : 7). (Although
Gen 1 : 27 states that he was created in the image of
God on the sixth day.) Adam was placed in the
Garden of *Eden and given a helpmate *Eve.
Tempted by her, he ate the *Forbidden Fruit of the
*Tree of the Knowledge of Good and Evil. Their
joint disobedience led to their *Expulsion from
Paradise. Their sons were *Abel, *Cain and *Seth.
According to one tradition, Adam was buried on
Mount Hebron, but another says that he was
interred at *Golgotha, 'the place of the skull',
where later the *Crucifixion of Christ took place.
At his death, Seth placed the seeds of the Forbid-
den Fruit under Adam's tongue and from them
grew the wood of the *Cross. Adam was released
from *Limbo at the time of Christ's *Descent into
Hell.

The *Greek letters of Adam's name were
thought to indicate the initials of the Greek names
of the four points of the compass, Anatole, Dysis,
Arctos, Mesembria. Adam thus symbolized all
mankind, in all quarters of the earth. Adam's
disobedience resulted in the *Fall of mankind, but
he was also an OT *type of *Christ, the *Second
Adam (Rom 5 : 14), agent of the *Redemption of
mankind.

The epiglottis is called Adam's apple because,
when Adam took a bite of the Forbidden Fruit, it
stuck in his throat and produced the protruberance
which now bears his name. The phrase, 'the Old
Adam', signifies the inheritance of *sin in unregenerate man. Water is called 'Adam's ale' because
it was the only beverage available before *Noah
planted the vine.

Adder Symbol of cunning, also of the *sin of envy
because the adder (or *serpent) was said to have
envied the happiness of *Adam and *Eve in
Paradise. It represents sin in the list of evil
creatures who will be overcome by *Christ, as
foretold in the text: 'Thou shalt tread upon the
*lion and the adder' (Ps 91 (90) : 13), in which the
lion is the *Antichrist and the adder the *Devil. On
the basis of the text: 'They are like the deaf adder
that stoppeth her ear; which will not hearken to the
voice of charmers' (Ps 58 (57) : 4-5), adders have
been ingeniously depicted with their tails pressed
to one ear and the other ear against the ground so
that they are unable to hear. This is interpreted as
signifying the sinful ones who will not listen to the
voice of God. Adders were frequently confused in
art with *asps, also symbols of envy.

Adelphotheos Greek for 'brother of God', used to
identify St *James the Less and written on the
scroll which he carries.

Adeste Fideles The opening words of a Latin

A tomb of the Herodian period in the Kidron
Valley, Jerusalem, dedicated to **Absalom.**

Eve, prompted by the serpent, tempts **Adam** to
eat an apple, the forbidden fruit (Albrecht Dürer,
1504).

*hymn, possibly of French origin and not earlier than the 17th century, that is translated as, 'O come, all ye faithful'. It summons Christians to *Bethlehem to worship the *Christ-Child.

Ad majorem Dei gloriam Latin for 'To the greater glory of God', abbreviated *AMDG.

Adoration An act of worship directed to God alone, as distinct from *hyperdulia* which is homage paid to St *Mary the Virgin as *Mother of God, and *dulia*, reverence paid to *angels and *saints. The word is used in art as a title for scenes which show St Mary the Virgin alone, or together with St *Joseph, worshipping the new-born *Christ-Child; the visitation of the *Shepherds; the adoration of the three *Kings; and the adoration of the *Lamb.

Adullam The cave in which the young *David took refuge from the anger of King *Saul; 'and every one that was in distress, and every one that was discontented, gathered themselves unto him' (1 Sam 22 : 2).

Advent In the Christian *calendar, a period of preparation for the 'coming' or 'arrival' (Latin *adventus*) of *Christ in the flesh at *Christmas. It foreshadows his *Second Coming on the Day of *Judgement. The season, originally consisting of six Sundays, now of four, begins on Advent Sunday, the Sunday following St Andrew's day (30 November), the first day of the Christian *year in *Anglican and *Roman Catholic calendars. It is some weeks earlier (mid-November) in *Orthodox Churches. In the Middle Ages, emphasis was placed on the wrath to come, making Advent a penitential season like *Lent. The present tendency is to promote the second theme, that of joyful anticipation. An Advent wreath, with four*candles, one to be lit on each of the four Sundays before Christmas, symbolizes the coming of Christ, the *Light of the World.

Adversary In general the OT word for an enemy of God, but by extension a synonym for *Satan, the enemy of mankind, as when *Job lamented, 'Oh that mine adversary had written a book' (Jb 31 : 35).

Advocatus diaboli Latin for *Devil's Advocate.

Agape A NT Greek word for 'brotherly love', or 'love of God' (as opposed to *eros*, 'sexual love'), used by the Early Christians as the name for their Love Feast, the common evening meal which was accompanied by prayers and the singing of *psalms (1 Cor 11 : 20-2; 33-4). *Agape* was translated into Latin as *caritas*, which becomes 'charity' in the AV version of St *Paul's famous hymn in praise of Christian love, 'And now abideth *faith, hope, charity, these three; but the greatest of these is charity' (1 Cor 13 : 13).

Agatha, St A well-born Christian virgin of Catania, Sicily, who possibly lived in the 3rd century. According to the 6th-century account of her death, she spurned the advances of the pagan Roman consul Quintinianus, who in revenge handed her over to a brothel-keeper called Aphrodisia. When she persisted in her refusal to accept his lewd suggestions, she was tortured and her breasts were either torn off or cut off (thus she is represented in art with pincers, tongs or a *knife and carrying her two breasts on a plate). St *Peter appeared to her in a vision of blinding light and healed her wounds. Her terrified jailors wanted to release her but she chose martyrdom, and in one legend was roasted over live coals. Her veil is said to have stopped the flow of lava from Mount Etna on the anniversary of her death, and she thus became the patroness of Catania. Because her inverted breasts on a dish were mistaken for *bells, she was also adopted as the patron saint of bell-founders. She is invoked against earthquakes and fires and is thus sometimes shown carrying a torch or a lighted candle.

Ages of the world Medieval exegetes and scholars divided world history into six ages, which begin with the *Creation, the *Flood, *Abraham, King *David, the *Babylonian captivity and the *Incarnation of Christ. The world is now in its seventh and last age, which will only terminate with the *End of the World.

Aggeus The Vg form of AV *Haggai, one of the *prophets who foretold the coming of the *Messiah.

Agnes, St A Roman maiden of thirteen who consecrated her virginity to *Christ, refused marriage and would not sacrifice to idols. When stripped naked and sent to a brothel, her hair miraculously fell to cover her nudity. Her *Guardian Angel then clothed her with a brilliant white robe. She was killed c.304 by being stabbed in the throat with a *sword after she had survived an attempt to burn her alive. Although her name was possibly derived from the Greek *agne*, 'chaste', its similarity to the Latin *agna*, 'ewe lamb', led to a *lamb being adopted as her attribute. A *pallium is made from the wool of two lambs blessed on her feast day (21 January, formerly also 28 January). There was a popular belief that a chaste maiden would dream of her future spouse if she prayed to her on the eve of her festival.

Agnus Dei 'Lamb of God', the opening Latin words of the invocation in the *Mass, based on the proclamation of St *John the Baptist, 'Behold the Lamb of God who takes away the sins of the world' (Jn 1 : 24). The original Latin text, first used in Rome c.700, was: *Agnus Dei qui tollis peccata mundi.* This was extended around the 10th century by the addition of the words : *miserere nobis, dona nobis pacem,* 'have mercy upon us, grant us (thy) peace'.

From the 8th century onwards it was the custom in Rome for the *Pope, on the Wednesday of *Holy Week in the first year of his reign and then in every seventh year, to bless small wax tablets (called 'Agnus Dei') bearing the image of the *Lamb of God. These were worn around the neck for protection against fire, flood, plague and the perils of childbirth.

A depiction of a lamb bearing a *cross or pennant (*vexillum) symbolizes *Christ as the sacrificial victim for the sins of mankind.

Agony in the garden Although 'agony' in this context contains the idea of 'suffering', it is the transliteration of the Greek *agonia*, related to *agon*, 'contest', and used to express the fears of a contestant before a combat. Jesus, knowing that his final hour of trial was near, retired to the Garden of *Gethsemane on the *Mount of Olives to pray that the cup (OT symbol [Is 51 : 17] for the punitive wrath of God, a cup which the guilty must drain to the dregs) might be taken from him, but if not, then he accepted his fate with the words, 'not as I will, but as thou wilt' (Mt 26 : 36). The trial is recorded in the *Synoptic Gospels (Mt 26 : 36-46; Mk 14 : 32-42; Lk 22 : 40-6), although the details differ. These variants have influenced representations of the scene in art.

Jesus was accompanied to the Garden by three of his *disciples : SS *Peter and the sons of *Zebedee, *James the Great and *John the Apostle. He went about a stone's throw away from them to pray, but when he returned, found them asleep. He said to Peter, 'Watch and pray that you may not enter into temptation; the spirit indeed is willing but the flesh is weak' (Mt 26 : 41; Mk 14 : 38). Nevertheless, when he returned a second and a third time they were asleep, 'for their eyes were heavy' (Mt 26 : 43). According to the *Gospel of Mark* and the *Gospel of Matthew*, Jesus fell on his face as he prayed, but he is mostly depicted kneeling, as stated in the *Gospel of Luke*, which also describes the physical effects of his suffering as he prayed: 'his sweat became like great drops of blood falling down upon the ground' (Lk 22 : 44). An *angel is shown descending from heaven to strengthen him and is sometimes depicted bearing a cup, or *chalice, as used in the *Mass. The *Instruments of the Passion may also be introduced into the picture. At the end of his period of trial, Jesus returned to his disciples and told them to save themselves because his betrayer was at hand (Mt 26 : 46; Mk 14 : 42). Thus some depictions show in the distance *Judas Iscariot and the High Priest's men advancing through the garden (*See* *Betrayal and Arrest of Jesus). The first of the sorrowful *Mysteries of the Rosary commemorates Jesus' suffering in the garden.

Ahab King of Israel (*c.*875 BC – *c.*853 BC) who made an alliance with the Phoenicians, which he confirmed by marrying *Jezebel, daughter of King Ethbaal of Tyre. By allowing her to introduce into his realm the cult of the god *Baal, he came into conflict with *Elijah, champion of the sole God of *Israel. Elijah also condemned Ahab's unjust seizing of his neighbour *Naboth's vineyard, and prophesied that he would suffer for his wickedness. The prediction was fulfilled years later when Ahab disguised himself in battle so as not to be a

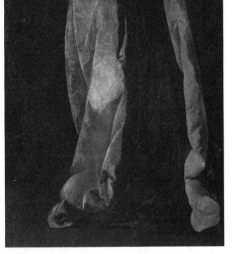

St **Agatha** displays on a salver her severed breasts, recalling the manner of her martyrdom (Zurbarán, 1631-40).

Judas leads the High Priest's men out of Jerusalem to Gethsemane where Jesus suffers his **Agony in the garden.** Angels display the Instruments of the Passion. SS Peter, James and John lie asleep (Mantegna, *c.* 1431-1506).

mark for enemy archers, but was killed by a man who 'drew a bow at a venture' (1 Kg 22 : 34). His daughter *Athaliah also died a horrible death, for worshipping Baal.

Ahasuerus King Xerxes I of Persia (486–465 BC). In the third year of his reign he assembled the great men of his realm in his capital Shushan (Susa). When he was drunk and in a boastful mood he sent for his wife *Vashti to show her beauty off to his guests. She refused his command, so he issued a decree forbidding her presence and sought another queen. Her place was filled by *Esther, through whom God brought about the deliverance of the Jews in Shushan from a planned massacre.

Ahasuerus was also one of the names given to the *Wandering Jew.

Aisle Popularly, but incorrectly (through confusion with the French word *allée*), the centre passageway (alley) up the *nave of a *church or *cathedral. In fact it is derived from the Latin *ala*, 'wing', and is applied to a division or divisions parallel to the nave, and separated from it by piers or columns supporting an arcade, or by series of arches.

Alb A white linen liturgical *vestment, the Latin *tunica alba*, 'white tunic', the 'best suit' of professional Greeks and Romans, adopted by the Early Christians as a distinctive dress for the celebration of the *Eucharist. It is a long white tunic, reaching from neck to ankles, with tight-fitting sleeves and a girdle, or *cincture, at the waist. It symbolizes the Seamless Robe or *Holy Coat worn by Jesus, and the purity of soul which should characterize the *celebrant at *Mass. As he puts it on, the *priest says a prayer beginning with the words, *Dealba me*, 'Make me white [i.e. pure] in heart'.

Alexis, St This patron of beggars (he is depicted in rags) is of doubtful historicity, but may have been an anonymous citizen of Edessa (Urfa), Syria, renowned for his charitable works, and called Alexis in a later Greek account of his life. A 10th-century Latin version said he was the son of a wealthy Roman patrician called Euphemian who lived in the reign of Emperor Honorius (395–423). Although he had made vows of chastity and service to *Christ, he was unwilling to disobey his parents and agreed to marry Ruth, the bride they had chosen for him. With her consent, he left her immediately after the ceremony. Dressed as a *pilgrim (with *scrip and *staff), he spent seventeen years as a beggar, giving to the poor the *alms which he received at church porches. When on his way to the church of St *Paul in Tarsus, storms drove his ship to Ostia and he returned to Rome unrecognized. Mistaken for a beggar, he was allowed to live under a stair or ladder (his *attribute) in his parents' house. He endured the insults of the servants, who threw slops over him, and spent his days in prayer. After many years he was found dying, clutching a letter which could not be forced from his hand. At the same time, Pope Innocent I (401–17) was celebrating *Mass

before the emperor, and was told by a heavenly voice to seek out the holy beggar. He arrived as Alexis was expiring, blessed him and took from his hand the letter in which his identity was revealed. On account of his sufferings, Alexis was regarded as a martyr and may thus be shown carrying a *palm. His body, together with the remains of St *Boniface, were said to have been discovered in 1216 when the church near the Aventine hill in Rome, now dedicated to both saints, was being rebuilt. The wooden stairway under which Alexis lived and the old well of his parents' house can be seen in the left *aisle of the church.

The life of St Alexis resembles the story of St John Calabyte ('the Cottager'), a hermit of Constantinople (c.450), who lived for many years unrecognized in a cottage on his father's estate.

Allegory An event or story in which the literal sense conceals a hidden meaning (Greek *allegoria*, 'something described by another thing'). Thus the OT was interpreted by 'allegory', whereby the surface meaning was shown to have also an allegorical or mystical significance: e.g. the apparently human love story narrated in the *Song of Songs was understood to represent the love of *Christ for his bride, the *Church.

Alleluia A liturgical ejaculation, 'Praise the Lord', from the Hebrew *hallelujah*; chanted in the *Divine office and *Mass, especially from *Easter to *Pentecost.

All Hallows The English name for *All Saints' Day (from the old English *hallow*, 'saint'). The evening before is *Hallowe'en.

All Saints The *feast celebrated by *Catholics on 1 November and by the *Orthodox on the first Sunday after *Pentecost, commemorating all *saints and *martyrs of the Christian faith. The day is also known in English as *All Hallows, and the evening before as *Hallowe'en. The following day is *All Souls. In art the saints are shown ranged in serried ranks, kneeling in adoration of the *Lamb.

All Souls Commemoration on 2 November (or on the following day if it is a Sunday) of all the faithful departed. The *feast was instituted by Abbot Odo (or Odilo) of Cluny, and was first observed in *Cluniac monasteries c.998. In some Latin countries lights are left burning throughout the previous night in churchyards and cemeteries in memory of the departed.

Alma redemptoris mater Latin for 'pure mother of the *Redeemer', the opening words of one of the *antiphons said or sung in honour of St *Mary the Virgin. It is thought to have been composed by Hermann the Cripple (d.1054), a *Benedictine monk of Reichenau, Germany.

Almond A *symbol of divine favour, as demonstrated by the flowering of *Aaron's rod (Num 17 :

1-8). Also a symbol of St *Mary the Virgin, who is depicted enclosed in an almond-shaped *aureole (or *vesica piscis*), also called *mandorla, from the Italian for 'almond'.

Almoner An official of a royal household, or a chaplain of an institution, whose function it is to distribute *alms to the poor.

Alms Assistance, usually monetary, given to the poor and needy. Alms-giving, prompted by *charity or Christian love for one's fellow-men, is one of the corporal *Works of Mercy. Alms are placed in an alms-box or alms-chest at a church door or collected on an alms-dish during *Mass and then dedicated at the *offertory.

Almshouse A house built and endowed for the care of the poor and aged.

Almuce An ecclesiastical *vestment consisting of a cloth *hood lined with fur, used mainly by *canons in the Middle Ages to protect the head and neck from cold when singing the *Divine Office in *choir.

Alpha and Omega The names of the first (A) and last (Ω or ω) letters of the *Greek alphabet which form the sacred *monogram *A – Ω (or ω). They symbolize *God the Son, the second person of the *Trinity, because the Lord said, 'I am Alpha and Omega, the beginning and the ending' (Rev 1 : 8).

Alphabet Symbol of complete knowledge because it comprises all the letters which form words. When a *bishop dedicates a *church, he traces letters of the *Greek and Roman alphabets with his *crosier, or *pastoral staff, on ashes strewn on the floor in the shape of a St *Andrew's Cross.

Altar A structure (Latin *altare*, 'place of sacrifice') on which the supreme act of Christian worship (*Mass, *Eucharist, *Holy Communion, or the *Lord's Supper), commemorating *Christ's sacrifice and the *Last Supper, takes place. A principal or *high altar, raised on three steps, stands in the *sanctuary at the east end of a *church, because 'the glory of the Lord came into the house by way of the gate whose prospect is toward the east' (Ez 43 : 4). Subsidiary altars are placed in the *Lady chapel and in *chantry chapels. In England before the *Reformation most altars were of stone, as in other *Catholic countries. Their upper surface (*mensa*, 'table') was inscribed with five *crosses (one in the centre and one in each corner) symbolizing the Five *Wounds of Christ and containing a *Confessio* in which were placed the *relics of a saint. *Puritans, who could not accept the sacrificial aspect of the Mass, objected to stone altars and substituted a *Holy Table or the *Lord's Table on which to commemorate the Last Supper. In the *Orthodox tradition there is one altar only, the word 'altar' also being used as the equivalent of *sanctuary. A *credence is nearby.

St Mary the Virgin holding the Christ-Child, enclosed within an **almond**-shaped aureole (St Cecilia's Church, Rome).

The Baroque high **altar** of the Franciscan Church, Salzburg, with central tabernacle.

Over an altar there may be a canopy (*baldacchino, *ciborium or tester) sustained by four columns. Side curtains (riddells) and a rear curtain (dossall) may surround it on three sides. To emphasize the supreme importance of the altar, a *reredos or ornamented screen may cover the wall behind and above an altar. An *altar-piece, sometimes standing on a *predella, may be at the back of an altar. The sides and front of the altar may be covered by a throw-over-cloth, often richly embroidered, the colour being the liturgical *colour of the season. A decorated *frontal or *antependium, a carved or painted panel, may face west towards the congregation. A *cross or *crucifix stands in the centre of the altar (above a *tabernacle, a receptacle for the *pyx in *Catholic churches), recalling the *Crucifixion. Two *candles, representing his two natures, human and divine, are placed one on each side of the cross. A white linen cloth on an altar recalls the *Holy Shroud in which Jesus was laid in the tomb.

For centuries the *celebrant positioned himself in front of the altar, his back to the *láity. Present *Anglican and *Roman Catholic liturgies require him to return to his earlier stance behind the altar, facing the congregation. This means that new churches must be designed so that the high altar occupies a central position. Where an existing building has to be adapted the tendency is to erect an altar in the *nave in front of the *chancel arch, so that it is nearer the people.

Altar-piece A carved or decorated screen, panel or panels, fixed or movable, standing on or behind an *altar and usually mounted on a *predella, a base or step. A group of three hinged panels is called a *triptych; of five or more, a *polyptych. From the 16th century onwards it was more usual to have one large picture either set in an architectural frame or hung on the wall behind the altar.

Amadour, St The legendary *hermit whose tomb was said to have been discovered in 1162 in a cave in a rock in Quercy, France, which became the *pilgrims' sanctuary of Notre-Dame de Roc-Amadour. It was explained that he was really *Zacchaeus who, after his encounter with Jesus in Jericho, became a servant of St *Mary the Virgin and married St *Veronica. After the *Crucifixion he and his wife sailed away from the *Holy Land, and guided by an *angel reached the estuary of the Gironde. Veronica became a recluse near Soulac and eventually died there. Amadour went to Rome where he witnessed the deaths of SS *Peter and *Paul and then returned to Gaul as a missionary before ending his days as a hermit at 'Rocamadour'.

Ambo In Early Christian *basilicas a raised platform (Greek *ambon*) in the middle of the *church (like a *bema), from the steps of which the *Epistle and the *Gospel were sung, sermons were preached and edicts announced. A later development, seen in the church of San Clemente, Rome, was to have two ambones (one on one side for reading the *Epistle, the other on the other side for intoning the *Gospel). They were later replaced by *pulpits and *lecterns.

Ambrose, St One of the four great Latin *Doctors of the Church (b.Trier 339), the others being SS *Augustine, *Jerome and *Gregory the Great. His future as an eloquent preacher was foretold when a swarm of *bees was seen to hover over his lips as he lay in his cradle. A beehive is thus his *attribute. He became a famous advocate and was prefect of the province of Aemelia when the *see of Milan fell vacant c.374. At the assembly to choose a new *bishop he tried to calm the rival *Arian and *Catholic factions, and a child's voice cried out, 'Ambrose shall be bishop!' Although a *catechumen (not yet baptized), he was elected by popular acclamation. His statesmanship and theological skills enabled him to convert pagans and to extirpate the Arian *heresy in his *diocese. (He is shown with a scourge with three knots, symbolizing the *Trinity, in his hand.) He became so powerful that he was able to impose a severe public penance on Emperor Theodosius I (346-95) for condoning the massacre of thousands of men, women and children following riots in Thessalonica in 390.

Ambrose converted and baptized St *Augustine of Hippo and was said to have been associated with him in the composition of the *Te Deum, known as the Ambrosian Hymn, although this is now thought to have been unlikely. Associated with his name also is the Ambrosian Chant, the manner of chanting the so-called Ambrosian *Rite, the ancient liturgy of the province of Milan. The fortuitous discovery of the remains of SS *Gervasius and Protasius provided Ambrose with *relics for the church of Sant' Ambrogio Maggiore which he founded in Milan. He was buried under its *high altar in 397 and his episcopal *throne may be seen in the present church. An ancient mosaic, possibly of the 9th century, shows him celebrating *Mass and also depicts the ancient cathedral of Tours, where he appeared in a vision to those assisting at the funeral rites of St *Martin.

Ambulatory A semicircular or polygonal 'walking-space' (Latin *ambulare*, 'to walk around') behind the *high altar, often with *chapels radiating from it, used in the Romanesque period and later for processions around the church, when *pilgrims visited altars dedicated to renowned *saints, or which contained their *relics. An ambulatory is also the name given to a covered walk on one of the sides of a *cloister.

AMDG The initial letters of the Latin *Ad Majorem Dei gloriam*, 'To the greater glory of God', a phrase in general Christian use but adopted as the motto of the *Jesuit Order.

Amen A Hebrew word indicating affirmation of belief, the equivalent of 'so is it', or 'verily', used in the *Septuagint as the equivalent of the Greek for 'truly'. In Christian, as in Jewish liturgical use, it is an affirmation which concludes a prayer. The Great Amen is the reply of the *choir or *server to the prayer at *Mass, beginning, *Nobis quoque peccatoribus*, 'And to us sinners'.

Amice In the *West a square or oblong white linen cloth with strings, worn around the neck by the *celebrant at *Mass to prevent his *vestments from becoming stained. Originally it may have been used to cover the head, because as the celebrant puts it on he says a prayer in which he refers symbolically to the amice as *galea salutis*, 'the helmet of salvation'.

Amnon Eldest son of King *David. He fell inconsolably in love with his half-sister *Tamar and contrived to seduce her by feigning illness. The king, wishing to aid his son's recovery, agreed to his request that Tamar should wait on him in his chamber. Amnon then raped her. Once he had satisfied his desires he was overcome with loathing and had her thrown out of his room. She took refuge with her brother *Absalom, who avenged her some years later when he had her seducer murdered at a sheep-shearing festival (2 Sam 3 : 2; 13 : 1-39; I Chr 3 : 1).

Amos One of the Hebrew *prophets. His prophesies are recorded in the *Book of Amos*. He is shown carrying a crook (because he was a sheep-farmer or herdsman of Tekoa), or a basket of figs (which he gathered from the Palestinian sycamore tree. [Am 7 : 14]). His vision of a basket of summer fruit (Am 8 : 1-3) indicated that the people of *Israel were ripe for destruction if they did not abandon oppression of the poor, extravagant living and corrupt practices. God would measure them with a plumb-line (Am 7 : 7-8) and lay waste their sanctuaries if they deviated from righteousness. He warned them that on the Day of the Lord, which would usher in the Golden Age, they could not expect to be especially favoured because they were the *Chosen People. Like the less favoured, they would be judged according to their deeds.

Amphisbaena (or Amphirena) A mythical poisonous *serpent with a head in its tail which it would half-swallow in order to turn itself into a hoop and thus roll in either direction. Its name is derived from the Greek words *amphi*, 'both ways', and *baino*, 'to go'. It lived in *Hell, its eyes shone like lamps, it fed on corpses, and it dedicated itself to performing evil deeds. Nevertheless, as it could look both ways, and as only one pair of its eyes slept at any one time, it could also symbolize vigilance.

Ampulla A bottle-shaped glass vessel found in the *catacombs, which although believed to hold the blood of *martyrs, actually contained perfume for sprinkling over corpses. The word was also applied to clay vessels for oil used to light the tombs of martyrs. They were decorated with symbols or portraits of *saints. Ampullae were later used to preserve consecrated or sacramental oils. St *Thomas of Canterbury is said to have received one from St *Mary the Virgin for use at the coronation of Henry II. *Pilgrims to his shrine

The **ambulatory** lies behind the altar at the east end of the church, linked with the aisles outside the columns that flank the nave and chancel seen here (Conques, France, early 11th century).

A lead **ampulla** with the Latin inscription, 'Thomas is the best healer of the holy sick', used for the holy water blessed at the shrine of St Thomas of Canterbury (13th century).

thus displayed an *ampulla*. The *Sainte Ampoule*, the Holy Ampulla, preserved in Rheims and used for centuries in the coronation of French kings, was brought by a dove to St *Remigius for the baptism of the pagan Clovis (496).

Amulet An object inscribed with words or images, worn as a charm against evil.

Ananias A deceitful member of the first Christian community in Jerusalem, and archetypal liar. He and his wife *Sapphira kept back part of the proceeds of the sale of their property instead of contributing the whole amount to the communal chest. When St *Peter reproached him in the assembly, Ananias fell dead and the young men of the community carried him out. Three hours later his wife came in, and when taxed with the same deception also fell dead (Ac 5 : 1-11). Ananias was also the name of the high priest who ordered St *Paul to be struck on the mouth (Ac 23 : 2) and of King *Abgar's messenger to Jesus.

Anastasia, St An early 4th-century martyr (*d.c.* 304) who is commemorated in the second *Mass of *Christmas in the *Roman Catholic liturgy. Little certain is known of her, but she is the subject of many legendary adventures. She was a noble Roman matron, converted by St Chrysogonus, arrested for helping Christian prisoners and put on an unseaworthy boat crowded with slaves. St Theodora appeared and guided the boat safely to land. The slaves had become Christians through Anastasia's exemplary steadfastness and were beheaded. Anastasia was taken to the Island of Palmaria (others say Sirmium, Yugoslavia) where she was tied with ropes to a St *Andrew's or *saltire cross, her breasts were cut off and she was burned to death. One version of her legend said that her relics were enshrined in Constantinople, another that she was buried in the garden of her friend Apollina on the Palatine hill in Rome where the church of Sant' Anastasia was erected in her memory, decorated with mural paintings of her life commissioned by Pope St Damasus I (366-84). In the *Orthodox Church she is given the title of *Pharmacolytria*, because she renders poisons harmless.

Anastasis Greek for 'resurrection', used for the *Resurrection of Christ and for that of the dead. It is also the *Orthodox name for the church of the *Holy Sepulchre at Jerusalem.

Anathema A Greek word meaning 'accursed' or 'separated', used to denote those excluded from the *Church and the *Sacraments on account of *heresy or contumacious behaviour. It thus signifies *excommunication. The sentence was pronounced on the person to be anathematized in a solemn ceremony performed by a *bishop, who wore a purple* cope and was accompanied by twelve *priests carrying lighted *candles, which they dashed to the ground at the conclusion of the ceremony (*See* *Bell, Book and Candle).

Anchor Symbol of hope which is grounded in faith, because God's promise to the faithful is 'as an anchor of the soul, both sure and stedfast' (Heb 6 : 18-19), also because it has the shape of a *cross. An anchor is also associated with St *Nicholas of Myra because he is the patron saint of seamen.

Anchoress A woman who chooses a solitary religious life under the same terms and conditions as an *anchorite.

Anchorite From the Greek word meaning 'to withdraw', applied to a man who withdraws from the world to devote himself to prayer and a solitary life. He differs from a *hermit in that the latter is free to move about but chooses to live in isolation, whereas the anchorite is confined to his *cell or dwelling. In the Middle Ages he was formally enclosed at a service performed by a *bishop. Cells were often attached to a *parish church and the anchorite was supported by gifts of food and other necessities from parishioners. The female equivalent of an anchorite is an *anchoress.

Ancient of days In Hebrew, a phrase meaning 'an old man', but used in the AV for *God the Father as judge of the world. The depiction of God as a majestic old man with white hair and white garments, seated on a throne and holding the books recording the deeds of men, is derived from *Daniel's Vision of the Great Day of *Judgement where the words are used three times to signify God (Dan 7 : 9, 13, 22).

Andrew, St A fisherman (a net is one of his *attributes), a follower of St *John the Baptist and the first (Greek *protokletos*) of the twelve *Apostles to be enlisted by *Jesus of Nazareth, who said he would make him and his brother Simon *Peter 'fishers of men' (Mk 1: 16-18). He found the boy whose scanty provisions enabled the miracle of *Loaves and Fishes (the Feeding of the Five Thousand) to be performed. An early tradition allocates Scythia (southern Russia) to him as his missionary field, another that he was active in Greece. The *c.*2nd-century *Acts of Andrew*, and later stories (many incorporated in the *Golden Legend*), make him the hero of miraculous happenings during and after his life on earth. He freed the citizens of Nicaea from the ravages of seven *demons who preyed on them in the shape of dogs. At Thessalonica, when thrown into the stadium, he survived the attacks of a succession of wild beasts. In the same town he so enraged the parents of a young nobleman whom he had converted that they set fire to the house in which St Andrew and their son were praying. The youth put out the flames by sprinkling water on them. When his father and mother tried to climb into his room through the window they were struck blind as they set foot on the ladder. Miraculously transported to Ethiopia, St Andrew restored the sight of the imprisoned St *Matthias (in some versions, St *Matthew). A *bishop devoted to St Andrew was tempted by the *Devil, disguised as a beautiful courtesan, but was saved from *sin when the saint appeared just as they were about to dine together.

Andrew's martyrdom was recounted in a late 4th-century *Letter of the priests and deacons of Achaia*, which was incorporated in the Roman breviary as a lesson for St Andrew's Day (30 November), the beginning of *Advent. At Patras in Achaia he cured and converted Maximilla, wife of the proconsul Aegeates (or Egeas), and the servant of her brother Stratocles, who also became a Christian. Aegeates, denied his marital rights by his Christian wife because he was a pagan, threw Andrew into prison, had him beaten with seven scourges and then condemned him to be crucified on the seashore. Refusing to be rescued by Stratocles, Andrew accepted his punishment, was bound to a *cross (a coil of rope is one of his *attributes) and remained alive for two days, preaching to the people continuously before yielding up his spirit. His cross was first in the conventional *T form, but from the late Middle Ages onwards was depicted as a *saltire cross, *X (probably recalling the *Greek letter *Chi for *Christos*, 'Christ'). He was taken down and buried by Stratocles and Maximilla. As he was well advanced in years at the time of his death, he is represented as white-haired with a long white beard.

The saint's coffin was taken to Byzantium (Constantinople) in 337 by command of Emperor *Constantine. When that city fell in 1204, his skull was taken to Amalfi and his face-bones to St Peter's, Rome. The *reliquary containing them was given by Pope Paul VI (1963-78) in September 1965 to the Ecumenical Patriarch Athenagoras of Constantinople as a token of fellowship.

Other *relics came into the possession of a *monk called Regulus (or Rule). An *angel ordered him in a dream to carry them northwards until he eventually reached the kingdom of Fife where, again in a dream, the angel told him to build a church to contain the relics at what is now the seaside university city of St Andrews. The Picts were converted, and were victorious in a battle against the English when St Andrew's cross appeared in the heavens. St Andrew thus became the patron saint of Scotland. His white saltire cross on a sky-blue background is the national flag, and also represents Scotland on the Union Jack of Great Britain. St Andrew is one of the *Seven Champions of Christendom and the patron saint of Greece and Russia.

Androcles A slave who ran away from his cruel master and hid himself in a cave. There he encountered a *lion, roaring in agony because it had a thorn in its paw. Androcles was recaptured and thrown to lions in the arena, but one of the lions recognized him as the man who had healed his paw and protected him from the other beasts. The spectators were amazed and Androcles was freed.

The story is first found in *Noctes Atticae* (5 : 14), 'Attic Nights', by Aulus Gellius (*c*.130-*c*.180).

Anemone Because of its three leaves, a *symbol of the *Trinity. It also symbolizes sorrow because anemones were said to have bloomed at the foot of

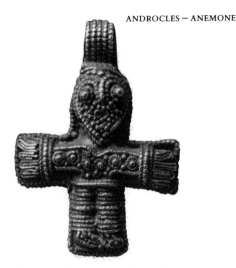

A cruciform **amulet,** worn as a charm, from Birka, Sweden, an example of the blending of pagan art with Christian themes.

The **Ancient of days,** surrounded by angels, sits on his judgement throne above the Four Horses (from Beatus' commentary on the *Apocalypse*, 1109).

the Cross in the evening after the *Crucifixion, the red spots on the petals being the blood which flowed from the *Wounds of Christ.

Angels Angels (from the Greek *angelos*, 'messenger', translating the Hebrew *malah*), are immaterial beings created before man and superior to him in intelligence and status. They were granted freedom of will. Those who willed good remained in a state of *grace and are conventionally called 'angels', the collective term for all these spiritual creatures. Those who chose evil and rebelled against God (the *devils, or *fallen angels, led by *Satan) were expelled from Heaven and condemned to eternal *damnation (*See* *Lucifer).

From many scriptural references (e.g. Col 1 : 16; Eph 1 : 21) it was deduced that there were many kinds of angels. St *Gregory the Great among others attempted to classify them. The most influential ordering was expounded in the *Celestial Hierarchies (De Hierarchia Celesti)*, attributed to Dionysius (or Denis) the Areopagite, who was converted by St *Paul (Ac 17 : 34) and was supposed to have written down what the Apostle had seen in a vision of the third heaven. (This textbook for artists was translated into Latin in the 11th century by Johannes Erigenda, and is now thought to be a Neoplatonist treatise of the 5th or 6th centuries.) Confusion arose in the Middle Ages because of the attribution of these mystical writings to St *Denis of Paris.

According to the *Celestial Hierarchies* of the pseudo-Dionysius angels were classified into nine choirs, grouped into three hierarchies each with distinctive qualities and functions:

1 *counsellors:*
*seraphim, *cherubim, *thrones, who stand in perpetual adoration around the throne of God and receive his glory from him. Their colour is *red, the symbol of love. They are sometimes shown bearing lighted *candles.

2 *governors of the stars and the elements:*
*dominions (or dominations), *virtues, *powers, who receive divine illumination from the first hierarchy and communicate it to the third, but remain aloof from mortals. Their colour is *blue, the symbol of light and knowledge.

3 *messengers:*
*principalities (or princedoms), *archangels (*Gabriel, *Michael, *Raphael), angels, who intervene in the affairs of mankind. ('Angel' is both the generic term and the name of the ninth choir.)

The artistic problem was to give visual expression to these spiritual beings. The Second Council of Nicaea (787) decided that it was lawful to represent angels in pictures, and this led to stylization of the members of the nine choirs, based on scriptural descriptions given in the visions of the prophets *Isaiah (Is 6 : 1-2) and *Ezekiel (Ez 1 : 4-14), and deductions from other biblical texts. (In Early Christian art, angels had been modelled on the Greek *nike*, the winged figure of victory, and on the Roman god Cupid. This tradition persisted into the Middle Ages.)

Angels were also thought to be supremely beautiful and were therefore portrayed as handsome boys and comely women, but as they were considered to be sexless, they were given an androgynous appearance. For modesty's sake they were clothed in a *dalmatic or other flowing garment which covered their feet. As St *Thomas Aquinas had deduced that angels were pure intelligences not united to bodies, and as intelligence resides in the head, the first two choirs, seraphim and cherubim, were represented from the late Middle Ages onwards simply as heads with wings.

Although exempt from suffering, angels sympathize with human sorrow and rejoice in good works and repentance. Their assistance may be invoked in times of need. Each baptized Christian has a *Guardian Angel to protect him.

Angelus A prayer said in the *West at six in the morning, at midday and at six in the evening, in honour of the *Incarnation. Its opening words are *Angelus Domini nuntiavit Mariae*, 'The angel [Latin *angelus*] of the Lord declared unto Mary . . .'. The words of the angelic salutation, *Ave Maria . . . (*Hail Mary) are repeated throughout. In many places an angelus-*bell is rung (three strokes, followed by nine) during the prayers. Although known in the Middle Ages, this act of devotion did not become widespread until the 17th century (*See* St *Bonaventure).

Anger Wrath (Latin *Ira*), one of the *Seven Deadly Sins.

Anglican From the medieval Latin *anglicanus*, 'English', an adjective used in the Middle Ages for the ecclesiastical province of Britain. It was revived in the 19th century to describe those reformed autonomous Churches, separated from Rome and in communion with the *see of Canterbury. It is now applied mostly to members of the *Church of England.

Anglo-Catholic A member of the *Church of England, whether of the *laity or the priesthood, heir of the *Oxford Movement, who emphasizes *Catholic tradition and ceremonial. Anglo-Catholicism has done much to deepen the devotional life of the *Anglican Church.

Animals The text: 'But ask now the beasts, and they shall teach thee; and the fowls of the air, and they shall tell thee' (Jb 12 : 7) has inspired commentators and preachers to draw ingenious moral lessons from the supposed habits of animals (in the broadest sense) and *birds. They derived their information not from direct observation but from what was said about them by Classical writers. The most influential of these were Pliny the Elder's *Naturalis Historia* ('Natural History') *c*.77; the 4th-century-BC *Historia Animalium* ('History of Animals') by Aristotle; and Isidore of Seville's *Etymologiarum sive originum* ('Etymology or Origin'), left unfinished at his death in 636. Treatises on the *Creation entitled *Hexameron* ('The *Work of Six Days'), especially those by SS

*Basil the Great (330-79) and *Ambrose (340-97),
were also influential. They were not necessarily
read in the original. Information they contained
was diffused through encyclopaedias and popular-
izations, like *bestiaries and the *Physiologus.
Many animals real and fictitious which appear in
the art and literature of the Middle Ages are
*symbolic, intended to recall moral teaching incul-
cated by sermons based on tales of beasts and
birds. Less attractive animals were used as warnings against bad habits and evil ways.

'Animals' which appear frequently in art are:
*adder, *ant, *antelope, *ape, *asp, *ass, *bear,
*boar (also *hog or *pig), *bull, *camel, *cat,
*crocodile, *deer (also *hart or *stag), *dog,
*elephant, *ermine, *fox, *frog, *goat, *hare,
*hedgehog, *horse, *hyena, *ibex, *lamb,
*leopard, *lion, *lynx, *monkey, *mouse,
*panther, *rabbit, *ram, *rat, *scorpion, *serpent
(or *snake), *sheep, *tiger (or tigress), *toad and
*wolf.

Some animals are associated with saints, e.g.
pig, St *Antony of Egypt; stag, St *Eustace. These
are noted under the appropriate entries. (For
fictitious animals and monsters, See *Fabulous
beasts.)

Anna An aged prophetess, widowed for eighty-
four years after only seven years of marriage, who
spent most of her time in the *Temple worshipping 'with fastings and supplications night and
day', awaiting the coming of the *Messiah who
would restore *Israel to greatness. She entered the
sacred court at the moment of the *Presentation of
Christ in the Temple. When *Simeon uttered his
prophecy, she realized that the child was the
promised *Saviour. She went about telling everyone in *Jerusalem of her discovery and is thus
depicted with a scroll announcing the good tidings
(Lk 2 : 22-38).

Annas The Jewish High Priest to whom Jesus was
brought for questioning before being sent on to
*Caiaphas, his son-in-law (Jn 18 : 13). (In fact
Annas had been succeeded by Caiaphas, but it is
assumed that his prestige was such that Jesus was
sent to him first.) SS *John the Apostle and *Peter
argued with Annas (Ac 4 : 14). Annas ordered the
death of St *James the Less (See *Trials of Jesus).

Anne, St (Anna) A rich lady of Bethlehem,
married to St *Joachim, and the mother of St
*Mary the Virgin. Childless for twenty years, and
grieved because her husband was not allowed in
the *Temple because he lacked a son and had
retired in sorrow to his sheepfold, she put on her
bridal attire and sat in the garden with her servant
Judith, watching with envy the sparrows feeding
their young in a laurel tree. An *angel appeared
and told her to hasten out to meet her husband as
her prayer had been answered and she would bear
a child. She met Joachim at the Golden Gate as he
returned with his flocks from the pasture. There
they kissed and in due time she bore Mary, whom
she dedicated to the service of the Lord (See
*Presentation of St Mary the Virgin).

Angels hover over the roof of St Bertin, St
Omer, to welcome into Heaven the soul of the
patron saint; a panel from the retable dedicated
1459, by Simon Marmion.

French peasants recite the **Angelus** as the
angelus-bell sounds from the distant church (Jean
François Millet, 1857-9).

This legend is not scriptural and resembles the story of *Samuel (1 Sam 1-2). It is first found in the *Book of *James* and was popularized in the *Golden Legend*. It was linked with the doctrine of the *Immaculate Conception of St Mary the Virgin, to explain how she came to be born without taint of *original sin. Thus a *dove is sometimes shown kissing Anne's lips, and the closed Golden Gate before which she greeted Joachim symbolizes non-human conception. Another legend, popularized by the *Carmelite Order, names Mary's parents as Stollanus and Emerentia, whom she accompanied on a *pilgrimage to Mount Carmel. Still another account, condemned by the *Council of Trent, accredits Emerentia with six husbands before she married Stollanus. Anne is said in the *Golden Legend* to have remarried twice after the death of Joachim and to have become the grandmother of SS John the Evangelist and James the Great, sons of *Zebedee; Simon, Jude, Joseph the Just and James the Less, sons of Alphaeus (See *Brethren of the Lord).

Anne, represented as a middle-aged matron, became the pattern of perfect motherhood because of the saintly way in which she educated Mary, teaching her to sew and to read (See *Education of St Mary the Virgin). At the hour of her death, Jesus (either as an infant or as a young boy) was at her bedside to comfort and bless her. She appeared (until this representation was condemned by the *Council of Trent) in a group of three, St Mary on her lap, and Jesus on Mary's lap. But later, *Holy Family groupings more frequently showed St Mary, the *Christ-Child and St Joseph.

The cult of St Anne began in the *East. A church was dedicated to her in *Jerusalem and another in Constantinople during the reign of Emperor Justinian I (483-565). It spread to the *West at the time of the Crusades when her head was brought to Chartres and her veil, said to have been brought to Provence by St *Mary Magdalene, was venerated as a *relic. St *Bridget of Sweden also brought back relics of St Anne from her pilgrimage to Jerusalem, and her Order, the *Brigittines, had a special devotion to the mother of St Mary the Virgin. Her feast day is 25 July in the East and 26 July in the West.

Annunciation to St Mary the Virgin The angel *Gabriel was sent to St *Mary, a young woman of Nazareth, when her cousin St *Elizabeth was six months pregnant with St *John the Baptist. He greeted her with the angelic salutation *Ave Maria . . .* ("Hail Mary") and told her that she had been chosen to bear the incarnate *Christ. She was afraid and wondered how that could happen, because although married to St *Joseph she was still a virgin. Gabriel told her that the *Holy Spirit would come upon her and the power of the Most High would overshadow her, so that the Son of God would be born. Mary assented, saying, *Ecce Ancilla Domini*, 'Behold the handmaid of the Lord', and at that moment the *Incarnation took place.

The *Gospel of *Luke* (Lk 1 : 26-38) records only one appearance of St Gabriel, but in the *Book of *James* he first came upon Mary when she was drawing water from a well in the courtyard of her house. She was frightened and ran indoors. This episode has generally been omitted in art, although the pitcher (or vase with *lilies, emblems of Mary's purity) included in the scene may be a reminiscence of this variant. Mary is usually shown reading (probably *Isaiah's prophetic words, *Ecce virgo concipiet*, 'Behold a virgin shall conceive' [Is 29 : 11-12]), or spinning (possibly the *veil of the Temple). A ray of light entering through the window indicates the virginal conception (because Mary remained intact just as the sunlight passes through glass without breaking it). For the same reason a flask of water, much favoured by Flemish artists, is another emblem of her purity. The setting may be a room in a house, or a church-like structure, indicating that the Christian era has begun. The event is commemorated on 25 March, *Lady Day, the Feast of the Annunciation, because it was supposed to have taken place on the same date as the *Creation of the World, and is nine months from the *Nativity of Jesus at *Christmas.

Anointing The anointing of parts of the body with holy oils to obtain divine *grace also *symbolizes consecration, as in *baptism, or the coronation of a monarch (See *ampulla, *David, *Saul). Those who are in danger of death or who are seriously ill are anointed on the eyes, ears, mouth and hands, either to prepare them for the trial to come or to give them strength to recover from their sickness (See *unction). *Christ is the Anointed One, the Greek *Christos*, corresponding to the Hebrew *Mashiyah*, 'Messiah' (See St *Mary Magdalene).

Ant Symbol of industry and thrift because of the proverbial advice, 'Go to the ant, thou sluggard, consider her ways, and be wise' (Prov 6 : 6). The ant was reputed to be able to distinguish wheat, which it ate, from barley, which it refused, thus symbolizing the wise man who perceives the truth and rejects false dogma. The ant was also said to increase its store by dividing seeds into two, teaching thereby that a distinction should be made between the letter and the spirit of biblical texts, 'for the letter killeth, but the Spirit giveth life' (2 Cor 3 : 6) (See *ant-lion).

Ant-lion A creature invented because of the misunderstanding of the *Septuagint's use of the word *mirmicoleon* instead of the more usual *myrmex*, 'Arabian lion', in the text: 'The old lion perisheth for lack of prey' (Jb 4 : 11). The beast was thought to be the result of the mating of a *lion, from which it derived its face and its carnivorous habits, and an *ant, which give it its body and its vegetarianism. According to one version, the strange hybrid perished because there was no suitable food for it, and such is the fate of the double-minded man. Another version transforms the *mirmicoleon* into a *formicaleon* (Latin *formica*, 'ant', *leon[em]*, 'lion'), a cunning animal which lies in wait for the industrious ant and robs him of his wheat grains.

Antelope (or Antalops) A swift animal, probably confused in the *Physiologus* with a reindeer, with beautiful eyes and two horns shaped like saws with which it cuts down trees. It meets its death when it goes to drink in the River Euphrates and, while playing with a shrub called herecine, entangles its horns, bellows as it attempts to get free, and is heard by the hunter who comes up and kills it. The wise man is thereby warned against getting entangled in the snares of wine and women, otherwise he will be slain by the wily hunter, the *Devil.

Antependium Hanging covering the front of the *altar which may be changed to accord with the liturgical *colour of the season.

Anthem Vocal music introduced into divine service, in *Anglican churches usually after the third collect at *Morning and *Evening Prayer.

Antichrist In a general sense all enemies of *Christ, especially *heretics (as in 2 Jn : 7) and persecutors of the faithful, but in particular the diabolical being opposed to the true *Messiah. The *End of the World will be heralded by his last desperate attempt to bring about the victory of the powers of evil, but he will be finally vanquished by Christ at the *Second Coming. Antichrist has been variously identified in different ages. One contender was the *Belial of Jewish eschatology, equated with *Satan and with the *Dragon of the *Revelation of St John the Divine* (Rev 12 : 9); another was *Simon Magus. Other suggested Antichrists were the *Beast of the Apocalpyse and Emperor *Nero, who was expected to return from the dead and once more persecute the Church. There was a strong belief in the Middle Ages that Antichrist would arise in Rome. This led the mystic Joachim of Fiore (c.1130/5-1201/2) to equate him with the *Pope.

Antiphon A verse of a *psalm or a short scriptural text sung by one choir in response to another, originating in Early Christian times when musical instruments were not allowed in church because they were considered pagan. Antiphons are now used in the *West to emphasize some special passage in a *psalm, or they may be short independent chants. In religious communities the psalms of the *Hours are sung as antiphonal chants. The book used is called the antiphonal or antiphonary.

Antiphons of St Mary the Virgin Four antiphons sung in her honour at the appropriate seasons: the one used through *Advent and until the *Purification of St *Mary the Virgin, *Alma redemptoris mater*; then, until Wednesday in *Holy Week, *Ave Regina coelorum*; next, until *Pentecost, *Regina coeli laetare*; finally, until Advent, *Salve regina*.

Antitype From the Greek *anti*, 'before', 'corresponding to', and *tupos*, 'mould', or 'type', a NT event which is prefigured in the OT (*See* typology).

A 16th-century depiction of the **Annunciation.** St Mary the Virgin acknowledges the Angel Gabriel's message; the Holy Spirit as a dove overshadows her; and the Incarnation of the Christ-Child takes place (Barthel Bruyn?, 1510-20).

A modern portrayal of the **Annunciation.** The Angel Gabriel floats into St Mary the Virgin's chamber on a golden cloud and presents her with a flowering rod of lilies (Dante Gabriel Rossetti, 1850).

Antonines (Antonians) Hospital Brothers of St Antony, or Hospitallers, a congregation founded by Gaston de Dauphiné in 1095 to care for *pilgrims and invalids. Their patron was St *Antony of Egypt and his cross in the shape of a *T (one of his *attributes) may be a reference to a cripple's crutch, symbolic of their concern for the infirm. In the same way, the *pig, shown as his companion in the desert, may refer to a special privilege from which they derived their funds, the right to allow their pigs, identified by a bell around their necks, to scavenge in the streets.

Antony of Egypt (Antony the Great, or Antony Abbot), St Founder of *cenobitical monasticism (251-356), born near Memphis, Egypt. At the age of twenty he sold all his possessions and went to live a solitary religious life in the Thebaid, in the desert of Lower Egypt. His ascetic existence inspired many others to settle near him and to accept his spiritual authority. He is thus depicted as a monk in cloak and *cowl, to indicate his influence on the development of the monastic system.

Despite prolonged *fasts, his wearing a *hair shirt and his severe *penances, St Antony suffered great temptations. The *Devil often put lewd thoughts into his mind by appearing as a beautiful woman. Devils also attacked him, disguised as *hyenas and other wild beasts, or inflicted severe blows on him. It is suggested that the *pig which accompanies him in art symbolizes his lustful thoughts and that the bell shown near him is there to frighten the Devil, but these *attributes are more likely to refer to his patronage of the *Antonines. The *Tau cross, one of his attributes, may also have a similar reference.

When St *Paul the Hermit, also a desert solitary, was over a hundred years old and close to death, St *Antony was told in a vision to seek him out and administer extreme *unction.

Antony of Padua, St A *canon regular of the Order of St *Augustine (b.Lisbon, 1195) who became a *Franciscan friar in order to evangelize Moslems in Morocco but was obliged through ill-health to remain in Italy. He gained renown as a preacher and is depicted holding a Bible, a symbol of his scholarship and of the fact that he was made a *Doctor of the Church. A *lily in his hand denotes the purity of his life. The *Christ-Child appeared to him in a vision while he was at his devotions and is shown in his arms. When *heretics in Rimini refused to listen to his sermon, he stood on the river bank and preached to fish which rose out of the water to hear him. A heretic in Toulouse said that he would not believe in the *Real Presence unless his mule (or *ass) knelt before the *Blessed Sacrament. It did so a few days later when St Antony passed by, carrying the *Host to a dying man. He preached at a miser's funeral on the text, 'For where your treasure is, there will your heart be also' (Lk 12 : 34). The miser's heart was found in his treasure chest when his heirs opened it in the saint's presence. In a fit of remorse for having kicked his mother, a young

man cut off his leg, but St Antony restored the limb. A young *friar stole a book from the convent which St Antony had founded at Brives. As he crossed a river he was confronted by a dreadful apparition which ordered him to return the volume. Possibly for this reason Antony is invoked for the restoration of lost property. Offerings from those whom he has favoured are used to provide food for the poor, called St Antony's Bread. A piglet at his feet recalls the custom of selling the first pigs of the season at St Antony's Fair, held on his *feast day in June. The name 'tantony' (i.e. St Antony) pig for the smallest pig of the farrow may have its origin in this custom, although there is a possible link with *Antonine pigs and St *Antony of Egypt.

St Antony died either at Vercelli or Padua in 1231. His *relics, including his tongue enshrined in a crystal *reliquary, a tribute to his eloquence, repose in the church of Sant' Antonio built in his honour in 1263 in Padua, where he is the patron saint.

Ape Symbol of *sin, cunning, evil, *lust and *sloth. In this it mirrors the failings of mankind, according to an etymological pun, for it is called in Latin simia, an indication of its similarity to man. It is associated with scenes of sexual licence because of its supposed addiction to copulation and voyeurism. An ape, like a *monkey, also symbolizes drunkenness because, in its antics, it resembles an intoxicated man. An ape was said to have offered *Eve the apple when the serpent tempted her to eat the fruit of the *Tree of Knowledge and thus, when shown holding an apple, represents the sense of taste. It lost its tail, its 'good end', when, like the *Devil, it fell from *Heaven because of the sin of *pride. *Satan assumes the shape of an ape when he tries to snare souls, depicted as birds, using an *owl as a decoy. Chained apes are shown held by saints who overcame evil. A woman who refused her husband his marital rights might find herself condemned to violation by apes in *Hell. Female apes who bore twins were said to love one more than the other and, if pursued, would escape up a tree with the favourite, abandoning the despised offspring to the hunter. Thus men cling to pleasure while sacrificing goodness (alternatively, God rescues the good man whom he loves, leaving the wicked one to the Devil). Female apes were supposed to be lascivious and to tempt the male by displaying their buttocks. They thus represent prostitutes or highly sexed women.

Apocalypse The Vg name for AV The Revelation of St *John the Divine, derived from the Greek word for 'unveiling' or 'revelation'. It belongs to a category of apocalyptic or revelatory writings of which there were many Jewish and Christian examples between 200 BC and AD 100. Visionaries, using their own or assumed identities, revealed the events which will herald the *End of the World and offered consolation to those who had retained their faith despite persecution, promising them heavenly bliss at the end of time. Visual representation of the visions which came to St John the

Divine when he was a prisoner on the Island of Patmos appeared frequently in art from the 10th century onwards, when fear of the Last *Judgement preyed on people's minds. Illustrations accompanying manuscript copies of a commentary on the *Apocalypse* written late in the 8th century (by Abbot Beatus of Liébana, in Asturias, Spain) are notable examples, as are the woodcuts of the *Apocalypse* (1498) by Albrecht Dürer (1471-1528). Among the many artistic themes derived from the Apocalypse are: the *Tetramorphs (Rev 4 : 6-9); the Twenty-Four *Elders (Rev 4 : 4; 5 : 8); the *Lamb with the book with seven seals (Rev 5 : 1); the *Four Horsemen (Rev 6 : 2-8); the opening of the Fifth Seal (Rev 6 : 9-11); the *Woman clothed with the sun (Rev 12 : 1-6); St *Michael conquering the dragon (Rev 12 : 7-9); the *Beast whose number is 666 (Rev 13 : 1-8); the gathering of the *grapes of wrath (Rev 14 : 17-18); the *winepress (Rev 14 : 19-20); the *Whore of Babylon (Rev 17 : 1-6); the New *Jerusalem (Rev 21 : 2-4); and much of the imagery descriptive of the End of the World.

Apocrypha Writings considered as inspired and sacred by early, Greek-speaking Jews, and included in their *Septuagint Bible. Called 'apocrypha' (Greek *apokryphos*, 'hidden things') because they were thought to contain esoteric teaching and therefore to have been withdrawn, or 'hidden away' from common use for centuries. There were some fourteen or fifteen writings in this category, composed over a period spanning the last two centuries BC and the 1st century AD. Among them were the books of *Tobit*, *Judith*, *Susanna*, *Bel and the Dragon* and the *First* and *Second Book of the Maccabees* (See *Judas Maccabaeus), works which have influenced Western art and literature. Aramaic-speaking Jews, who used the Hebrew scriptures, did not accept these apocrypha in their *canon.

Until the 4th century, Christians regarded works in the Septuagint as part of their *Bible, but when St *Jerome was preparing his *Vulgate (Latin) translation, he noted that the apocrypha were not in the Hebrew canon and placed them in a separate category. *Protestants at the *Reformation, who accepted for doctrinal purposes only Hebrew OT writings, claimed that the apocrypha were literature suitable for moral but not dogmatic instruction. They were therefore omitted from the so-called *Authorized Version. In contrast, at the *Council of Trent, these works were declared deutero-canonical, i.e. of authority equal with that of other books of the Bible. The *Eastern Churches took the same stance.

Apocryphal gospels and writings Works written from the 2nd century onwards which contain many strange and wonderful stories and hence gave rise to the adjective 'apocryphal' in the sense of 'untrue'. They have nevertheless provided material for artistic and literary works. They include many 'Gospels' or narratives (e.g. *Book of *James, Gospel of *Pseudo-Matthew*); 'Acts' of various apostles (e.g. *Acts of St *Andrew, Acts of St*

St **Antony of Egypt** beset by devils, one feeding the fires of lust with a bellows. An Antonine pig recalls that Order's privilege (mid-15th-century German engraving).

An angel with feet as pillars of fire, one on the sea and one on the earth, tells St John the Divine, writing his **Apocalypse** on Patmos, to eat the little book, the sweetest word of the Lord (Albrecht Dürer, 1471-1528).

Peter); 'Epistles' (e.g. *Abgar, *Lentulus*); and 'Apocalypses' (e.g. *Apocalypse of St *Paul*).

Apollonia, St A pious virgin of Alexandria (or according to a letter of the 4th-century Bishop of Alexandria, St Dionysius, an aged deaconess) *d*.249, whose teeth were torn out by a rioting mob who threatened to burn her alive unless she denied her faith. She threw herself into the fire rather than recant. She is the patron saint of dentists, is invoked against toothache, and is usually depicted holding a molar in a pair of pincers; or bound to a plank as one executioner holds her by the hair and another extracts her teeth.

Apollyon The 'destroyer', the Greek name of *Abaddon, *Beelzebub, king of the locusts in the *Bottomless Pit (Rev 9 : 11).

Apostles, Twelve The chief *disciples of *Christ whose names vary in the *Gospels and in the *Acts of the Apostles*. There are various accounts of their *calling. They are: SS *Andrew and *Peter, brothers from Bethsaida; *James 'the Great' and *John, sons of Zebedee; *Matthew and *James, sons of Alphaeus; *Simon the Zealot; *Jude, brother of James; *Thomas 'the twin'; *Judas Iscariot, who was replaced after his treachery and suicidal death by *Matthias. They represented one for each of the *Twelve Tribes of Israel to which their mission was initially directed. After the *Resurrection of Christ the title of 'apostle' was extended to others who proclaimed the faith. *Barnabas and *James 'the Less', the Lord's Brother, were so categorized. St *Paul also regarded himself as an apostle. In time, St James (son of Alphaeus) and St James 'the Less' were popularly thought of as one and the same person.

Apostles' Creed A concise statement of faith, used in the *West in the *liturgy and frequently set to music. It derives its name from the legend that, before departing on their respective missions, each of the *Apostles contributed a clause. They are therefore often shown bearing scrolls with the words of their credal statements inscribed on them. (The order in which they appear was established in the 5th century in a sermon incorrectly attributed to St *Augustine of Hippo.) St *Peter displays the words, *Credo in Deum patrem omnipotentem creatorem coeli et terrae* ('I believe in God the Father Almighty, maker of heaven and earth'); St *Andrew, *Et in Jesum Christum Filium eius unicum Dominum nostrum* ('And in Jesus Christ his only Son our Lord'); St *James the Apostle (or the Great), *Qui conceptus est de Spiritu sancto, natus ex Maria Virgine* ('Who was conceived by the Holy Ghost, born of the Virgin Mary'); St *John the Apostle, *Passus est sub Pontio Pilato, crucifixus, mortuus et sepultus* ('Suffered under Pontius Pilate, was crucified, dead and buried'); St *Thomas the Apostle, *Descendit ad inferna, tertia die resurrexit a mortuis* ('He descended into hell; the third day He rose again from the dead'); St *James (son of Alphaeus), *Ascendit ad coelos, sedet ad dexteram Dei Patris omnipotentis* ('He ascended into heaven, and

sitteth at the right hand of God the Father Almighty'); St *Philip, *Inde venturus est iudicare vivos et mortuos* ('From whence he shall come to judge the quick and the dead'); St *Bartholomew, *Credo in Spiritum Sanctum* ('I believe in the Holy Ghost'); St *Matthew, *Sanctam Ecclesiam Catholicam, Sanctorum communionem* ('The Holy Catholic Church, the communion of Saints'); St *Simon, *Remissionem peccatorum* ('The forgiveness of sins'); St *Jude, *Carnis resurrectionem* ('The resurrection of the body'); St *Matthias, *Et vitam eternam* ('And the life everlasting'). (There are variants.)

Appearance of Christ to his mother A legend originating in the *East, popularized in the *West in the later Middle Ages and declared official after the *Council of Trent, averred that before *Christ, after his *Resurrection, appeared to his *Apostles and disciples (See *Appearances of the Risen Christ), he showed himself to St *Mary the Virgin. He had given her this promise to console her as he hung on the Cross, and he sent St *Gabriel to tell her that he had risen from the tomb. Gabriel found her reading the prophecies of the Resurrection just as she had been reading the words of the Prophet *Isaiah at the *Annunciation. Christ then appeared to her, carrying his *Cross or the flag (*vexillum*) of the Resurrection (he is sometimes represented displaying his wounds), with only a loin cloth or wearing his shroud. Alternatively the appearance takes place after the *Descent into Hell. Christ, having released the *Just of the Ancient Law, presents them to his mother.

Appearances of the risen Christ The earliest record of the appearances of *Jesus between his *Resurrection and *Ascension was heard by St *Paul from the disciples: 'He was seen of Cephas [St *Peter], then of the twelve [*Apostles]. After that he was seen of above five hundred brethren at once; of whom the greater part remain unto this present, but some are fallen asleep. After that he was seen of *James ['the Less']; then of all the apostles' (1 Cor 15 : 5-7). This account differs considerably from that given in the *Gospels. The appearance to the five hundred may refer to the one in *Galilee (Mt 28 : 16) or on the *Mount of Olives (Lk 24 : 50). There is no reference in the Gospels to an appearance to James, although it was recounted in the lost *Gospel of the Hebrews* (See St *James 'the Less'). Likewise, there is silence concerning an appearance to St *Peter, although there were legends that after the *Crucifixion he took refuge in a cave where Christ appeared to him, as he did later on the Appian Way (See *Quo Vadis). St Paul's inclusion of the twelve and of 'all the apostles', may be intended to summarize a succession of appearances: to the disciples on the road to *Emmaus; to the *Eleven; to St *Thomas; to SS *Peter, *James 'the Great' and *John the Apostle by the lakeside (See *Draught of fishes). He does not mention the appearance to St *Mary Magdalene (See *Noli me tangere) nor to the *Holy Women at the Sepulchre. He concludes with a reference to his own conversion, 'And last of all he was seen of me also, as one born out of due time' (1 Cor 15 : 8), which was the basis of his claim to be an Apostle (*See also* *Appearance of Christ to his mother).

Apple The *Forbidden Fruit of the *Tree of Knowledge. Seen as an apple because of a pun on the Latin *malum* which means both 'apple' and 'evil'. St *Mary the Virgin is sometimes shown holding an apple because she is the new *Eve through whom mankind is redeemed from the *original sin of disobedience. The *Christ-Child may also be shown holding an apple to symbolize *redemption. Three apples are the *attribute of St *Dorothea. In art an apple is often represented by a *quince or a *pear.

Apple of the eye The pupil, thought of as the most precious part of the eye and therefore to be given the greatest protection, used as a metaphor for God's care for *Israel. In Hebrew the phrase means 'daughter of the eye' (Ps 17 (16) : 8).

Apse The vaulted semicircular or polygonal east end of a church. In Byzantine and Romanesque churches apses were decorated with mosaics or frescoes, usually portraying the glorified *Christ or St *Mary the Virgin.

Aquarius The water-bearer, the eleventh sign of the *zodiac, depicted as a man pouring water from a pitcher, presumably because the period from 20 January to 18 February over which he presides is a time of rain and flood. In the depiction of the *Labours of the Months this is the season when people remain indoors feasting, or venture out to fell trees for fuel. The earth is at present under the influence of Aquarius. Astrologers claim that persons born under this sign are open-hearted and friendly. The Age of Aquarius is therefore destined to be a new age of universal brotherhood.

Ara Coeli, Santa Maria in The ancient church on the Capitoline hill in Rome, built in the 7th century on the spot where Emperor *Augustus saw the vision of a Virgin and Child upon 'an altar in Heaven' (Latin *ara coeli*). This altar now stands in one of the side chapels, dedicated to St *Helena. The church also contains the *Bambino, an olive-wood statue of the *Christ-Child.

Ararat, Mount The mountain on which the *Ark built by *Noah came to rest after the waters of the *Flood had receded (Gen 8 : 4). The word is the Hebrew form of the Assyrian Urartu, the ancient kingdom in what is now part of Armenia, but the site of which has been disputed. Traditionally, Ararat is thought to be Mount Massis, called by the Persians 'the mountain of Noah', which stands on the bank of the Aras, a river which flows into the Caspian Sea.

Archangels The second choir of the third hierarchy of *angels, winged beings in human shape, clad in armour; also any angels of higher rank who

The Christ-Child, embraced by St Mary the Virgin, holds an **apple**, symbolizing redemption from Adam's sin (Carlo Crivelli, *d*. 1495).

Six **Apostles**, carved on the 12th-century tympanum of the porch of Malmesbury Abbey, England.

are directly concerned with the affairs of mankind. They appear frequently in art. Their number is seven because St *John the Divine speaks of 'the seven angels which stood before God' (Rev 8 : 2), but only four are named in the Bible: SS *Michael (also a prince of the *seraphim), *Gabriel, *Raphael and *Uriel. Traditional names for the other three are *Chamael, *Jophiel and *Zadkiel.

Archbishop A *bishop who presides over one or more *dioceses. In *Roman Catholic usage he may be styled *metropolitan if the area of his *see and jurisdiction includes an important city or ecclesiastical province. An archiepiscopal cross – with two horizontal bars – is carried before him on solemn occasions. There are two archbishops in the *Church of England, the archbishops of Canterbury and of York. The former is Primate of All England and takes precedence immediately after the blood royal.

Archdeacon In the *Anglican Church, an assistant to a *bishop, presiding over an administrative area known as an archdeaconry. There were archdeacons in the *Roman Catholic Church in the Middle Ages, but their duties were taken over by other clergy, following the reforms of the *Council of Trent.

Archer A sign of the *zodiac (See *Sagittarius).

Archimandrite A member of the monastic *clergy in the *Eastern Church. The title was formerly given only to the head of a religious community, or group of communities.

Architrinculus, 'St' Erroneously supposed to be the name of the chief steward at the wedding feast at *Cana.

Archpriest Before the reforms of the *Council of Trent, the special representative of a *bishop and head of a college of *priests. A number of archpriests constituted an archidiaconate, subject to an *archdeacon. Their duties later devolved upon *deans and other *diocesan functionaries.

Arian heresy A 4th-century *heresy propounded by Arius (256-336), a priest of Alexandria who in 318 began to disseminate a unitarian doctrine, asserting that there was only one person, *God the Father, not a *Trinity of distinct, equal and co-eternal persons in God. Jesus was the Son in that he was a man like the rest of mankind, although he was the greatest of them, chosen by God for the *Redemption of the world. Arius was vigorously opposed by St Athanasius (296-373), bishop of Alexandria, the outstanding theologian of the First Council of Nicaea (325), when the doctrine of the Trinity was reasserted and Arianism condemned. St *Ambrose vigorously opposed Arianism in his diocese of Milan. St *Basil put to shame the Arian Emperor Valens.

Aries The ram, the first sign of the *zodiac, said to govern the period from *c.*21 March to *c.*19 April. In the *Labours of the Months this is the time for preparing the ground for sowing by ploughing or digging and for pruning vines.

Aristotle Greek philosopher (384-322 BC) and tutor to Alexander the Great (356-323 BC). Despite his knowledge and wisdom he fell victim to the wiles of a woman. According to a legend current in the Middle Ages he warned Alexander that he should control his passion for his courtesan Phyllis (in some versions, Campaspe) because women had undone many heroes of antiquity. In revenge, Phyllis used her amatory skills to inflame the aged Aristotle with desire for her. She demanded, as proof of his passion, that she should be allowed to ride astride him. Aristotle is thus depicted on all fours, saddled, and with stirrups, Phyllis on his back urging him on with a whip. Alexander saw the philosopher's humiliation and learned thereby never to become infatuated with a woman.

Ark The boat built by *Noah at God's command to save his family and two of each kind of living thing from the *Flood. Because it floated safely above the waters, it is the symbol of salvation within the *Church.

Ark of the Covenant A gilded chest (Latin *arca*) of acacia wood which *Moses constructed to replace the *Golden Calf and to satisfy the wish of the *Israelites for some visible sign of the presence of the deity. It represented the covenant, or agreement, between God and his people and contained the *Tablets of the Law, a pot of *manna and *Aaron's rod. It was carried before the *Israelites in their battles and in their journey to the *Promised Land. It was finally placed in the *Holy of Holies of Solomon's *Temple. King *David danced before the Ark.

In Christian liturgies, the Ark symbolizes St *Mary the Virgin, whose body, the ark of flesh, sheltered *Christ, through whom came the new covenant between God and all mankind.

Arma Christi Latin for 'the arms of *Christ', the weapons with which he defeated the *Devil and death, namely the *Cross and the *Instruments of the Passion. These are depicted heraldically on coats-of-arms; on shields borne by *angels; and around pictures of Jesus as the *Man of Sorrows. They also appear in representations of Christ seated on his throne at the Last *Judgement.

Armageddon The name of the place where the kings of the lower world are to be gathered together by the *Beast, the *Dragon and the false prophet (*Antichrist) to make the final war on *Christ (Rev 16 : 16).

Arrow(s) *Attribute of many saints, notably SS *Augustine of Hippo, Edmund, *Giles, *Sebastian and *Ursula. St *Teresa of Ávila described how she felt the love of God enter her heart as though it had been pierced by an arrow, the subject of the sculpture by Gianlorenzo Bernini (1598-1680) in the Cornaro Chapel in Santa Maria della Vittoria, Rome.

Ars Moriendi Latin for 'the art of dying', the name given to illustrated treatises popular in the late Middle Ages on the way to make a good death and thus to be eligible for *Heaven through right living. They show a man on his death-bed assailed by the *Devil, who tries to make him despair of salvation because of his misdeeds, being consoled by an *angel who tells him of his *redemption through the blood of Christ.

Arts, liberal The seven arts taught in medieval universities, divided into two courses: *trivium* (hence 'trivia'), grammar, rhetoric, logic; and *quadrivium*, arithmetic, music, geometry, astronomy. Their personification and visual representation, especially in sculpture adorning Romanesque and Gothic churches, was derived from the treatise of Martianus Capella, *The Marriage of Philology and Mercury* (*c*.400-39), in which each art was represented by a female, accompanied by a notable practitioner of her particular art, e.g. Cicero for rhetoric and *Tubal-Cain for music.

Geometry and Music, two of the seven liberal **Arts,** carved on the pulpit in Pisa cathedral (Giovanni Pisano, *c*.1245-*c*.1314).

Ascension Day The commemoration of the *Ascension of Christ on the fortieth day after *Easter.

Ascension of Christ The earthly *Appearances of the Risen Christ ended when, as the *Apostles' Creed says, 'he ascended into Heaven'. The *Gospel of John* (Jn 20 : 17) places this event immediately following the *Resurrection; but at least since 400, the date of the formulation of the Toledo creed, it has been held to have happened forty days afterwards (the modern *Ascension Day), thus allowing time for *Christ's earthly appearances. The *Gospel of Luke* (Lk 24 : 50-3) records it as taking place on the way to Bethany, but traditionally the nearby *Mount of Olives (or Olivet) was preferred, where the marks of Christ's feet were said to be imprinted on a rock. Witnesses of the Ascension were the eleven *Apostles (Judas Iscariot having committed suicide and *Matthias not yet having been elected) and St *Mary the Virgin (assumed to have been there, although not mentioned in the *Gospels). A cloud took Jesus from their sight, when two men in white apparel (thought to be *angels) suddenly appeared standing near them and asked why they were gazing up into heaven, adding, 'this same Jesus, which is taken up from you into heaven, shall so come in like manner as ye have seen him go into heaven', a promise of the *Second Coming (Ac 1 : 9-12).

Early representations of the scene show the *Hand of God helping Christ to ascend. Later he is shown floating upwards with upraised hands, or only his feet are to be seen, the rest of his body being enveloped in a cloud. In some churches in the Middle Ages this event was dramatized by hoisting a figure of Christ, or a *crucifix, up to the roof.

Ash Wednesday The day following *Shrove Tuesday, the beginning of *Lent. It derives its name from the practice – which survived from the 4th to the 10th century – of the *bishop sprinkling

The risen Christ holds the *vexillum* and blesses St Mary the Virgin and the Apostles on his **Ascension** into Heaven (Mantegna, *c*.1464).

*ashes over the heads of penitents who appeared before him in a garment of *sackcloth. Later, as *penance became a voluntary and private act, the custom developed of a *priest making the *sign of the cross on the forehead of each member of the congregation with ashes made from *palms used on *Palm Sunday of the previous year.

Ashes *Symbol of penitence (See *Ash Wednesday and *sackcloth) and of the brevity of human existence, recalling the text, 'for dust thou art, and unto dust shalt thou return' (Gen 3 : 19).

Asmodaeus The evil *demon who beset *Tobias; thus one of the names borne by *Satan.

Asp The most venomous of the snakes, often confused with the *adder. It breathes out poison and its bite is fatal. In its head is a jewel which may be obtained if the asp is put to sleep by music. Thus the preacher enchants the sinner and wins his soul.

Aspen A tree like a poplar, but with tremulous leaves, a phenomenon given two contradictory explanations. In one legend, when the aspen heard that the *Cross was to be made of its wood, its leaves trembled in horror. A less sympathetic version makes the aspen a symbol of pride, because all the other trees bowed their tops when the *Crucifixion took place, but the aspen remained upright. As punishment, its leaves were condemned to tremble ever afterwards.

Asperges The rite of sprinkling with *holy water to symbolize purification, derived from the opening words of the psalm, *Asperges me, Domine, hyssopo* . . . ('Purge me with hyssop, O Lord, and I shall be clean: wash me, and I shall be whiter than snow') (Ps 51 : 7; Vg 50 : 9). It is performed by the priest holding an *aspergillum.

Aspergillum A small brush or perforated globe containing a sponge, used for aspersion (the rite of *asperges), sprinkling with holy water. It is an *attribute of SS *Antony of Egypt, *Benedict, and *Martha, who exorcized the *Devil with an aspergillum.

Ass An animal with both good and bad connotations. Because of the size of its penis it represents lechery or priapism. To be mounted backwards on an ass denoted degradation. Women taken in adultery, prostitutes and criminals were led in this fashion to their place of punishment. Asses were also reputed to be foolish, obtuse and incapable of understanding, and thus stood for those who refused to accept *Christ as *Messiah. An ass also symbolized *sloth (*accidie), one of the *Seven Deadly Sins.

In contrast, an ass is also the symbol of meekness and humility, because Jesus chose an ass on which to ride into Jerusalem (See *Entry into Jerusalem). It is said that the brown cross in fur on their backs commemorates this event. An *ox and

ass stand near the *crib in representations of the *Nativity. St *Mary the Virgin rode an ass on her way to *Bethlehem and on the *Flight into Egypt. St *Jerome had one as a faithful companion, and St *Antony of Padua caused an ass to kneel before the *Blessed Sacrament to convince an unbeliever of the mystery of *Transubstantiation (See Feast of the *Ass).

Ass, feast of the A celebration of the *ass on which St Mary the Virgin rode to *Bethlehem for the *Nativity of Jesus, and which carried her and her child on the *Flight into Egypt. It developed from the inclusion of *Balaam's Ass in the *Processus Prophetarium*, 'the procession of the *Prophets', a dramatic representation inserted into the *liturgy at *Christmas. By the 13th century it had become the occasion for so much mirth and ribaldry that it was forbidden by the ecclesiastical authorities.

Assumption of St Mary the Virgin The ancient doctrine, not defined as dogma until 1950 by Pope Pius XII (1939-58), that at the end of her life St *Mary the Virgin was taken up (assumed) body and soul into *Heaven. The event is not mentioned in the NT, but is deduced from tradition and scriptural references interpreted *allegorically. In art the Virgin is shown either rising bodily or borne up to Heaven by *angels from the tomb in which she was laid by the *Apostles after her *Dormition. Flowers (usually *roses and *lilies, the Virgin's *attributes) drop into the empty tomb. According to a legend popularized in Tuscan painting, the Virgin let her girdle fall into St *Thomas' hands to convince him of the truth of her Assumption. In the *Golden Legend* *Christ is stated to have appeared to the Apostles as they stood by the tomb. With him was St *Michael bearing the Virgin's soul which then re-entered her body as it rose into Heaven to be received by the angels. The event is commemorated on 15 August, the Feast of the Assumption.

Athaliah Daughter of *Ahab and *Jezebel. She ruled over Judah 841-835 BC, but since she promoted the cult of *Baal was opposed by priests and people. When her son was killed she ordered the death of all male children of the royal house of *David, but the priestly party saved Joash, her brother's son, and kept him hidden in the *Temple. When Joash was seven the priests conspired with the royal guard to have him proclaimed king. When Athaliah heard cries of rejoicing and shouts of 'Long live the king!' she rushed to the Temple crying 'Treason, treason!' but she was seized, dragged outside and put to death. Baal's altar and his images were then demolished (2 Chr 22 : 10-12; 23 : 1-17).

Atonement From Middle English 'at one', 'to make one', or 'reconcile'; the doctrine that Christ the *Redeemer, through his *Crucifixion and death, made full atonement to God for the *sins of the world which originated in *Adam's disobedience that led to the *Fall of mankind. The Atonement is symbolized by the *Crown of

Thorns, the Five *Wounds of Christ and the
*Instruments of the Passion.

Atrium The forecourt or entrance to a *basilica.
In Early Christian times it was a colonnaded court
with a fountain. It was connected to the church by
a portico, or *narthex.

Attribute An object (also called an emblem) used
in art to identify a *saint or OT *prophet. It is
usually connected with the manner of the saint's
martyrdom (a broken *wheel for St *Catherine, a
*spear for St *Thomas the Apostle); or a legend
associated with the saint (a tower for St *Barbara, a
*dragon for St *Margaret of Antioch); or, in the
case of a *prophet, a quotation from his prophecies
(a lantern for *Zechariah).

Augustine of Canterbury, St An Italian (d.c.
604) chosen in 596 by Pope St *Gregory the Great
(c.540-604) to be 'Apostle of the English' (although
early writers give this title to Gregory himself). He
converted King Ethelbert of Kent (whose wife
Bertha was a Christian) and is depicted baptizing
him. He founded the first cathedral at Canterbury
and established the monastery of SS Peter and Paul
nearby (later dedicated to him). Although he was
not a *Benedictine, St Augustine is sometimes
portrayed in the habit of that Order, but is more
frequently shown as a *bishop with *mitre, *cope
and *crosier.

Augustine of Hippo, St One of the four principal Latin *Doctors of the Church (354-430), the
others being SS *Ambrose, *Gregory the Great
and *Jerome, with whom he is often shown
talking, dressed in episcopal *vestments because he
became bishop of Hippo (North Africa) c.396.
Much that is known about his early life is found in
the first nine autobiographical books of his *Confessions*, written c.400. The title means not 'intimate
revelations of misconduct' (although he laments
his youthful dissipations) but thanks and praise to
God for his conversion through the influence of his
mother St *Monica. His great work was the *City of
God* (413-26), a compendium of the knowledge of
his times written to prove that the conquest of
Rome in 410 by Alaric, the Visgothic invader, was
not the result of the adoption of Christianity by the
Romans and the abandonment of their pagan gods.
He contrasted the misery of the temporal world
with the eternal joys of the New *Jerusalem.

Episodes of St Augustine's life together with
some legendary material are recapitulated in art.
He is shown being punished as a child at school in
his native Tregaste (Algeria); dressed as a young
medieval doctor of theology studying Rhetoric at
Carthage and discussing the claims of Christianity
with his mother; and departing for Rome, leaving
behind the mistress with whom he had lived for
fifteen years and by whom he had a son, Adeoda-
tus. His conversion was the result of a vision
which came to him when he was meditating under
a fig tree. He heard a child say in Latin, *Tolle, lege*,
'Take and read'. He opened his Bible at random
and read the words, 'Let us walk honestly, as in the

Apostles miraculously assemble for St Mary the
Virgin's **Assumption** into Heaven (German,
1495-9).

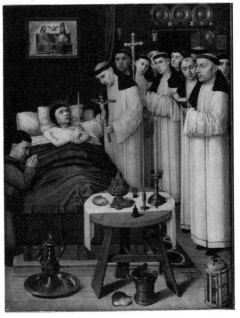

Augustinian monks at the death-bed of St
Augustine of Hippo. The picture of the Trinity
above, is a reference to his treatise on the subject
(Flemish, 15th century).

day; not in rioting and drunkenness, not in chambering and wantonness, not in strife and envying' (Rom 13 : 13). He was instructed in the faith and baptized in Milan by St *Ambrose. It was said that together they composed the *Te Deum.

He is shown giving his broken heart to the *Christ-Child as a symbol of his penitence, and writing in his study with his hand on his heart, a reference to his Confessions. A book denotes his theological writings, and in particular his treatise De Trinitatis, 'Of the *Trinity', although he realized the ultimate impossibility of explaining this mystery. This is symbolized by the legend that when meditating on the dogma of the Trinity by the sea shore, he saw a child (in some versions the Christ-Child) attempting to fill a hole in the sand with sea-water which it carried in a shell or spoon. When he remarked on the futility of trying to put the sea into such a small space, the child reproved him, saying that it was equally impossible for him adequately to explain the Trinity in the fifteen books of his treatise. When St Augustine is shown with his heart pierced by three arrows, or with the Trinity hovering above him as he celebrates *Mass, the reference is to his preoccupation with the meaning of this mystery.

St Augustine is most frequently portrayed as a *bishop with *mitre and *cope. He is also shown as a *monk in black *habit, with leather belt, and sometimes wearing a *canon's fur *almuce. This is a reference to *Augustinian communities who follow the *Rule of St Augustine, derived from his writings. *Austin friars and *Canons Regular may kneel near him and *heretics, defeated by his polemics, writhe beneath his feet.

Augustinian (or Austin) Canons *Canons Regular, religious communities dating from the 11th century, following the *Rule of St Augustine.

Augustinians Religious communities which follow the *Rule of St Augustine, derived from St *Augustine of Hippo's writings on the communal life. The earliest were the *Canons Regular, *Augustinian (or Austin) Canons, approved 1059-63. In 1256, groups of Italian hermits were united as Augustinian Hermits or *Austin Friars. Other notable *Orders which adopted the Rule are the *Premonstratensians and the *Jeronymites (Hieronymites).

Augustus Gaius Octavius (36 BC-AD 14), declared Emperor Augustus by the Roman Senate. According to the Gospel of Luke he was the Caesar Augustus who issued a decree 'that all the world should be taxed' (Lk 2 : 1), the reason for which St *Joseph went with St *Mary the Virgin to *Bethlehem to be enrolled in the census. There was a legend that at midnight on the day of the *Nativity of Jesus, Augustus went to the banks of the Tiber to consult the Tiburtine *Sibyl. He wished to know whether there was any ruler in the world greater than he and whether a greater person would ever be born. The Sibyl showed him in the sky the sun surrounded by a golden circle and in the midst a beautiful virgin suckling a child. This

child, said the Sibyl, would be greater than Augustus. A voice proclaimed in Latin, Haec est ara coeli, 'This is the altar of Heaven'. The emperor knelt in homage, refused to be deified by the Senate, and built the monument known as *Ara Coeli.

Aumbry A recess or cupboard in the wall of the *chancel or *sacristy of a church in which the *Blessed Sacrament was 'reserved' (i.e. 'kept'), or in which altar vessels, sacred books and sometimes *reliquaries were placed. If near a *font, an aumbry was used for the storage of oil and *salt used in *baptism. *Anglo-Catholic churches revived the use of an aumbry with a locked door for the reservation of the Blessed Sacrament. Since the *Council of Trent, a *tabernacle has served the same purpose in *Roman Catholic churches.

Aureole From the Latin aureolus, 'golden-coloured', an elliptical display of golden light (stylized as a *mandorla) which completely surrounds figures of the *Trinity (*God the Son and St *Mary the Virgin), thus differing from a *halo or *nimbus which crown the head (See *vesica piscis).

Ausculta fili Latin for 'Listen, my son', the opening words of the *Rule of St Benedict. In depictions of St *Benedict they may be inscribed on a book which he holds, or which is placed near him.

Austin Friars The English name for *Augustinian Friars or *Hermits, communities which follow the *Rule of St Augustine. They date from 1256 when Pope Alexander IV (1254-61) united groups of Italian hermits. In 1567 Pope Pius V (1566-72) attached them to the *Mendicant Orders. They wear a black *habit, leather belt, pointed cape and a priest's hat. The street name Austin Friars in the City of London recalls their friary on that site.

Authorized version of the Bible The name given to a translation of the *Bible proposed at the Hampton Court Conference (1604) of *Anglican *bishops and *Puritan leaders, presided over by King James I (1566-1625) and therefore known popularly as 'King James' Bible'. The first edition appeared in 1611, bearing on its title-page the words, 'Appointed to be read in churches', the basis of its claim to be called 'authorized'. Because of the majesty of its language and its superb prose, this translation became part of the linguistic heritage of the English-speaking world.

Auto de fe Spanish for 'act of faith' (in Portuguese, auto da fé), the public ceremony at which persons found guilty of error by the *Inquisition were paraded, wearing a conical cap and dressed in a *sanbenito. Those who accepted the 'decrees of mercy', the *penances imposed by the Inquisitors, were reconciled to the Church. Those who refused to recant were 'relaxed', handed over to the 'secular arm', the civil authorities, for punishment or to be judicially put to death.

Auxiliary saints Saints venerated for the special 'assistance' (Latin *auxilium*) which they grant to those who invoke their aid (*See* *Fourteen Holy Helpers).

Avarice From the Latin *avaritia*, 'greediness', the inordinate love of wealth, one of the *Seven Deadly Sins, personified as a man or woman with a *purse or *money bag, sometimes blindfold to indicate neglect of moral precepts. *Dives and *Judas Iscariot represent this vice, which is severely punished in *Hell. St *Paul warned that 'the love of money is the root of all evil' (1 Tim 6 : 10).

Ave Maria The opening words in Latin of the invocation addressed to St *Mary the Virgin, known as the *Hail Mary, or the angelic salutation because it is derived from St *Gabriel's greeting at the *Annunciation. The first two parts of the prayer, used as a devotion in the 12th century, are scriptural: *Ave (Maria) gratia plena; Dominus tecum; benedicta tu in mulieribus; et benedictus fructus ventris tui (Jesus)* (Vg Lk 1 : 28, 42); 'Hail, Mary, full of grace; the Lord is with thee; blessed is the fruit of thy womb (Jesus)'. To this the *Roman Catholic Church added, *Sancta Maria, mater dei, ora pro nobis, nunc et in hora mortis nostrae*, 'Holy Mary, mother of God, pray for us sinners now and at the hour of our death'. The form was standardized in 1568. (In the *East the version is, 'Hail, Mary, full of grace, maiden Mother of God, the Lord is with thee: blessed art thou among women and blessed is the fruit of thy womb, because thou hast brought forth Christ'.) The prayer is the response in the *Angelus, and the *bell indicating the *Hours when it is to be said is sometimes called the 'Ave bell'.

Ave, Maris Stella 'Hail, Star of the Sea', the opening words of the Latin 9th-century hymn by an unknown author, sung at *Vespers and on *feasts honouring St *Mary the Virgin.

Ave Regina coelorum Latin for 'Hail, Queen of the Heavens', the title and first line of the second of the *antiphons of St *Mary the Virgin, sung from *Compline of the feast of the *Purification until *Maundy Thursday.

Ave verum corpus Latin for 'Hail, true body (of Christ)', the opening words of the anonymous hymn of unknown date, frequently set to music and sung at the office of *Benediction.

Axe An *attribute of *saints and *martyrs beheaded or killed with one, notably SS *Jude, *Matthias, and *Thomas of Canterbury (shown with an axe in his head). St *Boniface carries an axe because he cut down the oak dedicated to the pagan god Thor as part of his campaign to convert the Germanic tribes. It may also symbolize St *John the Baptist who summoned the people to repentance, saying, 'the axe is laid unto the root of the trees: every tree therefore which bringeth not forth good fruit is hewn down, and cast into the fire' (Lk 3 : 9).

St **Augustine of Hippo** as a bishop, with his mitre and crosier, and a cope decorated with scenes from the life of Jesus (Piero della Francesca, *c.*1410-92).

Christ in majesty within an **aureole**, beside St Peter with his keys (Cluniac church, Payerne, *c.*1080).

Baal, massacre of the prophets of *Baal* is the Semitic word for a god, but it is applied particularly to the principal Canaanite sun god who controlled the elements and made the earth fruitful. Under the influence of his wife *Jezebel, King *Ahab built a temple to Baal and made worship there the court religion. This led to the famous conflict on Mount *Carmel between *Elijah, servant of God, and the prophets of Baal. Rival altars were set up, and each side called upon their deity to send fire to consume their sacrifices. Baal did not answer the invocations of his 850 priests, although they danced and mutilated themselves 'till the blood gushed out upon them'. Elijah drenched the ground around his altar with water. God then demonstrated his supreme power by sending down fire from heaven (prefiguring the tongues of the fire of the *Descent of the Holy Spirit at *Pentecost) to burn up the sacrificial bullock. On Elijah's orders, the prophets of Baal were slain at the brook Kishon (1 Kg 18 : 17-40).

Babel, tower of The OT myth explaining the diversity of mutually incomprehensible languages among mankind. It tells how *Noah's descendants all spoke the same tongue, but in their pride (and according to one legend, at the instigation of *Nimrod) they decided to make a name for themselves by building a city and a tower 'whose top may reach unto heaven'. Since a united people with one language could not be restrained from doing anything which they imagined they should do, God caused them to speak different tongues so that they could not communicate one with another and then scattered them abroad. The city they failed to complete was called Babel (translated 'Babylon', but actually a pun on the Hebrew word for 'to confuse', 'because the Lord did there confound the languages of all the earth'). The event prefigures the speaking in strange tongues on the *Descent of the Holy Spirit at *Pentecost (Gen 11 : 1-9).

Babylon The city on the Euphrates where the *Israelites were held in captivity and where *Nebuchadnezzar and *Belshazzar reigned. For the Early Christians it symbolized Rome, the city 'seated on seven mountains' which would be destroyed for its sins. In a vision of St *John the Divine 'a mighty angel took up a stone like a great millstone and hurled it into the sea and said, "Thus shall Babylon, the great city, be sent hurtling down, never to be seen again"' (Rev 17 : 5, 9; 18 : 21-4) (*See* Tower of *Babel).

Babylonian captivity The kingdom of *Israel was invaded several times by Assyrian or Babylonian kings, and the *Israelites carried off into captivity. The most notable invasion occurred in the first part of the reign of *Nebuchadnezzar (606-562 BC) when *Jerusalem was besieged, the first *Temple destroyed and the inhabitants de-

ported to *Babylon. The prophet *Jeremiah predicted seventy years of captivity (Jer 25 : 12) and this period was ended by the decree of King Cyrus of Persia (536 BC) which permitted the gradual return of some 42,360 *Israelites and their servants (Esr 1 : 2; 2 : 1-69). Those who remained in Assyria (*See* *Ten Tribes of Israel) were known as the *Diaspora*, or Dispersion, a word applied in NT times to Jews living in the Roman world and elsewhere away from Judaea. The phrase 'Babylonian Captivity' is also used figuratively with reference to the period 1309-77, which legitimate *Popes were obliged to spend away from Rome in Avignon, France.

Balaam's ass On their way to the *Promised Land, the *Israelites entered the Jordan Valley, the territory of the Moabites. The king of the Moabites sent a magician named Balaam to pronounce a curse on them, since they were too strong for him to overcome. As Balaam was riding his *ass through a vineyard, the beast three times refused to go forward and was thrice beaten. Then God 'opened the mouth of the ass, and she said to Balaam, "What have I done unto thee, that thou hast smitten me these three times?"' (Num 22 : 28). Balaam saw that an *angel with a raised sword was barring their way (prefiguring the appearance of Christ to St *Thomas the Apostle). He then decided to bless the Israelites instead of cursing them. When the king protested, Balaam prophesied that 'there shall come a Star out of Jacob, and a Sceptre shall rise out of Israel' (Num 24 : 17), understood as foretelling the *star which announced the birth of Christ and guided the three *Kings to Bethlehem.

The ass on which Christ entered Jerusalem was said to be descended from Balaam's mount. After the *Crucifixion it was taken to Verona where it died of old age. Its bones were preserved in the *cathedral of that city.

Baldacchino (Baldachino) A dome-like wooden, stone, or metal canopy (also called a *ciborium), supported by columns, standing over an *altar or tomb, the most notable example being over the *high altar in St Peter's, Rome, designed by Gianlorenzo Bernini (1598-1680). It is also a portable canopy held over the head of church dignitaries in processions. The word is derived from Baldacco, the Italian name for Baghdad, the city from which the costly materials used to make these canopies were imported.

Balls, three golden The attribute of St *Nicholas of Myra.

Bambino An olive-wood statue of the *Christ-Child, the *Santissimo Bambino* (Italian for 'Most Holy Babe'), brought from the *Holy Land in the 17th century, now in the *Franciscan church of *Ara Coeli in Rome. Its special virtue is to heal the sick. It is carried in procession at *Christmas and *Epiphany, and may be escorted by two Franciscan friars to the sickbed of a person with complete faith in its curative powers. The image of the

Christ-Child in a Christmas *crib is also called a bambino. This devotional custom was popularized by St *Francis of Assisi who set up a *Nativity scene in a *hermit's cave near Greccio and caused the story of the birth of Jesus to be enacted there at midnight *Mass at *Christmas 1223.

Banner Symbol of victory usually carried by military *saints. The resurrected *Christ bears a banner with a *cross to symbolize victory over death (*See *Vexillum*).

Banns Medieval Latin *bannus*, from the Germanic root *bann*, 'proclamation', used for the custom of publishing on three successive Sundays in a *parish church, or in each of the parishes in which the parties reside, of their intention to marry. The purpose is to discover whether anyone knows of 'any just cause or impediment', consanguinity or an existing marriage, to the proposed union.

Baptism The *sacrament by which a person is incorporated into the fellowship of the *Church. It is administered by a *bishop, *priest or *deacon, but in cases of emergency a *lay person may perform the rite. Ordinarily a child is baptized as soon as possible after birth. It receives its Christian name or names (*saint's names are advocated) and is sponsored by *godparents who make promises in the name of the child and assume special responsibilities for its Christian upbringing. Adults who are not Christians are also baptized when they accept the Faith. Baptism by pouring (called 'infusion') or sprinkling ('aspersion') of *Holy Water on the head now takes place at the *font. But in earlier times, when it was more usual to baptize adults, it was usually done by immersion in water. A special building called the *baptistery was constructed for this purpose. An adult candidate for baptism is known as a *catechumen.

Baptism of Christ The beginning of Jesus' public life, when his messianic mission was made plain at the time of his *baptism in the River Jordan by St *John the Baptist. Similar versions of the episode are recorded in the *Synoptic Gospels (Mk 1 : 9-11; Lk 3 : 21-2; Mt 3 : 13-17), but texts agree that four events took place: John baptized Jesus in the river; the heavens opened; the *Holy Spirit (represented as a *dove) descended on Jesus; and a divine voice was heard proclaiming that he was God's beloved son. There was much theological debate as to the need for the baptism of one who was sinless, but it was argued that, in submitting to the rite, Jesus was demonstrating his humility. He may therefore be shown kneeling rather than standing as John pours water over his head. (When John kneels before Jesus he is demonstrating visibly his protest, 'It is I who needs to be baptized by you'.) *Angels may stand by, their hands veiled as a sign of respect (not holding Jesus' clothes as is popularly supposed). In the *East, Jesus' baptism was regarded as one of his Manifestations (or *Epiphanies) and associated with the feast of Epiphany, on 6 January, or *Twelfth Night.

The tower of **Babel,** unfinished because the builders began suddenly to talk foreign languages (Hans Memlinc, *c*.1485).

The magnificent Baroque **baldacchino** surmounting the high altar of St Peter's, Rome (Bernini, 1598-1680).

Baptistery A round, rectangular or octagonal building with a large basin (the *piscina) in the centre, filled with running water. Attached to a church for the administration of *baptism and usually dedicated to St *John the Baptist. In the Middle Ages, when baptism was ordinarily by immersion, they were elaborately constructed and decorated and sometimes stood apart from the main building, as at Pisa. Until the 6th century baptism had to take place in a *cathedral church, but later the rite was permitted in *parish churches. This led to the *font replacing the baptistery, especially when baptism by immersion ceased to be customary and was replaced by sprinkling.

Barabbas A Jewish prisoner who was in the hands of the Romans when Jesus was brought to trial before *Pilate. According to the *Gospel of Mark* (Mk 15 : 6-15) he was a rebel 'who had committed murder in the insurrection'; while the *Gospel of Luke* (Lk 23 : 17-25) says he was a man who had been thrown into prison for an insurrection started in the city and for murder. In the *Gospel of John* (Jn 18 : 40) he is just a 'robber', possibly a bandit. It is now thought that he was a *Zealot, a resistance fighter, one of those dedicated to expelling the Romans by force.

Pilate believed Jesus to be innocent and a victim of the chief priests' envy and tried to avoid executing him. His expedient was to use the custom of releasing a prisoner at *Passover time. He asked the crowd whether he should free Jesus or Barabbas. (Point is given to the story in early manuscripts of the *Gospel of Matthew* (Mt 27 : 15-26) where, maybe through a scribal error, Barabbas is the surname of another Jesus.) Urged on by the chief priests and elders, the crowd yelled for Barabbas, and Pilate was therefore obliged to pass sentence on Jesus. It would appear that the motive behind the incident as recorded in the *Gospels is to put the blame for the *Crucifixion on the Jews instead of on the Romans who actually carried out the sentence.

Barbara, St One of the *Fourteen Holy Helpers, a late 3rd-century virgin martyr, daughter of Dioscorus, a rich noble of Heliopolis (or, in some accounts, of Nicomedia) who shut her up in a tower (one of her *attributes) to keep her away from her princely suitors. Contemplation of the heavens and philosophical studies (another of her attributes is a *book) led her to belief in a supreme God, and she was converted to Christianity by a disciple disguised as a doctor, sent by Origen, the Alexandrian Church *Father (c.185-254). In honour of the *Trinity, she caused a third window to be constructed in her tower, thus revealing symbolically to her father her renunciation of the pagan deities. To escape his wrath she took refuge at the top of the tower and was carried by *angels to a secret hiding place. A shepherd betrayed her and his flock was changed into grasshoppers. Dioscorus then sent Barbara to the Proconsul Marcian to be tortured, but she refused to abjure her new faith. In desperation, Dioscorus took his

daughter to a mountain top and beheaded her (a *sword is another of her attributes). A tempest arose and he was struck dead by lightning. Barbara is therefore invoked against thunderstorms and explosions and became the patron saint of gunsmiths and artillerymen (she may be shown with a cannon). She is also invoked by those who wish to make a good death, and for this reason is depicted carrying a *host and *chalice. She may also be shown with a *palm of martyrdom or with a *peacock's feather, a reference to the legend that the whips with which she was scourged turned to feathers, and also a symbol of immortality as the result of true faith.

Barlaam and Josaphat, SS Heroes of a Christian version of a Buddhist legend found in the works of St John of Damascus (c.675-c.749). Son of a 4th-century king of India who persecuted Christians, *Josaphat was shut up in a tower in order to foil the prophecy that he would renounce his right to the throne and become a *hermit. During his escape he learned about suffering and death through his encounters with a leper, a blind man and an old man. He was converted by the ascetic Barlaam, became king, but relinquished the throne and, as had been foretold, left to lead an eremitical life with Barlaam.

Barnabas, St Joseph, a *Jew of Cyprus, was given the surname Barnabas ('son of consolation') when he was converted to Christianity shortly after *Pentecost. He was not one of the original twelve *Apostles, although he was later granted the title of Apostle because of his association with St *Paul whom he introduced to the first Christian community. He was said to be the cousin of John Mark who may have been St *Mark, one of the *Evangelists. He accompanied Paul to Antioch, but later parted from Paul because of a disagreement and went with Mark to evangelize Cyprus. He is thought to have been stoned to death at Salamis in 61 (a heap of stones is one of his *attributes). A later tradition makes him the founder and first bishop of the church in Milan.

Barnabas and Paul, when preaching the Gospel at Paphos in Cyprus, were summoned to appear before Sergius Paulus the Roman governor, who wanted to hear their message. *Elymas, a sorcerer, tried to silence them, but was struck blind by Paul. At Lystra in Asia Minor they healed a cripple and were thought by the inhabitants to be Jupiter and Mercury. The priests of the temple of Jupiter brought oxen to sacrifice to them, but Paul tore his cloak in sorrow and by his arguments prevented the performance of the pagan rite. On his own, Barnabas cured a sick man by placing the *Gospel of Matthew* on his head, thus a book figures as another of his attributes (Ac 4 : 36; 9 : 27; 11 : 22; 13; 14; 15).

Bartholomew, St One of the twelve *Apostles. His name is the Greek version of the Aramaic for 'son of Tolmai' and may therefore be a patronymic. This has led to the supposition that Bartholomew also had a personal name, probably *Nathanael with whom he is identified. In the

*Synoptic Gospels he is closely associated with St *Philip and is said to have gone with him to Phrygia and to have preached in Hierapolis. According to *Eusebius he went to India, and left there the *Gospel of St Matthew* written in Hebrew. Bartholomew was described as an accomplished linguist with a voice like a trumpet. He was of medium height, white-skinned, with large eyes, a straight nose, black curly hair which came down over his ears, and a long beard. The Armenian Church claimed him as their founder because he was said to have been martyred in Albanopolis (Derbend). A more persistent tradition is that he was beheaded in India, possibly near Bombay, by order of King Astriagis. He was supposed to have been flayed alive before being executed. His *attribute is a large flaying knife, and he is sometimes shown (as in the Sistine Chapel) with his skin draped over his arm. For this reason he is the patron saint of tanners. In a procession of Apostles he carries a scroll inscribed with the words *Credo in Spiritum Sanctum* ('I believe in the Holy Spirit'), a clause which he contributed to the *Apostles' Creed. He is said to have brought back to life the son of the king of Armenia and to have driven a devil out of him, which he then chained. Another legend describes how he caused a *devil in India, with bristles like a hedgehog, to come out of an idol and run away howling. An apocryphal *Gospel of St Bartholomew* gives accounts of the *Annunciation, the *Descent into Hell, and the *Bottomless Pit.

Bartimaeus, healing of blind The story is told of the blind beggar of *Jericho who sat by the roadside and recognized Jesus as *Messiah by calling out to him, 'Jesus, Son of David, have mercy on me'. Versions appear in the three *Synoptic Gospels (Mk 10 : 46-52; Lk 18 : 35-43; Mt 20 : 29-34). He is named Bartimaeus in the *Gospel of Mark* (but the *Gospel of Matthew* has two blind men sitting by the roadside). When Jesus asked Bartimaeus (or the two beggars) what was required of him, he was told, 'Lord, that I may receive my sight' (or the two beggars requested, 'Lord, that our eyes may be opened'). Jesus restored Bartimaeus' sight with the words, 'thy faith hath made thee whole', but cured the two beggars' blindness by touching their eyes.

Basil the Great, St One of the four *Fathers of the Greek *Orthodox Church (the others being SS *John Chrysostom, *Gregory of Nazianzus [or Nazianzen] and Athanasius) who lived 329-80. Brought up in a saintly family, he had a brilliant academic career in Constantinople and Athens, but longed for a life of solitude. After extensive travels he gave away most of his possessions (hence he is shown feeding the poor) and then devoted himself to founding *cenobitic communities according to an austere *Rule which he drew up. The most celebrated event in his life was his contest with the *Arian Emperor Valens. When the latter was about to write his sentence of exile, the pen broke into three parts, symbolizing the victory of the *Trinity.

St **Barbara** studying philosophy, seated before the tower in which she was imprisoned by her jealous father (Jan van Eyck, 1434).

The donor of this German, *c*.1500 panel kneels before St **Bartholomew** who holds a flaying-knife, beside St Agnes.

Basilica Originally a Roman assembly hall, but adapted by the Early Christians as their meeting place when their religion was made legal. Basilican churches (seven of which were built in Rome under Emperor *Constantine) were oblong in shape, with an *apse at the east end for the *altar, a *nave with *aisles and a narthex at the entrance. The word now survives as a privileged title granted by the *Pope to certain ancient or historical churches, among the most famous being the basilicas of St Peter's, St John Lateran and St Mary Major (Santa Maria Maggiore) in Rome.

Basilisk A mythical creature and symbol of the *Devil, with the white-striped body of a *dragon or *serpent and the wings and head of a cock (often confused with a *cockatrice), supposedly hatched by a toad or a serpent from a cock's egg. Because its name resembles the Greek word *basileus*, 'king', or because it was supposed to have a crown-shaped white spot on its head, it was called 'the king of serpents' and was given a crown. Its smell would kill and its breath would burn up anything in its path. In desert places it would drive men mad from hydrophobia. A mere look from a basilisk's eye would also kill, penetrating first the brain and then the heart. (This is the source of the poetic conceit which calls a beautiful woman a basilisk because one glance from her has the power to slay her lover.) Moralists used the word as a synonym for a prostitute who destroys her customers with her looks. A basilisk thus symbolized *lust.

There were two ways of killing this creature. One, said to have been discovered by Alexander the Great (356-323 BC), was to hold before it a mirror or other reflecting object. Mistaking the image for an enemy, the basilisk would hiss and the poison would recoil on it and destroy it. Alternatively, according to Pliny the Elder (23/4-79), it would be frightened by its own reflection and would burst asunder with horror. The other way of disposing of the basilisk was to persuade two *weasels which had been fed on rue to bite it. Thus the Devil is overcome by those who digest the wisdom of the Old and New Testaments.

The victory of *Christ over the Devil is foretold in Vg Psalm 90 : 13, *Super aspidem et basiliscum ambulabis*, 'Thou shalt tread upon the asp and the basilisk'. (AV [Ps 91 : 31] has, 'Thou shalt tread upon the lion and adder'.) In art the Risen Christ is shown trampling on these creatures.

Bathsheba King David saw the beautiful Bathsheba, wife of *Uriah, one of his captains, bathing herself one evening, from his roof. Lusting for her, he sent messengers to her and she came to his bed. Later she told him that she was pregnant. David ordered his commander *Joab to put Uriah in the most dangerous part of the battle, where he was killed. David then married Bathsheba, but the child born of adultery sickened and died. The king was reproached by Nathan the prophet and did penance (a scene associated in art with the penitent St *Peter and St *Mary Magdalene). The second child born to David and Bathsheba was *Solomon (2 Sam 11; 12 : 1-25).

Beads Small beads are strung together to make a *rosary. Each one stands for a 'prayer' (Middle English *bede*) and 'to tell one's beads' is to 'count' (Old English *tellan*) prayers by fingering individual beads on the string. A beadsman was a person paid to say a number of prayers for someone, either alive or dead. He was usually an inhabitant of an *almshouse.

Bear Symbol of *lust – unlike other *animals, bears copulate face to face – and of greed – they have a voracious appetite for honey. The she-bear's period of gestation is thirty days, and she gives birth to small white forms which she has quite literally to lick into shape. (Thus the Christian faith reforms the sinner and the heathen.) Bears die from eating the fruit of the *mandrake, but may survive if they can ingest ants before the poison has time to work.

Beast of the Apocalypse One of the two beasts in the *Revelation of St *John the Divine* which symbolize the arch-enemies of the Early Christians. This one 'bears the number 666', which has given rise to many interpretations but which probably refers to *Nero redivivus*, the Roman Emperor *Nero, who was expected to return from the dead in the person of *Antichrist (Rev 13 : 18).

Beatification Permission by the *Pope for the veneration after death of an exemplary religious person who then receives the title of 'Blessed'. It may be a step towards *canonization.

Beatific vision The contemplation of the Divine Being in all his glory, the ultimate *grace which is granted to all redeemed Christians after death but which, by special favour, may be briefly enjoyed by mystics. *Moses (Ex 34 : 28-35), St *Paul (2 Cor 12 : 2-4) and St *Thomas Aquinas may have had this experience.

Beatitudes, eight The eight sayings, each beginning 'Blessed [meaning 'happy'] are they . . .', which in the *Gospel of Matthew* (Mt 5 : 3-10) Jesus pronounced in the course of his *Sermon on the Mount. The poor in spirit are happy, for theirs is the kingdom of heaven; they that mourn, for they shall be comforted; the meek, for they shall inherit the earth; they that hunger and thirst after righteousness, for they shall be filled; the merciful, for they shall obtain mercy; the pure in heart, for they shall see God; the peacemakers, for they shall be called the children of God; they which are persecuted for righteousness' sake, for theirs is the kingdom of heaven.

Beatus vir Latin for 'Blessed is the man', the opening words of the first *Psalm (Ps 1 : 1).

Beaver A gentle *animal hunted for its testicles which have a supposed medicinal value. When the beaver is pursued it bites them off to escape while the hunter stops to retrieve them. If it encounters another hunter it rears up to reveal that it lacks what is sought. (This is reinforced by the resemblance between the Latin word for 'beaver', *castor*, and 'castrate'.) The wise man learns to escape the *Devil by cutting himself off from lewdness and *lust. For this reason the beaver symbolizes chastity and victory over the desires of the flesh.

Bede, Venerable A *monk (673-735) who lived in Jarrow Monastery from the age of eight until his death, devoted to religion and scholarship. He is often shown holding a *book. He wrote learned commentaries on the *Bible, but is best remembered for his *Ecclesiastical History of the English People* (finished 731) which records the spread of Christianity in England. He lies in the *Galilee chapel of Durham Cathedral. It is possible that the title 'venerable' was derived from the Latin couplet inscribed on the stand supporting his *shrine:

Haec sunt in fossa
Bedae venerabilis ossa

'Here in the grave are the bones of the venerable [i.e. 'worthy'] Bede'.

Bedlam Popular form of *Bethlehem, the name of the hospital for the insane, founded in 1247 at Bishopsgate in London and dedicated to St Mary of Bethlehem. As a common noun it still signifies an uproar characteristic of an old madhouse.

Bee *Symbol of diligence because it is always busy storing up honey, also of eloquence because of the honeyed words which came from the mouths of great preachers like St *Ambrose and St *John Chrysostom. As bees were supposed never to sleep, they also symbolize vigilance.

Beehive The symbol of the Christian community because its members are united and industriously perform pious works. It may also represent the *Incarnation and *Virgin birth because bees were thought to reproduce by parthenogenesis. Also the attribute of St *Ambrose and St *Bernard.

Beelzebub 'Lord of the flies', the god of the *Philistine city of Ekron (2 Kg 1 : 1-16), and by extension *Satan, the prince of *devils. Jesus' enemies accused him of 'casting out devils by Beelzebub'. Jesus retorted by asking, 'How can Satan cast out Satan? If a kingdom is divided against itself, that kingdom cannot stand. And if a house be divided against itself, that house cannot stand' (Mt 12 : 24-6; Mk 3 : 22-6; Lk 11 : 15-18).

Bel and the Dragon Bel was a god worshipped by the king of Babylon. When *Daniel told him that the huge quantities of food and wine offered to the god were not consumed by Bel but by his priests, the king sealed the door of the temple. The next morning the provisions had disappeared but Daniel had strewn ashes on the floor and could show from footmarks that the priests and their families were able to enter by a secret passage and eat each night the offerings to the god. The king then ordered the idol and the temple to be destroyed.

A sacred dragon was also worshipped in Babylon, and Daniel undertook to kill it without using a

King David, from the roof of his house, espies the beautiful **Bathsheba** entering her bath (Hans Memlinc, *c*.1485).

The Christ-Child appearing in a **Beatific Vision** to St Antony of Padua (Murillo, 1656).

weapon. He made cakes of fat, hair and pitch and fed them to the dragon which burst and died. This caused a riot, and the king had Daniel thrown into the lions' den, after depriving the lions of their daily diet of two men and two sheep in order to make them more fierce. An angel appeared to *Habakkuk in Judaea as he was carrying bread to the harvesters and, seizing him by the hair, transported him to the lions' den. Daniel ate the food and thus survived until the seventh day, when the king was surprised to find him alive and well. He was released, his God praised, and his accusers thrown to the lions who devoured them before Daniel's eyes. In some Greek manuscripts these two stories are found attached to the end of the Book of Daniel, and are therefore included in the *Apocrypha of the English Bible although they are not in the Hebrew. They are treated as a separate work, Bel and the Dragon. In the *Vulgate this is placed at the end of the Book of Daniel (Dan 14). Another version of the incarceration in the lion's den is in Dan 6 : 10-24.

Belfry From the old French berfrei, not connected with bells but derived from the Latin berefredus, watch-tower. Strictly, it is the upper part of a tower or turret in which bells are hung, but by extension applied to the belltower itself.

Belial The wicked one, or the destroyer, the personification of uncleanliness and, for St *Paul, the equivalent of *Satan (2 Cor 6 : 15). In the OT the word is not a proper noun, 'son of belial' meaning 'a lawless person'.

Bell There is a tradition that bells were first used in church by St Paulinus (c.353-431), who was made bishop of Nola in Campania in 409, but it is possible that this is no more than a popular etymology for the two medieval Latin words for 'bell', nola and campana. Certainly bells were in use in the time of Pope St *Gregory the Great (c.540-604), who mentions them in his writings. A bell said to have belonged to St Patrick (c.390-c.460) is now in Dublin. By the 8th century, bells were generally part of church furnishings. They were placed in towers and *belfries to summon the faithful to church; rung at the elevation of the *Host; and tolled at 6 am, noon, and 6 pm so that people could join in saying the *Angelus (See *St Bonaventure). A 'passing-bell' announces the death of a *parishioner. A *Mass bell or the Sanctus bell is a small handbell rung at the *altar at the elevation of the Host, and a bell is carried by an *acolyte who accompanies a priest taking the *Blessed Sacrament to the sick or dying. In the Eastern *Orthodox rite, bells mark various points in the *liturgy. Bells are blessed with *holy water by a bishop, popularly called 'the baptism of bells', and prayers are offered in the hope that their sound may bring people to church and frighten away evil spirits. They are the attribute of St *Agatha. (See *Ave Maria.)

'Bell, book and candle' A phrase derived from the ceremony of greater *excommunication. In the presence of twelve *priests carrying candles, a *bishop read the sentence (*anathema), closed the 'book' (the Pontificale Romanum or 'the Roman Pontifical' which contained the words of the ceremony) and the priests threw their candles on the ground to symbolize the extinction of *grace in the soul of the person anathematized. A *bell was tolled as though for one who was dead.

Beloved Disciple An unnamed disciple of *Jesus, assumed to be St *John the Apostle, son of *Zebedee, who plays a central part in four episodes recorded in the Gospel of John. **1** During the *Last Supper he was at table 'leaning on Jesus' bosom' when St Peter beckoned to him to find out who it was that their master meant when he said that one of them would betray him. Then 'lying on Jesus' breast [as he is usually portrayed in depictions of the Last Supper] saith unto him, "Lord who is it?"'. Jesus took a morsel of bread and handed it to *Judas (Jn 13 : 23-6). **2** In his last moments on the *Cross, Jesus saw his mother and 'the disciple whom he loved' standing near and said to his mother, 'Woman behold, thy son!' and to the disciple, 'Behold, thy mother'. The disciple then took St *Mary the Virgin into his own home (Jn 19 : 26-7). In scenes of the *Crucifixion the two are shown standing one on each side of the Cross. **3** St *Mary Magdalene ran to St *Peter and 'the other disciple, the one whom Jesus loved' when she found the tomb empty on *Easter morning. As John was the younger he outstripped St Peter, but stood aside when the latter entered the *Empty Tomb and discovered the abandoned grave clothes. When he went in, he saw, and believed (Jn 20 : 2-8). **4** After the *Resurrection and the miraculous *Draught of Fishes, it was he who recognized the risen *Christ (Jn 21 : 3-7).

Belshazzar's feast King Belshazzar of *Babylon gave a great feast to a thousand of his lords, his wives and his concubines, filling with wine the golden vessels which his father *Nebuchadnezzar had pillaged from the *Temple in Jerusalem. As they drank and praised their gods, fingers of a man's hand wrote on the wall by the candlestick the words, 'Mene, mene, tekel, upharsin'. The king's magicians, astrologers and soothsayers failed to interpret the strange words, so *Daniel was sent for. He told the king that the message meant that he was 'weighed in the balances and found wanting' and that his kingdom would be divided up. That night the Medes invaded Babylon, Belshazzar was slain and Darius the Persian succeeded to his realm (Dan 5). This is the origin of the expression: 'The writing on the wall'.

Bema From the Greek word for a platform, or speaker's rostrum, applied in Early Christian churches to the raised part of the *apse where the *clergy stood. In *Eastern Churches it is used for the raised space at the east end containing the *altar and divided from the *nave by the *iconostasis.

Bench ends The partial enclosure of a *pew, often carved with symbolic decorations.

Benedicite The opening Latin word, 'Bless ye (the Lord)', of the canticle used in liturgical worship, derived from the song of praise uttered by the Three *Holy Children, *Shadrach, *Meshach and *Abednego, as they stood in the *Fiery Furnace. Their adventures were recounted in *The Song of the Three Children*, a short work accepted as canonical in the *Septuagint and *Vulgate Bibles and included in the *Book of *Daniel* (following Vg Dan 3 : 23), but placed among the *Apocrypha in English Protestant versions.

Benedict of Nursia, St Father of Western monasticism. The church of San Benedetto at Norcia (Nursia), near Spoleto, Italy, stands over the place where he and his twin sister St *Scholastica were born to a rich and noble family c.480. Benedict was aged sixteen when he was sent to study in Rome where he was much influenced by the teachings of SS *Jerome and *Augustine. To escape the immorality of those around him he retired to lead a *hermit's life in a cave near Subiaco. His reputation for sanctity attracted other solitaries whom he eventually organized into twelve communities, each governed by a superior. About 529 he settled at Monte Cassino where he became *abbot of the monastery built by him and his fellow *monks. For them he composed a *Rule with great insight and humanity, based on the faithful observance of the three monastic *vows of poverty, chastity and obedience. He is sometimes shown displaying its opening Latin words *Ausculta fili verba magistri*, 'Listen my son to the words of your master'.

The legends associated with St Benedict (depicted as an aged *Benedictine abbot), and his *attributes in art, are derived from episodes in his search for spiritual perfection in the context of community life. When he retired to his cave (*Il Sagro Speco*, now a church, the walls of which have frescoes dating from 1219) he was attended only by his faithful nurse. She borrowed a sieve (in some versions a tray) but unfortunately broke it. Benedict prayed and it was made whole again. He also brought to land the blade of a sickle which a peasant had lost in a stream. (In another version he dipped the broken end of a woodcutter's axe in the lake and made it perfect again.) A fellow hermit, called Romanus, brought him bread which he let down into Benedict's cave in a basket, first ringing a *bell. In an attempt to starve Benedict, the *Devil broke the bell, but Romanus contrived to continue to provide a daily supply of food. Benedict suffered severe sexual temptations which he overcame by rolling in a thorn bush which grew outside his cave. When St *Francis of Assisi went to Subiaco in 1216, the thorns changed to roses. Benedict's companions when he organized his first communities were Maurus and Placidus (later *canonized). Placidus fell into a lake and Benedict told Maurus to walk over the water to save him. Among Benedict's other miracles were the healing of a leper; driving the Devil out of a monk by hitting him with his pastoral staff; reviving a monk killed by falling masonry; and a gardener's son left for dead at the door of his monastery. When he became superior of a community of monks noted

Belshazzar, his concubines and guests, surprised by the fateful 'writing on the wall' (Rembrandt, 1606-69).

A **bench end** from the Chapel of St Nicholas, patron of mariners, King's Lynn, Norfolk, England (c.1415).

St **Benedict of Nursia** presenting to his Benedictine monks the book of his Rule, inscribed with the opening words *Ausculta o fili precepta* (Canterbury, early 11th century).

for their laxity at Vicovaro, they so resented his discipline that they tried to dispose of him with a cup of poisoned wine. Benedict made the *sign of the Cross over the cup and it broke to pieces. A raven carried off a poisoned loaf which they later left for him.

Benedict decided to found his monastery at Monte Cassino on the site of the Temple of Apollo. At his bidding, the populace destroyed the statue of the pagan god. When the foundations of the monastery were being dug a fire-breathing idol came to life, but was destroyed by Benedict's prayers. The Devil sat on a big stone to prevent it being used in the building, but Benedict put him to flight. King Totila of the Goths ravaged the countryside to test Benedict, disguising himself as his armourer when he went to Monte Cassino. Benedict easily penetrated his disguise, reproved him for his wicked ways, and told him that he would die within ten years.

Benedict died of fever on 21 March c.550. His remains were buried with those of St Scholastica under the *high altar of the church at Monte Cassino (destroyed during the Second World War and rebuilt), although it is claimed that they were later transported to Saint-Benôit-sur-Loire, France, where he is also venerated.

Benedictines Monks of the Order of St *Benedict, called *Black Monks after the colour of their *habit. They follow the *Rule of St Benedict and trace their origin to the monastery which he established at Monte Cassino, Italy, c.529. Although their emphasis is on community living and the daily performance of the *Divine Office in *choir, Benedictines have engaged in extensive missionary work and have always fostered the arts and learning. During the barbarian invasions of the early Middle Ages they kept alive the spirit of Western civilization. The original Benedictine abbeys which they founded, including the famous Abbey of Cluny (See *Cluniacs) established c.910, were autonomous and linked through the observance of the Rule of St Benedict. Reforms and administrative changes caused some Benedictine communities to reconstitute themselves as separate *Orders. Among these were *Camaldolese, *Carthusians, *Cistercians, *Maurists and *Trappists. Benedictine *nuns, once *enclosed, later emerged to engage in charitable and educational work. They follow the Rule and revere the memory of St Benedict and his sister, St *Scholastica.

Benediction A blessing (Latin benedictio) pronounced by a member of the *clergy. It is also the short name for a devotional service in the *Roman Catholic Church, the Benediction of the *Blessed Sacrament, in which the congregation is blessed with the *sign of the Cross made with the consecrated *Host enclosed in an *ostensorium, or in less solemn form, in a *ciborium.

Benedictus The first word of the canticle beginning Benedictus Dominus, Deus Israel, 'Blessed be the Lord God of Israel', derived from *Zacharias'

song of thanksgiving at the birth of St *John the Baptist (Lk 1 : 68-79). It is sung in the *Roman Catholic liturgy at *Lauds, and forms part of *Matins in the Anglican Book of Common Prayer (*Prayer Book) of 1662.

Benjamin The youngest son of *Jacob and the favourite younger brother of *Joseph, who was sold into slavery and then rose to be *Pharaoh's chief minister. When a famine struck Canaan, Jacob sent ten of his sons to buy corn in Egypt, but kept Benjamin with him in case harm might befall him. Though they did not know him, Joseph recognized his brothers (who years before had sold him to traders in the desert) and insisted that they should bring Benjamin to Egypt. When they returned, he showered favours on his younger brother, hid a silver cup in his sack of corn and then had him arrested as a thief in order to keep him in Egypt. When he finally made himself known to his brothers, they asked forgiveness for the evil they had done him. Jacob and all his family then left Canaan and settled in Egypt (Gen 42-6 : 1-7).

Bernard of Clairvaux, St Son of a Burgundian nobleman and his saintly wife who, when he was born in 1091, dreamed of a white dog with a black back. This foretold that Bernard would wear the white *mantle and black *scapular of the reformed Benedictine Order at Cîteaux, which he duly entered aged twenty-five, after studying in the University of Paris. When the abbey at Cîteaux became overcrowded, Bernard went with twelve companions to Clairvaux in the significantly named Valley of Wormwood (in Latin Vallis abstinthalis) near La Ferté, on the Aube. In 1115 he established a new *Cistercian community there, which by his death in 1153 had around 350 dependencies, 54 of which were in England. Bernard was canonized in 1174 and made a *Doctor of the Church in 1830.

Although he was active in preaching the second crusade in 1146 and was an eloquent controversialist (which earned him the title of 'the mellifluous doctor' [in Latin Doctor Mellifluus] and a *beehive as one of his *attributes), St Bernard is now remembered for his hymns, his devotional and mystical writings and his ascetic life. As a young man, when assailed by sexual desire at the sight of beautiful women, he threw himself into a half-frozen pond. His victory over other temptations is symbolized by a chained *devil at his feet. Three *mitres on the ground near him recall that he thrice refused to be a *bishop. He is also depicted holding a *cross on which the *Instruments of the Passion are displayed.

St Bernard had a vision of *Christ detaching himself from the Cross to embrace him. St *Mary the Virgin also appeared to him. Once when he was seated at his desk in his study yet unable to write of her perfections because he was ill and his inspiration had failed, she descended to encourage him. On another occasion she moistened his lips with milk from her breast so that his eloquence would be irresistible. It was said that she ordered that Cistercian monks should wear a white *habit in honour of her purity. He is depicted in this habit, and may also wear a *mitre and hold a *crosier because he was *Abbot of Clairvaux.

Bernardino, St Patron saint of his native city, Siena (1380-1444). Left an orphan at the age of seven, he was brought up by aunts in the country where he built a *chapel for prayer and meditation. He studied law in Siena and joined a brotherhood devoted to the care of the sick. He ministered to the victims of the plague which ravaged the city in 1400. Then, in response to a vision that he should look after men's souls as well as their bodies, he gave away all his possessions and became a *Franciscan friar. Later, wishing to live more in accordance with St *Francis' ascetic ideals, he joined a strict branch of the *Order, the *Osservanti*, or *Observants, which had been founded c.1360. The rest of his life was spent in exhausting missionary journeys throughout Italy. He thrice refused bishoprics (hence three *mitres are shown near him), and negotiated the conclusion of a civil war in Perugia where a chapel commemorates his skill as a peacemaker.

His principal *attribute is a tablet with the holy *monogram *IHS displayed in a circle of golden rays, with the words, *Manifestavi nomen tuum hominibus*, 'I have manifested thy name unto the men' (Jn 17 : 6). He used this device in his preaching and it led to his trial by the *Inquisition on a charge of encouraging idolatry. He was acquitted and the fame of his tablets spread rapidly. A man who had made his living making dice and printing playing-cards complained that St Bernard's preaching was depriving him of his customers. Bernard advised him to print instead cards depicting the sacred monogram. These sold in great quantities and the man made a fortune.

Bestiary A book that draws moral instruction from the supposed habits of real *animals and *fabulous beasts. The prototype was the *Physiologus*, mistakenly assumed by some to be the author and not the title of the work, first mentioned in the 5th century and pronounced heretical a century later. In the 11th century a scholar, Theobald, *abbot of Monte Cassino from 1022-35, arranged the information (or misinformation) under the headings of beasts, birds and fishes. These fictional accounts were popularized in medieval encyclopaedias, the main literary sources for *animal symbolism in literature and in art, and especially for the subject-matter of carvings on the underside of *misericords.

Bethany A village on the road to *Jericho, near *Jerusalem and on the east side of the *Mount of Olives. It was the home of SS *Lazarus, *Martha and *Mary Magdalene. According to the *Gospel of John* (Jn 12 : 4-7) it was there that Mary anointed Jesus before his *Entry into Jerusalem. The *Synoptic Gospels say that the anointing took place there at the house of *Simon the Leper (Mk 14 : 1-9; Mt 26 : 1-13) or at the house of *Simon the Pharisee at *Capernaum (Lk 7 : 36-50).

An early 15th-century stone statue of St **Bernard of Clairvaux** in the parish church of Fontaine-les-Dijon, France.

A realistic milking scene from a **Bestiary,** c.1200, illustrating the virtue of generosity.

Bethesda The name of the pool 'with five porches' near the sheep market in Jerusalem, where an *angel (said to be *Raphael) troubled the water at certain seasons. The blind, halt and lame waited around it because of the belief that the first to enter the pool when the angel appeared would be cured. Although it was the *Sabbath, Jesus healed a paralytic who had been lying in wait there for thirty-eight years, saying, 'Take up thy bed, and walk' (Jn 5 : 2-9).

Bethlehem A small town about five miles south of *Jerusalem, the native city of King *David and predicted by the *prophets to be the birthplace of the *Messiah. St *Mary the Virgin went there with her husband St *Joseph to be enrolled for taxation (See *Nativity of Jesus).

Bethsaida A fishing village on Lake Genasareth (Sea of *Galilee), possibly the home of SS *Peter, *Andrew and *Philip (Jn 1 : 44). It was there that the people brought a blind man to Jesus to be touched and healed. Jesus led him by the hand out of the village, spat on his eyes and laid his hands on him. Asked if he could see anything, the blind man replied, 'I see men as trees, walking!'. Jesus laid his hands again on his eyes and the man saw everything clearly (Mk 8 : 22-6).

Betrayal and arrest of Jesus After his *Agony, Jesus rejoined the disciples in the Garden of *Gethsemane and told them to make ready to depart because the one who would betray him was at hand. *Judas arrived while he was speaking, accompanied by a great multitude with swords, and by some slaves sent by the chief priests, the scribes and the elders of the people. (The *Gospel of John* adds that there was also a band of soldiers and that they came with lanterns, torches and weapons [Jn 18 : 3].) Judas had agreed with them that he would single out the man whom they were to arrest by saluting him in the way a disciple would greet his master, with a *kiss. He did so, saying 'Hail, Master'. Jesus said, 'Friend, wherefore art thou come?' (Mt 26 : 49-50). (The *Gospel of John* omits this episode, saying that Judas stood by when Jesus identified himself by proclaiming 'I am he'. Those who had come to arrest him retreated and fell to the ground [Jn 18 : 6].) Some of Jesus' followers who carried swords wanted to resist, and one of them (identified as Simon *Peter) struck off the right ear of the high priest's servant, whose name was *Malchus (Jn 18 : 10). Jesus healed his ear (Lk 22 : 51) and told his disciples to sheathe their swords, 'for all they that take the sword shall perish with the sword' (Mt 26 : 52). He asked the multitude why they should come to seize him with swords and staves, as if here were a robber, when they could have taken him openly in the *Temple where he taught daily (Mt 26 : 47-56; Mk 14 : 43-50; Lk 22 : 47-53; Jn 18 : 2-11, 20).

Jesus' disciples fled as he was led away. A young man (thought to be St *Mark) 'having a linen cloth cast about him over his naked body', followed. When the captors tried to lay hold on him, he ran away naked, leaving the linen cloth in their hands (Mk 14 : 51-2).

Betrothal and marriage of St Mary the Virgin The NT states simply that a virgin named *Mary was betrothed to a man of Nazareth whose name was *Joseph (Mt 1 : 18; Lk 1 : 26), but the account in the apocryphal *Book of *James*, which was popularized in the *Golden Legend*, emphasized not the betrothal or espousal, but the marriage.

Mary was brought up in the *Temple, but when she reached puberty at the age of twelve, *Zacharias 'the High Priest' feared that she would pollute the sanctuary and went to pray for guidance in the *Holy of Holies. An angel told him to assemble all the widowers of Judaea. Each man was to bring a rod or *wand to the Temple and give it to the High Priest. He would pray and hand back the rods and the one which flowered would indicate the man divinely chosen to be Mary's husband. Joseph, an old man with sons, received back the last rod. It flowered and a *dove came out of it and rested on his head. Joseph was reluctant to marry so young a maid, but was warned by Zacharias to remember the punishment of *Korah for disobeying the command of God. Joseph therefore took Mary to his house, but left for the hills to ply his trade as a builder without consummating the union.

The marriage is depicted as taking place in the Temple before the High Priest. Seven maidens serve Mary, and on the other side stand the rejected suitors holding their rods, some breaking them to show their disappointment. Joseph is represented as an old man, a dove hovering above him as Zacharias links his hands to those of the Virgin. A later scene may show the bride and bridegroom being escorted with trumpets to Joseph's house.

Bible A word derived through Latin from the Greek *biblia* 'books', the equivalent of 'the Scriptures', i.e. 'the writings' or *Holy Writ, and thus a collection of those sacred writings which have been accepted into the *canon of inspired works. Although it is a miscellany, the Bible is thought of as one book because it contains the whole plan of salvation, so is the one book for all Christians. It is divided into two parts, or *Testaments – covenants between God and mankind. The Old Testament (OT) is the record of the work of God before the *Incarnation, and the New Testament (NT) God's revelation in Jesus Christ. The original language of the OT was Hebrew, but a translation into Greek, the *Septuagint, was made for the benefit of Greek-speaking Jews. The NT was written in Greek. St *Jerome's Latin version, called the *Vulgate (Vg), was declared by the *Council of Trent to be the official Bible of the *Roman Catholic Church. There were various translations into English, but the version finally accepted was King James' Bible (1611), the so-called *Authorized Version (AV), 'appointed to be read in churches'.

Biblia Pauperum Literally the 'Bible of the Poor', but whether 'poor' in this context meant indigent priests and unlearned clerics with little Latin, or that the work was intended for the instruction of ordinary people, is uncertain. Each book consisted of about forty illustrations. In the centre of each picture was a NT scene with a *typological OT incident on either side, e.g. the *Last Supper is linked with *Melchizedek giving bread and wine to *Abraham, and the *Children of Israel in the wilderness being fed with *manna. Appropriate texts were inserted in the surrounding spaces. St Anschar of Bremen (801-65) was said to have invented the scheme. The invention of block-printing made possible the wide diffusion of these illustrated works.

Bird Symbol of the soul, when it is not particularized. When specified, it has a special reference (See *blackbird, *dove, *eagle, *falcon, *goldfinch, *lark, *owl, *partridge, *peacock, *pelican, *sparrow, *swallow).

Biretta A stiff cap with three or four ridges at the top, worn by clergy when entering or leaving the sanctuary. Rank is indicated by colour: black for *priests, purple for *bishops, red for *cardinals.

Bishop Literally 'overseer' (Greek *episkopos*), a successor of the *Apostles, who is head of a territorial unit of the Church, his *diocese or *see, and is responsible for its administration and the spiritual welfare of those in his charge. He has the authority to confer priestly orders (See *Holy Orders). In art a bishop wears a *mitre and holds a *crosier.

Black A liturgical *colour symbolizing mourning or grief, an alternative to *purple.

Blackbird Symbol of *sin, because of its colour, also of temptation to unchastity because of its sweet and alluring song, like other *birds.

Black Friars The name given in Britain to *Dominicans, members of the Order of St Dominic, who wore, outdoors, a black mantle over their white *habit. The London placename of Blackfriars recalls the location of a former Dominican monastery.

Black Monks The popular name for *Benedictines, who wear a black *habit.

Blaise, St A 4th-century bishop of Sebaste in modern Armenia who took refuge in the forest when Emperor Diocletian ordered the *persecution of Christians. Wild animals assembled fearlessly around his cave to be fed by him. He was discovered one day by hunters who, seeing him unharmed in the company of lions and bears, thought he was a magician and took him captive. In prison he saved the life of a boy who was choking on a fishbone. His mother rewarded Blaise with food and candles. This gave rise to the practice of placing two crossed candles (his *attribute) on the throat of a person suffering from a throat infection, and of invoking the aid of St Blaise. He is one of the *Fourteen Holy Helpers. He was martyred by beheading, first having his

High Priest Zacharias presides at the **Betrothal of St Mary the Virgin** (Master of Flemalle?, early 15th-century).

William Tyndale's translation of the **Bible,** for which he was burnt at the stake. Reprinted in 1537 and attributed to Thomas Matthew.

flesh torn by an iron comb, his chief attribute. For this reason he is the patron saint of wool-combers.

Blessed Sacrament The *Eucharist, one of the seven *sacraments, celebrated at *Mass, the central act of Christian worship. Also used for the consecrated *bread (and in some cases *wine) reserved for the communion of the sick (See *viaticum) in a *tabernacle, its presence denoted by a flame burning in a red lamp. For those who accept the doctrine of *Transubstantiation it is the object of *adoration.

Blind leading the blind A concise and humorous *parable by which Jesus sought to make his disciples aware of the foolishness of accepting instruction from those who were themselves ignorant. He said, 'And if the blind lead the blind, both shall fall into the ditch' (Mt 15 : 14; Lk 6 : 39).

Blue A *colour associated with St *Mary the Virgin, who is often depicted wearing a blue dress or mantle although the liturgical colour fixed for her feasts in the 16th century was white. Blue may have become popular because of its heavenly or sentimental associations.

Boanerges This Greek form of the Hebrew words for 'sons of thunder', was the name given by Jesus to two of his *Apostles, the brothers SS *James the Great and *John, sons of *Zebedee, who with St *Peter formed an intimate triumvirate, the inner circle of Jesus' disciples.

Boar Symbol of *lust (See *pig).

Boat The *attribute of St *Jude, either because he was thought to have been a fisherman or because of his missionary travels, and of St *Nicholas of Myra (or Bari), the patron saint of mariners and *ships.

Boaz One of the ancestors of *Christ who sometimes appears on the Tree of *Jesse and whose story is told in the *Book of Ruth. He was a rich landowner of *Bethlehem who saw *Ruth gleaning the barley left behind by his reapers. When he discovered that she was the widow of one of his kinsmen who had gone to the land of Moab, and that she had refused to abandon her impoverished mother-in-law Naomi, he took her under his protection. After ascertaining that a nearer kinsman was not prepared to fulfil his duty to a relative's widow, he married her himself.

Bonaventure, St A *Franciscan friar (1221-74) who wrote a life of St *Francis and became Minister-General of the *Order in 1257 when aged thirty-six. He devoted his energies to reconciling the various factions within the Order. At the Council of Lyons in 1274 he helped to bring about a temporary reunion between the *Roman Catholic and Greek *Orthodox Churches. His theological writings earned him the title of the Seraphic Doctor. He was canonized by Pope Sixtus IV (1471-84) in 1482 and declared a *Doctor of the

Church in 1588. One of the stories told about him is that he was named Bonaventura ('Good Fortune') because when seriously ill as a child he was laid at the feet of St Francis who prayed for him. He immediately recovered, and St Francis exclaimed *O buona ventura!*. St Bonaventure was so humble that he refrained from going to the altar to receive the *Blessed Sacrament, but an *angel brought it to him. When emissaries from the Pope brought his *cardinal's hat to his home, he told them to hang it on a tree until he had finished washing his dinner plate. He instituted the ringing of the *Angelus bell in honour of the *Annunciation.

Boniface, St A *Benedictine monk from Crediton in Devon, named Winfred or Winfrith (c.675-754) who became a missionary and devoted himself to the conversion of the Germanic pagans in Friesland, Hesse, Thuringia and Bavaria. He was consecrated *bishop in 722 and given the *see of Mainz in 745. He was active in promoting the disciplining of the *clergy in France and Germany, and in founding schools and *monasteries. He was murdered by a band of pagans on the bank of a river near Dokkum while preparing to *baptize a group of converts. His body was taken to Fulda which is the centre of his cult.

Boniface's best-known act was to defy the power of the pagan gods by felling a huge oak tree sacred to Thor. Many were converted when no disaster followed.

Book Symbol of learning when held by SS *Bernard of Clairvaux, *Catherine of Alexandria, *Thomas Aquinas and *Doctors of the Church. Saints who founded religious *Orders or who were renowned for their writings (such as SS *Augustine of Hippo and *Benedict of Nursia) hold a book and a pen. The four *Evangelists hold books representing their respective *Gospels. *Apostles carry gospel books to signify their missionary work. St *Mary the Virgin may hold a sealed book containing the names of the faithful, since 'in thy book all my members were written' (Ps 139 (138) : 16). The *Lamb (*Christ) holds a book with seven seals (Rev 5 : 7).

Book of Common Prayer The *Prayer Book of the Anglican Church, authorized in 1662.

Book of Hours A beautifully illustrated manuscript prayer book used by the laity (usually rich and noble) for devotional purposes. It contained a calendar of saints' days; *feast and *fast days; *psalms; prayers; *antiphons; the services of the canonical *Hours; and the *Hours of St Mary the Virgin (See Little *Office of St Mary the Virgin).

Boss An ornamental projection or knob placed at the intersection of the ribs of a vault or ceiling, often carved with foliage, angels, or other *symbolic figures.

Bottomless pit Either the grave (Jb 17 : 16) or *Hell, ruled over by *Apollyon (Rev 9 : 11).

Boy bishop On the feast of St *Nicholas of Myra (6 December), the patron saint of children, it was customary from the 13th century onwards for choirboys to elect one of their number to be a mock *bishop, whom they obeyed until the feast of the *Holy Innocents, or *Childermass (28 December). The attendant festivities became so scandalous that the practice was suppressed by the time of the *Reformation.

Boyhood of Jesus After spending some years in Egypt (See *Flight into Egypt), the *Holy Family returned to the land of *Israel. An angel had told St *Joseph in a dream that his enemies and *Herod were dead. But he feared the wrath of Archelaus, Herod's son and successor, and decided to go to *Nazareth in Galilee instead of to *Bethlehem, the place of the *Nativity of Jesus, which lay within Archelaus' jurisdiction (Mt 2 : 19-23). Nothing more is said about Jesus in the canonical *Gospels until he was twelve, when his parents took him to *Jerusalem for the *Passover festival (See The *Doctors and Jesus), but there are many apocryphal legends concerning the years between that event and his return from Egypt.

Patriarch Timothy of Alexandria was said to have written a *History of the Virgin Mary* which he claimed was based on information received from St *Mary the Virgin herself. According to this account, the Holy Family wished to travel home by sea, but a storm blew up and the boatmen refused to take them aboard. Jesus stilled the storm, and the rock on which they were waiting moved out of the harbour towards their intended destination. They were pursued at sea by the minions of a powerful sorceress who also followed them on land in a chariot, but Jesus miraculously vanquished them and the Holy Family reached the land of Israel.

(According to another legend, the Holy Family had set out from Egypt overland, St Mary on the *ass which had brought her from Bethlehem, and Jesus riding its foal on which he would eventually ride into Jerusalem on *Palm Sunday. *Salome the Midwife, who had shared their exile with them, is sometimes depicted with them. As they travelled near the River Jordan, villagers heard that Jesus was playing fearlessly with lions and their cubs. The waters of the rivers were held back so they could cross over to witness the strange sight.)

At Nazareth, St Joseph was befriended by a carpenter called Delanos who enabled him to set up business on his own account. Jesus learned the trade from his earthly father. He was a model child, helping his parents in their domestic duties. The *Gospel of the *Pseudo-Matthew* recounted how he made yokes for oxen, ploughs and bedsteads. He also enabled his father to rectify mistakes in his craft. When the king of Jerusalem ordered a throne, Joseph worked on it for two years, but when he fitted the pieces together he found that two were two spans too short. Jesus miraculously enlarged them so that they reached the required length. He once put cloth into a vat of indigo blue while the dyer was away. When he protested on his return that they should have been of a different

A dramatic rendering of the parable of the **Blind leading the blind** into a ditch (Pieter Brueghel the Elder, c.1525-60).

A **boss** from the ceiling of the muniment room, Westminster Abbey, London, showing St Michael slaying the dragon (mid-13th century).

St **Bonaventure** revealing to St Thomas Aquinas that the source of his great learning is contemplation of the passion of Christ (Zurbarán, 1629. Destroyed 1945).

colour, Jesus dipped them again and they came out in the colours the dyer had wanted.

*Gnostic legends depict a malevolent Jesus. He struck dead a child who had knocked him to the ground, and made blind the people who subsequently accused him of the deed. When St Joseph twisted his ear, he became angry and said, 'Do not vex me. Don't you know I am not your son?'.

At play on the *Sabbath he made twelve sparrows out of clay taken from a muddy pool. When his companions' fathers protested that this broke the Sabbath, he clapped his hands and the model birds came to life and flew away. He walked up a sunbeam, but when his playmates tried to imitate him, they fell to the ground and were hurt. They hid from him in an oven and he changed them into goats (in another version, pigs), but relented and turned them back again into children at their parents' request. He walked on the water of a deep pond, while those who followed him were drowned.

He confounded his teacher *Zaccheus by reciting the alphabet at the first lesson, and in one version caused his master to fall down dead when he hit him on the head. In contrast he healed two boys, one said to be the future St *James the Less and the other St *Simon the Zealot, of the bite of a serpent which attacked them when they were gathering straw (or, in another version, taking eggs from a partridge's nest).

Bramble Like the *acacia, thought to be the *burning bush in which God appeared to *Moses, and thus a symbol of the perpetual *virginity of St *Mary the Virgin, because it burned with fire but 'was not consumed' (Ex 3 : 2).

Brazen serpent The brass image of a *serpent set up on a *Tau or T-shaped pole by *Moses when the *Israelites in the wilderness were suffering from snake bites. All who looked at it were healed (Num 21 : 8-9). Jesus used it as an OT type of his own *redemption of mankind, saying, 'And as Moses lifted up the serpent in the wilderness, even so must the Son of man be lifted up' (Jn 3 : 14).

Bread Symbol of the body of *Christ, recalling his words at the institution of the *Eucharist at the *Last Supper, 'This is my body' (Mk 14 : 22; Mt 26 : 26; Lk 22 : 19). St *Philip, as patron saint of bakers, has loaves of bread as his *attribute.

Brendan, St An Irish abbot (c.484-c.577) born near Tralee, Ireland, called 'the Elder' to distinguish him from St Brendan of Birr, 'the Younger' (490-573). He made a missionary tour through Wales and Scotland. A tradition dating from the 9th century credits him with sailing westwards from Kerry, Ireland, on a journey lasting seven years during which he discovered a beautiful land thought to be part of the American continent.

Brethren of the Lord The *Synoptic Gospels mention four sons – James, Joseph, Judas and Simon – and four unnamed daughters as belonging to the family of Jesus in Nazareth. As Jesus was said to be St *Mary the Virgin's firstborn son (Lk 2 : 7) it was assumed by some that these were perhaps also her children, but this interpretation posed a problem for proponents of the dogma of Mary's perpetual *virginity and of the belief that she bore only one child, conceived by the *Holy Spirit. Their explanation was that 'firstborn' did not imply other children and that the Aramaic word for 'brethren' could also be used in the sense of 'kin'. The young males of the household were, therefore, either half-brothers or sons of St *Joseph by a former marriage (but the idea that he had other children was discounted after the 15th century, when St Joseph was revered as a model of *chastity) and the females were cousins; or all were cousins, sons of Mary, wife of Alphaeus. Another explanation, derived from *apocryphal writings, was that St *Anne (Anna) was married three times, her first union with *Joachim resulting in the birth of St Mary the Virgin. Two later marriages, first to Cleophas (Clopas) and then to Salome produced sons and daughters who in turn married and had children. These grandchildren of St Anne were the 'brethren' mentioned in the Gospels.

At the beginning of his ministry, Jesus' kindred were not convinced of his Messianic claims and even taunted him (Jn 7 : 3-5). At one time they thought he must be mad and tried to take him away from *Capernaum (Mk 3 : 21-31). After the *Resurrection they believed in his divine mission and joined the first Christian community (Ac 1 : 13).

Breviary, Roman A book containing the *Divine Office. It was a 'summary' (Latin *breviarium*) made in the 11th century of the original four volumes, one for each of the four seasons of the year, *Advent, *Christmas, *Lent and *Easter. The traditional Latin texts of 1568 (the *Breviarium Romanum*) and the arrangements of the *Hours at which each Office is said were revised in 1970.

Bridget (Birgitta) of Sweden, St Founder of the *Order of Brigittines and patron saint of Sweden (c.1303-73). She is represented in art in the *habit of her Order: black tunic, white veil, *wimple and a black or red band across her forehead. She may carry a *crosier to indicate that she was an *abbess. A *pilgrim's staff and scrip (or wallet) refers to her many pilgrimages, which took her to the shrine of St *James of Compostela, Rome and the *Holy Land. She was married at fourteen, bore eight children, became lady-in-waiting to the queen and, after her husband's death, devoted herself to a life of penitence and to the affairs of her Order. She ended her days in Rome and was canonized in 1391. Her relics are at Vadstena Abbey, where she had founded a community of *enclosed *monks and *nuns in 1346. She was renowned for her austerity, and slept on a bare mattress with only her cloak to cover her; would put gentian in her mouth on *Fridays; and drop wax on her palms (a candle or taper is one of her *attributes) to remind her of Christ's *wounds. She had the *Bible translated into Swedish and was granted many visions. Her *Revelations*, a book which influenced art, records her prophecies and contains communications from St *Mary the Virgin as to the manner of Jesus' birth and how she endured his *Passion.

Brief A letter, less formal than a papal *bull, issued by the papal chancery and signed with the Fisherman's *ring; usually requesting contributions for the building or maintenance of churches or for charitable objects.

In England, in the 17th and 18th centuries, briefs were sent under royal mandate to *parishes permitting collections for some special charitable purpose. These were read from the *pulpit and gifts were collected at the church door by the parish clerk.

Brigittines *Nuns of the Order of the Most Holy Saviour, founded by St *Bridget of Sweden in 1346, who follow the *Rule of St Augustine. They wear a grey or black *habit, are *enclosed and devote their time to contemplation and prayer for the relief of souls in *Purgatory. They have a special *Office which includes the recitation of the whole *psalter in the course of a week and lessons taken from St Bridget's writings. Each day at *Vespers the members of the two sides of the *choir ask each other's pardon for any offences which they may have committed one to another.

Bruno, St Founder of the *Carthusian Order (c.1033-1101). Of a noble family of Cologne, he studied and taught theology at Rheims. The death of his tutor, Raymond Diocrès, canon of the cathedral, who acknowledged his secret sins and said that he was justly condemned, had a profound affect on him. He denounced his *archbishop who had obtained his see by *simony, and was dismissed from his post. In 1046, seeking solitude, he went with six companions to La Grande Chartreuse, a remote and wild place in the mountains near Grenoble. St *Hugh, Bishop of Grenoble, having been warned of their coming when he dreamed of seven stars, gave them land to build their monastery. There they lived their solitary and austere life of fasting and penance, supporting themselves by copying manuscripts. Once it was reported to St Hugh that the monks had broken their vow not to eat meat. He found them in a trance before the untouched food which had been delivered to them in error. He made the *sign of the cross and the meat was turned into turtles which, being fish, they could eat.

Pope Urban II (1088-99), who had taught Bruno at Rheims, summoned him to Rome, but he was unhappy there, longing for his monastic solitude. He was offered and refused the *see of Reggio di Calabria (a *mitre is shown at his feet) and was then permitted to found another monastery at La Torre, near Squillace in Calabria. Other foundations followed, called after La Chartreuse, in English, *Charterhouse. Bruno died when on a visit to one of them at Stefano-in-Bosco. His sorrowing monks surrounded his bier.

Bull In the OT, a manifestation of the god *Baal. Its pizzle was a phallic symbol. Worship of the

An imaginary episode from the **Boyhood of Jesus**, by Sir J.E. Millais (1850). He has pierced his palm, foretelling the Crucifixion. SS Anne, Joseph and Mary the Virgin express concern and the youthful St John the Baptist brings a symbolic bowl of water.

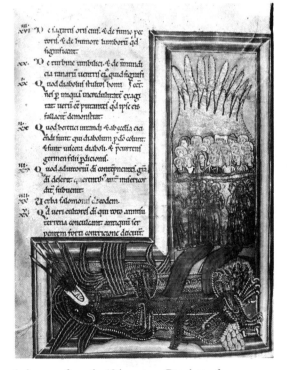

Index page from the 12th-century **Breviary** of St Hildegarde, Bingen, Germany, showing the dragon (sin and death) overcome and the virtuous saved.

horned bull-god was denounced by OT *prophets who abhorred the orgiastic rites with which it was associated.

In art a bull is the *attribute of St *Sylvester who confounded his opponents by restoring a dead bull to life and of St *Eustace who was roasted alive in a brazen bull. A similar story is told of St *Polycarp, although another version is that he was roasted in an oven when he refused to adore a pagan idol. A bull is also a sign of the *zodiac (See *Taurus).

Bull, papal A solemn and formal letter (distinct from a *brief or an *encyclical) in which a *Pope makes an official pronouncement on a matter of great importance. Each bull is named after the opening words of its text, so *Apostolicae curae* is the one issued in 1896 by Pope Leo XIII (1878-1903) which denied the validity of the *ordination of *Anglican clergy. The word 'bull' is derived from the lead seal (Latin *bulla*) which is attached to the document. The appointment of a *bishop is authorized by a papal bull.

Bulrush Because *Moses was hidden in the bulrushes by the River Nile and was rescued by *Pharaoh's daughter, the bulrush symbolizes salvation. It may also be a warning that those who forget God perish (Jb 8 : 11-13).

Burning bush Symbol of the perpetual *virginity of St Mary the Virgin because, as God spoke to *Moses from a bush (thought to be an *acacia or *bramble) which seemed to be on fire, but which 'was not consumed' (Ex 3 : 2), so Mary remained intact although she conceived a child by the Holy Spirit (See *Virgin birth of Jesus).

Burse A flat, square pocket or purse, covered with silk of the liturgical *colour of the season, in which the *corporal is kept.

Buskins Ceremonial silken socks of the liturgical *colour of the season, embroidered with gold thread, a *vestment worn by a *bishop at pontifical High *Mass.

Butterfly Symbol of the *Resurrection because it emerges from a chrysalis (See *wheel).

BVM Initial letters of *Beata Virgo Maria*, 'Blessed Virgin Mary', St *Mary the Virgin.

Caesar The family name of Caius Julius Caesar and the title of Roman emperors in the NT: *Augustus (Lk 2 : 1); Tiberius (Mt 22 : 21) and *Nero (Ac 25 : 8). The most notable reference to these hated rulers is in the scene concerning the tribute to be paid to Caesar (MT 22 : 15-22; Mk 12 : 13-17; Lk 20 : 20-6), when *Pharisees tried to trap Jesus into an admission which would compel the Roman authorities to take action against him as a rebel. They knew that he cared for no man but

taught the way of God, so they asked him whether it was in accordance with Jewish law to pay taxes to imperial Caesar. Jesus asked them to show him a Roman coin of the type used to pay the tribute and to tell him whose effigy was on it. When they replied 'Caesar's', he said, 'Then render to Caesar the things that are Caesar's and to God the things that are God's'. This silenced them.

Caiaphas, Joseph *Jewish High Priest (18-37) and son-in-law of *Annas. He presided over the *Sanhedrin when Jesus was brought for trial after his *betrayal by *Judas and arrest by the High Priest's men in the Garden of *Gethsemane. Fearful that the growing popularity of Jesus might cause the Roman occupying troops to act swiftly to put down an incipient rebellion, Caiaphas, as a conformist *Sadducee, had decided that it was expedient 'that one man should die for the people' rather than that the whole nation should perish (Jn 11 : 47-53). That night, in the presence of the elders and the scribes, and with Annas seated beside him, he attempted to trap Jesus into an admission of blasphemy, for which the punishment was death. False witnesses spoke against Jesus, but their testimonies were contradictory. When two men alleged that Jesus had claimed that he could destroy the *Temple and rebuild it in three days, Jesus remained silent. Caiaphas then put the crucial question: Was he the *Christ, the promised *Messiah?, to which Jesus replied, 'I am'. Caiaphas then tore his robes, as a sign that he had heard blasphemy, and the Sanhedrin declared Jesus guilty and deserving death. They had no power to carry out the sentence so, in the morning, after *mocking him, they bound him and took him for his trial before *Pilate (Mt 26 : 57-68; Mk 14 : 53, 55-64; Lk 22 : 54, 66-71; Jn 18 : 24, 28: these accounts differ in detail but are harmonized in art).

After the *Crucifixion, Caiaphas continued to persecute the Church. SS *Peter and *John were brought before him because of the miracle they had performed in the *Temple (Ac 4 : 5-22). He had St *Stephen, the first *martyr, put to death (Ac 7 : 59) and sent St *Paul (then called Saul) to extirpate the new heresy in Palestine and as far as Damascus (Ac 8 : 3; 9 : 1-2). The ruins of the High Priest's house in which the trial of Jesus took place, and containing the prison where Christians were punished, lie under the Church of St Peter in *Jerusalem. It seems likely that this *trial was interpolated to discredit the *Jews and clear the Romans (who perpetrated the *Crucifixion) of all blame.

Cain The first child of *Adam and *Eve, conceived after their *Expulsion from Paradise. He was a tiller of the soil. God rejected his sacrifice although he accepted that of his younger brother *Abel. Cain therefore slew Abel (traditionally with the jawbone of an ass) and was thus the first murderer. When God asked Cain where his brother was he replied 'I know not. Am I my brother's keeper?', but Abel's blood cried out for vengeance. God ordained that Cain would be accursed and become a wanderer on the face of the earth. Cain protested that his punishment was greater than he could bear and that he would be killed as an outlaw. God put a mark on his forehead to prevent this happening (not, as is popularly supposed, to brand him as a murderer – 'the mark of Cain'). Cain settled to the east of *Eden in the land of Nod, where he built a city which he called after his first son *Enoch (Gen 4 : 1-18). Abel was avenged when *Lamech, a hunter, mistaking Cain for a wild animal, slew him with an arrow – a legend based on his admission, 'I have slain a man to my wounding, and a young man to my hurt' (Gen 4 : 23).

Caladrius (Charadrius) A fabulous white bird with a neck like a swan, yellow legs and yellow beak (whence its power to cure jaundice, a disease which turns the skin yellow). Its droppings placed on the eyelids were said to be effective against blindness. To find out whether an invalid would live or die, a caladrius was to be placed by the sickbed. If it turned its back the patient would die. If it faced the patient, it would absorb the illness and the patient would live.

Calced An adjective from the Latin *calceatus*, 'shod', applied to certain branches of some religious *Orders, such as the *Carmelites, to indicate that they wear shoes or sandals. They are thus distinguished from their barefoot or *discalced brethren who follow the unmitigated *Rule of their Order.

Calendar, Christian A list of the seasons, weeks and feast days of the Christian *year. Fixed or immovable feasts occur on the same date each year, e.g. *Christmas, *Epiphany and *saints' days. Movable *feasts are those celebrated on dates which vary from year to year according to the calculation of the date of *Easter, e.g. *Maundy Thursday and *Whit Sunday.

In outline, the traditional Christian calendar (the 'Proper of Time' is based on the life of *Christ, as distinct from the 'Proper of the Saints' which lists the days on which saints are commemorated) is based on two cycles, *Christmas and *Easter, each with its period of preparation, as follows:

1 *Christmas cycle*
 *Advent
 *Christmas Eve
 *Christmas
 *Circumcision (or *Naming) of Christ
 *Epiphany
2 *Easter cycle*
 *Septuagesima
 *Sexagesima
 *Quinquagesima
 *Ash Wednesday
 *Quadragesima
 *Passion Sunday
 *Palm Sunday
 *The days of *Holy Week (including *Maundy Thursday, *Good Friday and *Holy Saturday)
 *Easter
 *Low Sunday

A Roman coin with the head of **Caesar**.

Cain, enraged because his sacrifice has been rejected (symbolized by the smoke from his altar turned earthwards), slays Abel with the jawbone of an ass (Lucas van Leyden, 1529).

*Ascension Day
*Pentecost (*Whitsunday)
*Trinity Sunday
*Corpus Christi

Calling of the Apostles *Jesus began his public ministry by assembling around him twelve *Apostles. The first to be called were the brothers SS *Peter and *Andrew, called when they were casting their nets into the Sea of *Galilee (of Genesaret, or of Tiberias). He said he would make them fishers of men. They left their nets and followed him. A little further on SS *James the Great and *John the Evangelist, sons of *Zebedee, were mending their nets. They too left their father and his hired servants and followed Jesus (Mt 4 : 18-22; Mk 1 : 16-20). The miraculous *Draught of Fishes (Lk 5 : 1-11) is a variant of this narrative. In the *Gospel of John*, St Andrew is stated to have been a disciple of St *John the Baptist. When the latter pointed to Jesus and said, 'Behold the Lamb of God' (*Ecce Agnus Dei*), he went home and brought his brother, St Peter, to Jesus (Jn 1 : 35-42).

Calvary, Mount The site, once outside the walls of *Jerusalem, where criminals were executed. The place of Jesus' *Crucifixion was called in Aramaic *Golgotha, the place of the skull (Latin *calvaria*, 'skull'), so named, according to one tradition, because *Adam's skull was found there.

Calvinist One who accepts the theological system expounded by John Calvin (1509-64) of Geneva, which is based on the belief that God predestines some to everlasting life and others to *damnation. Salvation comes through faith, not 'works' or deeds. But God's *grace is permanent.

Camaldolese A religious *Order founded at Camaldoli, near Arezzo, Italy, in about 1012, by St *Romuald of Ravenna (c.952-1027). He intended to provide within the Benedictine *Rule a hermit's life of penance and solitude as practised by the *Desert Fathers. Members of the Order wear a white *habit and white *scapular.

Camel Symbol of humility because it kneels to receive its burden. In particular indicative of the humility of *Christ who humbled himself to bear the sins of mankind. A camel also signifies temperance and prudence because it stores up water. Because it was believed that a female camel went on heat mad with *lust and that the coition of camels lasted a whole day, the camel also represented nymphomania or unrestrained sexual desire.

Cana, the wedding feast at Jesus, his mother St *Mary the Virgin and his disciples, attended a wedding feast at Cana (a village in *Galilee identified as the modern Kefr Kenna, northeast of *Nazareth). When the wine ran out, Jesus instructed the servants to fill six stone pots with water. When they drew off the water they found it had been changed into *wine. When he tasted it,

the chief steward (usually depicted as fat and jovial) said to the bridegroom, 'Every man setteth on first the good wine; and when men have drunk freely, then that which is worse; but thou hast kept the good wine until now' (Jn 2 : 1-11). The Latin for 'ruler of the feast', or 'chief steward' is *architrinculus*, but this word was ignorantly assumed to be his personal name when it appeared alongside him in paintings or stained glass. He is therefore sometimes described as 'St' Architrinculus.

The presence of Jesus at the feast signifies his sanctification of the institution of marriage. The miracle was one of his *Epiphanies or manifestations, and is thought to show the superiority of the New *Testament over the Old, in that the water of Judaism was changed into the wine of the *Gospel. The six stone jars, 'used for purification after the manner of the Jews', were understood to symbolize the six historical *ages of the old world (the seventh being the age of *Christ). Some commentators held that the bride was St *Mary Magdalene and the bridegroom St *John the Apostle, who was so impressed by the miracle that he left his wife and followed Jesus.

Cancer The crab, the fourth sign of the *zodiac, which presides over the period c.22 June to 22 July. In the *Labours of the Months this is a time for haymaking.

Candle Symbol of *Christ, the *light of the world; also of joy at the redemptive presence of the sun of righteousness. Candles of yellow or unbleached beeswax are used frequently in Christian worship. They are carried in processions, lighted during liturgical services and, since the 12th century, have been placed upon the *altar on either side of an altar cross or on the floor beside the altar, in *candlesticks. In the *Church of England altar candles were forbidden in 1549, but in 1890 the use of the two candles was stated to be legal. In the *Roman Catholic Church at least two candles are lit at *Mass, but six are permitted during the *Divine Office of the seven canonical *Hours, and twelve are required at the exposition of the *Blessed Sacrament. Seven candles are used at pontifical High *Mass, an allusion to the 'seven flaming lamps', the seven spirits of God (Rev 4 : 5). Votive candles are personal offerings placed before statues of St *Mary the Virgin and of the saints. A *paschal candle is lighted at *Easter.

Candlemas The popular name for the feast of the *Purification of St *Mary the Virgin, kept on 2 February (in *Roman Catholic and *Anglican calendars now designated the feast of the *Presentation of Christ in the Temple). It concludes the *Christmas cycle and derives its name from the ancient custom of processing on that day with candles, symbolizing the entry of Jesus into the *Temple and emphasizing the theme of the prayers used in the service: Christ as the *light of the world. The *Nunc Dimittis* and the *lumen ad revelationem*, 'a light to lighten the gentiles' are sung.

In the *Meditations on the life of Christ* the procession was understood to commemorate the conclusion of the presentation of Christ in the Temple, when Mary received back the child from *Simeon and she, St *Joseph, St *Anne and 'a vast company of people of all kinds', walked around the altar singing prophetic verses; 'a procession', it is added, 'that is today performed in the whole world'.

Candlestick A holder for a *candle when carried in procession or used liturgically. Romanesque candlesticks were often ornamented with scenes symbolizing the victory of light over darkness. A pendant in the shape of a wheel hanging horizontally from the roof with spikes for a number of candles, represented the city of God, the *Church, descending from *Heaven. Gothic candlesticks were simpler in design, but those of the Renaissance were more elaborate and were constructed on Classical architectural principles. The later seven-branch candlestick (also called *candelabrum*), which is also a symbol of Judaism, was made in imitation of the candlestick of the *Temple in Jerusalem. In his apocalyptic vision (Rev 1 : 12-20) St *John the Divine was shown seven golden candlesticks (the seven Churches of Asia) and in the midst of them one like the Son of Man (*Christ), holding in his right hand seven stars (the *angels of those Churches).

Canon Originally a Greek word meaning 'bar' or 'rod', 'canon' came to signify the rules of an art or a craft. In a Christian context it denotes: the rules regulating the life and discipline of the *Church (Canon Law); the books of the OT and NT regarded as inspired and from which doctrine may be deduced (Canon of Scripture, or *Bible); and the consecratory prayer of the *Mass (Canon of the Mass). As an ecclesiastical title, Canon denotes one of the secular *clergy attached to a *cathedral or collegiate church, either 'residentiary' in an institution, or 'non-residentiary', usually the *priest of a *parish but having certain duties at the cathedral. Canons regular are clerics who live in communities, usually following the *Rule of St Augustine, whence the name Austin (*Augustine) Canons.

Canoness A canoness regular is a member of a religious community of women, the female counterpart of a *canon regular. In France until the French Revolution, and in the Holy Roman Empire until 1806, there were secular canonesses, women of noble birth who lived in *convents and observed the *Divine Office, but who were free to leave and marry if they wished.

Canonicals *Vestments ordered by Church Law (*Canon Law) to be worn by the clergy while officiating.

Canonization Since the late 10th century the formal and solemn inscription in the catalogue (or 'canon') of *saints of the name of a deceased person who has already passed through the process of *beatification. The granting of saintly status rests

At the marriage feast at **Cana** Jesus turns water into wine (bronze column in Hildesheim Cathedral, Germany, c.1020).

Reconstruction of a 12th-century seven-branch gilt bronze **candlestick,** from St-Rémi Cathedral, Rheims.

with the *Pope and follows lengthy investigation by the Congress of Rites and the authentication of at least two miracles. Once canonized, the saint may be accorded liturgical veneration. In the *Orthodox Church canonization is usually made by a *synod of *bishops. (*See* *Devil's advocate.)

Canopy The structure covering an altar. (*See* *baldacchino); also the covering suspended over a throne or carried over a dignitary in a procession.

Canticle A sacred chant (other than a *psalm), with words from the *Bible, sung in the *Divine Office. 'Canticles' or 'Canticle of Canticles' is the Vg designation of the *Song of Songs.

Capernaum An important town (Tell Hum) on the northwest shore of the Sea of *Galilee where Jesus was active in the first part of his ministry following his rejection in *Nazareth. It was there that he cured the *Centurion's servant; caused the Temple *Tribute Money to be produced from the fish's mouth; and performed many other *miracles, including the raising of *Jairus' daughter.

Capital The uppermost part of a column or pilaster, in Romanesque and Gothic architecture often ornamented with symbolic designs, carved figures or scriptural and legendary scenes.

Capricorn The goat, the tenth sign of the *zodiac which governs the period from *c.*22 December to *c.*19 January. In the *Labours of the Months this is a time for salting pigs, baking, and preparing for the *Christmas feast. Capricorn is depicted as having the forepart of a goat and a curved or spiral fishtail. This possibly recalls the Greek legend of the god Pan, who hid in a river when he fled from the monster Typhon and emerged with his upper half changed into that of a goat and the part which had been in the water into the tail of a fish. (Pan is usually represented as a man with a goat's limbs.)

Capuchins *Observants (i.e. those who wished to observe the primitive and austere *Franciscan Rule) who were organized by Matteo di Bassi of Urbino (*d.*1552). The name by which they are popularly known is derived from their pointed *cowl (Italian *capuche*).

Cardinal Originally a *priest permanently attached to a *church. Later, priests of churches in Rome who came to compose a college in which, gathered in consistory or assembly, they advised the *Pope. Since 1179, when they took over the interim government of the *Roman Catholic Church, cardinals have the exclusive right of electing a new Pope. They themselves are nominated by the Pope, wear *red, and are in three ranks: cardinal-deacons, cardinal-priests and cardinal-bishops. Those who reside in Rome are called Cardinals of the Court. Notable cardinals depicted in art are SS *Bonaventure and *Charles Borromeo.

Carmel, Mount A sacred promontory on a range of hills at the foot of which lies Haifa. It was the scene of the contest between *Elijah and the prophets of *Baal. The *Carmelite order of friars, who claim Elijah as their founder, take their name from the mountain.

Carmelites Members of the Order of Our Lady of Mount *Carmel, an *Order which claims *Elijah as its founder. Its austere *Rule was granted in 1206 by St Albert, Patriarch of Jerusalem, to the Hermits of Mount Carmel. This Rule was mitigated in 1432 by Pope Eugenius IV (1431-47). The Order was reformed by St *Teresa of Ávila in the 16th century. Since then there have been two branches, the *Calced Carmelites who observe the mitigated Rule, and the *Discalced Carmelites who keep the primitive Rule (*See* *White Friars).

Carnation Symbol of pure love and thus associated with St *Mary the Virgin and with brides, bridegrooms and newly married couples.

Carnival A period of revelry and feasting before the rigours of *Lent. It ends at midnight on *Shrove Tuesday.

Carol Originally a medieval round dance accompanied by singing, later a song of the people to sing at church festivals at *Easter and, more especially in recent times, at *Christmas. Wynkyn de Worde printed the first English collection of carols in 1521. Many familiar carols were composed in the 19th century, e.g. 'Good King *Wenceslas'.

Carthusian Order A contemplative *Order which traces its origins to 1084 when St *Bruno and seven companions sought solitude in Chartrousse, a village near Grenoble in the Alps of Dauphiné. The mother-house of the *Order, La Grande Chartreuse, was built near the site. St *Hugh of Lincoln founded the first of the English monasteries, the *Charterhouse at Witham, Somerset.
Carthusians wear a white *habit with a white leather belt. Each lives in his *cell, fasts once a week on bread and water, abstains from meat and observes complete silence except on certain permitted occasions. The brethren assemble for *Mass, to chant the *Divine Office and to eat together on *feast days. Otherwise they spend their time in mental prayer, study and manual labour.

Cassock A long garment (from the Italian *casacca*, 'overcoat') reaching to the ankles. The official *dress of the *clergy, black for secular clergy (or white in tropical countries), violet or purple for a *bishop, red for a *cardinal and white for a *Pope. Other *colours are used by members of certain religious *Orders.

Cat One of the *animal forms assumed by the *Devil, hence the familiar of a *witch. As a cat tries to catch mice, so the Devil tries to capture the soul.

She-cats were thought of as promiscuous and thus represented lascivious women who relentlessly pursued men.

Catacombs The name given in Rome (and later elsewhere) to underground burial places. The first were on the road 'to the hollows' (Latin *ad catacumbas*) used by Jews and Christians for many centuries for the inhumations they preferred to the Roman custom of cremation. These cemeteries were accidentally rediscovered in 1578. They were labyrinthine galleries with niches in the walls for the bodies of the faithful departed. In semi-circular areas relatives and friends would gather for commemorative celebrations of the *Eucharist. Walls were decorated with symbolic and biblical scenes on the theme of salvation.

Catafalque A wooden structure (Italian *catafalso*, 'scaffold') covered with a black *pall, surrounded by six *candles, standing outside the *communion rails. It bears the corpse lying in state at a funeral or represents the deceased person when a requiem *Mass is said on the third, seventh and thirtieth anniversaries of death.

Catechumen An adult receiving instruction in the faith before *baptism.

Catharist From the Greek *katharos*, 'pure', a member of one of the *heretical sects, the best known being the Albigensians in southern France and the Bogomils in Constantinople, who from the 5th to the 11th century threatened the Catholic faith. They held that the material world was created by an evil god; that procreation was a sin because it resulted in a pure soul entering the evil world; and that the aim of life was to liberate the soul from the flesh through strict discipline. They were divided into the 'perfect' *(Perfecti)* who had received the *Holy Spirit and could accept the rigours demanded of them, and those who lived an ordinary life, until they neared death when they were granted the *consolamentum*, the reception of the Holy Spirit by the laying on of hands. If they recovered they were obliged to live like the 'perfect'. St *Dominic and the *Inquisition were charged with the suppression of this *heresy in Spain, France and northern Italy.

Cathedral A *church in which a *bishop has his chair (Latin *cathedra*) or *throne, symbolizing the bishop's authority as teacher. It originally stood in the centre of the curved wall of the *apse behind the high *altar, but is now generally placed in the sanctuary at the side of the high altar. *Popes speak *ex cathedra*, 'from the throne', when making an official pronouncement.

Catherine of Alexandria, St One of the *Fourteen Holy Helpers, among the most popular saints of the Middle Ages, but whose existence is doubtful (and whose feast was suppressed in 1969). Her story, diffused through the *Golden Legend*, may have been an elaboration of the account given by *Eusebius in his *Ecclesiastical History* (Bk viii.

A **Carthusian** monk outside his monastery holding a rosary (1695).

The west front of Chartres **Cathedral,** with rose window.

14) of the unnamed lady of Alexandria in the 4th century who withstood the lustful advances of Maximin, or Maxentius. ('Catherine' may be from the Greek *katharos*, 'pure'.) Legend made her the daughter of Princess Sabinella of Egypt and Costus, the son of Constantine Chlorus by his first wife. (His second wife, Empress *Helena, was the mother of Emperor *Constantine.) At Catherine's birth an *aureole was seen around her head. When she was fourteen her father died and she became queen (and wears a *crown), but she lived a holy life and devoted her time to the study of philosophy (a *book being one of her *attributes), ignoring repeated requests that she should marry. St *Mary the Virgin appeared to a hermit in the desert near Alexandria and ordered him to tell the queen that her husband would be Jesus. When he showed Catherine a picture of the Virgin and Child she was moved to love him and regarded herself henceforth as his bride. This is the origin of the *Mystic marriage of St Catherine*, a subject frequent in art since the 14th century. The *Christ-Child seated on the Virgin's lap inclines towards the kneeling figure of Catherine and places a ring on her finger, symbolizing her spiritual betrothal.

When Christians were being persecuted by Emperor Maxentius, Catherine pleaded with him to spare them. He summoned the most learned philosophers in his realm to debate the truth of her faith with her, but she confounded them with her learning and they were all converted to Christianity. Maxentius then cast her into prison, hoping to starve her into renouncing her beliefs, but *angels brought her food. The empress and her attendants, impressed by her courage, became Christians. They were executed, but Catherine was spared because the emperor lusted after her and offered to marry her. She refused because she was already betrothed to *Christ. (She may display the words, *Ego me Christo sponsam tradidi*, 'I gave myself as a bride to Christ'.) Maxentius, enraged by her steadfastness, ordered her to be torn to death between spiked wheels. (Her *attribute is a wheel with curved blades, the origin of the catherine wheel firework.) Fire from Heaven (or lightning, or angels) shattered the wheels (so her attribute is sometimes shown broken in half) and she was beheaded (a *sword is another of her attributes). Her body was placed in a marble *sarcophagus. It was carried by angels to the monastery of St Catherine at Mount Sinai, where it was discovered in the late 8th century.

Catherine of Bologna, St Patron saint of Bologna (1413-63), canonized by Pope Benedict XIII (1724-30). Her body reposes in the convent of the *Poor Clares (Strada San Mammolo) of which she became *abbess after being a maid-of-honour in the court of the prince of Ferrara. She wrote a book of prophecies published in 1511 which enjoyed considerable fame. She was an artist (her *attribute is a paint brush) and she may be shown painting a picture of the *Crucifixion or nursing the *Christ-Child, a reference to her vision one *Christmas Eve when St *Mary the Virgin appeared to her and placed the infant Jesus in her arms.

Catherine of Genoa, St Visionary and mystic (1447-1510), author of a treatise *On *Purgatory* and *A Dialogue between the Soul and Body*. Her noble family made her enter into a marriage of convenience at the age of sixteen with Julian Adorno, who disliked her and made her life wretched. Her prayers and the loss of his fortune brought him to the good life. They lived in continence until his death in 1497, Catherine devoting herself to the care of the sick despite her own severe illnesses. She was granted profound spiritual experiences in her later life. She is the patron saint of Genoa.

Catherine of Siena, St Mystic (1347?-80), renowned for her letters and other spiritual writings, canonized in 1461, patron saint of Siena, made *Doctor of the Church in 1970. The youngest of the numerous family of Giacomo Benincasa, a wool-dyer. Catherine experienced visions from an early age and became a *Dominican *tertiary when she was fourteen, living a life of great austerity in a room in her father's house, from which she emerged only to tend the sick. In time her saintly renown attracted followers and her insight into worldly affairs caused her advice to be sought by the powerful. Towards the close of her life she began to intervene in ecclesiastical politics. She went to Avignon in an attempt to persuade Pope Gregory XI (1371-8) to end the excommunication of the people of Florence and later influenced him to return to Rome. She secured support for Pope Urban VI (1378-89) in 1378 against the antipope who had been elected by French *cardinals. In Rome she promoted the reform of the Dominican Order.

Catherine never learned to write and is sometimes shown dictating to a clerk. She is dressed in the *habit of a Dominican tertiary (black cloak over a white robe), holding a book (her *Dialogue*, translated into English in the 15th century as *The Orchard of Syon*), or displaying the *stigmata which were imprinted on her hands and feet in Pisa in 1375 when she was meditating on the *Crucifixion. A *crown of thorns shown near her is a reference to how, when taunted by some jealous nuns, she told her sorrows to *Christ. He offered her the choice of a crown of gold and jewels or a crown of thorns, and she chose the latter in remembrance of his *Passion. A *lily is the emblem of her purity; a burning heart in her hand is a symbol of her mystical fervour; and a *rosary a reference to her Dominican devotions. On the Sunday after her festival (formerly 30 April but changed in 1969 to 29 April) Sienese children dressed as saints and angels escort her effigy through the city.

Catholic An adjective meaning 'universal', but with particular reference to the universality of the Christian faith, as in 'the Holy Catholic Church', meaning the whole body of Christians. At the time of the Eastern *Schism around 1054, which led to the separation of the Latin-speaking West and the Greek-speaking East, the adherents of the former described their tradition as Catholic and of the latter as *Orthodox. The *Reformation of the 16th century further divided the West into *Roman Catholics, who acknowledged the supremacy of the *Pope in Rome, and *Protestants of the Reform who did not accept his authority and referred to him as the Bishop of Rome. (Doctrinal differences, particularly with regard to *Transubstantiation, the *Immaculate Conception and the *Assumption of St Mary the Virgin also divide Roman Catholic and Protestant.) The Old Catholics separated from Rome because they could not accept certain definitions of doctrine (particularly papal *infallibility) by the First *Vatican Council (1869-70).

The *Church of England (*Anglican) considers itself to be both Catholic and Reformed, some of its members emphasizing the Protestant tradition (*Evangelicals, Low Church), others the Catholic (*High Church, *Anglo-Catholic). The *Oxford (or Tractarian) Movement which began in 1833, led to a revival of interest in Catholic theology and practice especially with regard to *vestments and ceremonial.

Cecilia, St A 2nd- or 3rd-century Roman virgin martyr (who holds a *palm branch). She was reputed to be the Christian daughter of Cecilus, a Roman patrician. Although wishing to remain chaste, she obeyed her father's command to marry a nobleman called Valerian. On their wedding night she told her husband that he must respect her vow of perpetual virginity otherwise he would be punished by an *angel who watched over her. He agreed on condition that he might see the angel, and was told that if he visited her mentor St Urban – who was instructing Christians in the *catacombs – he would see the angel on his return. When he came back he found the bridal chamber filled with the sound of heavenly music and the sweet fragrance of flowers. An angel presented him and his bride with a crown of roses and lilies (her earliest *attribute). He and his brother Tibertius were later baptized by St Urban, but were imprisoned because they preached the *Gospel. They converted Maximus, their jailor, and all three were put to death. Governor Almachius of Rome wished to obtain Valerian's property and ordered his widow to sacrifice to the pagan gods. When she refused, he had her shut up in her bathroom which was then made as hot as possible so that the steam would suffocate her, but she emerged unharmed. Next, an executioner was sent to behead her and failed three times (a fourth stroke was not allowed by Roman law). She is thus shown with three wounds in her neck. She lay for three days on the marble floor of her palace before her soul left her, and during that time was able to arrange with St Urban for the disposal of her wealth for the benefit of the Christian community.

Cecilia was buried in the catacomb of Callistus. In 817 a vision enabled Pope St Paschal I (817-24) to discover her white marble *sarcophagus. He placed it, together with the relics of St Urban, Valerian, Tiburtius and Maximus, in the crypt of the church of St Cecilia-in-Trastevere in Rome. When the church was being restored in 1599 Cecilia's sarcophagus was opened and disclosed

St **Catherine of Alexandria** in prison, blessed by her bridegroom, Christ, refuting the devilish arguments of a pagan philosopher (alabaster, Nottingham, England, 15th century).

Heavenly music and a crown of roses and lilies reward St **Cecilia** for observing her vow of perpetual virginity even in her bridal chamber (Bernardo Cavallino, 1645).

her beautiful uncorrupted body. Cardinal Sfondrato ordered the sculptor Stefano Maderno (1576-1636) to make a carving of the remains. The statue, showing her reclining on her side, was placed in the church.

In 1584 the newly founded Academy of Music in Rome chose Cecilia as its patron saint. St Cecilia's Day (22 November) became a yearly festival of music. Her patronage may derive from a misunderstanding of the word *organum*, Latin for 'musical instrument', in the *Acts* of her martyrdom, in which it was said that at her wedding feast 'as the musical instruments were sounding, she sang in her heart to the Lord', praying that she might remain unsullied. This gave rise to the legend that she invented the *organ, which she is shown playing. She may also be depicted with other musical instruments, or holding a scroll of music.

Cedar of Lebanon Symbol of St *Mary the Virgin because of its beauty; the healing virtues attributed to its sap; and its height, which raises it over all other trees, as the Virgin is exalted above all other women.

Celebrant The priest who says or sings *Mass or *Eucharist, as distinct from those who assist him. He may now be called the president because he presides at the celebration. When there is more than one celebrant it is called concelebration.

Cell A room in which a member of a religious community lives.

Cenobite (Coenobite) From the Greek *koimos*, 'common', and *bios*, life. One who, unlike a *hermit, lives in a religious community.

Censer Another name for a *thurible, the metal vessel in which *incense is burned. It is an *attribute of *Aaron.

Centaur A mythical creature, a man to its waist and a horse below. When depicted as an archer it represented virtue driving out vice. In contrast, because of its reputed predilection for women, it symbolized *lust. As a hunter it symbolized the *Devil who hunts souls.

Centurion, just *See* *Longinus.

Centurion's servant, healing the A miracle performed by Jesus in *Capernaum. A centurion who despite being in Roman service was well-disposed to the *Jews, begged Jesus to heal his servant who was lying paralysed at home in terrible distress. When Jesus said he would go to the centurion's house, the centurion protested that he was not worthy to receive Jesus under his roof and begged him but to say the word and the servant would be healed, adding, 'For I am a man under authority, having soldiers under me: and I say to this man, Go and he goeth, and to another Come and he cometh, and to my servant, Do this, and he doeth it'. Touched by his faith, Jesus healed the servant without seeing him. He used the gentile centurion's acceptance of him as the *Saviour to warn the Jews that, although they were the *Chosen People, they could well be shut out of the kingdom of heaven for, 'the first shall be last, and the last first' (Mt 8 : 5-13; Lk 7 : 1-10).

Chalice The *vessel in which the *wine is consecrated at the *Eucharist. Originally it was a cup (Latin *calix*). A knob or a stem was added so that it might be held up for adoration, and a base so that it could be set down without spilling its contents. The actual design has varied according to artistic fashions. From the 9th century onwards chalices were made of gold, or if of silver, the inside was plated with gold, and the outside decorated with scenes or symbols allusive to the *Last Supper. Enamel or precious stones, linked with the symbolism of *colours, were also used as ornaments. A chalice with a *serpent (representing poison) is the *attribute of St *John the Divine whose enemies tried to poison him. When St John made the *sign of the cross, the venom was neutralized. A chalice and *Host symbolize the *Eucharist.

Chamael (or Chemuel) The *angel of God's wrath and leader of the *principalities. He is said to have been the angel who wrestled with *Jacob and the one who brought the cup which Jesus prayed would be taken from him during his *Agony in Gethsemane (although another tradition says that this angel was St *Gabriel).

Chancel The eastern part of a church, in which the *altar is placed. It is reserved for *clergy and *choir, so is separated from the *nave where the congregation assemble by a chancel *screen or *rood screen, although strictly the word 'chancel' (Latin *cancellus*) means the screen, not the space which it encloses. When the chancel is out of alignment with the nave (whether deliberately or accidentally) it is called a 'weeping chancel', because it is said to symbolize Christ's head inclining towards his right shoulder as he hung in his last moments on the *Cross.

Chantry Either a *chapel or *altar endowed for the saying of *Mass for the soul of a departed benefactor, or the money set aside to pay the chantry *priest or priests for this service. In large *churches or *cathedrals the altar, together with the tomb of the founder, was in many instances enclosed with stone or wooden screens, making it a separate chapel.

Chapel From the Latin *capella*, 'a short cloak', the name first given to the *oratory in the court of the Frankish kings in which the cloak said to belong to St *Martin of Tours was kept. Later the word was applied to private oratories in castles and to oratories with *altars dedicated to various *saints placed in *churches and *cathedrals. A *chantry chapel is a small chapel within a cathedral or parish church, endowed for the saying of *Mass for the soul of the founder. It is often enclosed by tracery screens. A *Lady chapel is a chapel dedicated to *'Our Lady', St *Mary the Virgin.

Chapter The governing body of a *cathedral church, consisting of *canons presided over by a *dean. It meets in the chapter house. In monastic usage it is the choir where *monks assemble with their *abbot to hear a chapter of their *Rule read (hence the origin of the word) or to conduct the business of their house.

Charity The AV translation of the Vg *caritas*, Greek *agape*, meaning 'love', and especially love of one's fellow men. Because acts of brotherly love could be expressed through the relief of distress, 'charity' acquired the meaning of 'almsgiving', or 'clothing the naked', one of the *Works of Mercy. As one of the three theological *virtues, 'charity' means love of God.

Charlemagne King of the Franks (c.742–814), prominent in the epic *Chanson de Roland* ('Song of Roland') and regarded as the first of the royal saints (although never included in the Roman *Breviary) because he was canonized by the antipope Paschal III (1164–68) to placate Frederick Barbarossa. He was the first emperor (800–14) of the Holy Roman Empire. SS *Peter and *Paul were said to have given him his standard. St *Giles absolved him from a sin (supposed to have been his unnatural love for his sister) which he dared not confess. It was revealed to the saint as he celebrated *Mass by an angel who gave him a scroll on which the sin was inscribed. He is depicted wearing an imperial crown and holding an orb and a shield on which the French *fleur-de-lis is displayed. A church shown near him is the cathedral of Aachen (Aix-la-Chapelle), which he founded.

Charles Borromeo, St Patron saint of Bologna (1538-84), born at Arona, Lago Maggiore, of a noble Lombard family. As a youth he was distinguishéd for his saintly life and academic ability. When he was twenty-three, his uncle, Pope Pius IV (1559-65), made him cardinal bishop of Milan. When he inherited his family fortune, he gave it away to the poor. His attempts to revive the spiritual zeal of the clergy in accordance with the ideals of the *Council of Trent brought him many enemies. A *Franciscan friar even attempted to assassinate him when he was celebrating *Mass. During the plague of 1575 he went about Milan giving the *last rites to the dying and relieving distress. His *attribute is the *crucifix which he carried in the procession to intercede for the end of the plague. He founded the Order of *Oblates and was a patron of Palestrina. He used the *Inquisition to extirpate *Protestantism in his diocese. He is depicted in *cardinal's robes, barefoot, a rope around his neck (symbolizing penitence) and near him a crown with the word *Humilitas*, his family crest.

Charterhouse The English name for a *Carthusian religious house (from the French *maison chartreuse*).

A bronze Visigothic **censer** from Olot, Catalonia.

Reliquary of Emperor **Charlemagne,** in the Cathedral treasury, Aachen (Aix-la-Chapelle), c.1350.

Chastity Abstention from sexual relations, a Christian *virtue. Together with poverty and obedience, it is one of the three *vows taken by members of the monastic *Orders and of other religious communities.

Chasuble An outer garment, a *vestment made of silk, often ornamented with pictorial embroidery, or floral or other symbolic motifs, worn by the *priest during the celebration of the *Eucharist.

Cherubim Plural of cherub, the second choir of the first hierarchy of *angels. Their *colour is golden yellow or sapphire blue and they were at first represented as described in *Ezekiel's vision (Ez 10 : 1-12). They stand on winged wheels 'the colour of a beryl stone' and hold open books or scrolls because they represent the Wisdom of God. From the 16th century onwards they were depicted simply as smiling, chubby childs' heads with two wings, hence the adjective 'cherubic'. Their leader is *Jophiel. They guarded the Tree of Life in the Garden of Eden after the *Expulsion of *Adam and *Eve from *Paradise, and representations of them protected the *Ark of the Covenant in Solomon's *Temple at Jerusalem.

Childermas The old name for *Holy Innocents' Day.

Children, blessing of little As Jesus taught and healed in the 'borders of Judaea and beyond Jordan', people brought their little children to him so that he might lay his hands on them. His disciples disapproved and rebuked the parents, but Jesus was moved to indignation by their action and said, 'Suffer the little children to come unto me; forbid them not: for of such is the kingdom of God', and added the lesson, 'whosoever shall not receive the kingdom of God as a little child, he shall in no wise enter therein'. He then took the children in his arms and blessed them (Mt 19 : 13-15; Mk 10 : 13-16; Lk 18 : 15-17).

Children of Israel The collective name for the *Twelve Tribes, descendants of *Israel, the name given to *Jacob after he had wrestled with the angel. It is synonymous with *Israelites.

Chimaera A mythical monster which has never been seen and which might not exist, hence the adjective 'chimerical'. It was believed to breathe fire and to have the head of a *lion, the body of a *goat, and its rear part to be that of a *dragon.

Chimere A sleeveless silk or satin gown worn by *Anglican *bishops either as a liturgical *vestment or as full dress on ceremonial occasions.

Chi-Rho The symbolic *monogram composed by the imposition of the first two *Greek letters of *Christos* 'Christ', Chi (*X) on rho (P) (See figure) (See *Labarum).

Choir Architecturally that part of a church at the east end, separated from the *nave by a choir screen and raised above the rest of the building by three steps, symbolizing the *Trinity. It contains the *altar and is reserved for the *clergy (Latin *chorus*). As the clergy sang the proper of the *Mass, and were later augmented or replaced by trained singers called the *schola cantorum*, or 'group of singers', the word came to mean not the place, but the collective 'choir' in the modern musical sense. At first the choir stood around the altar, but as organs and other instruments came into use, they moved to the *rood screen, and later, when secular participants were introduced, to the back of the church. Elaborate baroque settings of the *liturgy led to the enlargement of choirs and to their duplication. The phrase in the Anglican *Prayer Book, or *Book of Common Prayer* of 1662, 'in quires and places where they sing', retains the old sense of 'choir' as the location and not the performers. The choir-office is the *Divine Office sung in the choir.

Choir-stalls Seats along both sides of the presbytery, that part of the church building around the *altar which is reserved for the *clergy or *choir. In the Gothic period choir-stalls were given elaborate settings and the seats, when raised, revealed carved decorations (See *Misericord; *Bench-end).

Chosen People In a general sense the *Israelites of the OT, who were chosen from among all peoples because of the promise God made to *Abraham that he would establish a covenant with his son *Isaac, 'an everlasting covenant, and with his seed after him' (Gen 17 : 19). Their election implied that through them he would reveal his ways to the rest of mankind and that the *Messiah would be born of their nation. Later, the *Jews.

Chrism, Holy Olive oil with a little balsam, consecrated by a *bishop on *Maundy Thursday. It is kept in a chrismatory or chrismal and used for *anointing.

Christ From the Greek *christós*, 'the Anointed One', a translation of the Hebrew *Messiah*, the long-expected deliverer of *Israel. It was originally the title given to *Jesus of Nazareth by his followers, 'Jesus the Messiah', but soon after his death was used in the Greek form, 'Christ', as a name by itself. The followers of Christ were thus known as *Christians.

Christ-Child The new-born Jesus, surrounded by rays of light (because he is the *Light of the World) either lying on the floor or sleeping in a *manger or *crib (See *Bambino and *Nativity). Also the infant Jesus on his mother's lap, a devotional picture. He may be surrounded by *saints or shown inclining towards a favoured saint (See SS *Antony of Padua and *Catherine of Siena).

Christians Followers of Jesus the *Christ, or *Messiah. The name was first applied to them by the people of Antioch who heard SS *Paul and *Barnabas preach about Christ (Ac 11 : 26).

Christina, St A legendary 3rd-century saint who enjoyed great popularity in the Middle Ages. The Christian daughter of a Roman patrician, she broke the family idols, gave the gold and silver pieces to the poor, and was thrown into prison where *angels ministered to her. She survived burning and an attempt to drown her by casting her into Lake Bolsena with a *millstone (her *attribute) around her neck. Torture with a knife and tongs failed to move her and she was finally killed with three *arrows. She is therefore often depicted in the company of St *Ursula.

Christmas The English name for the Feast of the *Nativity (Middle English *Cristes masse*, 'the festival mass of Christ'). There is no scriptural warrant for the celebration of the birth of Jesus on 25 December, nor is there any precise indication of the day in the birth narratives in the Gospels of *Luke* and *Matthew*. Speculation as to the time of year is not evident before the mid-2nd century, when there was a pressing need to emphasize *Christ's humanity in order to confound gnostic teachings that he only *appeared* to come in the flesh. Various dates were suggested, November being favoured by Clement of Alexandria (c.150-c.215). The first mention in the *West of a festival on the now traditional date is in an almanac of 354, which Furius Dionysius Philocalus, a calligrapher, illuminated for the use of Christians in Rome. It contained an entry under 25 December, *natus Christus in Betleem Judeae*, 'Christ was born in Bethlehem of Judaea'. This was also the date in the Julian calendar of the winter solstice, the day on which the sun is reborn, also celebrated by adherents of the oriental cult of the sun-god Mithras. It was the practice at the time of Emperor *Constantine (312-37) to syncretize pagan and Christian beliefs. As Christ was the *sol verus*, 'the true sun', it was appropriate that his birth should be commemorated on that day. It had the added advantage of being nine months from 25 March, the assumed date of the *Incarnation and of the *Creation of the World.

In the *East, according to the Alexandrian calendar, 6 January was the date of the winter solstice, and this was kept as the festival of the *Epiphany which included the manifestation of Christ at his birth. Epiphany on 6 January was adopted by the West and associated principally with the Visitation of the Three *Kings. The Feast of the Nativity, on 25 December, spread to the East and reached Antioch around 386, although it continued to be held on 6 January by Christians in *Jerusalem until 549, a practice still followed by the Armenian Church.

Christopher, St A giant who may have been martyred during the *persecution of Decius (250). He is depicted wading across a river, holding a huge staff and bearing the *Christ-Child, a Latin pun on his name *Christo-ferens*, 'Christ-carrier'. The legend explains that because of his strength he wished to serve the greatest king in the world. He met a *hermit (sometimes depicted near him, holding a lantern) who told him that he should

Cherubs at play. Detail of a late-15th-century carving from Rimini.

The **Christ-Child** seated on the lap of St Mary the Virgin, surrounded by the angelic host, blessing the world (Master of Moulins?, late 15th-century).

station himself on the bank of a swift-flowing river and help travellers across. One night, as he was bearing a child on his shoulders, the current became dangerously swift and the child seemed increasingly heavy with each step that Christopher took. When he succeeded in reaching the opposite bank, the child revealed himself as Jesus, and told Christopher that he had borne on his shoulder the weight of the one who had created the whole world. He was told to plant his staff in the ground by his hut and the next day it had turned into a palm tree bearing leaves, flowers and dates (which are sometimes shown on his staff).

Christopher was taken to the king in Lycia. He told him that his name before baptism was Reprobus and that he was a Canaanite. (This may explain why he sometimes appears in art with a dog's head, either a pun, or a confusion of the Latin *cananeus*, 'Canaanite', with *canineus*, 'dog-like', or 'canine'.) The king tried to persuade Christopher to renounce his faith, and imprisoned him with two prostitutes, but he converted them. He was then shot at with arrows. They all missed him, but one rebounded and pierced the king's eye. Finally Christopher was beheaded. As he died, he prayed that all who saw him and had faith would be saved from fire, storm and earthquake.

This explains his great popularity throughout the Middle Ages and even today. Travellers and motorists still carry a St Christopher medallion for protection, although his festival was suppressed in 1969. A *church was dedicated to him in Constantinople as early as 250 and his gigantic figure appeared in almost every *parish church, either as a statue or in a wall painting, usually opposite the south door, so that worshippers might see it as they entered. A doggerel couplet (there are many variants) explained why:

Christofori faciem die quacunque tueris
illa nempe die morte mala non morieris

'If you see the face of Christopher on any morning, you will be preserved throughout the day from sudden death'.

St Christopher is therefore one of the *Fourteen Holy Helpers.

Church The translation of the Vg *ecclesia*, meaning originally an assembly or, more specifically, a religious assembly, but extended to the building in which the faithful assembled for worship. In the abstract sense (the Church) it means the community of all those redeemed by the sacrifice of *Christ on the *Cross.

Church of England The established Church, of which the ruling monarch is Head. It is divided into two provinces, Canterbury and York, each with its respective *archbishop, and is part of the *Anglican communion. It is *Catholic, in that it is the continuation of the early Celtic Church and of the Roman Church established as the result of the mission of St *Augustine of Canterbury in 597; yet Reformed, in that it adopted *Protestant principles at the time of the *Reformation. In matters of doctrine, the Church attempted to achieve a compromise, expressed in the formulary known as

the *Thirty-Nine Articles of 1571, intended to put an end to bitter theological disputes. This aim was not entirely successful as it led to the Great Rebellion, or the Civil Wars of 1642-51; quarrels over the nature of the episcopacy; secessions; and the dependency of the Church on the state to enforce uniformity. A lack of spiritual fervour in the 18th century led to the *Methodists revival and their loss to the Church. In the 19th century, *Evangelicals attempted to maintain the Protestant position; Latitudinarians, a moderate attitude to doctrine and ceremonial; and the *Oxford Movement, an emphasis on the *Catholic tradition. Control by Parliament meant submission to the state in matters of worship and doctrine and led to the rejection of a revised *Prayer Book in 1927 and 1928, although more freedom was granted in 1965. Since the Church of England (Worship and Doctrine) Measure of 1974, greater liberty in forms of service and the question of assent to all clauses of the Thirty-Nine Articles has been possible, and more power given to the General Synod. Opinion is divided as to the advantages of being the established Church, with the right to crown the monarch and to have bishops in the House of Lords, and the freedom which would result from disestablishment. The Church of Rome does not recognize the validity of *Anglican orders.

Churchwardens Two Anglican *parishioners (one nominated by the *vicar) elected annually as representatives of the *laity. They are responsible for the movable property of their church; for the preservation of order and decency among the congregation; and for the promotion of cooperation between the *parish and the *incumbent.

Ciborium A vessel resembling a *chalice with a lid in which the *Host, the bread of *Eucharist is *reserved. Also the canopy supported by four columns over the altar, called the *baldacchino.

Cincture A girdle, worn with an *alb, symbolizing *chastity, in obedience to the injunction, 'Let your loins be girded about' (Lk 12 : 35) (*See *vestments).

Cinquefoil One of the small openings in Gothic tracery in the shape of five 'foils', or leaves.

Circle *Symbol of eternity because it is without beginning or end. Three interlaced circles represent the *Trinity.

Circumcision of Jesus Mosaic *law prescribed three ceremonies to follow the birth of a male child: circumcision; redemption (*See *Presentation of Jesus in the Temple); and the purification of the mother (*See *Purification of St Mary the Virgin). Jesus was assumed to have been brought up in the strict Jewish tradition and was circumcised 'at the end of eight days' (Lk 2 : 21). Accounts differ as to the place where the operation took place and who performed it. Those who accepted the tradition that Jesus was born in a cave, a shelter near an inn or a stable, claimed that he would have been

circumcised in one of these places by his earthly
father St *Joseph, as recorded by the apocryphal
Arabic *Gospel of the Infancy*. SS *Jerome, *Bernard
and the author of the *Meditations on the Life of
Christ*, basing their opinion on the *Book of Leviticus*
(Lv 12), held that Hebrew women circumcised
their own children and that Mary would have
circumcised Jesus. This tradition was evidently too
shocking to be widely adopted in art, although it
was incorporated in some manuscript illustrations.
The *Gospel of the *Pseudo-Matthew* harmonized the
traditions, saying that the child was circumcised
twice: in *Bethlehem on the eighth day and in the
*Temple in Jerusalem at the time of Mary's
Purification. This may be the origin of the
conflation in art of these two episodes.

Although the *Gospel of Luke* did not give details,
it was generally assumed that, as the account went
on to state that the Holy Parents were in Jerusalem
for Mary's purification, then the ceremony must
have been performed there in the Temple by a
ritual surgeon (or *mohel*) thought to be a priest.
The usual setting in art for this episode is therefore
a building resembling a church. A priest, dressed
in what was assumed to be Jewish garb, holds a
knife; Mary presents the child and Joseph stands to
one side. Jesus accepts the incision passively,
signifying his obedience to the Law of Moses
which he came not to destroy but to fulfil (Mt
5 : 17). He may comfort his mother by putting his
hand to her cheek, because this first shedding of his
blood is one of the Seven *Sorrows of the Virgin.
For the same reason the episode was for many
centuries the first of the *Stations of the Cross.
The *Foreskin of Christ became a holy relic. The
*knife used in the operation is included among the
*Instruments of the Passion. The event is associ-
ated typologically with the circumcision of *Isaac
and of *Samson and is commemorated on 1
January, the Feast of the Circumcision (or the
*Naming of Jesus).

Cistercians Members of the Cistercian *Order,
also called *White Monks because of the colour of
their *habit. They take their name from their
mother-house at Cîteaux (Latin *Cistercium*) near
Dijon, in Burgundy. St Robert of Molêsme
founded the first community there in 1098, in
order more strictly to observe the *Rule of St
Benedict. St *Bernard of Clairvaux became a
novice there in 1112. The movement spread
throughout the *West during the 12th century, one
of the earliest English foundations being the abbey
at Rievaulx (Rye Vale) near York.

Cities of the plain *Sodom and Gomorrah,
situated on the floor of the rift valley close to the
Dead Sea. The wickedness of the inhabitants made
God decide to destroy these cities, but *Abraham
pleaded with him not to kill the just together with
the unjust. Would God spare the cities if they
contained fifty just men? – or forty-five? – or
forty? – or thirty? – or twenty? – or ten?, he asked.
God made a concession as each number was
mentioned, and finally promised to restrain his
wrath if ten just men could be found. Even this

St **Christopher** bearing the Christ-Child across
a swift-flowing river (Quintin Massys, 1464/5-
1530).

In obedience to the Law of Moses, the infant
Jesus accepts **Circumcision** (Giovanni Bellini,
1455).

limited number of righteous ones could not be discovered. Early one morning Abraham looked across the plain towards Sodom and Gomorrah and saw smoke rising, like smoke from a furnace. The wicked cities were destroyed, but not before his nephew *Lot and his family were able to escape (Gen 18 : 16-33; 19 : 23-8).

Clare, St The greatest *Franciscan woman saint (1194-1253), founder of the Order of *Poor Clares. A daughter of the Count of Sasso Rosso who owned a palace in Assisi. She was attracted from an early age to a life of contemplation, and came under the influence of St *Francis. In 1211, on the night following *Palm Sunday, she abandoned her comfortable existence and joined him in the Porziuncola (See *Portiuncula), the mother-church of the Franciscan Order, into which she was received. A branch for nuns, the Order of the Poor Clares, was eventually created for her. She was allotted the church of San Damiano in Assisi and lived there a life of penance and severe discipline in company with other ladies who had forsaken their homes for a life of poverty. St Francis composed his *Canticle to the Sun* in the peace of their convent garden.

St Clare is depicted in the grey *habit of her Order, with a white coif and a black veil. About her waist is a rope girdle with three knots, symbolizing the three *vows of poverty, chastity and obedience. A *crosier indicates that she is an *abbess. A *monstrance in her hands and a turban on the ground with a cross above it, recall the story that when Saracen mercenaries of Emperor Frederick II were besieging Assisi, St Clare appeared before them bearing the *Blessed Sacrament whereupon they fled.

Before her death she had a vision of *Christ and St *Mary the Virgin. Her nuns later moved to the convent of Santa Chiara in Assisi where her body was enshrined in the crypt of the church.

Clerestory (or Clearstory) The upper storey of the *nave of a church with a series of windows giving light to the interior.

Clergy Christians dedicated to the service of God and to the performance of liturgical functions. They are set aside from the *laity through *Ordination. They may be distinguished by the wearing of clerical *dress and, in the *Roman Catholic Church, by the *tonsure. Clergy composed the *choir who sang the *Divine Office in the *chancel. Secular clergy are those who operate in 'the world' (Latin *saeculum*), as distinct from those who follow a *Rule and mostly live in *monasteries.

Cleric Any member of the *clergy.

Cloister A quadrangular area, covered and often vaulted, intended as a walk around an open green, or *garth, with a plain wall on one side and piers or columns often filled with tracery, or glassed-in on the other, outer side facing the green. In monastic buildings this passageway connects the *church to the *chapter house, *refectory and other domestic parts of the *monastery. As the medieval Latin name for enclosed monasteries, it has provided the word 'claustrophobia'.

Clover Because it is *trefoil (three-leaved), a symbol of the *Trinity.

Cluniacs Monks of the Order of Cluny, called after their mother-house at *Cluny, near Mâcon in Burgundy. They stressed the choir office and the strict observance of the *Rule of St Benedict, and exerted great influence during the Middle Ages.

Cluny The great *Benedictine *abbey near Mâcon, France, founded in 910 and closed in 1790 during the French Revolution. It was an independent *monastery, its *abbot elected by the *monks and responsible only to the *Pope. The first abbot, Berno of Gigny, set about establishing the Congregation of Cluny in 912, dedicated to the *Rule of St Benedict and to the performance of the *Divine Office with impressive ceremonial. It was at its most influential in the 11th century when *Cluniacs obtained the support of Henry III of France (1039-56). Over 300 monasteries, dependent on the mother-house of Cluny, their *priors appointed by the abbot, came into being and were responsible for much of the great architecture, art and learning of the Middle Ages in France and in Spain, where they settled in regions conquered from the Moors.

Cock *Symbol of vigilance because it crows to welcome the dawn. It is also associated with Jesus' *Passion because St *Peter, as *Christ had foretold (Jn 13 : 38), denied him three times before the cock crowed on the morning after his arrest.

Cockatrice A fictitious creature resembling a *basilisk, with which it is often confused. It is hatched by a serpent from a cock's egg and has the head, legs and wings of a cock, and a serpent's tail. Its eyes are fierce, its tongue is arrow-headed, its breath poisons, and its look kills. It *symbolized torment (Jer 8 : 17) and, on the authority of the text, 'The weaned child shall put his hand on the cockatrice's den' (Is 11 : 8), the conquest of evil.

Cockle A weed, *symbol of wickedness which can insidiously pervert a Christian community in the same way as the cockle creeps in among the barley (Jb 31 : 40).

Cockle-shell (or Scallop-shell) The *attribute (for which there is no satisfactory explanation) of St *James of Compostela, worn by *pilgrims to his shrine at Compostela, Galicia, Spain.

Coins One of the symbols of Christ's *Passion, because *Judas Iscariot betrayed him for thirty pieces of silver (Mt 26 : 15).

Colours, liturgical *Vestments, altar-hangings, chalice-veil, and certain other objects used in the liturgy, have conformed since the 12th century in the *West to colours deemed appropriate to the seasons, *fasts and *feasts of the Christian *year. In the *East, *white is used from *Easter to *Ascensiontide and dark colours for penitential seasons. In the West, colours have varied, but the present tendency is to use *red on *Palm Sunday, *Good Friday, *Pentecost (Whitsun) and on feast days commemorating *apostles and *martyrs. *Purple is used for *Holy Week; the penitential seasons of *Advent and *Lent; and for funerals. *Green characterizes Sundays after *Epiphany and up to Lent; and after *Trinity Sunday until Lent. White signifies feasts of virgin *martyrs, *confessors, St *Mary the Virgin, *Christmas and *Trinity Sunday.

Colours, symbolism of As well as being associated with the Christian *year (*See above* *colours, liturgical), colours have also general *symbolic references. Those most commonly cited are: *black, *blue, *gold, *green, *purple, *red, *violet, *white and *yellow.

Columbine Because of its association with Latin *columba*, '*dove', the plant is a symbol of the *Holy Spirit. Moreover, as there are seven flowers on each stalk it demonstrates the Seven *Gifts of the Holy Spirit.

Column One of the *Instruments of the Passion, because Jesus was scourged when tied to a column (or pillar). A broken column signifies the passing of the old order at the birth of Jesus, also death because the support of life has gone. A column is also the attribute of *Samson and St *Simon Stylites.

Communion One of the *Sacraments, commemorating the *Last Supper, at which the Christian receives the consecrated *bread (or wafer), which is the Body of *Christ. If Communion is in two kinds, as in Anglican and many other non-Roman Churches, he also receives *wine, the Blood of Christ. In the *Orthodox tradition, the communicant receives bread dipped in wine.

Communion of Saints A phrase, part of the ninth article of the *Apostles' Creed, meaning the spiritual union which exists between Christ and every Christian, living or dead, the three-fold *Church.

Communion of the Apostles The representation in art of the moment at the *Last Supper when Jesus gave *bread and *wine to the *Apostles, who were the first Christians to receive *Communion. In the *Eastern artistic tradition he may be depicted twice, administering bread to six Apostles on one side of an *altar and wine to six on the other side.

Communion rails Rails or balustrade separating the *sanctuary from that part of the church used by the congregation. The faithful kneel or stand there to receive *Communion.

St **Clare** and her nuns take leave of St Francis of Assisi as his cortège halts before her convent (Giotto, *c*.1266-1337).

Jesus consecrates the bread and wine, preparatory to the **Communion of the Apostles** (Bouts, *c*.1467).

Communion table At the *Reformation, *Protestants who objected to the sacrificial aspect of the *Mass, substituted a table for an *altar for the celebration of Holy *Communion.

Compline The last of the canonical *hours, said before retiring, as it completes the day. *Nunc Dimittis may be said or sung.

Conception of St Mary the Virgin See *Immaculate Conception.

Confessio In Early Christian days the tomb of a *martyr, later used for a *crypt beneath an *altar, containing a martyr's relics, the most famous being that of St Peter's in Rome.

Confessional Towards the end of the Middle Ages a chair was placed between the altar and *communion rails (or balustrade dividing the sanctuary from the nave) on which the priest might sit to hear confessions. In the 17th century a highly decorated, roofed structure was constructed in the body of the church to contain the priest's seat. These confessionals have a grille at the side through which the confessor may listen and speak to the penitent (See *St John Nepomucene).

Confessor A word used in two senses: **1** A male saint who was not a *martyr, but was a witness to the faith. In art these confessors are ranked as *Doctors of the Church, *bishops, *abbots and others. **2** A *priest who hears confessions and grants *absolution.

Confirmation One of the *Sacraments. A baptized Christian makes public confession of his faith and is confirmed in it ('strengthened', from Latin confirmatio, 'strengthening') by a *bishop (or in the *East by the *priest) by the laying on of hands. In the Roman *rite the candidate is also signed with the cross and anointed.

Confusion of tongues See *Babel.

Consecration The act by a *bishop of making a building or object sacred and dedicating it to the service of God. At first only *altars were consecrated, but in the early Middle Ages consecration was extended to *church buildings and their furnishings. Consecration is symbolized by a *cross. Twelve (one for each article of the *Apostles' Creed) are incised or painted on the exterior and interior walls of a church.

Constantine the Great Roman emperor (d.337), son of St *Helena and Emperor Constantius Chlorus. He was proclaimed emperor at York in 306, but faced the other contender, Maxentius, whom he defeated at the Battle of the *Milvian Bridge on 28 October 312. Thereafter he shared the rule, as senior, with Licinius, adopted the cause of Christianity and made it a tolerated religion (See *Edict of Milan). His aim was to use the forces of the new faith in the service of the state. To this end he sought a unified theology and achieved victory over the *Arian heresy by his personal intervention at the Council of Nicaea (325). By that time he had become sole emperor after defeating Licinius at Chrysopolis (324). He rebuilt the city of Byzantium, renamed it Constantinople (now Istanbul), and made it his capital in 330. This was the beginning of the breach between the Greek *East and the Latin *West.

Together with his mother St Helena he did much to further the cause of Christianity, building and endowing churches especially in the *Holy Land. In 321 he made *Sunday a public holiday, thus facilitating Christian worship. For these services he is venerated in the *East as a *saint on 21 May, among 'the holy, illustrious and great emperors, crowned by God and equal with the *Apostles'. The so-called *Donation of Constantine, granting extensive powers to the Church of Rome, was shown to be a forgery.

There are two contradictory accounts of Constantine's vision of the cross which led him to adopt the *Labarum with the *Chi-Rho symbol as his standard. One is given by *Eusebius in his Life of Constantine (c.337). Constantine was preparing to meet Maxentius' armies. Above the midday sun he saw a cross of light and the words In hoc vince, 'By this conquer'. That night *Christ appeared to him in a dream and told him to make this cross his standard. Sixty years later, Rufinus, in his translation of Eusebius' Ecclesiastical History, wrote that as Constantine slept he had a vision of the cross. He woke up in a cold sweat and an *angel appeared, predicting victory with the words, In hoc vince.

Although Constantine was sympathetic to Christianity, he was not baptized until shortly before his death. SS *Ambrose and *Jerome explained that he delayed because he wanted to be baptized in the River Jordan, like Jesus (See *Baptism of Christ). Nevertheless, as postponing *baptism was not looked upon with favour, he was later said to have been converted and baptized in miraculous circumstances by St *Sylvester.

Convent In popular speech a house inhabited by *nuns, but strictly the abode, or *monastery, of *monks, *friars or nuns.

Conventuals *Franciscans, or Friars Minor Conventual, who hold property in common, as distinct from *Observants who adhere strictly to St *Francis' ideal of absolute poverty.

Cope A semicircular cloak with a hood, reaching to the feet and held in place by a clasp or *morse. It is worn by a *bishop or *priest together with other *vestments on solemn occasions and when celebrating the *Eucharist, and is usually of silk or other costly material, finely embroidered with symbolic motifs which were seen by the congregation in the old *rite when the celebrant stood at the *altar with his back towards them.

Coral Red coral was thought to give protection against the evil eye or witchcraft, and was worn as a charm. Coral in the hand of the *Christ-Child signifies protection from the *Devil.

Corbel A projecting block of stone on the face of a wall, often moulded or carved with symbolic figures or monumental designs.

Coronation of St Mary the Virgin After her *Assumption, St *Mary the Virgin was crowned *Queen of Heaven. This event is not recorded in the NT, but was deduced by allegorical interpretation of certain scriptural texts, notably the Vg (not AV), 'Come, my bride, from Lebanon . . . thou shalt be crowned' (Sg 4 : 8). (A paraphrase in Latin, *Veni, electa mea, et ponam te in thronum meum*, 'Come my chosen one and I will put you on my throne', may be inscribed on a book held by *Christ in depictions of the Coronation.) Although discussed by Bishop Melitus of Sardis (*d.*381) and St Gregory of Tours (*c.*540-94), the Coronation was not a frequent theme until the Middle Ages when the cult of the Virgin was at its height.

In art, the Virgin may be shown seated on a throne beside *God the Son; kneeling before him; before *God the Father to receive the crown; or being crowned by all three persons of the *Trinity. She is always richly dressed and her robes may be embroidered with suns, moons and golden rays, recalling the 'woman clothed with the sun' seen in the vision of St *John the Divine (Rev 12 : 1). She may be surrounded by *angels and the whole court of *Heaven.

Corporal From the Latin *corporalis*, from *corpus* 'body', because it touches the body of *Christ. A square piece of linen on which the *Host and *chalice are placed. It is kept in a *burse.

Corpus Christi Literally 'the body of Christ', the name for the feast of the Veneration of the *Blessed Sacrament, instituted in 1264 and celebrated on the Thursday after *Pentecost (*Whitsunday). To emphasize the *Real Presence, the Blessed Sacrament is exposed in a *monstrance and carried in solemn procession through the *parish, town or city. In the Middle Ages, these religious processions were enlivened by tableaux, carried on carts and escorted by *allegorical figures and *carnival characters, including giants and dragons. The popularity of the feast was a potent factor in the development of religious drama. Guilds and other organizations participated in the festivities and provided secular entertainment.

Cosmas and Damian, SS Twin Arabian physicians of Aegae, in Cilicia, brought up by their mother as Christians. They refused to sacrifice to idols during the Diocletian *persecutions; were thrown into the sea; rescued by *angels; cast into fire, but emerged unscorched; stoned, but the stones rebounded on their executioners; and finally beheaded in 287. Their bodies were taken to Rome where a church in the Forum was dedicated to them in 526 by Pope St Felix IV (526-30). A mosaic in the *apse shows them being presented to *Christ by SS *Peter and *Paul.

The brothers owed their fame to their medical and surgical skill and their refusal to accept fees.

Jesus with St Mary the Virgin at her **Coronation** as Queen of Heaven, attended by her court (Fra Angelico, 1430-5).

SS **Cosmas and Damian** survive death by fire when flames from the pyre devour their executioners (Fra Angelico, *c.*1387-1455).

They are shown in the long red gowns of doctors, holding a box of *ointment, pestle and mortar, surgical instruments and sometimes examining urine in a flask. On one occasion they removed a man's diseased leg and replaced it with one from a negro who had just died. When the patient awoke he found that he had one black and one white leg. The wide diffusion of effigies or pictures of these saints is due to their ability to avert plagues and also to the fact that they were the patron saints of the Medici family. Michaelangelo Buonarroti (1475-1564) carved statues of them for the Medici Chapel in Florence.

Council of Trent The general or oecumenical council of the *Roman Catholic Church, held at Trent in the Austrian Tyrol, 1545-63. It was summoned in response to *Protestant secessions and attacks on matters of doctrine and Church government, and in order to redefine Catholic dogma, reform abuses and impose clerical discipline. The results of the lengthy deliberations set the pattern of Roman Catholic tenets and worship for almost the next 500 years, until the Second *Vatican Council (1962-5).

Decisions influencing the arts and literature were: insistence on the Seven *Sacraments; the *Real Presence and *Transubstantiation; *Purgatory; the invocation of *saints and the veneration of their *relics and images; and the renewed emphasis on clerical celibacy.

Counter-Reformation A name invented by historians for the reforming movement, against the *Reformation, within the *Roman Catholic Church, aiming to put into practice the decisions of the *Council of Trent. It represented renewed emphasis on the *Catholic tradition; an intensification of spiritual life; discipline of the clergy; foundation of new religious *Orders (especially the *Jesuits) to propagate the faith; and attempts to attract the *laity through art and music.

Cowl A dress with wide sleeves and a hood, part of the *habit worn in choir during the *Divine Office by the members of many monastic *Orders.

Crab A sign of the *zodiac (See *Cancer).

Crane Because it was believed that cranes form a circle each night to protect their leader or king, a crane symbolizes loyalty. It also represents vigilance because it keeps itself awake by standing on one leg and holding a stone in the other. If it nods, the stone falls and wakes it up.

Creation of the world There seem to be two accounts of the Creation in the *Book of Genesis* (Gen 1 : 1-2 : 3 and 2 : 4-25). They agree in ascribing the creation of the heavens and the earth to God, but differ as to the original state of the earth and as to the order in which things were made. In the first account, creation is the *Work of Six Days; in the second no period of time is stated and there are five separate operations to transform

the waterless waste of the earth: the creation of man; the planting of the Garden of *Eden; the growth of trees, including the Tree of Life and the *Tree of Knowledge of Good and Evil; the fashioning of beasts and birds, and their *naming by Man; and lastly the creation of woman, to whom *Adam gave the name *Eve. Traditional exegesis sees the accounts as continuous.

Considerable ingenuity was expended by many scholars, including Sir Isaac Newton (1642-1727), in attempts to establish a chronology to determine the exact moment of Creation. It was argued that when God divided the light from the darkness (Gen 1 : 4) he separated them into two equal parts. This would correspond to the vernal equinox, 25 March according to the Julian calendar, when day and night are of equal duration. Archbishop James Ussher (1581-1656) satisfied his contemporaries that the year of the Creation was 4004 BC, a date which was printed in the margin of the first chapter of *Genesis* in many editions of AV Bibles and accepted as late as the Darwinian controversies of the 19th century. Some *fundamentalist sects continue to defend it.

Creator The universe was created from nothing by God, but as he is three persons in one, he may be depicted in one of three ways: as *God the Father, an old man; as *God the Son, the Word Incarnate, a young man, because God said, 'Let there be light' (Gen 1 : 3); or as the *Holy Spirit, a *dove, because the spirit of God hovered over the watery waste (Gen 1 : 2). Alternatively, the three persons may be grouped into the *Trinity for the act of *Creation, because God said, 'Let *us* make man in our image' (Gen 1 : 26). On the authority of this last text, *angels are sometimes included in the scene because they formed part of the court of *Heaven.

Credence A small table or shelf near an *altar on which *bread and *wine for the celebration of the *Eucharist are placed.

Credo Latin for 'I believe', the part of the *Mass at which the *Nicene Creed is said or sung. The priest says or sings the first phrase, *Credo in unum deum*, 'I believe in one God', and the *choir or congregation join in with the second, *Patrem omnipotentem*, 'the Father, the Almighty'. The singular, '*I* believe', is used instead of the plural, '*We* believe', because this *creed was originally said by an adult at his *baptism. It came into general liturgical use after its acceptance by the Church of Rome in 1014.

Creed A definitive and concise statement of the essential tenets of the Christian faith. Each *Apostle was said to have contributed a clause to the *Apostles' Creed, although it dates from the 4th century and is first mentioned c.390 by St *Ambrose. The *Nicene Creed, resulting from the debates against the *Arian heresy at the First Council of Nicaea (325), is used in *Eastern and *Western liturgies. However, the East will not accept the so-called *filioque* (Latin for 'and the son') clause, referring to the procession of the *Holy Spirit, as this phrase was added in the West in the early Middle Ages (See *Trinity).

Crib, Christmas According to the *Gospel of Luke* St *Mary the Virgin laid her newborn child 'in a manger' (Lk 2 : 7) (See *Nativity). The *manger, a rack to hold fodder in a cowshed, was equated with the Old English 'crib', a basket, which was used for the same purpose. In Middle English, 'crib' was also used for a child's cradle, so that the *Christ-Child was shown in a wicker cradle. Supposed relics of the original crib were enshrined in the church of Santa Maria Maggiore (St Mary Major) in Rome. St *Francis of Assisi placed a model of the crib in the church in Greccio for the Feast of the Nativity in 1223. This may be the origin of the custom in the *West of constructing crib or Nativity scenes in churches for the octave of *Christmas (See *Bambino).

Crispin and Crispinian, SS Two noble Roman youths who would not live on the charity of the faithful, but worked at a trade, shoemaking, while preaching the *Gospel to pagans. They travelled through Gaul and settled at Soissons where they made shoes for the poor, refusing payment and receiving from *angels each night the leather which they needed next day for their cobbling. They are thus the patron saints of shoemakers and leather-workers. They were arrested by order of Emperor Maximian *c.*290. After having awls thrust into them, and surviving being thrown into the Aisne with *millstones round their necks, they were beheaded. St *Eligius (or Eloi) reconstructed their shrine at Soissons. A contrary tradition held that to escape the *persecutions they settled in Faversham, England. Their tomb in the *parish church there was for many centuries visited by *pilgrims.

Crocodile Like the *whale, a crocodile may represent *Hell because of the legend that the *hydrus, a water snake, covers itself with mud (as *Christ took on human flesh) and thus enters the crocodile's jaws (as Christ did in the *Descent into Hell) and emerges alive. It also symbolized hypocrisy because it was reputed to sob and sigh to make men take pity on it and approach near enough to be caught. It then wept over its victim, hence 'crocodile tears'. Because of its reputed sexual powers, the crocodile also symbolized *lust (See *Pachomius, St).

Crosier A *bishop's *pastoral staff (also used by some *abbots and *abbesses, probably originally a crook-shaped walking-staff, but later given symbolic value. It denotes authority as the shepherd of a flock.

Cross The pre-eminent symbol of the Christian faith, recalling the *redemption of mankind through the death of *Christ. It is estimated that the basic shape (a long vertical transversed at right angles by a shorter horizontal line) has almost 400 variants and elaborations. Of these the most

God presides over the **Creation** of the Garden of Eden, surrounded by sea, sky and planets, representing the world (Luther Bible, 1534).

a   b   c

d   e   f

g   h   i

Crosses

common are: the Latin Cross (see figure *a*) with the transverse arm about three quarters of the way up the vertical line; the Greek cross, in which the horizontal line bisects the vertical (see figure *b*); the *Tau cross in the shape of the letter *T (see figure *c*); the papal cross, with three transverse arms (see figure *d*) symbolizing the Pope's three-fold powers (*See* *tiara); the cross of the Eastern *Orthodox Churches, which has two vertical horizontal arms and a third one (the body of Christ) slanting (see figure *e*); the Celtic cross in which the arms are encircled (see figure *f*); the *crux ansata*, a Latin or Tau cross with a loop above (see figure *g*), said to derive from the ancient Egyptian symbol for Life; the *saltire, or cross of St *Andrew, in the shape of the letter *X; and the Maltese cross, four intersecting arrowheads (see figure *h*), symbol of the *Beatitudes and the insignum of the Knights of St John of Jerusalem. The cross of Lorraine, with a short transverse beam above the horizontal arm (see figure *i*), was developed from the Latin cross with the addition of the *titulus*, the inscription in three languages which *Pilate placed above the head of Jesus.

Cross, legends of the The typological correspondence between the tree in the *Fall of Mankind and the *Cross of his *Redemption, gave rise to many legends.

When Adam lay dying at the age of 900 years, he sent his son *Seth to *Paradise to beg for the oil of mercy. St *Michael guarded the entrance and told Seth that this could not be obtained until the *Crucifixion. Instead he gave him a piece of the wood of the *Tree of the Knowledge of Good and Evil which had borne the *Forbidden Fruit, saying that Adam would be saved when it flowered. From this wood the Cross was eventually constructed. It burst into bloom at the Crucifixion.

In another version St Michael gave Seth three seeds of the *apple, the cause of Adam's sin, and told him to place them under his father's tongue after he had died. From them grew a cedar, a cypress and an olive tree which were eventually used in the construction of the Cross. A variant of this story is that from these trees came the rod which *Moses used to strike the rock in the wilderness; the trees which King *David planted in his garden; and the timber with which Solomon proposed to build his *Temple in Jerusalem. Solomon's trees could not be used however hard his workmen tried, so he ordered them to be buried deep in the ground. The Pool of *Bethesda was formed on the site and, soon after *Palm Sunday, the trees floated to the surface and were used to make the Cross. Another version is that Solomon had the wood made into a footbridge. The *Queen of Sheba, on her visit to the wise king, realized that it was the wood from Paradise, refused to walk over it, and told Solomon to guard it carefully as the world would again tremble before it. The timber then sank, but resurfaced in *Holy Week and became the Cross (*See* finding of the *True Cross).

Crown A symbol of rank or sovereignty. Some

*saints are depicted wearing crowns to indicate that they are of royal blood. St *Mary the Virgin wears a crown to show that she is *Queen of Heaven (*See* *Coronation of St Mary the Virgin). A *crown of thorns is one of the *Instruments of the Passion. It is also an attribute of St *Louis of France who built the Sainte-Chapelle at Paris (1248) to contain the *relic of the original crown of thorns.

Crown of thorns One of the *Instruments of the Passion, recalling the episode when, after the *Scourging of Jesus, *Pilate's soldiers took Jesus into 'the palace', the *praetorium*. They stripped him and put on a scarlet (or purple) robe, plaited a crown of thorns and placed it on his head, put a reed as a mock *sceptre in his hand, spat upon him, and knelt down to pay him homage. They then dressed him again in his own clothes (the *Seamless Robe), struck him with the reed and led him out to his *Crucifixion.

In art these details are derived from a conflation of the accounts in the *Gospels (Mk 15 : 16-20; Mt 27 : 27-31; Jn 19 : 2-3), although the *Gospel of John* interpolates the *Ecce Homo* before the stripping of the garments. The scene is often confused with the *Mocking of Jesus. The crown of thorns became a *relic (*See* *Crown).

Crucifix A representation of the body of the crucified *Christ nailed to the *Cross (*See* *Rood screen).

Crucifixion 'Crucified under Pontius *Pilate' is the article of the *Apostles' Creed which expresses the supreme moment in the earthly life of *Jesus of Nazareth. The event is recorded in agonizing detail in all the *Gospels (Mt 27 : 33-56; Mk 15 : 22-41; Lk 23 : 33-43) and is the subject most frequently depicted in Christian art. In the earliest period it was alluded to in the form of a *Cross. Later the symbolic figure of the *Lamb was placed on the Cross to represent Christ, the sacrificial *Lamb. By the 6th century, possibly to confound the docetic *heresy which held that Jesus only *appeared* to die, his body was shown hanging on the Cross. His face turned upwards, his eyes open, looking towards his Father in Heaven, a moment of obedience to the Divine will and of triumph over death. Thereafter, the representation of the dying Christ varied according to the mood of the period. In times of war and suffering the emphasis was on his wounded, emaciated body. If he looked down, it demonstrated his compassion for the sinner who came repenting to the foot of the Cross.

Details were added to the central scene. St *Mary the Virgin and St *John the Evangelist standing on either side of the Cross recalled the moment when Jesus gave his mother into the care of his disciple (Jn 19 : 23-4). They also represent the old dispensation (OT) and the new (NT). The *titulus*, the superscription which Pilate, to the annoyance of the Jews, caused to be written in Hebrew, Latin and Greek, recording the charge on which Jesus was put to death, 'Jesus of Nazareth the King of the Jews' (Jn 19 : 19-22), may also be shown above his head (See *INRI). Through a misunderstanding of the Greek, the soldier who pierced Jesus' side with a lance (Jn 19 : 34) is given the name of *Longinus. He stands on the right, symbolizing the Church. The one who put a sponge full of vinegar upon *hyssop (Jn 19 : 29) is for the same reason called *Stephaton and stands on the left, representing the *Synagogue. The *Holy Women may also be shown nearby. Soldiers cast lots for his garments (Mt 27 : 35; Mk 15 : 24; Lk 23 : 34) and for his *Seamless Robe (Jn 19 : 23-4). The good and bad thieves, *Dismas and *Gestas, hang on either side of the Cross. The sun and the moon in the sky refer to the darkness (possibly an eclipse) which came over the whole land from the sixth to the ninth hour. The *veil of the temple which was 'rent in the midst' (Lk 23 : 45) may also be shown.

*Adam's skull at the foot of the Cross is a reference to the site of the Crucifixion, *Calvary, or *Golgotha, 'the place of the skull', and to the Legend of the *Cross that, as Adam was dying, he begged to be buried in the ground after the *Flood. Shem carried his coffin out of the *Ark and interred it on the hill of Golgotha. Adam's voice was heard to prophesy, 'The Logos [*word] of God will descend and will live with us, but he will be crucified where my body rests and he will wet my skull with his blood.' When Jesus' side was pierced with the lance, blood and water flowed down on Adam and he was baptized by the water and redeemed by the blood of Christ.

Crypt A vault or underground chamber beneath the *choir which originally contained a *saint's grave, later enlarged to form a vaulted church with one or more *altars and used as a burial place or for lesser liturgical services.

Curate A *priest who has the 'cure' or charge of an Anglican *parish, the *incumbent, who may be *rector, *vicar or perpetual curate. More popularly, the incumbent may have an assistant curate, so the word curate has been restricted to the assistant, his superior being the rector or vicar.

Cyclamen *Symbol of the Seven *Sorrows of St Mary the Virgin, because it has red markings at its centre or heart.

Cypress A tree which symbolizes mourning because of its dark hue, and death because once cut down it cannot grow again. A cypress branch surmounted by a *palm (symbol of victory) represents Christ's triumph over death.

Cyprian and Justina, SS Two late-3rd-century martyrs of Antioch. Cyprian was a magistrate (in some accounts a sorcerer) and fell in love with the Christian virgin, Justina. According to one legend, he sold his soul to the *Devil in order to obtain her by his magic, but was saved when she converted him to her faith. They were beheaded and their relics brought to Rome where they were placed in the baptistery of St John Lateran. (See St *Justina of Antioch for an alternative version of the legend.)

Two interpretations of the **Crucifixion,** symbol of suffering humanity: *(above)* by Mathis Grünewald (c.1470/80–1528) *(below)* by Georges Rouault (c.1918).

Cyriacus (Cyr, Quiricus) and Julitta (Giulietta), SS Cyriacus was the three-year-old son of Julitta, a widow of Iconium who fled to Tarsus c.300 to escape persecution. She was recognized as a Christian and brought before the governor who ordered her to be sawn in half (or beheaded, according to another version). Cyriacus ran towards his mother, shouting, 'I also am a Christian'. To silence him, the governor threw him down the steps of his rostrum. Mother and son were martyred at the same instant and fountains sprang from their blood. Their cult was widespread in Western Europe during the Middle Ages. Cyriacus, depicted as a *deacon in a *dalmatic, is one of the *Fourteen Holy Helpers and is invoked against diabolical possession.

Daffodil *Attribute of St *David, patron saint of Wales.

Dagger *Attribute of SS *Edward the Confessor and *Peter Martyr.

Daisy A flower which symbolizes innocence; by popular etymology, 'the day's eye' or the sun; and Jesus, 'the Sun of Righteousness' (Mal 4 : 2).

Dalmatic A long-sleeved outer garment with two parallel coloured or lace stripes running down its length, worn over an *alb by a *deacon. The name of this *vestment is derived from the Latin *tunica dalmatica*, a long white tunic originating in Dalmatia which was worn by Romans of high rank. Deacons have used a white dalmatic since the 4th century but from the 12th century onwards the tendency was to adopt the liturgical *colour of the season and to replace the two stripes by one central decorative stripe. Among the saintly deacons, shown in art wearing dalmatics, are SS *Stephen, *Lawrence and *Vincent of Zaragoza. *Angels are often dressed in dalmatics.

Damnation, eternal The final state of *demons, *devils and of persons who die in mortal *sin. They are condemned for ever to *Hell, and suffer the eternal 'loss' (Latin *damnum*) of the presence of God.

Dance of death The superstition that the dead (depicted as grinning skeletons) arise at night and dance on their graves, tempting the living to join them in death. The dance was linked in manuscript and book illustrations with the *Danse macabre*.

Dandelion A symbol of grief because it was assumed to be the bitter herb which the Israelites were ordered to eat on the night of the *Passover (Ex 12 : 8).

Daniel One of the four major *prophets, ranking with *Ezekiel, *Isaiah and *Jeremiah. His adventures and apocalyptic visions are narrated in the OT book which bears his name. Captured by *Nebuchadnezzar's soldiers and carried off with three other Hebrew young men (*See* *Fiery Furnace) to Babylon, he was educated for service in the court. His success in interpreting the king's dream of the golden image with feet of clay (Dan 2 : 31-45) and his prophetic gifts singled him out for a position of honour and influence which he retained under Nebuchadnezzar's successors. When other Jews returned to Palestine after seventy years of captivity, he remained in his adopted land. The famous episodes in his story are his incarceration in the *lions' den (Dan 6 : 10-14; and *Bel and the Dragon); the interpretation of the writing which appeared on the wall during *Belshazzar's feast; his defence of the chaste *Susanna; and the defeat of Bel and the Dragon. He is an OT type of *Christ and the personification of *Justice.

Danse macabre A procession of people of all ranks led by skeletons, depicted on church walls and in woodcuts, the most notable examples being by Albrecht Dürer (1471-1528) and Hans Holbein (1497/8-1543). It probably originated in an acted-out sermon on how death makes no distinction between people, whether high-born, ecclesiastics, common men or women. Jenkyn, a carpenter of London, is said to have paid for a *Danse macabre*, inspired by one in the cemetery of the Holy Innocents at Paris, to decorate the cloister of old St Paul's Cathedral, London (*See* *Dance of Death).

David, King One of the major OT figures (c.1085-1015 BC), king of *Israel and ancestor of Christ (thus he appears on the Tree of *Jesse). As the supposed author of the *Book of *Psalms*, he is shown as a crowned monarch with a musical instrument, usually a *harp, the instrument which he played to assuage *Saul's fits of melancholy (1 Sam 16 : 19). He was a shepherd boy, son of Jesse, unexpectedly and secretly anointed by the prophet *Samuel as the king of Israel when Saul had offended God. In the war against the *Philistines, David proved that he was fit to face and defeat their champion *Goliath by telling Saul how he slew the lion and the bear which had attacked his father's flocks. He formed a close attachment to Saul's son *Jonathan, and married Michal his sister, but when Saul became jealous of his popularity and caused him to flee the court, he married *Abigail. After Saul and Jonathan were killed at Gilboa, David became king and fought a number of wars to make Israel an independent kingdom with its capital at *Jerusalem. He brought the *Ark of the Covenant which had been captured by the Philistines to Jerusalem and, overcome with joy, danced naked before it, earning the disapproval of his first wife Michal who had observed him from a window (2 Sam 6 : 14-16). To obtain *Bathsheba, whom he had seen bathing, he caused *Uriah, her husband, to be killed in battle. His punishment was the death of his son *Amnon who had raped his half-sister *Tamar; the rebellion and death of his son *Absalom; and the intrigues of another son,

Adonias, who tried to prevent the succession to the throne of his brother *Solomon. He was one of the *Just of the Ancient Law released by Christ at the *Descent into Hell.

David, St Patron saint of Wales (known in Welsh as Dewi). Although he lived in the 6th century, his biography was not written until *c*.900, and is a somewhat unreliable document intended to prove that the primate of Wales was independent of the *see of Canterbury. David was said to have founded many monastic communities inhabited by men dedicated to a life of great asceticism. No wine was drunk, the daily diet was bread and vegetables, and monks were yoked to ploughs to till the fields. His most famous foundation was at St David's (formerly Mynyw or Menevia) on the coast of Pembrokeshire, where contact with Irish monasteries was maintained. His shrine at St David's became a centre of *pilgrimage in the 12th century, two visits there achieving the same merit as one pilgrimage to Rome.

St David is depicted as a *bishop, often standing on a mound which rose up for him to stand on, thus recalling his presence at the *synod at Brefi, in Cardigan. A *dove on his shoulder signifies the inspiration of the *Holy Spirit. This enabled him to preach so eloquently against the Pelagian *heresy that St Dubricius (who was reputed to have crowned King Arthur at Carleon) resigned his archbishopric in his favour. St David's Day, 1 March, is the national day of Wales. There is no satisfactory explanation for the custom of wearing leeks or daffodils on that day. It may be hazarded that the equivalent of David, 'Dafydd' (hence 'Taffy' for a Welshman) was linked with 'daffy' for 'daffodil', and that a leek, which is also bulbous, was a substitute for the flower. St David is one of the *Seven Champions of Christendom.

Day Star Christ, 'the morning star' (Rev 22 : 16), whom the faithful are exhorted to reverence, 'until the day dawn, and the day star arise in your hearts' (2 Pet 1 : 19).

Deacon At first one of the officers whose duty it was to serve the Christian community (Greek *diakonein*, 'to serve', *diakonos*, 'server', 'minister'), especially in charitable matters. Seven Greek-speaking deacons were appointed in Jerusalem to look after the needs of the Hellenistic Christians (Ac 6 : 1-6). One of these was St *Stephen, the first Christian martyr, who is usually depicted dressed as a deacon in *alb and *dalmatic, as are SS *Cyriacus, *Lawrence and *Vincent of Zaragoza. The diaconate is now a grade leading to ordination. The deacon assists the *priest in certain duties, including the distribution of *Communion. He may be entrusted with the *chalice, and leads the congregation in prayers and intercessions.

Deaconess In the early Church, a pious woman, usually a widow, who looked after the female sick, poor and elderly and assisted in the *baptism of women. They were ordained for their tasks by the laying-on of hands by the *bishop. With the

Eternal **damnation** awaits sinners in the bottomless pit, tormented by devils (Dieric Bouts, *c*.1415-75).

The boy **David** holding the stone with which he slew Goliath (Michelangelo, 1501-4).

decline of the baptism of female adults, their role was superseded. The title of deaconess had ceased to be used by the 10th century. The office was revived in the *Anglican Church in 1861.

Dean Originally the 'tenth' (Latin *decanus*) monk, who supervised nine others. Now the president of a cathedral *Chapter who is responsible for the services and the administration of the church.

Death of St Mary the Virgin Some theologians held that St *Mary did not die before she was taken up into Heaven; others that she was not immune from death and accepted the normal consequences of being human as did Jesus himself. Pope Pius XII (1939-58) defined the dogma of the *Assumption in 1950 by stating that when the course of St Mary's earthly life was finished, she 'was taken up body and soul into the glory of Heaven'. The explanatory gloss on this statement, advanced by those who believed that Mary actually died, was that as with all mortals her soul was separated from her body at the moment of death, but that it was reunited with her incorrupt body before she was taken up into Heaven.

This accords with tradition and with the account given in the *Golden Legend*. Although there is disagreement as to whether her death took place in Ephesus (where the *Beloved Disciple to whom Jesus had entrusted her was thought to live) or in *Jerusalem, where Mary spent her days weeping at the places associated with her son's last moments. When she was about sixty, she was visited by an *angel (thought by some to be *Gabriel, as the event was parallel to the *Annunciation; by others to be St *Michael, who guides souls to *Heaven). He presented her with a *palm from *Paradise, to be carried before her bier, saying that she would die within three days. The *Apostles were miraculously transported on clouds from their various missionary fields to her death-bed, where she lay with a candle in her hand. (Later versions say that she was given the *last rites by St *John the Divine, or by Jesus himself.) After taking leave of them she had a vision of her son, who came accompanied by *angels, *patriarchs and *prophets to carry her soul to *Heaven. (This moment is called the *transitus*, or Transition.) The Apostles escorted her body on a bier, St *John the Evangelist carrying the palm, to the valley of *Jehoshaphat (in some versions *Gethsemane) where she was to be entombed. Jews and their High Priest tried to stop the cortège, but the High Priest's hands stuck to the coffin and were only released when, on St *Peter's advice, he prayed to *Christ. (In another version St Michael cut off his hands, but acceded to St Peter's request and reaffixed them to his arms.) When she was laid in the tomb, Mary's soul was reunited with her body and she was carried up (or 'assumed') into Heaven for her *Coronation. Roses fluttered down into the empty sepulchre and her girdle fell into the hands of St *Thomas the Apostle who, true to his sceptical nature, had doubted the fact of her Assumption.

The site of the house in Jerusalem where Mary is said to have died was purchased in 1898 by Kaiser Wilhelm II and donated to German Catholics for the erection of the Church of the *Dormition (*See* *Falling asleep of St Mary the Virgin; *Koimesis).

Deborah A prophetess and *Judge of Israel who sat under a palm tree on mount Ephraim, 'and the Children of Israel came up to her for judgement' (Jg 4 : 5). She led the Israelites against the Canaanite forces under *Sisera, who held the fertile Jezreel (or Esdraelon) valley (modern Emek). The enemy assembled a large army and 900 chariots at the western end, but they were immobilized in mud when God caused the River Kishon to flood after torrential rain. 'The stars in their courses fought against Sisera' (Jg 5 : 20). He fled when the Israelites swooped down on his forces from Mount Tabor and was killed by a woman, *Jael. Deborah sang a song of triumph in which she recounted the victory (Jg 5).

Decalogue The liturgical name for the *Ten Commandments.

Decollation A word used in the *Calendar and in art for 'beheading', especially with reference to SS *John the Baptist, *Catherine of Alexandria, *Cecilia, *James of Compostela and other saints (e.g. *Denis, *Januarius, *Winifred) who were martyred in this way. They may be shown with a severed *head or a *sword as their *attribute.

Deësis The name given in the *Orthodox Churches to the depiction of *Christ enthroned, with St *Mary the Virgin and St *John the Baptist on either side pleading for the souls of mankind.

Defender of the faith The title granted to Henry VIII of England (1491-1547) in 1521 by Pope Leo X (1513-21) for his book *Assertio Septem Sacramentorum*, a defence of the seven *Sacraments against Martin *Luther (1483-1546). It is still used by British monarchs although Elizabeth I (1533-1603) was excommunicated by Pope St Pius V (1566-72) in 1570.

Delilah *Philistine harlot of the Vale of Sorek with whom *Samson fell in love. She was offered 1100 silver shekels if she could discover the secret of his strength. Samson deluded her three times: first by pretending that he would be rendered powerless if tied with seven new bow strings; then if secured with unused ropes; and finally if seven locks of his hair were woven into the warp of a web; and each time he escaped capture. Nagged by Delilah until 'his soul was vexed to death' (Jg 16 : 16), he later confided that his strength really lay in his hair which he had been forbidden to cut. When he slept with his head on her lap, Delilah called a man hidden in the chamber to shear his locks (in another version she did it herself). His strength left him and he was overcome by the Philistines. They blinded him and set him to work, 'eyeless in Gaza, at the mill with slaves' (Milton, *Samson Agonistes*), derided by the populace, thus prefiguring the *Mocking of Christ.

His hair began to grow again and his strength returned, but the unsuspecting Philistines, to

humiliate him further, took him to a festival in the
temple of their god Dagon, which was filled with
jeering crowds, while 3000 more men and women
stood on the roof. Samson persuaded a boy
(whom he warned to escape) to lead him to the
two middle pillars of the entrance, and calling on
God for help he put an arm around each pillar and
caused the building to collapse, killing him and all
the Philistines (Jg 16 : 4-31). His *attribute is thus
a broken *column. He is also the symbol of
fortitude. Delilah's betrayal of Samson for money
prefigures *Judas betraying Christ.

Delivery of the law This scene, also known by
its Latin name *Traditio Legis*, is without scriptural
foundation, but appears in art as early as the 4th
century on *sarcophagi and is repeated in mosaics
from the 5th century onwards. It shows *Christ
handing the scroll of his new law, the fulfilment of
the old (*See* *Ten Commandments), to St *Peter.
St *Paul stands alongside.

Delta The *Greek letter D symbolizes the *Trinity
because it has three equal sides, like an equilateral
*triangle (see figure), thus proclaiming the equality
and identity of the three persons.

Demon One of the *fallen angels; *devils who
serve *Satan and inhabit *Hell where they assist in
the torture of the damned. They tempt men to sin
and can take possession of a body, causing the
victim to act like a madman. Jesus exorcized
demons and the *Apostles and *saints were able to
cast them out in his name. Demons are condemned
to eternal *damnation.

Denis (Denys, Dionysius), St Patron saint of
France (*d.c.*250). A native of Italy, he was sent as a
missionary to Gaul. He was made bishop of Paris
and lived on an island in the Seine with his
companions, Eleutherius, a *deacon, and Rusticus,
a *priest. Their successful preaching incensed the
local pagan rulers and all three were beheaded on
Montmartre, 'the martyrs' hill'. According to
legend, Denis carried his head in his hands for two
miles to the spot where the abbey of St Denis, later
the burial place for the kings of France, was built
over his tomb. To enhance the fame of the abbey,
Abbot Hilduin in the 9th century wrote a treatise
to prove that St Denis was Denys the Areopagite,
actually a 5th-century Christian platonist, but
called Pseudo-Denys, because he identified himself
as the Dionysius of Athens who was converted by
St Paul (Ac 17 : 34). This had the effect of linking
St Denis with the early days of Christianity and
dating the foundation of the *see of Paris to late
apostolic times. St Denis' fame, promoted by the
*Benedictines, spread rapidly in the Middle Ages.
He is represented in episcopal robes and carrying a
head in his hands, although he is not usually
headless. He is one of the *Seven Champions of
Christendom and one of the *Fourteen Holy
Helpers.

De profundis Latin for 'Out of the deep', the Vg
opening words of the *psalm used on behalf of the

The **Death of St Mary the Virgin** in the
presence of sorrowing Apostles. Christ carries
her soul, depicted as a child, to Heaven
(Tympanum, south transept of Strasbourg
Cathedral).

In prison, St **Denis** receives his last communion
from Christ before being decapitated (15th
century).

dead, 'Out of the depths have I cried unto thee, O Lord' (Ps 130 (129) : 1).

Descent from the cross Jewish law prescribed that bodies of criminals should not hang on the gallows after sunset as this would 'defile the land'. It was also an act of piety to bury those who had been executed. These precepts conflicted with the Roman practice of allowing a corpse to rot on a cross or to be devoured by birds or wild beasts, unless a magistrate granted release of the body to relatives. Jesus died on *Good Friday at the ninth hour (three o'clock). As the *Sabbath would begin at sunset, it was necessary to have his remains buried as soon as possible. One of his followers, *Joseph of Arimathea, a rich man and a member of the *Sanhedrin, therefore petitioned Pilate to allow the body to be removed from the *Cross. As death by crucifixion usually occurred after two or three days, Pilate was surprised when he heard that Jesus was already dead and summoned the centurion who had been present at Golgotha. (The Just *Centurion thus appears with Joseph of Arimathea summoned before Pilate.) When the death was confirmed, Pilate released the body.

Although the *Synoptic Gospels (Mt 27 : 57-61; Mk 42-6; Lk 23 : 50-6) state simply that Joseph of Arimathea took the body down from the Cross, the episode, frequent in art since the 9th century, has been greatly elaborated. The Cross, which would have been about ten feet high, became taller over the years and the cross-piece proportionately longer, so that one, two and even four ladders were placed against it. Joseph, richly dressed as befitted his station and assisted by *Nicodemus who pulls out the *nails with a pair of pincers, lowers the body to the ground. (As the wealthy Joseph was assumed to have servants, they may also take part.) St *John the Evangelist stands close by and receives the nails from Nicodemus. St *Mary Magdalene, identified by her long hair, kisses Jesus' feet, and St *Mary the Virgin takes one of his hands or swoons at the foot of the Cross (one of the *Sorrows of the Virgin) (See *Entombment; *Lamentation over the dead Christ).

Descent of Christ into Hell (or Limbo) It is an ancient belief, already developed in the 2nd and 3rd centuries and enshrined in the fourth article of the *Apostles' Creed, that while Jesus' body remained in the tomb for the whole of the *Sabbath following his *Crucifixion, his soul went down into *Hell (or *Limbo). The descent was noted in the Acts of the Apostles (Ac 2 : 27-31) and was thought to be alluded to in other texts (1 Pet 3 : 18-19; 4 : 6; Ps 16 (15) : 10). As to the purpose of the descent, opinions differed, depending on the interpretation given to Hell or *Hades. If it meant the place of departed spirits, then Jesus was completing his course as a man, his spirit going to Limbo to await resurrection. On the other hand, if Hell meant the place of punishment, then he went there to triumph over *Satan in his own kingdom. This is the view taken in medieval drama and in art. The apocryphal Gospel of *Nicodemus supplied a detailed account of the Descent. Christ's body remained in the tomb, but his spirit went to a part of Limbo – the Limbo of the Fathers – where the *Just of the Ancient Law awaited his coming. His arrival was announced by St *John the Baptist and *Dismas the *Good (or Penitent) Thief. He came in a blinding light, bearing the flag (* Vexillum) of the *Resurrection, kicked down the gates of Hell which could not prevail against him, bound *Satan, and led out *Adam by the hand. (*Eve was not mentioned in the Gospel of Nicodemus, but she was included in the scene in medieval drama and in art.) *Abel (identified by his shepherd's crook), *Abraham (bearded), *Moses, *David and *Solomon (both crowned) were also released. (*Leviathan, slain by a thrust through the jaws with a beflagged lance, sometimes replaced Satan in the art of the Middle Ages.) Christ's soul then rejoined his body to await his *Resurrection. (For the *Orthodox Churches, the Descent is the *Anastasis, or 'resurrection'.) The event is associated typologically with *Jonah, *Joseph the Dreamer in the well, *Samson opening the lion's mouth and *David saving the lamb from the bear (See *Harrowing of Hell).

Descent of the Holy Spirit About the third hour (around nine o'clock in the morning) on the first day (*Sunday) of the Jewish Feast of Weeks or *Pentecost, the *Apostles were assembled in their house-church in *Jerusalem. A sound from Heaven 'like a rushing mighty wind' filled the whole house where they were seated and cloven tongues as of fire appeared to them and rested on each one of them. They were all filled with the *Holy Spirit and began to speak in strange languages. These ecstatic utterances, the *Gift of Tongues, the phenomenon known as glossolalia, are characteristic of people in highly emotional states. But St *Luke, who recorded the event in the Acts of the Apostles (Ac 2 : 1-43), believed that the Apostles were speaking coherently. Assembled in Jerusalem for Pentecost – one of the great pilgrimage seasons – were Jews of the Diaspora, or Dispersion, and many of them were attracted to the house by the great noise. To their astonishment, they heard the Aramaic-speaking Galilean Apostles tell them in their various native languages of the mighty deeds of God. The more sceptical among them mockingly claimed that the Apostles were full of new wine, but St *Peter told them that it was too early in the morning for them to be drunk. He then spoke to them of the approaching Last Days and of the *Crucifixion and *Resurrection of Christ. The result was that some 3000 were baptized. The Christian festival of *Pentecost (*Whitsunday) commemorates this happening.

The scriptural source does not mention the presence of St *Mary the Virgin, but it was assumed on the basis of the statement that she prayed with the Apostles (Ac 1 : 14) that she was in the house-church with them. She is therefore shown in art in the place of honour, in the centre of the group, which includes the newly elected *Matthias. A *dove, representing the Holy Spirit, hovers above her and tongue-like flames appear over the heads of those assembled in the upper room. The nationalities listed as being present (Ac 2 : 9-11) possibly corresponded to nations grouped by ancient geographers under the various signs of the *zodiac, which were supposed to control each particular country. In *Eastern art the diverse peoples may be represented by the single crowned figure of Cosmos, the World, or by an old man personifying the world, holding twelve scrolls, representing a gospel for each nation. The inclusion of a figure with a scroll bearing the words *Effundam de Spiritu meo super omnem carnem*, 'I will pour out my spirit on all flesh' (Jl 2 : 28) represents the prophet *Joel whom St Peter quoted in his address to the sceptical crowd. He also prophesied, 'your young men shall see visions, and your old men shall dream dreams' (Ac 2 : 17). The OT event that corresponds typologically to Pentecost is the *Confusion of the tongues, the punishment for human presumption in building the Tower of *Babel.

Desert Fathers *Hermits and *monks who inhabited the Egyptian desert in the 4th century. Some lived alone, others in groups of two or three, meeting for worship on *Saturdays and *Sundays. They were noted for their asceticism, strict fasts, mortification of the flesh and feats of physical endurance. They supported themselves by basket-making and weaving. St *Pachomius organized some of them into monastic communities and gave them a *Rule. Famous among the Desert Fathers were SS *Antony of Egypt ('the Great'), *Paul the Hermit and *Hilarion.

Devil Another name for a *demon, a minion of *the* *Devil, *Satan. Devils were represented in various guises, frequently as cats, dogs and monkeys, and appeared in the most horrid shapes, with faces in their abdomens and with serpent-like tails. They tempted saints by whispering in their ears lewd details of the sexual pleasures they had relinquished, but were chained or put to flight by these holy men.

Devil, the *Satan, chief of *devils and *demons (*See* *Lucifer).

Devil's advocate The popular name for the member of the Congregation of the Causes of Saints, whose duty it is to investigate critically the candidates for *beatification or *canonization.

Diamond The hardest of the precious stones. It could be cut only if moistened with goat's blood.

Dice Included in the *Instruments of the Passion, because the soldiers who stood around the *Cross after the *Crucifixion cast lots for Jesus' garments (Mt 27 : 35) (*See* *Holy Coat; *Seamless Robe).

Dies irae Latin for 'day of wrath', the opening words of the hymn attributed to the *Franciscan friar Thomas of Celano (*c*.1200-55), based on *Zephaniah's prophecy of the imminent 'day of

The **Descent of Christ into Hell** to rescue the Just of the Ancient Law. Dismas, the Good Thief, stands by, carrying his cross (Giovanni Bellini, *c*.1500).

The **Descent of the Holy Spirit** as a dove on the Apostles. St Mary the Virgin reads Joel's prophecy of the event (Flemish, 16th century).

wrath, a day of trouble and distress' (Zeph 1 : 15). It begins the *sequence proper to funeral and *requiem Masses, and is said or sung on *All Souls' Day.

Diocese A Roman governmental term adopted by Christians to denote a bishopric, or *see, the territory under the jurisdiction of a *bishop.

Diptych Two tablets of ivory, wood or metal (Greek *diptycha*, 'a pair of tablets'), the outer side carved with symbolic Christian illustrations, the inner surfaces covered with wax so that they could be inscribed with a stylus. They were hinged together. In early Christian days they were used to record names of illustrious living or dead persons to be read out during the church service. They fell into disuse in the *West but are still used in the Armenian and Syrian *liturgies.

Dirge A hymn of mourning, especially with reference to the music sung at funerals or in memory of the dead. The word is derived from the opening phrase of the *antiphon in the office for the dead, *Dirige Domine, Deus meus,* 'Guide O Lord my God', based on Ps 5 : 8 (9).

Discalced An adjective applied to austere members of religious Orders (particularly *Franciscans, *Capuchins, reformed *Carmelites) who go about barefoot (Latin *dis*, 'without', *calceus* 'shoe'), or wear sandals, with or without stockings. They differ from those who are *calced.

Disciple A follower of a religious teacher (Latin *discipulus*, 'student'); used in the NT for the followers of Jesus in general, from among whom the *Apostles were specially chosen. Jesus sent out seventy disciples two by two to prepare for his visitation of 'every city and place' (Lk 10 : 1).

Dismas The name given in the *Gospel of *Nicodemus* to one of the malefactors executed alongside Jesus at his *Crucifixion (the other being named as *Gestas). Because he rebuked his fellow criminal for railing at Jesus, saying that they were justly condemned, 'but this man hath done nothing amiss' (Lk 23 : 41), he became known as the Penitent Thief or the *Good Thief. As Jesus promised him, 'Today shalt thou be with me in *paradise' (Lk 23 : 43), he is shown carrying a *Tau cross among the *Just whom Christ released from *Limbo (*See* *Descent into Hell).

Distaff A cleft stick holding wool or flax; an *attribute of *Eve who was condemned to spin while *Adam dug the ground after their *Expulsion from Paradise; hence 'the distaff side' to indicate the female line.

Dives and Lazarus Jesus told a *parable (Lk 16 : 19-31) about a certain rich man who was 'clothed in purple and fine linen and fared sumptuously every day' (depicted as pot-bellied). He is not named, but has been known traditionally as Dives (the Latin for 'rich man', used here as a proper noun). Lazarus the beggar is covered with sores which the dogs licked, and lay at his gate desiring to be fed with crumbs from the rich man's table. Dives died and went to *Hell. When he lifted up his eyes, he was pained to see Lazarus in *Abraham's bosom. He begged for Lazarus to be sent below to give him a drop of water to cool his tongue, because he was suffering the torments of hell-fire. Abraham reminded him that he received his good things on earth whereas Lazarus had done badly, and added, 'now he is comforted and thou art tormented'. Dives personifies *gluttony or *Gula, one of the *Seven Deadly Sins. The parable is cited as the scriptural warrant for Particular *Judgement after death.

Divine Office A service, distinct from the *Mass, said or sung at stated times (*See* *Hours, canonical) either in *choir by members of religious communities (*monks, *friars, *nuns), or in church or privately by secular *clergy. The traditional Latin text of the Office, consisting of *psalms, *hymns, prayers and appropriate readings, is contained in the Roman *Breviary. Some religious *Orders (e.g. *Carmelites) have their own versions.

Doctors, Jesus and the According to the *Gospel of Luke* (Lk 2 : 41-50), Jesus was twelve years old when his parents, as was their custom each year, went from their home in *Nazareth to *Jerusalem for the feast of *Passover. On this occasion they took him with them, but on the return journey could not find him although they searched among their kinsfolk and acquaintances travelling with them. In great distress, they went back to Jerusalem. After three days they discovered him in the *Temple sitting among doctors and teachers of the *Law, listening to them and asking them questions. He astonished everyone by his understanding. His parents upbraided him for causing them such anxiety, and failed to understand the significance of his reply, 'Wist ye not that I must be about my Father's business?' (Lk 2 : 49).

This episode is one of the seven *Joys of St Mary the Virgin because she found her lost son (*See* *Rosary).

Doctors of the Church Principally four *Western saints, *Gregory the Great, *Ambrose, *Augustine and *Jerome, renowned for their theological acumen. Others were added later, including SS *Thomas Aquinas and John of the Cross, so that they now number around thirty. Greek doctors, commemorated by the *Orthodox Churches on 30 January, are: SS *Basil the Great, *Gregory Nazianzus ('The Theologian') and *John Chrysostom.

Dog The dog's reprehensible characteristics are mostly stressed. The word is used as a term of abuse; indicating copulation in dog-fashion; or as a symbol of evil (a hound of *Hell or the *Devil himself, who frequently assumes the shape of a dog). A lascivious woman is equated with a bitch, which is also a term of abuse. The howling of a dog portends death. Black dogs are the familiars of *witches. A dog baying at the moon signified the foolish man despising higher things.

In contrast, because of the dog's devotion to its master or mistress, it may also symbolize courage and fidelity. Opinion is divided as to the meaning of the dog carved at the feet of a recumbent figure on medieval tombs. It may be a substitute for a *lion, representing *Christ's victory over death as he trampled on the lion, or it may symbolize faithfulness unto death.

The mothers of two saints, *Bernard and *Dominic, dreamed prophetically of dogs before their birth, foretelling their sons' futures as propagators of the faith. A dog carrying a torch is one of St Dominic's *attributes. *Dominicans, by a Latin pun on the name of their Order, are *domini canis*, 'watchdogs of the Lord'. Dogs accompany *Tobias, St *Roch and St *Vitus. A dog is the attribute of St *Margaret of Cortona. As one of the *Five Senses, dogs represent the sense of smell.

Dolphin A symbol of salvation by *Christ, because a dolphin was said to rescue shipwrecked sailors by carrying them on its back to safety. Also of the *Resurrection because it was thought to be the great fish which swallowed *Jonah.

Dom Abbreviation of Latin *dominus*, 'master', the title of members of the *Benedictine, *Carthusian and *Cistercian Orders, originally applied to *bishops and later extended to *monks. It is also used by *Premonstratensian and other *canons regular.

Domine Quo Vadis The name of a church situated on the Appian Way in Rome where St *Peter is said to have encountered Christ returning to Rome to be crucified once more (See *Quo Vadis?).

Dominic, St Domingo de Guzmán (1170-1221), a Spaniard born at Calaruega, Old Castile, distinguished for his learning and for his missionary work among the Albigensian or *Catharist heretics in the South of France. To convince some of them of the truth of his arguments, he once cast into a fire a document containing his propositions (in another version, a *Bible) and it rose out unscorched.

About 1206 Dominic founded a *convent for nuns and encouraged the use of the *Rosary (St *Mary the Virgin is sometimes shown giving a rosary to him) as an aid to devotion for unlettered people. Around 1215 he went to Rome to obtain papal sanction for the foundation of a new Order of Friars Preachers (See *Dominicans) and was granted permission after Honorius III (1216-27) had a vision of two men saving his church from ruin (See St *Francis). Before he left Rome, while praying in St Peter's, Dominic saw SS Peter and Paul descend and present him with a staff and a book of the *Gospels. He met St Francis and gave him the *kiss of peace, symbolizing the united efforts of their Orders to spread the faith, Francis by emphasizing the love of God, Dominic through rational argument.

A **diptych** showing Adam naming the animals, and three scenes from the life of St Paul (4th-5th century).

St **Dominic** preaching from a wayside pulpit, the fire before him possibly indicating the punishment which awaits heretics (Lorenzo Lotto, *c*.1480-1556).

The rest of Dominic's life was spent in promoting the ideals of his Order and in giving theological advice to the *Inquisition. He was buried in Bologna in a small chapel in the Dominican convent there, but in 1267 his remains were removed to a magnificent tomb designed by Nicola Pisano (active c.1258-78) in the church of San Domenico. Fra Guglielmo, who assisted the sculptor, removed one of the saint's ribs for a relic. He confessed his theft on his deathbed.

St Dominic is represented in the *habit of his Order, a black cloak and hood over a white robe. A star on his breast recalls the tradition that a star shone over his head at his christening, and a *lily in his hand signifies his purity. A *dog with a flaming torch in its mouth is sometimes shown near him, referring to his mother's prophetic dream before he was born that the members of his Order, by a Latin pun, Domini Canis, 'watchdogs of the Lord', would carry the torch of faith throughout the world. St Dominic may also be shown holding the *Keys of the kingdom like St Peter, or in the act of receiving them – a reference to his appointment as Master of the Sacred Palace, or theologian to the *Pope, a post traditionally held by a Dominican.

Dominicans Friars preachers, or *Black Friars (called after the colour of their *habit – black cloak and hood to recall the death of *St Mary the Virgin, worn over a white robe), members of the Order of St *Dominic, founded by that saint in 1220-1 to spread the faith and to combat the *Catharist heresy through superior learning and power of argument. The tribunal of the *Inquisition was entrusted to them. They lived in poverty and depended on alms until 1475 when Pope Sixtus IV (1471-84) permitted them to hold property. Notable Dominicans represented in art are SS *Peter Martyr and *Thomas Aquinas.

Dominions (or Dominations) The first choir of the second hierarchy of *angels. They have human form, are crowned with a triple crown and carry an *orb, *sceptre, *cross and *sword. They represent the power of God and direct the *powers and the *virtues in their special tasks. Their leader is *Zadkiel.

Dominus vobiscum The Latin for 'the Lord be with you', a clerical *liturgical greeting to which the congregation replies, Et cum spiritu tuo, 'And with thy spirit', meaning 'and also with you'. This dialogue expresses the fellowship which unites *clergy and *laity.

Donation of Constantine A document forged c.750-850 in France or Rome by an unknown writer, purporting to grant great wealth and privileges to the *Pope and the *Church and claimed to have been drawn up by Emperor *Constantine. The first part, the Confessio, tells how Pope *Sylvester I (314-35) instructed the emperor in the faith, baptized him and cured him of leprosy. The second part, the Donatio, records the donation to the Pope and his successors of the city of Rome and all the West. The Italian

humanist, Laurentius Valla, proved the grant to be false in 1440.

Doom A mural or stained glass showing the Last *Judgement, usually sited on the *tympanum over the west door of a church, or forming the subject of the west window.

Dorcas A personal name meaning 'gazelle', the Greek equivalent of *Tabitha whom St *Peter raised from the dead in Lydda (Ac 9 : 40-2). Her life was full of good works and acts of charity and she made clothes for the needy. Like-minded *Anglican ladies thus formed Dorcas societies in their local churches.

Dormition of the Blessed Virgin Mary The name in the *Eastern Church for the feast on 15 August commemorating the *Death, or *Falling Asleep of St Mary the Virgin. It corresponds to the Feast of the *Assumption and *Koimesis.

Dorothea (Dorothy), St A maiden of Caesarea in Cappadocia who was martyred c.313 during the Diocletian *persecutions because she refused to marry a pagan and to worship idols. She is represented carrying a basket of *roses and *apples because Theophilus, the governor's secretary, jestingly asked her, on her way to be executed, to bring him the fruit which grew in the garden of her heaven. At the moment of her death an *angel appeared to Theophilus and presented him with three apples and three roses, although it was midwinter. He was converted by the miracle and was himself martyred.

Dove Symbol of the *Holy Spirit which was seen 'descending as a dove' at Jesus' *Baptism. Also of peace and reconciliation because a dove returned to *Noah's Ark with an *olive branch in its beak to indicate that the *Flood had receded and that God had forgiven mankind. A dove hovering over water refers to the Holy Spirit, the Spirit of God, which 'moved upon the face of the waters' at the time of the *Creation (Gen 1 : 2). Near an *evangelist, *apostle *or saint, a dove indicates divine inspiration. It also symbolizes purity because it was one of the few birds permitted as a sacrifice under Mosaic *law.

Doxology From the Greek words dotsa, 'glory' and logos, 'word', an expression of praise in honour of the *Trinity, 'Glory be to the Father and to the Son and to the Holy Ghost. As it was in the beginning, is now and ever shall be, world without end'. It is the *Gloria of the *Mass, the lesser doxology, so called to distinguish it from the greater doxology, Gloria in excelsis, 'Glory [to God] in the highest'.

Dragon A fictitious monster resembling a huge *crocodile, with fiery, poisonous breath issuing from its jaws and distended nostrils. It has a scaly body, bat-like wings and a knotted tail. Usually it dwells in a cave or in a fetid marsh. It symbolized evil, the spirit of evil, or the *Devil. In the Middle Ages it also represented *heresy. *Satan is 'the great dragon' (Rev 12 : 9) whom God will destroy at the end of time. The pregnant woman 'adorned with the sun, standing on the moon' who is beset by the huge red dragon in a vision seen by St *John the Divine (Rev 12 : 1-6), is assumed to refer to St *Mary the Virgin, although the writer probably had *Israel or humanity in mind.

The OT verse, 'the saints shall trample the devil under their feet' (Ps 91 (90) : 13), has given rise to many legends of the slaying of dragons by various saints, notably SS *George, *Andrew and *Martha. St *Margaret of Antioch was swallowed by a dragon, but on making the *sign of the cross she burst out of its belly and led the monster captive. The slaying of the dragon by the archangel *Michael is derived from *The Revelation of St John the Divine* (Rev 12 : 7-9), 'And there was a war in heaven: Michael and his angels fought against the dragon . . .'. The episode symbolizes victory over sin, as does an *elephant trampling on a dragon (See *serpent).

Draught of fishes, miraculous Two *miracles performed by Jesus involving unexpectedly large catches of fish are recorded in the NT.

The first (Lk 5 : 1-11) is an alternative version of the *Calling of the Apostles. To escape the crowd which pressed about him as he spoke to them on the shore of Lake *Galilee, Jesus got into a fishing boat and preached from there. He then told Simon (St *Peter), the owner of the boat, who had toiled all night without catching anything, to put out into the lake and lower the nets. So many fish were caught that Simon called his partners, James and John, sons of *Zebedee, to help. Both ships were so full that they began to sink. Simon fell on his knees and said, 'Depart from me; for I am a sinful man', but the boats were brought safely to shore. Jesus told the three fishermen that henceforth they would catch men, so 'they forsook all and followed him'.

The second miracle took place post-*Resurrection. SS Peter, *Thomas, *Nathanael, *James, *John and two other disciples, fished all night in Lake Galilee but caught nothing. A figure which they did not recognize stood on the shore next morning and asked if they had anything to eat. When they replied that they had been unsuccessful, they were told to cast their nets. The *Beloved Disciple recognized Jesus' voice, and Peter jumped out of his boat and waded ashore. They all made a meal of bread and fish cooked over a fire. Before he left them, Jesus said to Peter, 'Feed my sheep' (Jn 21 : 1-22).

Dress, clerical The garments worn by *clergy of all ranks on non-liturgical occasions, as distinct from the *vestments which they put on for the celebration of *Mass or *Eucharist. Some garments (such as the *cassock and *chimere) may serve for both. A *Church of England *bishop wore a black coat, breeches and gaiters outdoors, because he would ride on horseback around his *diocese. In the House of Lords or in Convoca-

St **Dorothy** with her basket of roses, and St Peter with his keys (German, late 15th century).

A **dove**, as the Holy Spirit, hovers over a cross that stands in a chalice (Ravenna, 6th century).

tion, he wore over his cassock a *rochet, with sleeves gathered in at the wrist, and a scarlet or black chimere. Around his neck he placed a *tippet or black scarf. Portraits of many 19th-century *Anglican divines show them wearing this dress.

Drunkenness of Noah After the *Flood had subsided and *Noah and his family came out of the *Ark, Noah became a husbandman and planted a vineyard. Unaccustomed to strong beverage (before the Flood only water had been drunk), he became intoxicated with the wine which he made from the grapes he had harvested. He lay naked in his tent. Two of his sons, *Shem and *Japheth, put a garment over their shoulders, walked backwards, and covered Noah's loins. *Ham, the younger brother, was cursed by Noah, presumably because he had derided him (Gen 9 : 20-7). The scene is therefore linked typologically with the *Mocking of Christ.

Dunstan, St Archbishop of Canterbury, b.909 at Baltonsborough near *Glastonbury, where he became a hermit after being expelled from the court of King Athelstan in 935, supporting himself by his craftsmanship (he is the patron of jewellers and goldsmiths). King Edmund of Wessex made him *abbot of Glastonbury and he devoted himself to the restoration of the *Benedictine Order in England. He was established in the *see of Canterbury in 960, from where he continued the reform of monastic life until his death in 988. His cult developed soon afterwards, although there was later a prolonged dispute – not settled until 1508 when his tomb at Canterbury was opened – as to whether his remains were there or at Glastonbury. He is known in art mainly through one episode. He was particularly skilled in the manufacture of golden liturgical objects, especially *chalices. The *Devil frequently appeared to him in his forge, hoping to tempt him away from his holy work. One night, losing patience, Dunstan seized the Devil's nose with red-hot tongs and held him until he swore to cease annoying him.

Dust *Symbol of mortality. Man was formed of dust (Gen 2 : 7) and will return again to dust (Jb 34 : 15). Also of grief, denoted by sprinkling dust and *ashes on the head of a mourner (Jb 2 : 12); and of rejection, as when SS *Paul and *Barnabas showed their disgust with the city of Antioch in Pisidia when 'they shook off the dust of their feet against them' (Ac 13 : 51).

Eagle Attribute of St *John the Evangelist (also *John the Divine) who is equated with the fourth of the living creatures, the one with 'the face of an eagle', seen in a vision of Heaven by Ezekiel (Ez 1 : 10) (See *Evangelists). Also symbolic of divine inspiration, which is why *lecterns – on which Holy Bibles, the word of God, are placed – are

designed in the shape of eagles with outstretched wings.

According to the *Physiologus, an eagle was able to look at the sun without blinking, and trained its young to do likewise, bearing them upwards on its wings and discarding those which failed the test. It thus represented *Christ, who gazes on *God the Father and raises men up to contemplation of the Godhead, rejecting those who cannot bear the divine brilliance. From the heights, the eagle would see a fish in the sea and dart down to capture it. In the same way, Christ rescues the sinner from the world. An eagle also symbolized rejuvenation, as in the text, 'thy youth is renewed like the eagle's' (Ps 103 (102) : 5). It was explained that when an eagle becomes old and its eyes are dimmed, it flies towards the sun, so that the film is burned away from its eyes and its plumage is renewed by the sun's scorching rays. It then dips itself three times in a pool of pure water and becomes young again. In the same way, man is born into new life through *baptism in the name of the Father, Son and *Holy Spirit.

The eagle's reputation for leaving half its prey for other birds has made it a symbol of generosity. But as a bird of prey it stood for evil, and an eagle's claw indicated rapacity. Because of its keen vision the eagle represented sight, one of the *Five Senses. Soaring upwards, the eagle symbolized Christ's *Ascension. An eagle with a *serpent in its beak indicated Christ's victory over *Satan.

Ear Symbol of the *betrayal of Jesus in the Garden of *Gethsemane, where St *Peter cut off the ear of *Malchus, one of the soldiers who had come to arrest his master. Because the *Word of God (Christ the Logos) enters the mind through the ear, and because the Psalmist said 'daughter . . . incline thine ear . . .' (Ps 45 (44) : 10), it was believed that St *Mary the Virgin conceived Jesus through her ear. A shaft of light is thus shown descending towards her ear (See *Incarnation). An ear of corn, or of *wheat, symbolizes the bread of the *Eucharist, the *Host.

Earth *Symbolized by an *orb or by the figure '4', the four corners of the globe. It is one of the *Four Elements.

East The Orient, the point of the compass where the sun (Christ) appears, hence the source of light and truth. Churches are therefore 'orientated', the altar being placed at the east end. About the 8th century, it became customary for the *celebrant to stand in front of the altar, facing eastwards. In the new *liturgy he presides at the *Eucharist in his original position, facing westwards towards the congregation from behind the *altar.

East, the A conventional term for the independent and occasionally national Churches which compose the *Orthodox 'Eastern' Churches.

Easter The most ancient of the feasts of the Christian *year, one of the two 'holy days of obligation' (the other being *Christmas) when all baptized Christians must take *communion. It is the culmination of *Holy Week, commemorating the *Resurrection of Christ on *Sunday, the first day of the week, symbolizing the victory of light over darkness and the defeat of sin and death. The Venerable *Bede (*c.*673-735) gave it as his opinion that the English name for the feast was derived from Eostre, the name of the Saxon spring goddess, but this is doubtful. Other languages use words derived from the Greek *paskha,* the transliteration of the Aramaic *pascha* (Hebrew *pessach,* 'to pass over'), the name of one of the great Jewish pilgrimage festivals (*See* *Passover), when only unleavened bread was eaten and the paschal lamb was slaughtered. The *Crucifixion took place at this time, but controversy as to the exact day divided Christians for centuries, as different methods were used in Alexandria and Antioch to calculate the date of the paschal moon, the first full moon of spring. Easter is thus a movable feast, as it can fall in different years between 21 March and 25 April. *Anglican, *Roman Catholic and Non-conformist Churches celebrate the feast on the same Sunday, the *Orthodox Churches a week later. The Easter egg, pagan symbol of rebirth, was given a Christian meaning when it became the practice to bring eggs, forbidden food during *Lent, to be blessed in church on Easter Sunday.

An **eagle** supporting the lectern on the pulpit of Pisa Cathedral (Giovanni Pisano, *c.*1245-*c.*1314).

Ecce Agnus Dei Latin for, 'Behold the Lamb of God', the words used by *John the Baptist as *Jesus approached the River Jordan for his *Baptism (Jn 1 : 36) (*See* *Agnus Dei*).

Ecce Ancilla Domini Latin for, 'Behold the handmaid of the Lord', the words used by St *Mary the Virgin when she accepted her divinely appointed role at the *Annunciation (Lk 2 : 38).

Ecce Homo Latin for, 'Behold the Man!', the words used by Pontius *Pilate when he presented *Jesus to the people of *Jerusalem, saying that he had found no fault in him (Jn 19 : 4-6). The episode is frequently depicted in art. Pilate emerges from the room where he has examined Jesus onto a balcony to address the surging crowd below. He points to Jesus who stands silent in the burlesque adornments of kingship which Roman soldiers have mockingly placed on him (*See* *Crown of thorns). The figure of *Christ alone, crowned with *thorns, holding a reed as a *sceptre, his wrists tied and manacled and the wounds from his scourging still visible on his body, is a devotional image, intended to incite the faithful to pity and repentance (*See* *Man of Sorrows).

Ecce virgo concipiet Latin for, 'Behold a virgin shall conceive', *Isaiah's prophecy (Is 7 : 14) of the *Virgin Birth of Jesus, often inscribed on a scroll which he holds.

Eden, garden of According to the second account (Gen 2 : 8) of the *Creation of the world, God planted a garden in Eden, a place which is vaguely stated to be 'in the east'. In the *Septuagint version

With the words, **Ecce homo,** Pilate presents the humiliated Jesus to the baying crowd (Lucas van Leyden, 1494?-1533).

of the OT, 'garden' is translated as *Paradise, a word which was later accepted as a proper name. The Garden of Eden is described as containing every kind of tree bearing fruit that is good to eat, and in the middle stand the Tree of Life and the *Tree of the Knowledge of Good and Evil. It is watered by a river which divides into four branches, the *Rivers of Paradise (named as Pishon, Gihon, Hiddekel and Euphrates), as it leaves the garden. Man and Woman lived in Eden in bliss, naked and unashamed, until they ate of the *Forbidden Fruit and thus incurred *Expulsion from Paradise (Gen 2 : 8-25).

Education of St Mary the Virgin There was some dispute as to whether St *Mary the Virgin, who spent her girlhood in the Temple, needed to be instructed. Since she was chosen before time, it was said, she must have possessed innately all knowledge. From the 16th century onwards, when the girl Mary became the model for good maidens to follow, there was recourse to the apocryphal legend, popularized by Jacobus de Voragine in his *Golden Legend, in which it was recounted that she was ministered to by *angels, and that her mother, St *Anne, taught her to read and to sew. When she pricked her finger with a needle, it foretold the *Sorrows which she would experience at the death of her son. Another version is that, under angelic instruction, she wove the *veil of the Temple which was rent at the time of the *Crucifixion.

Edward the Confessor, St The last of the Anglo-Saxon kings of England (c.1004-66; cd.1161), noted for his gift of second sight, for his ability to cure scrofula (the King's Evil) by touch, and for his pious refounding of Westminster Abbey, where his body still rests in a shrine set up in 1268 behind the high *altar. The title 'the *Confessor', bestowed on one whose saintly life is a witness to the Christian faith, was conferred on him by Pope Alexander III (1159-81) in 1161, and distinguishes him from St Edward the Martyr (c.962-78) who was murdered with a dagger on his stepmother's orders and whose body (entombed in a nunnery at Shaftesbury) was endowed with miraculous powers of healing. St Edward the Confessor's attribute is a *ring because when he attended the dedication of the church of Christ and St *John the Evangelist at Havering in Essex, a beggar asked him for alms and the king gave him all that he then possessed, the ring from his finger. Years later, English pilgrims in the Holy Land encountered the same beggar who said he was St John and asked them to return the ring to King Edward with the message that he would die within a year and meet St John in Heaven. This ring (or a substitute) was used at coronations until 1688 when it was stolen from James II (1633-1701) on his flight from England in 1688.

Egg One of the foods forbidden during *Lent and brought to church to be blessed on *Easter Sunday (hence Easter egg), also a symbol of rebirth and the *Resurrection. Because *Job (Jb 39 : 13-14) said

that the ostrich lays its eggs in the earth and leaves them to hatch by themselves, an ostrich's egg is a symbol of the *Virgin Birth of Jesus.

Eight A symbolic *number. It represents the *Resurrection because Christ rose from the tomb on the eighth day after his entry into Jerusalem; Holy *Baptism because eight persons were saved in Noah's *Ark (thus some *fonts are octagonal in shape); and the eight *Beatitudes. Jesus was circumcised and given his name on the eighth day after his birth. There are eight canonical *Hours.

Elders, four and twenty St *John the Divine saw in a vision twenty-four elders, clothed in white raiment with golden crowns on their heads, sitting around the Heavenly Throne (Rev 4 : 4). They worshipped the one on the throne, saying, 'Thou art worthy, O Lord, to receive glory and honour and power' (Rev 4 : 11). In art, they are shown in adoration of the *Lamb who stands on *Zion (Rev 14 : 3).

Elephant A gigantic *animal notable for its modesty and chastity. It was believed from the statement in the *Physiologus that since their sexual organs were reversed, elephants modestly preferred to look the other way during intercourse. They were faithful to one spouse, had little sexual desire and copulated only to reproduce their kind, as the chaste Christian is advised to do. To engender their offspring a pair would journey to *Paradise, where the female would eat the aphrodisiac fruit of the tree called Mandragora (the *Mandrake) and then give some to her mate to arouse his desire. (This recalled the fall of *Adam and *Eve after they had eaten the fruit of the *Tree of Knowledge, assumed to be the Mandragora.) The female would then give birth in a lake, just as *Cain was said to have been born 'upon the waters of tribulation'. The male would protect her by trampling on any *serpent that happened to come by, and would guard her from their enemy the *dragon. If it lies down, an elephant was said to be unable to get up as it has no joints, so it leans against a tree when it sleeps. A hunter partly saws through the tree so that when the elephant rests against it the tree collapses and the elephant can be captured. Not even a large elephant (the Mosaic *Law) or twelve more elephants (the *Prophets) can lift it up, but when the elephant shouts for help, a little elephant (*Christ) comes to its rescue.

Alexander the Great (356-323 BC) encountered armed men riding in howdahs carried on the backs of elephants when he tried to conquer India. This gave rise to the belief that an elephant had a castle on its back. The heraldic device of the Elephant and Castle thus symbolizes the impregnable Church supported on a firm foundation of faith.

Elevation of the Host The custom, dating from the end of the 12th century, whereby the *celebrant at *Mass lifts the *Host immediately after its consecration, so that the *Real Presence of Christ in the *Eucharist may be adored.

Eleven thousand virgins See St *Ursula.

Elias The NT and Vg form of *Elijah.

Eligius (Eloi), St A goldsmith of Limoges (*c*.588-660), renowned for his honesty. When called to Paris to make a golden throne set with jewels for Clotaire II (*d*.629), he constructed two thrones out of the material allotted him instead of retaining the surplus for himself. The next king, Dagobert, appointed him Master of the Mint and in 641, because of his piety, bishop of Noyon. He made many missionary journeys, one of which was to Bologna where he became the patron saint. He continued to work at his craft and made beautiful shrines and church ornaments, including decorations for the tombs of St *Martin in Tours and St *Denis in Paris. He was also a blacksmith, and while working at his forge one day became so exasperated with the *Devil who constantly taunted him that he seized him by the nose with his red-hot tongs. Eligius' attributes are a hammer, anvil and horseshoe because he cut off the leg of a restless horse brought to him to be shod, fixed the shoe, and then replaced the leg, making the *sign of the cross over it so that no trace of a wound could be seen.

Elijah (Elias) The Tishbite of Gilead, a 9th-century BC Hebrew *prophet who, like *Enoch, 'never tasted death' because he was taken up to Heaven in a whirlwind in a chariot of fire (2 Kg 2 : 11). An unkempt figure, dressed in a leather loincloth and cloak of hair (2 Kg 1 : 8), living in caves in the wilderness. He was the OT type of St *John the Baptist. He warned King *Ahab of the calamities which would overtake *Israel unless the nation forsook its evil ways, and he then took refuge by the brook Cherith, the limit of Ahab's jurisdiction, where he was fed by ravens (1 Kg 17 : 1-7). At Zarephath, he performed the miracle of the *widow's cruse which was never empty of oil and restored her sick son to health (1 Kg 17 : 8-24). He overthrew the prophets of *Baal in a contest on Mount *Carmel and fled to Horeb (Mount *Sinai) to escape the wrath of *Jezebel, their protector. There he was fed by an angel under a juniper tree. While sheltering in a cave from an earthquake and fire, he was made aware of the presence of God in 'a still small voice' (1 Kg 19 : 12). He denounced Ahab for coveting *Naboth's vineyard (1 Kg 21 : 17) and called down fire from Heaven on those who resisted God's commands (2 Kg 1 : 10). When he was taken up into the sky, his mantle fell on his successor, *Elisha (2 Kg 2 : 13). At the *Transfiguration, he appeared with Moses and was seen talking with Jesus. *Carmelites claim Elijah as the founder of their Order because he lived a solitary life in a cave on Mount *Carmel. He will appear with Enoch at the *End of the World.

Elisha A Hebrew *prophet. *Elijah came upon him when he was ploughing his father's land and cast his mantle over the youth's shoulders to indicate that he was to carry on his work of preventing *Israel from offending God (1 Kg 19 : 19-21). Elisha slaughtered his team of oxen for a farewell

The tomb of St **Edward the Confessor** (*c*.1250), Westminster Abbey, London, enclosed by altar rails and with an altar and candlesticks before it.

Elijah, on his long journey to Mount Horeb, falls asleep under a juniper tree in the desert, and is comforted and fed by an angel (Dieric Bouts, *c*.1415-75).

feast with his parents and followed Elijah until his mentor was taken up into Heaven in a fiery chariot. The prophet's mantle fell upon him (2 Kg 2 : 13). His main task was to aid King Joab against the Syrians. Like Elijah, he performed miracles, filling with oil a widow's empty jars; restoring to life a Shunammite boy suffering from sunstroke (2 Kg 4 : 1-37), in a prefiguration of the raising of *Lazarus; and feeding a multitude with twenty loaves of bread and some fruit (2 Kg 4 : 42-4). He cured the Syrian captain Naaman of leprosy by ordering him to bathe seven times in the mud of the River Jordan (2 Kg 5 : 1-14), and made iron float (2 Kg 6 : 5). Elisha was bald, and when some children taunted him shouting, 'thou bald-head', two she-bears came out of the wood and devoured them (2 Kg 2 : 23-4).

Elizabeth, St Kinswoman of St *Mary the Virgin and wife of *Zacharias. Although 'well stricken in years', she miraculously bore St *John the Baptist, as foretold by the angel (Lk 1 : 13-17). When Mary in her turn knew that she was pregnant, she went to Elizabeth who greeted her with the salutation, 'Whence is this to me, that the mother of my Lord should come to me?' (*See* *Visitation), and entoned the *Magnificat. She escaped the massacre of the *Holy Innocents by fleeing with St John into the wilderness where a huge rock opened up and concealed them both until the danger was past. She is depicted presenting St John as a child to the infant Jesus.

Elizabeth of Hungary (or of Thuringia), St Daughter of King Andrew II of Hungary, *b.*1207 and betrothed while still an infant to Ludwig the future landgrave of Thuringia, because this had been prophesied by Kilinsor, the court poet. The marriage turned out to be a happy one, despite constant attempts to humiliate her by the landgrave's relations who were jealous of her beauty. She nevertheless irritated her husband because of the time she spent caring for the poor, even to the extent of giving away her possessions. (Thus she is depicted in the midst of beggars.) Once she was left with only an old cloak to wear at a court function, but it was miraculously changed into a royal robe. In the depths of winter she was carrying food to the poor and was stopped by her enraged husband, but the food turned into roses, thus she is shown with an apron or basket full of *roses. A similar legend is told of St Elizabeth (Isabel), queen of Portugal (1271-1336). On another occasion she put a leper in her bed, but when the landgrave's mother tried to prove her guilty of infidelity, the leper was transformed into the figure of the crucified *Christ.

Ludwig died of plague at Otranto on his way to *Jerusalem on a crusade, and his brother usurped his rights. Elizabeth and her children were humiliated and forced to live in poverty in a small cottage. Although she was still young and beautiful, she refused offers of marriage and in 1228 became a Franciscan *tertiary. Conrad of Marburg, her spiritual director, treated her so harshly, sending her children away and imposing severe

fasts and penances on her, that she died in 1231 in her twenty-fourth year. She was canonized in 1235 and the church in Marburg which contained her shrine was a centre of pilgrimage until the mid-16th century.

Elmo, St The popular name of St *Erasmus.

Elymas Magician at the court of Sergius Paulus, Roman governor of Paphos in Cyprus. He tried to prevent St *Paul from speaking and was struck blind (Ac 13 : 6-12).

Ember days Fast days 'about' or 'around' (Old English *ymbren*) four seasons of the Christian year: the third week in *Advent; the first in *Lent; the *octave of *Pentecost; and the week after the third Sunday of September. *Clergy are ordained at these seasons (*See* *Holy Orders).

Emmanuel The *Septuagint spelling of Immanuel (Is 7 : 14), Hebrew for 'God is with us', the name prophesied to be that of the *Messiah, and later given to Jesus (Mt 1 : 23).

Emmaus, road to An unidentified location, 'about threescore furlongs' from *Jerusalem. Perhaps Latrun. After the *Crucifixion, some of Jesus' disciples, including Cleophas, left Jerusalem. As they walked along the road near Emmaus they were accosted by a stranger who surprised them because he did not seem to know what had happened in the city. Later he revealed himself as the risen *Christ when he supped with them in the inn. They recognized their Lord in the breaking of the bread, symbol of the *Eucharist (Lk 24 : 13-32). Because the Latin *peregrinus* could mean both 'stranger' and 'pilgrim', Christ in this scene is often depicted in *pilgrim's garb with staff and scrip. Emmaus is called in the Vg a *castellum* and is therefore sometimes pictured as a castellated town.

Empty Tomb The fact of the *Resurrection of Christ was affirmed by the discovery early on the first day of the week that the tomb in which he had been laid the previous *Good Friday (*See* *Entombment of Christ) was empty. Details of the event differ in the *Gospels (Mk 16 : 1-8; Mt 28 : 1-8; Lk 24 : 1-12; Jn 20 : 1-18). Early in the morning, the *Holy Women, St Mary Magdalene, Mary the mother of James, and Mary Salome (or Joanna and others, according to *Luke*), brought aromatic oils to anoint the body. (Purchase of these oils from an itinerant spice-seller is a comic episode in medieval drama.) They found the stone which *Joseph of Arimathea had placed at the entrance to the tomb already rolled back (but *Matthew* says there was an earthquake and an angel descended and rolled back the stone). The women saw a youth sitting inside on the right of the tomb (*Mark*); or sitting on a stone outside (*Matthew*); or two men standing inside (*Luke*). They were told not to be afraid (or asked, 'Why seek the living among the dead?' *[Luke]*; or *[John]* 'Why do you weep?') and were informed that Jesus was not there (*non est hic*, 'he is not here') but that he was risen from the dead (*surrexit*, 'he is risen'). The Easter sepulchre for the repose of the *Host was devised to provide for the liturgical enactment of this event which was the central dramatic episode in the medieval Easter cycle.

St Mary Magdalene, according to *John*, hastened to tell St *Peter and the *Beloved Disciple (supposed to be St John) who both came running to the tomb. Peter (who was outstripped in the race) went into the tomb first (and thus represents the Ancient Law of the OT) and saw the linen cloths in which the body had been wrapped lying on the ground and also the cloth that had been over Jesus' head (*See* *Holy Shroud) rolled up in a place by itself. John, who reached the tomb first, waited outside and then followed Peter. He thus symbolizes the new dispensation of the NT.

Enclosed An adjective used to describe members of a religious community who have vowed to remain within the enclosure or confines of their *convent, access to them being forbidden except on strictly limited occasions.

Enclosed garden In Latin, *hortus conclusus*, the words used in the *Song of Songs* to describe the beloved, 'a garden inclosed is my sister, my spouse' (Sg 4 : 12), understood as a reference to St *Mary the Virgin. An enclosed garden is thus one of her *attributes.

Encyclical From the Latin *encyclicus*, 'circular', a letter or document sent by the *Pope to *bishops in which he commemorates a special event or expresses the teaching of the *Roman Catholic Church on a particular topic of immediate interest. Encyclicals are named after their opening Latin words. Recent examples are *Pacem in Terris* (1963), 'Peace on earth', issued by Pope John XXIII (1958-63), and *Humanae Vitae* (1968), 'Of human life' (birth control), sent by Pope Paul VI (1963-78).

End of the world The *Second Coming of Christ, the *parousia promised at his *Ascension (Ac 1 : 11), will herald the End of the World, the conclusion of finite time. When this second *Advent will happen is not known, but throughout the centuries the scriptures have been searched for clues to the future. It was believed that the esoteric imagery of the *Book of Daniel*, much of which was adapted in the *Apocalypse (*The Revelation of St John the Divine*), and the complicated numerological symbolism of apocalyptic writings, if correctly interpreted would provide the answer. Also taken into account were the so-called 'Little Apocalypse' (Mt 24 : 3-28), Jesus' escatological predictions of the rise of false prophets; wars and rumours of wars; nation rising against nation; brother betraying brothers, fathers and sons; and the *Abomination of Desolation set up in the *Temple in Jerusalem. Other indications would be the return of *Nero from the dead and the appearance of the *Wandering Jew and *Antichrist.

St **Elizabeth of Hungary** distributes her jewels and plate among the poor. A painting by Master Pepin of Antwerp, representing one of the Works of mercy.

At the inn in **Emmaus**, the risen Christ reveals himself to his astonished disciples when he breaks bread at supper (Caravaggio, *c*.1598).

The Archangel *Gabriel told *Daniel in a vision that God had allowed seventy weeks (thought to be 'weeks of years', i.e. 70 × 7 = 490 years) for man 'to make reconciliation for iniquity' (Dan 9 : 24). It was calculated that sixty-nine of these weeks (483 years) had elapsed by the time of the *Crucifixion. We are now said to be in the seventieth week, the latter half of which is the period of 'great tribulation', as predicted by Jesus (Mt 24 : 21). At some time in this period, either before, half-way through or after the 'great tribulation' (opinion is divided on this point), *Christ will descend and meet his Church, those who have died in Christ and the living faithful, and take them to *Heaven. His return will be signalled by the *Signs of the Times. The armies of the *Beast will be overthrown and the 'false prophet' (thought by some to be Antichrist) will be cast into a 'lake of fire burning with brimstone' (Rev 19 : 20). *Satan will be bound for a thousand years (the *Millennium), during which time Christ will reign over the world. Then *Satan will be set free and will attack with an army as numerous as 'sand of the sea', but they will be destroyed by fire from Heaven and cast into the lake of fire to 'be tormented day and night for ever and ever' (Rev 20 : 7-10). The Last *Judgement will then take place; the New *Jerusalem will descend (Rev 21 : 1-4); and Christ and his servants shall 'reign for ever and ever' (Rev 22 : 1-5). This is the outline of events, but the details have been the subject of much debate and reinterpretation.

Enoch The name of probably two OT persons. One is the eldest son of *Cain (Gen 4 : 17), the other the father of *Methuselah (Gen 5 : 21), described as 'the seventh from *Adam' (Jude 5 : 24). As *seven is symbolic of perfection, this may imply that he represented a perfect man. Enoch 'walked with God: and he was not; for God took him' (Gen 6 : 24). This was understood to mean that he did not die but was taken up to *Heaven like *Elijah. Enoch and Elijah are thus regarded as 'the two witnesses' who will appear at the *End of the World and fall before the *Beast (Rev 11 : 3).

Entombment of Christ After Jesus' body had been taken down from the Cross (See *Descent from the Cross), it was wrapped in a linen *shroud and carried to an unused tomb recently hewn out of living rock, a resting-place which *Joseph of Arimathea had probably prepared for himself. In the *Gospel of John* (Jn 19 : 41) the tomb was said to be situated in a garden near the place where Jesus had been crucified. The corpse was laid on a slab and Joseph rolled a great stone over the entrance to the tomb. The event was witnessed by the *Holy Women who had followed Jesus out of Galilee (Lk 23 : 55), including St *Mary Magdalene and 'the other Mary', presumably Mary the mother of James and Joses (Mk 16 : 1). Although not mentioned in the Gospels, *Nicodemus, St *John the Apostle and St *Mary the Virgin were assumed to have been present and are depicted among the mourners. They are grouped as in the *Pieta –

Nicodemus and Joseph respectively at the head and foot of the body (behind the tomb when it is represented not as a cave but as a grave) and between them St John and the Virgin, overcome by grief. St Mary Magdalene is in front of the tomb, either kneeling before it or bending over it. The episode is the fourteenth of the *Stations of the Cross. After the burial all the mourners left the garden. According to the *Meditations on the Life of Christ* St John took the Virgin to his own home.

Entry into Jerusalem The first episode in the *Passion of Christ, commemorated on *Palm Sunday when Jesus entered Jerusalem on an *ass and was acclaimed by the crowd as the expected *Messiah.

Envy One of the *Seven Deadly Sins, in Latin *invidia*.

Epiphany From the Greek *epiphaneia*, 'manifestation', a festival older than *Christmas, originating in the *Eastern Church in the 3rd century and celebrated on 6 January. It commemorated four manifestations of Jesus: his appearance to the *Shepherds; to the three *Kings; his *Baptism in Jordan; and his first miracle at *Cana in Galilee, where he changed water into wine. The feast was adopted by the *Roman Catholic Church about the 4th century and observed on 6 January, a date which coincided with pagan New Year festivities, the revelry perpetuated in the celebrations of *Twelfth Night.

Epistle From the Latin *epistola*, 'letter', an extract from one of the NT letters, the first NT lesson at *Eucharist or *Mass (the second lesson being the *Gospel). It is read or intoned from the epistle-side, the right side of the altar from the viewpoint of the congregation.

Erasmus (Elmo), St A bishop of Syria (*d.c.*303) who fled to Mount Lebanon to escape *persecution during the reign of Emperor Diocletian. He was fed by a raven, but left because the Archangel *Michael ordered him to preach the gospel in Italy. There he was put to death by having his entrails wound around a windlass (his *attribute). A cathedral in Mola-di-Gaetà (Formiae) between Rome and Naples is dedicated to him and marks the place of his martyrdom. He is the patron saint of sailors because an *angel once guided him across the Mediterranean when he escaped from his persecutors. Electrical discharges seen on mast-heads during storms are called 'St Elmo's fire' because it is believed that the saint has taken the ship under his protection. He is invoked against sea-sickness and bowel trouble and is one of the *Fourteen Holy Helpers.

Ermine Symbol of purity because it can be captured if surrounded with mud, as it would rather submit to its pursuers than dirty itself by trying to escape; whence its association with the motto, 'Better death than dishonour'. Because it was reputed to conceive through the ear, the ermine also represented the *Incarnation of Christ in the body of St *Mary the Virgin.

Esau A hairy man and a hunter, son of *Isaac, who sold his birthright for a mess of pottage, a dish of lentil soup (Gen 25 : 24-34), and was tricked out of his inheritance by his brother *Jacob, a shepherd and 'a smooth man' (Gen 27 : 1-45).

Esther The beautiful *Jewess who became queen of King *Ahasuerus of Persia (Esther means 'star' in Persian). Her story is told in the *Book of Esther*. She was the adopted daughter of *Mordecai, one of Ahasuerus' court officials, and was one of the maidens placed in the harem so that the king could choose a successor to his consort *Vashti who had offended him. When Ahasuerus saw Esther, he was so taken with her 'that he set the royal crown upon her head and made her queen', an act typologically linked with the *Coronation of St *Mary the Virgin as *Queen of Heaven. When Haman, the king's chief minister, issued an edict for all Jews to be slaughtered and their possessions seized, she appeared before Ahasuerus to plead for her people, an episode which prefigured St Mary the Virgin interceding for mankind before the heavenly throne at the Last *Judgement. Haman was later hanged (See *Mordecai). On Esther's orders the Jews commemorated their deliverance each year with the Feast of Purim, 'a day for gladness and feasting' (Est 9 : 19).

Eucharist From the Greek *eucharistein*, 'to give thanks'; the central act of worship and sacrament of the Christian Church, otherwise the *Mass, Holy *Communion, or the *Lord's Supper (See *Last Supper).

Eugenia, St Probably a Roman virgin-martyr of the 3rd century, buried in the cemetery of Apronian on the Via Latina. But according to the *Golden Legend* she was daughter of Duke Philip of Alexandria and famous for her learning. Wishing to lead an eremitical life, she dressed as a man, was admitted to an Egyptian *monastery and later became its *abbot. Accused of adultery, she was brought before her father for trial, but proved her innocence by revealing her identity. She later went to Rome where she was beheaded by order of Emperor Severus.

Eusebius 'The Father of Church history' (*c*.260-*c*.340), so called because of his *Historia Ecclesiastica*, 'History of the Church', or 'Ecclesiastical History' (finished *c*.324), which is an account, based on earlier writings and original research, of Christianity from its beginnings to his own day. He also wrote a *Life of *Constantine*. Eusebius was bishop of Caesarea from *c*.315. He was present at the Council of Nicaea (325).

Eustace (Eustacius), St Patron saint of huntsmen. Before his conversion he was called Placidus, captain of the Guards of Emperor Hadrian (or Trajan). While out hunting he encountered (as did St *Hubert) a white stag with a bright light in the

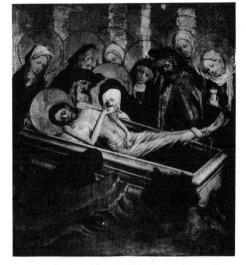

The **entombment** of Jesus by Nicodemus and Joseph of Arimathea. St Mary the Virgin kisses Jesus' hand. St Mary Magdalene with her pot of ointment and the other Holy Women are also present (Master Franke, 1424).

Haman and his ten sons, their eyes concealed so as not to offend the Mosaic aniconic law, are hanged in place of Mordecai because of **Esther**'s pleading with Ahasuerus (German, 1344).

form of a cross between its horns, and on the cross the figure of Christ (his *attribute). He was baptized together with his family and took the name of Eustace. He was warned by Christ that he would suffer trials as harsh as those of *Job. He lost his home and his possessions and fled to Egypt, where the captain of the ship impounded his wife because Eustace was unable to pay the fare. She was later captured by pirates. A lion carried off one of his sons, a wolf another, and he himself was obliged to work for fifteen years as a farm labourer. Then the emperor recalled him to his former position in Rome where he was united with his wife who had escaped from her captors, and then joyfully discovered that his sons, rescued by ploughmen from wild beasts, were serving under his command. When the four of them refused to sacrifice to idols, they were roasted inside the statue of a bull made of brass. St Eustace is one of the *Fourteen Holy Helpers.

Evangelical The name given to those members of the *Church of England who, from the mid-18th century onwards, have sought a deeper spiritual life through emphasis on salvation, through faith and the experience of a personal conversion. They avoid ceremonial, stress simplicity in worship and incline to the *Protestant tradition.

Evangelists, four The supposed authors of the four canonical *Gospels, symbolized in art by emblematic figures (the *Tetramorphs) derived from the vision of *Ezekiel (Ez 1 : 4-10) and the *Revelation of St John the Divine* (Rev 4 : 6-7). St *Matthew is represented as a human face or as a man, sometimes winged, because his Gospel begins with the human ancestry of Christ. St *Mark appears as a *lion, often winged, because the lion dwells in the desert and Mark's Gospel begins with the mission of St *John the Baptist, 'the voice of one crying in the wilderness' (Mk 1 : 3). St *Luke is a winged *ox, a sacrificial animal, because his Gospel opens with the story of *Zacharias entering the Holy of Holies to sacrifice. St *John is an *eagle, a bird which soars into the skies, because his Gospel opens with the words 'In the beginning', thus carrying the reader into the Heavens. These Tetramorphs are sometimes shown as animal heads on human bodies. They first appeared in Christian art in mosaics in the late 4th century. St *Jerome gives the symbols as above, but St Iranaeus (c.130-c.200) makes John a lion and Mark an eagle. St *Augustine and the Venerable *Bede described Matthew as a lion and Mark as a man.

Eve The name which *Adam, the first man, gave the first *Woman, his wife, 'because she was the mother of all living' (Gen 3 : 20) (Eve is in Hebrew *Hawwah*, possibly from the root *hayah*, 'to live'). Sin entered the world through Eve's disobedience to the divine command not to eat of the fruit of the *Tree of Knowledge of Good and Evil. Redemption came through another woman, St *Mary the Virgin, who is therefore called the 'new Eve'. The first word of the angelic salutation *Ave Maria* was read symbolically backwards as *Eva* (Eve), thus reversing the sin of Eve. Eve's punishment, painful childbirth, was inherited by womankind (Gen 3 : 16).

Evensong A medieval name for the canonical *Hours of *Vespers and *Compline, retained in the *Church of England as the equivalent of Evening Prayer. The service consists of prayers, OT and NT readings, *psalms, the *Apostles' Creed, the *Magnificat* and the *Nunc Dimittis*, the last two said or sung in English.

Exaltation of the Holy Cross The *feast on 14 September (Holy Cross Day) which commemorates the return to Jerusalem in 630 of a relic of the Holy *Cross.

After she discovered the *True Cross, St *Helena left one piece of it in Jerusalem where it was kept in the Church of the Holy Sepulchre until it was carried off in 615 by King Chrosröes (Khrosrow II) of the Persians. Legend had it that he put it on the right side of his throne and ordered that he should be worshipped as *God the Father. According to the *Golden Legend*, Emperor Heraclius (c.575-641) defeated the Persian army on the banks of the Danube, punished Chrosröes with death for his impiety, and took the relic of the Cross back to Jerusalem. As he was about to enter the city by the gate through which Jesus had passed on his way to *Calvary, the stones of the parapet fell down and barred his royal progress. An *angel appeared on the wall, holding a cross, and told him that Jesus had entered that city humbly on an ass (See *Entry into Jerusalem), not in royal state. Heraclius dismounted, took off his shoes, stripped himself to his shirt, and humbly carried the piece of the Cross towards the gate, whereupon the stones moved away to let him pass.

Unfortunately Heraclius was defeated by an Arab army in 636 and returned to his Byzantine capital, Constantinople, taking some of the wood of the Cross with him.

Ex cathedra Latin for 'from the chair', i.e. the papal *throne, a phrase used for an official pronouncement by the *Pope on faith or morals and thus, because of the dogma of *infallibility, binding on the faithful (See *cathedral).

Excommunication The exclusion from communion at the *Eucharist and from other *sacraments of persons unrepentant of some grievous and notorious crime or *heresy.

Exodus from Egypt The 'going out' or escape of the *Israelites from captivity in Egypt, the event which marked their beginning as a nation. They were saved from the last of the Ten *Plagues on the night of the *Passover, and led by *Moses over the *Red Sea, to spend many years *wandering in the Wilderness until they came finally to their permanent home, the *Promised Land.

Exorcism A command in Christ's name given to the *Devil to leave a person or place. It is performed by a *priest before *baptism and in cases of proven demonic possession.

Exposition of the Blessed Sacrament The placing of the consecrated *Host in a *monstrance for the adoration of the faithful. The ceremony originated in the 14th century after the establishment of the feast of *Corpus Christi.

Expulsion from Paradise As punishment for eating the *Forbidden Fruit, *Adam and *Eve were driven out of *Paradise. *Cherubim and a flaming sword were placed at the east of the Garden of *Eden to guard the way to the Tree of Life (Gen 3 : 23-4). This scene is the OT prefiguration of the *Expulsion of the traders from the Temple. A *Life of Adam and Eve* of Jewish origin and written early in the 1st century before the destruction of the *Temple, lists the penances which Adam and Eve suffered in the hope of expiating their sin.

Expulsion of the merchants from the Temple Enraged by the mercenary traders who desecrated the Temple precincts and made his Father's house 'a den of thieves', Jesus overturned their tables and drove them and their animals (with a whip according to Jn 2 : 14-16) out of the courtyard. The *Gospel of John* places the episode at the beginning of his ministry, the other gospels (Mt 21 : 12-13; Mk 11 : 15-17; Lk 19 : 45-6), just before the last events of his life. Typologically, the scene is linked with the *Expulsion from Paradise.

Ex voto An object, usually a *candle, offered in fulfilment of a vow and placed near an altar or in a sanctuary.

Eye The all-seeing eye of God (based on Prov 15 : 3). Enclosed within a *triangle it is the symbol of the *Trinity. Eyes on a platter are the attribute of St *Lucy, who plucked out her eyes and sent them to her suitor.

Ezekiel A Hebrew *prophet of the 6th century BC who lived in exile in Babylon. His visions and prophecies are set out in the *Book of Ezekiel*, which encourages the *Israelites to turn again to God and keep his commandments, because he has promised that 'they shall be my people and I will be their God' (Ez 11 : 20). Three of Ezekiel's visions have influenced art: the four beasts (the *Tetramorphs) which he saw around the throne of God (Ez 1 : 10), understood to symbolize the *Evangelists; the vision of the dry bones in the valley which were clothed with flesh and brought again to life (Ez 37 : 1-14), held to prefigure the resurrection of the dead at the Last *Judgement; and his vivid description of the four creatures each with a wheel (Ez 1 : 4-11), a basis for the portrayal of *angels. His text, *Porta haec clausa erit; non aperietur*, 'This gate shall be kept shut; it must not be opened' (Ez 44 : 2), which he sometimes displays on a scroll, was thought to refer to the Perpetual *Virginity of St Mary the Virgin, so that a closed door (*porta clausa*) is one of her *attributes.

The **Expulsion from Paradise** of Adam and Eve (Masaccio, early 15th century).

The **Expulsion from the Temple** of the money-changers, whose tables are overturned, and of the merchants whom Jesus drives out with a whip (St Stephen's Church, Vienna).

Ezra A Hebrew word meaning 'help', and also the name of two books of the *Bible, the Vg form being *Esdras*. The second book is also called in the AV *Nehemiah* (Vg *Nehemias*), after the author, cup-bearer of the Persian King Artaxerxes, sent by him to rebuild *Jerusalem. Ezra narrates in the first book the return of the Jews from their *Babylonian captivity. Two books of the *Apocrypha (III and IV *Esdras*) bear Ezra's name. From the latter comes the liturgical text, 'Eternal rest grant them O Lord' and the words, 'the seventh part, namely where the water was gathered' (2 Esd (Vg IV) 6 : 50), on which Christopher Columbus depended for his calculation of the width of the Atlantic Ocean.

Fabulous beasts As well as using real animals and *birds as symbols and vehicles for moral instruction, it was the practice in the Middle Ages to draw on fantasies from the *bestiaries, the *Physiologus* and similar works (See *animals). Those strange creatures which figured most prominently were: *amphisbaena, *ant-lion, *basilisk, *caladrius, *centaur, *cockatrice, *dragon, *griffin, *hydrus, *manticora, *mermaid, *phoenix, *salamander, *sciapod, *siren, *satyr, *unicorn, *wild man (or *woodwose), *wyvern and *yale.

Faith, Hope and Charity The three theological *virtues, as distinct from the natural, or cardinal virtues: prudence, temperance, fortitude and justice. These virtues are extolled by St *Paul, 'And now abideth faith, hope and charity, these three; but the greatest of these is charity' (1 Cor 13 : 13). 'Charity' in this context is the equivalent of 'love' (See *agape).

Faith, Hope and Charity are also saints, three 2nd-century Roman martyrs, daughters of Sophia (Greek for 'wisdom'), whose Greek names were Pistis ('Faith'), Elpis ('Hope') and *Agape ('Charity'). All four were put to death during the reign of Emperor Hadrian (117-38) and buried on the Aurelian Way. Four martyrs with similar Latin names, *Sapientia* ('Wisdom'), *Spes* ('Hope'), *Fides* ('Faith') and *Caritas* ('Charity') were buried on the Appian Way in the *catacomb of St Callistus.

Falcon The wild falcon symbolizes evil or unregenerate man because it is a bird of prey. Tamed, the falcon symbolizes the converted pagan.

Fall of mankind God created mankind in the persons of *Adam and *Eve and set them in the Garden of *Eden. There they lived in a state of innocence and grace, free from concupiscence, naked and unashamed. They were allowed to eat any fruit in the garden, except for that of the *Tree of Knowledge of Good and Evil. The *Serpent, 'the most subtle of the beasts of the field', tempted Eve to eat the *Forbidden Fruit, saying that the prohibition was due to God's fear that the man and

or woman who ate this fruit might 'become as gods, knowing good from evil'. Desirous of this knowledge, Eve ate some of the fruit, believed to be an *apple, and gave some to her husband. Then their eyes were opened and they saw that they were naked, so they sewed *figleaves together and made themselves aprons, or loin-cloths (Gen 3 : 1-7).

Frightened, they hid from God among the trees as he walked in the Garden in the cool of the day. When he asked why they avoided him, Adam explained that they had hidden because they were naked. God then knew that they had disobeyed his command because they had realized that they were unclothed (Gen 3 : 8-13). This was man's first disobedience, his *Original Sin, and fall from *grace. Mankind would ultimately be freed from the inheritance of this sin through the sacrifice on the *Cross. The punishment of Adam and Eve was *Expulsion from Paradise.

Fallen angels *Angels, led by *Satan, who rebelled against God and who, after their defeat by St *Michael and his host, fell from *Heaven. They lost their angelic qualities and were transformed into *devils (See *Lucifer).

Falling asleep of St Mary the Virgin The name in the *Orthodox and *Anglican Churches for the feast commemorating the *death of St Mary the Virgin (also entitled in Latin *Dormitio* and in English *Dormition). In the *Roman Catholic Church it is called the Feast of the *Assumption (15 August).

Fanon A *vestment worn by the *Pope at solemn *Mass, a cape with a hole for the head, made from two oval pieces of white silk striped with red and gold.

Fasting Complete or partial abstention from food (and, before Holy *Communion, drink) for religious or disciplinary reasons. At certain periods or on certain days, strictly until sunset, but usually for one meal. It may involve giving up meat on a Friday or other fastdays, or foregoing certain personal indulgences during *Lent.

Fathers of the Church Writers on the Christian faith, renowned for their saintly lives and the soundness of their doctrines and teaching, who lived during the first twelve centuries of the Church's existence. Among those so regarded, and who appear most frequently in art, are SS *Augustine, Cyril of Alexandria, Ephraem and *Jerome. In the *West, St *Gregory the Great (*d.*604) is held to be the last of the line; in the *East, St John Damascene (*d.*754).

Fátima, Our Lady of the Rosary of A *shrine near Cova da Iria in central Portugal where St *Mary the Virgin appeared six times from 13 May to 13 October 1917 to four peasant children. She told them that the faithful should pray the *rosary, do penance and hold processions in honour of the *Immaculate Conception so that the world would escape punishment. On her last appearance, 70,000

people saw the sun darken. Pope Paul VI (1963-78) visited the shrine in 1967. Pope John Paul II (1978-) celebrated *Mass there on 13 May 1982, when an attempt was made on his life.

Faun A hairy, lascivious man of the woods, the symbol of *lust, one of the *Seven Deadly Sins.

Feast day A day of commemoration. *Sunday is the principal feast and kept weekly. Other feasts are fixed, or immovable, e.g. *Christmas and *Epiphany; or movable, e.g. *Easter and *Pentecost (Whitsunday), because they depend on the date of Easter (See *Calendar; *Year, Christian).

Feeding of the five thousand See *Loaves and fishes.

Fiacre, St An Irish hermit who went to France in 628 and founded a monastery at Breuil, near Meaux (where his *relics repose in the *cathedral). His *attribute is a spade, because his *bishop told him that he could have as much land for his community as he could dig in one day. He is therefore the patron saint of gardeners. Cab drivers used to congregate outside the Hôtel de St-Fiacre in Paris, thus a cab was called a *fiacre*.

Fiery furnace When King *Nebuchadnezzar of Babylon captured Jerusalem he carried off to his capital *Daniel and his three companions Hananiah, Michael and Azariah, better known by their Chaldean names, *Shadrach, *Meshach and *Abednego. Nebuchadnezzar set up a huge golden image, and ordered that when music was played in its honour everyone should bow down and worship it on pain of being cast into a 'burning fiery furnace'. Strict monotheists, and trusting in their God, the three refused. They were bound and cast into the furnace which had been heated seven times more than usual and was so hot that it killed the men who threw the Hebrews in. An *angel joined them in the fire and they walked out unharmed (Dan 3 : 1-30). They are an example of salvation through faith (See *Benedicite*).

Fifteen A *number symbolizing progress, recalling the fifteen steps of the *Temple which St *Mary the Virgin ascended when she took leave of her parents (See *Education of St Mary the Virgin).

Figleaf When *Adam and *Eve ate the *Forbidden Fruit of the *Tree of Knowledge of Good and Evil they realized that they were naked and sewed figleaves together to make aprons, or loincloths to cover their bodies. In the *Geneva Bible the translation is, 'They made themselves breeches', so that Bible is called the Breeches Bible (See *Fall of Mankind).

First parents *Adam and *Eve.

Fish In Early Christian art the *symbol of *Christ, because he was the fisher of souls for their salvation and because the initial letters of the Greek

St Michael drives the **Fallen Angels** into Hell (Pieter Bruegel the Elder, c.1525-69).

Shadrach, Meshach and Abednego, with a dove holding an olive branch hovering over them, are saved from the flames of the **Fiery Furnace** (Catacomb of St Priscilla, Rome, 3rd century).

word for 'fish' IXOYC *(ichthos)* formed an acrostic which could be read as 'Jesus Christ, Son of God, the Saviour'. St Clement of Alexandria (*c*.150–*c*.215) recommended his fellow Christians to use on their seals Christian symbols such as a fish, a dove or a ship instead of pagan devices. In sermons, Christians were also spoken of as fish because they lived in the waters of baptism. Five fish also had a eucharistic significance, a reference to the miracle of the *loaves and the fishes. Fish is a sign of the *zodiac (*See* *Pisces).

St *Peter, a fisherman, has a fish as one of his *attributes or symbols; so also has *Tobias, who cured his father's blindness with the gall of a fish.

Five A symbolic *number, recalling the Five *Wounds of Christ and the five *Wise Virgins.

Flagellation of Jesus *See* *Scourging of Jesus.

Fleur-de-lis A variety of *lily, symbol of purity and in particular of the purity of St *Mary the Virgin. It is also the emblem of the city of Florence, of which city Mary is the patron saint, and of the French royal line because King Clovis (*c*.466–511) chose it after his baptism to signify his purification. When modelled on crowns or sceptres, the fleur-de-lis indicates that the saint is of the French royal house, notably *Louis IX (1215–70) and his nephew Bishop Louis of Toulouse (*d*.1297), the patron saint of Perugia, Italy (*See* St *Ursula).

Flight into Egypt The Three *Kings returned to their own countries without informing King *Herod where they had discovered the infant *Messiah. In his wrath, Herod ordered the Massacre of the *Holy Innocents, the slaughter of all male children who were two years old or under, hoping in this way to kill his potential rival. The angel of the Lord, assumed to be St *Gabriel, warned St *Joseph in a dream to take *Mary and Jesus into Egypt and to stay there until the danger was past (Mt 2 : 13-18). Joseph set his wife and child on an ass and led it from Bethlehem. (In art, an ox, angels, Joseph's three sons by a former marriage, and *Salome the midwife may be included in the procession.)

Miracles occurred on the journey which are recounted in the *Gospel of the *Pseudo-Matthew*. Dragons came out of a cave where the *Holy Family hoped to rest, but departed when the child got down from his mother's lap and stood before them. Lions, leopards, wolves and other wild beasts escorted the Holy Family, bowing their heads and wagging their tails in reverence. On the third day of their journey, Mary was overcome by the heat of the desert and they rested in the shade of a *palm-tree. They lacked water and food, but the fruit on the palm was too high for Joseph to reach. Jesus ordered the tree to lower its branches (*angels are sometimes shown pulling them down) and caused a spring to gush out from its roots. As a reward, angels were told to plant one of the branches in *Paradise to await the coming of the saints (who are therefore depicted with palms).

Joseph then decided to leave the desert and travel along the coast so that they might rest in the cities. Jesus therefore arranged for them to complete in one day a journey which would have taken thirty. They reached the region of Hermopolis and entered an Egyptian city called Sostinen, where there was a temple with 365 idols, one to be worshipped on each day of the year. But as Mary and the Holy Child entered the city the idols fell to the ground and were shattered. Afrodisius, the city governor, came up with all his army intent on avenging the sacrilege, but perceived that here was a God mightier than his idols and worshipped Jesus.

A later legend tells that on the first day of their flight the Holy Family passed a field being sown with corn. That night the corn sprang up, and next day, when Herod's pursuing soldiers asked the husbandman when the Holy Family had gone by, they were told that it was when the corn was being sown. Thinking that they had missed them by a season, the soldiers returned to Jerusalem.

In the Arabic *Gospel of the Infancy* there are other legends connected with the Flight into Egypt. A woman washed the infant Jesus in sweet-smelling water which she then kept in a jar. When she poured the water over a girl whose skin was white with leprosy, the girl was cured. In a desert place, the Holy Family fell into the hands of two robbers, Titus and Dumachus. Touched by compassion, Titus persuaded his companion to let them go. Jesus prophesied that thirty years later they would be crucified on either side of him, but that Titus, the *Good Thief on his right, would be with him in *Paradise.

After some years, the angel of the Lord told Joseph that Herod was dead and that the Holy Family could return in safety to their native land. They settled in Nazareth (Mt 2 : 19-23). On the way back they met St *Elizabeth and the infant St *John the Baptist, who is depicted playing with Jesus.

Flood, the Because of the wickedness of the first men and women, God decided to loose the waters which were above the firmament to rain upon the earth so that they would all perish in the Flood. *Noah, a righteous man, found favour in God's eyes and he, his wife, his three sons, *Ham, *Shem and *Japeth with their wives, and pairs of animals, birds and creeping things were saved in the *Ark which God had commanded Noah to build. As the Flood abated, and the mountain-tops began to appear, Noah sent out a raven to see if they could disembark, but the raven returned because there was not sufficient dry land. After a lapse of seven days he sent out a *dove, but it too returned. Seven days later he sent out the dove again and it returned with a fresh *olive branch (symbol of peace between God and mankind) in its beak. Seven days later Noah let the dove loose once more, but it did not return, a sign that they could now leave the Ark which had come to rest on Mount *Ararat.

Noah's first act was to build an altar and make a sacrifice to God, who blessed him and his children

and said, 'Be fruitful and multiply, and replenish the earth' (Gen 9 : 1). He made a covenant with Noah and signified it by placing his *rainbow in the sky. Noah became a husbandman and was the first man to plant the vine, becoming intoxicated with the juice of the grapes (See *Drunkenness of Noah) (Gen 6, 7, 8, 9).

Flowering rod A symbol with three references. The first is to *Aaron's rod which blossomed and produced ripe almonds when placed before the *Ark of the Covenant, thus indicating that the privileges of priesthood belonged to the tribe of Levi of which Aaron was a member. In the same way, St *Joseph was singled out as the chosen husband of St *Mary the Virgin when his rod flowered when he placed it on the High Priest's altar (See *Betrothal of St Mary the Virgin). Thirdly, a rod which burst into flowers, usually lilies, is also an *attribute of St Mary the Virgin, a pun on the Latin words *virga*, 'a branch' and *virgo* 'a virgin'.

Flowers Frequent in art because of their symbolic as well as decorative value. The most usual are: *anemone, *carnation, *clover (*trefoil), *columbine, *cyclamen, *daisy, *dandelion, *iris, *lady's bed-straw, *lily, *lily of the valley, *rose and *violet.

Fly Symbol of evil because it brings pestilence, and of sin and the *Devil (or *devils) because *Satan is 'Lord of the flies' (*Beelzebub). Swarms of flies and other insects were sent to punish *Pharaoh's obstinacy (See *Plagues of Egypt).

Font From the Latin *fons*, 'spring of water'. A basin on a stand, usually of stone, which contains the *Holy Water for *baptism. It is placed symbolically in some churches near the entrance, to indicate the beginning of a new life. It is also the symbol of baptism.

Forbidden fruit The fruit of the *Tree of Knowledge of Good and Evil, supposed to be an *apple, forbidden food for *Adam and *Eve. Eating it caused their *Expulsion from Paradise (See *Mandrake).

Foreskin of Christ It was said that after the *Circumcision of Jesus, St *Mary the Virgin kept the foreskin and later gave it to St *John the Evangelist. But according to the Arabic *Gospel of the Infancy* an old Hebrew woman, identified as *Salome the midwife, retrieved it and embalmed it 'in a vase of old oil of spikenard'. She entrusted it to her son who was a perfumer, saying, 'Take care not to sell this vase of ointment of spikenard, even if 300 pence should be offered for it'. This was the ointment with which St *Mary Magdelene anointed Jesus at Bethany.

In the Middle Ages, a number of churches claimed to possess the foreskin as a holy *relic. According to Jacobus de Voragine in the *Golden Legend*, an angel brought it to *Charlemagne, who placed it in the church of St Mary at Aix-la-

St Joseph and his children, the brethren of the Lord, escort St Mary the Virgin and the Christ-Child on the **Flight into Egypt** (Giotto, c.1304–13).

A bronze **font,** showing the baptism of Jesus. The oxen recall the twelve oxen supporting the molten sea of bronze in Solomon's Temple (early 12th century).

Chapelle (Aachen). The *Historia Scholastica* says that it was first taken to Charroux (derived by popular etymology from *caro rubra, chaire-rouge* or 'red skin') and then to the chapel of Sancta Sanctorum in the church of St John Lateran. Jacobus mentioned an inscription there which read: 'Here is the foreskin, navel and sandals of Jesus Christ', adding, 'If all that is true, it must be admitted that it is wonderful!' A further version is that the foreskin was placed in a *reliquary adorned with enamels showing scenes of the infancy of Jesus (the reliquary is now in the Vatican Museum), but this was stolen during the sack of Rome in 1527, reappearing later in the parish church of Calcata, near Viterbo, where it is said it may still be seen.

Forty martyrs of Sebastea Christian soldiers stationed at Sebastea (now Sivas) in Armenia who, in the year 320, refused the command of Emperor Licinius to abandon their religion. They were driven naked into a frozen pond but in sight of warm baths which awaited those who denied their faith. All remained steadfast except one, whose place was taken by a pagan soldier, encouraged by a vision of *angels to become a Christian and join his comrades. Those of the faithful who were not dead by the next morning were killed and their remains burned. Meletius, one of their number, left an account, *Testament of the Forty Martyrs of Christ*, giving their names, last wishes and their encouraging message to fellow Christians to follow their example. Their martyrdom is frequently depicted in early *Orthodox art.

Fountain An *attribute of St *Mary the Virgin, derived from the allegorical interpretation of two texts, 'a fountain sealed' (Sg 4 : 12), thought to refer to her perpetual virginity, and, 'for with thee is the fountain of life' (Ps 36 : 9; Vg Ps 35 : 10). Also Jesus, the *fons vitae*, 'fountain of life'.

Four A symbolic *number recalling the four corners of the globe (hence the *earth); the four *Rivers of Paradise; the four *Evangelists; the *Four Horsemen of the Apocalypse; the *Four Elements; the four *Last Things; the four cardinal *Virtues; and the four *Gospels.

Four elements The constituents of all created matter. They are (with their symbols in brackets), Fire (*salamander); Air (*eagle); Earth (*lion); Water (*dolphin).

Four horses (horsemen) of the Apocalypse In a vision of St *John the Divine, God is described as seated on a throne and holding in his right hand a scroll sealed with seven seals. When the first four are opened, four horses appear, white, red, black and pale, or piebald (Rev 4 : 5). They are usually depicted with riders and symbolize conquest, slaughter, famine and death, all of which will ravage the earth before the end of time.

Fourteen holy helpers A group of saints who were especially responsive to prayers for help in recovery from illness and for those who made a good death. Their names varied: SS *Anthony of Padua, *Leonard, *Nicholas, *Sebastian and *Roch sometimes appear as alternatives in the following more usual list: *Achacius, *Barbara, *Blaise, *Catherine of Alexandria, *Christopher, *Cyriacus, *Denys, *Erasmus, *Eustace, *George, *Giles, *Margaret of Antioch, *Pantaleon and *Vitus. An altar was dedicated to these saints collectively in Krems, Austria in 1284. Their cult appears to have been at its height about the time of the Black Death, the plague which decimated the population of Europe between 1347 and 1351. In 1445 or 1446 a shepherd boy of Langheim, Germany, saw the Fourteen in a vision and was ordered to build a church there in their honour.

Fox A crafty *animal, symbol of astuteness and trickery and thus appearing in anticlerical satires, although foxes may also denote heretics. A fox lies on its back, with its mouth open, pretending to be dead, so that it may snap up the fowls and *birds which come curiously to inspect it, just as the *Devil lies in wait to trap the unwary. It never runs straight ahead but always follows a tortuous path and thus represents a man whose ways are devious.

Franciscans Originally *Friars of the First Order of St Francis, which St *Francis of Assisi formed with eleven companions between 1207 and 1208 and which was legally established in 1210 by Innocent III (1198–1216). According to legend, the Pope was impelled to do so because of a prophetic dream in which he saw the *Lateran basilica, his personal church, about to collapse and being propped up by a small and despised man. (In another version, St *Dominic was also present. Their *Rule, first composed by St Francis, rewritten in 1221 and confirmed in its final form in 1223 by Honorius III (1216–27), stressed absolute poverty for individual friars and their Order, and an intense spiritual life.

Two factions emerged as the Order grew, the Spirituals, who wanted the Rule to be strictly observed, and those led by Elias of Cortona (c.1180–1253), one of St Francis' companions, who sought to mitigate its harshness. The dispute continued into the 14th century, and was lost by the Spirituals when their insistence on complete poverty and no property was declared heretical in 1323. This did not satisfy the more fundamentalist Franciscans, who in 1368 grouped themselves into Observantines, or *'Observants' of the primitive Rule. The other branch in contrast, the Friars Minor *Conventual, followed the Rule but obtained certain dispensations on the matter of poverty and property held in common. They were formally separated from the Observants in 1517, adopted a new constitution in 1625, and were known as Black Franciscans from the colour of their *habit.

The Observants themselves were divided when the followers of Matteo di Bassi of Urbino (d.1552) sought an even more perfect observance of the primitive Rule. They wore the original grey

Franciscan habit and were called Friars Minor
Capuchin, or *Capuchins because of their pointed
*cowl (in Italian *capuche*). They drew up their strict
and austere constitution in 1529. Their numbers
grew, although their houses were restricted to
Italy until 1574, after which they were permitted
to extend abroad. Their influence was greatest in
the 16th and 17th centuries as a result of their
charitable works and their overseas missions.
Their constitutions were approved in 1638 and
modified and again approved in 1909. *Nuns of
the Second Franciscan Order are called *Poor
Clares.

Meanwhile, other groups of Franciscans who
sought various reforms had been united in 1517 as
the Friars Minor of St Francis, or of the Regular
Observance. (The use of 'Minor' signifies their
humility, they are 'little brothers'.) Over the
centuries there were added to them other reformist
bodies, including the Alcantarines (1496), the
Reformati (1532) and the *Recollects (formed in
France c.1570). Each body had its own statutes,
but obeyed one General. They were active as
missionaries, preachers and *inquisitors. They
were united in 1897. They dress in a dark brown
habit and wear around the waist a white cord with
three knots, symbolizing their three *vows of
poverty, chastity and obedience. Sandals are usually worn. Small Anglican groups for men and
women, inspired by Franciscan ideals, have been
formed in England since 1931.

Franciscans promoted the dogma of the
*Immaculate Conception for centuries before it
was formally defined in 1854. They also encouraged popular devotions such as the *Angelus, the
*Christmas Crib and the *Stations of the Cross.

Francis de Paola (or Paula), St Robert Mar-
tolella, founder of the Order of *Minims, *b.*1416 of
humble parentage at Paola, Calabria, Italy. He was
vowed in infancy to a nearby Franciscan *friary
when he was thirteen, went on a pilgrimage with
his parents to Assisi and Rome, and, taking the
name of Francis, lived as a *hermit in a cave by the
sea. He attracted others to settle in cells near him,
and in 1435 they banded together as *mendicant
friars, calling themselves Minims, 'diminutive
ones', as a sign that they were even more humble
than 'Minor' *Franciscans. They were approved
by the Pope in 1474. In 1482 they spread to France
when Louis IX, who had heard of Francis'
miracles, was cured of an illness by him. Francis
spent the rest of his life in France and was adviser
to Charles VIII and Louis XII. He died at Tours in
1507 and was canonized in 1519. By then Minims
had established themselves in Spain and Germany.
They were renowned for their austerity and severe
penances. For fifty-seven years after their foundation they did not have a written *Rule but lived in
accordance with the principles laid down by St
*Francis of Assisi for his Franciscans. They were
given one in 1493, based on the Franciscan model.
It was revised in 1501 and again in 1506, when it
was confirmed by Julius II (1503-13).

St Francis de Paola is shown in the dark brown
*habit of the Order of Minims. On his breast is the

Christ waits in Heaven to receive the souls of the
Forty Martyrs of Sebastea (Byzantine ivory,
10th or 11th century).

The **Four Horsemen** of the *Apocalypse* ravage
the earth, bringing conquest, slaughter, famine
and death (Greek icon, 1625).

word *Caritas*, *'Charity', surrounded by a *halo, because he and his followers professed love for all human kind. A cloak near him or spread on the sea recalls how he once could not pay his fare from Sicily to the mainland so floated over on it. An ass beside him refers to the miracle that occurred when a blacksmith became abusive when Francis could not pay him for putting new shoes on his ass. Francis told the animal to shake off the shoes and they fell to the ground.

Francis of Assisi, St Founder of the Order of Friars Minor (*Franciscans), born *c*.1181 in Assisi, son of a rich cloth-merchant, Pietro Bernardone. He was christened Giovanni, but was called Francesco (Francis) either because the name belonged to his mother's side (her surname was Pica and her family were Provençal), or because his father traded in France. At first a carefree, dissipated youth, he was moved by his experiences as a prisoner-of-war in Perugia and a serious illness which followed, to devote himself to the care of the poor and of lepers. One day he exchanged his rich clothes for the beggar's cloak worn by one of his former wealthy acquaintances who had been reduced to poverty. That night he dreamed of a magnificent palace filled with fine garments and superb arms, all marked with a cross. At first he thought that it meant that he should become a soldier, but the voice of *Christ told him, 'These are the riches reserved for my servants, and the weapons which I give those who fight for me.'

While praying in the ruined church of St Damian, Francis heard the crucified Christ order him to repair it. He sold some of his father's goods and offered the proceeds to the parish priest, who refused the money. He hid in a cave to escape his father's anger, was thought to be insane, and was taken to the *bishop, before whom he tore off his clothes to reveal a *hair shirt. The bishop covered him with his cloak, as a sign of his acceptance into the religious life. Disowned and disinherited, Francis lived in a cell near the church of Santa Maria degli Angeli, a chapel in which (the *Porziuncola) became the place where he used to meet a group of twelve followers, among them St *Clare, daughter of a noble family, and later founder of the *Poor Clares. Once, on his way to Siena, Francis met three poorly dressed maidens who all resembled each other and who greeted him with the words, 'Welcome, Lady Poverty!', before they vanished. Francis symbolically took Poverty as his bride. This did not free him from the temptations of the flesh, but he repressed them by rolling naked in the snow and throwing himself into a thorn bush. Roses sprang up where drops of his blood bespattered the earth.

Wishing to found a new Order, the Brotherhood of Poverty, Francis went to Rome in 1210. Innocent III (1198-1216) only gave his permission for it to be established after he had had a vision in which he saw the church of St John Lateran (the Pope's church as Bishop of Rome) tottering and being propped up by Francis and St *Dominic (whose *Dominican Order was also constituted at that time).

In 1219, Francis went on a missionary journey to the *Holy Land where he attempted to convert the Soldan of the Saracens by proposing an ordeal by fire. The Imams refused to accept his challenge to walk through the pyre and emerge unscathed. Back in Italy, he encouraged the growth of his Order through his example, living in poverty, weeping for the sins of the world, and spending much of his time in prayer and contemplation. His belief in the kinship between men and nature enabled him to perform many miracles, preaching to the birds who acknowledged his message by flying away in the form of a cross, and taming the *wolf which ravaged the town of Gubbio by persuading him to sign a treaty under his dictation.

While on a retreat at La Verna in 1224, he prayed that he might feel in his body the agony of Christ on the Cross and was rewarded with the *stigmata, purplish marks on his hands and feet recalling the wounds inflicted by the nails at the *Crucifixion. He also had a vision in which he heard music made by angels. After patiently enduring great suffering in his last days, he asked his companions to place him on the earth and he died (1226) intoning, 'Bring my soul out of prison, that I may praise thy name' (Ps 142 (141) : 7). His last request was that his body should be buried with the remains of criminals at the Colle d'Inferno, outside the city walls of Assisi, but his fellows buried him in the church of San Giorgio. St Clare and her nuns came out to bid him farewell as the cortege passed their convent of St Damian. It was said that when his tomb was opened his body was found standing upright, his eyes still open in contemplation. He is depicted in brown *Franciscan habit, exhibiting the stigmata or gazing on a skull. His chastity is denoted by a *lily and his devotion to prayer by a *crucifix. He was canonized in 1228.

Francis Xavier, St Famous *Jesuit missionary, apostle of India and of Japan. He was born in 1506, of a noble Basque family of the castle of Xavier, near Sangüesa, Navarra. Sent to study in Paris in 1525 he met St *Ignatius of Loyola and joined him in the formation of the Society of Jesus. After receiving *Holy Orders in 1537, he went first to Goa and then to Ceylon in 1542. He reached Mindanao in the Philippines, and Japan in 1549 where he endured many hardships before being expelled the following year. He died in 1552 on an island in the Canton River on the way to evangelize China, and was canonized in 1622. From his pioneer work developed the Jesuit missions in the Far East. His *Letters* are a fascinating account of the methods by which he sought to spread the Faith.

St Francis Xavier appears in art bareheaded with a short black beard, holding a *lily, symbol of his chastity, and a *cross, representing his missionary zeal. A crab or lobster with a *crucifix in its mouth recalls the legend that his previous crucifix fell overboard but was restored to him by one of these creatures. He may display a scroll with the words, *Satis est, Domine*, 'It is enough, O Lord'. He composed the hymn, *O Deus ego amo te*, 'O God, I love thee'.

Frankincense From the Old French *franc encens*, 'pure incense', the sweet-smelling resin of the balsam tree, originating in Arabia. It symbolizes divinity, and was thus the gift (presented in a *censer) offered by Melchior, one of the Three *Kings, to the *Christ-Child.

Fraticelli The Italian for 'little friars', applied in general to *mendicant friars, but more particularly to groups which broke away from the *Franciscans between the 13th and the 15th centuries because they wished to return to the original concept of absolute poverty. Some of the *fraticelli* added certain heretical ideas such as the rejection of all spiritual and temporal authority and the belief that a sinful priest invalidated his priestly functions. They were persecuted and eventually suppressed with great brutality.

Free Churches *Protestants who claim freedom from binding creeds and from all ecclesiastical authority, e.g. *bishops. The emphasis is on the right of the local congregation to manage its own affairs.

Free-will Men and women, because they are rational creatures, are endowed with freedom to choose of their own will between good and evil.

Friar From the Latin *frater*, 'brother', French *frère*, Italian *fra*; a title applied from the 13th century onwards to members of the *mendicant (or 'begging') *Orders, distinguished from monks living in monastic communities in that they worked in the world outside. At first they lived entirely on voluntary contributions and were not allowed to have personal or corporate possessions. But, with the exception of the *Capuchins and the Friars Minor (*Franciscans), they were permitted by the *Council of Trent to hold property collectively. The best-known orders of friars are the Franciscans (Grey Friars); *Dominicans or Friars Preachers (Black Friars); *Augustinians (Austin Friars); *Carmelites (White Friars); *Servites (Order of Servants of Mary); *Capuchins; and Discalced *Trinitarians (*See *Friary).

Friary A community of *friars and the house in which they live, although the word has fallen into disuse. It was mostly applied to *Augustinians, *Carmelites, *Dominicans, *Franciscans and *Servites.

Friday The day of the *Crucifixion is commemorated weekly by an act of *penance or *fasting. Abstinence from meat on Fridays (fish was permitted) is no longer obligatory for *Roman Catholics. In some churches a Friday-bell is rung at 3 pm, recalling the 'ninth hour', when Jesus died on the Cross (*See *Crucifixion).

Frog An amphibian used as a *symbol of evil, because a mass of them was one of the *Plagues of Egypt. On the other hand it hibernates and reappears in the spring, so may signify the *Resurrection.

St **Francis of Assisi** receives the stigmata. Below are Pope Innocent's dream; the establishment of the Franciscan Order; and St Francis preaching to the birds (Giotto?, early 14th century).

A portrait of St **Francis Xavier** when he went to Ceylon in 1542.

Fruit A cluster (or basket) of fruit *symbolizes the *twelve fruits of the *Holy Spirit, 'love, joy, peace, long-suffering, gentleness, goodness, faith, meekness, temperance' (Gal 5 : 22-3), to which are added patience, modesty and chastity.

Individual fruits have their own symbolic values (See *almond, *apple, *cherry, *chestnut, *fig, *gourd, *grapes, *lemon, *orange, *peach, *pear, *pomegranate and *strawberry).

Fundamentalism The insistence by some *Protestant sects on the literal truth of the *Bible, religious and scientific. They also hold that the Bible is the inspired word of God in a literal sense and that it contains the fundamentals of his revelation.

Gabriel, St The second in rank of the *archangels, one of the seven angels who stand ever-ready to enter the presence of God and be his messenger to mankind. He interpreted for *Daniel the vision of the Ram and the He-Goat (Dan 8 : 1-27) which foretold the destruction of the Persian Empire by Alexander the Great (356-323 BC), and explained the prophecy of the seventy-two weeks (Dan 9 : 1-27) which promised the freeing of *Israel from captivity and the approach of the Messianic age. According to tradition he announced to *Joachim and *Anna the impending conception of St *Mary the Virgin and told *Zacharias that he would become the father of St *John the Baptist (Lk 1 : 13-20). His supreme task was as angel of the *Annunciation, when he was sent to tell Mary that she was the woman chosen to bear Jesus. In this episode he may be shown wearing an *alb or a *dalmatic and carrying a herald's baton (or a sceptre); a *lily, symbolic of Mary's virginity; or an *olive branch, signifying peace between God and mankind through the *Incarnation. He may also display a *phylactery, or scroll, with the words of the angelic salutation, *Ave Maria, 'Hail, Mary', or Ave Maria, gratia plena, Dominus tecum, 'Hail, Mary, full of grace, the Lord is with you'. In early representations, Gabriel and Mary are shown standing, or Mary takes up a pose of humility, indicating thereby her acceptance of the divine will. Later, as the cult of the Virgin developed, Gabriel kneels to acknowledge her as *Queen of Heaven, or Queen of the Angels. Although not named, Gabriel is also assumed to be the angel who announced the birth of *Samson to his mother, and the one who brought the glad tidings of the birth of the *Messiah to the *Shepherds. According to tradition, it was Gabriel who comforted Jesus during his *Agony in the Garden of Gethsemane.

Gabriel watches over childbirth and, since 1921, is the patron saint of television and telecommunications. With St *Michael, he guards church doors against the *Devil. He is also revered in Islam because he dictated the Koran to Mahomet.

Gad A seer and prophet who told *David to leave the cave of *Adullam to avoid capture by Saul (1 Sam 22 : 5). When David angered God by taking a census (the reason why some *fundamentalist sects refuse to make census returns), Gad told him that he could choose one of three punishments, defeat in battle, famine or plague. David chose the last, but after the death of thousands of this people, he prayed that the pestilence might end. Gad told him to confess his fault and build an altar to God on the threshing floor of Araunah the Jebusite (2 Sam 24 : 10-25). This was later the site of the *Temple.

Gadarene swine When *Jesus and his disciples were in the Gadarene (or Gerasene) country, they encountered a mad man called Legion, because of the many devils within him (described as two men in the Gospel of Matthew). Jesus transferred the unclean devils to a herd of swine, which then ran off a cliff into the sea (Mt 8 : 28-34; Mk 5 : 1-13; Lk 8 : 26-33). 'Gadarene swine' became a proverbial expression for those who rush headlong to their doom.

Galilee The most northern of the three provinces of Roman Palestine (the others being Samaria and Judaea), where Jesus had his home and where he began his ministry. Thus *Julian the Apostate's acknowledgment of his supremacy, 'Thou hast conquered, O Galilean', refers to Jesus as a native of that province. Jesus recruited his first disciples on the shores of the Sea of Galilee, a lake in the floor of the Jordan Valley, and performed many miracles there. The Galilean accent differed from that of Jerusalem, and was immediately recognized by the maid-servant who challenged St *Peter as he stood in the courtyard while Jesus was being tried before Pilate (See *Trials of Jesus).

Galilee The architectural term (equivalent to *narthex) for a vestibule or chapel above the porch at the west end of a *church.

Gamaliel A *Pharisee Rabbi, or doctor of the *Law, and mentor of St *Paul (hence the use of 'Gamaliel' to signify master or teacher). He urged the *Sanhedrin not to put St *Peter and his companions to death (Ac 5 : 34-40), and there is an early tradition that he was eventually converted to Christianity and that he appeared in 415 to a priest named Lucian to tell him where he would find the tomb of St *Stephen.

Gargano The name of a man of Sipontum, Italy, who in 530 went along the slopes of the mountain seeking his lost bull. He found the animal at the mouth of a cave and when it refused to move, shot at it with an arrow. The arrow rebounded and killed him. His family asked Laurentius, their *bishop, for help. He prayed for three days, and then St *Michael appeared to say that the cave had been used for the worship of a pagan god Calchas and that it must be consecrated as a *church. The church was duly built deep in the cavern and is reached by a stairway. Monte Gargano is now a resort for *pilgrims on 8 May, the *feast commemorating the appearance of St Michael. Chips of stone from the site are believed to be effective against cholera.

Gargoyle A rain spout emerging from the mouth of a grotesque animal or human figure projecting from the walls at the level of the roof gutters of a *church or other medieval buildings. Also, similar strange figures which ornament outside walls and presumably symbolized the evils of the world, in contrast to the spiritual safety offered within the church.

Garth The central open space of a convent *cloister, usually a lawn or garden. The word is derived from the Old English *geard*, 'yard'.

Gate A symbol of St *Mary the Virgin, who is the 'gate of heaven' (Latin *janua coeli*). She was also the 'closed gate' and ever-virgin (*See* *porta clausa*).
   A gate also symbolizes death, a reference to the gates of death (Ps 9 : 13; Vg Ps 9 : 14), and the entrance to Hades (*See* *Descent into Hell*).

Gaudete Sunday The third Sunday in *Advent, so named because the *antiphon *Gaudete in Domino semper*, 'Rejoice in the Lord always', is sung at *Mass.

Gehenna A valley beside *Jerusalem associated with the idolatrous rites of Moloch, involving fires for child immolation until abolished by King Josiah (2 Kg 23 : 10). It was later the place where the corpses of outcasts were burned, the fires burning continuously to prevent infection. The name (a corruption of the Hebrew 'Valley of Hinnom') thus became a synonym for *Hell or *Sheol.

Gelasian Decree A document, probably of the 6th century, wrongly attributed to Pope St Gelasius I (492-6). It distinguished *canonical from *apocryphal writings.

Gemini The twins, the third sign of the *zodiac, governing approximately the period 21 May to 21 June. In the *Labours of the Months it is the time for hawking.

Genesius, St Patron saint of *actors, martyred *c.*286 during a *persecution, when he was converted to the Christian faith after performing the role of a rich man who was seeking eternal life and heard of *Christ.

Geneva Bible An English translation of the *Bible published in Geneva in 1560, the first version in which the text was divided into verses for ease of reference. It was known as the 'Breeches Bible' because of the rendering, 'they [*Adam and *Eve] made themselves breeches' instead of 'aprons' (Gen 3 : 7).

Geneviève (Genovefa), St Patroness of Paris, born at Nanterre. She may have been a shepher-

St **Gabriel**, the angel of the Annunciation. (From the St Bavon Altarpiece, Ghent, early 15th century, by Jan and Hubert van Eyck.)

A 17th-century **gargoyle** on the campanile of the church of St Maria Formosa, Venice.

dess, but she is sometimes shown with a spinning-wheel. She was called at an early age to a religious life by St Germanus, bishop of Auxerre (c.378-448), her ambition being to become a bride of *Christ. Her mother became blind when she slapped her child, but Geneviève restored her sight. She took the veil when she was nearing fifteen and lived a life of prayer and extreme austerity, subsisting on two meals a week of bread and beans. It is said that when she went to pray at night she was able miraculously to light her candle without the aid of flint or fire. The *Devil would try to blow it out with his breath and then with the aid of bellows, but an *angel always kept it alight. Her prayers and her exhortations to the citizens of Paris caused Attila and his Huns to turn back in 451 from their proposed attack on the city. She discovered through prayer the lime needed to build a church to contain the remains of St *Denis and his companions. After her death c.500, she continued to protect Paris from plague and other disasters. When her relics were carried in procession through the city in 1129 an outbreak of grain disease (that poisoned bread) subsided. King Clovis founded a church in her honour, but her shrine was destroyed during the French Revolution and the Panthéon built on the site.

Genuflexion The act (from the Latin *genu*, 'knee', *flectere*, 'to bend') of touching the ground with the right knee, a gesture of obeisance used in the *West (but not in the *East) since the Middle Ages, to indicate reverence, homage or veneration of the *Blessed Sacrament or of the *Cross. Double genuflexion is kneeling on both knees, bowing, and rising again.

Geometrical figures *Symbols of various tenets of the Christian faith (See *circle, *trefoil, *triangle, *triquetra).

George, St Protector of women, pattern of chivalry, but a saint whose existence is disputed. One tradition preserved in the *Golden Legend* says that he was a late-3rd-century Roman centurion of Cappadocia, Asia Minor; a Christian, but in the service of a pagan emperor. Travelling through Libya he found the city of Silene (in other versions, Beirut in the Levant) living in terror of a *dragon which had eaten their sheep and could only be appeased by the daily sacrifice of a maiden chosen by lot. It was the turn of Cleodolinda, the king's beautiful daughter, who was awaiting her fate dressed as a bride at the mouth of the dragon's cave by the sea. George rode up on his white charger, overcame the dragon, bound it with the princess's girdle (or garter), and told her to lead it back to the city. Her father and 15,000 of his people were astounded by their miraculous deliverance and agreed to become Christians. George then killed the dragon and went on to Palestine where he refused to recognize the divinity of Emperor Diocletian and was tortured to death at Lydda. He did not feel the pain when he was first dragged along the highway by wild horses, then roasted in a brazen bull and finally beheaded.

St George is the patron of Venice, Genoa, Portugal, Catalonia and Greece. He replaced St *Edward the Confessor as patron saint of England in 1222 after the Crusades, when he appeared to Richard Coeur de Lion before the siege of Antioch and promised him victory. The cry, 'St George for England', also proved effective in enabling Edward III (1327-77) to beat the French. His red cross represents England on the Union Jack, and his feast day, 23 April, is the English national day. The St George's Channel (or Irish Sea) is so named because he is said to have visited England by that route. As patron of the Order of the Garter, he is sometimes shown in the robes of that Order, and the church where the members' banners are placed, St George's Chapel, Windsor, is dedicated to him. He is one of the *Fourteen Holy Helpers.

Gervase and Protase (Gervasius and Protasius), SS The first *martyrs of Milan. Their supposed remains were discovered by St *Ambrose in 386 as the result of a vision, and transferred to a new *church which he was about to dedicate. Blind men, sick people and demoniacs were healed as they touched the *relics. In the 6th century their *shrines were taken to Paris and were greatly venerated, their cult continuing well into the 18th century. They were twins put to death by *Nero, and are shown as youths bearing the instruments of their martyrdom, Gervase with a scourge with leaded thongs, and Protase with a whip. One legend says that they were the sons of St *Vitalis and that after their parents were martyred they sold their property and lived as *hermits until they were executed for refusing to serve in the army.

Gestas The supposed name of the Bad Thief crucified with Jesus (See *Dismas).

Gethsemane, garden of A plot of land on the *Mount of Olives in *Jerusalem where an oil-press (Hebrew *gat*, 'a press' and *shemen*, 'oil') was located. Here, Jesus used to meet his disciples, later suffered the *Agony in the Garden, and was finally arrested (Mk 14 : 32-52). Exegetes saw it as the parallel to the Garden of *Eden in the plan for the *redemption of mankind. One unreliable tradition locates the tomb of St *Mary the Virgin in the Valley of Gethsemane (other accounts place it in the Valley of *Jehoshaphat or in Ephesus).

Giant Two giants appear in Christian art, *Goliath, and St *Christopher with the Child Jesus on his shoulder. According to the *Book of Genesis*, between the *Expulsion from Eden and the *Flood 'there were giants in the earth' (Gen 6 : 4).

Gideon (Gedeon) The fifth of the *Judges of Israel, depicted as a soldier in armour because he subdued the nomadic Midianites in the 12th century BC. He is important for the symbolic significance of certain events in his military career. A humble farmer, he was threshing corn in a winepress to hide it from marauding Midianites, when an *angel appeared under an oak tree with a message from God that Gideon had been chosen to deliver the people of *Israel (Jg 6 : 11-40). (This foretold the *Annunciation and the angel that spoke to Jesus during the *Agony in the Garden.) Incredulous (like St *Thomas the Apostle), Gideon asked for proof of the divine call and was granted three signs. Unleavened bread and meat wetted with broth were consumed with fire when the rock on which they were placed was touched by the angel's staff. Dew wetted a sheep's fleece placed on the threshing floor so much that Gideon squeezed the water into a drinking-cup, but the ground around was dry (symbolizing the virginal conception [*Incarnation] of Jesus). The following night the ground was wet but the fleece remained dry.

Convinced, Gideon led a successful campaign against the Midianites, three episodes of which have been singled out for illustration in art. So that victory should be seen to be the work of God, Gideon reduced his force from 10,000 to 300, rejecting those who knelt to drink from the spring of Harod and selecting only those who showed they were wary and alert by scooping up the water in their hands. (As the Greek numerical sign for 300 is *T, the shape of the *Tau Cross, the episode symbolizes the victory of the Cross over the heathen.) Gideon then won a surprise night attack by ordering his men to spread confusion by blowing trumpets and breaking the pitchers concealing their torches when they were upon the enemy encampment, so Gideon's *attribute is a broken pitcher (Jg 7 : 2-23). The punishment by beating with thorns and briars which Gideon inflicted on the seventy-seven elders of Succoth who refused his soldiers food (Jg 8 : 4-16) foretold some of the torments which the wicked could expect in *Hell.

Gifts of the Holy Spirit, seven As prophesied by *Isaiah (Is 11 : 2), the spirit of God (the *Holy Spirit) would bestow seven gifts on the *Messiah. These, symbolized by seven doves, lamps or flames, are *Sapientia*, 'Wisdom'; *Intellectus*, 'Understanding'; *Consilium*, 'Counsel'; *Fortitudo*, 'Might'; *Scientia*, 'Knowledge'; *Pietas*, 'Piety'; and *Timor Domini*, 'Fear of God'.

Gift of tongues At *Pentecost, the Apostles astonished men of many nations assembled in Jerusalem for the festival by speaking in a variety of languages (Ac 2 : 4-12). This ecstatic gift, called glossolalia, speaking with tongues under supernatural influence, was a feature of the worship of the early *Church and still appears in some sects. Typologically, it parallels the confusion of tongues following the building of the Tower of *Babel and demonstrates that mankind, once divided linguistically, is united through faith in *Christ.

Giles (Aegidius), St One of the *Fourteen Holy Helpers, a *Benedictine abbot (*d.c.*710), depicted with a *crosier or *pastoral staff and dressed in Benedictine *habit. Born into a noble Athenian family, he early felt called to a solitary life and built a *hermitage in wild country near the mouth of the

St **George** rescuing the princess by killing the dragon who was about to devour her. The sheep for which she was a substitute stands near her (15th century).

People from many lands hear the Apostles speaking foreign languages as they receive the **Gift of tongues** (Giotto?, early 14th century).

River Rhône. From there he moved to a forest near Nîmes where for years his only companion was a hind (his *attribute). This hind had taken refuge with him when pursued by King Wamba. The king shot an arrow at his quarry but missed his mark and hit Giles in the leg, crippling him. He is thus the patron of cripples. Giles later decided to follow the *Rule of St Benedict and to found a *monastery at Saint-Gilles (Provence), a centre of *pilgrimage in the Middle Ages. His cult was associated with hospitals where lepers and cripples were cared for (recalled in St Giles, Edinburgh and St Giles, Cripplegate, London). Because he was said to have absolved Emperor *Charlemagne of a sin which he dared not confess, he was also invoked by those who feared to go to confession.

Girdle Symbol of chastity and as such bestowed upon St *Thomas Aquinas. St *Mary the Virgin granted her girdle to St *Thomas the Apostle to still his doubts at her *Assumption. Three knots in the corded girdle of *Franciscans recall their three *vows, poverty, chastity and obedience (See *cincture).

Glastonbury abbey A *Benedictine foundation in Somerset, England, endowed in the 8th century by King Ina of the West Saxons and restored by St *Dunstan after its destruction by Danish invaders. It enjoyed great renown in the Middle Ages as a *pilgrimage centre because, according to the chronicler William of Malmesbury (d.c.1143), it was once the island called in Celtic Ynyswritrin, later said to be the mysterious Avalon, where St *Joseph of Arimathea landed bearing the *Holy Grail and where St *Patrick established a *cenobitic community. According to the historian Giraldus Cambrensis (1146?-1220?), King Arthur's tomb was discovered in the reign of Henry II (1154-89) in the *monastery grounds, with an inscribed cross recording his burial there with his queen, Guenevere. The *abbey was destroyed in 1539 at the time of the dissolution of the monasteries, and its *abbot and two *monks hanged on the nearby Tor. The abbot, Richard Whiting (1460-1539), was *canonized.

Glastonbury thorn A variety of hawthorn which flowers in May and at Christmas, said in the legend to be the shoot of the staff which St *Joseph of Arimathea brought with him from the *Holy Land and which flowered when he stuck it in the ground on Wearyall Hill (then an island), a sign that he should build the first British Christian church there. The legend was fostered by the monks of *Glastonbury Abbey and was mentioned in a letter to Thomas Cromwell in 1535. The original tree was destroyed in 1653 during the Civil War, but a tree said to have been grown from a cutting survives in the nearby church of the Holy Trinity.

Glebe A portion of farmland set aside in England for the maintenance of a *parish priest who lived in the glebe-house, or *parsonage.

Globe Symbol of the world, or of sovereignty over it (See *orb). At the feet of St *Mary the Virgin, as in depictions of the *Immaculate Conception, it shows her to be *Queen of the World. Surmounted by a cross, it is held by Christ as *Saviour of the World.

Gloria in excelsis Deo The Latin for 'Glory to God in the highest', the opening words of the angels at the Annunciation to the *Shepherds (Lk 2 : 14), incorporated into a hymn of praise used at every festive *Mass. It was originally intended to be sung by the congregation, but because of its length and the complexity of its music, was taken over by the choir, especially in Baroque settings. It has now been restored to the people in the revised liturgy and is sung on *Sundays and festivals except in *Advent and *Lent.

Gloria Patri The Latin for 'Glory be to the Father', the opening words of the prayer, called the lesser *doxology, used at the conclusion of *psalms in the *liturgy, except on the last three days of *Holy Week and in *Masses for the dead.

Glory An *aureole or *nimbus, especially when it surrounds the whole body, as though it were radiating light. The figures of *Moses, *Elijah and of Christ at the *Transfiguration are presented in this way. The word is derived from the Latin gloria, 'splendour' or 'glorification'.

Gluttony One of the *Seven Deadly Sins, usually designated in art by the Latin word *gula, 'gullet'. It may be personified by a pot-bellied man, or by *Dives, the Rich Man of the parable.

Gnostic, gnosticism A *heresy which taught that salvation was to be obtained through 'knowledge' (Greek gnosis) of the secrets of the universe. Gnostics believed that the world was created by a malevolent god and that matter was evil and hostile to the spirit. They used Christian writings selectively and adapted them to their teachings, thus giving rise to a number of *apocryphal gospels.

Goat The sharp-sighted mountain goat represents *Christ who seeks his beloved, the *Church, or God who is all-seeing. The wild goat is also said to eat only good grass and to reject unwholesome weeds and to prosper like those who choose virtue instead of vice. A wounded goat cures itself by eating the herb dittany, or pepperwort, also called herb-o'grace because it cures like the *grace of God when sought by the sinner.

But the domestic goat was renowned for the size of its phallus and was identified with procreation and *lust. The hot blood of a lascivious goat, it was said, would dissolve a diamond, the hardest of the precious stones. The *Devil assumes the shape of a he-goat when he attends a *witches' coven but is recognized by his cloven hoof. Goats (sinners) are separated from sheep (the redeemed) at the Last *Judgement (Mt 25 : 32).

As *capricorn, a goat is the sign of the *zodiac for December, and in representations of the *Labours of the Months controls the tasks of winter (See *Scapegoat).

God the Father The first person of the *Trinity. To represent him in art presented many difficulties, not only because the *Ten Commandments forbid graven images of the Deity. 'No man hath seen the Father', said Jesus (Jn 6 : 46; 14 : 8-9), and the record in the OT of his personal contact with mankind, otherwise than through an *angel as a messenger, bore this out. His voice was heard by *Adam and *Eve, 'walking in the Garden [of *Eden] in the cool of the day' and he spoke to many of the *Patriarchs. But he never revealed himself in bodily form as did *God the Son incarnate. As it was impossible to give visual representation to a voice, artists resorted to another device to reveal his presence. The *Hand of God symbolized his intervention in a particular episode. The Greek letter O for *on*, 'I am that I am' (Ex 3 : 14), or the sacred *Tetragrammaton were also used to symbolize the presence of God.

From the 11th century onwards, after the ending of the *Iconoclastic controversy (See *iconoclasm), artists were less inhibited. As God had created man in his own image (Gen 9 : 6) it was deduced that he must resemble a man, and as he was God the Father he must be advanced in years. Daniel's vision of the *Ancient of Days provided the model. An old man with white hair and a long beard became the artistic convention for the depiction of God the Father.

With the growth in power and prestige of the papacy, the link between the Chair of St *Peter and the throne of *Heaven was demonstrated by showing an enthroned God the Father as a *Pope (his representative on earth) but wearing a five-crowned *tiara (five being the symbol of earth plus heaven), in contrast to the Pope's three crowns. God the Father, whose works are recorded principally in the OT, was also thought of as a supernatural High Priest and is shown wearing a *mitre-like headdress which was thought to be like that of the Aaronic priesthood. In Renaissance art God the Father was sometimes equated with Jupiter (or Zeus), the supreme god. The *Calvinist tradition forbids any representation of God, in accordance with the Mosaic law (Ex 20 : 4).

God the Son The second person of the *Trinity. At first he was represented symbolically as a *lamb, as the *Good Shepherd, as *Orpheus, or as a young philosopher. When it became necessary to combat docetic heresy (the belief that Jesus only 'seemed' to be a man) by emphasizing his humanity, he had to be shown as a man, but the problem was to decide what he looked like in his human form. One tradition, derived from an OT reference, was that the *Messiah would be ugly: 'He hath no form or comeliness' (Is 53 : 1-2). This gave place to a more acceptable deduction from the Psalmist's statement, 'Thou art fairer than the children of men' (Ps 45 (44) : 3), so that Jesus was depicted as a handsome and usually bearded youth,

The ruins of **Glastonbury Abbey** where King Arthur was allegedly buried.

The resurrected Christ surrounded by angels, set in a **glory** (Masaccio, early 15th century).

a convention much in vogue from the 7th century onwards and continued in a degenerate form in sentimental and popular religious art. When Jesus' suffering was emphasized, he was shown as the *Man of Sorrows (See *Ecce Homo), wounded and bleeding and wearing the *crown of thorns. There were also legendary accounts of Christ's features. St *Luke was said to have painted him as a child in the arms of St *Mary the Virgin. Ananias, the emissary of King *Abgar, having failed to paint Jesus' portrait because he was overcome by the splendour of his countenance, was rewarded with a likeness miraculously imprinted on a napkin, as was St *Veronica. *Nicodemus was also said to have carved the *Holy Face on a crucifix, the famous *Volto Santo of Lucca in Italy. Christ's features were described in the letter which Publius *Lentulus, a friend of Pontius *Pilate, was said to have sent to the Roman Senate.

Godparent At *baptism, the person who sponsors the person to be baptized and accepts the obligation to assist in the development of his or her spiritual life. If the candidate is an infant, as is now usual, the godparent carries the child at the font and answers the priest's or minister's questions on its behalf.

Gog and Magog The names given in the *Revelations of St John the Divine* (Rev 20 : 8) to the leaders of the armies which will make the final ineffectual assault on the followers of *Christ. As they were thought to be *giant warriors, their names were awarded to the two huge wooden figures outside the Guildhall in London (alternatively, one was said to be Gogmagog, leader of the giants of Albion, and the other Corineus who overcame him and threw him into the sea, acquiring Cornwall as his patrimony). The statues were destroyed in the Great Fire of London (1666), replaced in 1709, lost in the bombing of 1940, and replaced by replicas.

Gold *Symbol of purity, divinity and kingship, and as such one of the gifts offered to the Christ-Child by the Three *Kings.

Golden calf When *Moses was with God on Mount Sinai and left his brother *Aaron in command, the people of Israel rebelled against the monotheistic and aniconic leadership and demanded that Aaron give them an idol to worship. They donated gold ornaments and Aaron cast in one night a model of a golden calf to which the Israelites made sacrifices. Moses returned from the mountain and was so angered at the sight of their idolatrous feasting and drinking that he dashed to the ground the *Tablets of the Law which he had received from God. He then destroyed the image, reducing the gold to powder which he spread upon water and made the people drink (Ex 32). To replace the idol he constructed the *Ark of the Covenant (Ex 36 : 1-6). Worship of the Golden Calf now symbolizes a materialistic approach to life and the accumulation of money, the *Mammon of Unrighteousness (Lk 16 : 9).

Golden Legend The *Legenda Aurea*, a work giving the legends of the *saints and stories associated with the chief events of the Christian *year, compiled from a variety of earlier sources by *Jacobus à (de) Voragine (Jacopo de' Varazze), 1230-98, *archbishop of Genoa.

Golden rose A spray of roses made of gold, symbolizing spiritual joy, the central rose containing a small cup of balsam and musk, blessed by the *Pope on the fourth Sunday in *Lent, and donated to a person or institution in recognition of outstanding services.

Golden sequence A name given to the hymn *Veni, Sancte Spiritus, 'Come, Holy Spirit', sung on *Whitsunday (*Pentecost).

Goldfinch A bird supposed to feed on thorns, thus an emblem of suffering. When held in the hand of the *Christ-Child, it foretells his *Passion.

Golgotha The site of the *Crucifixion (See *Calvary), so called because its shape resembled a skull (Aramaic *gulgulta*).

Goliath The *Philistine *giant, 'Six cubits and a span high', shown wearing a helmet, a breastplate and greaves of brass. He was the champion of the army which faced the forces of King *Saul across a stream in the Valley of Elah. Neither side dared attack, and Goliath each day challenged the *Israelites to decide the battle by single combat, but they could not find anyone to match him. *David, then a young shepherd boy who had brought food for his soldier brothers, scorned the offer of Saul's armour because he trusted in God, and, armed only with round pebbles taken from a stream, went out to meet Goliath. After exhausting the giant by nimbly evading his grasp, he stunned him by hitting him on the forehead with a stone from his sling. He then took Goliath's sword and cut off his head. The Philistines fled, and David was carried in triumph, bearing aloft Goliath's severed head which he presented to Saul in his tent. The women of the cities came out to meet him with harp and lute, singing 'Saul has killed his thousands, but David his ten thousands' (1 Sam 17 : 4-58; 18 : 6-7).

The fight between David and Goliath represents the victory of the weak who have God on their side, against the wicked who are strong; also *Christ overcoming the *Devil. David's triumphant return foreshadows Christ's entry into Jerusalem on *Palm Sunday.

Good Friday The day of Christ's *Crucifixion, kept in *Holy Week as a solemn day of fasting and *abstinence. Altars are stripped of cloths, *crucifix and *candles to symbolize mourning. It is customary to have a three-hour service from noon onwards to commemorate the time that Jesus hung on the Cross. The ninth hour (3 pm) is the hour of Christ's death, and there may be the *Veneration of the Cross, followed by the Mass of the *Presanctified; or these may take place before noon.

Good Samaritan Samaritans inhabited Samaria, the former northern kingdom of Israel, and accepted only the *Pentateuch, the five *Books of Moses*, while rejecting the *prophets and other writings of the OT, and had their own sanctuary on Mount Gerizim. For these reasons orthodox Jews excluded them. In answer to a lawyer's question, 'Who is my neighbour?', Jesus told the story (Lk 10 : 29-35) of a man (by implication a Jew) on the road between Jerusalem and Jericho who had fallen among thieves, 'who stripped him and beat him and went away leaving him half dead'. A priest and a Levite went down the road but 'passed by on the other side' when they saw the injured man. In contrast, a despised Samaritan had compassion on the victim, bound up his wounds, set him on his own beast and took him to an inn, leaving the innkeeper two *denarii* (pence) for his lodging and promising more on his return if this proved to be insufficient. Jesus then asked the lawyer, 'Which now of these three thinkest thou, was neighbour unto him that fell among the thieves?'. The lawyer replied, 'He that shewed mercy on him'. 'Go, and do thou likewise', said Jesus.

Good shepherd Jesus is shown in the art of the *catacombs carrying on his shoulders a lost sheep, the redeemed soul. The image is derived from the parable of the lost sheep (Mt 18 : 12-14), the one member of the flock of one hundred which has strayed. The good shepherd leaves the ninety-nine which are safe and goes in search of the one which is lost and needs his care, and when he has found it, he brings it back rejoicing. The parable illustrates the unique value of the individual soul.

Good thief The thief, sometimes called the Penitent Thief, whose name was said to be *Dismas. With another robber, *Gestas, he was crucified with Jesus. He is the patron of criminals and of those condemned to death (*See* *Descent of Christ into Hell).

Goose A *symbol of vigilance because a legend recalls that the cackling of geese in the Capitol saved Rome from invasion by Gauls. Also an attribute of St *Martin of Tours (because he hid to avoid being made *bishop but was given away by a goose) and of St *Werburga who stopped geese eating up villagers' crops. Geese listening to a *fox preaching, on a *misericord, represent credulous people duped by a false *friar.

Gospel In general the 'glad tidings' or 'good news' of the redemptive work of *Christ; in particular the record of this work as written down under the guidance of the *Holy Spirit by the four *Evangelists. Extracts from these writings, called 'The Gospel', are read at *Eucharist or *Mass as the second lesson (the first being the *Epistle). *The Gospel-book (or evangelistiary) is carried with candles and incense to the gospel-side (the right side of the altar from the view point of the congregation) in the *Western rites, or to the *ambo in the *Eastern rites. At the announcement

The Christ-Child accepts the symbolic **goldfinch** presented by the infant John the Baptist (Raphael, 1483-1520).

Marble statue of Christ as the **Good Shepherd** (Rome, late 3rd or early 4th century).

of the reading, the people respond: *Gloria tibi Domine*, 'Glory be to thee, O Lord', and at the conclusion say: *Laus tibi Christe*, 'Praise be to thee, O Christ'. The book may be kissed to indicate the presence of Christ in the words of the Gospel. The 'last Gospel' is the name given to the *Gospel of St John*, thought (although this is now doubted) to be the last of the four to be written. It is also the name for the passage of scripture, usually from the first chapter of St John's Gospel, which is read at the end of Eucharist or Mass, except during *Lent and at certain other specified times (*See* *Synoptic Gospels).

Gourd A symbol of the *redemption of mankind, in contrast to the *apple which brought about the *Fall. It may also represent the *Resurrection, possibly because of the gourd which God caused to spring up to shade *Jonah and 'deliver him from his grief' (Jonah 4 : 6).
    As a hollowed-out gourd was used by travellers to carry water, it may also be an *attribute of *pilgrims and pilgrim saints, notably St *James of Compostela, also of the Risen Christ on the Road to *Emmaus.

Grace From the Latin *gratia*, 'favour', assistance freely and gratuitously given by God to man with a view to his eternal life and sanctification. Habitual grace is the gift of God conveyed in the *Sacraments. To be in a state of grace is to be sanctified by grace for the reception of the *Blessed Sacrament. Grace at meals is a *Sacramental act, the word 'grace' in this case being derived from Latin *gratiae*, 'thanks'.

Gradual A chant sung after the reading or singing at *Mass of the *epistle, so called because it was sung or declaimed by the precentor from a lower step (Latin *gradus*) of the *ambo. Also the name of the book which contains these chants and the sung parts of the Mass.

Grapes A bunch of grapes symbolizes the wine of the *Eucharist, the blood of *Christ, the true *Vine.

Greed Inordinate desire or lust for power, personified as *Gula, one of the *Seven Deadly Sins.

Greek letters Certain Greek letters are used in writing and in art because of their *symbolic value. Single letters include *alpha, *delta, *ipsilon, *omega, *omicron and *Tau. Combinations include *A, *Chi-Rho, *IC, and *IHS *monograms.

Gregorian chant Also called *plainchant, the mode of diatonic choral singing without instrumental accompaniment used in singing the Latin *liturgy. The invention of its melodies was wrongly ascribed to Pope St *Gregory I 'the Great' (590-604) because of his work in rearranging the texts of the *antiphonary. In medieval times it was the usual form of chanting in monasteries, but it declined with the vogue for polyphony and the composition of more elaborate Baroque settings.

St Pius X (1903-14) ordered the universal use of the Gregorian chant, in 1903, which he stated to be the supreme form of sacred music. Plainchant is now in favour not only in seminaries but also among amateur singers, as the longterm result of the work of the French Benedictines of the Abbey of Solêmnes who, at the beginning of the 20th century, began the publication of new editions of the old chant-books.

Gregory of Nazianzus (Gregory Nazianaen), St A *Doctor of the Greek Church (329-89). Convinced by a vision in his childhood that he must follow a religious vocation, he studied in Athens and lived for a time in the desert. He preached against the *Arian heresy, was made *bishop of Constantinople, but was so overcome by the dissentions within the Christian community that he retired to live a life of great austerity in his home town of Nazianzus. He wrote poems and many theological works. He is depicted holding a book, and is sometimes accompanied by the personified figures of Chastity and Wisdom (*Sophia) who appeared to him as he was reading.

Gregory the Great, St One of the Four *Fathers of the Latin Church, often depicted with SS *Ambrose, *Augustine and *Jerome, distinguishable from them by his papal *tiara and his *crosier with double or treble transverses. A *dove near his ear symbolizes the inspiration of the Holy Spirit which enabled him to write distinguished theological works, including a commentary on the *Gospel of St Luke*, whose winged *ox emblem is sometimes shown near him. He lived 590-604, covering a notable period in the expansion of the Roman Church. He was of rich parentage, but abandoned a promising political career, gave away his possessions and became a *monk. He devoted his considerable abilities to founding *monasteries, representing successive Popes in Constantinople, and was finally himself called to the papal throne. At first he refused (he is shown praying, a tiara on the ground beside him), but was told in a vision to accept the office. As Pope he was a great administrator. He came to terms with the Lombard invaders, insisted on clerical celibacy, disciplined the *clergy, reformed the *calendar and the *liturgy, and established choir-schools where the so-called *Gregorian chant was taught. The sight of some youthful fair-haired Yorkshire captives exposed for sale in the slave market inspired him to send St *Augustine of Canterbury to convert the English.
    Miraculous events associated with him are: the appearance of *Christ as the thirteenth pauper at a supper which he was accustomed to give to twelve poor men; the release from *Purgatory through his prayers of the soul of a monk who had been refused *last rites because he had concealed three golden coins in his *cell; and the deliverance from *Purgatory of the soul of Emperor Trajan by promising that in compensation he himself would either endure two days there or suffer ill-health for the rest of his life. When Gregory gave the shroud of St *John the Evangelist as a precious *relic to

Empress Constantia, she refused it as unauthentic. Gregory cut the cloth with a knife and it dripped with blood as proof that it was genuine. The Mass of St Gregory, frequently depicted, is a late legend which tells how a woman who doubted the doctrine of the *Real Presence of Christ in the Eucharist was convinced when she saw the bleeding figure of the Redeemer appear over the *Host as Gregory celebrated *Mass at the altar.

Gremial An apron (Latin *gremium*) laid over a bishop's lap at liturgical ceremonies, formerly of embroidered silk of the liturgical *colour of the season but now of white linen.

Grey Friars The name given in Britain (and perpetuated in the names of districts where there were *Franciscan monasteries) to Franciscan friars, whose brown habit was formerly grey.

Gridiron The emblem of St *Lawrence who was martyred by being roasted on a gridiron. Also of St *Vincent of Zaragoza who died in the same way.

Griffin A mythical quadruped, thought to be one of the unclean beasts 'going upon all four' forbidden in *Leviticus* (Lev 11 : 20). It had the head and wings of an eagle, and a lion's body. It hated horses and carried men off to its nest in its talons. Because the griffin was reputed to be able to discover and hoard gold, it came paradoxically to symbolize either *Scientia* (Knowledge) or Usury. Dante used the griffin as the symbol of *Christ, possibly because he thought of it as a combination of the qualities of the *lion and the *eagle.

Guardian angel An ancient belief explained in the writings of Honorius Augustodunensis (*d.*1151) is that every person, during his earthly existence, has assigned to him an *angel who will pray for him, protect him and guide his steps throughout his life. Pope Clement X (1670-6) made the Feast of the Guardian Angels (now on 2 October) universal in 1670. The model for the Guardian Angel is Archangel *Raphael, who looked after *Tobias.

Gula The Latin for the personification of *Gluttony, one of the *Seven Deadly Sins.

Habakkuk (Habacuc) One of the minor Hebrew *prophets whose oracles are preserved in the OT book bearing his name. He was thought to be bald, bearded and stooping (or hunchbacked, as in his statue in Genoa Cathedral). His hope that the *Messiah would appear 'in the midst of the years' (Hab 3 : 2), reads in the *Septuagint version, *in medio duorum animalium* ('between two beasts'), and was understood to foretell the presence of the *ox and the ass beside the manger in which *Jesus was laid. When Habakkuk complained of God's apparent indifference to the sufferings of the righteous,

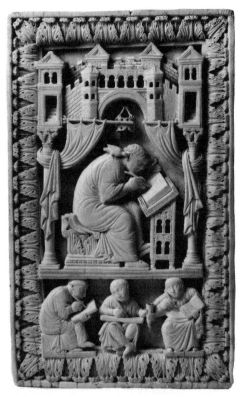

Scribes copy the works of St **Gregory the Great,** who writes under the inspiration of the Holy Spirit, represented as a dove perched on his shoulder (Germany, 9th or 10th century).

The first tone of the **Gregorian chant,** on a capital in the Abbey church of Cluny (1088-95).

he was instructed to write legibly on tablets – 'that he may run that readeth' (Hab 2 : 2) – that the faithful would be rewarded and wicked oppressors punished by one who would appear at the appointed time. This promise was included in the *Advent liturgy as it was understood to point to the *Second Coming of Christ. Habakkuk was also assumed to be the prophet of Judaea who was taking a basket of bread to some harvesters when he was seized by the hair by an angel and carried off to Babylon to feed *Daniel in the lions' den (Dan 14 : 33-9). He thus prefigures Christ at the *Last Supper.

Habit, religious Clothes worn by members of religious *Orders, each of which has its distinctive garb, the variations being in *colour and style. *Monks and *friars generally wear a tunic, belt (or *girdle), *hood and *scapular. A long cloak may be worn by some friars in *choir or out of doors. Monks wear a *cowl in choir. *Sandals are used by some Orders, depending upon whether they are *calced, or *discalced. (*Jesuits are the exception in that they could always wear civilian dress.) *Nuns' habits are basically similar, but they may wear a white *wimple and a black or a white veil. Black, brown, or white were colours usually chosen. Formerly habits were always worn by monks, friars and nuns, but in recent times the tendency is to wear the habit of the Order in the *monastery and civilian dress outside.

Hades The temporary abode or state of the dead, where departed spirits await the Last *Judgement. Christ visited Hades after his *Crucifixion (See *Descent into Hell). It is derived from the Greek *Haidēs*, 'the underworld', which translates the Hebrew *sheol* in the OT.

Hagar An Egyptian maidservant whom the barren *Sarah gave as a concubine to her husband *Abraham. When Hagar became pregnant she despised her childless mistress. In revenge, Sarah treated Hagar so badly that she ran away, but an angel found her on the road to Shur by a desert spring and told her to return to her mistress and to endure her abuse. Hagar bore Abraham a son, *Ishmael, who made Sarah jealous after she had miraculously given birth to *Isaac. Abraham therefore gave Hagar some bread and water and sent her and her child away. She wandered aimlessly in the desert of Beer-Sheba until the water was exhausted and then, unwilling to watch her son die, she placed him under a shrub and sat sobbing some distance away. Moved by the child's cries, God sent an angel (traditionally St *Michael) to lead Hagar to a well where she refilled the water-skin and saved Ishmael's life (Gen 21 : 9-21). Abraham was said to have married Hagar after Sarah's death.

Haggai (Aggeus) One of the minor Hebrew *prophets, supposed author of the early-6th-century BC book called after him. Because of the confusion of *Aggeus*, the Latin form of his name, with *angelus* ('angel'), he is sometimes represented as an *angel. His *attributes are a money-bag, recalling God's words, 'Gold and silver belong to me' (Hag 2 : 8), or an axe and a plank of wood because he obeyed God's command (Hag 1 : 8) to go up into the hills to bring wood to rebuild the *Temple in Jerusalem, so that the prosperity of the Jews who had returned from exile in *Babylon would be restored and the Messianic age brought nearer. He also predicted the Last *Judgement (Hag 2 : 22).

Hagioscope A small hole or opening in a church wall or partition which allowed the high *altar and the celebrant of the *Eucharist to be seen from the aisles or side chapels, also called a squint.

Hail Mary A prayer in honour of St *Mary the Virgin, derived from the salutation of the angel *Gabriel (Lk 1 : 28) and the greeting of St *Elizabeth (Lk 1 : 42) (See *Ave Maria).

Hair shirt A garment of coarse cloth, originally made in Cilicia from goat's hair, and because of its irritant quality worn either as a girdle or as a shirt for penance or mortification. *Carmelites and *Carthusians wear it by *Rule.

Hallelujah (alleluia) An ejaculation of praise in Hebrew, 'Praise ye *Yah(weh)', found at the beginning or end of certain *psalms and adopted in the Christian *liturgy as an expression of joy.

Hallowe'en The evening of All Hallows (Old English *hallow*, 'saint'), 31 October, and the evening before *All Saints' Day when traditional games and customs, some originally pagan, are indulged in.

Halo The popular name for a refulgence of light or a circle or globe of light around the head of a sacred or sanctified figure, technically a *nimbus. Living persons (such as saintly donors) were given a square or rectangular halo.

Ham One of the three sons of *Noah, apparently the second in age, supposed ancestor of the black peoples of Africa.

Hammer and nails *Instruments of the Passion used for nailing Jesus to the *Cross, and associated with *Nicodemus who was said to have been a blacksmith and to have assisted in taking down the crucified body (See *Descent from the Cross).

Hand of God The presence of *God the Father, the First Person of the *Trinity, was frequently indicated in early-Christian art by a hand appearing from a cloud. Usually the fingers of the hand were arranged as though in the act of blessing. This convention was derived from the double meaning of the Hebrew word *yad*, which means either 'hand' or 'power', so that a hand (as in the *Baptism of Christ or in the stoning of St *Stephen) expressed the power of God to intervene in human affairs or to bestow* grace. Diminutive figures held in a closed hand represent the souls of the righteous, as expressed in the text, 'the righteous . . . are in the hand of God' (Eccl 9 : 1).

Hanuel (Haniel) Leader of the *virtues, the fifth choir of the *angels.

Hare *Symbol of lust. It was believed to be able to change its sex at will. As it was thought to reproduce its kind by parthenogenesis, it also symbolized the *Virgin birth of Christ.

Harp A stringed instrument associated with King *David, who as a youth at court played the harp to calm King *Saul's outbursts of madness. A harp in King David's hands also refers to the belief that he composed and sang the *Book of Psalms*. In exile by the rivers of *Babylon the *Israelites refused to sing, hung their harps on the willows and wept when they remembered their homeland, *Zion (Ps 137 (136) : 1-2).

Harrow *See* *Hearse.

Harrowing of Hell The medieval English phrase for the *Descent of Christ into Hell. 'Harrowing' is used in the sense of 'robbing', or 'despoiling'.

Hart Symbol of the Christian who seeks the water of eternal life, a reference to the text, 'As the hart panteth after the water brooks, so panteth my soul after thee, O God' (Ps 42 (41) : 1). As a hart was thought to be able to scent a *snake in its lair and then to trample it to death, it also symbolized Christ who seeks out the *Devil to destroy him.

Harvest, great A parable given in slightly different forms in the *Gospel of Matthew* (Mt 9 : 37) and the *Gospel of Luke* (Lk 10 : 2). In the former, Jesus is moved by the sight of the multitude who have no one to care for them. He said to his disciples, 'The harvest truly is plenteous, but the labourers are few'. In the latter, he enjoins the seventy-two *disciples whom he is sending out to spread the *Gospel.

Harvest thanksgiving A service of thanks for the harvest, possibly stemming from the medieval English custom of offering a loaf of new corn at *Lammastide. It was revived in 1843 by the Vicar of Morwenstowe, Cornwall, after which it caught the popular imagination and became an annual occurrence in many parishes.

Head Christ is described by St *Paul as the head of the mystical body of the *Church (Eph 4 : 15). A head on a platter, or charger, is the head of St *John the Baptist (*See* *Salome) and a head on a napkin is the imprint of Christ's features (*See* St *Veronica). Saints martyred by decapitation are sometimes depicted holding their heads before their truncated bodies. Three heads joined at the back, the middle one frontal and the others in profile, symbolize the *Trinity. (This representation appears carved on *bench ends and columns but was condemned by Pope Urban VIII (1623-44) in 1628.)

St Agnes with a **halo,** holding an *agnus dei* (Duccio, early 14th century).

The **Hand of God** rejecting Cain's wheat sheaf (from the bronze doors of Hildesheim Cathedral, *c.*1015).

Hearse Originally a triangular frame or stand (named after its resemblance to a *harrow, Latin *hirpex*) which usually held fifteen candles and was used at *Tenebrae. It also surmounted the bier on which the coffin was placed at funeral services, hence the modern extension of the word to the car or carriage in which coffins are carried to burial.

Heart *Symbol of affection, love, devotion and charity, one of the theological *virtues. A heart transfixed by a *sword and surrounded with a wreath of roses is the Heart of St *Mary the Virgin; pierced by seven swords, the emblem of the Seven *Sorrows of the Mother of God; with three nails, encircled with thorns and surmounted by a *cross, the *Sacred Heart of Jesus as seen in the vision of St Margaret Mary Alacoque (1647-90). St *Augustine of Hippo is sometimes shown with a flaming heart because of his religious zeal.

Heaven Popularly located above the sky and inhabited by God, his *angels and his *saints, where the redeemed will ultimately dwell in eternal bliss (See *Abraham's bosom). Jesus' saying, 'In my Father's house are many mansions' (Jn 14 : 2), is understood to mean that in Heaven there are many degrees of happiness because, 'Every man shall receive his own reward according to his own labour' (1 Cor 3 : 8).

Hedgehog *Symbol of prudence (like other *animals), because it rolls on grapes which fall from the vine, makes them stick to its bristles and then carries them back to its young. This also imparts a moral lesson: unless a man cares for his spiritual garden, the *Devil will carry off the good fruits that he has cultivated.

Helena (Helen), St According to the chronicler Geoffrey of Monmouth (*d.*1154) she was the daughter of King Coel of Colchester ('Old King Cole'), but she was most probably of humble parentage and born *c.*255 at Drepanum (Helenopolis) in Bythinia, Asia Minor. She became the wife of Constantius Chlorus ('the Pale') and is thus shown as an empress wearing a *crown. After twenty years of married life Constantius divorced her for political reasons. This was resented by her son *Constantine, who when he was proclaimed emperor in York in 306 honoured his mother in every possible way.

At first hostile to the Christian faith, Helena was converted after her son's victory over his rival Maxentius at the battle of the *Milvian Bridge. She used her wealth and power to promote her new religion, and it may have been through her influence that Constantine issued his edict in 312 making Christianity a tolerated religion. When she was nearly eighty Helena made a *pilgrimage to the *Holy Land, where she died *c.*330 after helping to found a number of churches, including the Church of the *Holy Sepulchre, on sites connected with Christ's life and passion. It was thought that a vision helped her to discover the *True Cross, so a cross borne to her in a dream by an angel is her *attribute. Among other relics which she is said to have found was the *seamless robe worn by Jesus at his *Crucifixion (the *Holy Coat), some of the Holy *Nails and the Holy Stairs (See *Scala Santa). Her own relics are under the altar of the Cappella Sant' Elena in the church of *Ara Coeli, Rome, built on earth which she brought from *Jerusalem. One of the pillars supporting the dome of St Peter's, Rome, is dedicated to her and has her statue near it.

Hell In the strictest sense, the place of eternal punishment for the damned, the infernal regions where *devils and *demons dwell and where *Satan rules. It is located under the earth, and is filled with flames and sulphurous fumes from eternal fires. In its midst is a lake of brimstone and burning pitch. In a broad sense (as in the *Apostles' Creed, 'he descended into Hell') it is the equivalent of the *Limbo of the Fathers (Latin *limbus patrum*) where the souls of the *Just who died before the *Incarnation awaited their release by Christ. It may also signify *Purgatory where those who die in venial *sin are cleansed by suffering before being admitted to *Heaven. Hell is symbolized by the mouth of a *whale, recalling *Jonah in the belly of a great fish, or *Leviathan, the sea monster mentioned by *Job (Jb 41 : 1).

Héloïse An orphan (1101-64), niece of Canon Fulbert of Notre-Dame, Paris, in whose house Peter *Abélard lived. This girl of lively intelligence was given lessons by the young theologian who became her lover. After the birth of their child, they entered into a secret alliance because marriage would hinder Abélard's career. (Another version is that they were actually married.) Fulbert revenged himself by hiring villains to castrate the seducer. Héloïse retired to a convent and corresponded with Abélard in Latin. Eight letters survive and are frequently translated, although they are possibly improvements on the originals. The first is to a friend, giving Abélard's account of his tragic affair; the others contain spiritual and moral advice in response to questions put by Héloïse as head of the Convent of the Holy Paraclete, which he had founded and donated to her. Abélard and Héloïse were romanticized as the pattern of true love which develops from the physical into the spiritual. They are reputed to be buried in the same grave.

Heresy Literally a 'choice' (Greek *hairesis*) of any opinion or belief, but now restricted to one contrary to the accepted and authoritative teachings of the Church. A distinction is made between 'formal heresy' – the contumacious adherence to a condemned heresy which may involve *excommunication – and 'material heresy', the innocent acceptance in good faith of opinions at variance with defined doctrine (See *Arian; *Catharist).

Heretic One who has accepted the faith, but rejects one or more of its dogmas in favour of a *heresy.

Hermit Like an *anchorite, one who chooses to live alone in a hermitage in order to devote himself to prayer and meditation. The word is derived from the Greek *eremites*, 'desert-dweller', because in the 4th century, many were attracted by the example of St *Antony of Egypt (the Great) to this type of solitary existence in the Theban desert. St *Hilarion fomented a similar movement in the Gaza desert.

Herod The family name of many rulers in Palestine mentioned in the NT. Herod the Great (73-4 BC) was first made governor of Galilee by the Romans and in 40 BC, king of Judaea. He ruled at the time of the birth of Jesus and ordered the massacre of the *Holy Innocents. His fatal union with *Mariamne is recounted by the Jewish historian *Josephus. His son, Archelaus, ruled as ethnarch over half his father's kingdom, but incurred religious opposition by marrying his brother's wife and was exiled to Gaul in AD 7. It was through fear of him that the *Holy Family settled in Nazareth, outside his territory, on their return from Egypt. Another son, Antipas, was Tetrarch of Galilee (4 BC-AD 39) and put St *John the Baptist to death because he had condemned his marriage to *Herodias, his half-brother's wife. Jesus was tried by him before his *Crucifixion. Herod the Great's grandson, Agrippa I, spent some time in Rome as a prisoner of Emperor Tiberius, but was made king again in 37. He died in 44, consumed by worms. It was under him that St *James the Less, the Lord's brother, was beheaded and St *Peter imprisoned. St *Paul appeared before his son Agrippa II who was titular king of Judaea at the time of the fall of Jerusalem.

As the name Herod was associated with the persecution and deaths of so many NT figures, it was inevitable that they should be confused and assumed to be one raging tyrant. This conflation of persons was reinforced in the popular mind through the influence of medieval religious drama.

Herodias Daughter of Aristobulus, son of *Herod the Great (73-4 BC) and *Mariamne. She was first married to Herod Philip and then to his half-brother, Herod Antipas, Tetrarch of Galilee. The condemnation of this adulterous union by St *John the Baptist provoked her fierce hatred of the prophet and led her to plot his death by exploiting Herod's infatuation with her daughter *Salome. She accompanied Antipas when he was exiled to Lyons.

Hexagram Two equilateral triangles, one inverted, intersected to form a star-like shape (see figure). Modern symbol of Judaism and of divine protection (*see* *Solomon).

High Altar The principal *altar in a church, placed centrally in the east end.

High Church *Anglicans who adhere to the *Catholic rather than to the *Protestant tradition of the Church of England and emphasize the

An angel locking damned souls up in **Hell,** depicted as a whale's maw (Psalter of Henry of Blois, *c*.1150-60).

The head of St John the Baptist brought to **Herod** Antipas (Donatello, 1425).

*Eucharist and the importance of *vestments and ceremonial.

High Mass The chief *Mass of the day, in Latin *Missa Solemnis*, the complete rite performed by the *priest, assisted by *deacon and subdeacon, with *choir, incensing and full ceremonial. Many notable musical settings were commissioned for it. Pontifical High Mass is solemnly sung by a *cardinal, a *bishop in his own *diocese, or by an *abbot in his own *abbey.

High Priest In the OT the chief of the Levites, the priesthood descended from the tribe of Levi who officiated in the *Temple sanctuary. In NT times he was head of the Judaean state appointed by the Romans, as well as being the supreme religious functionary. After his arrest Jesus was taken before the High Priest as a potential political criminal as well as a religious agitator.

Hilarion, St The founder of eremitical life in Palestine was born near Gaza *c*.291 and converted to Christianity while studying in Alexandria. A visit to St *Antony of Egypt in the desert stimulated him to follow a life of solitude. On his return home he found that his parents had died, so he gave his inheritance to the poor and went to live in a hut in the Gaza desert, existing on fifteen figs a day, eaten at sunset, and supporting himself by weaving baskets. He achieved fame through his exorcisms and cures and was so beset by would-be disciples and followers that he fled first to Dalmatia and then to Cyprus where he died in 371. He appears in art as naked, emaciated, with a long beard. His *attribute is a *dragon, recalling the episode where he overcame one by making a *sign of the cross.

Hilary of Poitiers, St Born at Poitiers *c*.315 of wealthy pagan parents and converted to Christianity through his philosophical studies. When he was about thirty-five, he was elected *bishop of his native city, although he was married and had a daughter Abra (who also became a *saint and is sometimes depicted beside him). His learning and talents as an orator were devoted to combatting the *Arian heresy. He did so with such success that he was banished to Phrygia in 356 by the Arian emperor Constantius II, where he composed a voluminous treatise on the *Trinity (which is why he is depicted as a bishop writing at his desk). Uninvited, he appeared at the Council of Seleucia in 359, and legend describes how, when he was refused a seat, the earth rose up to form a mound for him to sit on. He was sent back to Gaul as a trouble-maker in 360. On his way to Poitiers he rid the island of Gallinaria (near Genoa) of serpents by planting his staff in the ground (a miracle also attributed to St Hilary of Arles). His extensive theological writings, including a famous commentary on the *Gospel of Matthew*, filled the rest of his time until his death *c*.367, and led to his being proclaimed a *Doctor of the Church in 1851. He is not the patron saint Hilary of Parma, but may have acquired this status because some of his relics were

thought to repose in the cathedral there. His name is given in England to legal and university terms which used to begin on his feast day, formerly 14 January.

Hippolytus the soldier (or the jailor), St A Roman soldier who acted as jailor for St *Lawrence and who was converted to Christianity by the example of his prisoner. He revealed his secret adherence to the forbidden faith by burying the martyr's body. For this, nineteen members of his family, his old nurse Concordia, and he himself were put to death. The story of his martyrdom is probably derived from a popular interpretation of his Greek name, 'killed by a horse'. He is said to have met his end either by being tied to the tail of a wild horse, or by having horses attached to each limb and being torn apart. He is the patron of horses.

Holly The association of holly oak *(ilex)* twigs and leaves with *Christmas has been variously explained. One legend states that when the *Holy Family was fleeing *Herod's soldiers (See *Flight into Egypt), they took refuge beneath a holly tree which spread its branches to conceal them. St Mary the Virgin blessed it and said that it would be 'evergreen', hence it symbolizes immortality. Another legend is that the *Cross was made of holly wood because it was the only tree which allowed itself to be cut down. Prickly holly leaves also symbolize the *Passion, and the *Advent wreath recalls how *Easter is implicit in Christmas. On the other hand the use of holly may be a pagan survival, because it was a Roman custom to send branches of holly as a sign of good wishes at the time of the new-year festivals.

Holy Children, Three See *Fiery Furnace; *Benedicite*.

Holy Coat The *seamless garment worn by Christ, for which Roman soldiers cast lots at the *Crucifixion. Said to have been woven for Jesus by his mother when he was a child, it grew with him so that he was able to wear it throughout his earthly life. The relic was discovered in the *Holy Land by St *Helena and sent to Trier, Germany, where a 6th-century tablet commemorates the gift. On the other hand, a document of 1156 attests the presence of the tunic of the *Christ-Child at Argenteuil, France.

Holy Communion See *Communion.

Holy Cross Day The *feast of the *Exaltation of the Holy Cross on 14 September.

Holy Face The supposed imprint of Jesus' features on the napkin which St *Veronica handed him on his way to *Calvary (See *Volto Santo).

Holy Family The earthly Trinity, St *Mary the Virgin, *St Joseph and the *Christ-Child, usually depicted together in their household in *Nazareth. The cult of the Holy Family developed in the 17th century, and the second Sunday after *Epiphany became a popular feast (hence the increase in the number of paintings of this subject). It was instituted as a feast of the Universal Church in 1921 by Pope Benedict XV (1914-22) in order to foster family life through devotion to Mary, Joseph and the Christ-Child. St *Anne, the mother of St Mary the Virgin, and St *John the Baptist as a child are sometimes added, the latter playing with his cousin Jesus.

Holy Father The title given to the *Pope as father of all Roman Catholics. It is the English equivalent of the Latin *Beatissimus Pater*.

Holy Ghost The English alternative name for the third person of the *Trinity, the Holy *Spirit (Old English *gast*, 'spirit').

Holy Grail Either the dish on which the paschal lamb was placed at the *Last Supper, or the cup (*chalice) containing the wine which Jesus blessed on that occasion. The vessel was used by St *Joseph of Arimathea to catch the blood of Christ as he hung on the Cross. Legend claims he later took it to *Glastonbury, England, where it was buried and the location forgotten. The search for the Holy Grail is the subject of a large number of medieval romances linked with the Arthurian legend. The story, probably originating in the *Gospel of *Nicodemus, was exploited by the monks of Glastonbury Abbey in the 12th century (they also discovered King Arthur's tomb there) to encourage *pilgrims to visit their *monastery.

Holy Innocents The children of Bethlehem 'from two years old and under' who were slaughtered at Herod's command in an attempt to get rid of the infant Jesus whom he regarded as a rival to his throne (Mt 2 : 16-18). The event is commemorated on Holy Innocents' Day, 28 December (*Childermass).

Holy Land In Latin *terra sancta*, the name given to the *Promised Land, and particularly *Galilee and Judaea in the Middle East, associated with the life of Jesus and the Early Church and containing the *Holy Places.

Holy Maccabees (Machabees) Seven brothers, their mother and the aged Eleazer, who suffered terrible tortures and were put to death in the 2nd century BC for refusing to obey laws imposed by Antiochus Epiphanes with the intention of ending Jewish religious observances (2 Mac 6-7). They are the only OT *saints honoured in the *liturgy, as examples of steadfastness under persecution. Their supposed *relics (which have now been shown to be bones of dogs) were kept in the church of San Pietro-in-Vincoli (St Peter-in-chains), Rome.

Holy Nails *Relics, supposed to be the nails extracted by *Nicodemus from the body of Jesus on the *Cross.

Holy Name, feast of the Veneration of the Holy Name of Jesus on the Sunday between 2 and 5

The martyrdom of St **Hippolytus,** horses attached to each limb (Dieric Bouts, *c.*1415-75).

Sir Galahad sees the **Holy Grail.** A romantic interpretation by Sir Edward Burne-Jones (*c.*1890).

Rachel (in the background) weeps for her children, the **Holy Innocents,** slain by Herod (Poussin, 1593/4-1665).

January, or 2 January if a Sunday, fostered by the *Franciscans and by St *Bernardino of Siena, and appointed a feast day by Pope Innocent XIII (1721-4) in 1721. It commemorates the *Naming of Jesus at his *Circumcision and *Presentation in the Temple.

Holy Office The Roman Catholic Congregation, popularly the *Inquisition, established in 1542 as the final court of appeal in matters of *heresy. Its name was changed in 1965 to the Congregation of the Doctrine of the Faith.

Holy of Holies A Hebrew idiom meaning 'the most holy', applied to the innermost room of the Tabernacle in the *Temple of Jerusalem. A *veil (the one 'rent in twain' [Mt 27 : 51] at the hour of the *Crucifixion) separated it from the outer room, and it was entered only once a year on the Day of Atonement by the *High Priest who offered an animal sacrifice on behalf of the people.

Holy Oils Oils blessed by a *bishop in his *cathedral on *Maundy Thursday.

Holy Orders Grades of the ministry conferred by 'the laying-on of hands', the imposition of a *bishop's hands on the head of the man to be ordained, one of the Seven *Sacraments. The major orders are those of bishop, *priest and *deacon (episcopate, priesthood and diaconate). In the *Roman Catholic Church, until the Second *Vatican Council, the sub-diaconate was also considered to be one of the major orders. For centuries also, *acolyte, reader (or lector), exorcist and doorkeeper (or porter), were in minor orders. In 1973 acolyte and reader were placed in the category of special ministries for which a liturgical ceremony was provided.

*Anglican Orders (bishop, priest and deacon) were declared by the *bull *Apostolicae Curae* (1896) of Pope Leo XIII (1878-1903) to be invalid, because they were said to be defective in form (lacking historical continuity) and intention (in the way the *Sacraments are administered). This major obstacle to reunion, the historical and theological basis of which is doubtful, is now being actively discussed.

Holy Places Those places in the *Holy Land associated with events in the life, ministry and death of Jesus. Since at least the 4th century they have been centres of *pilgrimage. Chief among them is the *Holy Sepulchre in Jerusalem, *Calvary, *Gethsemane, the grotto of the *Nativity in Bethlehem, and the *Via Dolorosa.*

Holy Rood The cross or *rood on which Christ died (See *Crucifixion) or reproductions of it.

Holy Saturday The Saturday of *Holy Week, commemorating the day when Jesus was in the tomb before his *Resurrection on Easter Sunday morning. Because of St *Mary the Virgin's faith in his promise to rise again from the dead, the day is consecrated to her.

Holy See The Apostolic See of Rome, the seat of the *Pope.

Holy Sepulchre The tomb hewn out of rock in which the body of Jesus was laid after the *Crucifixion. It was in a garden (Jn 19 : 41) outside the city of *Jerusalem, but its precise location went unrecorded until 326 when St *Helena, possibly relying on local tradition, rediscovered the site and Emperor *Constantine erected a *basilica over it. The Church of the Holy Sepulchre (properly the Church of the Resurrection) now stands there.

Holy Shroud *See* *Shroud of Turin.

Holy Spirit Otherwise, *Holy Ghost (Old English *gast*, 'spirit'), third person of the *Trinity, one in being with *God the Father and *God the Son, coequal and coeternal but distinct. Whether the Holy Spirit 'proceeds from the Father *and the Son*' (the *filioque* clause inserted by the *West in the Nicene *Creed) was for centuries a matter of controversy between West and *East.

In art, the Holy Spirit is depicted as a *dove, because at the *Baptism of Christ the Holy Spirit was said to have descended on Jesus 'in a bodily shape like a dove' (Lk 3 : 22). A dove may therefore appear at the *Creation of the world, when 'the Spirit of God moved upon the face of the waters' (Gen 1 : 2); settling on St *Joseph's flowering rod; descending on St Mary the Virgin at the *Incarnation; hovering over Jesus at his *baptism; and above the Apostles and St Mary the Virgin at *Pentecost. A dove perched near the ear of a *saint or *Doctor of the Church signifies divine inspiration. Seven doves symbolize the seven *Gifts of the Holy Spirit. The colour of the Holy Spirit is *red.

The Holy Spirit is also called the Holy *Paraclete (Greek *parakletos*, 'comforter', 'advocate') because Jesus promised his disciples that after his death he would pray his Father to give them 'another Comforter' (Jn 14 : 16).

Holy Thursday The name given to the Thursday preceding *Easter. In the evening the *Washing of the disciples' feet is commemorated. From the words of the first antiphon of this ceremony, *mandatum [novum]*, 'a [new] command', is derived the English *Maundy Thursday. Altars are stripped on this day and the *Holy Oils are blessed by a *bishop in his *cathedral.

Holy Water Water blessed by a *priest and used liturgically as a sign of cleansing and sanctification. The faithful bless themselves with holy water from a stoup or font at the entrance to a church, and the *celebrant symbolically sprinkles all present before the *High Mass (See *Asperges). Holy water is also used symbolically in dedications, exorcisms and burials.

Holy Week The last week in *Lent, beginning with *Palm Sunday and ending on Easter Saturday (*Holy Saturday), during which the events of the last days in *Christ's earthly life are commemorated.

Holy Women The three *Maries (*Mary Magdalene, *Mary Cleophas (Clopas) and *Mary Salome) who were near Jesus at his *Crucifixion and who came to his tomb early on *Easter morning bringing spices (See *Resurrection).

Holy Writ The *Bible, the Sacred Scriptures or Holy Writings (Old English *writan*, 'to write').

Holy Year A year during which the *Pope grants special *indulgences to *pilgrims who visit Rome. It begins with the Pope opening the Holy Door in St Peter's, and ends with its closing. Originally, in the 14th century, it was intended to be celebrated every hundred years, but now it happens every twenty-five years or so.

Homobonus, St *See* *Omobuono, St.

Hood A conical headdress, usually part of a cloak, worn by *monks and mendicant *friars in the Middle Ages and still used in *choir by certain of the older religious *Orders. It survives in secular usage in academic *hoods worn over the shoulders, the colour of the lining denoting the University and Faculty which granted the wearer's degree.

Hope One of the three theological *virtues (the others being *faith and *charity (love)) symbolized by an *anchor.

Horologion The office-book of the *Orthodox Church containing the choir *antiphons for feast days.

Horse *Symbol of virility and lust. According to popular belief it loses its sexual powers when its mane is cut, and is the only *animal which can show sorrow, because it weeps for its dead master.

Hosanna A shout of joy (Hebrew *hoshi'a na*, 'save me, please') originating in a *psalm (Ps 117 (116)) which was intoned daily during the Jewish Feast of Tabernacles. On the seventh day, when verses 25-26 were recited, the people waved palm branches and myrtle and cried, 'Hosanna!', an expression of Messianic hope. It is thought that this was the motive behind the rejoicing at Jesus' entry into Jerusalem on *Palm Sunday, when he was hailed as the expected *Messiah.

Hosea (Osee) One of the minor *prophets, whose words are recorded in the book bearing his name. At God's command he married a harlot (Hos 1 : 2) whom he bought for fifteen shekels and a bushel-and-a-half of barley (Hos 3 : 2). He continued to cherish her despite her infidelities, thus symbolizing God's enduring love for *Israel, and *Christ's for the *Church. In art, the skull at his feet recalls his prophesy (Hos 13 : 14) of Christ's triumph over death, 'O Death, where is thy sting?' (1 Cor 15 : 55).

The **Holy Rood,** a 14th-century German sculptured crucifix.

The angel tells the **Holy Women** that Christ is risen (Duccio, *c*.1308-11).

Host Bread (unleavened in the *West, leavened in the *East), as cut from ordinary loaves or in the form of a wafer, used for the celebration of the *Eucharist, but more particularly the bread or wafer after consecration – the body of Christ, the 'victim' or 'hostage' (Latin *hostia*) for the sins of mankind. As an emblem in art it is associated with St *Barbara who takes the Last Sacraments to the dying, St *Clare of Assisi who dispersed the Islamic army by displaying a host in a *monstrance, and St *Yves who was devoted to the Body of Christ.

Hour glass Symbol of the passage of time, of the inevitability of death and of the vanity of human existence. It is associated with a scythe, symbolizing Death, the reaper, who claims all in time.

Hours, canonical The divine office to be recited at different hours of each day by those in *Holy Orders and members of religious *Orders who observe the Office of *Choir. There are seven daily services embracing the greater hours: matins and lauds (said together), and vespers; and the little (or lesser) hours: prime, terce, sext, none and compline. Each has a reference to events in the *Passion of Christ: matins, Christ before *Caiaphas; lauds, Christ condemned by Caiaphas; prime, Christ before *Pilate; tierce, Christ scourged and crowned with thorns; sext, Christ on the Cross and the Seven Last *Words; none, Christ's death; vespers, the *Descent from the Cross and the *Entombment.

Hubert, St A wild young nobleman of Aquitaine, born *c.*656, much given to the pleasures of the court and the chase – so much so that he went out hunting on *Good Friday in the forest of the Ardennes. Suddenly a milk-white *stag with a *crucifix between its horns stood before him. The shock of this apparition made him repent of his follies (a similar story is told of St *Eustace). After his wife's death, he gave his money to the poor and spent his days trying to convert the bands of robbers and idolators who infested the forest. He then studied for the priesthood and eventually became bishop of Liège. Thirteen years after his death (728), his remains were found to be in perfect condition and his robes unstained. He is the patron of hunters. Dogs were sprinkled with *holy water on his feast day as a prophylactic against hydrophobia.

Hugh of Grenoble, St Born near Valence, 1053, and a pupil of St *Bruno at Rheims. He was created *bishop of Grenoble in 1080 aged only twenty-seven. He is famous for his vision of seven stars (his *attribute) which heralded the arrival of St Bruno and six companions, who founded the monastery of La Grande Chartreuse on diocesan land which he made over to them, also receiving their *habits from him. When news was brought to St Hugh that the *monks were eating roast fowl, prohibited by their *Order, he entered the refectory to find St Bruno and his monks in a trance: the forbidden food inadvertently served to them lay untouched on the table before them. St Hugh made the *sign of the cross and the chickens were changed into turtles, which as they were thought to be fish they were allowed to eat. St Hugh died in 1132 and was canonized two years later by Pope Innocent II (1130-43).

Hugh of Lincoln, Little 'St' The scandalous excuse for an anti-Jewish riot at Lincoln in 1255. He was a child whom a Jew named Copinus (or Koppin) was said to have enticed into his house, disembowelled, crucified and then thrown into a well. A similar slander, with the same regrettable consequences, was earlier told of the twelve-year-old 'St' William of Norwich (*d.*1144).

Hugh of Lincoln, St Born at Avalon in Burgundy *c.*1135, he became a *Carthusian monk and was sent *c.*1178 to take charge of the *Charterhouse (the English for a Carthusian monastery) at Witham, Somerset, where he remained for seventeen years before being made *bishop of Lincoln, then an extensive *diocese. He rebuilt Lincoln Cathedral, defended the rights of the people against oppressive forest laws and did his best to prevent the endemic anti-Jewish riots. He died at Lincoln's Inn, London, in the year 1200 and was canonized in 1220. He is shown with his pet *swan which always accompanied him and which announced his death by refusing to eat. He is also depicted holding a *chalice containing the figure of the *Christ-Child which once materialized when he was saying *Mass.

Humility (Humilitas), St Founder of the *Vallombrosan nuns, the feminine counterpart of the religious society created by St *John Gualberto in 1038. A married woman, she convinced her husband that they should both adopt a conventual life. They received their *habits, and Humility entered the convent of St Perpetua where, although she was illiterate, she was able to take her turn to read in the refectory because the *Holy Spirit, in the form of a *dove, whispered the words in her ear. She was later ordered by an *angel to seek admission to the convent of St Chiara (*Clare) and from then on was able to perform miracles. She walked dryshod over the River Lamone; cured with the *sign of the cross a *monk's gangrened limb when he refused to have it amputated; stopped a *nun's haemorrhage which doctors had been unable to cure; and revived a dead child by prayer. She helped build the convent for her nuns with her own hands and is thus depicted as an *abbess loading bricks on an ass. In her last illness (she died 1310) nuns were able to relieve her suffering with ice which they found, at her bidding, in a well although it was mid-August.

Hydrus A water-serpent said to live in the Nile. It would contrive to get itself swallowed by a *crocodile, feed on its entrails and then swim out of its mouth. It thus typifies Christ's *Harrowing of Hell.

Hyena A loathsome *animal said to live in graveyards and feast on corpses. It is able to imitate the human voice and thus to lure men and animals to their death. It can change its sex and therefore resembles a double-minded and inconstant man. It can also paralyse an animal by walking around it three times. In its eye is a stone which will enable the man who can obtain it and keep it under his tongue to foretell the future.

Hymn A song of praise, from the Greek *hymnos*.

Hyperdulia Homage paid to St *Mary the Virgin, greater than that paid to a saint, but less than that paid to God.

Hyssop A plant with diuretic powers, that therefore symbolized penitence and forgiveness of sins to those who truly repent. As a symbol of spiritual cleansing it was also used to sprinkle *holy water, as in the text, 'Purge me with hyssop, and I shall be clean: wash me, and I shall be whiter than snow' (Ps 51 : 7; Vg 50 : 9).

Ibis A fabulous *bird which kills *serpents in order to feed its young. It also feasts on corpses.

Icon (or ikon) From the Greek *eikon*, 'image'. A religious picture painted on wooden panels. Used in the *Eastern Church, usually displayed on the *iconostasis, or image screen.

Iconoclasm The destruction of images in churches (pictures, statues, stained glass and so on) by those opposed to 'idolatry'. In the *Eastern Church such attacks were the result of the iconoclastic controversy which raged at intervals from *c.*726 until 842. In the *West, particularly in the Netherlands and England, much damage was done in the 16th century in the course of the *Reformation and the break with Rome.

Iconostasis In *Orthodox churches a wall of wood or stone (the word is derived from the Greek for 'image screen') on which *icons are placed. It divides the *Sanctuary from the body of the church and has three entrances, the one in the north leading to the Offertory-chapel, that in the south to the *Sacristy, and in the centre are the great Holy (or Royal) Doors, with a curtain and a veil behind them giving access to the *altar. To the north of the Holy Doors is the image of St *Mary the Virgin, to the south that of *Christ with an open book, and next to that the image of the saint to whom the *church is dedicated.

IC *Greek capitals, the first and last letters of *IHCUC*, pronounced 'Iesus', Jesus (the Greek letter *sigma* also being written as *C*).

IC XC NIKA One of the most ancient of the sacred *monograms. These *Greek capitals, usually arranged between the arms of a Latin *Cross in groups of two, are the first and last letters of

Death with an **hour glass** warns a knight of his approaching end (Dürer, 1513).

A Greek **icon** showing St Anne with St Mary the Virgin.

IHCUC, pronounced 'Ieusus', Jesus, and of *XPICTOC*, pronounced 'Christos', Christ, together with the word *NIKA*, conqueror.

Ignatius of Antioch, St Second or third bishop of Antioch, said to have been a disciple of one of the *Apostles, probably of St *John the Evangelist, but possibly of St *Peter or St *Paul. Thought to be the child whom Jesus set in the midst of his disciples to teach them humility when they were disputing as to who should be greatest in the kingdom of heaven (Mt 18 : 1-6; Mk 9 : 33-7). He is also said to have instituted *antiphonal singing of *psalms and *hymns, because he had a vision of *angels singing in this manner. He refused to obey the order of Emperor Trajan to sacrifice to idols and was taken prisoner to Rome. On the way he wrote seven letters to the Christian communities of the various towns through which he passed with his escort of ten brutal soldiers. These writings are informative on Early Christian ways and doctrines and place him among the *Fathers of the Church. He was martyred *c.107 in the Colosseum, so is depicted standing in the arena between two lions. His surname Theophorus means 'God-bearer', so he is said to have carried God in his heart and is shown with the image of *Christ on his breast. A legend states that this image was found on his heart when his body was dismembered. For this reason he is shown carrying a heart inscribed with the sacred monogram *IHS. He may also hold a fiery globe. In one account of his martyrdom he died before the lions could touch him; in another they left only his bones which were taken back to Antioch by his followers. When the Arabs captured that city in 637 the *relics were removed to Rome, where they were deposited under the *high altar of San Clemente. Frescoes there illustrate his life.

Ignatius of Loyola, St Founder of the Society of Jesus (*Jesuits), born Iñigo (Latin *Ignatius*) at Loyola in the Spanish Basque country *c.*1491. He was wounded during the French siege of Pamplona and spent his long convalescence reading many devotional books, after which he decided to devote himself to the service of *Christ. He made a *pilgrimage to *Jerusalem, humbly studied Latin with schoolchildren in Barcelona, took his degree in the University of Paris and gathered around him a small company of followers, including St *Francis Xavier, who vowed to become missionaries. These formed the nucleus of the new *Order which was approved by Pope Paul III (1534-49) in 1540. Its members were dedicated to the promotion of the Faith, particularly in education and in overseas missions. Ignatius was canonized by Pope Gregory XV (1621-3) in 1622, the year of his death. His *Spiritual Exercises*, much used in religious retreats, was aimed at training the soul in the way of perfection. His remains are in the church of the Gesù in Rome. There is no contemporary portrait of him but his death mask survives. He is depicted bearded, in Jesuit *habit (black with a high collar and small tonsure on the back of the head); or in Mass *vestments, holding the book of the Rule of his Order; with the Jesuit motto *Ad Majorem Dei Gloriam* ('To the greater glory of God); the sacred monogram *IHS (adopted by the Jesuits) inscribed on his breast. A *dragon at his feet symbolizes his victory over *sin and his casting out of *devils. He is also shown healing miraculously. Christ carrying his cross appeared to him on his way to Rome saying, *Ego vobis Romae propitius ero*, 'I will stand by you on your way to Rome', and an angel showed him a tablet with the words *In hoc vocabitur tibi nomen*, indicating the name of the Order.

IHC **(or *IHS*)** The first three letters of the *Greek *IHCUC* (sometimes *IHSUS*, because Greek *C* could stand for *sigma*), pronounced 'Ieusus', Jesus. They appear in depictions of Emperor *Constantine's victory at the *Milvian Bridge because they were wrongly thought to be the initial letters of the Latin words *In hoc signo (vinces)*, 'in this sign thou wilt conquer'. They were also wrongly interpreted as signifying the Latin *Ieusus hominum salvator* ('Jesus the saviour of mankind'), and are thus an *attribute of St *Bernardino of Siena who used to display these letters on a plaque when he preached. The *Jesuits adopted the monogram as their device because they were the Society of Jesus (*See* St *Ignatius of Antioch).

Ildephonsus (Ildefonsus), St *Archbishop of Toledo 657-67, and before that *abbot of the *Benedictine monastery there, said to have studied in Seville under St *Isidore. He wrote a treatise on the perpetual *virginity of the Blessed Virgin and was rewarded with visions of St *Mary the Virgin. Once, when he entered the *cathedral, he saw her sitting in his episcopal chair surrounded by angels, who at her orders arranged a *chasuble made in Heaven around his shoulders (or in some accounts gave him the *vestment herself). A *cardinal's hat near him indicates that he would have been a cardinal had the office then existed.

Ilex (*Holly) Its prickly leaves make it a symbol of the *crown of thorns placed mockingly on Jesus' head *(See *Ecce Homo)*.

Immaculate Conception The dogma that St *Mary the Virgin, by special grace and privilege, was kept free from all stain of *original sin from the first moment of her conception (*See* SS *Anne and *Joachim). In the Middle Ages it was the subject of acrimonious dispute between *Franciscans who defended it and *Dominicans who opposed it, but from the 16th century onwards it was generally adopted in Latin countries following the institution in 1476 of the Feast of the Immaculate Conception, to be kept on 8 December. The doctrine was finally defined in 1854 by Pope Pius IX (1846-78).

Imprimatur The Latin for 'let it be printed', a declaration that a book has been approved for publication by a censor. In the *Roman Catholic Church all works on theology or morals require this licence from a censor appointed by a diocesan *bishop.

Incarnation of Christ At the *Annunciation, when the angel *Gabriel told St *Mary the Virgin of God's plan for the birth of *Christ, she accepted her role with the words, 'Behold the handmaid of the Lord; be it unto me according to thy word'. At that moment of assent, God the Son, the *Word of God, took flesh in her womb (Lk 1 : 38).

The scene of the Incarnation is usually combined in art with that of the Annunciation. After hearing Gabriel's words, Mary crossed her hands on her breast as a token of obedience, and a *dove symbolizing the *Holy Spirit came gliding towards her on a ray of light. This caused some commentators to explain that Mary conceived through her ear, preserving her virginity intact. The event was thought to have taken place on 25 March, commemorated as *Lady Day, the date of the Spring equinox in the old calendar and the supposed date of the *Creation of the World. It was also nine months before *Christmas, the assumed date of the *Nativity of Jesus.

Incense A mixture of aromatic resins (originally derived from a single species of pine indigenous to Arabia) which is burned in a *thurible or *censer that is swung to give off a pleasing fragrance. It symbolizes the spirit or prayer of humanity ascending to God. The practice in church services of censing the *celebrant or the *altar, during blessings or consecrations, is intended as a mark of honour and sanctification. Five grains of incense are inserted in the pascal *candle (which stands near the altar from *Easter to *Ascension Day) to symbolize the Five *Wounds of Christ.

Incumbent The holder of a benefice, a *rector, a *vicar or a *parish priest.

Indulgence From the Latin *indulgentia*, 'remission', a mitigation of the penances imposed for grave *sins. It may be plenary, remitting the whole of the punishment (applicable also to souls in *Purgatory), or partial, whereby part of the punishment may be suspended for a period. The mercenary sale of indulgences in the Middle Ages (*See* *pardoner) helped to provoke the *Reformation.

Infallibility, papal The First *Vatican Council of 1870 affirmed that the *Pope, when he speaks *ex cathedra* (officially, from his 'chair') on matters of faith and morals and defines a doctrine to be held by the whole Church, is 'infallible', or free from error.

Infancy Gospels A number of *apocryphal narratives, some tainted with *gnostic heresies, which aimed to make up the lack of material in the canonical *Gospels concerning the birth and early years of Jesus. They are the sources of many later legends. The most influential were the *Book of *James (*Protevangelium)* and its derivative the *Gospel of the *Pseudo-Matthew*, probably of the 8th

St **Ignatius of Loyola** holds a monstrance with the monogram IHS, symbol of the Jesuit Order (Spanish, *c.*1622).

The Woman clothed with the sun, a supposed reference to the **Immaculate Conception** (Giovanni Battista Tiepolo, 1696–1770).

or 9th century. The latter was also influenced by the *Gospel of Thomas the Israelite*, *c*.125. Latin, Arabic and Armenian infancy Gospels circulated in the Middle Ages which reproduced and added to this material, incorporated indirectly in the *Golden Legend*.

Inquisition An ecclesiastical tribunal set up in 1229 by Pope Gregory IX (1227-41) to enquire into cases of *heresy and to prevent its spread. The work was entrusted mainly to learned *Dominicans and *Franciscans. The use of torture to procure evidence was sanctioned in 1252 by Pope Innocent IV (1243-54), partly in response to the spread of the *Catharist heresy in the south of France and northern Italy, which St *Dominic and his followers actively attacked. The notorious Spanish Inquisition came into being in 1479 to combat apostasy among *marranos* (converts from Judaism), *moriscos* (Moorish converts) and, in the next century, *Protestants. It lasted until 1808 when it was suppressed by Joseph Bonaparte, the French 'intruder king'. The restored Ferdinand VII revived it briefly from 1808-14 (*See* *auto de fe, *Holy Office, *sanbenito*).

INRI The initial letters of *Ieusus Nazarenus Rex Judaeorum*, 'Jesus of Nazareth, King of the Jews', the Latin phrase, together with a translation in Hebrew and Greek, which Pilate caused to be put on the Cross at the *Crucifixion of Jesus (Jn 19 : 19). It was inscribed on the *titilus*, or plaque above his head, and is sometimes represented by this sacred *monogram.

Instruments of the Passion Emblems of the *Passion of Christ borne on shields by *angels, carved on roof bosses, or otherwise depicted. As well as referring to the various episodes of the *Trials and *Crucifixion, some of them had a symbolic meaning: thirty pieces of silver (betrayal, covetousness); lantern (the dark night of sin); vinegar and gall (the poison of sin); and spitting (hatred). Other Instruments include the *pillar or *column where Christ was scourged, St *Peter's *cock, *dice, the *seamless robe, *hyssop, *ladder, *lance, *hammer, *nails and *pincers.

Introit A chant (Latin *antiphona ad introitum*, 'antiphon on the entry') sung by the *choir to accompany the entry of the *clergy into the church, or a fragment of a *psalm said by the *celebrant after his prayers at the foot of the *altar, as he goes up to the altar to begin the *Mass.

Invention of the Cross *See* Finding of the *True Cross.

Ipsilon The name of the *Greek letter, written 'y'. It symbolizes the *Trinity because it is composed of three strokes which make one figure; also free will because of the choice offered at the intersection of the two arms.

Iris One of the flowers associated with St *Mary the Virgin. It is called 'sword lily' after the shape of its leaf, so it symbolizes the *Sorrows of the Virgin.

Isaac Son of *Abraham and the second of the *Patriarchs. His name in Hebrew, *Yitzchak*, means 'he laughed', and was given him, it was said, because his father, then ninety-nine years old, laughed when told by God that his aged wife *Sarah would bear him a son (Gen 17 : 16). Abraham circumcised Isaac when he was eight days old (Gen 21 : 4) foreshadowing the *Circumcision and the *Presentation of Christ in the Temple. Told by God that through Isaac his line would be made great, Abraham gave him preference over *Ishmael, son of his concubine, *Hagar. His faith was put to the test when God ordered him to sacrifice Isaac (prefiguring the *Crucifixion). In complete obedience to the divine command, he bound his son, placed wood on the altar for the burnt offering, and raised his knife to kill Isaac, but an angel stayed his hand and indicated that a ram, caught in a nearby thicket, should be sacrificed in his place (Gen 22 : 1-13).

When he was forty years old Isaac married *Rebecca (Rebekah) (Gen 24 : 62-7), who proved barren until, in answer to Isaac's prayers, she gave birth to twins, *Esau, covered with red hair, and *Jacob, who came out of the womb clutching his brother's heel (Gen 25 : 20-6). To escape a famine in Canaan, Isaac moved his family and flocks to Gerar, ruled over by Abimelech. But fearing that the *Philistines would kill him in order to acquire his beautiful wife, he passed her off as his sister. The ruse was discovered when Abimelech, looking through a window, saw Isaac making love to Rebecca, and realized that he could not take the wife of a guest into his harem. He therefore ordered that Isaac and his family should not be molested on pain of death (Gen 26 : 1-11).

When Isaac was old and almost blind, Jacob (his mother's favourite) obtained his father's last blessing by deceit. Isaac loved his hunter son *Esau and asked him to kill a deer and to make a favourite stew. Rebecca, who had overheard the request, covered Jacob's hands and neck with wool, so that he could pass himself off as his brother, a hairy man, and arranged for him to present the dish of meat to his father. Deceived, Isaac gave Jacob his blessing. When he discovered the truth he could not give Esau back his inheritance, but he prevented strife between the brothers by sending Jacob to his mother's home in Haran (Gen 27 : 1-45). The two sons buried Isaac in a cave when he died aged 108 (Gen 35 : 29).

Isaiah One of the great Hebrew *prophets who lived in the kingdom of Judah in the latter part of the 8th century BC. His prophecies and visions are contained in the OT book which bears his name (although only the first thirty-five of the sixty-six chapters are thought to be by him). They are prized because many are understood to refer to the coming of *Christ and to the inauguration of the Messianic age. Prophetic texts often inscribed on scrolls carried by him include: 'For out of Zion shall go forth the law, and the word of the Lord from Jerusalem' (Is 2 : 3); 'Behold a virgin shall conceive and bear a son, and shall call his name Immanuel' (Is 7 : 15); 'And there shall come forth a rod out of the stem of Jesse' (Is 11 : 1); 'For unto us a child is born, unto us a son is given: and the government shall be upon his shoulder: and his name shall be called Wonderful, Counsellor, The mighty God, The everlasting Father, The Prince of Peace' (Is 9 : 6); 'the wolf shall dwell with the lamb . . . and a little child shall lead them . . . for the earth shall be full of the knowledge of the Lord as the waters cover the sea' (Is 11 : 6-9); and 'Comfort ye, comfort ye my people, saith your God . . . The voice of him that crieth in the wilderness, Prepare ye the way of the Lord . . .' (Is 40 : 1-3). Isaiah's assurance that there will eventually be universal peace – 'and they shall beat their swords into ploughshares . . . nation shall not lift up sword against nation, neither shall they learn war any more' (Is 2 : 4) – is inscribed on the United Nations building in New York.

Isaiah is most frequently depicted with a scroll inscribed with the words *Ecce virgo 'concipiet et parium filium*, 'Behold a virgin shall conceive and bear a son' (Is 7 : 15), foretelling the *Incarnation. If he holds a branch, the reference is to the Tree of *Jesse. A saw or a scythe refers to the legend given in *De ortu et obitu patrem*, and attributed to St *Isidore of Seville, that he met his death by being cut into two.

Ishmael Son of *Abraham and his concubine *Hagar. Abraham sent him and his mother into the desert to escape the wrath of his wife Sarah after she had borne *Isaac. Without food or water, Hagar placed Ishmael under a bush to die, but the miraculous discovery of a well saved them (Gen 21 : 9-19). They lived in Paran, in the Sinai desert, where Ishmael became a skilled bowman. The angel had foretold before his birth he would be a wild man, his hand 'against every man and every man's hand against him' (Gen 16 : 12). He thus personifies the outlaw. His wife came from Egypt and he was the ancestor of the nomadic tribes of the Arabian peninsula.

Isidore of Seville, St *Bishop of Seville (*c*.560-636), who organized the Catholic religion in Spain as well as completing the conversion of the Visigoths from the *Arian heresy. His writings are an encyclopedia of the knowledge of his time and influenced medieval literature and art. He is depicted with a pen and a book. He was canonized in 1598 and declared a *Doctor of the Church in 1722. Devoted to acts of charity, he is said to have died on the steps of the *altar after donating all his worldly possessions to the poor. He is sometimes shown with his brothers SS Leander and Fulgentius, his sister St Florentina, and with Ferdinand of Castile at his feet.

Isidore the Farm Labourer (or Ploughman), St Patron saint of Madrid (*c*.1070-1130) canonized 1622 in acknowledgment of his helping Philip III to recover from an illness in 1617. He and his wife Mary (also revered in Spain) were devout but

St Dominic presides over a tribunal of the **Inquisition** which sentences heretics, dressed in sanbenitos, to be handed over to the secular authority for burning. The *auto de fe* is in the foreground (Berruguete, 1450–*c*.1504).

An angel indicates the ram in the thicket which is to be sacrificed instead of **Isaac.** (Bronze model for the Florence Baptistery doors by Lorenzo Ghiberti, 1378-1455).

impoverished peasants working for a master who begrudged them the time they devoted to religious observances. He was once about to upbraid Isidore for kneeling in prayer when he should have been working, when he perceived two *angels doing the ploughing for him. (Isidore's *attribute is a sickle or a plough.) He performed many miracles, including restoring to life his master's child after it had fallen into a well, and causing water to flow from a rock by striking it with a goad.

Israel The name (meaning 'God fights') given to *Jacob after he had wrestled with an *angel (Gen 32 : 28) and again bestowed on him by God at Bethel (Gen 35 : 10). His twelve sons became the heads of the *Twelve Tribes of Israel, the word thus later signifying the Hebrew nation, still later the *Jews.

Israelites The *Children of Israel, descendants of *Israel.

Ite missa est The Latin words of dismissal (Latin *missa*) spoken to the congregation by the celebrant at the conclusion of Low *Mass or sung by the deacon at High Mass, meaning 'Go, you are dismissed' (and the origin of the word *Mass).

Ives of Brittany, St *See* Yves, St.

Ivy Symbol of friendship or fidelity because of its tendency to cling, and of eternal life because it is forever green.

Jacob The third of the Hebrew *Patriarchs from whose twelve sons the *Twelve Tribes who occupied the *Promised Land after its conquest by *Joshua traced their descent. His name was changed to *Israel after he had wrestled with an angel (*See* *Jacob and the Angel). His descendants were known as the *Children of Israel. As Israel was the ancient name of the *Holy Land, it was chosen for the new Jewish state founded in 1948.

Jacob was the younger of twin sons born to *Isaac and *Rebecca. He came out of the womb clutching the heel of his brother *Esau (Gen 25 : 26). His mother favoured Jacob and contrived to have him blessed by Isaac and thus obtain Esau's inheritance (Gen 27 : 21-9). To escape his elder brother's vengeance, Jacob left his home in Beer-Sheba and sought a wife in Haran, where his mother's brother *Laban lived. (This prefigured the *Flight into Egypt.) On the way he had a vision of angels ascending and descending a ladder which reached to *Heaven, and he received a promise from God that his descendants would return from exile to occupy the Promised Land (*See* *Jacob's ladder).

At Haran, Jacob fell in love with Laban's beautiful younger daughter *Rachel and agreed to work seven years for her. On the wedding night, Laban substituted the elder, less favoured sister

*Leah, claiming that it was the custom that the elder should be married first. A week later Rachel was given to him as his second bride on condition that he worked seven more years for Laban (Gen 29 : 21-8). At the end of that time he became rich by out-witting his father-in-law. It had been agreed that Jacob should have for himself all the streaked goats and dark-fleeced sheep born to the flocks. Jacob cut wands, peeled white streaks in them and set them before the goats at the drinking trough so that they bore speckled offspring (Gen 30 : 27-43).

Jacob decided to return to his home country and while Laban was away sheep-shearing he left surreptitiously with his wives, concubines and flocks. Rachel took with her the teraphim, or household gods. Laban pursued them and searched Jacob's tents for the teraphim. Rachel hid them under her camel's furniture and sat on the saddle, pretending that she could not get up because 'the custom of women' was upon her, so that she was unclean. Laban was thwarted, but he and Jacob were later reconciled and went their separate ways (Gen 31 : 17-55).

As he neared his home country, fearing Esau's wrath, Jacob sent messengers with presents to find out whether his brother was still angry, and learned that he was advancing towards him with 400 men. To his relief the generous Esau ran to meet him and fell on his neck and kissed him (Gen 32 : 13-20; 33 : 1-15). Jacob then settled in Shechem in the land of Canaan.

Jacob gave *Joseph, his favourite son, the coat of many colours. His affection for this child caused his other sons to attempt to dispose of Joseph. This led to Joseph's adventures in Egypt, his rise to fame there and the migration of Jacob and his family to the kingdom of *Pharaoh because 'there was corn in Egypt' (Gen 42 : 1). They were well received and settled there. When Jacob died, Joseph had his body embalmed and escorted it in great style to Canaan as his father had requested. It was buried in the cave of Machpelah which *Abraham had bought near Mamre (Gen 50 : 1-13).

Jacob and the angel After he had been reconciled with *Laban and resumed his journey to Canaan, his homeland, *Jacob arrived at a ford across a tributary of the River *Jordan. He sent his family and flocks across and remained alone beside the stream. A man wrestled with him all night but was unable to defeat him. He touched the hollow of Jacob's thigh and Jacob said he would let him go if he blessed him. He was told, 'Thy name shall be called no more Jacob, but *Israel: for as a prince hast thou power with God and with me and hast prevailed'. (The new name means 'God fights'.) When Jacob crossed over the ford at daybreak, the sun shone upon the hollow of his thigh and it shrank (Gen 32 : 22-32).

Who the mysterious man was has not been satisfactorily explained. Because he refused to give his name, Jacob thought he was God. In art he is represented as an angel, possibly *Chamael or *Uriel. The story was interpreted allegorically as

the combat between *Virtue and Vice and between the *Church and the *Synagogue.

Jacob's ladder In obedience to his father *Isaac's command that he should not take a wife from the Canaanite women, *Jacob left Beer-Sheba, his home, and set out for Haran in Mesopotamia (North Syria) where his maternal uncle *Laban lived. When the sun went down, he stopped at a place called Luz and went to sleep using a stone for a pillow. He dreamed that he saw 'a *ladder set up on the earth, and the top of it reaching to heaven . . . and the angels of God ascending and descending on it'. God stood above it and Jacob heard his voice saying that his descendants would be spread over the earth, finally to be gathered together again in the land he had allotted them, the *Promised Land. When Jacob woke he made a pillar of the stone on which he had slept, poured oil over it and renamed the place Bethel, saying, 'this is none other than the house of God, and this is the gate of heaven' (Gen 28 : 10-22). The Stone of Scone, on which Scottish kings were crowned and which now rests beneath the Coronation Chair in Westminster Abbey, London, is said to be the stone which Jacob used as a pillow. The consecration of the stone is a symbol of the Christian *altar.

Jacob's ladder was said to have fifteen rungs, symbolizing the cardinal and derived *virtues.

Jacob's Well A well, fed by an underground stream, a day's journey out of *Jerusalem near the village of Sychar (or Askar), so called because the Samaritans believed that the patriarch *Jacob watered his cattle there and gave the 'parcel of ground' to his son *Joseph (Jn 4 : 5-6). It was there that Jesus rested 'about the sixth hour' (at noon) and encountered the *Woman of Samaria. The well is now in the crypt of a chapel built by Crusaders, over which an *Orthodox church has been erected.

Jacobus de (à) Voragine (James of Viraggio), the Blessed Archbishop of Genoa, *b.c.*1230 in Viraggio, now Varezze, and *d.*1298 in Genoa. He became a *Dominican in 1244 and gained a great reputation for learning and piety. Although he was reluctant to accept the dignity, he was made archbishop in 1292 and spent much of his time in a vain attempt to reconcile the warring Guelph and Ghibelline factions. He left a large collection of sermons, a defence of the Dominican Order and a chronicle of Genoa, but his fame resides in his *Legenda aurea*, popularly known as the *Golden Legend*, the most notable source book for sacred art. He was beatified in 1816. His *relics are in the church of Santa Maria di Castello, Genoa.

Jael The wife of Heber the Kenite, who was at peace with Jabin, the Canaanite king of Hazor. When the Canaanites attacked the *Israelites, the prophetess *Deborah encouraged the *Children of Israel to defeat Jabin's army led by *Sisera. Sisera sought refuge with Heber and was met by Jael who took him into her tent, gave him milk to

Jacob and the angel wrestle all night at the ford (Eugène Delacroix, 1857-60).

Angels ascend and descend **Jacob's ladder** in his dream as he sleeps with a stone for a pillow (Milton's *Poetical Works*, 1794-7).

drink, put a coverlet over him and told him to rest. When he was asleep she took a tent-peg (the erection of tents was a woman's duty) and drove it into his temple with a hammer. In this way she fulfilled Deborah's prophecy (Jg 4 : 9) that he would be killed by a woman, a dishonourable death. When the Israelite leader Barak arrived in pursuit of Sisera, she showed him the body of his enemy (Jg 4 : 17-22).

Deborah's song of victory commemorated the event, but gave a different version of Sisera's death, according to which Jael struck him down at the entrance to the tent (Jg 5 : 24-7). There is no explanation why Jael killed him as she was not an Israelite. But because of her deed in defence of Israel she figures as one of the heroines of the OT.

Jairus' daughter Jairus, one of the rulers (administrators) of the synagogue in *Capernaum, begged Jesus to heal his twelve-year-old daughter who was on the point of death. On his way to the house Jesus was delayed by the *Woman with the issue of blood, and news was brought that the child had died. When Jesus entered Jairus' house he told the mourners not to weep because the damsel was 'not dead but sleepeth'. They 'laughed him to scorn', but he took the girl by the hand and said in Aramaic, *Talitha cumi* (one of the few recorded phrases of Jesus speaking in his native tongue), 'Damsel, I say unto thee, arise', and she sat up, cured. Jesus was accompanied in the house by SS *Peter, *John the Apostle and *James the Great, who are depicted standing with him by the girl's bed (Mk 5 : 22-3; 35-43; Mt 9 : 18, 23-5; Lk 8 : 41-2; 49-56).

James, Book of An apocryphal work dating from the 2nd century. Also known as the *Protevangelium* because it narrates earlier events than those in the canonical *Gospels, notably the story of the parentage, birth and girlhood of St *Mary the Virgin. It also amplifies details of the birth of *Jesus and the escape of St *John the Baptist at the time of the Massacre of the *Holy Innocents. Although not accepted as authentic, it was the source of many later apocryphal writings and of the stories incorporated in the *Golden Legend (See *Infancy Gospels).

James of Compostela, St A hermit living early in the 9th century near the River Sar in Galicia, in northwest Spain, was told by *angels in a dream that the body of St *James the Great reposed in a tomb in the woods near his cell. At the same time peasants observed a star shining over a thicket and heard heavenly music when they approached the place. These events were reported to Bishop Teodomiro of Iria Flavia. He had the site excavated and discovered a ruined chapel, in the crypt of which were human remains. These he did not hesitate to designate as relics of St *James the Great. The place was called Compostela, supposedly a corruption of the Latin *Campus Stellae*, 'the field of the star', although more likely to be related to *compostum*, 'burial place'. Alfonso II of León built a church on the spot and declared St James patron of Spain in the fight to reconquer the land from the Moors. The saint demonstrated his support of the Christians when he appeared sword in hand, on a white horse, on the eve of the Battle of Clavijo in 930 and led the Spaniards to victory against a greatly superior Moslem army. He was therefore known in Spain as *Santiago Matamoros*, 'St James, Killer of Moors'.

When *Benedictine communities from *Cluny in France began to be established during the 10th century in Spanish lands reconquered from Arabic-speaking invaders, Compostela was transformed from a local shrine into the goal of *pilgrimages from France, England and other parts of Western Europe, rivalling Rome and Jerusalem in popularity. *Pilgrims came by sea, or by roads across France (the Way of St James) which converged on the pass of Roncevaux (Roncesvalles) in the western Pyrenees. They returned bearing a scallop-shell or *cockle-shell as their insignium. St James of Compostela is thus depicted in the dress of a pilgrim, wearing a characteristic floppy hat, carrying a scrip, or *wallet, and supporting himself with a staff.

How St James the Great came to be associated with Spain, when there is no NT record of his having been there, was explained by a legend first noted by the 8th-century Spanish monk Beatus of Liébana in his commentary on the *Apocalypse (The Revelation of St John the Divine). He stated that after the *Crucifixion, St James preached the *Gospel in Spain and that St *Mary the Virgin brought him the marble *Pillar of Our Lady which is now enshrined in the cathedral of Zaragoza. After his martyrdom in Jerusalem, St James' disciples, guided by angels, brought his body by sea to El Padrón in Galicia. There it was placed on a stone which miraculously opened to receive it. The pagan Queen Lupa, wishing to be rid of the relic, ordered twelve wild bulls to be attached to the stone, hoping to destroy it when they were driven into the sea. The bulls were tamed when the *sign of the cross was made over them, and they pulled the stone back to the queen's palace. She was converted and built the shrine, which in the course of time was lost in the woodlands, to be rediscovered miraculously in the 9th century when Spain was in need of a saint to help them against the Moors. He is thus one of the *Seven Champions of Christendom.

St James performed many miracles to help pilgrims on their way to his shrine. One was frequently depicted even as late as the 16th century, and tells how the daughter of an innkeeper lusted after the chaste son of a pilgrim family, and when he refused her advances, hid a golden cup in his scrip and had him arrested and hanged for theft. When the sorrowing parents returned from Santiago de Compostela they found their son alive on the gallows, where St James had held him up. The magistrate, who refused to believe that the boy was any more alive than the two chickens he was about to eat, saw the birds stand up and cackle.

James the Great (James Major), St One of the two sons of *Zebedee, a Galilean fisherman, the

other being St *John the Apostle. The two brothers were among the first to be called to follow Jesus (*See* *Calling of the Apostles), and were nicknamed by Jesus *Boanerges, 'sons of thunder'. Together with St *Peter they were preeminent among the disciples and witnessed the raising of *Jairus' daughter, the *Transfiguration and the *Agony in the Garden. James and John were reproved by Jesus when they asked to sit on either side of his throne when he came into his Kingdom (Mk 10 : 39).

James' death, *c*.44, is recorded in the *Acts of the Apostles* (Ac 12 : 1-3) which states that he was beheaded (a *sword is his *attribute) by order of *Herod Agrippa I. (Another, non-canonical, version is that he was stoned to death.) The 3rd-century historian Abdias wrote that before his death James converted two magicians. Hermogenes and Philetus. The latter, sent to spy on James to learn the secret of his seemingly magical powers, sought baptism when he witnessed the miracles James performed. Hermogenes ordered his *devils to bring James and Philetus to him, but James forced them to bring Hermogenes to him instead. The magician sued for pardon and was told to disburse in charity the money which he had obtained through his fraudulent sorcery.

St Clement of Alexandria (*c*.150-*c*.215) described in his *Institutions* how the soldier who escorted St James to his trial was so impressed by his behaviour and his defence of his faith that he also confessed to being Christian and begged James to forgive his sins. James said, 'Peace be with you!', kissed him and they were executed together. This is said to be the origin of the *Pax vobiscum* in the *Eucharist.

St James is called 'the Great' (or 'Major') to distinguish him from the other apostle named St *James the Less (St James Minor). (For St James' supposed association with Spain, *See* St *James of Compostela.) He contributed the clause *Qui conceptus est . . .* to the *Apostles' Creed.

James the Less (James Minor), St One of the eleven *Apostles who were in the *Upper Room, according to the Gospels (Mt 10 : 3; Mk 3 : 18; Lk 6 : 15), when St *Matthias was chosen to replace Judas Iscariot (Ac 1 : 13), but otherwise difficult to identify. His name is linked with that of *Thaddaeus and of *Levi (Matthew), a 'son of Alphaeus' (Mk 2 : 14). Attempts have also been made to identify him as the James 'the younger', the son of the Mary who witnessed the *Crucifixion (Mt 27 : 56; Mk 15 : 40; Lk 24 : 10), but this Mary was *Mary Cleophas (Jn 19 : 25).

Traditionally he is James 'the brother of the Lord' (in Greek *Adelphotheos*), which may mean that he was his cousin, or the son of St Joseph by an earlier marriage (*See* *Brethren of the Lord). Like the rest of the family he thought that Jesus was mad, but he was convinced of his divinity when Jesus appeared to him after the *Resurrection (1 Cor 15 : 7). St *Jerome, in his *De viris illustribus* ('Of famous men'), quoted an account of this appearance to St James from the lost *Gospel according to the Hebrews*.

Two depictions of St **James of Compostela** as a pilgrim, with his staff and his scallop-shell insignium: *(above)* by Simone Martini (*c*.1284–1344) *(below)* a late-15th-century Burgundian stone sculpture.

James became the leader (or first bishop) of the Christian community in Jerusalem. He was so assiduous in his attendance at the *Temple and so fervent in his prayers that his knees became as hard as those of a camel. His death in 62 is recorded both by the Jewish historian *Josephus in his *Antiquities of the Jews*, and by *Eusebius. After the death of the procurator Festus, the *Sanhedrin was persuaded by the High Priest *Annas to seize the opportunity to have James thrown down from the Temple wall into the valley of *Jehoshaphat. A fuller then beat him to death with his fuller's club (St James' *attribute).

There is a legend that St James was so distressed by the *Crucifixion that he vowed to *fast until the *Second Coming. Jesus appeared, prepared a meal for him, blessed it and absolved him from his vow. James contributed the clause *Ascendit ad coelos . . .* to the *Apostles' Creed.

Januarius (Gennaro), St Patron of Naples; *b.c.*305 at Benevento where he was *bishop during the Diocletian *persecutions. He was arrested, brutally tortured, and then beheaded near Pozzuoli (Puteoli) together with his companions, Festus and Desiderius. His *relics, after being moved to Benevento and then to Monte Virgine, now rest in a chapel of Naples *cathedral where they were brought in 1497. The famous 'Miracle of St Januarius' occurs there eighteen times each year. After his martyrdom a poor woman collected his blood in two glass *ampullae*, or phials. These are placed on the altar, and one is brought near the saint's head after prayers have been said, whereupon the dried-up clots of congealed blood are seen to liquify. The saint saved Naples on several occasions from threatened eruptions of Mt Vesuvius, when his relics were carried in procession through the streets.

Japheth Youngest son of *Noah. His father blessed him after he and his brother *Shem had covered Noah's nakedness (See *Drunkenness of Noah), and promised that God would 'enlarge' him (a pun on his name which means 'enlargement' in Hebrew), meaning that he would multiply his descendants (Gen 9 : 27). Japhet is the ancestor of the Japhetic, or European, peoples (See *Races of Mankind).

Japhkiel Leader of the *thrones. He is said to have guided the Israelites in the Wilderness after the *Exodus from Egypt, although another tradition names this *angel, who is depicted with a golden crown in his right hand and a scourge with three cords in his left, as Jehudiel.

Jasmine *Symbol of St *Mary the Virgin because of its pure white colour and sweet smell.

Jehoshaphat, Valley of The site where the Last *Judgement will take place according to the prophet *Joel who quotes God's proclamation: 'Let the heathen be wakened, and come up to the valley of Jehoshaphat: for there will I sit to judge all the heathen round about' (Jl 3 : 12). Jewish,

Christian and Moslem commentators identify it as the Valley of the Cedron (Kidron), a ravine between *Jerusalem and the *Mount of Olives, where for centuries the dead were buried or cremated. Nevertheless, as *jehoshaphat* means in Hebrew 'the Lord has judged', it is possible that Joel did not have a particular place in mind.

Jehovah An artificial reconstruction of the incommunicable name of God to protect it from abuse, made by the Masoretes, Jewish scholars who from the 6th to the 10th centuries endeavoured to establish a standard text of the Hebrew Bible. They combined the *Tetragrammaton (the four consonants *YHWH) with the vowel signs from the Hebrew *Elohim*, 'God' and *Adonai*, 'My Lord', to make YeHoW(or V)aH. Anglicized as Jehovah, the name was used from the *Reformation onwards for the God of the OT.

Jehu Tenth king of Israel (841-814 BC), anointed by a disciple of the prophet *Elisha who told him that God had appointed him to extirpate the house of *Ahab and his wicked queen *Jezebel. In obedience to the divine command, Jehu mounted his chariot and rode with his followers to Jezreel. A sentry reported that he saw men approaching and that the driving was like the driving of Jehu, 'for he drives furiously' (2 Kg 9 : 20). Cabmen were often humorously dubbed 'Jehu'. Jehu treacherously slayed the two kings who had come to meet him, killed Jezebel and threw her body to the dogs as had been foretold. In a series of bloody killings Jehu then ended the worship of *Baal in Israel.

Jehudiel See *Japhkiel.

Jephthah (Jephte) One of the *judges of Israel, although he was the son of a harlot and cast out from his people because of his illegitimate birth. Chosen by the elders of Gilead to lead the attack against the besieging Ammonites, he made a rash vow that if victory were granted him, he would sacrifice the first person to meet him on his return. When he came back in triumph, his daughter and only child came out dancing to the sound of timbrels. Jephthah tore his clothes in sorrow, but his daughter insisted he should fulfil his sacred oath. She spent two months in the mountains lamenting her virginity (equated with the *Education of St Mary the Virgin in the *Temple) and was duly sacrificed by her father, although medieval Jewish commentators held that he dedicated her to live in the Temple in perpetual virginity (Jg 11 : 1-12; 7) (See *Shibboleth).

Jeremiah A Hebrew *prophet (*c.*650-*c.*585 BC) who earned the appellation 'dismal' because of his perpetual fulminations against successive kings of *Israel whom he threatened with disaster if they compromised their monotheistic faith. The denunciations in the book of his name gave rise to the word 'jeremiad' to describe a tirade or doleful complaint against the evils of the times. His *Lamentations* is a short work of five chapters that is doubtfully ascribed to him. It mourns the desolation of Judah after the capture of Jerusalem by *Nebuchadnezzar and the destruction of the *Temple in 586 BC. Its dirges were given Christian interpretation and are quoted with reference to the *Passion of Christ in the services of *Tenebrae during *Holy Week. For this reason Jeremiah is depicted holding a *cross, his chief *attribute. A *manticore – a fabulous man-eating creature said to dwell in the deep – may also accompany him. This recalls Jeremiah's punishment at the instigation of the false priests for proclaiming that the Babylonian army would take Jerusalem. He was let down with cords into a dungeon and sank into the mire which covered its bottom. He was rescued by an Ethiopian eunuch who lowered 'old cast clouts and rotten rags' for Jeremiah to put under his arms, and then pulled him to the surface (Jer 38 : 1-13). There is a tradition that after the destruction of the Temple, Jeremiah was taken to Egypt and stoned to death because of his predictions.

In the procession of prophets and in sequences of *Apostles and prophets, Jeremiah corresponds to St *Peter and exhibits a scroll with the words, *Patrem invocabitis qui fecit et condidit coelos*, 'You shall call him Father who made and founded the heavens'. This is a conflation of two texts, 'Thou shalt call me, My Father' (Jer 3 : 19), and 'Ah Lord God! behold thou hast made the heaven and the earth' (Jer 32 : 17).

Jeremiah's vision of 'a rod of an almond tree' (Jer 1 : 11), depicted as a flowering branch, was understood to refer to the *Church which would flourish in the new age.

Jericho An ancient Canaanite city about five miles from the north end of the Dead Sea, destroyed by *Joshua when he led the *Children of Israel out of the *Wilderness and into the *Promised Land. The gates of this strongly defended walled city were shut against the *Israelites, but at God's command Joshua ordered seven priests escorted by armed men to march at dawn with the *Ark of the Covenant around the city, blowing on seven rams' horn trumpets. This they did for six days, and on the seventh day, when the priests blew the trumpets, Joshua ordered his people to shout, and 'the wall fell down flat'. The Israelites then pillaged and burned the city, killing all the inhabitants except *Rahab the harlot who had protected the Israelite spies (Jos 6 : 1-25).

*Herod the Great (37-4 BC) founded a new Jericho. This was the city through which Jesus passed on his last journey to Jerusalem (*See* *Entry into Jerusalem). At its gates he healed two blind men (Mt 20 : 29) and called to *Zacchaeus, who had climbed into a tree to see him, that he would dine with him that night (Lk 19 : 1-6).

Jeroboam King of Israel (*c.*931-910 BC) whose exploits are recorded in the *First Book of Kings* (1 Kg 11-14). He is best remembered because he was 'a mighty man of valour' (1 Kg 11 : 28) and thus gave his name to a 'jeroboam', a huge winebottle which contains the equivalent of eight to ten bottles of usual size.

King **Jehu** bringing tribute to the Assyrian Shalmaneser III (841 BC).

Jeremiah displaying his prophetic scroll in a stained-glass window (French, mid 12th century).

The seal of Shema, servant of **Jeroboam** (8th century BC).

Jerome (Hieronymus), St One of the four great Latin *Doctors of the Church, born (c.341) at Strido, near Aquileia, in Venetia. A pupil of the grammarian Donatus, he studied the Classics at Rome. He was baptized when about nineteen and travelled through Gaul, becoming a monk when he lived for a time in Trier. He set out on a *pilgrimage to the *Holy Land and at Antioch decided to retire to the Syrian desert where he spent some years as a *hermit. He suffered temptations of the flesh and recounted in one of his letters how, alone in the heat of the sun with no other companions than scorpions and wild beasts, he imagined Roman maidens dancing before him. He threw himself in tears before a *Crucifix, beat his breast with a stone (one of his *attributes), and fled away from his cell into the desert, striving to master his desires. This episode of St Jerome Penitent is associated in art with two other penitents, SS *Peter and *Mary Magdalene.

Jerome had a vision in which he was brought before *Christ. Angels whipped him for being a Ciceronian (because he loved the Latin of the Classics more than the barbarous language of the OT prophets, whom he had read in the Greek version of the *Bible). This made him decide to learn Hebrew. He returned to Rome in 382 as secretary to the aged Pope St Damasus I (366-84) and was ordered to produce the standard text of a Latin Bible, revised according to Hebrew and Greek sources. This task, completed after he had left Rome on the death of Damasus and had settled in *Bethlehem, culminated in the production of the *Vulgate Bible, declared by the *Council of Trent to be the official *Roman Catholic version. He also composed commentaries on some OT and NT books, his discussion of the *Gospel of Matthew* being the most renowned of these works. He is therefore frequently represented as a scholar at work in his study. Although he was never a *cardinal (an office not yet founded), a red cardinal's hat shown near him presumably indicates that he would have been one had this been possible. In later art he may be shown listening to a trumpet, a motif based on a misunderstanding of a sentence in a letter (wrongly attributed to him), in which the writer said that whether asleep or awake he always heard the trumpet of the Last *Judgement.

St Jerome is usually accompanied in his study by a *lion (his *attribute) because when explaining a text to his monks (he was regarded as the founder of the *Jeronymite Order) a lion once approached them. The monks fled, but Jerome saw that the lion had a thorn in its paw, causing it to limp. He pulled out the thorn and the grateful beast settled down near his cell and became Jerome's servant, his special task being to look after the monastery ass. One day a caravan of merchants passed by and stole the ass. Jerome upbraided the lion, believing that it had eaten its companion, but the lion followed the trail of the caravan, put the merchants to flight and rescued the ass.

When he was ninety, St Jerome received his last *communion in the presence of his disciples, a theme frequent in art after the *Council of Trent

when emphasis was placed on the seven *Sacraments. He was buried (420) under the Church of the Nativity in Bethlehem, near the graves of SS *Paula and Eustochium whom he had inspired to join him in the Holy Land.

Jeronymites *(Hieronymitae)* A religious *Order, the Hermits of St Jerome, the members of which took as their example St *Jerome who spent four years alone in the Syrian desert struggling against worldly temptations. They were originally followers of the Blessed Thomas of Siena, a Franciscan *tertiary who came to Spain around the middle of the 14th century. At first they lived as *hermits, but later opted for a coenobitical (community) life in accordance with the *Rule of St Augustine, an arrangement approved by Pope Gregory XI (1371-8) in 1374. Similar communities under the patronage of St Jerome were established in Italy. These were the Hermits of Fiesole, founded by Carlo di Montegraneli (b.c.1340), but suppressed by Clement IX (1667-9) in 1668; the Hermits of the Blessed Pietro of Pisa, founded by Pietro Gambacorli (1355-c.1377) at Montebello; and the Hermits of Lombardy, or of the Observance, founded in the mid-15th century by Lope de Olmedo, a Spaniard, who desired a more strict observance of the Rule.

The Jeronymite Order flourished most in Spain and Portugal, twenty-five communities attending the first general chapter in 1415. As the special concern of the *monks was care for the dying and saying masses for the repose of their souls, their Order received considerable endowments which enabled them to build monasteries which are among the architectural wonders of Europe. They also adorned their houses with works of art by the great masters. The fine convent of Our Lady of Guadalupe in Estremadura gained fame because of its miracle-working image. It also contained notable works by Zurbarán. At Belem, near Lisbon, a magnificent convent was built to enshrine the tombs of the Portuguese royal family. When Emperor Charles V (1516-58) abdicated, he retired to the monastery of St Jerome at Yuste, near Placencia. Philip II of Spain built the monastery of San Lorenzo del Escorial near Madrid as his royal mausoleum and gave it in charge to the Jeronymites.

Jerusalem The ancient and holy city which contains places sacred in the Jewish, Christian and Islamic traditions. Its commanding hill-position at the heart of the whole country was constantly celebrated by OT writers. The *Psalmist placed there the habitation of God, from which 'he looked upon all the inhabitants of the world' (Ps 33 (32) : 14). Its kings were 'higher than the kings of the earth' (Ps 89 (88) : 27). In medieval maps Jerusalem was placed at the centre of the known world and it was expected that the *Second Coming would take place in the *Jehoshaphat valley near the city.

The destruction of Herod's *Temple in AD 70 by the Romans under Titus was a national disaster which Jews mourn to this day. Their hope is the gathering together again of their dispersed peoples in a reconstructed Jerusalem. A great Islamic sanctuary, the Dome of the Rock, now stands on the site of the Temple.

For Christians, Jerusalem is the city hallowed by the earthly presence of *Christ. Sites traditionally associated with him, many confirmed by recent archaeological discoveries, are places of *pilgrimage and devotion, the most notable being the Church of the *Holy Sepulchre on the western hill, on the spot where Emperor *Constantine claimed that the rock containing Jesus' tomb had been found. The *Via Dolorosa follows the route supposedly taken by Jesus on his way from Pilate's court to *Calvary.

Jerusalem, New In his final escatological visions, St *John the Divine saw 'the holy city, new Jerusalem, coming down from God out of heaven, prepared as a bride adorned for her husband' (Rev 21 : 2). This is the city where the *saints – those who have remained faithful witnesses – will enjoy eternal bliss when the first heaven and the first earth have passed away and have been replaced by a new heaven and a new earth. There 'God shall wipe away all tears from their eyes: and there shall be no more death, neither sorrow, nor crying, neither shall there be any more pain: for the former things are passed away' (Rev 21 : 4). The New Jerusalem thus symbolizes the ultimate hope of all the faithful.

Jesse, tree of Jesse was the grandson of *Boaz and father of King *David, and thus an ancestor of Jesus. His importance in art is that he demonstrates the descent of Jesus, the *Messiah, from the royal house of David, as foretold by the prophet *Isaiah, 'And there shall come forth a rod out of the stem of Jesse, and a Branch shall grow out of his roots: and the spirit of the Lord shall rest upon him' (Is 11 : 1-2). Jesse is depicted lying on his back, asleep, or experiencing a vision of the future. A genealogical tree grows out of his loins with scrolls naming the ancestors of Jesus placed on the branches. This is the Tree of Jesse which appears in manuscripts and most notably in stained glass, the so-called Jesse Window.

Jesuits Popular name for members of the Society of Jesus, a religious *Order of clerics regular founded at Montmartre, Paris, in 1534 by St *Ignatius of Loyola. They have a small *tonsure on the back of the head and wear a black habit with a high collar when not in secular dress. Their rule was approved by Pope Paul III (1534–49) in 1540 and St Ignatius was elected their first general the following year. His *Spiritual Exercises* were the basis of their constitutions which he drafted and which were adopted in 1558. Their motto is *Ad Majorem Dei Gloriam*, 'To the greater glory of God', often abbreviated to *AMDG, signifying that their work is directed towards preaching, teaching and spreading the faith. They were active in combatting *Protestantism during the period of the *Counter-Reformation, and utilized the dramatic aspects of Baroque art and ceremonial to

St Jerome writing in his cell, accompanied by the lion who was his constant companion (Albrecht Dürer, 1514).

Jerusalem lies at the centre of this medieval world map, the model for the New Jerusalem, the spiritual world to come (English psalter, early 13th century).

attract the laity to church. Painting, sculpture and plays were used as media for the propagation of the doctrines which differentiated *Roman Catholic from Protestant. Jesuits were also notable for their missionary work, especially in China. Between 1542 and 1549, St *Francis Xavier evangelized Goa, Ceylon, Malacca and Japan. Other Jesuit missions were established in Abyssinia, Persia, Mexico, and Central and South America, the most famous being the settlements in Paraguay which constituted what was almost a theocratic state under Jesuit rule.

The Jesuits were expelled from Portugal, Spain and France in the mid-18th century and suppressed in 1773 by Pope Clement XIV (1769-74). Pius VII (1800-23) restored the Society in 1814.

Jesus of Nazareth Founder of Christianity, *God the Son incarnate, *Christ (or *Messiah), whose advent (coming) was foretold by the *Prophets and *Sibyls and whose life, teaching, death and resurrection form the essentials of the Christian story. The facts of his earthly existence have to be inferred from the *Gospels, but although constructed basically on a chronological pattern, they were probably not intended to be biographical. They are essentially theological interpretations of Jesus' coming into the world. These Gospels relate at length the events leading to Jesus' *Crucifixion and contain much of what he did and said between his *Baptism and his last *Entry into Jerusalem, but the accounts differ in detail and their harmonization presents exegetical problems. The Gospels of *Matthew* and *Luke* add material about Jesus' birth and early years.

Independent contemporary evidence of the incidents of Jesus' life is lacking, but a disputed passage in the Slavonic version of the Jewish historian *Josephus' *History of the Jewish War* may be authentic, although expanded by later Christian editing. The information given in the *apocryphal gospels is legendary and consequently suspect, although these works have influenced profoundly Christian art and literature. The principal writings in this category are the *Book of *James (Protevangelium)*, a probably 2nd-century narrative of the infancy of Jesus; and the *Gospel of *Nicodemus*, which contains an account of the *Passion and the *Descent into Hell. Much of the information in these apocryphal works was utilized by medieval encyclopedists and popularized in the *Golden Legend.*

The following entries cover most aspects of his life in detail: *Advent; *Agony in the garden; *Apostles; *Appearances of the risen Christ; *Ascension; *Barabbas; *Beatitudes, eight; *Betrayal and arrest of Jesus; *Boyhood of Jesus; *Brethren of the Lord; *Caiaphas; *Calvary; *Capernaum; *Children, blessing of little; *Crucifixion; *Descent from the cross; *Doctors, Jesus and the; *Ecce Homo*; *Emmaus, road to; *Entombment of Christ; *Epiphany; *Flight into Egypt; *Good Samaritan; *Good shepherd; *Herod; *Holy Coat; *Holy Grail; *Holy Sepulchre; *Incarnation of Christ; *Instruments of the Passion; *Lamb; *Last supper; *Lazarus; *Lord's Prayer; *Man of sorrows; *Messiah; *Miracle; *Mocking of Christ; *Naming of Jesus; *Nativity of Jesus; *Parable; *Passion of Christ; *Pharisees; *Pilate, Pontius; *Presentation of Jesus in the Temple; *Resurrection of Christ; *Second Coming; *Shepherds, manifestation to the; *Stations of the Cross; *Temptation in the wilderness; *Transfiguration; *Trials of Jesus; *Via Dolorosa*; *Washing of the disciples' feet; *Widow's mite; *Woman of Samaria; *Woman taken in adultery; *Woman with the issue of blood; *Words from the cross; *Wounds of Christ.

Jew Originally a term applied to an inhabitant of the land of Judah, that part of the *Promised Land allotted to the tribe descended from Judah, fourth son of *Jacob and Leah. Later the word was used to designate an inhabitant of the Roman province of Judaea who professed the ancient religion of Judaism which reached its full development in Early Christian times. The conflict between Judaean adherents of Judaism and proponents of the new Christian faith led to unedifying disputes. The blame for the death of *Christ was shifted from the Romans to the Jews and made the excuse for execration and persecution for centuries after Christianity became the dominant religion. The injustice of this attitude is now recognized and amends are to be made.

In art Jews are represented with conical hats and wear what were thought to be oriental robes.

Jezebel Wife of King *Ahab of *Israel, whom she dominated, and mother of *Athaliah. Her depravity made her name a synonym for a tyrannous and abandoned woman. She also symbolized *Lust, one of the *Seven Deadly Sins. A Phoenician, she promoted in Israel the worship of her god *Baal and the cult of Ashtaroth, a fertility goddess. Those Israelites who remained faithful to their God or who opposed her were killed or forced to go into hiding. To prove the power of God the prophet *Elijah staged a contest with her priests of Baal on Mount Carmel and they were defeated and slain.

When Ahab wished to incorporate into the gardens of his palace at Jezreel a vineyard belonging to *Naboth, who refused to sell, Jezebel arranged to have him arrested for blasphemy and stoned to death. His property then passed to the king. For this unjust act she was denounced by *Elijah who prophesied the fall of the house of King Ahab and the death of his queen, proclaiming, 'The dogs shall eat Jezebel by the wall of Jezreel' (1 Kg 21 : 23).

This prophecy was fulfilled when *Jehu, commander of the army, murdered Ahab's son and seized the throne. When Jezebel heard that Jehu was approaching the palace of Jezreel, 'she painted her face, and tired her head, and looked out at a window' (2 Kg 9 : 30), thus making herself the eponymous harlot. Jehu ordered two eunuchs to throw her down, and her blood bespattered the wall and his horses as she was trampled underfoot. After he had dined, Jehu ordered his men to bury her body, but the dogs, as Elijah had prophesied, had eaten her flesh and 'they found no more of her than the skull, and the feet, and the palms of her hands' (2 Kg 9 : 35).

Joab A kinsman of King *David and general of his army in the victorious fight against the forces of the rebel Ishbosheth, led by *Abner (2 Sam 2 : 12-17). Joab treacherously killed Abner by stabbing him in the back after he had changed sides. Although David resented the death of Abner, Joab became the king's commander-in-chief and helped him to dispose of *Uriah by placing him in the front line of battle, thus enabling David to marry Uriah's wife, *Bathsheba (2 Sam 11 : 6-26). He was also responsible for the death of *Absalom who rebelled against David (2 Sam 18 : 14-33). When David was nearing his end, Joab made the mistake of supporting the claim to the throne of Adonijah instead of *Solomon, David's nominee, and was later killed before the altar at Gibeon where he had sought sanctuary (1 Kg 2 : 34).

Joachim, St According to the apocryphal *Book of *James*, Joachim was the husband of St *Anne and father of St *Mary the Virgin. He was an exceedingly rich man of *Nazareth, of the royal house of *David. He lived righteously – dividing his wealth into three portions, one part for the service of the *Temple, one for the poor and strangers, and the rest for his household – yet he was childless. This was the cause of public reproach because it was assumed that it was due to a sin which he had committed. When Isacaar the High Priest refused his offering in the Temple, although he had brought double what was required of him, he retired to his sheepfold in the wilderness. There he built a hut and fasted for forty days and forty nights. An angel, said to be *Gabriel, told him to return to his wife. The two met at the Golden Gate in *Jerusalem, kissed, and the child was conceived without taint of original sin (See *Immaculate Conception). St Joachim, depicted as an old man, is sometimes shown gazing in wonderment in scenes of the birth of St Mary the Virgin and standing by the Temple with his wife as Mary ascends the steps (See *Presentation of St Mary the Virgin). According to legend, St Anne had other husbands after his death (See *Brethren of the Lord).

Joan of Arc, St The Maid of Orléans, national saint of France, b.1412 at Domrémy, Lorraine. While watching her father's sheep she heard voices telling her that she was destined to save France from the English invaders. She then went to Chinon where she assumed the leadership of the forces of Charles the Dauphin (she is depicted as a female warrior in armour, holding a banner and brandishing a sword). After raising the siege of Orléans and seeing the Dauphin anointed as Charles VII at Rheims Cathedral, she was captured at Compiègne by the Burgundians and handed over to the English. She was tried in an Inquisitorial court for witchcraft and *heresy, and when she refused to recant was handed over to the secular

Jews and Christians debating rival interpretations of biblical texts (Dutch, 16th century).

St **Joachim**, despondent because his Temple offering had been refused, retires to his sheepfold (Giotto, c.1304-13).

arm to be burned at the stake in the market square of Rouen.

Joan, Pope According to the chronicles of Martin of Troppau, *c*.1250, a woman who passed herself off as a man was elected *Pope and given the title of John VIII. She is not mentioned in the *Liber Pontificalis*, 'the Papal Book', and there is no way of fitting her into the known succession of Popes, although it was alleged that she held the office for just over two years between 855 and 858.

Another account, that of Stephen of Bourbon, a 13th-century French Dominican, places Joan's election *c*.1100 and says that she gave birth on the way to the *Lateran. A Latin joke was said to have circulated among the populace, *non papa sed mama*, 'not a Pope [or father], but a mother'. A more romantic version is that she was a 9th-century English girl (although some said she was born in Mainz, Germany) who fell in love with a *Benedictine monk, dressed as a man in order to travel with him, gained fame for her learning and became first a *cardinal and then Pope.'

Job The supreme OT example of *fortitude, the patience of Job being proverbial. Job is the hero of the *Book of Job*, a work of great antiquity, dating back at least to the 4th century BC and ascribed by some to *Moses. The story may be the rewriting of a folktale in an attempt to answer the question, 'Why do the righteous suffer?'.

Job was an exceedingly rich man in the land of Uz, but 'perfect and upright, and one that feared God, and eschewed evil' (Jb 1 : 1). *Satan, the embodiment of evil, came from 'going to and fro in the earth, and from walking up and down in it' (Jb 1 : 7) and claimed that Job only served God because he was protected by him and was therefore prosperous. If he suffered adversity, he would curse God to his face.

God gave Satan power to put Job to the test. Messengers brought Job news of disaster upon disaster. Sabeans had carried off his cattle and slaughtered his servants; lightning had killed his sheep and his shepherds; Chaldeans had made away with his cattle; and a tornado had blown down his elder brother's house in which his children were feasting and they had all died in the rubble. Job rent his mantle and shaved his head in grief, but accepted these tragedies with resignation, saying, 'Naked came I out of my mother's womb, and naked shall I return thither: the Lord gave and the Lord hath taken away; blessed be the name of the Lord' (Jb 1 : 21).

Satan then proposed another test. 'Skin for skin, yea, all that a man hath will he give for his life'. He 'smote Job with sore boils from the sole of his foot to the crown of his head', but Job 'took him a potsherd to scrape himself withal; and he sat down among the ashes' (Jb 2 : 7-8). In the Vulgate version 'ashes' is given as *stercor* 'dunghill'. Job is therefore depicted sitting on a dungheap. His wife, who advised him unsuccessfully to 'curse God, and die', is shown standing by, holding her nose. In accordance with the anti-feminist attitude of the Middle Ages, she may also throw water over his

boils, or whip him, thus foretelling the *Scourging of Jesus.

Job lamented, wishing he had been born dead so that he would then have been where 'the wicked cease from troubling and the weary be at rest' (Jb 3 : 17). His four friends came to console him. Three argued at length that his suffering was the result of sin, saying that 'man is born unto trouble, as the sparks fly upward' (Jb 5 : 7). Job acknowledged that, 'man that is born of a woman is of few days, and full of trouble. He cometh forth like a flower, and is cut down: he fleeth also as a shadow, and continueth not' (Jb 14 : 1-2). He refuted his friends' arguments, saying 'miserable comforters are ye all' (Jb 16 : 2), the origin of the proverbial phrase, 'Job's comforters'. Elihu, the fourth friend, in face of Job's denials of sin, suggested that suffering is not necessarily an indication of God's displeasure but a means of refining the spirit.

Then God spoke to them out of a whirlwind, asking, 'Who is this that darkeneth counsel by words without knowledge?' (Jb 38 : 2). How can man presume to understand the ways of God and the majesty of his creation? Where was Job 'when the morning stars sang together and all the sons of God shouted for joy?' (Jb 38 : 7). He demanded, 'Canst thou draw out *leviathan with a hook?' (Jb 41 : 1). Overwhelmed, Job acknowledged his impotence, saying, 'Therefore have I uttered that I understood not; things too wonderful for me, which I knew not' (Jb 42 : 3). Job repented in dust and ashes, saying, 'I have heard of thee by the hearing of the ear: but now mine eye seeth thee' (Jb 42 : 5). He prayed for his friends. God then restored his fortunes, gave him twice as much as he had before, and granted him seven sons and three daughters. He saw four generations of his children, and died 'being old and full of days' (Jb 42 : 17).

Joel One of the minor *prophets who lived in Judah *c*.400 BC. He recounted the signs which would herald the Last *Judgement, including invaders with teeth of a lion (one of his *attributes) (Jl 1 : 6); swarms of locusts who would devour everything in their path and darken the sun, moon and stars; and an age of plenty (hence his *cornucopia) (Jl 2 : 24-7), when 'your sons and daughters shall prophesy, your old men shall dream dreams and your young men see visions' (Jl 3 : 28). Then the sun will be turned to darkness and the moon to blood before the great and terrible Day of Judgement dawns. Joel's words, 'I will pour out my spirit in those days' (Jl 3 : 2) were taken as foretelling the *Descent of the Holy Spirit at *Pentecost.

John the Apostle, St Son of *Zebedee and brother of St *James the Great, possibly his younger brother, as he is usually mentioned after him in the NT when the two names are linked together. It is inferred that his mother was *Mary Salome, who may have been the sister of St *Mary the Virgin. This would make him the cousin of *Jesus of Nazareth, thus providing a basis for identifying him as 'the disciple whom Jesus loved'

(Jn 13 : 23) (See *Beloved Disciple). He and his brother obeyed the call to leave their nets and to follow Jesus of Nazareth who named them *Boanerges, 'sons of thunder' (Mk 3 : 17) (See *Calling of the Apostles). The two of them and St *Peter formed a triumvirate who were singled out from the other *Apostles to accompany Jesus on three significant occasions: the raising of *Jairus' daughter (Mk 5 : 37); the *Transfiguration (Mk 9 : 2); and the *Agony in the Garden of Gethsemane (Mk 41 : 33). John and Peter were sent into *Jerusalem by Jesus to seek out the man carrying a water-pot who would show them the *Upper Room where he and his disciples would eat the *Last Supper (Lk 22 : 8). After Jesus' death, John and Peter were among the leaders of the community in Jerusalem. They were dismissed by *Annas the High Priest as 'unlearned and ignorant men' when they boldly proclaimed that Jesus had risen from the dead (Ac 4 : 14).

Except for references to John's participation in the affairs of the early *Church in Jerusalem, there is no direct evidence in the NT as to his subsequent history. Later unreliable tradition held that he was martyred in Jerusalem at the same time as his brother James. A contrary tradition, for which there is the evidence of Polycrates, *bishop of Ephesus towards the end of the 2nd century, affirms that John was the Beloved Disciple who took St Mary the Virgin into his own home, and that after being a witness to the *Resurrection and a teacher of the Faith, 'he fell asleep at Ephesus'. It was there, according to Irenaeus (c.130-c.200), that he wrote the fourth Gospel (See St *John the Evangelist) and died in the reign of Emperor Trajan (98-117). This is the reason for one of the ways in which John is represented in art, as a very old man with a long grey beard, and the *eagle which accompanies him as his *attribute. His vigorous proclamation of the Gospel in Ephesus and his contests with heretics within the Christian community may explain his supposed exile to the island of Patmos and his authorship of the *Revelation of St John the Divine* (the *Apocalypse). He was said to have contributed the clause, *Passus est sub Pontio Pilato*, 'he suffered under Pontius *Pilate', to the *Apostles' Creed.

When St John is represented as a handsome young man, he is intended to be the Beloved Disciple. In this guise he also appears as the bridegroom in the marriage feast at *Cana (his bride was said to be St *Mary Magdalene). He is shown leaning on Jesus' breast at the *Last Supper; and standing with St Mary the Virgin at the foot of the *Cross (See *rood). (For legends concerning St John's life and miracles at Ephesus, See St *John the Divine.)

John Chrysostom, St One of the four Greek *Doctors of the Church, b.c.347 at Antioch. His widowed mother intended him to be a lawyer, but he decided to join a community of monks c.373. He lived in a cave in the mountains until his health suffered and he returned in 381 to his native city where he was ordained and where he devoted himself to the care of the poor. (He is shown

Job and his miserable comforters are silenced when God speaks to them out of a whirlwind (William Blake, 1825).

St **John the Apostle,** from a mosaic in Daphni, Greece, c.1100.

distributing *alms.) He also gained fame through the eloquence of his preaching and was named *Chrysostom*, 'honey-mouth'. A *beehive – his *attribute – is a reference to this oratorical skill. Nevertheless, this generated a further legend: it was said that when the devil upset his inkwell, he dipped his pen in his mouth and it was covered with gold.

In 397 he was made *archbishop of Constantinople. In that city he continued to protect the interests of the poor. He also set about reforming the clergy and improving public morals. This brought him into conflict with Empress Eudoxia, who had him exiled for calling her a *Jezebel because she painted her face. An earthquake struck at that very moment and was taken as a sign of divine wrath at his banishment, so he was recalled only to be banished again in 404. He died in 407 while being escorted by soldiers along the road to Pontus. Years later his body was brought back to Constantinople and entombed in the church of the Apostles. The Greek *Orthodox Liturgy of St Chrysostom is attributed to him, but was probably composed after his lifetime.

There is a late-medieval legend, the subject of an engraving by Albrecht Dürer (1471-1528), which recounts that when St John Chrysostom was a hermit he seduced a girl, killed her and her child, and buried their bodies. Filled with remorse, afraid to look up to *Heaven, he went about on all fours and lived like a beast until a newborn son of a queen (presumably the *Christ-Child) pronounced his pardon after he had confessed his crime. The girl and her bastard child were restored to life.

John Climacus, St Abbot of the monastery of St *Catherine (of Alexandria) at Mount Sinai (*d*.649), who owes his appellation *climacus*, *'ladder' (his *attribute), to his treatise, *The Ladder to Paradise*, a description of the steps which monks must climb on the ascent to Heaven. This was summarized pictorially in *icons which show monks, encouraged by angels, negotiating each step of a ladder which – like *Jacob's ladder – extends from earth to *Heaven. Those who fail fall off and become prey to *devils.

John Damascene, St Theologian (*c*.657-*c*.749) of Damascus, famed for his *De Fide Orthodoxa*, 'On the Orthodox Faith', and declared *Doctor of the Church in 1890. He became involved in the iconoclastic controversy (*See* *iconoclasm), writing vigorously in defence of statues of St *Mary the Virgin. This may have given rise to the legend, originating in Damascus, that he was denounced to the Moslem caliph under whose jurisdiction he lived. His hand was cut off and nailed to the city gate, but was miraculously rejoined to his arm by St Mary the Virgin in recompense for his defence of her image. His *attribute is thus a severed *hand.

John de Matha, St Founder, with his friend Félix de Valois, of the Order of the Holy Trinity for the Redemption of Captives (*Trinitarians, but renamed Mathurins after him). Born in Provence in

1160, he studied for the priesthood in Paris. When saying his first *Mass he had a vision of an *angel whose hands rested on the heads of two prisoners. In Rome, he and his friend found that the *Pope had been granted a similar vision, except that the chained captives were a Moor and a Christian; but he was ready to support their plans to found an Order dedicated to the release of prisoners in enemy hands. They soon attracted many followers. Wearing their white *habit with a red and blue cross on the breast, Trinitarians ranged the shores of the Mediterranean ransoming captives. John was once returning with prisoners whom he had freed, when outraged local inhabitants tore the sails and broke the rudder of his ship. He hoisted his cloak, with others following his example, and the vessel arrived safety at Ostia. He died at Rome in 1213 and was canonized in 1632. The Rue des Mathurins in Paris is named after a convent of his Order which stood there.

John Gualberto, St Founder of the *Vallombrosan Order (985-1073); a Florentine who entered the *Benedictine monastery at San Miniato after sparing the life of his brother's assassin, and seeing the figure of *Christ on the *crucifix before which he was praying, bend its head towards him. After some years he went with some other monks to found a new Order at Vallombrosa in Tuscany, the place from which the Order took its name.

John Nepomucene (Nepomuk), St Bohemian martyr, *b*.Nepomuk 1330, *d*.1393. He became *confessor to Princess Joan of Bavaria, wife of King Wenceslaus IV, a jealous husband who treated his wife outrageously. Although imprisoned and tortured, John consistently refused to reveal the innocent queen's confessional secrets to the suspicious monarch. He is therefore represented with his finger to his lips, or with his lips padlocked, and is the patron saint of the *confessional. He is also invoked against slander.

Outraged by his stubborn silence, the king ordered John to be thrown over a bridge into the Moldau. (A statue was later erected at the spot.) As John sank to his death, five *stars (his *attribute) were seen to rise above the waters. St John Nepomucene is therefore the patron of bridges, and has shrines in mountainous districts where bridges may be washed away by floods and torrents.

John of God, St Founder of the Brothers Hospitallers of Granada, whose *attribute is therefore a *pomegranate (in Spanish *granada*). Born in Portugal in 1495, he fought as a mercenary, became a shepherd in Andalusia, peddled books in Granada and suffered a period of madness from which he was cured when he heard the Blessed John of Ávila preach. In 1539 he opened a house for the sick and the poor and devoted the rest of his life to their care. He died in 1550 before the altar in his house, after being helped by an *angel to rescue a beggar from a flooding river. After his death, his followers were constituted as a religious *Order and given a brown *Franciscan habit with a large cape and *capuchin hood. He had a vision in which St *Mary the Virgin and St *John the Evangelist placed a *crown of thorns (another attribute) on his head.

John and Paul, SS Two brothers who were Roman officers. According to one tradition they were on a campaign in Thrace when they promised victory to their general Gallicanus if he became a Christian. When he agreed, *angels dispersed the enemy. They then refused to attend the court of Emperor *Julian the Apostate, were put to death and buried in their garden on the Coelian Hill in Rome. Another version describes them as eunuchs who were given by Emperor *Constantine to his daughter Constantia; Paul to be master of her household and John to be her chief steward. On her death, Constantia left the two of them a large fortune as a reward for faithful service. Emperor Julian the Apostate took away their possessions, and had them tortured and beheaded (*c.*362) when they refused to renounce their faith. A church was built to enshrine their remains, decorated with frescos telling their story, on the site of Constantia's house on the Coelian Hill. SS John and Paul are represented together as Roman soldiers. A *sword, the instrument of their martyrdom, is their *attribute. Their feast on 26 June was deleted from the Roman Calendar in 1969.

John the Baptist, St In the Christian tradition the last of the OT *prophets and forerunner (Greek *podromos*) of *Jesus. In early-Byzantine art he may be depicted with wings, like an *angel or a divine messenger, as in the text, 'Behold, I send my messenger' (Mk 1 : 2). He was the 'voice of one crying in the wilderness, "Prepare ye the way of the Lord, make his paths straight"' (Mk 1 : 3), and may therefore display a scroll with the words of *Isaiah's prophecy, *Vox clamantis in deserto*. He is depicted carrying a cross with a long stem, is dressed in a garment of camel's hair 'with a girdle of a skin about his loins' (Mk 1 : 6), and holds or has near him a lamb with a *nimbus about its head *(See *Agnus Dei)*. He points to the lamb, reflecting his words as he was baptizing *Jesus in the River Jordan, *Ecce Agnus Dei*, 'Behold the Lamb of God'. A honey-pot near him recalls his diet of locusts and wild honey in the wilderness. He may also be shown preaching to the multitude on 'the baptism of repentance for the remission of sins', and baptizing them as they 'flee from the wrath to come'. He told them that 'the axe is laid unto the root of the tree (Lk 3 : 3-9).

John's chief role is as baptizer of the *Messiah *(See *Baptism of Christ)*. He had proclaimed that one would come who would be mightier than he, 'the latchet of whose shoes I am not worthy to stoop down and unloose' (Mk 2 : 7). When he acknowledged Jesus to be the expected saviour, many of his disciples, including SS *Peter and *Andrew, left him to follow the young man from Nazareth. *Herod Antipas imprisoned John because he had denounced his incestuous marriage to *Herodias, his half-brother's wife. He was ex-

St **John Climacus** visualizes the metaphorical ladder which his monks must climb to reach Heaven. St Catherine's monastery, Mount Sinai, is in the background (Greek icon, 1663).

St **John the Baptist** baptizes Jesus in the River Jordan. In the background he is shown preaching and warning the people that the 'axe is laid to the root of the tree' (Gerard David, *d.*1523).

ecuted and his head presented to Herodias because of Herod's infatuation with *Salome, her daughter.

The *Gospel of Luke* makes John a close relation of Jesus. His mother St *Elizabeth was St *Mary the Virgin's cousin. John's birth was miraculous, as she was past the age of childbearing. Her husband *Zacharias was punished because he refused to believe that she would bear a child and that he would be called John. When she was six months pregnant Mary came to see her (*See* *Visitation) and the 'babe leaped in her womb' (Lk 2 : 44). According to legend, Zacharias was killed at the time of the Massacre of the *Holy Innocents, but Elizabeth hid the infant John in a cave where they were found by the *Holy Family when they returned from the *Flight into Egypt. John then played with the child Jesus in *Nazareth until he left his parents' home for the wilderness (Zacharias' death appears to have been forgotten as he is shown in representations of the leave-taking).

After his execution in Herod's fortress (thought to be Machaerus on the Dead Sea), John's body was buried by his disciples at a place believed to be Sebaste in Samaria, where his tomb was revered until it was destroyed by Emperor *Julian the Apostate. His feast day, 24 June, coincides with the pagan midsummer festival and is associated in many countries with bonfires and other customs.

John the Divine, St The visionary writer exiled on the island of Patmos, who was 'in the Spirit on the Lord's day' (Rev 1 : 10). He recorded what he then heard and saw in the *Revelation of St John the Divine (*Apocalypse)*. Until the present century it was generally accepted that he was the same as three other NT persons: the *Beloved Disciple, St *John the Evangelist and St *John the Apostle. His attribute is therefore an *eagle. Because *Jesus said to St *Peter, 'If I will that he tarry till I come, what is it to thee?' (Jn 21 : 22), it was believed that John, 'the disciple whom Jesus loved', lived to a great age. In *Eastern art he is therefore represented as an old man with a flowing beard. It was also thought that like *Enoch and *Elijah in the OT he did not die but was assumed into *Heaven. According to legend, when he was told by *Christ that his end was near, he dug his grave in the form of a cross and lay down in it. The disciples who stood by were blinded by a great light and when their sight was restored they were astonished to find John's body no longer there, and that a sweet odour arose from *manna (or in some versions, a *Host) in the tomb.

In the *West, St John appears more frequently as a handsome young man. When Jesus on the cross commended St *Mary the Virgin to his care, 'he took her unto his own home' (Jn 19 : 27), presumably in Jerusalem. There is a tradition that they moved to Ephesus. There he witnessed the *Falling asleep of St Mary the Virgin and her *Assumption. (In these scenes he is shown holding a *palm.) In a legend noted by Tertullian (*c*.160-*c*.220), Emperor Domitian (51-96) ordered him to come to Rome. John refused to acknowledge the emperor's divinity there and was thrown naked into a cauldron of boiling oil from which he emerged unscathed. This took place outside the Latin Gate, where the church of San Giovanni-in-Olio was later built to commemorate the miracle.

Back in Ephesus, John was challenged by Aristodemus, High Priest of the temple of Diana, to prove the superiority of his God by drinking out of a poisoned cup. When John made the *sign of the cross over the cup the poison emerged in the shape of a *serpent, and he drank the contents unharmed. (A cup or *chalice with a serpent in it is thus the chief *attribute of St John the Divine.) Aristodemus fell dead at his feet and John then restored to life two criminals who had been made to test beforehand the efficacy of the poison and had succumbed to its effects. He also recalled to life Drusiana, a widow with whom he had lodged and who had longed to see him on his return to Ephesus. As her funeral procession passed by she sat up in her coffin at his command and went off to her house to prepare a meal for him. Miracles like this, it was said, caused him to be arraigned as a magician and exiled to the island of Patmos where he experienced his visions of the end of time.

Tradition also connected St John with the conversion of several young men. According to St Clement of Alexandria (*c*.150-*c*.215), he began to instruct in the faith a promising youth but was obliged to leave him in the care of a *bishop when he went to Rome. On his return, he found that the young man had become the leader of a band of robbers. John sought him out, kissed the hand that had committed so many crimes, and reconverted him. On another occasion two rich young men who had sold their possessions and followed him regretted their decision. John sent them to gather faggots and stones which he then gave back to them in the form of jewels and gold. In another version of this story, the young men were followers of a philosopher called Craton. To show their contempt for worldly things they ground their diamonds into powder. John then turned the powder back into precious stones. Craton was converted by the miracle.

St John performed a special favour after his death for Empress Galla Placidia. On her way from Constantinople to Ravenna, fearful of perishing in a storm, she vowed to the saint to build a church in his honour. When she had fulfilled her promise, she prayed for a *relic. St John then appeared to her in a vision. She kissed his feet and he vanished, but he left one of his sandals on the ground, a relic for the church of San Giovanni Evangelista, Ravenna.

John the Evangelist, St Traditionally the author of the *Gospel of St John* and believed to be the same person as the *Beloved Disciple, St *John the Apostle and St *John the Divine, although these identifications have been challenged by scholars. His *attribute is, like theirs, an *eagle, because his sublime Gospel carries the reader up to *Heaven (*See* *Tetramorphs). He may hold a book, indicating his writings, and display a scroll inscribed with the opening words of his Gospel, *In principio erat verbum*, 'In the beginning was the Word' (Jn 1 : 1).

Jonah A *prophet whose story is told in the short but subtle OT book bearing his name. He is there said to be the son of a certain Amittai, although there is a tradition that his mother was the widow of Sarepta and that *Elijah restored him to life. God ordered Jonah to go to the city of Nineveh to denounce the wicked ways of the inhabitants. Fearing a hostile reception, Jonah tried to avoid the command by boarding a ship at Joppa bound for the Phoenician city of Tarshish where he believed that God's writ did not run. God raised a tempest and it seemed the ship would break in two. To discover who on board had provoked the storm, the sailors cast lots 'and the lot fell upon Jonah' (Jonah 1 : 5) – 'a Jonah' is now one who brings bad luck. Jonah told them to appease the divine wrath by throwing him overboard. As he fell into the sea he was swallowed up by a great *fish, assumed to be a *whale, a *dolphin, *Leviathan, or a sea-serpent. He was in the belly of the fish for three days and three nights. Typologically this symbolizes both the *Entombment of Jesus and the *Descent into Hell, a parallel made by Jesus himself, 'For as Jonas was three days and three nights in the whale's belly; so shall the Son of man be three days and three nights in the heart of the earth' (Mt 12 : 39). Jonah then prayed to God who spoke to the fish and 'it vomited out Jonah upon the dry land' (Jonah 2 : 10). This is both a symbol of the *Resurrection and of the salvation of the individual Christian. Jonah and the whale thus appear frequently in Early Christian art.

Chastened, Jonah went to Nineveh and preached so eloquently against their evil ways that the inhabitants repented. God then did not punish them as he had intended. This angered Jonah, and he built a shelter for himself outside the city and sat in its shade. God caused a gourd plant to grow up to give him additional protection from the sun and this pleased Jonah. That night God prepared a worm which attacked the plant and it withered the next morning. Jonah was sorry for the gourd, and God used this as a lesson that he must have compassion for all men, just as God had had pity for Nineveh 'that great city, wherein are more than six-score thousand persons that cannot discern between their right hand and their left hand; and also much cattle' (Jonah 4 : 11).

Jonathan Eldest son of King *Saul. A resourceful soldier and a skilled archer, he campaigned against the *Philistines, and at Michmash rescued his father whose army had been reduced to six hundred men (1 Sam 13 : 3; 14). When the young *David was brought to *Saul to be rewarded for slaying *Goliath, 'the soul of Jonathan was knit with the soul of David, and Jonathan loved him as his own soul' (1 Sam 18 : 1). They became devoted to each other and are therefore quoted as models of masculine friendship. Jonathan gave David his armour and his bow and tried to protect him when Saul turned against him.

Jonathan and Saul died on Mount Gilboa when Saul's army was defeated by the Philistines (1 Sam 31 : 2). When David, still in hiding from Saul, learned of the death of the king, he lamented,

St **John the Divine** on Patmos writes of the beast with seven heads which rises out of the sea (French, late 15th century).

St **John the Evangelist** with his attribute, an eagle (in Pisa Baptistery, by Giovanni Pisano, c.1245-c.1314).

Jonah is cast into the sea, swallowed by a great fish, vomited forth, and falls asleep under a gourd plant (on an Early Christian sarcophagus).

'How are the mighty fallen . . . Tell it not in Gath, publish it not in the streets of Askelon . . . lest the daughters of the uncircumcised triumph' (2 Sam 1 : 19-20). Weeping over Jonathan, he cried out, 'I am distressed for thee, my brother Jonathan; very pleasant hast thou been unto me: thy love to me was wonderful, passing the love of women' (2 Sam 1 : 26).

Jophiel (or Zophiel) Leader of the *cherubim and representative of the splendour of God (his name means in Hebrew, 'the beauty of God'). His symbol is a flaming *sword because he drove *Adam and *Eve out of *Eden and guarded the gate to prevent their re-entry. He protects those who seek the truth.

Jordan, River The great river of the *Holy Land, fed by three streams from Mount Hermon and flowing through the Sea of *Galilee into the Dead Sea. 'Crossing over Jordan' was a metaphor for going to *Heaven, because the Israelites led by *Joshua were miraculously enabled to go over the river dryshod on their way to the *Promised Land. At God's command the priests carried the *Ark of the Covenant towards the river and as soon as their feet touched the shore, the waters were cut off and the Israelites passed over on dry ground (Jos 3 : 7-17). This is an OT type of *baptism and is associated with the crossing of the *Red Sea.
    *Elisha was able to walk across the bed of the river when he 'smote the waters' with *Elijah's mantle which had fallen upon him when his master was caught up by a whirlwind into Heaven (2 Kg 2 : 13-14). The leper Naaman was cured when Elisha told him to bathe seven times in the Jordan (2 Kg 5 : 1-14). Jesus went to the Jordan for his baptism by St John the Baptist (See *Baptism of Christ).

Josaphat Son of a 4th-century king of India who kept him in seclusion because it had been prophesied that he would be converted to Christianity. The hermit *Barlaam contrived to teach him the new faith and also to convert the king. Josaphat ruled his father's kingdom for a while and then abdicated in order to join Barlaam in the desert. The legend appears to be a Christian version of the story of Buddha.

Joseph, St For those who do not accept the dogma of the *Virgin Birth, Joseph was the father of *Jesus of Nazareth; for those who do, he was the divinely chosen husband of St *Mary the Virgin with whom he lived in perfect chastity (hence he is shown with a *lily). He was a descendant of the royal house of *David (Mt 1 : 15; Lk 2 : 14), from which it had been foretold the *Messiah would be born. In the Greek NT he is described as *teckton*, 'craftsman', but this is rendered as 'carpenter' in the AV and other translations. A 5th-century apocryphal work which claims to be autobiographical in part is entitled *History of Joseph the Carpenter*, and it is as a carpenter that Joseph is usually depicted. He is identified by the tools of his trade which are shown near him. He is also shown

instructing the boy Jesus in his craft. Because the family was able to offer only two turtle-doves to the High Priest (See *Presentation in the Temple), Joseph was thought to be a poor man.
    In the Middle Ages Joseph was not held in high esteem. At worst he was stigmatized as the 'divine cuckold'; at best as one destined to be on the margin of events, always apart from the central scene, pondering the significance of what was taking place. To explain why he did not participate in the child's conception he was described as an old man. According to St Epiphanius (c.315-403) he was eighty-nine when he was divinely chosen to be St Mary the Virgin's bridegroom (See *Betrothal and Marriage of St Mary the Virgin). The crutch which he carries in early depictions symbolized his impotence. He was also said to be a widower. Jesus' brothers and sisters were therefore held to be his children by a former marriage (See *Brethren of the Lord).
    A change of attitude became apparent in the 16th century. It was argued that as Joseph had lived so close to the *Christ-Child and had practised to perfection the virtues of poverty, chastity and obedience, he was an example to all, and especially to members of religious *Orders. St Teresa of Ávila dedicated the first convent of her *Carmelite reform to him. *Franciscans and *Jesuits were also devoted to his memory. In 1621 Pope Gregory XV (1621-3) declared 19 March to be a universal feast day in his honour, and this encouraged the spread of his cult notably in Spain and French Canada. He was promoted as the perfect father and artisan, singled out to be the protector of the Christ-Child until the boy was ready to undertake the work of his divine Father. St Joseph thus ceased to be an impotent old man and becomes a strong and determined workman, aged around thirty-two at the time of the *Nativity, according to the *Revelations* of the Spanish *Franciscan nun St María de Agreda (1602-65).
    The narrative scenes in which Joseph participates were derived from the *Gospels, but amplified by much non-biblical material. After his betrothal to St Mary the Virgin he took her to his own home. When he discovered that she was pregnant, but as he was a just man, he sought to divorce her without publicity before only two legal witnesses, the minimum required by rabbinical law. An *angel appeared to him in a dream and reassured him that the child had been conceived by the *Holy Spirit (Mt 1 : 18-25). Icons of the Nativity show his doubts about Mary's virginity being whispered to him by the *Devil in the form of a wild man of the woods.
    St Joseph appears in the *Flight into Egypt; the *Circumcision and *Presentation in the Temple; and the finding of Jesus among the *Doctors. As St Joseph is not mentioned in the NT after Jesus' *baptism, he is assumed to have died long before the wedding feast at *Cana. A legend which appears to have originated in the Coptic fragment of the *History of Joseph the Carpenter* stated that Jesus was present with St Mary the Virgin at Joseph's death bed. This is quoted as the supreme example of *Ars bene morendi*, the way to make a

good end. The risen *Christ is shown presenting him with a chaplet of roses, a parallel to the *Coronation of St Mary the Virgin and reward for the part which he played in the divine plan.

Joseph the dreamer One of the *Patriarchs, according to Christian tradition. His history concludes the *Book of Genesis* (Gen 30-50) and he also appears in the *Koran*. In processions of Patriarchs and *prophets he is distinguished by a sheaf or blade of wheat (his *attribute) – a reference to his foresight in storing up corn in Egypt against a threatened famine. Typologically he prefigured *Christ in many ways.

Joseph was the son of *Jacob by his second wife *Rachel. His younger brother was *Benjamin. When he was seventeen he incurred the envy of his older half-brothers when his father gave him a long-sleeved coat, 'the coat of many colours' (Gen 37 : 3). They were also angry when he told them of two dreams which foretold that he would be superior to them. In one, as they were binding sheaves in the countryside, Joseph's sheaf stood upright and the brothers' sheaves gathered around and bowed to it. In the other, the sun (his father), the moon (his mother) and eleven stars (his half-brothers) did obeisance to him.

The brothers decided to kill Joseph in vengeance, but one brother, Reuben, hoping to save him later, persuaded them to throw him into an empty well (prefiguring Christ's *Entombment and *Descent into Hell). Seeing a caravan of Ishmaelites approaching, they took him out of the well (the *Resurrection) and sold him to them for twenty pieces of silver (the *Betrayal of Jesus). (In another version Joseph was rescued by some Midianites.) They dipped Joseph's coat in goat's blood and sent it to Jacob as proof that he had been eaten by wild beasts. (Joseph's coat was said to be of one piece [like Jesus' *Holy Coat, the seamless robe] and of diverse shades, like the skin of a panther, hence it was called a 'coat of many colours'.)

Joseph was taken to Egypt where his misadventure with *Potiphar's wife caused him to be cast into prison. He escaped when he interpreted *Pharaoh's dreams and rose to high favour when he saved the land from famine. He was later reconciled with his brothers, who now recognized his ascendancy over them, when they came despairingly to buy corn in Egypt. Jacob and his family then settled in Egypt under Joseph's protection. Their descendants remained there until a later Pharaoh enslaved them (*See* *Exodus).

Joseph of Arimathea A respected member of the *Sanhedrin, from Arimathea (thought to be present-day Ramlah), 'a good and righteous man' who was looking for the *Kingdom of God (Lk 23 : 50-1). He became a disciple of *Jesus but kept his allegiance secret 'for fear of the *Jews' (Jn 19 : 38). He did not vote with other members of the Sanhedrin for Jesus' death, and after the *Crucifixion he begged *Pilate for permission to bury his body. With *Nicodemus he took down Jesus' body from the Cross (*See* *Descent from the

St **Joseph,** a carpenter, fashions a mousetrap to ensnare the Devil, in part of a triptych by Robert Campin (*d.*1444).

Cross); wrapped it in a linen cloth (See *Holy Shroud); and laid it on a slab in an unused tomb which he had bought for his own use (See *Entombment). As he is described as 'a rich man' (Mt 27 : 57), he is shown in depictions of these scenes wearing costly robes. According to the Gospel of *Nicodemus he helped to found the first Christian community at Lydda, near his home town.

The alleged association of Joseph of Arimathea with *Glastonbury is unrecorded before the time of William of Malmesbury (c.1080-c.1143), who wrote that Joseph went with SS *Mary Magdelene and *Lazarus to Gaul and was sent from there by St *Philip the Apostle to found the first Christian church in Britain on the Isle of Avalon. Walter Map in 1200 wrote that Joseph brought with him the *Holy Grail, the *chalice used in the *Last Supper that later contained Jesus' blood, and buried it at Glastonbury. From his staff sprang the *Holy Thorn of Glastonbury.

Joseph of Cupertino, St An Italian mystic (1603-63) of Cupertino, Italy. Of humble birth and little education, he started out as a shoemaker's apprentice. In 1620 he became a *lay brother in the *Capuchin monastery near Tarento and later entered a *Franciscan convent near his home town as an *oblate. He was ordained *priest in 1628. He lived a life of great austerity, was favoured with many visions, and had the gift of levitation. When in a state of ecstasy he would elevate himself above the ground and was once observed to fly from a church door over the heads of the congregation and alight on the *altar. Once he flew into an olive tree and remained for an hour sitting on a branch. He was an innocent, open-hearted friar, eccentric in his behaviour and with the gift of healing. It was said that he recognized sinners because their faces appeared black to him and that he knew who were perverts and sexual offenders because they gave off an unpleasant smell.

Josephus, Flavius Jewish historian (b.c.37, d. early 2nd century). The son of a priest, he spent some time in the desert and was associated with the Essenes, a Jewish ascetic sect. At the age of nineteen he joined the *Pharisees. He visited Rome in 63. He then advised against the Jewish revolt (which eventually broke out in 66) although he later commanded the Jewish resistance force in Galilee. When the Romans captured Jotaphata he thought the Jewish cause was lost and surrendered after surviving a suicide pact which he had made with forty of his companions who had taken refuge in a cave. The Roman commander Vespasian later accepted him as an ally. When Vespasian's son Titus besieged *Jerusalem, Josephus acted as his interpreter. After the city fell in 70 he settled in Rome, adopting the surname Flavius, the same as the Roman emperor. He spent the rest of his time writing about the Jewish people in an attempt to rehabilitate them in Roman esteem, demonstrating that historically and culturally they were equal to the Greeks. His History of the Jewish War – a summary of Jewish history from 168 BC to

AD 66 – and the twenty books of his Jewish Antiquities – the story of the Jewish people from the Creation to his own times – were among the chief sources for later Christian writers and commentators on the NT period. Of special importance were his references to St *John the Baptist (Antiquities 18 : 166ff) and to St *James the Less, 'the Lord's brother' (Antiquities 18 : 200). The Slavonic version of the History of the Jewish War contained a controversial passage referring to Jesus. Some consider this to be a later insertion, but it is possible that it is basically authentic, although inflated by later Christian editing.

Joshua Son of Nun, an Ephraimite, successor to *Moses and conqueror of Canaan. He led the Children of *Israel on the last stage of their journey to the *Promised Land, which Moses was not permitted to enter. He was one of the twelve young men representing the Israelites who were sent to spy out the land of Canaan. They returned with the report that it was 'a land flowing with milk and honey' (Num 14 : 7-8), but the people refused to trust Moses and were condemned to wander for forty years in the desert.

When Moses was near death, he handed over the leadership to Joshua, a man 'full of the spirit of wisdom' (Dt 34 : 9). When the Israelites reached the Jordan Valley, they besieged the city of *Jericho. Joshua sent two men to spy out the city and they were protected by *Rahab the Harlot. God then held back the waters of the River *Jordan so that the Israelites were able to pass over and surround the city (Jos 3 : 6-17). An angel of the Lord, dressed as a warrior and holding a drawn sword (thus thought to be St *Michael) appeared to Joshua as he stood before Jericho, saying that he was the commander of the army of God. He told Joshua to take off his shoes for the place on which he was standing was holy (Jos 5 : 13-15). Joshua commemorated this miraculous event by erecting a cairn of twelve stones, representing the *Twelve Tribes and foreshadowing the Twelve *Apostles.

Joys of St Mary the Virgin, seven The seven *Sorrows of St *Mary the Virgin are compensated by seven joyful events in her life. They are: the *Annunciation; *Visitation; *Nativity of Jesus; *Adoration of the Three Kings; finding of the boy Jesus in the Temple (See *Doctors, Jesus among the); the *Resurrection; and the *Assumption. Five, twelve or fifteen joys used to be ennumerated. The events chosen varied and included the suckling of the infant Jesus; his healing of the lame; curing blindness; raising the dead; the Resurrection and the *Ascension. Reduction to the symbolic number of *seven was the result of *Franciscan teaching in the 15th century, the most active proponents being SS *Bernardino of Siena in Italy, and John of Capistrano (1385-1456), his companion in Germany. The *rosary of the Seven Joys is called the Franciscan Crown, or the Seraphic Rosary, after St *Francis of Assisi.

Jubal A descendant of *Cain and son of *Lamech by his first wife Adah. He was 'the father of all such as handle the harp and organ' (Gen 4 : 21) and is thus the first musician.

Jubilate The Latin for 'O be joyful' (not related to *jubilee), the opening words of the psalm (Ps 100 (99) : 1) sung at Anglican Morning Prayer as an alternative to the *Benedictus. 'Jubilate Sunday' is the third Sunday after *Easter, and was so named because the *Introit of the Latin *Mass began with the words *Jubilate Deo, omnis terra* (Vg Ps 65 : 1). The AV version is 'Make a joyful noise unto God, all ye lands' (Ps 66 : 1; 100 : 1).

Jubilee Probably derived from the Hebrew *jobel*, 'ram's horn', the trumpet which signalled a time of pardon and rejoicing ('A jubilee shall that fiftieth year be unto you' (Lev 25 : 11)), but confused with the Latin *jubilare* 'to shout with joy'. It was used from *c*.1300 for a period marked by *pilgrimages to Rome, for which a special *indulgence was given. This was repeated every twenty-five years and marked by the opening at the beginning, and the closing at the end, of the holy doors in the *basilicas of St Peter and St John Lateran. It now signifies an anniversary, usually the sixtieth, called the 'diamond' jubilee, but also the 'golden' (fiftieth), and the 'silver' (twenty-fifth) jubilees.

Judas Iscariot Archetypal traitor, who betrayed his master; originally one of the twelve *Apostles of Jesus. Legend describes him as small, with red hair and wearing a *yellow robe. He was said to have lived in Calabria, Sicily. The scriptural designation 'Iscariot' may have meant that he came from Kerioth in southern Judaea, but he may have been a *sicarius*, 'dagger-man', hence a *Zealot, who sought to overthrow Roman rule by guerrilla action. In art he was represented as the treasurer of Jesus' band of followers, carrying the bag or chest which contained their funds. He was reputed to be consumed by greed, and to pilfer from the common stock. His meanness was demonstrated when he protested at the anointing of Jesus at Bethany by St *Mary Magdalene, with ointment which could have been sold for thirty pence. Legend has it that he wanted the proceeds of the sale for himself.

Tempted by *Satan, he conspired with the High Priest *Caiaphas to betray Jesus for thirty pieces of silver. At the *Last Supper, when Jesus told his disciples that one of those eating with him at table would betray him, Judas asked, 'Is it I, Master?'. Jesus replied, 'You have said so'. St *Peter asked who would be the traitor, and Jesus answered, 'It is he to whom I shall give this morsel when I have dipped it', and he handed it to Judas, saying, 'What you are going to do, do quickly'. Satan entered into Judas and he hurried out into the night (Jn 13 : 21-30).

Judas led the High Priest's men to the Garden of *Gethsemane where Jesus had gone to pray. He told them to seize the man whom he would *kiss. Going up to Jesus he said, 'Master', and kissed him on his cheek, or in some versions on his lips (*See* *Betrayal and arrest of Jesus).

After the *Trials of Jesus, Judas was overcome

Joshua led twelve young men to spy out the Promised Land, and returned with giant grapes as evidence of its fertility (Rheims, *c*.1240).

The High Priest's men know whom to arrest when **Judas** identifies Jesus with a kiss, the archetypal betrayal (Giotto, *c*.1306).

by remorse and took the thirty pieces of silver back to the chief priests and the elders saying that he had sinned in betraying innocent blood. They refused the 'blood-money', whereupon Judas threw the coins on the floor. The chief priest used the money to buy a potter's field, later called *Aceldama, 'The Field of Blood', after Judas hanged himself (traditionally on a fig tree) (Mt 27 : 3-10). In another version it was Judas who bought the field (Ac 1 : 16-20). He fell over, his bowels burst open, and he died. He is shown in *Hell suffering terrible torments, condemned to be chewed eternally by the *Devil.

Typological scenes associated with Judas are: *Joseph sold into slavery by his brothers; *Samson betrayed by *Delilah; and *Abner treacherously killed by *Joab.

The Cainites, a *gnostic sect which held that the God of Israel was the god of evil, and celebrated those who opposed him, had a *Gospel of Judas*. They regarded him as a saint and a hero like other OT rebels, *Cain and *Korah.

Judas Maccabeus A 2nd-century BC warrior of Judaea. His second name is derived from the Hebrew *makob*, 'hammer'. He was the leader of the Maccabean revolt against King Antiochus IV, the Seleucid who dominated the Israelites from his Syrian capital at Antioch and tried to suppress their faith. Because of Judas' exploits, first as a guerrilla fighter and then as a military commander (recounted in the *First Book of Maccabees*), he was regarded in medieval times as a model soldier and was included among the Nine Worthies. His most celebrated exploit was the liberation of Jerusalem when he destroyed the heathen altars, cast down the statue of Jupiter which had been set up in the Temple and rebuilt and rededicated the Temple altar. This is commemorated at the Jewish feast of Hanukkah, also called the Feast of Lights, because of the relighting on that day of the seven-branched *candlestick or candelabrum, the *menorah*. This event was made possible by the discovery of a small jar of the special oil which had been hidden after the conquest by the last high priest and which was miraculously increased so that it was sufficient to keep the lights burning for eight days, the time required to prepare more oil. It is now the duration of the feast.

Jude, St One of the *Apostles, usually called 'Judas, brother of James' (Lk 6 : 16; Ac 1 : 13) and 'Judas, not Iscariot' (Jn 14 : 22); thought also to be the same person as *Thaddaeus (Mk 10 : 3), and as the Lebbaeus of the 4th-century *Apostolic Constitutions*, as the word could be a nickname meaning 'big-chested'. He questioned Jesus at the *Last Supper and was told that the *Holy Spirit would be sent to teach the Apostles all things (Jn 14 : 22-7). He was present at *Pentecost, but is not otherwise mentioned in the NT. Legend makes him the Thaddaeus whom Jesus sent to King *Abgar of Edessa, and links him with St *Simon the Zealot in evangelizing the twelve provinces of Persia. He was beaten to death in the city of Suanir with a club or a stick (his *attributes) when,

together with Simon, he drove two devils out of the pagan temple.

St Jude helps those in trouble and assists in locating lost objects. The NT *Epistle of St Jude* is attributed to him.

Judgement, Last Scripture and the teaching of the Church describe how, at the end of time, *Christ, in the language of the *Creed, 'will come again in glory to judge both the quick [the living] and the dead'. This terrible moment has inspired some of the greatest artistic works: sculptures on the *tympana of the west front of churches; and *Doom paintings and frescoes on west walls.

A trumpet will sound and the dead will awake. Their *souls will be united with their bodies, and they will all be in a state of physical perfection, aged thirty, the age of Jesus when he was crucified (*See* *Resurrection of the Dead). The 'sign of the son of man' (Mt 24 : 30) will appear in the skies, but there is no indication what this will be. Some *Fathers were of the opinion that the sun, the planets and the stars will be darkened, followed by the 'sign' – a blaze of light that will herald the coming of Christ in Glory. Others held that the 'sign' would be the appearance of the Cross in the skies, its fragments gathered from the ends of the earth. Christ will then come in the clouds (Mt 26 : 64), accompanied by his angels (1 Cor 3 : 13). He will take his seat on his throne and the good will be brought to his right hand and the bad to his left, the separation of the *sheep from the *goats (Mt 25 : 31-3). St *Mary the Virgin and St *John the Baptist will plead on behalf of all those brought to judgement. Those to whom mercy has been granted will go to eternal bliss or *Paradise, but the unredeemably wicked will be cast into *Hell to suffer eternal torment, in accordance with the words of the parable 'Come, ye blessed of my Father, inherit the kingdom prepared for you from the foundation of the world' (Mt 25 : 34), and 'Depart from me, ye cursed, into eternal fire, prepared for the devil and his angels' (Mt 25 : 41). It is assumed that, as 'all' will be judged, *angels as well as men, women and unbaptized infants will be answerable. The twelve *Apostles will sit near the judgement seat (Mt 19 : 28). According to some, the place of judgement will be the Valley of *Jehoshaphat.

Judgement of Solomon Two harlots who lived in the same house appeared before King *Solomon. Each had borne a child at about the same time but one of the infants had died. It was then claimed that the mother of the dead child had substituted it for the one which had survived while her companion slept. To decide which was the rightful parent, Solomon ordered a sword to be brought and said, 'Divide the living child in two, and give half to the one, and half to the other'. One woman agreed to the division, revealing that the child was not hers, but the real mother was prepared to relinquish it to save its life. Solomon awarded her the baby (1 Kg 3 : 16-28).

Solomon appears as judge in a medieval legend of similar theme. Two men claimed the inheritance of a dead man. To decide which was the son, Solomon ordered the corpse to be tied to a stake and told them to shoot arrows at it. The false claimant prepared to do so, but the true son and heir refused to dishonour his father's body.

Judgement, Particular It is a belief, long held and confirmed by the Council of Florence (1438-45), that immediately a soul in a state of *grace leaves the body at death, it appears before God for Particular (or individual) Judgement. Souls which are perfectly pure are received immediately into *Heaven; those in need of purification are sent to *Purgatory; and those who have departed this life in mortal sin are consigned to *Hell. All await the Last (or General) *Judgement. The scriptural warrant for this teaching is the parable of the Rich Man (*Dives) and Lazarus. In art, Particular Judgement was represented by the soul (shown as an infant because it is reborn into eternal as opposed to temporal life) being carried upwards by angels to stand before the throne of God where its good and bad deeds are weighed, or where it is accused by *devils and defended by its *Guardian Angel (*See* *Abraham's bosom).

Judges of Israel Leaders of the Israelites after the death of *Joshua, who ruled over the *Promised Land until the establishment of the monarchy under *Saul. They were called 'judges' because they assumed moral as well as military authority. Their histories are narrated in the *Book of Judges*, the most notable among them being *Deborah, *Gideon, *Jephthah and *Samson.

Judith One of the biblical heroines, or 'worthy women'. Her story is told in the OT apocryphal *Book of Judith*. She was the young and beautiful widow of Manasseh, living in seclusion in her country estate, faithful to her husband's memory. (She is sometimes depicted accompanied by a *dog, emblem of fidelity.) She was also pious and strict in her observance of the Mosaic code and dietary laws. *Nebuchadnezzar, who reigned over the Assyrians in Nineveh, sent his general Holofernes against the Jews who had refused to help him in his war against King Arphaxad of the Medes. Holofernes laid siege to Bethulia, a city so far unidentified, which blocked his route to *Jerusalem, and cut off its water supply. Its despairing inhabitants were persuaded by their chief priest Ozias to surrender. Judith heard of it, came to Bethulia, admonished Ozias and said that she would save the people.

Abandoning her widow's weeds, she dressed herself in all her finery and went with her maid to the enemy camp. She informed Holofernes that the Jews of Bethulia were about to lose the protection of their God because they had broken his laws, and that she would tell him the exact moment when this would happen so that he could conquer them. She was therefore allowed to go freely in and out of the encampment. Holofernes was captivated by her beauty and made a feast for her in his tent. His commanders then discreetly withdrew. Judith plied Holofernes with wine that

The dead arise from their graves as Christ comes in Glory at the **Last Judgement** (Italian, 15th century).

her servant had brought in a skin. Before he could carry out his intention to ravish her, Holofernes fell into a drunken stupor. Seizing him by the hair, Judith severed his neck with two blows of his sword, wrapped his head in the canopy of the couch, handed it to her servant who put it in her bag and carried it through the enemy lines back to Bethulia. Judith then stood on the walls of the city and showed the severed head to the Assyrians. They fled in terror as the Israelites attacked them. Judith sang a hymn of thanksgiving, part of which was included in the Roman *Breviary for recitation at *Lauds.

Julian the Apostate Flavius Claudius Julianus (331-63), Roman emperor. His statue is in the Musée du Louvre, Paris. Son of Julius Constantius, half-brother of Emperor *Constantine the Great, he was brought up as a Christian but later reverted to paganism and persecuted the faithful. He wrote a bitter attack on Christianity, *Adversus Christianos* ('Against the Christians'). He died fighting the Persians at Ctesiphon, near modern Baghdad, wounded by a spear which pierced his liver. According to legend this was the posthumous act of St Mercurius, an officer in his army whom he had put to death because he was a Christian. Julian rode at the head of his army when a pale warrior (St Mercurius) mounted on a white charger, thrust a lance into him and vanished. He was carried to his tent and as he died he scooped up a handful of the blood which was flowing from his wound and cried, *Vicisti Galilaee!* ('Thou has conquered, Galilean!'). St *Basil the Great was told in a vision to go to the tomb of St Mercurius, and there he found the blood-stained lance. It was revealed that the saint had killed Julian the Apostate at the behest of St *Mary the Virgin who had arranged for him to rise temporarily from his tomb to do the deed.

Julian the Hospitator (Hospitaller), St A 9th-century nobleman who lived in great luxury and spent his time hunting. One day, a *deer (his *attribute) which he was about to run down turned and said, 'You who are pursuing me to my death will cause the death of your father and mother'. To escape the curse, Julian fled to another country and married Basilissa, a rich widow. His parents, dressed as pilgrims, went in search of him and eventually arrived at his house while he was absent. His wife, on hearing who they were, received them kindly and put them to rest in the matrimonial bed. Julian returned and finding two people in his bed thought that his wife was unfaithful. He drew his sword and killed them, thus fulfilling the prophecy.

Overcome with remorse, Julian and his wife left their home and built a cell near a dangerous mountain river where Julian devoted himself to ferrying travellers across, refusing payment for his arduous task. One stormy night he responded to a cry of distress and found on the opposite bank an exhausted leper, whom he brought across and put to sleep in his bed. The next morning, when the leper arose, his face shone like that of an *angel. He told Julian that his time of penance was over and that he and his wife could die in peace.

Just of the Ancient Law Those righteous persons who lived before the *Incarnation and who were released by Christ on his *Descent into Hell. They include *Adam, *Abel, *Abraham, *David, *Solomon and *Moses.

Justice One of the four cardinal *virtues (the others being Prudence, Temperance and Fortitude). When personified as a woman (*justitia*, 'justice', is a feminine noun in Latin) she carries a *sword signifying temporal power, scales representing the balancing of right against wrong or the two sides of a case, and is blindfold indicating impartiality. *Daniel symbolizes Justice.

Justina and Rufina, SS Patron saints of Seville, whose special care was the Giralda, the Moorish tower there, which they preserved from damage during a fierce thunderstorm in 1504 and which therefore appears in paintings of them. They were the Christian daughters of a potter of Seville. They earned their living by selling his wares, keeping only what was sufficient for their bare necessities and giving the rest to charity. When asked to supply vessels to be used in the worship of Venus, they broke the pots (broken pots are their *attribute) and destroyed the statue of the goddess. They were brought to trial before the Roman prefect, tortured and condemned to death. One version is that Justina died on the rack and that Rufina was strangled, another that they were both thrown to the lions. A *lion is therefore sometimes shown with them.

Justina of Antioch, St A virtuous early-4th-century Christian maid of Antioch (her *attribute is a *unicorn, emblem of *chastity). A pagan nobleman called Aglaïdes fell in love with her. To win her, he employed a magician named Cyprian who no sooner saw Justina than he wanted her for himself. He used necromancy to fill her mind with lustful visons, but she resisted temptation. He even conjured the *Devil to tempt her, but she remained obdurate. Her constancy, and the fact that her God was more powerful than the Devil, led Cyprian to seek *baptism after confessing to Justina his attempts on her chastity. During the persecutions, the two were thrown into a cauldron of boiling pitch but survived. They were then sent to Nicomedia, and were there beheaded on the orders of Emperor Diocletian. (*See* SS *Cyprian and Justina for an alternative version.)

Justina of Padua, St Patron saint of Padua and of Venice, appearing in many paintings commissioned in those two cities. The presence of a *unicorn – emblem of *chastity – in some of them betrays confusion with St *Justina of Antioch whose *attribute it is. She was the daughter (early 4th century) of the pagan King Vitalcino, and was brought up as a Christian by St Prosdochimus, first *bishop of Padua. One day she was arrested by soldiers on the bridge over the Po. She knelt to pray for courage (the marks of her knees are said still to be seen on the bridge) and was taken before Maximian who ordered her to be put to death. Her attribute is a *sword thrust through her side.

Kentigern, St Kentigern (*d*.612), also known as Mungo, was bishop of Strathclyde. He converted the inhabitants of Glasgow, and his *relics now repose in that city in the *crypt of the *cathedral (a Church of Scotland church). He is also said to have founded the *monastery of St Asaph (Llan Elwy), in North Wales. The fish with a ring in its mouth which appears on the arms of Glasgow recalls a legend in which Kentigern saved the queen of that region from the wrath of her husband. She had given her husband's ring to her lover, but it had been thrown into the sea. Out of compassion for her, Kentigern arranged that one of his *monks should catch the salmon which had swallowed the ring. It was restored to the queen before her fault could be discovered.

Key A key is an *attribute of SS *Martha, a housewife with a *ladle, *Zita (or Sitha), a servant with a *rosary, and *Peter to whom were given the *Keys of the Kingdom.

Keys of the Kingdom In response to Jesus' question, 'whom do men say that I the Son of Man am?', St *Peter alone among the disciples acknowledged that he was the *Christ, the expected *Messiah. Jesus replied, punning on the Greek word *petra*, 'rock', 'thou art Peter [*Tu es Petrus*], and upon this rock I will build my church; and the gates of hell shall not prevail against it'. He went on to say that he would give Peter 'the keys of the kingdom of heaven', adding, 'and whatsoever thou shalt bind on earth shall be bound in heaven: and whatsoever thou shalt loose on earth shall be loosed in heaven', meaning that Peter was given authority to interpret what was forbidden or what was permitted to Christians (Mt 16 : 13–20 and with variations in Mk 8 : 27–30; Lk 9 : 18–21). This episode forms the basis of the claim of the *Pope, as Bishop of Rome and successor to St Peter, to supreme authority over the Church. Crossed keys figure in papal heraldry because of the tradition that St Peter was given a golden key and a silver key to symbolize his dual powers to bind or loose and absolve or condemn, which are crossed because these powers originate in the one divine grant. Because he has charge of the keys, St Peter is also cast in the role of doorkeeper of *Heaven.

Kingdom of God (Heaven) Central to Jesus' teaching, expressed in his *parables and sayings, is the *Gospel, the good news of the Kingdom of God. As an eschatological concept based on OT prophecy, it meant the establishment of God's universal rule through the defeat of the wicked on the Day of *Judgement, or Day of the Lord, and

A marble statue of **Justice** holding a sword, representing the power of the state, and on her breast scales, signifying impartiality, the heart of right judgement (Giovanni Pisano, *c*.1245–*c*.1314).

The risen Christ takes Adam by the arm, in order to lead him, Eve and the **Just of the Ancient Law** out of the jaws of Hell, a whale's maw (alabaster relief, Nottingham, England, 15th century).

eternal life for the righteous following the *Second Coming of Christ. St *John the Baptist proclaimed that the Kingdom of God was at hand (Mt 3 : 2) and recognized in Jesus the promised *Messiah. Jesus, although tacitly accepting this role, declared that the Kingdom was a present as well as a future reality, and said, 'the kingdom of God is within you' (Lk 17 : 21). He taught that those hoping to enter God's realm, a spiritual, not a political kingdom, must undergo a profound religious conversion and be 'born again' in a spiritual sense.

Kings (or Magi), adoration of the The central scene of the story of the Three *Kings (or Magi) who were led by a star to the place in *Bethlehem where the *Christ-Child, the *Messiah, had been born (See *Nativity). They found him in a cave, according to a tradition recorded in the Book of *James, or, following the account in the Gospel of Luke, in a stable or shelter attached to an inn. There are two views on the age of the Christ-Child when the Three Kings came to worship him. One was that the visit followed close on the Adoration of the *Shepherds, so the child is represented as a new born babe, the kings kneeling before him. Others point out that because Herod's Massacre of the *Holy Innocents applied to all children under two, the Child must have been approaching that age. He is therefore shown sitting up on his mother's knee, often in the act of blessing the king (usually the oldest), who kneels before him and who, following the account in the *Meditations on the life of Christ, kisses his foot. St *Joseph stands to one side in an attitude of wonderment, or receives the gifts brought by the kings. These gifts have symbolic significance. *Gold (offered by Gaspar) is a tribute to the Child's kingship, and *frankincense (offered by Balthazar), used in worship in the *Temple of Jerusalem, represents prayer. *Myrrh (presented by Melchior) is a spice used in burial and for embalming, and thus foretells not only the *Crucifixion but also the *Resurrection. (In later art, myrrh is contained in a *ciborium, the vessel which enshrines the eucharistic body of *Christ.) Theologically the Adoration of the Kings is one of the theophanies or manifestations of Christ, in this case his revelation to the Gentiles. It is commemorated on the feast of the *Epiphany on 6 January.

Kings (or Magi), three The Gospel of Matthew (Mt 2 : 1-12) records that there was great consternation in *Jerusalem when wise men from the east enquired where they could find the *Messiah. They had seen the *star which was to herald his birth and had come to pay him homage. *Herod summoned the *Sanhedrin, who quoted the prophet *Micah's statement (Mic 5 : 1) that the *Messiah would be born in *Bethlehem of Judaea. After carefully questioning the wise men as to the exact time when they had seen the star, Herod was convinced that a rival had appeared in his kingdom. Cunningly, he asked the wise men to seek the child in Bethlehem and to return to him with news of his abode so that he also might do him homage. The star reappeared and led the wise men to a place in Bethlehem where they found St

*Mary the Virgin and the child 'wrapped in swaddling clothes and lying in a manger', as had been predicted (See *Nativity). They worshipped him, opened their treasure chests and presented him with symbolic gifts of *gold, *frankincense and *myrrh. An angel warned them in a dream not to go back to Herod in Jerusalem, so they returned to their own country by a different route. Outwitted, Herod tried to dispose of his unknown rival by ordering the Massacre of the *Holy Innocents, the slaughter in Bethlehem of all male children under two years of age. The *Holy Family escaped (See *Flight into Egypt).

This story is one of the most popular of the NT narratives, and the central episode, the Adoration of the *Kings (See above), is among the earliest and most frequently represented subjects in art. At first, the wise men (Greek magoi, 'sages'; Latin, magi) are depicted as oriental (possibly Persian) astrologers or Zoroastran priests. From the 4th century onwards they are shown as kings, the most usual manner in which they are thereafter depicted. This change resulted from the assumption that the wise men who came to worship the *Christ-Child were the kings referred to by the Psalmist, 'The Kings of Tarshish and the isles shall bring presents; the Kings of Sheba and Seba shall offer gifts' (Ps 72 (71) : 10). Their number, unspecified in the Gospel of Matthew, varied at first from two to four, but was finally fixed at three because each king presented one of the three gifts. By the 9th century their names had been standardized as Gaspar (who gives gold or gold coins), Balthazar (who offers frankincense), and Melchior (who presents myrrh). They were supposed to come from different parts of the earth, so they were later assumed to represent the three *Races of Mankind, so that one king (usually Balthazar) is black and African. They are also depicted as the three ages of man: youth, manhood and old age. As the star appeared to each of them separately in their own countries, the kings are supposed to have travelled independently to Jerusalem and to have met at *Golgotha where later the *Crucifixion was to take place. After their audience with Herod and their adoration of the Christ-Child, they heeded the angel's warning and went back to their homelands 'by a different way'. One tradition was that they took a ship from Tarshish and that Herod, in revenge, ordered that all the ships in the harbour should be burned.

According to a late-medieval legend, the wise men were so moved by the sight of the Christ-Child that they went to India and devoted themselves to good works and prayer. There St *Thomas encountered them on his way to evangelize the east and consecrated them as *archbishops, which is why they are sometimes depicted wearing *mitres. After leading exemplary lives and converting many heathens, the kings expired one by one. In one version their bodies came to rest in the same *sarcophagus, in another they died in different regions of the east, where their bodies were eventually discovered by Empress *Helena and brought to Constantinople. Their marble coffin was later moved to Milan at

the request of Eustorgus, a noble Greek and eloquent preacher who succeeded St *Ambrose as *bishop of that city. In 1164, after Frederick Barbarrosa had captured Milan, their remains were transported to Cologne Cathedral where their golden *shrine may still be seen.

Kiss A sign of greeting, love, fellowship or veneration of a person or an object associated with a person. Pious Christians kiss the *relics of *saints or the *shrines containing them, and *rings of *bishops and *cardinals. The custom of kissing a *Pope's foot (or the jewel set in a ceremonial slipper) originated in Byzantine court etiquette. The kiss of *Judas expresses betrayal under the guise of friendship. The kiss of peace (or *Pax) is a sign of greeting and of Christian fellowship, expressed as a reciprocal embrace between officiating clergy at solemn *High Mass or *Eucharist. It may be passed on by the congregation in this way or as a handshake. The *celebrant initiates the exchange with the words, 'The peace of the Lord be with you always' (in Latin, *Pax domini sit semper vobiscum*).

Knife The *attribute of *Abraham who was prepared to sacrifice *Isaac, and of St *Bartholomew who was flayed alive with a knife. A *Dominican with a knife (or knife wound) in his head is St *Peter Martyr. SS *Agatha, *Wenceslaus and many other saints killed with a knife may also be shown with this attribute. A knife also symbolizes the *Circumcision of Jesus.

Knock (Cnoc Mhuire) A village in County Mayo, Republic of Ireland, where on the evening of 21 August 1879 a number of the faithful claimed to have seen over a period of an hour and a half on the wall of the church, about two feet above the ground and bathed in light, the figures of St Mary the Virgin, St *John the Evangelist and St *Joseph. A *shrine was constructed, miraculous cures reported, and Knock was visited by thousands of *pilgrims. Pope John Paul II (1978-) prayed at the shrine on the centenary of the occurrence.

Knot Franciscans and members of some other religious orders wear corded girdles with three knots to remind them of their three vows, poverty, chastity and obedience. St *Ambrose is sometimes shown wielding a scourge with three knots to symbolize the dogma of the *Trinity and his contest with the unitarian followers of Arius, who denied the concept of the triune God.

Koimesis The *Orthodox Church's name for the *feast of the *falling asleep of St Mary the Virgin.

Korah, punishment of Korah led two hundred and fifty members of the priestly tribe of Levi in a rebellion against the primacy assumed by *Moses and *Aaron saying, 'You have gone too far! For all the congregation are holy'. Challenged to offer incense to God – a function reserved to priests – they were consumed by fire which leaped out from their *censers. The earth 'opened its mouth' and

The three **Kings**, symbolizing the three ages of man and the three known continents, present their gifts to the Christ-Child. The ruins in the background signify the ending of the old order and the beginning of the new (Gerard David, c.1484).

The three **Kings**, shown here as Orientals travelling on camels, find the Christ-Child in a stable with animals nearby (Rubens, c.1624).

swallowed them, their followers and their households (Num 16 : 1-35). This episode foreshows the punishment of the wicked in *Hell and, in particular, the fate of *heretics and of those who rebel against papal authority.

Kyriale The name given to the Latin liturgical book which contains the musical chant for the Ordinary of the *Mass, so called because it opens with the *Kyrie eleison.

Kyrie eleison The Greek for 'Lord, have mercy', the opening words of the liturgical petition 'Lord, have mercy, Christ have mercy [Christe eleison]. Lord have mercy', which is either recited or sung alternately by *celebrant and *server or congregation at *Mass. The threefold repetition of each phrase is in honour of *God the Father, *God the Son and God the *Holy Spirit.

Laban Brother of *Rebecca (Rebekah) and father of *Rachel whom *Jacob sought in marriage. By substituting his less-favoured daughter *Leah on the wedding night, he tricked Jacob into working for him for a further seven years (Gen 29 : 15-30). In compensation he agreed to give Jacob every speckled and spotted sheep or goat and every black lamb which would be born in his flock. Jacob peeled white streaks in fresh rods of poplar, almond and plane and set them before the flock as they came to drink in the stream, with the result that their offspring were speckled and spotted and fell to his portion (Gen 30 : 25-43). In this way he grew rich and left secretly for his homeland with his wives, but Rachel stole the household gods and Laban went in angry pursuit of the fugitives, but was mollified by Jacob's protestations of kinship (Gen 31 : 1-55).

Labarum The military standard adopted in 312 by Emperor *Constantine after his vision of a cross of light before the battle of the *Milvian Bridge. It was a purple banner with the words In hoc vince and the *Chi-rho monogram – composed of the intersecting Greek letters X and P (see figure), the first two letters of ΧΡΙΣΤΟΣ or ΧΡΙCΤΟC, Christos 'Christ' – carried on a long golden spear. Fifty soldiers were assigned to guard it.

Labourers in the vineyard A *parable (Mt 20 : 1-16) told by Jesus to illustrate the nature of the *Kingdom of Heaven, where generosity is as important as justice. A householder hired various labourers at different times throughout the day to work in his vineyard, and at the end paid them all the same wage, a penny. When those who had been hired first complained that they had 'borne the burden and heat of the day' but had received no more than those who had come at the eleventh hour, the good man of the house replied that he had made a bargain with them for one penny and had kept his word, adding that he could do as he

wished with his own money. Jesus concluded, 'So the last shall be first, and the first last: for many be called, but few chosen'. One allegorical interpretation of the parable which influenced its artistic presentation, was that the first labourers were the people of *Israel and the latecomers Christians, the New Israel. Another was that those hired first were the *Patriarchs of the OT, the next the *Prophets and the last the *Apostles.

Labours of the months Depictions of the tasks to be performed each month of the year, often coordinated with the twelve signs of the *zodiac. The following is a typical arrangement:

January	*Aquarius	Spinning, digging and feasting
February	*Pisces	Sitting by the fire, gathering logs
March	*Aries	Pruning vines, sowing seeds
April	*Taurus	Scaring birds
May	*Gemini	Hawking
June	*Cancer	Mowing
July	*Leo	Haymaking
August	*Virgo	Reaping
September	*Libra	Threshing, hunting
October	*Scorpio	Treading grapes
November	*Sagittarius	Killing pigs
December	*Capricorn(us)	Salting meat

Labyrinth A design often composed of broken concentric circles which form a winding and intricate passageway, blocked at various points so that there is only one correct path from the entrance on the outer circle to the centre. Outlined in coloured marble or mosaics, labyrinths were a feature of pavements in the nave in some French *cathedrals (labyrinthes de pavé, as at Chartres) and were said to represent the way to the Holy City of *Jerusalem, located at the centre of the supposedly flat and circular earth. Pilgrims would walk the circular paths, the blocked ways symbolizing the snares of the *Devil, in order to attain their heavenly goal at the centre. Labyrinths or mazes decorated roof bosses in many churches.

Ladder One of the *Instruments of the Passion, recalling the *Descent of Christ from the Cross. A ladder placed against a house refers to the attempt by pagan parents to regain possession of their son whom St *Andrew had converted to Christianity. St *Romuald had a vision of his fellow monks in white robes ascending a ladder to Heaven. Thereafter monks of the *Camaldolese Order wore white *habits. (For Jacob's vision of angels ascending and descending a ladder See *Jacob's ladder.) St *John Climacus described the way to *Heaven as a ladder.

Ladle *Attribute of St *Martha of Bethany, who, in contrast to her sister, busied herself with household tasks.

Lady Chapel A chapel dedicated to St *Mary the Virgin, 'Our Lady', in larger English *churches and *cathedrals, usually located in an *apse at the east end behind the *high altar. In smaller churches it may be in an *aisle.

Lady Day Formerly *feast days commemorating events in the life of *Our Lady, but in later English usage the feast of the *Annunciation, 25 March, a quarter-day in popular and legal reckoning. In *Roman Catholic countries it was *Dies Mariae Deiparae*, 'the Day of Mary Mother of God', 15 August (now the Feast of the *Assumption), recalling the decree of the Council of Ephesus *c.*431 which declared her *Theotokos, 'God-bearer', or 'Mother of God'. Other Lady Days were 8 December, *Conception of the Virgin, and 8 September, *Nativity of the Virgin.

Lady's bed-straw A wild flower, claimed in a legend to have grown in the straw which St *Joseph spread on the floor of the stable to make a bed for St *Mary the Virgin when she was about to give birth to the *Christ-Child. Another version is that it grew in the straw in the *manger (*See* *Nativity of Christ).

Laetare **Sunday** The fourth Sunday in *Lent, so called from the first Latin word of the *introit, *laetare*, 'rejoice'.

Laity Those members of churches who are not *clergy.

Lamb Principally the symbol of Christ (the *Lamb of God), the sacrificial victim for the sins of mankind; also from early times the redeemed Christian, either shown as carried on the shoulders of the *Good Shepherd, or as one of the flock pastured by Christ. A lamb also signifies innocence or meekness and is the *attribute of St *Agnes. As an attribute of Pope St Clement (*d.c.*100) it recalls the story of how a lamb led him to a spring of water when he was dying of thirst. St *Joachim was a shepherd and may also be depicted with a lamb or lambs. St *Geneviève may be shown with a lamb near her as she was said to have been a shepherdess.

Lamb, adoration of the One of the visions of St John the Divine in the *Apocalypse* (Rev 7 : 9-17), on the basis of which a lamb (Christ) is depicted with an *aureole around its head and either recumbent, as if slain, or standing on a book with seven seals. The Lamb bears a flag or *Vexillum*, a banner with a red cross (symbol of the *Resurrection) and is worshipped by twenty-four *Elders with harps, four beasts (the *Evangelists) and a great number of people from different nations, 'clothed with white robes, and palms in their hands'. These are the *martyrs (their palms symbolizing their victory over death) 'who have washed their robes, and made them white in the blood of the Lamb'. Their reward is that the Lamb shall feed them and shall lead them unto living fountains of waters: and God shall wipe away all tears from their eyes'.

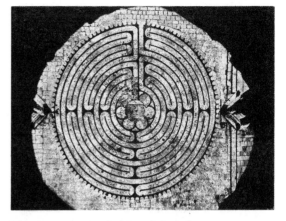

The tortuous way to the heavenly Jerusalem, sited at the centre of a symbolic **labyrinth** in Chartres Cathedral. Only the virtuous can avoid the blocked paths.

All the company of Heaven – saints, martyrs, confessors and angels – join in the **Adoration of the Lamb** (Jan and Hubert van Eyck, *c.*1426-32/4).

Lamb of God Christ was identified with the Suffering Servant, the *Messiah, who would be 'led as a sheep to the slaughter and dumb as a lamb before his shearer' (Is 53 : 7). St *John the Baptist recognized *Jesus as Messiah when he proclaimed, 'Behold the Lamb of God' (Jn 1 : 29), words which have become a liturgical formula (*See* *Agnus Dei*). In Early Christian art it was thought to be sacrilegious to show the human figure of *Christ on the Cross, so the emblem of the Lamb was sometimes substituted.

Lamech A descendant of *Cain and supposedly the first polygamist (Gen 4 : 19-24). He said to his wives Adah and Zillah 'I have slain a man to my wounding and a young man to my hurt', and a legend arose that he became blind and when he was out hunting mistook Cain, who was hiding in a thicket, for a wild animal. He slew him, and when he discovered his mistake he also killed his son *Tubal-Cain who had pointed out the lair to him. His other sons were *Jubal and Jabal. He is said to have been the father of *Noah.

Lamentation over the dead Christ The scene in art, called by the Italian name *Pietà*, 'pity', 'compassion', which shows the body of *Christ after it had been taken down from the Cross, stretched out on a block of stone or on the ground, or on the knees of St *Mary the Virgin, mourned either by his mother alone or by the faithful followers shown in the *Descent from the Cross.

Lamentations of Jeremiah Selected passages from elegiac poems taken from the *Book of Lamentations* which the prophet *Jeremiah composed, sung during the office of *Tenebrae during *Holy Week.

Lammas Day The first day of August, one of the four legal quarter-days, so named because the first loaf made from newly harvested wheat was offered in church on that day. It means 'loaf-festival' (Old English *hlaf*, 'loaf'; *maesse*, 'festival').

Lamp Symbol of enlightenment, knowledge and guidance. Five upright lamps are borne by the *wise virgins of the *parable to indicate that they are full of oil, whereas the lamps carried by the foolish virgins are inverted because they are empty. Clay and bronze lamps bearing Christian symbols have been found in the *catacombs and other centres connected with the early Christians. It became customary in the 13th century to place a lighted lamp before the altar where the *Blessed Sacrament was reserved. This practice was made obligatory in *Roman Catholic Churches after the *Council of Trent. St *Lucy has a lamp as one of her *attributes. Seven lamps may symbolize the seven *Gifts of the Holy Spirit.

Lance One of the *Instruments of the Passion, recalling the lance or spear with which Jesus' side was pierced (supposedly by St *Longinus) after he had died on the Cross (Jn 19 : 34). It was found by St *Helena in *Jerusalem. The bro..en point was

taken to Constantinople in 615 and to Paris in 1241, where it was preserved as a *relic until it was lost during the French Revolution. A lance (or spear) is also the emblem of SS *Matthew and *Thomas who were killed with this weapon.

Lantern An architectural structure at the top of a dome, intended to give light or ventilation. Also an enclosed lamp, the *attribute of St *Christopher because he lights the way for travellers. Lanterns may be carried by the *wise and foolish virgins in place of *lamps. One of the *Sibyls may hold one.

Lark Symbol of the good priest because it flies high and sings as it goes heavenwards.

Last rites *See* *Unction, Extreme; *Viaticum.

Last supper The final meal – recorded in all the *Gospels (Mt 26 : 20-30; Mk 14 : 17-26; Lk 22 : 14-23; John 13 : 1-30) – which Jesus took in company with his *Apostles in the *upper room of a house in *Jerusalem, during which he instituted the *Eucharist, hence the popularity of the subject in art. If the act of institution is emphasized, Jesus is shown in the centre of a long table, his hands touching *bread and *wine. Before him there may be a dish with the pascal *Lamb (signifying his sacrifice) or, less frequently, a *fish (also his symbol). The *Beloved Disciple sits beside him, either leaning towards him or with his head resting on his bosom. The other Apostles are ranged on either side, but *Judas (sometimes identified by his yellow hair or yellow robe) sits apart at the end of the table or rises as if he is about to leave hastily to betray his master.

Last things, four Death, *Judgement, *Heaven and *Hell, the finality of all mankind, as defined in the branch of systematic theology called eschatology (Greek *eschatos logos* 'discussion of the uttermost, or end').

Latria The homage and service (Greek *latreia*) due exclusively to God, distinguished from *hyperdulia due to St Mary the Virgin, and *dulia due to the Saints.

Lauds Originally 'morning praises' (Latin *matutinae laudes*) sung at dawn, but since the early Middle Ages the canonical *hour which follows *Matins. It included Psalms 148, 149 and 150, the so called 'praise psalms' in which the Latin word *laudate*, 'praise ye (the Lord)', is a recurring refrain, hence the English name, 'Lauds'. The Anglican *Book of Common Prayer retained parts of the monastic Lauds in the service of Morning Prayer.

Laurel A symbol of eternity because it is an evergreen; of triumph because Roman victors were given a laurel crown; and of virtue because it was sacred to the Vestal Virgins of Rome.

Lavabo The ceremony of washing the hands or symbolically of the fingers (Latin *lavabo*, 'I will wash'), performed by the *celebrant after the

*offertory and before proceeding with the
*Eucharist, when he recites the words *lavabo inter innocentes manus meas*, 'I will wash my hands in innocency' (Ps 26 (25) : 6). Also the dish or font where the celebrant washes his hands.

Law of Moses The social, moral and religious precepts set out in five books of the *Pentateuch and traditionally ascribed to *Moses. The basis is the *Ten Commandments (Ex 20 : 1-17) and their extension in detail (Ex 20 : 22-30; 38). Additions and elaborations were made in *Leviticus* (Lev 11 : 20) and *Deuteronomy* (Dt 5 : 1-21) with respect to the moral law, and there is much to be found *passim* in these books and in *Numbers* with regard to ceremonial requirements. Jesus said that he had not come to destroy the law but to fulfil it (Mt 5 : 17). St *John the Evangelist commented, 'For the law was given by Moses, but *grace and truth came by Jesus Christ' (Jn 1 : 17).

Lawrence (Laurence), St An Early Christian *deacon (depicted in a *dalmatic) ordained by Pope Sixtus 11 (257-8), born late 2nd or early 3rd century near Huesca, Spain, renowned for his miraculous cures and also for his humility – he imitated *Christ by washing the feet of members of the persecuted Christian community in Rome. When ordered to hand over to the Imperial authorities the Church property and monies which had been placed in his charge by the martyred Pope, he assembled the poor to whom he had given all the wealth in alms saying, 'These are the treasures of the Church'. He is thus the patron of the poverty-stricken masses. As he looked after the Church service books and scriptures, he is also the patron of librarians. He was martyred in 258, being first scourged and then roasted on a *gridiron (his *attribute) in the presence of Emperor Decius, to whom he said, 'You have done me on one side, turn me over on the other so that you may eat me well done'. (These words in Latin, *Assasti unam partem, gira et aliam et manduce*, are sometimes included in portrayals of his martyrdom.) One theory advanced to explain this unusual method of execution is that it arose from an error in copying the account of his death: the scribe substituted for *passus est*, 'he suffered', *assus est*, 'he was roasted'. During his imprisonment Lawrence's patience so impressed his jailor *Hippolytus that the latter became a Christian and was subsequently martyred. St Lawrence was reputed to have the special privilege of leading a soul out of *Purgatory each Friday. When his tomb in Rome was opened 400 years after his burial to receive the body of St *Stephen, he is said to have moved over to make room for the corpse, hence his title, 'the courteous Spaniard'.

Lay brother A member of a religious *Order, 'one of the people' (Greek *laikos*), who is not a *choir monk, bound to the recitation of the *Divine Office, but who occupies himself with the secular business of the *monastery. The grade seems to have originated in Italy in the 11th century when a distinction was made between, on

Christ, the sacrificial **Lamb of God,** bringing victory over death and reconciliation between God and mankind, symbolized by the wreath in the dove's beak (from a 6th-century sarcophagus).

St **Lawrence** holding the gridiron on which he was martyred, and a book to signify his patronage of librarians (German, *c*.1502).

the one hand, those wishing to lead a conventual life who were intellectually capable of learning the Latin choir office or taking *Holy Orders, and, on the other, those who were more fitted to manual or practical tasks. The female equivalent is lay sister.

Layman A churchman, one of the people, or *laity, who is not a *cleric.

Lay reader In the *Anglican Church a *layman, since 1866 (and since 1969, a lay woman), who may be licensed by the *bishop to preach or conduct certain services, or otherwise assist in a *parish or *diocese.

Lazarists The Congregation (or Priests) of the Mission, founded in 1625 by St *Vincent de Paul. Their first establishment was the College of St Lazare in the Place de St Lazare, Paris. They are also called Vicentians after their founder.

Lazarus The brother of SS *Mary and *Martha of Bethany, and an intimate friend of Jesus. When he fell ill his sisters sent for Jesus, and Martha went out to meet him. Mary followed with the news that Lazarus was dead, but Jesus told them to have faith, 'thy brother is not dead but sleepeth'. At the tomb where Lazarus had lain for four days, Jesus called in a loud voice, 'Lazarus, come forth', and he came out alive, still bound in his grave clothes (Jn 11 : 1-44). Legend tells how after the *Crucifixion Lazarus went with Mary to Gaul, where he became the first *bishop of Marseilles and where he was martyred; but the *Orthodox tradition is that he became bishop of Kition in Cyprus.

Lazarus is also the name of the beggar in the parable of *Dives and Lazarus, and the two were frequently assumed to be one and the same person, so that Lazarus of Bethany is sometimes depicted as a bishop, sometimes as a leper, because the Lazarus of the parable was covered with sores.

Leah The eldest daughter of *Laban and substitute bride for *Jacob, who was tricked into serving an additional seven years in order to obtain her younger sister *Rachel, whom he loved for her beauty.

Leaven A substance such as yeast which causes dough to rise. Jews were enjoined to eat un-leavened bread during the *Passover as a symbol of sinlessness. Jesus likened the *Kingdom of Heaven which conquered the world imperceptibly to leaven 'which a woman took and hid in three measures of meal, til the whole was leavened' (Mt 13 : 33; Lk 13 : 20-1). This is 'the leaven in the lump' of popular phraseology.

Lectern A reading desk on which the *Bible or other liturgical books are placed. If fixed, lecterns are constructed of wood or marble and often elaborately ornamented; if moveable they are of wood, brass or bronze. In English churches since the 13th century, a stand surmounted with the symbolic figure of a *pelican or more frequently an *eagle with open wings.

Lectionary A volume containing scriptural passages which are declaimed or chanted in church services. Also the table of OT and NT readings approved for these services.

Lent The fast before *Easter, whose name is derived from the Old English *lencten*, 'Spring'. It comprises forty fasting days (excluding Sundays) of penance and *abstinence, recalling the forty days which Jesus spent in the desert (See *Temptations in the Wilderness), beginning on *Ash Wednesday and ending on *Holy Saturday. The modern pious custom of 'giving up something for Lent' is a mitigation of the more rigid observance of the fast in earlier centuries when only one meal a day (fish and meat being excluded) was permitted.

Lentulus Publius Lentulus, allegedly governor of Judaea before Pontius *Pilate, who was said to have written a letter (a 13th-century forgery) to the Roman Senate, describing Jesus as a man of middling stature with a reverend countenance and curling hair of the hue of an unripe hazelnut.

Leo The lion, the fifth sign of the *zodiac, ruling the period c.23 July to c.22 August. In the *Labours of the Months this is the time for haymaking.

Leonard, St A Frank at the court of King Clovis of France, who established a *monastery at Limoges and dedicated himself to the relief of prisoners, whose patron saint he is. Grateful prisoners kneel at his feet. His *attribute is a chain or fetters. He is one of the *Fourteen Holy Helpers.

Leopard *Symbol of sin and a destroyer because of the text, 'And the beast I saw was like unto a leopard' (Rev 13 : 2). Said to be born of a lion (Greek *leon*) and a panther or pard (Greek *pardus*). The text, 'Can the Ethiopian change his skin or the leopard his spots?' (Jer 13 : 23) has become proverbial.

Leper A low window (or *hagioscope) was placed in the *chancel wall of medieval churches for lepers to see the *Mass (not only those suffering from leprosy, for the term was applied to most skin diseases). In the Middle Ages lepers were strictly segregated in leper houses or 'Lazaries' (called after Lazarus, the beggar covered with sores who is the hero of the parable of *Dives and Lazarus). They were compelled to sound wooden clappers to warn people of their approach.

Levi Son of Alphaeus, a tax-gatherer, 'sitting at the receipt of custom', and called by Jesus to be his disciple (Mk 2 : 13-17; Lk 5 : 27-32), but identified in the *Gospel of Matthew* (Mt 9 : 9-13) as the publican (public official) who became St *Matthew. When Jesus ate at his house in company with other publicans and sinners, the scribes and

*Pharisees protested that this could not be the conduct expected of the *Messiah. Jesus silenced them with the words, 'They that are whole have no need of the physician but they that are sick: I came not to call the righteous, but sinners to repentance' (Mk 2 : 17).

Leviathan The monster with which God confounded *Job, emphasizing his impotence by asking, 'Canst thou draw out leviathan with an hook?' (Jb 41 : 1). In the *Vulgate the word is rendered *draco*, 'dragon', or 'serpent', but as Leviathan's home was said to be this great and wide sea (Ps 104 (103) : 25-6) it was identified with the 'great fish' or *whale in which *Jonah spent three days and three nights, and was thus equated with *Hell.

Libra The balance, the seventh sign of the *zodiac, governing the period *c*.22 September to *c*.23 October. In the *Labours of the Months this is the time for threshing the corn and hunting. Libra is shown as a balance or a pair of scales, alone or held by a woman who may originally have represented Astrea, the Roman goddess of justice.

Light of the world *Christ's description of himself, 'I am the light of the world: he that followeth me shall not walk in darkness, but shall have the light of life' (Jn 8 : 12).

Lilith According to the Talmud, the name of the first woman given to *Adam before the creation of *Eve. She refused to submit to him and vanished into the upper air from which she returns to haunt the night.

Lily The *lilium candidum*, the pure white lily, is said to have grown from the tears of *Eve as she left *Paradise (*See* *Expulsion from Paradise). It is the symbol of purity and virtue, and is the emblem of St *Mary the Virgin. Lilies included in scenes of the *Annunciation and *Incarnation indicate her Perpetual *Virginity, even in conception. St *Gabriel presents her with a lily for the same reason. A lily held by a *saint, or presented to one by the *Christ-Child, is a tribute to chastity. SS *Antony of Padua, *Clare, *Dominic and *Francis of Assisi are thus honoured. Associated with St *Joseph, it recalls the belief that he lived chastely with Mary for the whole of their married life (*See* *fleur-de-lis, St *Zenobius).

Lily of the valley Symbol of St *Mary the Virgin because 'I am the rose of Sharon, and the lily of the valleys' (Sg 2 : 1) was assumed to refer to her. The whiteness of the flower represents her purity and its scent the sweetness of her nature.

Limbo The outskirts of *Hell, from the Latin *limbus*, 'fringe'. It was said to be divided into two sections, the *Limbus Patrum*, 'Limbo of the Fathers', otherwise *Abraham's bosom, where the *Just of the Ancient Law awaited their release by Christ (*See* *Descent into Hell); and the *Limbus Infantium*, 'Limbo of Children', where infants who

Lazarus in his grave clothes emerges from his tomb at Jesus' command. A bystander holds his nose because of the smell of putrefaction, proof that Lazarus was really dead (Duccio, 1308-11).

Christ, holding a lantern to show that he is the **Light of the World,** knocks at a door (the sinner's heart, choked by evil weeds), a summons to repentance (W. Holman Hunt, 1853-6).

had committed no sin, but could not enter *Heaven because they were unbaptized, remained without experiencing suffering. The existence of the *Limbus Infantium* was much debated in the Middle Ages and has never been defined by the *Roman Catholic Church.

Lion This *animal figures in many different contexts. Winged, it represents St *Mark (*See* *Tetramorphs) and is the emblem of Venice whose patron saint he is. It is also associated with saints who lived in the desert and particularly with SS *Antony, *Jerome, *Mary of Egypt and *Paul the Hermit. A lion may signify *Christ, ruler of the world, because it is king of the beasts, or because St *John the Divine said that Christ is the 'Lion of the tribe of Judah' (Rev 5 : 5). In contrast, because 'the devil, as a roaring lion, walketh about, seeking whom he may devour' (1 Pet 5 : 8), it represents *Satan. The text, 'Thou shalt tread upon the lion' Ps 91 (90) : 13) foretells Christ's victory over evil. *Samson killed a lion by forcing open its jaws. Bees hovering in the mouth of a lion refers to his riddle, 'out of the strong came forth sweetness' (Jg 14 : 14).

The account in the *Physiologus* of the habits of a lion provided many parallels with Christ. When it perceives hunters approaching, it swishes its tail to obliterate its footprints so that they cannot find its den. Thus Christ hid his divinity from the *Devil when he entered the Virgin's womb. The lion always sleeps with its eyes open, so Christ seemingly slept the sleep of death on the Cross but he was even then awake in *Heaven. A lioness's cubs are born dead, but after three days the lion wakes them by roaring and brings them to life by breathing on them. Thus *God the Father brought his son to life at the *Resurrection.

A lion is shown with St Jerome, who removed a thorn from its paw, and with *Androcles, an escaped Christian slave who performed the same service and was rewarded when the lion in the arena recognized his benefactor and refused to kill him. *Daniel was saved from death in the den of lions (*See* *Bel and the Dragon). A lion is a sign of the *zodiac (*See* *Leo).

Litany A series of supplications to God, the *saints or St *Mary the Virgin, said or chanted by the *priest, with the congregation making a fixed response to each petition. In *Anglican churches the *priest recites the litany as he kneels at a low litany desk usually placed in the *nave. There is a special litany of *Loreto.

Liturgy In the strict sense, the service of the *Eucharist or *Mass, but used broadly for authorized church services in general. There were and are many liturgies, including the Coptic, Persian, Gallican, and Mozarabic, but those which have had perhaps the greatest cultural influence are the *Roman Catholic, *Anglican and *Orthodox rites. Orthodox Churches do not permit instrumental music so use plainchant. In the Roman Catholic liturgies, *Gregorian chant and plainsong are also used, but more elaborate and notable orchestral

and choral settings were commissioned from the 17th century onwards.

Loaves and fishes, miracle of the A *miracle performed by Jesus when crowds, which followed him far from their homes to listen to his preaching, became hungry. There are duplicate accounts of this incident, varying in detail, but so similar that they are usually conflated in art. In one account (Mk 8 : 1-10; Mt 15 : 29-39) 4000 are fed from seven loaves and a few small fish, and seven baskets full of the broken pieces are left over. In the others (Mk 6 : 31-44; Mt 14 : 13-21; Lk 9 : 10-17; Jn 6 : 1-14) 5000 ate from five loaves and two fish, and twelve baskets were left filled with the broken pieces. The narrative is symbolic of the *Eucharist.

In art Jesus is shown in a desert place, men and women grouped around him as he blesses the loaves and the fish. 'A lad' (Jn 6 : 9), said to be St *Mark as a youth, stands nearby as the miracle is performed on the provisions he brought. The OT *types are the *manna in the wilderness and the *Widow's cruse.

Longinus, St The soldier in the *Gospel of John* (Jn 19 : 34) who wounded the side of the crucified Jesus. He used a spear or lance – Greek *longké* – a word which was later understood to be his name. He was said to be blind, or suffering from an eye disease, and was cured when he rubbed his eyes with the hand stained with the blood of *Christ which had run down his spear. He was confused with the centurion who according to the *Gospel of Matthew* was in charge of the *Crucifixion, and who exclaimed when he saw the strange events which then occurred, *Vere filius Dei erat iste*, 'Truly, this was the Son of God' (Mt 27 : 54). Longinus is therefore sometimes depicted standing on one side of the Cross dressed as a centurion and carrying a spear, or mounted on a horse. His companion *Stephaton is on the other side. He is also said to be one of the soldiers who guarded the tomb in which Jesus was laid (Mt 27 : 65). Another tradition states that he was blinded at the Crucifixion but regained his sight at the *Resurrection. He was so impressed by the miracle that he became a Christian, was baptized by the *Apostles, preached in Caesarea and was martyred because he refused to make the conventional sacrifice to the emperor's deity. Before his execution, Longinus promised the blind Roman governor that he would regain his sight after he was beheaded. It happened accordingly and the governor became a Christian. There is a statue of Longinus in St Peter's, Rome, because his spear or *lance (his *attribute) is said to have been deposited in that church. He is the patron saint of Mantua because he took to that city a *pyx in which he had caught drops of Christ's blood.

Lord, the Jesus Christ, *'Our Lord'.

Lord's Day An alternative name for *Sunday, the day on which *Christ the Lord arose from the dead. It was in use in Early Christian times, as the opening words of the *Revelations of St John the Divine* say he was 'in the Spirit on the Lord's Day' (Rev 1 : 10).

Lord's Prayer The prayer beginning *'Our Father' (*Pater noster*), until today said by all Christians because it was taught by Jesus to his disciples as a model of the way in which they should pray. In the NT it is given in two forms with only slight variations, a shorter one (Lk 11 : 2-4), and a longer version more commonly used (Mt 6 : 9-13). The concluding *doxology, not used in some traditions, was added at least as early as the 2nd century. The traditional English form (now revised) is derived from the Great *Bible of 1539, made by Miles Coverdale (1488-1568).

Lord's Supper The name (based on 1 Cor 11 : 20) given by some *Protestants to *Holy Communion, or *Eucharist.

Lord's Table A *Protestant name for an *altar.

Loreto, holy house of A small stone and brick structure, now encased in white marble and enshrined in a domed *basilica, situated in the town of Loreto, south of Ancona, Italy. It is said to be the house where St *Mary the Virgin was born and where she was visited by the angel *Gabriel at the time of the *Annunciation of the *Incarnation of Christ, hence the name Holy House, or *Santa Casa*. From the mid-12th century onwards Loreto was a place of *pilgrimage, because its church contained an image of the Virgin which angels were believed to have brought there from the *Holy Land. By the end of the 15th century, the reputation of the town as a centre for miracles was enhanced by the story that in 1291, to save it from the infidels, *angels had transported Mary's house from Nazareth to Tersato, near Fiume, and then to Loreto. It was first placed in a grove near the town, but the place became the resort of robbers. The house was therefore moved to its present position. Thereafter the sanctuary became internationally famous, enjoying *indulgences, the favours of successive *Popes, a local *feast day (10 December) in commemoration of the translation (or removal) of the Holy House from Palestine, and a special *litany named after it. Because the Holy House was brought through the air to Italy, Pope Benedict XV (1914-22) declared Our Lady of Loreto to be the patron of airmen in 1920. The truth of the legend has been contested, but its defenders adduce as proof of its authenticity the fact that the Holy House is built of materials found in Palestine but not near Ancona; that it lacks proper foundations; and that numerous miracles have occurred at the *shrine.

Lot The son of Haran, brother of *Abraham, Lot was with Abraham in Canaan. Their herdsmen quarrelled over the sparse grazing in the hill country, so Lot settled in Sodom, one of the *Cities of the Plain of the River Jordan (Gen 13 : 5-12). He was captured by the forces of four

Jesus multiplies the **loaves and fishes** brought to him by his disciples, a miracle foretelling the Eucharist (6th-century ivory).

St **Longinus** holding the spear which pierced Jesus' side, amazed at recovering his sight (Bernini, *c*.1628, St Peter's, Rome).

kings who came raiding from the north, but Abraham rescued him and sent him back to Sodom with his possessions (Gen 14 : 12-16).

Because of the wickedness of the men of *Sodom and Gomorrah, God sent two angels to destroy the cities. Lot met them at the gate of Sodom and, thinking they were travellers, offered them lodging for the night. The homosexual men of Sodom surrounded his house and demanded that the strangers be handed over to them. Lot, believing that the laws of hospitality were superior to the protection of women, offered his two virgin daughters instead. The Sodomites, objecting to Lot, a foreigner, setting himself up as judge of their actions, started to attack his house, but the angels blinded them and they could not find the door. The angels warned Lot that the Cities of the Plain would be destroyed and told him to seek refuge in the hills with his family, but his future sons-in-law thought it was a joke and refused to accompany him. As Lot and the rest of his family fled by night, they were ordered by the angels not to turn round. When the sun came up, God rained down brimstone and fire which destroyed Sodom and Gomorrah. Out of curiosity, Lot's wife disobeyed the angelic order and looked back. She was changed into a pillar of salt (Gen 19 : 1-26).

Lot sought refuge in the little town of Zoar, but not daring to remain there, took his two daughters to the hill country where he made his home in a cave. The daughters, thinking that no men other than their aged father remained alive, sought to continue the race through incest. They made their father so drunk that he did not realize what he was doing and the eldest slept with him that night. She bore Moab, the ancestor of the Moabites. The next night Lot was again plied with wine and the second daughter stayed with him. She bore Amon, the father of the Amonites (Gen 19 : 30-8).

Louis of France, St Louis IX (b.1215), king of France (1226-70), who led the Seventh Crusade, was taken prisoner, and died of plague at Tunis in 1270 when on the Eighth Crusade. He was canonized in 1297. He is the patron saint of Paris and is usually depicted crowned and with a robe embroidered with *fleur-de-lis, the emblem of the French royal line. He sometimes carries a *crown of thorns and three nails from the *True Cross, as he built the Sainte-Chapelle (often shown with him) to house the *relics which he brought back to France when he returned from his Crusade in 1248.

Low Sunday The first Sunday after *Easter, named after the simplicity of its services compared with the elaborate ceremonies of the previous Sunday (See *Quasimodo).

Lucifer The morning star. Used by the early Church *Fathers as a synonym for *Satan, prince of the *fallen angels, who fell from his high place in *Heaven when he led the revolt against God. The prophet *Isaiah was thought to have alluded to him in the text, 'How art thou fallen from heaven, O Lucifer, son of the morning' (Is

14 : 12). Jesus said, 'I beheld Satan as lightning fall from heaven' (Lk 10 : 18), thus equating Lucifer with Satan.

Lucy, St A virgin of Syracuse who went with her mother Eutychia on a *pilgrimage to the tomb of St *Agatha at Catania, Sicily. When her mother was miraculously cured there, she gave all her money to charity. Her pagan suitor, the Consul Paschasius denounced her as a Christian and she was ordered to be placed in a brothel, but the four oxen who were to drag her there refused to move. To save herself from shame, she plucked out her eyes (her *attribute) and sent them to Paschasius on a plate. Another version is that she was condemned to death in 304 during the Diocletian *persecutions, her teeth and eyes were pulled out, and when she would not burn on a pyre, she had her throat cut with a *knife or dagger (another of her attributes). The lamp which she carries may be a pun on the Latin accusative form of lux – lucem, 'light' and Lucia (Lucy).

Luke, St One of the four *Evangelists, author of the Gospel of Luke and the Acts of the Apostles. His attribute is an *ox, a sacrificial animal, because he emphasized the sacrifice of *Christ. (The ox is usually winged, a reference to the *Tetramorphs.) He was said to be a physician because St *Paul greeted him with that title (Col 4 : 14); and an artist because he was believed to have painted a portrait of St *Mary the Virgin and the *Christ-Child who appeared to him in a vision. He is therefore the patron saint of artists. Luke was a follower of St Paul, and after his master was put to death he was thought to have evangelized Egypt and Greece and to have been crucified with St *Andrew at Patras.

Lust One of the *Seven Deadly Sins, the inordinate pursuit of sexual gratification, particularly outside marriage. It is personified with the Latin name of Luxuria.

Luther, Martin Progenitor of the *Reformation, b.1483 at Eisleben, Saxony. His father, a pious copper-miner, intended him to become a lawyer. Instead, in 1506, he joined the *Augustinians at Erfurt, after graduating as master of philosophy at Magdeburg, and was ordained priest in 1507. He received his doctorate in theology in 1512 at the recently-founded University of Wittenberg, to which he was attached as professor until his death in 1546.

Apart from his voluminous theological tracts and polemical writings, and his translation of the Bible into German (1522-34), Luther is noteworthy for two acts which were instrumental in bringing about the ultimate division between *Protestant and *Roman Catholic. The first was his attack on abuses within the Church, particularly the sale of *indulgences, which began when he proclaimed his Ninety-Five Theses at Wittenberg on 31 October 1517, some of which were condemned as heretical. The other, resulting from his obsession with his own sinfulness and a revelation to him *c*.1512-15, was his elaboration of the doctrine of justification (or salvation) through faith alone, not through works (or deeds). He also denied freedom of the will and held that rulers were supreme in matters of religion.

Luther was *excommunicated in 1521 for refusing to recant his heretical teachings. He married Catherine von Bora, a *nun who had renounced her obedience to her *Order.

Lux Mundi Latin for *Light of the World.

Lynx An *animal noted for its keen sight, reputed to be able to see through stone walls and other solid objects, hence symbolic of vigilance and of the all-seeing eye of God. Its urine, which it covered with sand, turned into precious stones.

St **Luke** paints the portrait of St Mary the Virgin and the Christ-Child, whom he has seen in a vision. A characteristic architectural setting by Mabuse (*d.c.*1533).

M The letter M with a crown over it is the *monogram of St *Mary the Virgin. MA DI is the abbreviation of *Mater Dei*, 'Mother of God', *Theotokos; the title granted to Mary at the Council of Ephesus in 431.

Madonna Italian for 'my lady', but specifically a synonym for St *Mary the Virgin. *La Madonna* is the equivalent of 'Our Lady'. 'Madonna' is used in English as the title of a work of art (usually of Italian origin), together with a descriptive phrase, e.g. Leonardo's 'Madonna of the Rocks'. It may also be used adjectivally, as in 'Madonna lily', the white *lily of the *Annunciation.

Magi The plural of the Latin *magus*, 'magician', the Vg for the AV 'Wise Men' who came from the East to worship the *Christ-Child and who were later described as the three *Kings. The Greek historian Herodotus said they were men of the tribe of the Medes who exercised a priestly function in the Persian Empire. From the *Book of Daniel* (Dan 1 : 20; 2 : 27; 5 : 15) it was inferred that they were astrologers who interpreted dreams and watched the stars for a sign that a redeemer was about to be born (*See* *Star of Bethlehem).

Magnificat The hymn (Lk 1 : 46-55) entoned by St *Mary the Virgin when she was greeted by her kinswoman Elizabeth (*See* *Visitation). Its name comes from the opening word of the Latin text, *Magnificat anima mea Dominum*, 'My soul doth magnify the Lord'. It expresses Mary's joy that God had chosen a humble maiden to bear the *Redeemer, and forms part of *Vespers in the Roman Catholic rite; *Evensong in the Anglican *Book of Common Prayer*; and *Lauds in the Orthodox *rite.

Magpie A *bird of evil omen because of its *black feathers.

Malachi (Malachias) One of the prophets of the 5th century BC and supposed author of the *Book of*

A 15th-century wooden **Madonna** which opens to reveal in her womb the Trinity worshipped by saints.

Malachi. His name means 'my messenger' and he is thus sometimes assumed to have been an *angel. He complained about the religious slackness of the Israelites, and condemned mixed marriages and divorce. He promised that God's messenger (identified as *Elijah and later as St *John the Baptist) would prepare the way for *Messiah (Mal 3 : 1). He is depicted holding a scroll with the inscription, *Cum odium habueris, dimitte,* 'When thou shalt hate her, put her away' (Vg Mal 2 : 16).

Malachy, Prophecies of A work apparently composed *c.*1590, but claiming to be by the Irish St Malachy (1094-1148). It lists the attributes of Popes past and those to come, the last one to fit the given description will hold office at the *End of the world.

Malchus The High Priest's servant whose ear was cut off by St *Peter (See *Betrayal and arrest of Jesus).

Malo (Macutus), St A 6th(?)-century *bishop, probably of Welsh origin, who was educated in Brittany and founded the church of Aleth (Saint-Servan) in Saint Malo, a city which is named after him. He travelled throughout the region to bring spiritual comfort to remote villages, singing psalms as he rode along the wild countryside. He was once cut off by the rising tide, but was saved from drowning when a mass of seaweed miraculously appeared and carried him ashore.

Mammon A transliteration into NT Greek of the Aramaic *mamona,* 'wealth' or 'profit'. Jesus pointed out that attachment to wealth estranged man from God because 'No man can serve two masters . . . Ye cannot serve God and mammon' (Mt 6 : 24). He also urged, 'Make to yourselves friends of the mammon of unrighteousness' (Lk 16 : 9), that is, avoid dishonest gain and use your money to benefit your fellow-men.

Man The first of the two accounts of the *Creation of the world (Gen 1; 2 : 1-4) stated that the first Man was made on the sixth day in the image of God, and was appointed master of the fish of the sea, the birds of heaven, all animals and reptiles, and all seed-bearing plants. The second account (Gen 2 : 5-7) said that he was created immediately after the earth, when God fashioned Man (*Adam) out of dust and breathed into his nostrils the breath of life.

Man of sorrows The depiction of Christ wearing his *crown of thorns, his arms either crossed on his breast in an attitude of submission, or extended with palms open to show the holes made by the nails at his *Crucifixion. Blood is sometimes shown flowing from the wound in his side. The artistic intention is to create a devotional image which will remind the faithful of the sufferings of Christ on their behalf *(See *Ecce Homo).* It recalls the prophecy of Isaiah (Is 53 : 3).

Mandeylion, Holy According to an Armenian tradition the image of *Jesus' features were im-

pressed on a napkin which he sent to King *Abgar the Black in Edessa. The Syrian version is that it was painted by Hannan, Abgar's emissary. An *icon, purporting to be the portrait of Jesus, was in Edessa in 544, taken to Constantinople in 944, stolen by Crusaders in 1207 and, according to one account, lost at sea. It (or a copy) reposed in the church of San Silvestro in Capite, Rome, but the Vatican, Genoa and Venice also claimed to possess the icon (See *Abgar's letter; *Holy Face; *Veronica; *Volto Santo).

Mandorla The Italian for *'almond', used for the almond-shaped *aureole or *glory surrounding figures of Christ, especially in depictions of the *Transfiguration; of St *Mary the Virgin in the *Assumption; and of St *Mary Magdalene when angels carried her to Heaven (See *vesica piscis).

Mandrake (or Mandragora) The male of this fictitious plant has leaves like a beetroot, and the female leaves like a lettuce. Both have roots of human shape. If it is pulled out of the ground it utters a cry which kills anyone who hears it. It could only be obtained if a dog were tied to it and then called from a safe distance, after covering both ears with the hands. The dog would wrench out the plant and then fall dead from hearing the shriek. A mandrake-root mixed with wine kills pain. It is also an aphrodisiac and thus is thought by some to be the *Forbidden Fruit. A female *elephant would feed a mandrake to her mate in order to arouse its desire.

Manger of Bethlehem When Jesus was born in *Bethlehem (See *Nativity), his mother 'wrapped him in swaddling clothes, and laid him in a manger; because there was no room for them in the inn' (Lk 2 : 7). A manger in Palestine would have been a stone ledge, trough, or a niche in the wall of the stable on which fodder was placed, but it was traditionally assumed to have been a wooden rack, or *crib, as used in Europe. The Santa Maria Maggiore church in Rome claimed to possess five pieces of wood from Jesus' crib. The custom of setting up a Christmas crib in churches was fostered by the *Franciscans (See *Bambino).

Maniple A band of silk worn over the left arm, over the *alb, by the *celebrant at *Mass, symbolizing the cord used to bind Jesus after his *Arrest, but also fidelity and penitence.

Manna A 'small round thing', whitish like hoarfrost and tasting like honey, which the Israelites found each morning after the dew had gone, except on the *Sabbath, in the Wilderness of Sinai. This 'bread from Heaven' sustained them during their forty years *wandering in the desert before they reached the *Promised Land. It was believed to be called 'manna' because, when the Israelites first saw it they asked, 'What [Aramaic *man*] is it?' (Ex 16 : 14-15, 31; Num 11 : 7-9). Jesus drew the typological parallel between the Israelites who ate manna but eventually died, and himself, the *bread of life. Whoever eats of that bread lives for ever (Jn 6 : 35, 51).

Manticore A monster with the body of a lion, head of a man, three rows of teeth and a scorpion's tail. The name is derived from the Old Persian for 'man-eater', indicating the manticore's special liking for human flesh. It symbolized the *Devil. *Jeremiah's *attribute is a manticore.

Mantle A sleeveless outer garment reaching to the knees and fastened at the neck, or a cloak (Latin *mantellum*).

Margaret of Antioch, St A legendary virgin martyr whose story was popularized in the *Golden Legend*. She attracted considerable devotion in the Middle Ages and later, but she is not included in the revised *Calendar of 1969. A daughter of Theodosius of Antioch, a pagan prince. She was a delicate child and was put in the care of a country woman who was a secret Christian. Governor Olybrius of Antioch one day saw her as she was herding sheep and fell in love with her, but she refused him because she had become a Christian. He therefore ordered her to be tortured and thrown into prison where a fierce *dragon (her *attribute) appeared and swallowed her up. She made the sign of the cross, and a cross materialized, grew larger, and eventually split the dragon in two, so that Margaret was able to walk unharmed out of its belly (she is thus the patroness of women in childbirth). In some versions she led the dragon through the city and more than 5000 people were converted by the example of her constancy. She was subjected to further trials and then beheaded. In art she may wear a *crown inset with pearls (a pun on her name, in Latin *margarita*, 'pearl'). She is one of the *Fourteen Holy Helpers.

Margaret of Cortona, St Born 1247 at Laviano, near Cortona. Her stepmother treated her so badly that she left home and became the mistress of the lord of the castle of Montepulciano. She lived with him for nine years and bore him a son. One day her *dog (and *attribute) pulled at her skirts and led her to a bush where she discovered her murdered lover's body. Overcome by horror, and believing that her beauty had caused his death, she decided to live a life of penitence. Carrying her son, and walking barefoot with a rope around her neck, she begged admission at the Franciscan convent at Cortona. She was received as a *Tertiary and spent the rest of her life in poverty (she is known in Tuscany as *La Povorella*, 'the poor little woman'), caring for the sick and helping the poor. One day, as she was kneeling in ecstasy before a *crucifix, the figure of Christ inclined towards her, an indication that her sin of loving too much was forgiven. She died in 1297 and was canonized in 1728. Her shrine, decorated with scenes of her life, is in the church of Santa Margherita, Cortona, on the site of a building which she helped to restore.

Mariamne Wife of *Herod the Great who, according to the Jewish historian *Josephus, put her to death with their two sons Alexander and Aristobulus in a fit of jealousy.

Christ as the **Man of sorrows** moves to repentance the sinner who contemplates his suffering. An engraving for the *Passion of our Lord Jesus*, 1511, by Albrecht Dürer.

St **Margaret of Antioch,** a prince's daughter, dressed as a shepherdess because she was nursed in the countryside, (Zurbarán, 1631-40).

Marigold A flower which, as its name implies, is dedicated to St *Mary the Virgin. Sometimes depicted in the tracery of circular windows.

Mark, St One of the four *Evangelists, supposed author of the *Gospel which bears his name. He is thought to be the John Mark, cousin of St *Barnabas, who accompanied Barnabas and St *Paul on their mission to Cyprus. He left them, but was later reconciled, and helped St Paul when he was in prison in Rome (Col 4 : 10). The historian *Eusebius, in his *Ecclesiastical History* (*Historia Ecclesiastica* Bk III. 39), quotes a tradition that he was St *Peter's interpreter and that his Gospel was based on Peter's reminiscences. The two are thus sometimes shown together, Peter dictating, or preaching, and Mark writing down his words. Mark is also depicted with a scroll bearing the opening words of his Gospel, *Initium evangelii Jesus Christi filii dei*, 'Here beginneth the gospel of Jesus Christ, the Son of God' (Mk 1 : 1). His emblem or *attribute is a winged lion (*See* *Tetramorph) either because he wrote of Christ, the 'Lion of the tribe of Judah', or because a *lion is a symbol of the *Resurrection, the episode with which his Gospel ends.

When Mark is shown as a *bishop, the reference is to the tradition that he was the first bishop of Alexandria and that he was martyred there after appointing Anianus as his successor, a cobbler with an injured hand whom he had healed. Before Mark was put to death, Christ appeared to him in his cell. After his execution, as his body was being dragged through the streets, a violent thunderstorm scattered the pagans, thus enabling his followers to rescue his remains and give them Christian burial.

According to legend, St Mark's connection with Venice began when he was preaching on the shores of the Adriatic. A storm compelled his ship to seek refuge on the island in the lagoon now called San Francesco della Vigna. An angel appeared and told him that a great city, Venice, would be built there in his honour. Mark also founded a church at Aquileia in the lagoon. Venetian sailors discovered his body in Alexandria in 815 and smuggled it back to their city, hiding it under evil-smelling pork which the Moslem guards would not touch. His relics came to rest under the high altar of the cathedral of San Marco, built in his honour and ornamented with mosaics recounting his life and miracles. One mosaic shows Mark's descent from Heaven to rescue a slave who was devoted to his shrine and who was being led through the streets of Venice to be executed. Another depicts the famous legend of the fisherman's ring. It relates how, at the height of a storm, a stranger (St Mark) persuaded a fisherman on the Piazzetta to take him first to the island of San Niccolo di Lido, where they picked up St *Nicholas of Myra, and then to the island of San Giorgio Maggiore, where St *George came aboard. The fisherman was ordered to make for the open sea, where they encountered a galley filled with *demons who intended to destroy Venice. The saints overcame them, and were then taken back to their respective islands,

but when the fisherman asked for payment, St Mark told him to ask the Doge for the money and gave him the ring from his sanctuary as proof of his story. The storm was caused by a schoolmaster who had sold himself to the *Devil and who had later hanged himself. Paintings based on these events are to be seen in the *Accademia* in Venice.

Marriage at Cana *See* *Cana, wedding feast at.

Martha, St One of the two sisters of *Lazarus of Bethany and prototype of the busy housewife, hence her *attribute is a *ladle or a bunch of *keys. She complained to Jesus that her sister Mary (traditionally identified as St *Mary Magdalene) sat at his feet and listened to his teaching, leaving her to do the housework. Jesus told her that she was 'anxious and troubled about many things' (Lk 10 : 38), but one thing was needful and Mary had chosen it. Although the last part of the statement is a gloss, on the evidence of the Western text of the *Gospels, it has been used to justify the contemplative as opposed to the active life. Possibly Jesus was commending Martha but warning her not to detract from her merit by self-pity. Martha was present at the raising of Lazarus (Jn 11 : 1-46), and served Jesus again in Bethany in the house of *Simon the Leper (Jn 12 : 1-2). She is thus said to have been Simon's wife. There is no other mention of her in the Gospels, but legend has it that she was forced to sail from Joppa with Lazarus and Mary in a leaky boat. They eventually reached the Rhône estuary and evangelized the country around Marseilles. She rid Tarascon in Provence of a *dragon by sprinkling holy water over it (she is shown with an *aspergillum) and then leading it with her sash to Arles where it was killed. In the Orthodox tradition, she is included among the *Holy Women who brought spices to the *Holy Sepulchre.

Martin of Tours, St Born in Hungary *c.*315, he was educated at Pavia where his pagan father was military tribune. He became a Christian and wished to live in a monastery, but was made to join the imperial cavalry, according to legend being knighted by *Constantine the Great. At Amiens, in the bitter winter of 362, he encountered a shivering beggar and cut his cloak in two with his sword to share it with him (thus he is the patron of tailors). That night Christ appeared to him in a dream to say that he, Christ, was the beggar. Later Martin applied to leave the army to devote himself to a contemplative life, but Emperor *Julian the Apostate taunted him with cowardice. Martin offered to stand naked in front of the enemy armed only with a cross to prove his courage. He was not put to the test because the foes sued for peace, due, it was said, to divine intervention. Martin then became a disciple of St *Hilary at Poitiers and later retired to an island near Genoa. Much against his will, he was appointed bishop of Tours. He attempted to hide, but was betrayed by the cackling of a goose (one of his *attributes). At Tours he lived simply in a cell outside the city, where the monastery of Marmoutier now stands, devoting himself to combatting paganism and the Gnostic *heresy. In revenge, devils tormented him in various disguises, frequently appearing in the forms of beautiful women.

Martin was renowned for his charity and humility. Celebrating *Mass one day, he gave his fine *vestments to a naked beggar. At the elevation of the *Host, his arms were seen to be covered with gold and a ball of fire shone over his head. At a banquet the emperor handed him a cup of wine to honour him, but Martin, scorning favours, passed it to a poor priest nearby. He is thus the patron of wine-bibbers and drunkards. When he died in 387, angels carried his soul to *Heaven and many heard them singing as they went. His *feast day, 11 November (*Martinmas) coincided with the season when pigs and cattle were slaughtered and salted for the winter. Servants were also hired at that time. A period of fine weather occurring then is known as St Martin's summer.

Martinmas See St *Martin of Tours, whose feast day (11 November) it is.

Martyr Literally a witness (Greek *martus*) to the Christian faith, but in the first centuries it meant particularly one who chose death rather than denial of belief in Christ. The word is thus used for anyone who suffers death for the faith. Lists of martyrs with accounts of their martyrdoms were kept by the early Churches in their martyrologies, one of the earliest surviving examples, the Hieronymian, dating from the 5th century.

Mary Magdalene, St The archetypal repentant woman sinner, absolved from her sins through her love for Jesus. In legend since the time of St *Gregory the Great she has become the conflation of three NT persons. One was Mary, called Magdalene because she was of Magdala, a village near the sea of *Galilee, out of whom Jesus drove seven devils (Lk 8 : 2). She stood looking from far off when he was crucified (Mk 15 : 10) and was a witness to the *Resurrection (See *Noli me tangere). Another was Mary of Bethany, sister of *Lazarus and *Martha. The third, according to St Gregory the Great, was the unnamed woman in the city, 'which was a sinner', who brought an alabaster box (or jar) of ointment (her attribute) to *Simon the Leper's (or the Pharisee's) house where Jesus was dining 'and began to wash his feet with tears, and did wipe them with the hairs of her head, and kissed his feet, and anointed them with the ointment' (Lk 7 : 36-8). She was converted from her evil ways when Jesus said, 'Her sins, which are many, are forgiven; for she loved much' (Lk 7 : 47). The *Eastern Churches keep these three persons distinct and separate. Mary is also said to have been the bride of St *John the Apostle at the marriage at *Cana.

One tradition says that Mary Magdalene died at Ephesus, perhaps as a martyr, but a Provençal legend dating from the 9th century states that Mary, Martha and Lazarus were cast adrift in a rudderless boat. They reached Marseilles, where

St **Mark's** throne in the basilica dedicated to him in Venice. The Tree of Life is carved on the backrest.

An old woman counsels a rebellious servant-girl to behave like St **Martha,** seen in the background with her sister, St Mary (Velázquez, c.1618).

Lazarus became the first bishop of that region. Mary retired to the desert where she spent thirty years in penitence in a cave, refreshed by celestial food and the songs of angels who carried her daily up to Heaven, an *assumption witnessed on one occasion by a hermit. At her death, angels (or in some accounts St Maximin) gave her the last communion. Her remains, together with those of Lazarus, were discovered north of Toulon, at a place now called St Maximin, where a church was built to house their relics, although Vézelay also claimed those of St Mary Magdalene (*See* *Descent from the Cross; *Entombment).

Mary [of] Cleophas (Clopas), St One of the *Holy Women who followed Jesus from *Galilee and who stood by the Cross. St *John the Evangelist described her as sister of St *Mary the Virgin and 'wife of Cleophas' (Jn 19 : 25). She was identified as 'Mary the mother of *James the Less and of Joses' (Mk 15 : 40; Mt 27 : 56; Lk 24 : 10). Tradition made her the daughter and not the wife of Cleophas, who was said to be St *Anne's second husband, thus she was the step-sister of St Mary the Virgin. According to this version, she married Alphaeus and was the mother of James, Joses, Simon and Jude (*See* *Brethren of the Lord).

Mary of Egypt, St A 4th-century Alexandrian prostitute who joined a pilgrimage to Jerusalem hoping to earn money on the way by plying her trade. A mysterious force prevented her from entering the Church of the *Holy Sepulchre with the pilgrims and she perceived that she was standing by a statue of St Mary the Virgin. She vowed to the Virgin that she would give up her trade if she were allowed to go inside, and as she passed unhindered through the doorway she heard a voice telling her that she would find rest on the other side of the Jordan. She took three loaves (her *attribute) and spent years alone in penitence in the desert living on berries, and when her clothes rotted, her hair grew to cover her nakedness. A priest called Zosimus, who had come to observe *Lent in the wilderness, one day saw her from the opposite bank of the river. He made the sign of the cross and she walked over dry-shod and received the *Blessed Sacrament from him. When he returned the following year, he discovered her bones and a message written on the sand to say that she had died on the very night that he had given her *Communion. A *lion (sometimes shown with her) dug a grave and Zosimus buried her remains.

Mary Salome, St One of the three *Holy Women present at the *Crucifixion according to St Mark (Mk 15 : 40; 16 : 1), and presumably the mother of SS James the Great and John, the sons of *Zebedee (Mt 27 : 56). One legend says that she went with St *Mary Magdalene to Provence (in another version, to Spain) where she converted many pagans.

Mary the Virgin, St Called the *Blessed Virgin Mary, *Madonna, *Mother of God, *Our Lady,

*Queen of Heaven, and many other titles; a young woman of the line of King *David, living in *Nazareth, divinely chosen to bear *Christ. Information about her in the Gospels is confined to her betrothal to St *Joseph; the conception and birth of Jesus (*See* *Annunciation; *Incarnation; *Visitation; *Nativity; Adoration of the *Shepherds; *Adoration of the *Kings; *Presentation of Jesus in the Temple; *Flight into Egypt); his early years and ministry (*See* Jesus and the *Doctors; Wedding feast at *Cana); and her presence at the *Crucifixion when Jesus commended her to the care of the *Beloved Disciple. These events are commemorated in devotional exercises (*See* *Joys and *Sorrows of St Mary the Virgin; *Mysteries of the Rosary; *Stations of the Cross) and expanded for artistic representation (*See* *Descent from the Cross; Pietà; *Lamentation; *Mater Dolorosa; *Deposition; *Entombment). It was deduced that St Mary witnessed the *Ascension and the *Descent of the Holy Spirit.

Pious legends supplemented these slender accounts. The *Book of *James supplied details of her parentage and birth (*See* *Joachim; St *Anne); her early years (*See* *Presentation of St Mary the Virgin in the Temple; *Education of St Mary the Virgin); and her *Betrothal and Marriage. It was believed that Jesus took leave of his Mother before his *Passion and that he came to her again after the *Harrowing of Hell (*See* *Appearance of Christ to his Mother). The circumstances of her death were recounted in detail (*See* *Falling asleep of St Mary the Virgin).

*Types of St Mary the Virgin were found in the OT. She was the second *Eve, through whom came *redemption from *original sin; *Abishag, the young virgin who was brought to King David; *Bathsheba who was placed on a throne by her son (*See.* *Coronation of St Mary the Virgin); and *Judith and *Esther, the heroines who saved their people. In the NT she was the *Woman clothed with the sun. Among OT personages associated with her are: *Aaron with his *flowering rod; *Daniel who saw the stone 'cut out of the mountain without hands' (Dan 2 : 45); *David as ancestor; *Ezekiel who said, 'This gate shall be shut' (Ez 44 : 2) (*See* *porta clausa); *Gideon who beheld his fleece wet with dew; *Moses who saw the *Burning Bush; and *Isaiah who foretold that a virgin would bear a son.

Dogmatic truths concerning St Mary the Virgin have been defined as her divine motherhood (*See* *Theotokos); her *Immaculate Conception; her Perpetual *Virginity; and her *Assumption. She may be venerated, invoked for aid, and her images honoured. Prayers, *hymns and *antiphons are addressed to her (*See* *Alma redemptoris mater; *Angelus; *Ave Maria; *Ave, Maris Stella; *Ave, Regina Caelorum; *Magnificat; *Regina Caeli; *Salve Regina; *Stabat Mater). Among her many shrines are *Knock, *Loreto and *Walsingham.

Among the many *attributes of St Mary the Virgin are the *Ark of the Covenant, *Cedar of Lebanon, *Enclosed Garden, *Fountain, Spotless *Mirror, and *Tower of David. The principal flower associated with her is the *lily, emblem of her purity. The *marigold, and an infinite number of wild flowers, e.g. lady-fern, lady's mantle, lady's slipper, maidenhair fern and lady's thimble (hairbell), recall her name. Her *colours are white, gold, silver and blue.

Legends of St Mary the Virgin abounded in the Middle Ages, many of them appearing in collections like the *Golden Legend and the Miracles of the Blessed Virgin Mary by John Herolt (d.1468). Tales which have influenced literature are: the tumbler (or juggler) who was rewarded with a smile when he performed his tricks before the Virgin's statue, and the nun who ran away with her lover but was not missed because the Virgin took her place. Another famous legend is that of Our Lady of the *Snow.

Representations of St Mary the Virgin in art show her with the *Christ-Child, surrounded by *angels and saints (See *Sacra Conversazione), and as Mother of Mercy (Madonna della Misericordia) spreading her mantle over members of religious *Orders or brotherhoods specially devoted to her.

St Anne teaches St **Mary the Virgin** to read (Eugène Delacroix, 1842).

Mass The traditional *Catholic name for the liturgy of the *Eucharist, dating from the 4th century when it was also known as dominicum ('the Lord's') sacrificio, 'sacrifice', mysterium, 'mystery' and oblatio, 'oblation' or 'offering'. 'Mass' is thought to be connected with the Latin missio, 'dismissal', as the words, Ite, missa est, 'Go, you are dismissed', were addressed to those preparing for *baptism, and to penitents before the beginning of the consecration of the *bread and the *wine. Another possibility is the influence of the phrase used at the conclusion of the service, Et missae fiant, 'And let the dismissals be made'.

The structure of the Mass has varied throughout the centuries, but the form established by the *Council of Trent, the Latin Tridentine Mass, has had the greatest artistic influence. The basic elements are: (1) the Ordinary of the Mass, the invariable part (*Kyrie, *Gloria, *Credo, *Sanctus, *Benedictus, *Agnus Dei, *Communion, are the sections most frequently chanted or set to music); (2) the Proper of the Mass, the part which is 'proper to the occasion' and thus varies according to the season (e.g. *Introit, *Gradual, *Alleluia, *Offertory).

Two types of Mass are the most frequent: Low Mass is said and has little ceremonial, while High Mass (Solemn Mass, *missa solemnis) is sung with full ceremonial. Pontifical Mass is sung by a *cardinal, *bishop or *abbot. Midnight Mass is the first of the three Masses of *Christmas Day (See *Requiem Mass).

Mater Dolorosa Latin for 'Sorrowing Mother', the title of St *Mary the Virgin as she mourns the death of her son, especially when she stands at the foot of the *Cross (See *Stabat Mater).

Matins (Mattins) From the Latin matutina (hora), 'the early morning (hour)', the first of the canonical *Hours, originally said at midnight, then moved by the *Benedictines to 2 am, and later

An angel brings a stole to St Hubert for him to celebrate **Mass.** The chalice and paten lie ready on the altar ('Master of the Life of the Virgin', c.1485/90).

towards daybreak. It is followed by *Lauds. The name was retained in 1549 for the *Anglican service of Morning Prayer, constructed from matins and *prime.

Matthew, St One of the *Apostles, supposed author of the *Gospel of St Matthew* and of an apocryphal *Gospel of the *Pseudo-Matthew*. As one of the four *Evangelists he is represented as a man, either because he gives the genealogy of Jesus, which stresses his humanity (Mt 1 : 1-17), or because one of the 'four living creatures' (Rev 4 : 7) 'had a face as of a man' (*See *Tetramorphs). Alternatively he is shown as an angel, recalling the appearance of an angel to St Joseph (Mt 1 : 12-4). In the AV he is one of the 'publicans' (AV Mt 9 : 10), from the Latin *publicani*, 'tax collectors', possibly customs officers, a hated profession in NT times. One of his *attributes is a money bag. Jesus saw him sitting in his office in the town of Capernaum and said, ' "Follow me". And he rose and followed him'. He sat at table with Jesus and other 'publicans and sinners', and is thus identified with *Levi who feasted in similar circumstances according to the other Gospels (Mk 2 : 14-17; Lk 5 : 27-32). When the *Pharisees reproached Jesus for eating in such unholy company, he replied: 'Those who are well have no need of a physician, but those who are sick; I have not come to call the righteous, but sinners to repentance' (Lk 5 : 29-32).

According to the historian *Eusebius, in his *Ecclesiastical History* (*Historia Ecclesiastica* Bk III. 24. 6), St Matthew preached 'to the Hebrews' and wrote his Gospel for them before he left to continue his mission. Where he spread the good news – whether in Ethiopia, Persia, Parthia or Macedonia – is uncertain, but legend attributes a variety of strange adventures to him, particularly in the land of the cannibals, often confusing him with St *Matthias. The Jewish Talmud recorded a tradition that he was put to death on the orders of the *Sanhedrin, but an apocryphal *Acts of Matthew* said that he died in Myrna, 'the city of the man-eaters'. He had annoyed the king by converting his consort, putting the devils who supported him to flight, and making his people ashamed of their nakedness and their cannibalism. One version is that he was martyred on a pyre, another that he was beheaded (with an *axe, his attribute). He may be shown holding a set-square, possibly through confusion with St *Thomas, or displaying the Latin words, *Sanctam ecclesiam catholicam, sanctorum communionem*, 'The Holy Catholic Church, the communion of saints', phrases which he was said to have contributed to the *Apostles' Creed.

Matthias, St The twelfth *Apostle, a shadowy figure who is mentioned only once in the NT (Ac 1 : 23-6) when he was chosen by lot to take the place of *Judas Iscariot. He had been a disciple of Jesus since his baptism and was a witness to his *Resurrection. There was a tradition, recorded by *Eusebius in his *Ecclesiastical History* (*Historia Ecclesiastica* Bk I. 12. 3), that he was one of the disciples sent out two-by-two to spread the Gospel

in Galilee, and that his election to the apostolate was foretold at *Pentecost when a ray of light shone on him. A Coptic fragment stated that he was the rich man who forsook all to follow Jesus (Mt 9 : 9), and equated him with St *Matthew. This led to Matthias being styled a 'publican' (or tax-gatherer) like Matthew, and to a further confusion with *Zacchaeus (Lk 19 : 1-10) who was also of that profession. (For this reason a money bag is one of his attributes.) Clement of Alexandria (*c*.150-*c*.215), in his *Miscellanies* (*Stromateis*, Bk II. 26. 3), said that Matthias, like Matthew, was a vegetarian.

The apocryphal 6th-century *Acts of Andrew and Matthias* narrates that the land of the anthropophagi (man-eaters) or cannibals, was allotted to Matthias as his mission field. He was captured, blinded, and imprisoned, and was to be eaten on the thirtieth day, but Jesus appeared to him and told him that his sight would be restored and that he would be rescued. In a distant country St *Andrew was told in a vision to take a ship (which turned out to be navigated by Jesus) and to sail to the city of the cannibals. There he made the sign of the cross before the door of the prison where Matthias was confined, released the Apostle, and took him (and the 270 men and 49 women whom he had converted) on a cloud to the mountain where St *Peter was teaching. Matthias was later martyred outside Jerusalem, the *axe or halbard with which he was beheaded thus figuring as his attribute. Empress *Helena brought his relics to Rome. They were removed to Trèves in the 11th century. The church dedicated to him there became a centre of pilgrimage. His supposed contribution to the *Apostle's Creed, inscribed on a scroll which he carries, is *Et vitam eternam. Amen.* 'And the life everlasting. Amen'.

Maundy Thursday The word 'maundy' is derived from the Latin *mandatum*, the 'command' which Jesus gave at the time of the *Washing of the Disciples' feet. On Maundy Thursday (Holy Thursday), *bishops wash the feet of twelve poor men, and the British sovereign gives a purse of maundy money to the elderly.

Maurice, St Commander of the Theban Legion, composed of 600 (or according to the *Golden Legend*, 6660) Christian soldiers. At Martigny near Lake Geneva in *c*.290, Emperor Maximian ordered them to sacrifice to the pagan gods. When they refused and withdrew to Agaunum (now St Moritz, St Maurice-en-Valais), every tenth man was condemned to be beheaded. As each soldier persisted in disobedience, every tenth man again was executed until they were all dead. Maurice remained in their midst, encouraging them to be steadfast, until it was his turn to die. At Veriolez may be seen the stone on which he knelt for his execution. In art he is depicted as a Roman knight with a banner or an axe and wearing a martyr's crown. He may be shown as dark skinned, in a pun on his name, Latin *maurus*, 'Moorish'. An eagle near him or on his banner indicates the eagle of Austria, of which country he is the patron saint.

Meditations on the Life of Christ An anonymous work probably written by a Franciscan monk who lived in Tuscany in the second half of the 13th century. Originally attributed to St *Bonaventure, now more usually listed as by 'Pseudo'-Bonaventure. It consists of a series of pious reflections as an aid to contemplation on all episodes of the life, death and *Resurrection of *Jesus of Nazareth and the life of St *Mary the Virgin. Narratives are elaborated and humanized by the addition of imaginary details and fictional episodes which were nevertheless accepted as fact and incorporated into many works of art.

Melchizedek King and high priest of Salem (he may be depicted as a warrior) who met *Abraham when he returned from rescuing *Lot. He blessed Abraham and gave him food and wine (Gen 14 : 18). As Melchizedek was both priest and king, and as his name means 'king of righteousness', he is the OT type of Christ. His encounter with Abraham foreshadows the *Eucharist because he offered *bread and *wine.

Mendicant friars Members of religious *Orders who are forbidden to own property in common, and are therefore required to beg (Latin *mendicus*, 'beggar') outside their *monasteries. The best known are *Carmelites, *Dominicans, *Mercedarians, *Franciscans and *Servites.

Mercedarians Members of the *Order of Our Lady of Mercy, founded in 1218 by St Peter Nolasco for the ransom of captives held by the Moors. Although now primarily dedicated to preaching and the care of the sick, Mercedarians still make a vow to offer themselves as hostages. They wear a white *habit, tunic belt, *scapular and *hood with a small shield round their necks with five red crosses, depicting the *Wounds of Christ.

Messiah The Hebrew word for *'anointed', denoting the person specially chosen by God. It was rendered into Greek as *Christos*, *Christ, which becomes the attributive title of *Jesus of Nazareth. When the Israelites suffered persecution and exile, they were promised by their *prophets, notably *Isaiah, *Jeremiah, *Malachi, *Nahum, *Micah and *Ezekiel, that Messiah, the Anointed One, a king of the house of *David, would appear to rescue them from their oppressors and restore them to their former prosperity. This expectation was still alive in NT times. Although during his lifetime Jesus kept this fact secret, his followers realized, especially after his *Resurrection, that he was in fact the Messiah, *Redeemer and Deliverer, particularly because he had come to free not only Israel but mankind from the bondage of sin.

Methodist Originally a follower of the brothers John (1703-19) and Charles (1707-99) Wesley who began in Oxford in 1729 to try to revivify the *Church of England through deepening its spiritual life, evangelization and charitable works. They were active in missionary work in England and America. By the end of the 18th century,

St **Matthew,** inspired by the Holy Spirit, writes his Gospel (from a Gospel-book, *c*.820).

St **Maurice** and his captains agree to die rather than betray their faith. He blesses them while angels wait above to crown the souls of the martyred Theban legion (El Greco, 1580-4).

differences over the role of *bishops, the place of the *laity, preaching and the nature of the *Eucharist led to their separation from the Church of England and the foundation of what became a great world-wide Methodist connection.

Methuselah Son of *Enoch and grandfather of *Noah. He lived to the great age of 969 years (Gen 5 : 27). Hence 'as old as Methuselah' signifies a great age.

Micah (Michaes) One of the *prophets who lived in Judah in the 8th century BC, whose tirades are contained in the OT book bearing his name. He sided with country poor who were exploited by rich landowners, and with the ordinary people of Jerusalem oppressed by their priests and rulers. He promised the advent of the Messianic era when swords would be beaten into ploughshares, nation would not fight nation, there would be no more training for war and each man would sit 'under his vine and under his fig tree' (Mic 4 : 3-4). He also prophesied that *Messiah would be born in *Bethlehem of Judah (Mic 5 : 2). He may carry a scroll inscribed with the words, *Invocabunt omnes eum et servient ei*, 'All shall call upon him and shall serve him', a text in fact from Zephaniah (Zeph 3 : 9).

Michael, St First of the seven *archangels, leader of the Hosts of Heaven who defeated *Lucifer when he revolted against God. In one of *Daniel's visions, he appeared as the great prince who defended the people of Israel (Dan 10 : 13, 21; 12 : 1) and, according to the *Epistle of St Jude* (Jude 9), there was a legend that he preserved the body of *Moses from the devil who had claimed it because Moses was guilty of murdering an Egyptian. Michael also led the angelic host which defeated the *dragon (the *Devil), shown at his feet (Rev 12 : 7-9). He is depicted as a winged warrior because he fights against the powers of darkness. In another role, he rescues souls from *Limbo and *Hell and leads them to *Heaven. In representations of the Last *Judgement he is shown holding the *scales or balance in which good deeds are weighed against bad. He also protects high places, and many St Michael's Mounts, as in Brittany, *Gargano and Cornwall, are named after him. When the people of Rome were dying of plague in 590, St *Gregory the Great organized a penitential procession. At the tomb of Hadrian, St Michael appeared and, by sheathing his sword, indicated that the plague was over. Gregory built a chapel on top of the tomb, now the Castel Sant'Angelo, the Castle of the Holy Angel. His principal feast day, 29 September, Michaelmas, a quarter-day, coincided with the migration of geese, hence the custom of eating a Michaelmas goose.

Michaelmas The feast of *St Michael, 29 September.

Millennium The *Revelation of St John the Divine* (Rev 20 : 1-10) describes a period of 1000 years, the 'millennium', in which Satan is bound and Christ reigns with the saints before the Last *Judgement. When this will occur has long been the subject of dispute. There was a widespread belief in the Middle Ages that it would happen about the year 1000, but as this did not come about, there was much further speculation on the date, based on numerological and allegorical interpretations of biblical texts (See *End of the World).

Millstone One of the *attributes of St *Vincent of Zaragoza whose body was attached to a millstone and thrown into the sea, but miraculously washed ashore and given Christian burial.

Milvian Bridge The bridge over the Tiber where Emperor *Constantine defeated the forces of his rival Maxentius on 28 October 312. A vision the previous night, in which he saw a cross in the sky and heard a voice saying *In hoc signo vinces*, 'By this sign shalt thou conquer', led to his favouring the Christian cause and to his use of the *Chi-Rho monogram on his coins and on his *Labarum, or standard. There are two versions of Maxentius' death. One account states that Constantine killed him with a thrust of his lance. *Eusebius claimed that the bridge collapsed as Maxentius fled across it and that he was drowned.

Minims The *Order of Minim Friars founded in 1435 by St *Francis de Paola, called 'minim' (Latin *minimus*, 'the least') to signify their humility. They devote themselves to contemplation, preaching and to complete abstinence from dairy products, eggs, meat and fish.

Minster From the Latin *monasterium*, '*monastery', indicating a church which prior to the *Reformation was served by clergy who were *monks, as in York Minster.

Miracle An effect or event independent of the laws of nature, the result of the intervention of God either directly or through a particular person. Before such a person can be *beatified it must be proved that at least two miracles have been performed through the candidate, either when alive or through his or her intercession after death. Two more proven miracles are required before *canonization.

Jesus performed many miracles as signs of his divinity. He drove *devils out of the *Gadarene demoniacs and out of the woman tormented with seven devils (See St *Mary Magdalene). He cured St *Peter's mother-in-law and the *Woman with the issue of blood. He healed blind *Bartimaeus; the cripple at *Bethesda; the *Centurion's servant; raised *Jairus' daughter; and brought back *Lazarus from the tomb. His command over nature was shown by the changing of water into wine at *Cana; *walking on the water; promoting the miraculous *Draught of Fishes; multiplying the *Loaves and the Fishes; and producing the *Tribute Money from the fish's mouth.

Miriam Sister of *Aaron and *Moses. She (although unnamed) was the sister who suggested to *Pharaoh's daughter that she would find a Hebrew nurse for the baby Moses, who had been found in a cradle or basket made of *bulrushes among the reeds on the banks of the Nile, and brought his mother (Ex 2 : 1-10). For this she was honoured as one of the saviours of the *Children of Israel. She was also a prophetess and led the women in singing and dancing after the crossing of the *Red Sea (Ex 15 : 20-1). Because she objected to the divinely ordained marriage of Moses to an Ethiopian woman, she was smitten with leprosy, but was cleansed through Moses' intercession after she had been shut out of the Hebrew camp for seven days (Num 12 : 1-15).

Mirror An *attribute of St *Mary the Virgin, who was *specula sine macula*, 'the unspotted mirror of the power of God and the image of his goodness' (Wis 7 : 26).

Miserere The first Latin word of the penitential *psalm beginning, *Miserere mei Deus, secundum magnam misericordiam tuam* (Vg Ps 50), 'Have mercy on me, O God, according to thy great mercy' ('Have mercy upon me O God, according to thy loving kindness [AV Ps 51]). It is used at *Lauds and *Tenebrae*. *Monks of austere religious *Orders – e.g. *Cistercians – mortify themselves with a discipline on Fridays for the time taken to say the psalm. It is incorrect to use this term for *misericord.

Misericord From the Latin *misericordia*, 'mercy', a projecting piece of wood on the underside of a hinged seat of a *choir-stall, intended to give merciful relief to those required to stand during lengthy *choir services. Misericords were often carved with humorous or symbolic figures.

Missal The book containing the Ordinary and Proper of the *Mass, often beautifully illuminated.

Mitre From the Greek *mitra*, 'turban', the head-dress of a *bishop (and of some *abbots in the *West). It is said to have been derived in the West from the *camelaucum*, a hat of camel hair, worn outdoors by a *Pope. In the *East, the shape is that of a crown ornamented with embroidery or medallions. It is modelled, it is said, on the crowns worn by Byzantine emperors. The Western mitre appeared in its present shield-like shape in the 11th century. It is worn at all solemn functions, but is removed for prayers and for the celebration of the *Eucharist, or *Mass. Three mitres on the ground or near SS *Bernard of Clairvaux and *Bernardino indicate that they three times refused to be made bishops.

Mocking of Christ Either before his examination by *Caiaphas (Lk 22 : 63-5) or after the High Priest had found him guilty of blasphemy and deserving death (Mk 14 : 64-5; Mt 26 : 65-7), the men who had arrested Jesus mocked and beat him. They struck him and slapped him (a hand is one of the *Instruments of the Passion), spat on him, blindfolded him and shouted 'Prophesy!' (Mk

St **Michael** victorious over the dragon. Jacob Epstein's dominating sculpture, 1955-7, for the rebuilt Coventry Cathedral, England.

Two griffins carry Alexander the Great into the sky so that he can survey the world. A **misericord**, *c*.1340, from Wells Cathedral, England.

14 : 65), 'Prophesy unto us, thou Christ, who is he that smote thee?' (Mt 26 : 68), or 'Prophesy, who is it that smote thee?' (Lk 22 : 65).

In art this scene resembles the mock coronation of Jesus with the *Crown of Thorns, but is distinguished from it in that in the latter the mockers are Roman soldiers, not Jews; and Jesus, dressed in a scarlet or purple robe, holds an *orb and *sceptre.

Mole An *animal which lives underground, reputed to be blind and deaf and thus representing the *heretic, or one who is blind to the *Gospel.

Monastery The house of a religious community. In popular speech incorrectly restricted to *monks, while 'convent' is used for a house of *nuns.

Money bag Symbol of *avarice (See *Judas Iscariot).

Monica, St A woman of saintly character (c.330-87), model of devout wife and mother, who devoted her life to her son, St *Augustine, following him to Rome and guiding him towards his conversion to Christianity, as he narrates in his *Confessions*. She died in Ostia on her way home to Africa, a few days after her son had been baptized by St *Ambrose. Her relics were translated to the church of Sant'Agostino, Rome, c.1420. She is revered by the *Augustinians and is depicted in the black or grey robe of a widow, or nun, usually alongside St Augustine.

Monk A member of a male religious community who has vowed himself to poverty, *chastity and *obedience.

Monkey A mischievous *animal, symbol of cunning and evil (See *ape).

Monograms, sacred Combinations of initial letters of words referring to *Christ. Latin capitals are: *IHS and *INRI; Greek, *A-O (or A- ω), AMO (or AM ω), *ICO ωC, *ICXC, IHC, *X, XC, X-P. God is symbolized by the Greek capitals ωC, the first and last letters of Θ EOC, *theos* 'God'. The letters of a monogram may be intertwined or combined with others in an intricate design. Some monograms may have a horizontal line over them to indicate that they are abbreviations. Monograms of St *Mary the Virgin are *M and *MDI.

Monstrance The vessel, also called *ostensorium, which is used to expose the *Host for veneration. It is of gold or silver, finely wrought, with rays radiating from a central circular glass panel through which the Host may be seen. A monstrance is the attribute of St *Clare who put Saracen mercenaries to flight when she appeared bearing this vessel.

Mordecai A devout Jew living in Shushan (Susa), capital of the Persian Empire, where he was an official in the court of King *Ahasuerus. His story is told in the *Book of Esther*. His cousin and adopted daughter, *Esther, under his guidance became queen and through her he was able to warn the king of a plot to assassinate him, a service which was recorded in the court annals. When Haman, the chief minister, ordered all persons to bow down before him, Mordecai refused, saying that this honour belonged only to God. Haman revenged himself by obtaining the king's permission to slaughter all the Jews and to hang Mordecai on the following day. That night, Ahasuerus was unable to sleep and had the court annals read to him. He realized that he had not rewarded Mordecai for saving his life. He consulted Haman, without naming the proposed recipient, as to the best way of rewarding one whom he wished to honour. Haman, thinking it was he who was to be fêted, proposed an elaborate ceremony. Esther, when she heard what was happening, arrayed herself in her jewels, dined with the king, and denounced Haman, who was thereupon hanged on the gallows which he had prepared for Mordecai. Mordecai was made next in rank to the king, Jews were allowed to carry arms in self-defence and, on the very day which Haman had appointed for their massacre, they turned on their enemies and slaughtered them. The expression, 'A Mordecai at your gate', meaning an importunate person, refers to Mordecai's persistence in walking every day before 'the court of the women's house' (Est 2 : 11), where Esther was living as a concubine, to obtain news of her.

Morse A metal or gold clasp (Latin *morsus*, 'buckle') used to fasten a *cope.

Moses The greatest figure of the OT, deliverer of the *Children of Israel whom he led out of captivity in Egypt (See *Exodus) and guided to the *Promised Land. He is depicted with horns on his forehead because of the confusion of the Hebrew words for 'rays of light' (which shone on his forehead) with the Latin *cornu*, 'horn', in the text *et ignorabat quod cornuta esset facies sua* (Vg Ex 34 : 29. AV:) 'Moses wist not that the skin of his face shone'.

At the time of his birth the descendants of the Children of Israel who had settled in Egypt in the days of *Joseph the Dreamer were enslaved. To end their line, *Pharaoh decreed that all male Hebrew babies should be drowned. His mother hid him in a basket in the reeds and *bulrushes by the Nile where he was found by Pharaoh's daughter who brought him up as her own, although unwittingly engaging his mother as nurse (See *Miriam). He was 'slow of speech', but his stammer, according to a Jewish legend, was due to his burning his tongue with a live coal when Pharaoh's ministers sought to have him put to death because one of them had dreamed that he would one day seize the crown. He was presented with two cups, one containing a ruby ring, to choose which meant death, and the other a live coal. An angel guided him to the right choice.

When he grew up, Moses' sympathies lay with his enslaved people. He killed an Egyptian overseer who was maltreating an Israelite, and fled into the desert where he married Zipporah, daughter of Jethro, 'priest of Midian' (Ex 2 : 11-22). For twenty years he lived as a shepherd, but God manifested himself in the *Burning Bush, and he returned to his kinsmen in Egypt (Ex 3-6). God sent Ten *Plagues on the Egyptians to enable Moses and his brother *Aaron to convince Pharaoh that he should free the Israelites. They escaped on the night of the *Passover, and when Pharaoh pursued them, he and his soldiers perished in the *Red Sea.

The Israelites spent forty years on their *Wanderings in the Wilderness. They were saved from starvation when *manna fell from *Heaven (Ex 16 : 12-15), and from thirst when Moses turned bitter water into sweet (Ex 15 : 23-5) and caused water to gush out from a *rock when he struck with his *wand (Ex 17 : 1-8). To ensure victory over the raiding Amalakites, he kept his arms extended all day (Ex 17 : 8-16), foretelling the *Crucifixion. He received the *Tablets of the Law from God on Mount Sinai, was angered when the Israelites in his absence worshipped the *Golden Calf, and he replaced it with the *Ark of the Covenant which was housed in the *Holy of Holies of the *Tabernacle. To save the Israelites from a plague of serpents, he held up a *Brazen Serpent and all who looked at it were cured.

When in sight of the Promised Land, Moses sent *Joshua to spy out the terrain. Terrified by the report which he brought back, the Israelites revolted against Moses and were condemned to spend more years in the Wilderness before finally settling in the Promised Land. Moses himself, because he had doubted the power of God to bring water out of the rock in the desert, was not permitted to enter it (Num 20 : 12), but was allowed sight of it from Mount Pisgah before he died (Deut 32 : 49). According to legend, to prevent the Israelites from worshipping Moses, God had him buried in a secret place. St *Michael with his sword warded off the *Devil who tried to steal the corpse.

Moses is the reputed author of the *Pentateuch, the five Books of Moses containing the *Law. He was granted the *Beatific Vision and was one of the *Just of the Ancient Law released by *Christ on his *Descent into Hell. He appeared with *Elijah alongside Jesus at the *Transfiguration.

Mother of God In Greek *Theotokos and in Latin *Mater Dei, the title given to St *Mary the Virgin at the Council of Ephesus (431).

Mothering Sunday The fourth Sunday of Lent (*Laetare Sunday), possibly named after the custom of visiting the *cathedral, the mother church of a *diocese, and of visiting one's mother on that day.

Mount of Olives A hill to the east of *Jerusalem and higher than the city, the 'mount called Olivet' (Ac 1 : 12) where the *Agony in the Garden and the *Betrayal and Arrest of Jesus took place. *Gethsemane stood at its foot. On the central ridge

The body of Christ, the host, was displayed in the window at the centre of the star of this gold **monstrance** (Peru, 17th century).

Michelangelo's statue of **Moses,** c.1513, for the tomb of Pope Julius III. He is horned because of a misunderstanding by the translators of the Hebrew for 'rays of light'.

is the church of the *Ascension, and nearby the rise called *Viri Galilaei*, 'Men of *Galilee', because of the tradition that it was there that the angel appeared to the *Apostles at the *Ascension and promised the *Second Coming with the words, 'Ye men of Galilee, why stand ye gazing up into heaven? This same Jesus, which is taken up from you into heaven, shall so come in like manner as ye have seen him go to heaven' (Ac 1 : 11).

Mouse A highly fertile *animal, symbol of female lasciviousness and of greed *(*Gula)* because of its appetite. It gnaws in the darkness, thus symbolizing the *Devil who secretly corrupts the human soul.

Mozetta An article of ecclesiastical *dress, a silk or wool cape, reaching to the elbows and buttoned in front, with a small hood attached, signifying jurisdiction or privilege, the *colour indicating status. The Pope's is *red (*white at *Easter); a *cardinal's red (*purple at *Lent); a *bishop's purple or black. *Dominicans, *Franciscans and *Trinitarians wear a *mozetta* as part of their *habit.

Mungo, St The name given in Scotland to St *Kentigern.

Mustard seed, the grain of Jesus likened the *Kingdom of Heaven to a grain of mustard seed, insignificant in size, but which grows into a great tree, with birds nesting in its branches (Mt 13 : 31-2; Mk 4 : 30-2; Lk 13 : 18-19).

Myrrh An aromatic gum of a species of balsam used in embalming. It was presented symbolically to the *Christ-Child when the three *Kings brought him gifts, as a prophecy of his death.

Myrtle Symbol of the people whom Jesus came to save, derived from an allegorical interpretation of a vision of *Zechariah in which he saw a man (Jesus) riding upon a red horse through a grove of myrtle trees (men of the world), 'and behind him were red horses, speckled and white' (Zech 1 : 8). These were the army of the saints and martyrs who would bear witness to the faith.

Mystery From the Greek *mysterion*, 'secret', used in two senses:
1 a divinely revealed truth which cannot be fully understood by the rational mind but which is not contrary to reason, e.g. the *Incarnation or the *Trinity.
2 'mystery of faith' (Latin *mysterium fidei*), the mystery of the Holy *Eucharist, the moment of *Transubstantiation at the consecration of the *bread and the *wine.

Mysteries of the rosary Fifteen events, each group of five being recalled in a chaplet of the *Rosary and frequently illustrated in art:
1 Joyful Mysteries: *Annunciation; *Visitation; *Nativity of Jesus; *Presentation of Jesus in the Temple; Finding of Jesus among the *Doctors
2 Sorrowful Mysteries: *Agony in the Garden;

*Scourging of Jesus; *Crown of Thorns; *Way of the Cross; *Crucifixion
3 Glorious Mysteries: *Resurrection; *Ascension; *Descent of the Holy Spirit; *Assumption and *Coronation of St Mary the Virgin.

Naboth's vineyard Naboth the Jezreelite owned a vineyard close by King *Ahab's palace. Ahab wanted it for a herb garden, but Naboth would not exchange it for a better one because God had forbidden him to give away the inheritance of his fathers. The refusal caused Ahab to take to his bed and refuse to eat. To cure him, Queen *Jezebel arranged that Naboth should be stoned to death, on false evidence, as a blasphemer. Thus Ahab acquired the vineyard on the pretence that it had belonged to a criminal. The prophet *Elijah was sent by God to tell Ahab that he would be slain in the very place where Naboth had been executed, and the dogs would lick his blood and eat his queen's body. 'Has thou found me, O mine enemy?' said Ahab in anguish (1 Kg 21 : 1-20).

Nahum One of the OT *prophets, whose fulminations against Nineveh are contained in the book, written around the mid-7th century BC, which bears his name. Nineveh is the 'bloody city, all full of lies and booty' (Nah 3 : 1), which God will destroy. It is like a pool whose waters are draining away (Nah 2 : 8); its fortresses will be shaken and fall like ripe figs into the mouth of the eater (Nah 3 : 12). He earned his place in the Christian tradition because he prophesied the advent of *Messiah: 'Behold upon the mountains the feet of him that bringeth good tidings, that publisheth peace!' (Nah 1 : 15).

Nails, Holy Nails which transfixed the body of *Jesus when he was nailed to the Cross and which were pulled out by *Nicodemus after the *Crucifixion. It is uncertain whether there were four (one through each limb) or three (one through each palm and one through the crossed feet). They were discovered by St *Helena, who, according to tradition, had one nail worked into a crown for Emperor *Constantine and another incorporated into a bridle for his horse. Holy nails were venerated as relics in the Middle Ages in more than thirty *churches, including the Sainte-Chapelle in Paris, where they were placed by St *Louis IX (1215-70) who has three nails as his *attribute. Three nails are also included among the *Instruments of the Passion.

Naming of Jesus In accordance with Mosaic *law, the *Circumcision of Jesus took place eight days after his birth. This meant that, in the old inclusive way of counting, if Jesus was born on 25 December (*See* *Christmas), commemoration of the ceremony would fall on 1 January, the day of outrageous pagan celebrations which disgusted the early Christians. The Church was therefore for long reluctant to institute a festival on that day, and the earliest mention of one is in the proceedings of the Second Council of Tours in 567. Thereafter, 1 January was kept as a feast day in Gaul and in Spain (in the Mozarabic *rite) but was not observed in Rome until the 11th century. This may account for the late appearance of the depiction of the circumcision in art.

At the time of circumcision, a Jewish male is given his name. The *Gospel of Luke* (Lk 2 : 21) stated that the child was to be called Jesus (the Greek equivalent of the Hebrew 'Joshua' or 'Yeshua', meaning 'the Lord is Salvation') in obedience to the command 'given by the angel before he was conceived in the womb' (*See* *Annunciation). The day of the naming of Jesus (as the equivalent of Christian baptism) was therefore given special emphasis by the *Jesuits as signifying also the naming of their Order. A painting of the circumcision was placed above the high altar of their church of the Gesù in Rome, a custom followed by many Jesuit churches and the cause of the increase in the number of representations of the event from the 17th to the mid-18th century when Jesuits were expelled from many countries.

In recent times, possibly because of the unpleasantness of the subject, emphasis has been more on its baptismal significance and its place in the cult of St *Mary the Virgin. In 1960, 1 January was styled the 'Octave of Christmas', and in the 1969 *Roman Catholic Calendar it is called *Solemnitas S. Dei Genetricis Mariae*, 'Solemnity of Holy Mary, the Mother of God'. In the *Anglican calendar it is the Feast of the Naming of Jesus.

Naming of living things According to the second account of the *Creation of the world (Gen 2 : 19-20), God brought all the birds, cattle and wild beasts to the first man (*Adam), so that he might give each a name.

Nathanael, St One of the twelve *Apostles, 'an Israelite indeed, in whom there is no guile' (Jn 1 : 47), equated with St *Bartholomew because it is assumed that 'Nathanael' was his first name, and 'Bartholomew' – meaning 'son of Tolmai' – his patronymic. He lived in Cana, a devout Jew who looked forward to the coming of *Messiah. Returning from his *Baptism in the River Jordan, Jesus saw Nathanael sitting under a fig tree where he had gone to pray. He enlisted him as one of the first of his band of disciples, promising him that he would 'see heaven open, and the angels of God ascending and descending on the Son of man' (Jn 1 : 51). After the *Resurrection, Jesus appeared to Nathanael and six others by the Sea of *Galilee when they made the miraculous *Draught of fishes (Jn 21 : 5-14).

Nativity of Jesus A tradition recorded in the apocryphal *Book of *James* states that Jesus was born in a cave. St *Joseph, in compliance with Caesar Augustus' decree that all the inhabitants of Judaea should be enrolled for taxation purposes, set out for *Bethlehem, the pregnant St *Mary the Virgin seated on his ass, one of his sons by his first

IHS, the monogram representing the name of Jesus, received at his **Naming,** adopted by the Jesuits because they work for the glory of his name (title-page of a centenary volume of the Society, 1640).

St Mary the Virgin genuflects in obedience to God's command and the Christ-Child appears in a blaze of light (German 15th-century **Nativity**).

marriage leading, Joseph and his other son following behind. In a desert place, half way to the city, Mary knew that her time to give birth was near. Joseph found a cave and there the child was born (*See* *Salome, the midwife*).

The other tradition, elaborated from the statement in the *Gospel of Luke* (Lk 2 : 7) that since there was 'no room for them in the inn' at Bethlehem Mary laid her son 'in a manger', held that the birth took place in a stable, or shelter, alongside the inn. The shelter is often shown in ruins, symbolizing the ending of the old Jewish *Law, or, if classical ruins, of the pagan world.

These two accounts are harmonized in the *Gospel of the *Pseudo-Matthew (*See* *Infancy gospels) in which the child is born in a cave and taken by Mary on the third day to a stable where he is laid in a *manger. This Gospel is the first to mention the *ox and the ass as kneeling to worship the child in fulfilment of the Messianic prophecies: 'The ox knows his owner and the ass his master's crib' (Is 1 : 13), and in the *Septuagint, 'Between two beasts are you known' (Hab 3 : 2). The ass was said to have been the one on which Mary rode to Bethlehem from her home in *Nazareth.

As to the manner of the birth of the Christ-Child, there are three versions. The oldest shows the Virgin resting on a bed or pallet, in accordance with the ancient belief that she suffered in the normal way of women. This tradition persists in the *Orthodox Church, but was replaced in the *West after the end of the 14th century by the account given in the *Revelations* of St *Bridget of Sweden. The Virgin knelt to pray (or genuflected) and the child appeared in a blaze of light. This is the source of the depiction of the Christ-Child portrayed as lying on the ground with Mary kneeling in adoration.

The third version is derived from the *Meditations on the Life of Christ* of the Pseudo-Bonaventura. Joseph and Mary were in a stable when she felt the birth pangs. Mary leaned against a pillar, Joseph spread hay at her feet and the child appeared in a blaze of light on the floor (*See* *lady's bedstraw*).

Nativity of St Mary the Virgin A frequent genre scene in art, based on the account given in the apocryphal *Book of *James and popularized in the *Golden Legend*, of the birth of Mary. St *Anne, her mother, is shown sitting up in bed being washed or being given soup or gruel by a servant; midwives bathe the new-born child; the father St *Joachim stands nearby in wonderment; and neighbours bring gifts. *Angels may be seen descending from *Heaven to greet the baby. The event is commemorated on 8 September, a *feast day which may have originated in the Greek *Orthodox Church soon after the Council of Ephesus, 431, when Mary was declared *Mother of God. It was mentioned in a hymn, by St Romanus (536-56).

Nave The central portion of a *church, set aside for the congregation, lying west of the chancel or choir and often separated from it by a screen of wood or stone. The word is derived from the Latin *navis*, 'a ship', because the Church was compared to a ship in which the faithful would be saved.

Nazareth A town in Galilee in a hollow between the hills of northern Israel, where St *Mary the Virgin lived and to which the *Holy Family returned after their sojourn in Egypt. There Jesus spent the first thirty years of his life before his *Baptism in the River Jordan. The present church of the Annunciation was built in the 1960s on the traditional site of Mary's home, where Emperor *Constantine had erected the first *basilica.

Nebuchadnezzar King of Babylon (605-562 BC) who destroyed Jerusalem and carried off most of the inhabitants. *Daniel was one of the Hebrew captives, who rose to power in his kingdom through interpreting the king's dream of the golden image with feet of clay (Dan 2 : 32-3). Three other Hebrews, *Shadrach, *Meshach and *Abednego refused to worship the golden image and survived the ordeal of the *Fiery Furnace (Dan 3 : 19-30). Nebuchadnezzar paid no attention to Daniel's interpretation of his dream of a tree cut down to its stump, meaning that he would be humbled if he did not repent. A year later, when the king was boasting of his power, he went mad. As Daniel had foretold, 'he was driven from men, and did eat grass as oxen' (Dan 4 : 33). The terraced roof gardens, the Hanging Gardens of Babylon on the top of Nebuchadnezzar's palace, were one of the seven wonders of the ancient world.

Nero Roman emperor (54-68), loathed for his brutality and his *persecution of Christians whom he blamed for the destruction of Rome by fire in 64. Outlawed after he had failed to quell revolts in the provinces, he committed suicide. It was believed that he would return from the dead (hence his title, 'Nero Redivivus') to herald the end of the world. He was thought to be the *Beast of the Apocalypse because the Hebrew letters of 'Neron', if given numerical value, add up to 666. According to tradition, he had a vision in which he was scourged by St *Peter. This caused him to cease persecuting Christians.

Nicene Creed The creed recited at *Mass or *Eucharist which came into use after the Council of Constantinople (381), replacing the earlier creed issued in 325 by the Council of Nicaea, hence its (not strictly correct) name. It is a more elaborate statement of faith than the *Apostles' Creed and defines the 'procession' of the *Holy Spirit as from the Father 'and the Son', the so-called *filioque* clause (*See* *Trinity) which is not accepted in the *East.

Nicholas of Myra (or Bari), St A saint whose existence is doubtful, although he is said to have been present at the First Council of Nicaea (325) and to have been bishop of Myra, Asia Minor. The child of wealthy parents, he revealed his saintly destiny when he stood up and praised God the moment he was born. He also refused his mother's breast every Friday and *fast day. When he inherited his father's fortune, he gave his money away to the poor. His most celebrated act of generosity was when he heard an impoverished gentleman lamenting that his three daughters would have to become prostitutes because he could not support them honourably. On three successive nights he threw through their window a bag of gold (or a golden ball) for their dowries so that each might find a husband. When St Nicholas became the patron saint of pawnbrokers, three golden balls (his *attribute) were adopted as their insignia and displayed outside their shops. His *feast day, on 6 December, within the *Christmas season, led to his being confused with another generous person, a character of folklore who rewarded good children by bringing them gifts secretly in the night. He is thus the archetypal Father Christmas, or Santa Claus (a 19th-century North American invention).

St Nicholas is the patron saint of children and choirboys, because during a famine he discovered that a certain innkeeper had stolen little children, killed them and salted them in a tub with the intention of serving them up as meat for his guests. He made the *sign of the cross over the tub and three children stood up, restored to life and health. (This legend may have arisen through confusion with another miracle when St Nicholas appeared in a dream to Emperor *Constantine and per-suaded him to release three innocent princes from prison.) He brought back to life the child of his landlady at Myra, who had fallen into the fire and had been burned to ashes while his mother was attending Nicholas' consecration as *bishop. He relieved a famine in his diocese by inducing the captains of some Alexandrian ships to unload their grain, promising that when they reached Constan-tinople they would find that their holds had been miraculously replenished. He also resurrected a man who had been unjustly hanged.

One of St Nicholas' attributes is an *anchor, because he was adopted as the patron saint of sailors when he answered the prayers of some mariners lost in a storm, joining them in their sinking ship and bringing them safely to land. Many harbour *churches are therefore dedicated to him. His association with the sea is commemo-rated annually at Bari, Italy, where part of his relics were transferred from Myra in 1087. His image is taken out in a boat on his feast day and brought back to his church at night, escorted by a torchlight procession. His relics exude a curative and sweet-smelling oil, the *Manna di San Nicola*, and he is therefore also the patron of perfumers.

Nicholas of Tolentino, St An *Augustinian friar who lived an austere and pure life (hence shown holding a *crucifix entwined with lilies). He was named after St *Nicholas of Myra because his parents had prayed to him that they might have a son. At his birth, *c.*1246, a star appeared and is shown on his breast. He holds a girdle because he rescues souls from *Purgatory and he is also invoked against plague. A partridge recalls the

Nebuchadnezzar, humbled and an exile from men, eats grass because he failed to heed the allegorical meaning of his dream about an angel cutting down a tree to its stump (Spanish, Alba Bible, 15th century).

St **Nicholas of Bari** restores to life a dead man and three murdered children (Dieric Bouts, *c.*1415-75).

story how, when he became ill through fasting, his superior sent him a roasted bird (or two pigeons, according to another version). Unwilling to break his fast, Nicholas made the *sign of the cross over the dish and the bird flew away. The Virgin appeared to him to say that her house had been translated from Nazareth to *Loreto. After his death, in 1306, a German friar cut off the saint's arms as *relics to take back to his country, but after walking all night he found that he was still in the same place. The arms are now restored to his body (which rests in the Madonna Chapel of the Cathedral of San Nichola in Tolentino) and are said to bleed whenever danger or misfortune threaten the city. He was canonized in 1446.

Nicodemus A *Pharisee and a 'ruler of the Jews' – meaning a member of the *Sanhedrin – who perceived that Jesus was a 'teacher come from God' and wished to know more about him. Unwilling to compromise himself, he sought out Jesus secretly by night and questioned him. During their conversation Jesus predicted his *Crucifixion, saying: 'As Moses lifted up the serpent in the wilderness, so must the son of man be lifted up'. He also puzzled Nicodemus by saying that unless a man were born again of water and the spirit, he could not enter the *Kingdom of Heaven. 'The wind bloweth where it listeth' and 'so is everyone that is born of the Spirit' (Jn 3 : 1-15).

After the arrest of Jesus, Nicodemus defended him before the Sanhedrin, protesting that it was not right to try a man in his absence (Jn 7 : 50-2). When Jesus expired on the Cross, Nicodemus assisted *Joseph of Arimathea to take down the body (See *Descent from the Cross), traditionally pulling out the Holy *Nails – which is why he was thought to have been a blacksmith. In scenes of the *Lamentation over the dead Christ and of the *Deposition or laying in the tomb, he is shown at the feet of the body, near St *Mary Magdalene, having brought spices to be placed in the shroud (Jn 19 : 40). Nicodemus is also said to have been a sculptor and to have carved in a vision (or Christ carved it for him while he slept) the *Volto Santo, the *crucifix venerated at Lucca, Italy. It is said that some merchants brought his remains to Pisa in the 12th century and that they repose in the *cathedral of that city.

Nimbus From the Latin for 'cloud', the technical name for *halo, light surrounding the head of a holy figure, or of persons who are renowned for their great piety. The light or rays of light may be enclosed in a circle, as in portrayals of St *Mary the Virgin; a *triangle, especially for the three persons of the *Trinity; or a square, for saints, donors, less exalted but devout men and women, and living people. One of the sacred *monograms may be combined with the nimbus around *Christ. Stars are sometimes inset in the nimbus of the Virgin. Each of the four *Evangelists, or their symbolic figures, has a nimbus.

Nimrod (Nemrod) A descendant of *Noah; a

giant and 'a mighty hunter before the Lord' (Gen 10 : 9) because, according to legend, he wore the skins which God had made for Adam after his *Expulsion from Paradise and which had been preserved in Noah's *Ark. At the sight of these skins, all beasts surrendered to him. The root of his name was thought to be Hebrew *marad*, 'he revolted', and he was therefore thought to have instigated the building of the Tower of *Babel.

Nine A symbolic *number, representing the nine choirs of *angels, and the nine fruits of the Holy Spirit, 'love, joy, peace, long-suffering, gentleness, goodness, faith, meekness, temperance' (Gal 5 : 22-3).

Noah (Noe) Son of *Lamech. A righteous man who 'walked with God' and was 'perfect in his generations' (Gen 6 : 9), that is, far better than his fellow-men whom God decided to punish for their wickedness by drowning them in the *Flood. He and his sons, *Shem, *Ham and *Japheth, with their wives, and accompanied by two of each kind of living thing were saved in the *Ark which God ordered him to build. When the flood abated and the family and beasts came out of the Ark, Noah built an altar and made a sacrifice to God. A covenant was concluded between them, and God placed a *rainbow in the sky as a perpetual reminder of his promise (Gen 9 : 9-17). Noah planted a vineyard (Gen 9 : 20), but got drunk and lay naked in his tent (See *Drunkenness of Noah), to the discomfiture of his sons.

Nocturns From the Latin *nocturnus*, 'by night', originally the night Office, now a part of Matins (See *Hours).

Noli me tangere Latin for 'touch me not', the words spoken by the risen *Christ to St *Mary Magdalene as she stood weeping by the *empty tomb. She mistook him for the gardener (he is represented in this guise, carrying a spade or a hoe) and asked what had happened to the body of her Lord. When Jesus called her name, she recognized him and exclaimed, 'Rabboni; which is to say, Master'. He told her, 'Touch me not; for I am not yet ascended to my Father' and ordered her to tell the disciples that he would meet them in the city (Jn 20 : 11-18).

None From the Latin *nona*, 'nine', the office of the ninth hour in Roman counting (about 3 pm) (See *Hours).

Norbert, St A frivolous nobleman (c.1080-1134) of Xanten on the lower Rhine, who was converted when a ball of fire fell at his horse's feet. He became a missionary, attracted many followers, and St *Mary the Virgin appeared c.1120 in a vision in the Forest of Courcy and indicated a meadow (*pré montré*, 'the meadow pointed out', according to popular etymology) where he was to found the community which eventually became the *Premonstratensian Order. The Virgin told

Norbert that their habit was to be a black tunic with a white cloak and a *biretta. He was made archbishop of Magdeburg in 1126. A *chalice with a spider in it alludes to the story that, when celebrating *Mass, he swallowed a poisonous spider along with the consecrated wine but survived unharmed.

Novena In the *Roman Catholic Church, nine days of special devotion, either public or private. It derives its name from the nine days which the *Apostles spent in prayer between the *Ascension and *Pentecost.

Novice A person who, having been admitted into a religious *Order and having passed successfully his period of probation as a *postulant, is undergoing a further trial (his novitiate).

Numbers, mystical At least from the time of the *Fathers of the Church, numbers occurring in the *Scriptures were particularly attributed with mystical significance. Three represents the *Trinity, the thrice-holy God and the eternal God, past, present and future. Four is the material created world. Seven (3 + 4) is the union of God and mankind. For the same reason the seventh day (the *Sabbath), the seventh year and the forty-ninth year (7 × 7) are holy. Eight denotes completion. Twelve (3 × 4) represents God's chosen people, gathered from the four quarters of the earth by the Trinity. Much ingenuity was devoted to discovering the symbolism of each cardinal number, especially the prime numbers (*See* *Five, *Four, *Nine, *One, *Seven, *Six, *Ten).

Nun A female member of a religious *Order who takes either simple or solemn *vows and devotes herself either to contemplation or to personal perfection and works of charity or education. Nuns who restrict themselves to simple vows are called 'sisters'. All wear *habits appropriate to their Order.

Nunc dimittis The Latin opening words in the Vg version, *Nunc dimittis servum tuum Domine*, of the song of *Simeon, 'now lettest thou thy servant depart in peace, for mine eyes have seen thy salvation' (Lk 2 : 29-32), when he beheld the *Christ-Child at the *Presentation in the Temple. It is sung in the Roman *rite on 2 February, *Candlemas, and at *Compline; in the *Eastern rite at *Vespers; and in accordance with the Anglican *Book of Common Prayer* at *Evensong. The words, 'and a sword shall pierce her heart', were understood to refer to the *Sorrows of the Virgin.

Nuncio From the Latin *nuntius*, 'messenger', the representative of the *Pope at the seat of a foreign government who acts in the same way as an ambassador or accredited minister in matters arising between that government and the Holy Apostolic *See of Rome. He is by courtesy dean of the diplomatic corps.

Noah stands in a box in this detail from a late-3rd-century sarcophagus because it recalls the sacred chest (Latin *arca*), the Ark of the Covenant, symbol of the presence of God and salvation. A dove brings him an olive-branch.

St Mary Magdalene mistook the risen Christ for a gardener as she wept by the empty tomb. He forbade her to touch him, saying, **Noli me tangere** (Albrecht Dürer, 1471-1528).

Oak Symbol of endurance and strength. Some authorities held that it was the wood from which the *Cross was made.

Obadiah (Abdias) One of the Hebrew *prophets. His book, a single chapter of twenty-one verses, is the shortest in the OT. He looked forward to the day when the people of Israel would be restored to their rightful homeland and 'the Kingdom shall be the Lord's' (Ob 1 : 21). In the Middle Ages he was confused with the 9th-century-BC pious head of King Ahab's household who hid in a cave a hundred priests of God whom *Jezebel sought to kill (1 Kg 18 : 4). He fed them on bread and water, so his attributes are a pitcher and a loaf.

Obedience One of the three monastic *vows, the others being poverty and chastity. It is symbolized by a kneeling *camel, an ass patiently moving a millstone, and a *yoke recalling Jesus' words, 'Take my yoke upon you, and learn of me; for I am meek and lowly in heart' (Mt 11 : 29).

Oblate A layman who offers himself (Latin *oblatus*, 'offered') as an associate of a religious *Order, undertaking to follow its rule as far as possible, although living outside the monastery. Until the practice was condemned by Pope Innocent III (1198-1216), parents in medieval times 'offered' their children as oblates, binding them to a monastic life, whether or not they had experienced a vocation.

Observants *Franciscans who followed the primitive and more austere *Rule of St Francis in respect to poverty, in contrast to the *Conventuals who held property in common. In 1897, by a *bull of Pope Leo XIII (1878-1903), they were united with their offshoots, the *Recollects and others, as *Friars Minor.

Octave A period of eight days (Latin *octavus*, 'eighth') consisting of certain special feast days (*Christmas, *Easter, *Pentecost) and the seven days following, on each of which the feast day is commemorated.

Odilia (Ottilia), St A royal *abbess (dressed in *Benedictine habit trimmed with ermine) *d.c.*720, patroness of Alsace and Strasbourg. The daughter of Duke Adalric of Alsace, who tried to dispose of her because she was born blind. She was rescued by her faithful nurse and carried off to the convent of Baûme-les-Dames, near Besançon. Bishop Erhard of Bavaria, having been warned in a vision to go to her aid, sought her out, baptized her and she immediately recovered her sight (she is depicted with her two eyes on a platter or a book). She was reconciled to her father, who left her all his wealth when he died (she is shown at her death bed). With this money she founded two convents, Höhenburg (modern Odilenburg, a place of pilgrimage) in the hills, and Niedermünster in the

valley. (These two foundations are shown with her.) Through her prayers, she released her father's soul from *Purgatory.

Odium theologicum The Latin for 'theological hatred', the bitterness engendered between proponents of contrasting theologies.

Office of St Mary the Virgin, Little The association of the canonical *Hours with events in the life of St *Mary the Virgin. The usual scheme, as illustrated in a *Book of Hours is:

*Matins	*Annunciation
*Lauds	*Visitation
*Prime	*Nativity
*Tierce	Annunciation to the *Shepherds
*None	*Presentation of Jesus in the Temple
*Vespers	*Flight into Egypt
*Compline	*Assumption, or *Coronation

Ointment, jar of The *attribute of St *Mary Magdalene, who anointed the feet of *Jesus with a pound of ointment of spikenard (Jn 12 : 3) and later went to the *Holy Sepulchre to anoint his body (Mk 16 : 1). A jar or box of ointment is also associated with the doctor saints *Cosmas and Damian with the Archangel *Raphael who cured *Tobit's blindness.

Olive branch Symbol of peace. It recalls the olive branch brought back by the dove to *Noah in the Ark, which signified that the waters which covered the earth were receding and that God's anger against mankind had abated. Carried in the hand of the Archangel *Gabriel, it indicates that he bears the message announcing the coming of *Christ, the Prince of Peace. The popular phrase 'to show the olive branch' is derived from the ancient custom of displaying an olive branch when an army was seeking a truce.

Omega The last letter of the *Greek alphabet, written Ω, and thus symbolizing 'the end' (*See* *Alpha and Omega).

Omicron A letter of the *Greek alphabet, written O and symbolizing the *Trinity, because, like a *circle, it is a unity.

Omobuono (Homobonus), St A wealthy merchant of Cremona, Italy, of which city he is the patron saint, renowned for his charity. He was prophetically baptized Uomobuono, 'good man'. Although his wife feared that his generosity to the poor would impoverish his family, the more he gave away, the more prosperous he became. On a journey, he once distributed all his provisions, including his bread and wine, among some poor *pilgrims. His bags were replenished with bread by *angels and when he took his wine flasks (his *attribute) to a spring to refill them, the water turned into wine. He died (1197) in the church of St Egidius as he knelt before a *crucifix while the choir was singing the *Gloria in Excelsis*, and was canonized by Pope Innocent III (1198-1216) in 1199. He is depicted in a merchant's tunic, wearing a fur-trimmed cap and distributing *alms to the poor.

Onan Grandson of *Jacob and son of Judah. When compelled to fulfil his duty under the *Law and marry his deceased brother's widow in order to raise up children to his brother, 'he spilled it [his seed] on the ground'. As he had frustrated the purpose of the Law, 'God slew him because he did a detestable thing' (Gen 38 : 8-10). Although Onan's act was *coitus interruptus*, onanism also became a synonym for masturbation and was extended to the condemnation of any form of birth control which frustrated procreation, the divine purpose of matrimony.

Onuphrius, St A 4th-century *hermit, said to have been a prince, who left his native Thebes, in Egypt, to spend sixty years in the desert without seeing another human or uttering a word except in prayer. He dressed in leaves, his hair grew long and his beard remained uncut. He overcame many temptations and was ministered to by a raven which carried food to him, and by *angels who brought him Holy *Communion each Sunday. At the end of his life, the saintly Bishop Paphnutius of Upper Thebes arrived to comfort him, and found him crawling on his knees like a beast. When Onuphrius died, Paphnutius covered him with his cloak and two lions came out of the desert to dig his grave.

Opus Dei Latin for 'the work of God', the *Benedictine name for the *Divine Office, the seven monastic *Hours, because prayer is the work which the religious offer to God.

Orange tree Because of its white flowers, the orange tree (or orange branch) symbolizes purity, and the chastity of St *Mary the Virgin.

Orans A female figure praying (Latin *orare* 'to pray') standing up with arms outstretched, found depicted on the walls of catacombs. It is assumed to represent the soul of the departed Christian interceding in *Heaven for those left behind on earth.

Oratorio A musical composition for solo voices, chorus and orchestra or organ, the words set to music being derived from passages of *Scripture. The form was said to have originated among the community of the *Oratory of St Philip Neri in Rome at the end of the 16th century.

Oratory A 'place of prayer' (Latin *oratorium*) which is not a *parish church, where prayer and the celebration of *Mass is permitted. It may be in a private house, an institution or a religious community.

Oratory of St Philip Neri The Order of Oratorians, communities of secular priests, founded by St *Philip Neri in Rome in 1575, and promoted by Gregory XIII (1572-85), for prayer, preaching and the administration of the *Sacraments. Their rule

The Soul of a departed Christian, **orans,** with arms outstretched, the usual attitude for prayer in the Early Church. The figure is in female garb possible because the Latin for 'soul', *anima,* is a feminine noun. (Romano-British villa at Lullingstone, Kent.)

A priest of the Order of the **Oratory of St Philip Neri** (17th century).

was approved in 1612 by Paul V. Their name probably derives from their first place of meeting, the *oratory of the church of St Girolamo in Rome. Their purpose was to spread the ideals of the Catholic reformation (*See* *Counter Reformation) and to encourage a deeper spiritual life among the laity. One of their chosen means to this end was sacred musical drama, the *oratorio, which would attract the public to church. The first of these, the *Disputa della Anima e Corpo* ('Debate between the Soul and the Body'), was set to music by Emilio de Cavaglieri and performed in the church of Santa Maria in Vallicella in 1600. The Oratory was introduced into England in 1847 by Cardinal (then Dr) Newman who, following his conversion to *Roman Catholicism (*See* *Oxford Movement), had been impressed by what he saw of the work of the Order in Rome.

Orb A globe surmounted by a cross, held in the hand to symbolize sovereignty and power. It is carried by Christian monarchs at their coronation and by the *Christ-Child when seated on his mother's lap, or by Christ as *Pantocrator, ruler of the world. A cross is placed on top of the globe to demonstrate Christ's supremacy over temporal things.

Ordeal by water When the priests of the *Temple, where St *Mary the Virgin had spent her girlhood, heard that she was pregnant, they assumed that St *Joseph had had relations with her while she was still in their charge and had thus violated the sanctity of the Temple. According to the *Book of *James*, to prove their innocence, Joseph and Mary had to drink bitter (or purgative) water administered by the High Priest, who is sometimes identified as *Zacharias. They were then sent to the mountains, and when they returned without having become ill, they were acquitted of fornication. In the *Gospel of the *pseudo-Matthew* the accused couple had to prove their innocence by walking seven times around the altar in the Temple without becoming ill.

Order, religious The name was first applied in the early 12th century to a religious society of *canons regular, *monks, *friars or *nuns, based in a *monastery, *convent or *friary. The members of the society take solemn *vows after a probationary period as *postulants, are distinguishable by their *habit, swear obedience to their *superior (*See* *abbot, *abbess) and follow the *rule of their Order. A majority of male members of religious Orders may be *priests in *Holy Orders, although some may be *lay brothers.

The earliest *Western religious societies – later defined by *canon law as Orders – were the *Benedictines, founded by St *Benedict of Nursia at Monte Cassino, Italy, c.529. His sister, St *Scholastica, established a similar community for women, Benedictine nuns. The most famous early-medieval Benedictine monastery was the abbey of Cluny (909), imitated by many *Cluniac congregations in fostering the arts. Other Benedictines became independent Orders, the chief patrons of the arts being the *Camaldolese (1009), *Vallombrosians (1039) and Cistercians (1098). A Cistercian reform produced the *Trappists (1664).

In the 12th and 13th centuries, religious enthusiasm engendered by the Crusades, by the *Catharist heresy, and by the desire to serve mankind, inspired more *Orders. *Premonstratensians (1120) devoted themselves to penance and saving souls. *Carmelites (claiming Elijah as their founder), *Trinitarians, *Mercedarians (1218), who ransomed Christian captives of the Moors in North Africa, *Servites (1233), a *mendicant Order, and *Brigittines (1233), for monks and nuns, soon appeared.

Possibly the greatest 12th-century foundations were the *Dominicans (1205-16) and the *Franciscans (1207-09), the latter dividing on the questions of property and austerity in 1415 into *Conventuals and *Observants (from which the *Recollects seceded), the *Minims in 1435 and the *Capuchins in 1625.

Protestantism inspired reform within the Roman Catholic Church. Traditional catholicism was defended by new Orders, notably *Theatines (1524), *Jesuits (1514) and *Visitandines (1610). *Oratorians (1575) were strictly a congregation and not an order.

Ordinary, the A diocesan *bishop, so called because he is the successor of the *Apostles *de jure ordinario*, 'by common [or ordinary] right'.

Ordination The conferring of *Holy Orders by the imposition of a *bishop's hands; one of the Seven *Sacraments.

Organ The *attribute of St *Cecilia, patroness of music, thought to be her invention.

Original sin The consequences of the first or 'original' sin of disobedience to God's command not to eat of the fruit of the *Tree of Knowledge, committed by *Adam. The result was that he lost for himself and his descendants his supernatural state, and condemned mankind to concupiscence and death. Nevertheless, the redemption of the human race through the sacrifice of Christ is implicit in the divine plan. It was argued by some Church fathers, and by medieval schoolmen, that this inheritance of guilt was transmitted through the sexual act, which they thus condemned.

Orpheus In Classical mythology a poet who drew wild beasts to him when he played on his lyre. In the art of the *catacombs he stands for *Christ who draws all men to him.

Orthodox Church A family of self-governing and autonomous Churches, conveniently if somewhat incorrectly termed the *East in the present work, because apart from the ancient Patriarchates of Jerusalem, Antioch and Alexandria, the Greek-speaking Patriarchate of Constantinople was the most influential in the Middle Ages in the *West. In 863, SS Cyril and Methodius began the conversion of the Slavs, with the result that the lands of

Russia became equally important, with Moscow as the new Constantinople (Byzantium).

By calling themselves 'Orthodox', the members of these Churches proclaim that they hold the right belief in *Christ and practise the right worship of him. They acknowledge the *Seven Sacraments; lay great stress on the spiritual life; the veneration of images (See *icon, *iconostasis); and believe in the *Assumption of St Mary the Virgin, although they do not accept the dogma of the *Immaculate Conception. Clerical celibacy is not held to be necessary but a *bishop must be celibate. Monasteries, particularly those on Mount Athos and Sinai, have exerted great influence both spiritually and theologically (See *Schism).

Orthodoxy Right belief (Greek *orthodoxia*), acceptance of the doctrines of the one true Church as founded by *Christ.

Osee The Vg name of the prophet *Hosea.

Ostensorium (Ostensory) An ornamented vessel of gold or silver with a transparent centre in which the *Host is placed to be exposed, or 'shown' (Latin *ostensum*, 'shown') for adoration or for carrying in processions; otherwise called a *monstrance. It is an *attribute of St *Thomas Aquinas, who composed the office of the *Exposition of the Holy Sacrament, and of St *Clare of Assisi who put Saracen mercenaries to flight by displaying the Host in an ostensorium.

Ostrich The text, 'the ostrich . . . which leaveth her eggs in the earth, and warmeth them in the dust' (Jb 39 : 13-14) provided the moral lesson that worldly concerns should be abandoned, like the ostrich looking up to *Heaven.

Otter Usually a symbol of the *Devil, but also of the *Resurrection of *Christ when identified with the *hydrus, a small fish which would cover itself with mud and thus escape alive from the *crocodile's belly, in the same way as Christ came out safely from the nether regions after his *Descent to Hell.

Our Father The opening words (in Latin *Pater noster*) of the *Lord's Prayer (Mt 6 : 9-13), taught by Jesus, and since apostolic times the prayer said by all Christians and given unique status in the liturgy. In the *Roman Catholic tradition, it ends with 'but deliver us from evil'. *Protestants may add, 'For thine is the kingdom, the power and the glory', which some take to be an interpolation.

Our Lady Since at least the 8th century, when it was used by Cynewulf, the first English poet, the most usual way of referring to St *Mary the Virgin.

Owl A nocturnal bird, thought to be blind and thus to represent the *Jews on the basis of the text, 'darkness hath blinded his eyes' (1 Jn 2 : 11), because they did not accept *Christ as their *Messiah and 'to turn . . . from darkness to light' (Ac 26 : 18). When present in scenes of the

The Abbey of Cluny before its destruction during the French Revolution. This Benedictine monastery was where the Cluniacs originated, one of the most influential medieval religious **Orders.** (An 18th-century view of the church from the east.)

Orpheus with his lyre charming the beasts, and Hercules, who accomplished many symbolic tasks: two pagan heroes adopted as types of Christ (late-4th-century ivory pyxis).

*Crucifixion, an owl emphasizes the fact that Christ came 'to give light to them that sit in the darkness and in the shadow of death' (Lk 1 : 79). Because it chose the night for its activities, the owl also symbolized those who 'loved darkness [*sin] rather than light' (Jn 3 : 19). As the owl was used as a decoy to trap birds for the hunter, it also stood for the *Devil who ensnares souls.

Ox A sacrificial *animal. When winged it represents St *Luke, whose *Gospel emphasizes the sacrifice of Christ (*See* *Tetramorphs). Its presence together with an *ass near the manger in *Nativity scenes is first mentioned in the 8th- or 9th-century *Gospel of the* *pseudo-Matthew, and is intended to show that the child was the expected *Messiah, proved by the texts: 'The ox knoweth his owner, and the ass his master's crib' (Is 1 : 3); and 'Between two beasts are you known' (Hab 3 : 2 in the *Septuagint version). These two animals were said to have accompanied the Holy Family on the *Flight into Egypt, Mary riding on the ass, and the ox being led by Joseph's sons from a former marriage. The ox is also an attribute of St *Thomas Aquinas, who as a boy was called 'dumb ox' by his companions, and of St *Sylvester who brought an ox (or bull) back to life by making the *sign of the cross.

Oxford movement The movement in the *Church of England to reassert the *Catholic tradition. It dates from 14 July 1833, when John Keeble (1792-1866) preached the controversial Assize Sermon before the University in the Church of St Mary the Virgin, Oxford. The principles were set out in the series *Tracts for the Times* (1833-41), hence the name Tractarians for Keeble's associates, among whom were J. H. Newmán (1801-90), later, after his conversion to Rome in 1845, Cardinal Newman. Another collaborator was E. B. Pusey (1830-80) whose followers were called 'Puseyites'. Their ardent advocacy of *High Church principles, emphasis on the *Eucharist and on ceremonial, brought new life into the Anglican community, attracting not only intellectuals but many from the poorer quarters of the great cities.

Pachomius, St Born in Memphis, Egypt (*c*.292), a pagan, he was converted to Christianity while serving as a conscript in the army. A disciple of St *Antony of Egypt (the Great), he spent some time as a *hermit. He then assembled a community of *monks at Tabennisi, an island in the Nile, who elected to follow the coenobitical way, or 'common life', instead of the solitary eremitical life which was then practised in the Theban desert. Before his death (*c*.346), Pachomius had drawn up a *Rule and established an *Order which lasted until the 11th century. His sister presided over the first nunnery of the Order. Pachomius is depicted as an *abbot, or as a hermit dressed in palm leaves.

He is shown crossing the Nile on a crocodile, a feat attributed to him in a pious account of his life, and being told by an angel to found his first monastery.

Pall From the Latin *palla corporalis*, 'a cloth for the body [of Christ]', recalling the *Holy Shroud in which his corpse was wrapped in the tomb. It is made of several layers of linen, or of a square piece of cardboard covered with linen, which should be white, although other liturgical *colours are sometimes to be seen. (The Baroque practice of using embroidered silk is now discouraged.) A pall is placed over a *chalice at the *Eucharist. A cloth beneath a chalice is called a *corporal.

By extension, a pall is a black or violet cloth spread over a *catafalque or coffin.

Pallium A narrow circular white band embroidered with six black crosses, worn on the shoulders, with two twelve-inch weighted pendants, one hanging down over the breast, the other over the back. It is made in Rome by the nuns of the Torre de' Specchi from the wool of two lambs which are blessed while the *Agnus Dei is being sung on St *Agnes' Day (21 January) in the church of Santa Agnese fuori le mura ('St Agnes without the walls'), which is dedicated to her. Finished bands are placed for a night on the tomb of St *Peter in the Vatican and retained there in a niche. A symbol of authority derived from the badge of superior Roman officers, the pallium has been worn by *Popes since the 4th century. It is granted to *archbishops, who must petition for it before they can exercise their authority. They wear it over a *chasuble on certain ceremonial occasions and it is buried with them. A similar *vestment, called *homophorion*, is given by *Orthodox patriarchs to their metropolitans.

Palm A pagan symbol of victory, adopted by the Early Christians to signify the triumph over death of their *saints and *martyrs who would eventually appear before *Christ 'clothed in white robes, and palms in their hands' (Rev 7 : 9). These palms would be given to them by angels who had gathered them from palm trees in *Paradise.

A palm tree sheltered the *Holy Family when they rested on their *Flight into Egypt. Palms were spread before Jesus on his *Entry into Jerusalem to welcome him as *Messiah. St *Michael brought a palm to St *Mary the Virgin to herald her approaching death, and she handed it to St John who carried it before her bier (*See* *Falling asleep of St Mary the Virgin). Also an *attribute of the Virgin, because 'This thy stature is like a palm tree' (Sg 7 : 7).

Palm Sunday The Sunday before *Easter, the beginning of *Holy Week, recalling Jesus' triumphal *Entry into Jerusalem. It is marked by the blessing of palm branches followed by the *Eucharist (or the *Mass of the Passion). The custom of carrying palm branches blessed in procession may have originated in Jerusalem as early as the beginning of the 5th century, when it was customary to parade, with the *bishop playing the part of Jesus, from the *Mount of Olives to the Church of the Resurrection. It was also a festival in Gaul in the late 7th century, when a cross decorated with flowers was carried to the accompaniment of hymns and psalms to the principal church in the city. The day was called in Latin *Pascha Floridum*, 'Flower Easter', in German *Blumensontag*, 'Flower Sunday', and in Spanish *Pascua florida*, which gave rise to the name of the State of Florida, USA, which was discovered on that day. In Germany, the procession included a carved figure of Jesus seated on a *palmesel*, a wooden ass with wheels so that it could be pulled along. In the Alps, the procession began at a *crucifix or rural chapel, designated 'Mount of Olives', and moved to the main church. In Normandy, box (French *haie*) may be displayed. It was customary to sing *Gloria, laus, et honor*, 'All glory, laud [praise] and honour', composed by Bishop Theodulf of Orleans (*c*.720-81), as one of the processional hymns.

A winged **ox,** attribute of St Luke (from an altar-piece by Donatello, 1386-1466).

Panagia Greek for 'All Holy', the title given in the *Orthodox Church to St *Mary the Virgin and applied to her *icon contained in a small case which Orthodox *bishops wear on their breasts.

Pancras (or Pancratius), St There are two saints of this name. The earlier is a 1st-century *martyr who was said to have been sent by St *Peter to evangelize Sicily and was stoned to death in Taormina by robbers who resented his preaching. The other, St Pancras of Rome, supposedly came from Phrygia and was beheaded in the 4th century, during the Diocletian *persecutions, when he was only fourteen years old. His body was retrieved by Christian women and a church was built in his honour on the Via Aurelia. He was believed to wreak immediate justice on anyone breaking an oath and was thus the guarantor of treaties. The London railway terminus derives its name from the church in the vicinity dedicated to him. He is one of the *Fourteen Holy Helpers.

Pange lingua The opening words of the *Corpus Christi hymn, *Pange lingua gloriosi corporis mysterium*, 'of the glorious Body telling', composed by St *Thomas Aquinas.

Pantaleon, St One of the *Fourteen Holy Helpers, a native of Nicomedia in Bithynia, son of a pagan father and Christian mother. A talented physician, he practised in the court of Emperor Galerius, forgot his Christian upbringing for a time, but was reconverted before the beginning of the Diocletian *persecutions. Denounced for his faith, he was tortured and beheaded *c*.303 at the foot of a barren olive tree (his *attribute) which bore fruit as soon as his blood reached its roots. (A phial of his blood, preserved in the cathedral at Ravello, Italy, liquifies on his feast day, 27 July.) His name was wrongly said to be derived from *Pianta Leone*, 'Plant the Lion', the warcry of Venice, where he was especially venerated. Actually it comes from the Greek *panteleimon*,

Children spread **palms** before Jesus as he enters Jerusalem on an ass, an event commemorated on *Palm Sunday* (Maestà altar-piece in Siena by Duccio, 1308-11).

'all-merciful', a reference to the help which he gave to the sick and needy. His relics are in the *abbey of St Denis, near Paris.

Panther A beautiful and excessively kind animal, the friend of all, identified with *Christ because, after feeding until it is replete, it sleeps for three days in its den (as Christ spent three days in the tomb). When it wakes it belches out a sweet smell like allspice (the sweet words of the *Gospel) which attracts other wise animals (the godly) but puts to flight the dragon (the *Devil).

Panthera The name of the soldier who, according to an early slander, was the real father of Jesus.

Pantocrator The representation of *God the Son as ruler of the world, as he will appear at the end of time. In Romanesque art he sits on his throne at the Last *Judgement of mankind, holding an open book inscribed with the symbols A - Ω or A - ω (*Alpha and Omega) or the words *Ego sum lux mundi*, 'I am the light of the world'.

Paphnutius, St A 4th-century *bishop of the Upper Thebaid (*d.c.*360), sometimes depicted as a musician because, when he prayed that he might know his value in the sight of God, he was told that it was the same as that of an itinerant flute-player. Paphnutius was sent to console the hermit St *Onuphrius in his last moments. His attribute is a palm tree because he was crucified on one in the desert.

Parable A short story based on human experience, used to illustrate a moral, religious or spiritual truth. Jesus used parables to explain to the people the mysteries of the *Kingdom of Heaven, telling his disciples that he did so 'because they seeing see not; and hearing they hear not, neither do they understand' (Mt 13 : 13) (*See* *Blind leading the blind; *Good Samaritan; *Good Shepherd; *Mustard seed; Hidden *Talents; *Thief in the night; *Wheat and the tares; *Wise and foolish virgins).

Paraclete From the Greek *paraklitos*, 'advocate'. The word is used in the *Gospel of John* as a synonym for the *Holy Spirit. Jesus promised to send his disciples 'another Paraclete' after his *Ascension (Jn 14 : 16). In the AV this reads as 'another Comforter'.

Paradise From the Old Persian for an enclosed garden. The *Septuagint Greek version of the Hebrew OT translated 'garden' (of *Eden) (Gen 2 : 8) as 'paradise' and this word was made into a proper noun. It was the earthly place where *Adam and *Eve, the first Man and Woman, lived in a state of innocence, and which was said to have been rediscovered by St *Brendan. Because Jesus said to *Dismas, the Good Thief, 'Today shalt thou be with me in paradise' (Lk 23 : 43), it was thought to be the intermediate states of *Limbo or *Purgatory. A contrary view was expressed in the apocryphal *Acta Pilati* ('Acts of Pilate') where it was said that while *Enoch and *Elijah, the two OT personages who did not taste death but went straight to *Heaven, were conversing, they saw a man carrying a cross on his shoulder. In reply to their questioning, he said, 'I am the thief who was crucified with Jesus. He promised that I should be with him in Heaven and gave me this cross so that the keeper of the gate would let me in'. Dismas is therefore shown waiting at the door of Paradise in depictions of the Last *Judgement, or identified by a cross among the blessed who are already within. Thus Paradise signified Heaven where the faithful will dwell after death, in accordance with the promise, 'To him that overcometh, will I give to eat of the tree of life which is in the midst of the paradise of God' (Rev 2 : 7).

Paralipomenon From the Greek for 'things left out', the title given by the *Septuagint translators to the first and second books of *Chronicles* which they thought supplemented the books of *Samuel* and *Kings*.

Paralytic sick of the palsy In the early days of his ministry, *Jesus was preaching in a house in Capernaum when four men let down through the roof, on a bed, a man paralysed with the palsy. Seeing their faith, Jesus, after an altercation with the Pharisees over his power to forgive sins, said to the cripple, 'Arise, and take up thy bed, and go thy way to thine own house' (Mk 2 : 1-12). A parallel to this miracle is the healing of the paralytic at the Pool of *Bethesda (Jn 5 : 1-15). In the art of the *catacombs the paralytic is shown carrying his bed on his back, symbolizing salvation and the forgiveness of sins.

Pardoner The name given in the Middle Ages to itinerant preachers who raised money for the Crusades, for the construction of churches or simply for alms, by selling *indulgences – the remission of temporal punishment after the forgiveness of a sin. Their methods were often so reprehensible that they were frequently satirized in literature. The sale of indulgences was forbidden by the *Council of Trent.

Pardons In Brittany, pilgrimages made between *Easter and *Michaelmas to certain churches where an *indulgence, or pardon, is granted. The poor are associated with St *Yves at Tréguier; singers, at Our Lady of Rumengol; fire, at St Jean-du-Doigt; mountains, at St Ronan; and the sea, at St Anne de la Palude.

Parish Originally the ecclesiastical division (Greek *paroikia*, 'district') controlled by a *bishop (in modern terms his *diocese), but later applied to the subdivisions cared for by *presbyters, or *priests. In England it is the district, often coterminous with a village or a section of a town, ministered to by an *incumbent, a *Church of England clergyman.

Parishioner One who lives in a *parish.

Parousia The Greek for 'arrival', or 'presence', used in the NT for the *Second Coming of Christ who will appear in glory for the Last *Judgement.

Parson In popular speech, the name for any clergyman of the *Church of England, but more correctly in the past restricted to the *rector, one who enjoyed the full rights of a benefice.

Partridge The prophet *Jeremiah likened the partridge, a *bird which 'sitteth on eggs and hatcheth them not', to him 'that getteth riches, and not by right' (Jer 17 : 11). The partridge thus symbolizes theft, deceit, or the *Devil, who is the chief deceiver of mankind.

Paschal candle A large *Easter (Latin *Pascha*) candle, inscribed with a cross, the year, the symbols *A Ω, florally decorated, and in which are inserted five grains of incense symbolizing the five *wounds of Christ. It is blessed on *Holy Saturday, carried that day in the blessing of the baptismal water, lighted on Easter Day and placed on the *Gospel side of the altar where it remains until after the Gospel on *Ascension Day. It symbolizes the Risen Christ, the *light of the world.

Passion music The musical setting of the narratives of the *Passion of Christ. In the *Catholic tradition, three persons, usually *deacons, stand in front of the *altar; one declaiming the words spoken by the members of the *Sanhedrin or *Pilate; the other the replies of Jesus; and the third, the shouts of the crowd.

Passion of Christ From the Latin *passio*, 'suffering', a word used to cover the events of *Holy Week from Jesus' *Entry into Jerusalem on *Palm Sunday until he suffered death on the Cross on *Good Friday. The narrative, as told in each of the four *Gospels, is read during the week as follows: Sunday (Mt 26 : 36-27 : 60); Tuesday (Mk 14 : 32-15 : 46); Wednesday (Lk 22 : 39-23 : 53); Friday (Jn 18 : 1-19; 42). It is also the basis for *Passion plays. In art, the incidents are treated separately, or as a sequence which may extend to the events of *Pentecost (Whitsunday). *Passion music, the setting to music of the Gospel texts recounting Jesus' suffering, reached its finest expression in the works of Schütz (1585-1672) and Johann Sebastian Bach (1685-1750). Its origin may be traced to the 5th century, or earlier, when the harmonized Gospel narratives of the Passion were declaimed in Church during Holy Week. In the 10th century the text was sung dramatically by three singers. Medieval *Passion plays developed from this liturgical practice.

Passion play A dramatic representation of events in the *Passion of Christ, originating in chanting or reading the Gospel accounts, together with interpolations, as part of the liturgy. The substitution of the vernacular for Latin; of laymen for clergy who declaimed the parts; and the introduction of secular and comic episodes; led to the production of plays outside the church, often

The stern face of Christ as **Pantocrator,** ruler and judge of the world, as he will appear at the end of time (Daphni, Greece).

The **Passion** of Christ symbolized by the Instruments of his suffering (wayside calvary at Roccamandolfi, Italy, 1910).

sponsored by Guilds or similar associations in towns and villages. By the 17th century they were in decline, frowned on by the *clergy because of the licence associated with them. The 20th century saw a revival with performances once again taking place in church. The most famous passion play is that of Oberammagau, in the Austrian Tyrol, performed by villagers every ten years in thanksgiving for deliverance from the plague.

Passion Sunday The second Sunday before *Easter and the fifth in *Lent, appointed for meditation on the *Passion of Christ. Altars, statues and crucifixes are draped in violet. It begins *Passiontide.

Passional A book which contained the lives of saints, or accounts of their acts and martyrdoms, to be read at *Matins on their *feast days. The word was also used for a book containing the narratives of the *Passion of Christ taken from the four *Gospels.

Passiontide The last two weeks of *Lent, from *Passion Sunday until *Holy Saturday. Since the 13th century, crosses and statues in churches have been veiled with purple cloths during these two weeks. Readings in the liturgy recall the *Passion of Christ.

Passover The *Jewish commemoration of the *Exodus, the deliverance of the Israelites from Egypt (Ex 12 : 1-13), when their forefathers were commanded to be in readiness to depart at a moment's notice from their oppressors. They were to slay a male lamb at sunset and stain the side posts and lintel of their houses with its blood (traditionally they made the *Tau sign) so that God would 'pass over' them when he slew the firstborn sons of the Egyptians. They were to roast the lamb, eat it with unleavened bread and bitter herbs, and to burn the remains. In the Christian context, 'Christ our passover is sacrificed for us' (1 Cor 5 : 7).

Passus est sub Pontio Pilato 'He suffered under Pontius Pilate', the opening Latin words which St *John the Apostle was said to have contributed to the *Apostles' Creed and which he displays on a *scroll.

Pastoral staff A *crosier, carried by *bishops and some *abbots and *abbesses.

Paten A flat circular silver plate, symbol of the dish used at the *Last Supper, on which the bread of the *Eucharist is placed.

Pater noster Latin for *'Our Father', the opening words of the *Lord's prayer. Also a bead in the *rosary which indicates where a 'paternoster', the Lord's Prayer, is to be said.

Patience Long-suffering, a Christian virtue, from the Latin *patiens*, 'enduring'. When personified, patience is depicted as a woman, usually accompanied by a lamb (gentleness), or less frequently by an ox (sacrifice and endurance). *Job is an example of patience because he bore his troubles with fortitude.

Patriarch A title of honour, dating from the 6th century and denoting a 'father over fathers', giving precedence over *bishops and those above them. The *Pope is the patriarch of the West. In the *Orthodox Churches there are patriarchs of various rites, Armenian, Maronite, Chaldean and Melchite. A patriarchal cross has two crossbars and is carried before a patriarch in a procession.

Patriarchs, the The 'Heads of the fathers, by their generations, chief men' (1 Chr 8 : 28), that is, founders of clans. They were numerous, but those singled out for special mention are *Abraham, *Isaac and *Jacob, and his twelve sons who founded the tribes of Israel. King *David is sometimes included because he was called 'the patriarch' by St Peter (Ac 2 : 29-30) when he recognized him as an ancestor of Jesus Christ.

Patrick, St St Patrick (*c.*390-*c.*461), according to his *Confessio* or autobiography, was the son of Calpurnius, a Roman tax collector, at Banavem Tabernia, probably on the Welsh side of the River Severn. He was taken captive when a boy by raiders and carried off to Ireland where he was sold as a slave to Milchu, a chieftain of Antrim. After six years he escaped and went to Gaul. He studied for the priesthood at Auxerre and was then sent back to Ireland as a missionary because he spoke the Irish form of the Celtic tongue. He founded the see of Armagh and spent the rest of his life spreading the Christian faith. He is thus the patron saint of Ireland. His feast day, 17 March, is kept as the Irish national holiday. The *shamrock is the Irish national emblem because St Patrick converted the pagan King Loigaire by using clover, its three leaves separated, yet united in one stem, to demonstrate the mystery of the *Trinity. He rid Ireland of serpents (his *attribute) by driving them out with his staff, said to have been given him by *Christ. His name was popularly supposed to have been derived from Patritius or Patercius, a corruption of the title *Pater civicus*, 'father of the land', said to have been bestowed upon him by Pope Celestine. He is depicted with fire burning before him because he confounded King Loigaire by miraculously kindling the Pascal Fire on *Easter Eve and because he caused the flames of *Purgatory to rise from a hole which he made in the ground. At the Last *Judgement, it is said, he will have the privilege of leading the souls of the Irish to the Judgement Seat. He is also reputed to have the power to release seven souls from Purgatory every Thursday and twelve each Saturday.

Paul, St The *Apostle of the Gentiles, supposed author of the NT epistles which bear his name, some of which are certainly his. His name was Saul, born at Tarsus in Cilicia, and thus 'a citizen of no mean city' (Ac 21 : 39). He was of Jewish

parents who had also the advantage of being
Roman citizens, a fact which would later give him
the right to be sent to Rome for trial. He was
brought up as a strict *Pharisee and studied in
Jerusalem under *Gamaliel. His hatred of the new
Christian sect caused him to take part in the
stoning of St *Stephen, the first martyr (Ac
8 : 1-3). He heard the young *deacon pray for his
executioners and this led to the great event in his
life, his conversion, which took place when he was
on the road to Damascus, 'breathing out threaten-
ings and slaughter against the disciples of the
Lord'. He was blinded by a light from Heaven and
heard a voice saying, 'I am Jesus whom thou
persecutest: it is hard for thee to kick against the
pricks' (the goading of conscience) (Ac 9 : 6). He
was cured of his blindness in Damascus by
Ananias, a Christian, who was told in a vision to
visit him. He was baptized, took the name of Paul,
and retired to the desert to meditate. He had
previously sought ferociously to drive Christians
out of the synagogues, but he returned to Damascus to preach Christ with equal vigour. Strict Jews
'took counsel to kill him' and watched the city
gates hoping to capture him, but Christian disciples let him down from the walls by night and he
escaped to Jerusalem. There it was necessary for St
*Barnabas to vouch for him because the *Apostles
could not believe that Paul was the same man who
had previously ill-treated them (Ac 9 : 1-31). It
was agreed that Paul's field of activity should be
among the gentiles. He came into conflict with St
*Peter at Antioch over the question of the cir-
cumcision of gentile converts, which the Church
in Jerusalem insisted on, but which was finally
resolved in Paul's favour (Gal 2 : 11-14).

Among the many events in Paul's active missionary life, the following are most frequently
illustrated in art: his healing of *Elymas the
sorcerer who was struck blind when he tried to
prevent Paul and *Barnabas preaching to Sergius
Paulus, the Roman governor of Cyprus (Ac
13 : 6-12); the curing of the paralytic at Lystra,
when the two missionaries were thought by the
inhabitants to be the pagan gods Zeus and Hermes
(Ac 14 : 8-18); his imprisonment with Silas at
Philippi when an earthquake destroyed the doors
of the jail, and the jailor was converted to
Christianity (Ac 16 : 16-40); his preaching before
the Areopagus about the *Unknown God (Ac
17 : 16-34); and the conversion of the magicians at
Ephesus who then burned their books (Ac 19 : 19-
20). When St Paul and his Christian companions
(one of whom may have been St *Luke) were
being escorted to Rome to stand trial, their ship
was wrecked on the Island of Melita (possibly
Malta). A viper fastened itself on to Paul's hand,
but he shook it off into the fire (Ac 27; 28 : 1-7).

The vivid account of Paul's missionary journeys
given in the *Acts of the Apostles* ends with his
preaching the *Gospel in Rome for two whole
years while awaiting his trial. The 2nd-century
Acts of Paul and Thecla add further details which
may have basis in fact. Paul (his name means
'little') is described as small of stature. with a bald
head and crooked legs, his nose somewhat

The bejewelled shrine containing the bell used by
St **Patrick** (*c*.1100).

A 15th-century carving of the arrest of St **Paul,**
protesting that as a Roman citizen he is free to
stand trial in Rome.

hooked, his eyebrows meeting, but his face full of friendliness, 'for now he appeared like a man, and now he had the face of an angel', a description which influenced his representation in art. His conversion of St *Thecla at Iconium caused his imprisonment, from which he emerged to have many other adventures. He was thrown to the wild beasts in the stadium at Ephesus but he was protected by a lion which he had baptized, and was saved by the onset of a violent hailstorm. The account ends with Emperor *Nero ordering Paul's execution. When his head was struck off, milk spurted over the executioner's clothes. Paul returned from the dead to tell Nero that he was alive in God.

St Peter and St Paul are depicted together as the founders of the Church of Rome. They were said to have been executed on the same day and are shown taking leave of each other, or being put to death together. St Paul's *attribute is the *sword which cut off his head (this was his right as a Roman citizen). It is also a reference to the 'sword of the spirit' (Eph 6 : 17). His severed head bounded three times, and at each point where it touched the ground, three fountains (*Trei fontane) gushed forth. He returned from the dead to give back to Plantilla, a Christian follower, the veil which she had given him to bind his eyes before his execution. In art St Paul is usually shown holding an inverted sword, but he may hold a book or scrolls to represent his epistles. When twinned with St Peter, he stands for the Church of the Gentiles and St Peter the Church of the Circumcision. Paul's emphasis on justification through faith caused him to be considered by *Protestants as their champion. Thus St Paul's Cathedral, London, is in some ways intended to contrast with St Peter's, Rome, the Church of the *Counter-Reformation.

St Paul's statement that he was 'caught up into paradise, and heard unspeakable words, which it is not lawful for a man to utter' (2 Cor 12 : 4) was elaborated in the apocryphal *Apocalypse of Paul* into a vision of the torments of Hell, which was so vivid that it influenced the representation in art of the Last *Judgement. He himself was afflicted with a mysterious illness, 'a thorn in the flesh, the messenger of Satan to buffet me, lest I should be exalted above measure' because of the mystical vision which he had been granted (2 Cor 12 : 7).

Paul the Hermit (Paul of Thebes), St Cited by St *Jerome, his biographer, as the 'founder of the monastic life' (Letter XXII. 36), and certainly the first Christian *hermit. To escape the *persecutions of Emperor Decius (c.250), he took refuge, while still a boy, in the Theban desert. There he lived for nearly a hundred years as a hermit, a palm tree (his *attribute) providing him with shelter, and its leaves his clothes. A raven brought him half a loaf of bread each day. When he was near death (c.345), St *Antony of Egypt was sent to administer his last *communion. A lion (or two lions) dug his grave.

Paula, St A noble and wealthy Roman matron who was consoled by St *Jerome after the deaths of her husband and daughter (the church of San Girolamo della Carità is said to be on the spot where her house once stood). She and her other daughter, Eustochium, made a pilgrimage to the *Holy Land and settled at *Bethlehem. There she assisted Jerome in his literary work and founded, on strict ascetic lines, a monastery, a convent and a guest house for pilgrims. After a life of great austerity, for which she was reprimanded by Jerome, she died (404) at the age of fifty-six, making the *sign of the cross on her lips. She was buried in the crypt of the Church of the Nativity.

Pax Latin for 'peace', the name of the moment in the *Eucharist when the *celebrant gives the *kiss of peace to the deacon who passes it on to the congregation. A pax brede, or *osculatorium*, a small ivory, metal or wooden plate with a cross or lamb carved on it, was used in the Middle Ages to convey the pax, or kiss of peace. A bishop salutes the faithful with the words *Pax vobis*, 'Peace be unto you'.

Peace of the Church The period which followed the so-called *Edict of Milan (313), a rescript drafted by Emperors *Constantine and Licinius, which accorded Christianity full equality with the other religions in the Empire. It led to the cessation of the *persecutions which had caused the death of more than 20,000 Christians since the time of *Nero (64-8).

Peacock Symbol of *pride ('proud as a peacock') because it displays its magnificent tail-feathers. Also of the *Resurrection because it was believed that its flesh was incorruptible, even if it had been buried for three days.

Pearl Attribute of St *Margaret of Antioch, a pun on her name which resembles the Greek *margarites*, 'pearl'.

Jesus in his teaching used the simile of the pearl on two notable occasions. In the course of the *Sermon on the Mount he said, 'Give not that which is holy unto the dogs, neither cast ye your pearls before swine, lest they trample them under their feet and turn again and rend you' (Mt 7 : 6). Later, as he sat by the lakeside, he told the multitude who thronged about him that the *Kingdom of Heaven 'is like unto a merchant man seeking goodly pearls: who, when he found one pearl of great price, went and sold all that he had and bought it' (Mt 13 : 45-6).

Pectoral cross A *cross of fine metal, ornamented with precious stones, suspended by a chain over the breast (Latin *pectus*). If it contained a *relic, it was offered to the faithful to kiss. Worn by *bishops.

Pedilavium The Latin name for the ceremony of the *washing of the feet, performed on *Maundy Thursday in memory of Jesus' humble act before the *Last Supper.

Pelagia, St There are three saints of this name. The first was a young maiden of Antioch (d.c.311) who preserved her virginity from the soldiers who had surrounded her house by throwing herself into the sea. Another was a 4th-century actress of the same city who renounced her profession, dressed as a man and lived a life of penitence in a cave on the *Mount of Olives. The third (c.304?) came from Tarsus and was martyred because she refused to become the emperor's concubine.

Pelican A sea-bird which, according to the *Physiologus*, becomes angry with its young and kills them. Then, repenting of the deed, it tears its breast with its long beak and brings its fledglings to life again with its blood. It thus represents the sacrifice of Christ and the blood of the Redeemer offered to the faithful in the cup of the *Eucharist.

Penance One of the Seven *Sacraments, from the Latin *paenitentia*, 'repentance'. The person confesses his sins to God through a priest (*See* *Confessional), atones for them, and is granted *absolution. The nature of the penance imposed for atonement depends on the priest's assessment of the case.

Pentateuch The five OT books, *Genesis, Exodus, Leviticus, Numbers* and *Deuteronomy*, traditionally ascribed to *Moses but drawn from various sources dating from the 9th to the 4th centuries BC.

Pentecost The feast to commemorate the *Descent of the Holy Spirit on the *Apostles, called in England *Whitsunday. It originated in the *East in the 3rd century and is probably the Christianization of the Jewish Feast of Weeks, originally a thanksgiving for the wheat harvest but later linked to the giving of the *Tablets of the Law to Moses on Mount Sinai. This feast took place fifty days (Greek *pentikosti*, 'the fiftieth day') after *Passover. The Christian festival is therefore fifty days after *Easter.

In numerological and eschatological symbolism Pentecost is also linked with *seven, as it concludes Pascaltide (the period from Easter to Pentecost) which contains seven times seven days. Thus the Descent of the Holy Spirit, the consummation of Christ's redemptive work, foreshadows the final act of salvation, the *Second Coming, which will take place at the end of the seven times seven 'days' of the world.

Pentecost (Whitsunday) ranks after Easter as the second festival of the Church. The liturgical *colour is red. The hymn *Veni Sancte Spiritus*, 'Come Holy Spirit' is usually sung (now attributed to Stephen Langton, Archbishop of Canterbury [d.1228] and not to his friend Pope Innocent III). In the Middle Ages, to dramatize the event, an effigy of a dove might be lowered in church, a dove let loose, or a shower of roses made to descend on the congregation.

Pentecostarion A book containing prayers and readings for the period from *Easter Sunday to the

St **Paul** on the road to Damascus falls from his horse, blinded by a light from Heaven. He is converted when he hears Jesus' voice (Michelangelo's fresco in the Vatican, 1542-5).

The Apostles take off their sandals for the **Pedilavium.** St Peter asks Jesus to wash his head as well as his feet, to cleanse him thoroughly (Maestà altar-piece, Siena, by Duccio, 1308-11).

Sunday after *Pentecost, used in the *Orthodox Church.

Perpetua and Felicity, SS Two Carthaginian women who were martyred in 203. Vibia Perpetua was a wealthy married lady with a son; Felicity the wife of a slave. They were arrested and thrown into prison together with other Christians: Saturus, Saturninus, Secundulus and Revocatus. When they refused to sacrifice to the gods they were condemned to be killed at the games. While awaiting their ordeal Felicity gave birth to a daughter. Her patient endurance of a painful labour converted her jailor Pudens. Saturus and Perpetua were consoled by visions. In the amphitheatre they were attacked by beasts and Perpetua was mauled by a cow (her *attribute), but they survived and were later beheaded. St *Augustine of Hippo preached sermons to honour their memory. A stone bearing their names was excavated in 1907 in the Basilica Maiorum in Carthage.

Persecutions, Roman Intermittent attacks, leading to confiscation of property and martyrdom, on Christians in the Roman Empire who refused to acknowledge the emperor's divinity. They began with *Nero in 64 when he held Christians responsible for setting fire to Rome. Christians continued to be persecuted by later emperors: Domitian (94–6); Trajan (98–117); Marcus Aurelius (166–80); Septimus Severus (202–11); Maximinus Thrax (235–8); Decius (249–51); Valerian (247–59); Aurelian (275); Diocletian (303–c.5). They ended with the *Peace of the Church, which began in 313 when a rescript of toleration was issued by Emperors *Constantine and Licius.

Peter, St The most prominent of the *Apostles and the one most frequently represented in art. He played a leading part in the ministry of *Jesus and in the life of the first Christian communities in Jerusalem and Rome. He and his brother St *Andrew were the sons of Jonah, or John (Greek *Joanes*), Galilean fisherman of Bethsaida (Jn 1 : 44) and Capernaum (Mk 1 : 21). They were summoned by Jesus to be 'fishers of men' (*See* *Calling of the Apostles). Peter was married and took his wife with him on his missionary journeys (1 Cor 9 : 5). His first name was Simon. When he recognized his master as the *Christ, Jesus conferred on him the punning title of Peter, saying, 'thou art Peter [Greek *Petros*] and upon this rock [*petra*] I will build my church' (Mt 16 : 18). The exegesis of this statement has divided Christendom. One interpretation, accepted by many *Protestants, is that put forward by Origen (c.185–c.254): 'Rock means every disciple of Christ'. From the *Roman Catholic point of view, 'Thou art Peter' (Vg *Tu es Petrus*) substantiates the claim of the *Pope, as St Peter's successor, to be the father of all Christians. This right is considered to be reinforced by the granting to Peter of the *Keys of the Kingdom of Heaven, *Tibi dabo claves regni coelorum* (Mt 16 : 19 Vg), and the post-Resurrection commission, 'Feed my sheep' (Jn 21 : 17). St Peter's principal *attribute is therefore a key – or two keys, one silver, one gold, usually crossed. Other attributes are a boat, alluding to his trade and to the *ship of the Church; a *fish because he was a fisher of men; and a *cock because of his denial of Jesus while he was being tried before the High Priest (Mk 14 : 72). Chains refer to his imprisonment in *Jerusalem when an *angel appeared in a blaze of light, freed him from his chains and led him past the sleeping guards to the house of Mary, mother of John Mark (thought to be St *Mark) where his fellow-Christians were praying for his safety (Ac 12 : 1-19). They also recall his imprisonment in the Mamertine prison in Rome (as narrated in the *Acts of Peter*, an apocryphal work of the end of the 2nd century) from which he was also released by an angel. The chains which then bound him were discovered by St Balbina and placed in the church of San Pietro-in-Vincoli (St Peter-in-Chains) in Rome.

Although there is no direct scriptural reference to St Peter living in Rome, there is early testimony to that effect dating from the 2nd century, and he is closely associated with that city in tradition. A portable chair, believed to be the one he used, is preserved at the *Vatican. The Feast of the Chair of St Peter on 18 January was established at an early date to commemorate his first preaching in Rome. (A similar feast at Antioch celebrated the belief that he was the first *bishop of that city.) According to the *Acts of Peter*, St Peter was martyred in Rome, either on the Janiculum Hill where the church of San Pietro in Montoro now stands, or in the circus, between the *metae*, the two turning-points of the racecourse. He desired to be crucified head downwards so that he would be seen to be lower than his master. As he hung there he pronounced a discourse explaining the symbolic significance of the *Crucifixion. There is evidence of an early *cultus* (shrine) of St Peter under the present St Peter's in Rome, but excavations at his supposed tomb have not revealed true relics.

After his martyrdom, Emperor *Nero was said to have seen St Peter in a vision and felt that he was being scourged by him. Thereafter Nero refrained from persecuting Christians.

Peter Martyr, St A *Dominican friar, b.c.1205 in Verona, Italy, of which city he is the patron saint. In 1232 he was made *Inquisitor in Milan (where he is buried and where he is also the patron saint). He was so brutal in his pursuit and persecution of *Catharist heretics in northern Italy that they decided to murder him. In 1252, when Peter and a fellow friar were going through a wood on their way from Lake Como to Milan, they were set upon by men led by Carino de Balsamo, who split his skull with a dagger and stabbed him in the breast. He died praying for his assassin, while tracing on the ground with his own blood the words *Credo in Deum*, 'I believe in God'. Carino repented of his crime and became a postulant in the Dominican convent in Forli, where Peter's brother received him and forgave him. After leading an examplary life, he was eventually beatified as the Blessed Carinus.

Peter was canonized in 1253 by Pope Innocent IV, a year after his death. He was soon depicted in Dominican habit, a wound in his head, or a dagger or knife cleaving his skull. In some representations his finger is laid to his lips, a gesture which is difficult to explain. It may refer to the fact that he kept silent about a vision which he had of SS *Mary the Virgin, *Agnes, *Catherine and *Cecilia.

Many posthumous miracles were attributed to St Peter Martyr. He brought to life a child whose mother had gone back on her promise that he should become a Dominican, and revived the stillborn child of a woman whose husband threatened to kill her if she did not produce a live heir. Paralytics, cripples and the sick were also cured when they prayed at his tomb. In his lifetime he stopped with a gesture a runaway horse which threatened to run down a crowd listening to him preach. He also unmasked a *devil who had appeared in a Catharist church in the shape of St Mary the Virgin in order to justify their heresy.

Pew Wooden benches fixed in English churches from about the 13th century onwards for the comfort of worshippers who had previously stood, or if infirm, sat on stone seats around the nave. *Bench ends enclosing pews were often carved with symbolic devices.

Pharaoh In the OT the generic title of the kings of Egypt. They are not identified, but three are deeply involved in the history of the people of *Israel. A *pharaoh fell in love with *Sarah, Abraham's wife, who had been passed off as his sister (Gen 12 : 14-20). *Joseph interpreted another *pharaoh's dreams and was raised to high office (Gen 41 : 1-45). A new pharaoh, 'who did not know Joseph' (Ex 1 : 8), enslaved the descendants of the *Israelites who had settled in his land. The *Plagues of Egypt forced him to let the Israelites depart. He regretted his decision, pursued them, and perished in the *Red Sea.

Pharaoh's dreams When *Joseph was imprisoned on a false accusation of attempted rape made by *Potiphar's wife, he earned the trust of the head jailor and was put in charge of the other prisoners. Two of them, *Pharaoh's butler and baker, had troublesome dreams, the former that he had filled the ruler's cup with wine from the grapes of three vines, the latter that he carried three baskets of bread on his head and birds ate the loaves in the top one. Joseph forecast correctly that, within three days, the butler would be restored to favour and the baker hanged (Gen 40 : 1-22). They are thus equated typologically with *Dismas and *Gestas, the Good Thief who went to Paradise, and the Bad Thief who was sent to Hell.

Two years later, Pharaoh had two dreams. In one, seven fat cows came out of a river and grazed in a meadow. They were followed by seven thin cows who devoured them but did not get fat. The next dream was of seven full ears of wheat on one stalk which were eaten up by seven ears blasted by the east wind. None of Pharaoh's magicians could

St **Peter** was crucified head-downwards because he wished to be lower than his Master (Masaccio, early 15th century).

St **Peter** with the gold and silver keys of the Kingdom of Heaven (12th-century statue from Cluny).

Catharist heretics murder St **Peter Martyr** and his companions in a wood on their way to Milan. Carino, St Peter's assassin, was converted when he saw his exemplary death.

interpret the dreams, but the butler remembered Joseph. He was taken from his prison, bathed, shaved and given clean clothes and brought before Pharaoh. His explanation of the dreams was that Egypt would have seven years of plenty, to be followed by seven years of famine. He advised that one fifth of the produce of the prosperous years should be collected and stored in anticipation of the years of starvation. Pharaoh was so impressed with Joseph's wisdom that he made him supreme in the land next to himself, allowed him to ride in the second processional chariot (linked typologically with Jesus' *Entry into Jerusalem) and married him to Asenath, daughter of the High Priest (Gen 41 : 1-45).

Pharisees From the Hebrew for 'the separate ones', a Jewish religious party who held aloof from worldly things and were respected by the people because of their support for the nationalist cause against the Roman oppressors. Led by scribes, or lawyers, they are reported to have opposed Jesus because he appeared to flout the *Laws of Moses. (Yet two of their number, *Nicodemus and *Gamaliel sided with Jesus.)

Jesus annoyed some of them when he told a parable which ridiculed their pretensions. Two men went into the *Temple to pray. One, a Pharisee, thanked God that he was not as other men and boasted of his virtues and strict religious observances. The other stood humbly afar off and 'smote upon his breast', saying, 'God be merciful to me a sinner'. He was the one who returned home justified, 'for', said Jesus, 'every one that exalteth himself shall be abased: and he that humbleth himself shall be exalted' (Lk 18 : 9-41).

On the Feast of the Dedication of the Temple, as Jesus walked in Solomon's porch, Pharisee extremists threatened to stone him for blasphemy because, being a man, he made himself out to be God (Jn 10 : 21-39). This scene is linked typologically with Ahab ordering *Naboth to be stoned to death.

Philip the Apostle, St A fisherman of Bethsaida on the Lake of *Galilee (Jn 1 : 44), a village which was also the home of SS *Andrew, and Simon called *Peter. He was the third of the twelve *Apostles to adhere to *Jesus of Nazareth, who had seen him among the crowd assembled around St *John the Baptist on the banks of the River Jordan. In turn he brought *Nathanael (or Bartholomew) to Jesus and is thus associated with him in art. He took part in the Feeding of the Five Thousand (See *Loaves and fishes) (Jn 6 : 5), and thus has five loaves as his *attribute. He was probably fluent in Greek as well as Aramaic because he was approached by Greek-speaking Jews who had come to Jerusalem for the *Passover and wished to see Jesus (Jn 12 : 21). At the *Last Supper he asked Jesus to show him the Father and was told, 'He that hath seen me hath seen the Father' (Jn 14 : 9).

Philip was with the other Apostles when *Matthias was chosen to replace *Judas but is not mentioned thereafter in the NT, although an apocryphal *Gospel according to Philip* was one of the collection of papyri discovered at Nag Hammadi in 1945. *Eusebius, in his *Ecclesiastical History* (Bks 3 : 31; 5 : 24), referred to the tradition that Philip and his two aged virgin daughters were buried at Hierapolis in Phrygia and that another daughter was interred at Ephesus, but there was some confusion about this among early historians because *Philip the Deacon, who also had daughters, was identified as Philip the Apostle.

Legends of Philip's career after *Pentecost do in fact associate him with Hierapolis where he ordered the devil, who had taken the shape of a *dragon, to leave the plinth of a statue of Mars. The dragon fled, breathing out fiery poison which killed the son of the pagan high priest, tribunes and many other bystanders. In consequence, Philip was stoned (stones, sometimes confused with five loaves, are his other attribute) and crucified head downwards like St *Peter. But he was tied to his cross, whereas Peter was nailed.

Philip the Deacon (or the Evangelist), St One of the seven disciples who were chosen by the Church in Jerusalem to look after the needs of Greek-speaking widows (Ac 6 : 5). After the martyrdom of St *Stephen he evangelized Samaria where he healed the sick, cast out evil spirits and converted *Simon Magus (Ac 8 : 5-12). On the road from Jerusalem to Gaza he encountered 'an eunuch of great authority under Candace, queen of the Ethiopians, who had charge of all her treasure, and had come to Jerusalem for to worship'. He was reading the prophecies of *Isaiah, and invited Philip to sit beside him in his chariot to explain them to him. When Philip demonstrated that Jesus Christ was the *Messiah foretold by Isaiah, the eunuch asked to be baptized and became the first Ethiopian Christian (Ac 8 : 26-40). This episode was portrayed in the 17th century as illustrating the sacrament of *baptism.

Philistines A piratical seafaring people who settled in the coastal plain of Palestine and came into conflict with the Israelites on many occasions. *Samson fought with them (Jg 13-16); *Saul and *Jonathan waged war on them (1 Sam 13 : 14); and *David made them vassals (2 Sam 8 : 1), although they afterwards gained their independence. The name 'Philistine' thus came to mean 'enemy' and was applied by German university students to their despised enemies, the materialist townsfolk, who lacked their respect for culture. It was in this sense that Matthew Arnold (1822-88) adapted the word into English to signify a person with a bourgeois dislike of art and literature.

Phoenix According to the Greek historian Herodotus (5th century BC), the phoenix was a bird like an eagle, with red and golden plumage, and which inhabited Arabia. Only one could be alive at any time, and every 500 years it came to Heliopolis, constructed an altar, set fire to itself on it, and rose again, beautiful and young, from the ashes of the pyre. It was therefore a symbol of the *Resurrection and an emblem of immortality.

Phylactery In art, a narrow streamer bearing an inscription, usually part of a text relative to the event portrayed. The word was first used for an amulet, a safeguard (Greek *phylacterion*) against evil, and then applied to the capsules containing scriptural texts worn on the forehead and arm by pious Jews at morning prayer. These were attached by long leather ribbons and this may have suggested the use of the word to describe streamers bearing texts or inscriptions.

Physiologus The Greek *physiologos*, 'a discourse on nature', is the title of a work probably of the 3rd century, but was thought to be the name of the author, 'the naturalist'. It is a collection of strange tales about the curious habits of animals, real and mythical, from which moral instruction could be deduced. These allegories became the exempla included in the numerous *bestiaries composed in the Middle Ages.

Pietà Italian for 'pity', the name given in art to devotional representations of the sorrowing St *Mary the Virgin who holds the body of the dead *Jesus across her knees. The theme, first found in Byzantine art, was later elaborated and popularized as the result of the *Revelations* of St *Bridget of Sweden. The most famous *Pietà* is Michelangelo's statue in St Peter's in Rome. When other figures are added, a *Pietà* resembles the *Lamentation over the dead Christ.

Pig A loathsome *animal, unclean in Mosaic law, the symbol of greed and lust. A pig accompanies St *Antony of Egypt (the Great), possibly to signify the sins of the flesh which he had to overcome. If the pig has a bell, it is a reference to the *Antonines, an order of Hospitallers (founded 1095) who looked after the sick and *pilgrims, and who were named after St Antony. Their pigs were allowed to scavenge in the streets and were identified by a bell hung around their necks.

Pilate, Acts of An apocryphal account, not earlier than the 4th century, of the examination of Jesus before *Pilate, his *Crucifixion and *Resurrection. It purports to be a translation made from the Hebrew by a lawyer called Ananias (or Aeneas, or Emaus) of *Nicodemus' record of the trial and Passion. Around the 14th century, an account of the *Descent of Christ into Hell was attached to it and given the title, *Gospel of Nicodemus*.

Pilate, Pontius, Eponymous villain – because of the part he played in the *Trials of Jesus of Nazareth and his *Crucifixion. He was cited in the *Apostles' Creed, the clause 'suffered under Pontius Pilate', presumably being inserted to emphasize the historical fact of Christ's death and to contradict the docetic view that he only 'seemed' to suffer.

Pontius Pilate, an equestrian or upper-class Roman, was appointed *praefectus* of Judaea in 26, a title commemorated in Caesarea on an inscription discovered in 1961. He was later called *procurator*

When criticized for making St Mary the Virgin look younger than her son in his marble **Pietà** (1498-9, St Peter's, Rome), Michelangelo replied that her purity afforded her eternal youth.

Philistine prisoners in Egypt. A relief from Thebes.

by the Roman historian Tacitus and by the Jewish writer *Josephus, who records the many ways in which Pilate antagonized the Jews and provoked tumults and uprising which he brutally suppressed. Some of Jesus' followers may have been resistance fighters or *Zealots, who fought against Roman rule as represented by this insensitive procurator.

Pilate's final act of brutality was the slaughter of Samaritans who had gathered on Mount Gerizim, lured there by a false prophet who said that he would reveal where Moses had hidden the sacred vessels used by the priests. He was sent to Rome c.37 to defend his conduct. There is no record of what happened to him there, but *Eusebius (*Ecclesiastical History*, Bk 2 : 7) wrote that he committed suicide in the reign of Emperor Gaius (37-41). Legends suggest that *Nero ordered his execution, or that he had been banished to Vienne in Gaul where he died a horrible death, his body being consumed by worms. The anti-Christian polemical work, *Acts of Pilate*, was circulated under Emperor Maximinus and answered by a Christian *Acts of Pilate* which was the source of many later legends. Tertullian (c.160-c.220) wrote that Pilate sent a letter to Emperor Tiberius which told of Jesus' miracles. Jesus was there presented in such a favourable light that it was believed in some quarters that Pilate must have been a secret Christian. The Ethiopian Church made him a saint.

It was not usual for a procurator's wife to accompany him when he was posted abroad, but it would appear that Pilate's wife Claudia Procula (Procla), granddaughter of Emperor *Augustus, was with him in Jerusalem. When Pilate sat in his *praetorium* or 'judgement seat' to try Jesus, he received a message from her in which she said, 'Have thou nothing to do with that just man: for I have suffered many things this day in a dream because of him' (Mt 27 : 19). Procula's dream is made into a terrifying nightmare when it is depicted in art.

Pilgrim One who undertakes a *pilgrimage to a sacred place or *shrine as an act of devotion. He is shown with a staff and scrip, or *wallet. If he has visited the shrine of St *James of Compostela in Spain, he wears a scallop *shell in his hat. The disciples on the road to *Emmaus are sometimes depicted as pilgrims, as are St *Bridget of Sweden and St *Roch.

Pilgrimage A journey made by a *pilgrim to a *shrine, in order to discharge a vow or obligation; to worship; or to seek spiritual aid and comfort. Pilgrimages to the sacred places of the *Holy Land became frequent after St *Helena's visit c.325. Medieval Rome, the tomb of St *James of Compostela and the shrine of St *Thomas of Canterbury were the great pilgrimage centres, especially when the hardships of the journey were regarded as penance or canonical punishment imposed for sins or crimes. Present-day centres enjoying great popularity are Lourdes in France, *Loreto in Italy, *Fátima in Portugal and *Walsingham in England.

Pillar, Holy The marble column to which Jesus was tethered for his *scourging, one of the *Instruments of the Passion. Half of the column remained in Jerusalem, the remainder, made of oriental jasper, was brought to Rome in 1223 by Cardinal Giovanni Colonna and placed in the church of Santa Prassede (St Praxedes).

Pillar, Our Lady of the In Spanish, *Nuestra señora del Pilar*, the name of the splendid Baroque church (completed 1681) in Zaragoza which contains a shrine with a statue of St *Mary the Virgin and the Child on a pillar, called *La Virgen del Pilar*, said to have been brought there by Mary herself and left with St *James 'the Great' who is said to have built the sanctuary, although the earliest record of it belongs to the 12th century. She was made patroness of the Spanish army and her statue was crowned in 1905 with a crown containing a diadem of great worth. Spanish girls, especially those from Aragón, are given the name of (María del) Pilar. Her feast day is 12 October which is also the *Día de la raza*, the festival of all Spanish-speaking peoples, coinciding with Columbus Day in the USA.

There is also the Vièrge du Pilier, the 15th-century 'Black Virgin' of Chartres Cathedral.

Pisces The twelfth sign of the *zodiac, governing the period from c.19 February to c.20 March, is represented by two fishes, either joined by their tails or by a line linking their mouths. They may refer to the episode in Greek mythology when Aphrodite (Venus) and Eros (Cupid) escaped from the monster Typhon by jumping into a river, and were either changed into two fishes or rescued by them. In the *Labours of the Months, pisces is associated with the time for gathering logs and sitting by the fire waiting for Spring.

Piscina A stone basin with a drain, placed in a niche in the wall of the *sanctuary for the priest to perform *ablutions – to rinse his hands or wash liturgical vessels after use.

Plagues of Egypt, ten To convince *Pharaoh that he should allow the *Children of Israel to depart from their enslavement in Egypt, God caused ten plagues to devastate the land. After each of the first nine plagues Pharaoh agreed to let the *Israelites go on condition that the plague was abated. Then his heart was hardened and he withdrew his promise. The tenth was so severe that the Israelites were permitted to leave.

The ten plagues were: all the water in Egypt as well as the Nile 'were turned to blood', the fish died and the river stank (Ex 7 : 14-25); frogs swarmed all over the land and into people's houses, ovens and kneading-troughs (Ex 8 : 1-15); the dust turned into lice which crawled over man and beast (Ex 8 : 16-19); swarms of flies corrupted the land (Ex 8 : 20-32); 'a very grievous murrain' afflicted cattle, horses and camels (Ex 9 : 1-7); boils covered the skin of man and beast (Ex 9 : 8-12); hail, rain and thunder devastated the crops (Ex 9 : 13-35); locusts ate up everything that remained (Ex 10 : 1-20); 'thick darkness' covered the land for three days (Ex 10 : 21-9); and 'all the firstborn in the land of Egypt', human and animal, died (Ex 11 : 1-10). The Children of Israel, because of Pharaoh's obduracy in the face of these disasters, were told by God that they would be immune from the tenth plague (See *Passover) and that the Egyptians would hasten to get rid of them, loading them with gifts to encourage them to depart. They went after they had 'spoiled the Egyptians' of their goods (Ex 12 : 31-6).

Plainchant (plainsong) Unadorned ritual music used in the Middle Ages, before the advent of polyphony, to accompany the liturgy. It is associated with SS *Ambrose and *Gregory the Great who were said to have invented the mode.

Plough Monday The first Monday after the feast of the *Epiphany (6 January) when prayers are said for the successful ploughing of the land which begins about that time.

Pluviale The old name for a *cope.

Polycarp, St Bishop of Smyrna, said to have been converted by St *John the Divine; martyred when an old man c.155 because he refused to take the required oath to the Roman emperor's deity and curse *Christ. 'I have served him for eighty-six years and he has done me no harm. How can I blaspheme my King and Saviour?', he asked. The proconsul ordered him to be burned alive, but the flames billowed around him like the sails of a ship filled with the wind. He was then stabbed to death. His fellow-Christians gathered up his remains, one of the early examples of devotion to a saint's *relics.

Pomegranate A fruit usually shown cut in half with its seeds displayed. As these are tightly packed, St *Gregory the Great said that they demonstrated the unity of all Christians. When held whole in the hand of the *Christ-Child, a pomegranate foretells his *Resurrection because it heralds the return of Spring. It was one of the fruits promised to the Children of Israel when they reached the *Promised Land (Dt 8 : 8), so it also symbolizes the joys of Heaven which await the faithful. It is the *attribute of St *John of God.

Pontifex Maximus A Latin title of the *Pope who is the head of the hierarchy of priests.

Pontiff A *bishop. The Supreme Pontiff is the *Pope. Pontifical Mass is solemn *Mass celebrated by a bishop with full ceremonial. Pontificals are the eight *vestments (*mitre, *dalmatic, *tunicle, *pectoral cross, *ring, *gloves, *buskins and *sandals) worn by *cardinals, bishops and *abbots when celebrating Mass with full solemnity.

Poor Clares The popular name for the Sisters of St Clare, the Second Order of St Francis, founded in 1212 at the convent of San Damiano, Assisi, Italy, by St *Clare under the inspiration and

The chief priests bring Jesus to **Pilate** who finds no fault in him and sends him to Herod (Duccio's Maestà altar-piece, 1308-11, in Siena).

Pilgrims crawling in and out of the shrine of St Edward the Confessor where they touch his relic, a rib (French illustration to the history of his life, 13th century).

direction of St *Francis of Assisi. They were originally an enclosed contemplative *Order, devoted to a life of poverty, mortification, prayer and meditation. In 1804, their *Rule was modified to permit the *nuns to engage in charitable work. Poor Clares wear a black veil, cloth sandals on bare feet, and a habit resembling that of the *Franciscans, and belong to the most austere of the women's orders.

Pope According to the doctrine of the *Roman Catholic Church, as defined at the First Vatican Council in 1870, the successor to St *Peter who established the papacy in Rome, and through him the heir to the supreme authority over the whole Church which was given to him by *Jesus. The title, the Anglicization of *papa*, 'father', was first applied to all *bishops who were the spiritual fathers of their people, but in the *West from the 6th century onwards it was reserved exclusively for the bishop of Rome. *Orthodox and *Protestant Churches do not recognize the supreme authority of the Pope, although some would be prepared to grant primacy should there be a reunion of Christians.

Porta clausa Latin for 'closed gate', an *attribute of St *Mary the Virgin, symbolizing her perpetual *virginity. It is derived from *Ezekiel's vision of the gate 'which looketh toward the east; and it was shut'. He was told by God, 'This gate shall be shut, it shall not be opened, and no man shall enter in by it; because the Lord, the God of Israel, hath entered in by it' (Ez 44 : 1-2). Ezekiel sometimes displays the opening words, *Porta clausa erit*, on a *scroll.

Portiuncula The Latin form of the Italian *porziuncola*, 'small portion', the piece of land on the outskirts of Assisi on which stood the small chapel of Santa Maria degli Angeli ('St Mary of the Angels') where St *Francis and his companions used to meet and which is thus the birthplace of their *Order. It is now enclosed within the basilica, the fine Franciscan church reconstructed after the earthquake of 1832.

Postulant A person who wishes to become a member of a religious community and is 'asking' (Latin *postulare*, 'to ask') to be admitted. The person then becomes a *novice.

Potiphar's wife The Midianites who bought *Joseph from his wicked brothers resold him in Egypt to Potiphar, *Pharaoh's captain of the guard, who was so pleased with Joseph that he made him overseer of his household (Gen 39 : 1-7).

Joseph was a handsome young man and soon attracted the attentions of Potiphar's wife. (In Islamic tradition she is called Zuleika, but she was also known as Saphira in Europe in the Middle Ages.) She begged him to lie with her (one explanation for her lustful conduct was that Potiphar was a eunuch) but Joseph, conscious of the favours which his master had granted him,

refused to betray his trust. One day, when the men of the household were absent, Joseph went into the house on business. Potiphar's wife caught him by his garment and again tried to get him to lie with her. He fled, leaving his robe in her hands. To be revenged for her humiliation in the hands of a slave she denounced Joseph, saying that he had tried to rape her but had run away when she shouted for help. She produced his garment as evidence. Potiphar cast Joseph into the king's prison, from which he was eventually released in order to interpret *Pharaoh's Dreams (Gen 39 : 1-20).

An Islamic version of this story adds the additional detail that Potiphar's wife and her women attendants were peeling oranges when they first caught sight of Joseph and were so overcome by his beauty that they cut their fingers. Their blood stained the fruit and that is why today there are blood oranges.

In Christian exegesis, Joseph is an example of *chastity and a forerunner of St *Joseph whose relationship with St *Mary the Virgin was also chaste.

Powers The third choir of the second hierarchy of *angels. They carry flaming swords with which they protect mankind and conquer *devils. Their leader is *Raphael.

Prayer Book The *Book of Common Prayer* of 1662, authorized by the Act of Uniformity to be the official service book of the Church of England. It was inspired by the Archbishop of Canterbury Thomas Cranmer (1489-1556) and his associates, who wished to compose a simplified English version of the Latin service books which *priest and people could use in common. It became part of the English spiritual and literary heritage, with felicitous phrases, familiar from church, passing into everyday use. Although archaic by the mid-20th century, so that it had ceased to fulfil Cranmer's ambition that it should be entirely 'understood of the people', the House of Commons in 1928 rejected a revised version which had been accepted by the *Anglican Church. After many years of liturgical experiments, services authorized for use in conjunction with the *Book of Common Prayer* have now been published in the *Alternative Service Book 1980*, albeit against some vocal opposition. Much of this has come from non-Anglicans and from many Anglicans who claim to dislike merely the language of the new services.

Predella The Italian for 'kneeling stool', and by extension an altar step on which the priest knelt. It was later applied to a raised shelf at the back of an altar on which a picture was placed. When larger altar-pieces became fashionable the word was used for the series of smaller paintings at the base of the main picture or pictures. The scenes depicted on them were usually related to the theme or main subject of the altar-piece.

Prelate From the Latin *praelatus*, 'one preferred', applied to ecclesiastical officials of high rank, *bishops, some *abbots and certain superiors of religious *Orders.

Premonstratensians Members of the Order of Canons Regular of Premontré, also called Norbertines after their founder St *Norbert. Because of the *colour of their *habit they were known in England as White Canons.

Presanctified, Mass of the The *Mass celebrated on *Good Friday includes no consecration, and a *Host previously consecrated ('pre-sanctified') is used for *Communion. In the *East this Mass is celebrated on Wednesdays and Fridays in *Lent.

Presbyter In the early Church an 'elder' (Greek *presbuteros*) of the community whose function seems to have been the same as that of the *bishop (Greek *episkopoi*). The latter appears to have taken precedence from the 2nd century onwards and to have claimed authority as a successor to the *Apostles. The word 'priest' is a contraction of 'presbyter'.

Presentation of Jesus in the Temple According to Mosaic law (Ex 13 : 12), a firstborn male had to be redeemed by an offering of five shekels made in the *Temple in Jerusalem (Num 18 : 15-17). This could be done at any time after the first month of the child's life, but it was assumed that the infant Jesus was brought to the Temple, in accordance with Jewish custom (Lv 12 : 1-6), when his mother went there for the ceremony of *Purification (Lk 2 : 22-39). The two events are thus closely connected in art and sometimes conflated. They precede the *Circumcision of Jesus.

When the presentation is the subject, the High Priest stands behind the altar, ready to receive the child from St *Mary the Virgin. St *Joseph is nearby, often depicted searching in his purse for shekels, or counting coins in his hand. Two doves, ready to be presented at the Purification are included in the scene. They may be carried by a woman companion of the Virgin, assumed to be St *Mary Salome. The aged prophetess *Anna is present, as is *Simeon, although according to the apocryphal *Book of *James* he had replaced Zacharias as High Priest. He is therefore given this role in some depictions and is shown holding the child in his arms as he declaims the *Nunc dimittis*. Simeon's prophecy, 'Yea, a sword shall pierce through thine own soul' (Lk 2 : 35), led to the inclusion of the presentation in the sequence of the Seven *Sorrows of the Virgin.

Presentation of St Mary the Virgin in the Temple According to the apocryphal *Book of *James*, St *Mary the Virgin's mother promised to dedicate her child to God, and placed her in the *Temple when she was three years old (although she is usually depicted as somewhat older). According to *Josephus in the *Jewish War*, there were fifteen steps leading from the court of women to the Temple. Mary is therefore sometimes shown ascending that number of steps

Pope St Leo the Great (440-61) rides out to confront Attila, the invader Hun. He wears an anachronistic tiara (Raphael's decoration for the Vatican *stanze,* early 16th century).

Potiphar's wife complains to her husband that Joseph, model of chastity, has tried to rape her (Rembrandt, 1606-69).

towards *Zacharias the High Priest who stands waiting to receive her. SS *Joachim and *Anne, her parents, watch from below. A feast commemorating the event (21 November) was introduced in the *East in the 7th century, possibly following a custom which originated in the Church of the Mother of God in Jerusalem *c.*543. It came to the *West in the 14th century, was abolished by Pius V (1566-72), and reestablished in 1585 by Sixtus V (1585-90).

Prester John A legendary priest (*presbyter) and king said to rule over a fabulously rich Christian kingdom in the Orient. The traveller Marco Polo identified him as Uric (or Gor) Khan, the Chinese prince who vanquished the Sultan of Persia in 1140. In the 15th century Portuguese merchants in *Jerusalem came into contact with some Ethiopian priests and assumed that Abyssinia (often confused with India) was the realm of Prester John. One of the motives which inspired Portuguese exploration of the African coastline, begun by Prince Henry the Navigator (1394-1460), was to forge a link with this supposedly Christian king and thus circumvent Islamic control of the Mediterranean trade-route to India.

Pride One of the *Seven Deadly Sins, symbolized in art by a woman looking into a mirror (where the *Devil is reflected); a rider falling off a horse (pride coming before a fall); and a *peacock ('proud as a peacock').

Prie-dieu A kneeling-desk for private devotions, where it is possible to read prayers from the book which rests on the shelf.

Priest The ordained minister of the *Sacraments, with authority to preach, bless and care for souls.

Prime First of the little monastic *Hours, to be said at sunrise, the first hour of the day, 6 am.

Prince of Darkness *Satan, who rules over *Hell, the place of 'outer darkness' (Mt 22 : 13).

Prince of Peace The title given by the prophet *Isaiah (Is 9 : 6) to the expected *Messiah, Christ, whose rule will be one of peace.

Principalities (or Princedoms) The first choir of the third hierarchy of *angels, represented as winged and in human form, clad in armour and carrying a sceptre, a lily, a cross, or palms. They protect rulers and are led by *Chamael.

Prior The general term for a superior of a small male monastic community, usually a *priory, which depends on an *abbey, although originally it meant the elder (Latin *prior*) *monk who ranked next to the *abbot.

Prioress The deputy of an *abbess, or the superior of a women's monastic community.

Priory A monastery with a *prior as *superior.

Procla (Procula) The name of *Pilate's wife in an appendix to the *Gospel of *Nicodemus, or *Acts of Pilate*. She warned Pilate when he was sitting on his judgement-seat with Jesus before him, 'Have thou nothing to do with that just man: for I have suffered many things this day in a dream because of him' (Mt 27 : 19). According to the apocryphal account she went with her husband to Rome when *Caesar (Tiberius) summoned him to explain why he had allowed Jesus to be crucified. When Pilate was condemned to death he asked pardon for her. When his head was cut off, an *angel took it away (which may be the reason why some sects believed Pilate to be a *saint). Procla saw the miracle, was filled with joy, and fell down dead. They buried her with Pilate.

Prodigal son The most moving of all Jesus' parables, illustrating God's love and mercy. It is in two parts. The first (Lk 15 : 11-24) tells how a younger son requested his share of inheritance and went off to a distant country where he 'wasted his substance with riotous living'. (He is depicted gambling in a bawdy house in the company of thieves and two courtesans, who drive him out when he has frittered away his wealth.) Friendless and poor in a strange land ravaged by famine where 'no man gave unto him', he was obliged to hire himself out as a swine-herd, the most despised of occupations, and was so hungry that 'he would fain have filled his belly with the husks that the swine did eat'. He resolved to return home and to ask forgiveness, saying, 'Father, I have sinned against Heaven, and before thee, and am no more worthy to be called thy son: make me as one of thy hired servants'. His father saw him in the distance 'and had compassion, and ran, and fell on his neck and kissed him'. He ordered his servants to dress him in the best robe, to put a ring on his hand, and shoes on his feet, to kill the fatted calf and be merry, 'For this my son was dead, and is alive again; he was lost, and is found'.

The second part (Lk 15 : 25-32) teaches that justice must yield to the *grace of God. The elder brother returned from his work in the fields and protested that although he had served his father faithfully, he had never been fêted like his erring brother. His father replied that his love for his elder son would never change, but that it was right that they should all rejoice at the return of the prodigal who had repented of his folly.

Promised Land The land of Canaan which God granted to *Abraham and his descendants after he had parted from *Lot (Gen 13 : 14-17). Its limits were later demarcated by God when he spoke to *Moses on Mount Sinai, saying, 'I will set thy bounds from the Red Sea even unto the sea of the Philistines, and from the desert unto the river' (Ex 23 : 31). The *Children of Israel, wandering in the desert after their *Exodus from Egypt, were told that if they kept God's commandments and had no other gods but him, they would be given tenure of this land, described as, 'a good land, a land of brooks of water, of fountains and depths that spring out of valleys and hills; a land of wheat, and barley, and vines, and fig trees, and pomegranates; a land of oil olive, and honey; and a land wherein thou shalt eat bread without scarceness, thou shalt not lack anything in it' (Dt 8 : 7-9). It was 'a land that floweth with milk and honey' (Dt 26 : 9). Christians interpreted these delights symbolically, so that the Promised Land became a metaphor for *Heaven, the ultimate home of the faithful.

Prophets Inspired men of *Israel who made known the will of God, and through whom the *Holy Spirit foretold the Christian era. Their prophesies were contained in the OT books bearing their names, classified according to length into a group four major works: *Daniel, *Ezekiel, *Isaiah and *Jeremiah; and twelve minor writings: *Hosea (Osee), *Joel, *Amos, *Obadiah (Abdias), *Jonah (Jonas), *Micah (Micheas), *Nahum, *Habakkuk (Habacuc), *Zephaniah (Sophonias), *Haggai (Aggeus), *Zechariah (Zacarias) and *Malachi (Malachias). The major prophets parallel the four *Evangelists, the minor ones (with some variations) the twelve *Apostles, supporting them on sculptured frontals or lower registers, and displaying *scrolls or *phylacteries on which are inscribed their prophetic utterances. *Attributes referring to outstanding characteristics or events in their lives (sometimes portrayed on the plinths of statuary) serve to identify them. A procession of prophets, each proclaiming a text foretelling the advent of the *Messiah, was a feature of medieval liturgical Christmas plays.

Protestant An adherent of those *Western Churches which separated from Rome following the *Reformation of the 16th century. The word was first used to describe the *Protestatio*, the protest of the representatives of certain German princes and free cities, against the *Catholic majority at the Diet of Speyer (1529) who wished to reaffirm the edict of the Diet of Worms (1521) which condemned the teachings of Martin *Luther. Protestants reject the supremacy and authority of the *Pope (whom they regard as the bishop of Rome); believe in the universal priesthood of all believers; accept the *Bible and not tradition as the only source of dogma and teaching; propound the doctrine of justification by faith as opposed to works; and object to ceremonial. Emphasis is placed on the preaching and hearing of the Word of God and on the commemorative aspect of the *Eucharist.

Protevangelium of James The title given to the 1552 edition of the Latin translation of the *Book of *James*, an apocryphal *infancy narrative, because it deals with events before those recorded in the canonical *Gospels.

Psalms From the Greek *psalmoí*, 'songs to be sung to the accompaniment of a stringed instrument'. The OT *Book of Psalms* contains 150 such songs (the Psalter), traditionally thought to have been composed by King *David. He is therefore depicted playing a harp or some other musical instrument. It is nevertheless obvious that these

Starving among the swine after dissipating his fortune, the **Prodigal son** resolves to seek his father's forgiveness (Albrecht Dürer, 1498).

Protestants led by Prince Mauritz fish for souls (allegorical Dutch painting, 1614).

psalms belong to different periods and must be attributed to many unknown composers. Whatever their original meaning, they have been interpreted in Jewish and Christian traditions alike as the sublime collective expression of the relationship of God to mankind and are sung liturgically by both faiths. Words from a psalm, 'My God, my God, why has thou forsaken me?' (Ps 22 (21) : 1) were on the lips of Jesus as he died.

The first Christians found prophetic references in the psalms to the life and death of their Lord and continued the Jewish custom of singing psalms at their assemblies. At least as early as the 4th century the Psalter, sung responsorially with the congregation participating, was a regular feature of church services. *Antiphonal singing of the psalms characterized the *choir office of religious communities. When church music developed as a complex art-form, psalms became the preserve of *clerics (the choir) but the *Reformation reestablished the participation of the people. The singing or chanting of psalms is thus a constant feature of public worship in most traditions.

Psalter The book containing the *psalms sung in the liturgy.

Pseudo-Matthew, Gospel of The name given to the 8th- or 9th-century apocryphal narrative of the birth and *infancy of Jesus, attributed to St *Matthew. It contains much that is to be found in the *Book of *James* but is notable for being the first account of the *ox and ass at the manger. It is also the source of legends associated with the *Flight into Egypt.

Pulpit A raised dais reached by steps and surrounded by a parapet, from which sermons are preached. It has a sounding-board over it. The word is derived from the Latin *pulpitum*, 'platform'. In the Middle Ages it replaced the *ambo. It was made of wood or stone and was often carved with symbolic scenes. Pulpits usually stand on the north side of the *nave, but there are examples on the exterior of a church, used for open-air sermons. In non-conformist chapels and churches, where emphasis is placed on the preaching of the word, pulpits may occupy the centre of the east end, behind a *communion table.

Purgatory A place of cleansing (Latin *purgare*, 'to cleanse') through suffering, the temporary abode of those who die in a state of grace but who require purgation from venial or remitted mortal sins before they can enter *Heaven. Souls are punished by knowing that they have been excluded for a time from the *Beatific vision (*poena damni*, 'punishment of the condemned'). In the *West it is also believed that they are purged by fire (*poena sensus*, 'the punishment of the senses'), although this view is not accepted in the *East. *Protestant reformers rejected the idea of Purgatory as being without scriptural basis.

How long individual souls must spend in Purgatory is not known, but they may be helped by the prayers and pious works of the faithful and by *Masses said for them, according to the doctrine defined at the Council of Florence (1438-45) and reaffirmed by the *Council of Trent.

Purification of St Mary the Virgin In the Mosaic *law (Lv 12 : 2-4) a mother was unclean after the birth of a male child and disqualified from touching any hallowed thing for forty days. She completed her purification by offering in the *Temple a yearling lamb and a pigeon or a dove. If poor, another dove or pigeon might be substituted for the lamb. St *Mary the Virgin came to the *Temple at the appropriate time with St *Joseph and the *Christ-Child (Lk 2 : 22-4). This event was commemorated in the *Calendar on 2 February with a feast, the Purification of St Mary the Virgin, also called *Candlemas. It was later conflated with the *Presentation of Jesus in the Temple, the name now given to the feast in the revised *Roman Catholic calendar of 1969 and in the new *Anglican lectionary.

Puritan In the strict and historical sense it denotes a member of the group of *Protestants who rejected Queen Elizabeth's religious compromise of 1560 as betraying the principles of the *Reformation. They demanded the 'purification' of the *Church of England by the abolition of *bishops, ceremonial, *vestments and religious imagery. They were not, as is popularly supposed, implacably opposed to the arts or music, but they insisted that these should have a high moral purpose.

Puritan emphasis on a virtuous life lived in accordance with the dictates of a 'Puritan conscience', the 'voice of God in the heart' and the 'inner light', gave rise to the second meaning of the word – one who advocated an extremely strict religious and moral existence and who, by extension, was a killjoy.

Purple A liturgical *colour, an alternative to *violet, symbolizing sorrow or *penance. It is used during the penitential seasons of *Advent and *Lent, except that rose may be used on *Gaudete* Sunday, the third Sunday in Advent, and *Laetare* Sunday, the fourth Sunday in Lent.

Pyx (Pyxis) From the Greek *pyxos* (plural *pyxides*), 'box tree'; originally the name for a jewel or toilet case made of boxwood and later of ivory or metal. From the 4th century onwards circular pyxides, small gilded wooden boxes, were used by *Christians as sacred containers for the reserved *Host or a saint's relics. They were ornamented with symbolic scenes and devices. In the early Middle Ages a pyx was usually made of ivory and was circular in shape, with a pointed lid. It resembled a tower and was referred to in Latin as *turris eburnea*, 'ivory tower'. Gothic pyxides were mostly polygonal. In the 13th century, Limoges became the centre for the production of beautifully enamelled copper pyxides. The modern pyx, used to take *communion to the sick, is a small round gold or silver-gilt case, gold-plated inside, and large enough to hold four or five Hosts. A larger vessel of similar shape with a removable lid and a pedestal, also called a pyx, or *ciborium, is used to reserve the *Blessed Sacrament in the *tabernacle. It is covered with a *corporal, or linen cloth, so called because it holds the body of *Christ.

Quadragesima The Latin for 'fortieth', applied to the first Sunday in *Lent, the fortieth day before *Easter, and to the whole of the lenten season.

Quail A bird which, because of its supposed sexual insatiability, symbolizes lasciviousness.

Quasimodo Sunday Low Sunday, the first Sunday after Easter, so called from the opening word of the office for that day, *Quasimodo geniti infantes*, 'Like new-born babes' (1 Pet 2 : 2).

Quattro Incoronati The name of the church in Rome dedicated to the late 4th-century saints called Severus, Severianus, Carpophorus and Victorinus – the Four Crowned Brothers. They were famous sculptors who as Christians refused Emperor *Diocletian's order to carve statues of pagan gods. Along with five other craftsmen they were put to death. They are patron saints of masons and sculptors.

Queen A title bestowed on St *Mary the Virgin (the equivalents in Latin being *domina* and *regina*; and in Greek *basilissa* and *despoina*) and used in liturgies of the *Roman Catholic and *Orthodox Churches. Mary was crowned Queen of Heaven (*Regina caeli*) after her *Assumption (See *Coronation of Mary the Virgin). The Feast of Mary the Queen, on 31 May, was instituted in the Roman Catholic Church by Pope Pius XII in the Marian year 1954. Mary is hailed and depicted as Queen of angels, *patriarchs, *prophets, *apostles, all *saints, *confessors (i.e. witnesses to Christ), virgins, and peace.

Queen of Sheba Ruler of Sheba (Saba), a country in southern Arabia, although the Jewish historian *Josephus cites her as queen of Ethiopia and Egypt (*Antiquities* Book VI, 5). She was given the name of Bilkis, or, in some sources, Nictoris. Hearing of King *Solomon's great wisdom, 'she came to prove him with hard questions', possibly riddles, but Solomon answered every one of them. She was astonished by his wisdom, his great wealth, the magnificence of his palace and the number of his servants. This was proof for her that God favoured the Israelites. After presenting gold, spices and precious stones to Solomon (the OT type of the visit of the Three *Kings to the *Christ-Child), she left Jerusalem with her great train of camels and attendants (1 Kg 10 : 1-13). *Allegorical interpretations of this episode equated Solomon with *Christ the King, and the queen of Sheba with St *Mary the Virgin whom he placed on the throne beside him (See *Coronation of St

A **pulpit** sculpted by Giovanni Pisano (*c*.1245–*c*.1314) for St Andrew's Church, Pistoia, Italy.

A 5th-century Italian **pyxis**.

Mary the Virgin). It also represented pagans acknowledging Christianity.

There are additional non-biblical versions of the visit. One is that the queen had exceptionally hairy legs and hoped to obtain a depilatory recipe from the wise king. Another is that Solomon had heard rumours that she had hirsute limbs and webbed feet. To discover the truth, he caused her to walk over a floor of polished crystal and she, mistaking this for a pool of water, raised her skirts. It was also said that the wood of the *Tree of Knowledge had been used to bridge a stream in Jerusalem. In a vision, the queen of Sheba had been told that this would be the *True Cross. She refused to walk over the bridge, worshipped the wood, and forded the stream barefoot. The Ethiopians, who named the queen as Makeda, held that she married Solomon and established their royal line with their offspring.

Quentin, St The fifth child (Latin *quintus*) of Zeno, a Roman senator who was converted to Christianity early in the 4th century, relinquished his command in the army, and went to evangelize Gaul. He worked in the region of Amiens where he was accused before the prefect Rictius Varus, had red-hot nails driven through his head and shoulders, and was eventually martyred by being impaled on an iron spit and then beheaded. A *millstone was tied around his neck and his body thrown into the River Somme. Half a century later it floated uncorrupted to the surface and was brought ashore by a blind woman called Eusebia who had been warned in a vision where the corpse was to be found so that she might give it Christian burial. She recovered her sight when she touched the body, and carried it to a hill where the city of Saint-Quentin was ultimately built and where a church was constructed to house the relics which St Eloi (*Eligius) miraculously discovered in 651. Some time afterwards, a man of the town was condemned to death for stealing a horse. A priest who had defended him, and had failed to secure a pardon, prayed before the tomb of St Quentin (or, in another version, the robber himself prayed) and when the hanging took place, the rope broke and the man was saved.

Qui conceptus est de Spiritu Sancto 'Who was born of the Holy Ghost', the clause supposedly contributed to the *Apostles' Creed by St *James the Great and displayed by him on an inscribed tablet or *phylactery.

Quince A fruit which, because its shape resembles an *apple, the *forbidden fruit, symbolizes sin.

Quire The alternative word for *choir (retained in the Anglican *Prayer Book of 1662, 'in quires and places where they sing'), denoting the part of the church within the chancel-screen, where the choir of singers sits.

Quiricus (Cyr), St The three-year-old child of Julitta, a Christian widow of Iconium who fled to Tarsus in Cilicia to escape *persecution but was arrested and tortured. Seeing his mother suffering, Quiricus cried out, 'I also am a Christian!'. In an attempt to keep him quiet, the governor pushed him down the marble steps of his tribune. The child fell with such force that he died. More elaborate deaths appear on Romanesque altar-frontals, including being sawn in half and boiled in oil.

Quo vadis? It is related in the late 2nd-century *Acts of Peter* that St *Peter's preaching of the virtue of purity so impressed many Roman matrons, including Xantippe the wife of Albinus 'the friend of Caesar', that they refused intercourse with their husbands. Their spouses were so angered that they plotted St Peter's death. Xantippe warned Peter and he finally agreed – much against his will – to flee Rome in disguise in order to protect his fellow Christians. As he went out of the city gate he saw Christ entering and asked him, 'Lord, whither goest thou?' *(Domine, quo vadis?).* Jesus replied that he was going to Rome to be crucified again. Peter came to himself, saw the Lord ascending into Heaven, and returned to Rome, encouraged to face martyrdom. The vision is commemorated in the church of *Domine quo vadis on the Appian Way.

Rabbit Symbol of timidity, but also of sexual love (a pun on the female generative organ because of the similarity of the Latin words *cunnus*, 'cunt' and *cuniculus*, 'coney', 'rabbit').

Rachel The younger daughter of *Laban and sister of *Leah. When *Jacob fled his home to escape the vengeance of his brother *Esau, whom he had deprived of his birthright, he met Rachel at a well in Haran and helped her to water her father's sheep. He wished to marry her because she 'was beautiful and well favoured', agreed to serve Laban for seven years in order to obtain her, but was tricked on his wedding night when Laban substituted the elder sister for the bride. He was obliged to serve a further seven years before she became his wife (Gen 29 : 1-30). Rachel was barren, but eventually God 'harkened to her, and opened her womb'. She bore *Joseph the Dreamer (Gen 30; 22-4). When Jacob parted from Laban, she stole her father's household gods and hid them in her 'camel's furniture' when Laban searched for them (Gen 31 : 19; 33-5). She died giving birth to *Benjamin and was buried 'in the way to Ephrath, which is *Bethlehem'. Jacob 'set a pillar upon her grave' (Gen 35 : 16-20).

Radegonde of Poitiers, St Born 518, daughter of the king of Thuringia. She was captured by Clothaire I of France whom she eventually married (thus she wears a crown, or has one at her feet to show her contempt for worldly pomp). She left her husband when he murdered her brother, became a *deaconess and later founded the convent of the Holy Cross at Poitiers (thus she is depicted as an *abbess). She was renowned for her charitable works. In response to her fervent prayers, fetters (her *attribute) dropped off the limbs of some suffering prisoners. She died in 587 and her tomb is in the crypt of the church of St Radegonde in Poitiers. In a niche in the nave of that church is a flagstone with the imprint of the feet of *Christ, brought from her cell where the Lord appeared to her as she was kneeling before a *crucifix, praying that her earthly crown could be exchanged for a *crown of thorns. She is patroness of Jesus College, Cambridge.

Rainbow Symbol of peace and concord between God and man. When *Noah came out of the *Ark, and built an altar and sacrificed ritually clean beasts and fowl, God promised he would never again curse the ground because of mankind's disobedience to his commands. As token of this covenant he set his bow in the sky, so that it would be seen when the clouds and rain came and be a reminder of his promise (Gen 20-2; 9 : 8-17).

Races of mankind All humans, except *Noah and his family who took refuge in the *Ark, perished in the *Flood. Post-diluvian mankind is therefore descended from Noah's sons: *Ham is the progenitor of the Hamitic or African race, *Shem of the Semitic or Asian, and *Japheth of the Japhitic or European. The discovery of America posed the difficult problem of fitting the American Indians into this scheme. One theory was that they were descended from the Lost *Ten Tribes of Israel, another that their ancestor was Canaan, son of Ham, whom Noah cursed and made a servant to the others (Gen 9 : 25).

Rahab the harlot *Joshua sent two of his men to spy out the city of *Jericho. They hid in the house of Rahab, a harlot. The king of Jericho heard that they were there and sent his men to capture them, but Rahab hid them on the roof of her house under stalks of flax. Her house stood on the walls of the city, and when the city gates were shut she let them down by a cord through the window and they escaped. They promised that if she bound a line of scarlet around the window, she and her household would be spared when the *Israelites attacked Jericho (Jos 2 : 1-18). Rahab is the OT type of St *Mary the Virgin because through her men were saved. The scarlet thread symbolized redemption through the blood of *Christ.

Ram One of the signs (*aries) of the *zodiac, and associated with the *Labours of the Month of March. It is also a symbol of virility and sexual power.

Raphael One of the three *archangels named in the Bible (Tob 12 : 15), the others being *Gabriel and *Michael. He is also one of the seven angels who stand in the presence of the Lord. As his name means in Hebrew, 'God heals', Raphael was said to be the angel who stirred the waters of the Pool of *Bethesda. As he protected *Tobias on his journey, he is the model of the *guardian angel. He is

In answer to St Peter's question, **Quo vadis?**, Christ points to Rome where he will be crucified again (Annibale Carracci, 1560–1609).

The Archangel **Raphael** tells Adam and Eve that God forbids them to eat the fruit of the Tree of Knowledge (William Blake's *Paradise Lost*, 1808).

also the protector of travellers and *pilgrims and is thus sometimes depicted as a winged wayfarer with staff and scrip (or wallet). When he carries a fish, the reference is to his adventures in company with Tobias. A jar of ointment recalls his cure of *Tobit's blindness (Tob 11 : 7-8) and indicates that Raphael is the patron of apothecaries.

Rat A white rat symbolizes day, a black rat night. Gnawing rats are a reminder of the way in which the years of a man's life are eaten away by the passage of time.

Raven A *bird of ill-omen, but in some instances of hope. The raven which *Noah put out of the *Ark brought back bad news (Gen 8 : 7), but a raven carried bread to *Elijah and SS *Antony Abbot, *Benedict and *Paul the Hermit. Ravens also protected the body of St *Vincent of Zaragoza.

Raymond Nonnatus, St Patron of Catalonia, born 1204, and given the title of *non natus*, 'not born', because he was delivered by Caesarian section after his mother had died. He was one of the early members of the *Mercedarian Order and was elected General, but died in Barcelona in 1240 on his way to Rome to be made a *cardinal. It was said that *Christ gave him his last communion. A *monstrance thus appears as one of his *attributes, the other being chains, recalling his work in Algiers where he went to ransom Christian captives. When his funds ran out, he took the place of one of the prisoners. The Moors padlocked his lips to stop him preaching the Gospel and he endured many years of suffering before he was released.

Real Presence, doctrine of the The *Catholic doctrine (not accepted by *Protestants) that in the *Eucharist, after the consecration of the *bread and the *wine, *Christ is truly, really and substantially present in these elements.

Rebecca (Rebekah) Wife of *Isaac and mother of *Jacob and *Esau. When *Abraham 'was old and well stricken in age', he sent his servant Eliezer to his homeland in Mesopotamia to find a wife for Isaac. Eliezer made his camels kneel beside a well outside the city of Nahor, and prayed that the first woman who would give this stranger a drink from her pitcher would be the divinely chosen bride for his master's son. Rebecca not only gave him drink but also drew water for his camels (Gen 24 : 1-28). The meeting of Eliezer and Rebecca is a frequent subject in art because it prefigured the *Annunciation, with Eliezer telling Rebecca, as *Gabriel told St *Mary the Virgin, that she had been chosen for a divine purpose. The marriage of Isaac and Rebecca (Gen 24 : 67) is the OT type of the union of Christ with his bride, the Church.

When Isaac sought refuge from famine in the land of the *Philistines, he passed his wife off as his sister in case the men should kill him to obtain her. King Abimelech wanted her for his harem, but when he looked out of a window he saw Isaac 'sporting with Rebekah' and discovered the deceit (Gen 26 : 6-11).

Rebecca favoured her son *Jacob and helped him to trick his elder brother *Esau out of his birthright (Gen 27 : 1-40).

Recollects A branch of the *Observants, those *Franciscans who followed the primitive *Rule of St Francis in contrast to the less austere practices of the *Conventuals. They are now *Friars Minor.

Rector In the *Church of England, originally an incumbent who was entitled to the whole *tithes of a *parish, and who might have a considerable income and live in a large rectory, thus differing from a *vicar, part of whose income was supplied by a body which received the tithes. Financial arrangements are now identical. In the *Roman Catholic Church, a rector is the head priest of a parish. The title is also applied to the head of a college or similar educational institution.

Red A *colour symbolizing blood, thus the liturgical colour for the commemoration of *martyrs whose blood is the seed of the Church, and for the feast of the *Holy Innocents. As red is also the colour of fire, it is used at *Pentecost because tongues of fire appeared above the assembled *Apostles. Red (called 'the sacred purple') is the colour for *cardinals, who wear in art red hats with two sets of fifteen tassels.

Red Sea, crossing of the When *Pharaoh allowed the *Children of Israel to leave Egypt, they were led by God who was hidden in a pillar of cloud by day and in a pillar of fire by night until they reached the Red Sea. Pharaoh caught up with them there and they feared death. But 'Moses stretched out his hand over the sea; and the Lord caused the sea to go back by a strong east wind all that night and made the sea dry land, and the waters were divided' (Ex 14 : 21). The *Israelites walked across, but when Pharaoh and his host followed close upon them, God trapped the Egyptians by taking the wheels off their chariots. He then told Moses to stretch forth his hand again. The waters returned and drowned the host of Pharaoh, his chariots and his horsemen (Ex 14 : 9-30). This story symbolizes the salvation of the faithful through *Baptism and the blood of *Christ (the 'Red' sea), and the punishment of the wicked.

Safe on the other shore the Israelites sang praises to God, and *Miriam the prophetess, Moses' sister, took a timbrel and danced and sang, her song foretelling the *Magnificat (Ex 15 : 1-21).

Redeemer Jesus *Christ, through whom came the *Redemption of mankind.

Redemption The restoration of mankind to communion with God through the *Incarnation and Death of Jesus Christ (See *Crucifixion), whereby all were delivered from *sin, brought into the world by the disobedience of *Adam and *Eve (See *Fall of Mankind).

Refectory The dining-hall of a religious community, the place of refreshment (Latin *refectum*, 'refreshed'). It is customary to eat in silence at dinner and supper while listening to a reading from an edifying text. *Carthusians assemble in their refectory only on *Sundays and great festivals, eating alone in their *cells on other days.

Reformation The movement against certain abuses in the *Roman Catholic Church – notably the loose life of some of the *clergy, their excessive wealth, neglect of their spiritual duties, and the sale of *indulgences – which was intensified after Martin *Luther's protest in 1517 and his subsequent attacks on the supremacy of the *Pope. It culminated in the secession of *Protestant Churches which did not acknowledge the jurisdiction of the Pope and would not accept certain doctrines, such as *transubstantiation (See *Counter-Reformation).

Regina Caeli Latin for 'Queen of Heaven', the opening words of the fourth of the *antiphons sung in honour of St *Mary the Virgin from *compline on *Holy Saturday until *none on the Saturday after *Pentecost. Of unknown authorship, it probably dates from the 12th century.

Relics Remains of the bodies of *saints, instruments of their martyrdom or objects which they used in their lifetimes. They are placed in an altar when it is consecrated and inserted in a *Roman Catholic *bishop's pectoral cross. Relics may be offered for veneration if there is proof of their authenticity or if they have been accepted as authentic since time immemorial. The earliest references to relics is the account of the martyrdom of St *Polycarp in 156, when Christians of Smyrna gathered up his remains. The translation (or transfer) of a martyr's bones to a church and the yearly commemoration of his death (really his birth – *dies natalis* – into the kingdom of God) encouraged the cult of relics from the 4th century onwards, but remains were left intact until the 7th century. To discourage their dispersal, a cloth called a *brandeum* was laid on the saint's grave and used as a substitute relic which could be carried away. Barbarian incursions meant that tombs were no longer secure from disturbance. It therefore became the custom to distribute relics, and their acquisition became a matter of the greatest importance to the rulers and clergy of nascent Christian kingdoms. By the 10th century, relics were being placed in shrines and in church and cathedral *reliquaries, which became centres of *pilgrimages.

Reliquary A vessel, often beautifully ornamented, intended to contain or display a sacred *relic. Also a chest, casket or *shrine for a relic.

Remigius (Rémi), St The 'Apostle of France' (*c*.438-530). He studied at Rheims, was ordained priest in 457, and because of his great abilities was soon elected archbishop. He baptized and anointed Clovis as king of the Franks in 496 – a crism containing holy oils, *la Sainte Ampoule*, was brought to him by a dove and is his *attribute –

Rebecca, divinely chosen to be Isaac's bride, gives Eliezer water from the well, prefiguring the Annunciation (Murillo, 1617-82).

A **reliquary** of St Francis of Assisi displaying his stigmata (13th century).

Figures of Holy Roman emperors adorn niches along this gold-embossed **reliquary** of Charlemagne in the treasury of Aachen Cathedral (*c*.1200).

and gave him the power to touch for 'the king's evil', or scrofula. His relics now repose in the *Benedictine Abbey of St Rémi, Rheims. Among the miracles attributed to him is the blessing of an empty barrel which then overflowed with wine and flooded the cellar of a relative's house where he was dining. When devils started a fire which threatened to destroy Rheims, he put it out by raising his hand. Sparrows ate at his table without fear. While still a child at his mother's breast he restored the sight of a blind *hermit by moistening his eyes with her milk.

Reparata of Florence, St Patron saint of Florence where the cathedral (the Duomo) was dedicated to her and called by her name from 680-1298. It was then renamed Santa Maria del Fiore and rededicated to SS *Mary the Virgin and *John the Baptist. She was said to be a 3rd-century virgin martyr of Caesarea in Palestine, who was horribly put to death when she was twelve after being paraded naked through the city. When she was beheaded a *dove (her *attribute) flew out of her mouth (or her truncated body).

Requiem The Latin for 'rest', the first word of the *Introit of the *Mass celebrated for the dead, *Requiem aeternam dona eis Domine* 'Rest eternal grant him, O Lord'.

Requiescat in pace Latin for 'may he [or she] rest in peace' (abbreviated RIP). The plural is *requiescant in pace*, 'may they rest in peace'. It is said at the end of a *requiem Mass and at the conclusion of prayers for the dead.

Reredos An *altarpiece, a screen of stone or wood at the back of the altar and connected with it by means of a *predella. The side facing the nave is called the *retable; the other side, the counter-retable. Reredos became common in the 12th century when they were attached to altars containing relics; predella and reredos being fitted with panels decorated with religious scenes and narratives of the life of the saint to whom the altar was dedicated. Later, more elaborate and beautifully decorated reredos were constructed, displaying large-scale paintings and with statues placed in niches.

Reservation The custom of retaining the *Blessed Sacrament in a *tabernacle or other suitable place for the communion of the sick or (in *Roman Catholic usage) for the adoration of the faithful. Its presence is usually signified by a lighted red lamp.

Resurrection of Christ That Jesus rose from the dead on the third day (Sunday, counting inclusively in ancient style) after his *Crucifixion on Friday, is a fundamental Christian belief and is enshrined in the *Apostles' Creed, but the event is reported, not described, in the *Gospels. Depictions of the Resurrection are therefore based on deductions from the scriptural accounts of the *Entombment and on the reports of the *Holy Women who discovered the *Empty Tomb. It is stated (Mt

27 : 62-6) that the chief priests and the *Pharisees asked *Pilate to have the sepulchre made secure so that Jesus' disciples should not be able to steal his body and then claim that he had fulfilled his prophecy that he would rise from the dead. Pilate put a guard at their disposal and these soldiers are shown by the tomb, either asleep or falling back, blinded by cosmic light as Jesus emerges from the grave. He carries a flag *(*vexillum)* with the red cross of the Resurrection, symbolizing victory over death, and either rests one foot on the edge of the tomb, preparatory to stepping out (a posture not favoured after the *Council of Trent) or stands in front of it. When he is shown in a *mandorla in the sky above the tomb, it may be a reference to the belief that his spirit returned to his body after his *Descent into Limbo and before the Resurrection.

Resurrection of the dead A tenet of the Christian faith, an article of the *Apostle's Creed, that at the end of time there will be a general resurrection of all who have died, good and bad, preparatory to the Last *Judgement.

Retable A shelf or ledge (also called a *gradine) at the back of an *altar on which a *cross or *candlesticks may be placed; also a structure (especially one forming part of an altarpiece or *reredos) which contains painted panels or carvings.

Reverend Abbreviated Rev., from the Latin *reverendus*, 'worthy of respect', the usual English courtesy title for the *clergy.

Rich man and Lazarus *See* *Dives and Lazarus.

Ring A symbol of eternity, as it is a complete circle. Three interlaced rings represent the *Trinity. A ring also symbolizes union, as in the exchange of wedding rings. As an emblem of authority and as a signet, a ring is worn by *cardinals and *bishops. The *Pope wears the 'fisherman's ring', indicating that he is the successor of St *Peter, the fisherman. A *nun wears a ring to show that she is a bride of *Christ.

Rite The words and actions prescribed for a liturgical or sacramental act, e.g. *Mass or *baptism. In the Early Christian centuries different regions had their own rites – Gallican in France, Mozarabic in Spain and Celtic in Ireland and parts of England for instance – but these local rites gave way to the Latin rite as *Roman Catholicism spread and the supremacy of the *Pope was acknowledged. In the *East the prevailing influence was the Greek rite of Constantinople (Byzantium).

Ritual Strictly, the words prescribed for a religious service, but popularly extended to include the ceremonial acts which accompany them. A 'ritualist' was thus a term of abuse used in the 19th and early 20th centuries in England by those who did not approve of *High Church clergy who sought to revive *Catholic ceremonial and the wearing of *vestments.

Rivers of Paradise The garden in which the first man and woman lived was watered by a river from *Eden which divided into four as it flowed out of *Paradise. These rivers were: Pishon, said to encircle the land of Havilah (Arabia), where pure gold, aromatic resin and onyx are found; Gihon (thought to be the Nile), which flows round the land of Cush (Upper Egypt); the Tigris, 'which flows to the east of Ashur'; and the Euphrates (Gen 2 : 10-14). These rivers appear on medieval world maps.

Road to Emmaus *See* *Emmaus, road to.

Roch, St A saint invoked for protection from plague, cholera and other infectious diseases. Born in Montpellier, France, in 1293, his wealthy parents died when he was twenty, leaving him their money, but he was converted to a religious life, sold all his worldly goods for the support of hospitals and the poor, and set out on a pilgrimage to Rome (hence he is depicted in a *pilgrim's garb and carries a staff). At Acqua Pendente he found the city ravaged by plague and spent some time there nursing the sick. He was infected at Piacenza (a plague spot is shown on his bared leg) and would have died had not a faithful dog (shown as his companion) brought him food each day from his master's table. When he returned to Montpellier he was so emaciated that he was unrecognized and thrown into prison as a spy. He spent five years in a dungeon where an angel comforted him. Before he died in 1327 he wrote an account of his life. When the manuscript was discovered he was rehabilitated and buried with great honours by his repentant fellow-citizens.

Rochet A *vestment, a sleeved tunic of white linen, the lower part being lace, reaching to the knees and worn over the *mozzetta in *choir by *bishops, *abbots and *prelates who are not members of religious *Orders.

Rock Symbol of St *Peter and of the *Church, because of *Christ's pun on the word 'Peter', which also means rock – 'thou art Peter and upon this rock will I build my church' (Mt 16 : 18). The *parable of the wise man who built his house on a rock, not on sand, so that it was not washed away when the floods came (Mt 7 : 24; Lk 6 : 47), illustrates the need for firm and consistent faith. *Moses striking the rock in the desert to bring water to the thirsting *Israelites (Ex 17 : 6; Num 20 : 10) may symbolize the *Eucharist, because of the piercing of Christ's side on the Cross (but it also means the *Gospel, which refreshes the faithful).

Roman Catholic Church The Church of all Christians in communion with the *bishop of Rome, whom they acknowledge as *Pope and Vicar of Christ – the visible head of the Church founded by Christ. At the time of the *Reformation, *Protestants disputed the Pope's

An ancient and a modern interpretation of the **Resurrection:** *(above)* a medieval alabaster plaque made in Nottingham, England *(below)* a detail from Sir Stanley Spencer's huge **Resurrection of the dead** (1922-7), set in his native village of Cookham.

right to be so regarded, so ceased to be in communion with his Church.

Romuald, St Founder of the *Camaldolese Order. Born at Ravenna *c*.952, he became a *Benedictine monk at the age of twenty to expiate a murder committed by his father, and was elected *abbot of the *monastery of St Apollinare-in-Classe in 998. A year later he resigned, saddened by the laxity of his fellow monks. After some time spent in travel, he retired to live as a *hermit at Camaldoni, near Florence. His way of life attracted many followers, who became the first monks of his Order. He had a vision of his monks dressed in a white *habit and ascending a ladder into heaven, and he took this as a divine indication that they should wear white. He is depicted as a venerable hermit or abbot with a long white beard, carrying a staff and a skull to indicate his asceticism.

Rood From the Old English for 'wood' and hence (wood of) the *Cross; a *crucifix, usually with the figures of St *Mary the Virgin and St *John the Evangelist placed on either side. Usually placed in medieval English churches on a rood beam laid across the front of the *chancel arch. Below this was a rood screen, beautifully carved and with paintings or carvings of *apostles, *prophets and *saints in the panels at the base. A rood loft above the screen could be reached by spiral stairs, and from there the *Gospel was read or sermons preached, drawing attention to the sacrifice on the Cross.

Rosary A string of 150 small *beads and fifteen larger ones, divided into fifteen sets of ten small and one large bead, used to keep count of prayers. (The word 'bead' is derived from the Old English *bede*, 'prayer'.) The first large bead denotes the *Lord's Prayer, the small ones *'Hail Mary', said ten times, and the next large bead a *Gloria*. Each set is dedicated to meditation on one group, joyful, sorrowful and glorious, of the fifteen *mysteries of the faith. Two large beads may be added, one each for the *Apostles' Creed and the Lord's Prayer, and three small beads for repetition of the *Ave Maria* or the *Salve Regina*. A *crucifix may also appear. Five decades make a corona or chaplet, the third part of the Rosary.

The use of stones or beads to count prayers is ancient and possibly non-Christian in origin, but according to legend it was first devised by St *Dominic, to whom St *Mary the Virgin presented the first rosary in a vision. The word 'rosary' is derived from the Latin *rosarium*, 'rose-garden', and St Mary the Virgin is sometimes shown in a garden full of roses. The rosary in monastic use in the *Eastern Church consists of 100 or 107 beads. The Feast of the Rosary on the first Sunday in October was instituted as an act of thanksgiving for the victory over the Turks at the battle of Lepanto, 1571.

Rose A white rose symbolizes purity, a red rose martyrdom or blood (as when the drops of blood from the wounds of St *Francis of Assisi turned into roses when they touched the ground). The *flower is also sacred to St *Mary the Virgin, the Rose of Sharon (Sg 2 : 1). She is also called the Rose without a Thorn because she is without taint of *original sin, as the rose was when it grew in *Paradise. It acquired thorns (sins) when it was planted on earth after the *Fall of Mankind. St *Elizabeth of Hungary displays an apron full of roses, and St *Dorothea (or Dorothy) carried a basket with roses and apples.

Rose of Lima, St The first *saint to be canonized (in 1671) in the Americas. Born in Lima, Peru, of poor parents in 1586, she supported them by her embroidery, needlework and by cultivating flowers for sale. She refused offers of marriage, and at the age of twenty became a *tertiary of the Third Order of St Dominic (*Dominicans). She lived austerely in a hut in her garden and was rewarded with mystical experiences. Her severest mortifications were the wearing of a *crown of thorns and sleeping on a bed of broken glass. It was said that the *Vatican was showered with roses as a sign that she should be made a saint.

Rose window A circular window with tracery radiating from the centre, filled with stained glass and usually placed at the west end of a *church or *cathedral. Each section contained an illustration, frequent subjects being *doves or *lamps representing the Seven *Gifts of the Holy Spirit.

Rubrics Ritual or ceremonial directives written in red (Latin *rubrica*, 'red earth') in *missals and other service books, to distinguish them from the text which is to be spoken or sung.

Rule From the Latin *regula*, 'norm', 'measure'; the regulations prescribed for the daily life and conduct of members of religious communities. Rules are named after *saints who founded religious *Orders based on them, even if the clauses were later revised. Some have fallen into disuse, like the Rule of St *Pachomius, the first rule written for *monks living in the nine *monasteries which Pachomius founded in Egypt (315-46). It prescribed strict, almost military discipline, hard manual labour and constant study of sacred texts.

Rules followed by long-established communities vary to meet special needs or circumstances. They may be classified under four heads. **1** All monks of the *East follow the Rule of St *Basil, and for this reason are sometimes called Basilians. This Rule was revised by St Theodore of Studion (759-826). It is austere and emphasizes manual work, study and the regular observance of the canonical *Hours. **2** The Rule of St *Augustine (in Latin *Regula Sancti Augustini*) is derived from a letter which he composed in 423 describing the way of life to be followed by monastic communities. It was codified towards the end of the 11th century, its distinctive precepts being individual

215

RUTH

poverty, all property to be held in common and communal prayer. This Rule is followed by *Austin Friars (*Augustinians), *Augustine Canons (*Canons Regular), *Dominicans and *Servites. 3 The Rule of St *Benedict, written by that saint in the early 6th century for his monks at Monte Cassino, set the pattern for *Western monasticism and was adopted by *Benedictines, *Camaldolese, *Cluniacs and *Vallombrosans. It enjoins strict obedience to the *abbot or *abbess, the *Opus Dei (the observance of the canonical *Hours in *choir), abstinence from meat and a day divided between manual work, prayer and study. 4 The original Rule of St *Francis was written by St Francis in 1209, but lost, rewritten in 1221 and given final form and approval in 1223 by Pope Honorius III (1216-27). Poverty for the community and for its individual members was strictly enjoined, together with chastity and obedience. In 1279 Pope Nicholas III (1277-80) decreed that 'poverty' meant that the community could have 'moderate use' of the necessities of life, provided there was no ownership. Begging and manual labour was to produce the means of existence. This question of ownership led to the formation of distinctive groups of *Franciscans: the *Observants (later *Friars Minor) have no corporate property, *Conventuals permit it, and *Capuchins emphasize poverty and austerity. Franciscan *nuns, or *Poor Clares, are divided into the strictly *enclosed Colettines founded by St Colette (1406-34) who do not possess property, and Urbanists who follow a modified rule, approved in 1263 by Pope Urban IV (1261-4), which permits them to undertake work outside their convent.

*Carmelites, *Carthusians and *Jesuits have their own constitutions which express their particular objectives.

Ruth The Moabite heroine of the *Book of Ruth*, who insisted on accompanying her mother-in-law Naomi to her native Bethlehem after the death of the men of the family in Moab, saying 'for where you go I will go, and where you lodge, I will lodge; your people shall be my people, and your God my God' (Rt 1 : 16). Destitute, she gleaned – 'in tears amid the alien corn' – what was left by the reapers on the land of Naomi's late husband's kinsman, Boaz. Aware of her devotion to her mother-in-law, Boaz secretly ordered his men to leave grain for her and she returned home with a bushel of barley. Naomi saw her opportunity and advised Ruth to go at night to the threshing-floor where Boaz used to sleep after the day's harvesting. When he awoke in the middle of the night, she begged him: 'spread your skirt over your maidservant, for you are next of kin' (Rt 3 : 9). Struck by her virtuous conduct, and having persuaded another nearer relative to swear in the presence of ten elders that he relinquished his right to her under the Levirite law, Boaz married Ruth. Their son, Obed was the father of *Jesse, the father of King *David. Ruth and Boaz are therefore ancestors of *Christ, and Boaz thus sometimes figures in the Tree of Jesse.

St **Romuald** is seen here being blessed by a bishop before departing on a pilgrimage (Flemish, c.1490).

The **rose window** on the west front of the church of San Rufino, Italy (early 13th century).

Sabaoth Hebrew for 'hosts', 'armies'. The word is left untranslated in the *Te Deum* in the Anglican *Book of Common Prayer* (1662) where 'Lord God of Sabaoth' or 'Lord of Hosts' means *God the Father, who commands the hosts of *angels.

Sabbatarianism The strict observance of *Sunday as a day for church-going, devotional reading and moral recreation, so that it approximates in spirit to the Jewish *Sabbath. A characteristic of the *Reformation in England and Scotland, Sabbatarianism was enforced by *Puritan legislation in the 17th century, relaxed somewhat when the monarchy was restored under Charles II, and revived by *Evangelicals in the late 18th century, culminating in the Lord's Day Observance Act (1781). In the 19th and early 20th centuries Sabbatarianism accorded well with the religious attitudes of English, Welsh and Scottish middle classes who scorned a 'Continental Sunday'. Their view is stoutly defended by the Lord's Day Observance Society as a bulwark against secularism.

Sabbath From the Hebrew *shabbat*, 'rested', 'desisted from toil'. The seventh day of the Jewish week, recalling the day when God rested from the *Work of Six Days of Creation. He blessed the seventh day and sanctified it (Gen 2 : 1-3). Jews therefore abstain from work on this day and gather for worship, in obedience to the fourth of the *Ten Commandments (Ex 20 : 8; Dt 5 : 12). Christians at first followed this tradition, but later observed the first day of the week, *Sunday, the Lord's Day, as their day to meet for prayer and for the celebration of the *Eucharist in commemoration of the *Resurrection.

Sabina, St A wealthy Roman widow, converted to Christianity by her servant Serapia who was put to death for her faith. Sabina's social position protected her for a while but she practised her religion so fervently and openly that she was arrested and martyred in Rome *c.*126. Her relics were enshrined in the 4th century in the *basilican church dedicated to her on the Aventine Hill. It contains early wooden carvings recounting her history. She is shown wearing a martyr's *crown and carrying a *palm.

Sackcloth A coarse cloth made of goat's hair, used for making sacks, but also for garments worn by mourners as a sign of grief. *Ashes were added to complete the symbolism. Thus *Mordecai put on 'sackcloth with ashes, and went into the midst of the city, and cried with a loud and a bitter cry' (Est 4 : 1).

Sacra Conversazione Italian for 'holy conversation', the name given in art to a type of painting, which came into prominence in the 14th century, in which St Mary the Virgin enthroned and holding the *Christ-Child, or the Virgin of the *Assumption, are depicted surrounded by saints.

These saints may belong to different periods, but are linked by a single theme and may include *Doctors of the Church, saints revered by a particular religious *Order, or saints bearing the same Christian name as the donor.

Sacramentals Religious practices, such as *grace at meals, making the *sign of the cross, wearing *vestments, imposition of *ashes on the forehead to signify penance, and carrying blessed *palms on *Palm Sunday. They confer spiritual significance on an occasion.

Sacraments, seven A sacrament (from the Latin *sacramentum*, 'a sacred obligation') is an outward sign, divinely instituted, signifying and conferring *grace. *Roman Catholics and *Orthodox Churches recognize seven of them. These were frequently depicted in *Western art, especially after the *Council of Trent when it became necessary to emphasize differences from *Protestant Churches which then accepted only two as instituted by Jesus: *Baptism and the *Lord's Supper. The seven are: Baptism; *Confirmation; *Mass or *Eucharist; *Confession (Penance); *Holy Orders (for *clergy); Matrimony (for lay persons); Extreme *Unction. The last five are recognized as lesser sacraments in Article 25 of the *Thirty-Nine Articles of the *Anglican Church.

Sacred Heart of Jesus A *Roman Catholic devotion to the *heart of Jesus, observed on the Friday of the week following *Corpus Christi. It gained popularity through the visions of St Margaret Mary Alacoque (1647-90), a nun of the contemplative Visitation Order (*Visitandines) founded by St Francis de Sales (1567-1622) and St Jane Frances de Chantal (1572-1641).

Sacristan A church official or *cleric, or where that is not possible a *layman, who looks after the *sacristy, the room where *vestments, sacred *vessels and other furnishings are kept and where the *clergy robe. His duty is to make all the necessary preparations for the ceremonial of the *liturgy.

Sacristy A room in the charge of a *sacristan, adjoining a church or chapel, where the *clergy put on their *vestments and where the liturgical *vessels are stored. It derives its name from the medieval practice of reserving the *Blessed Sacrament in that room (*See* *vestry).

Sadducees A conservative and worldly *Jewish sect in NT times; pro-Roman and centred on the *Temple cult. Their name is probably derived from *Zadok, high priest in the reign of King *David. *Pharisee thought admitted of change and had popular appeal; Sadducees recognized only the written *Law. They refused to believe in the resurrection of the dead or in the existence of spirits or angels, because the Law did not mention them. Jesus had frequently to contend with their opposition to his liberal teaching. They caused SS *Peter and *John the Apostle to be arrested (Ac 4 : 1-4). Their power and influence waned after the fall of *Jerusalem in AD 70.

Sagittarius The *archer, the ninth sign of the *zodiac, which the sun enters around 22 November. This constellation is to be distinguished from the *centaur, half man and half horse, who is shown shooting an arrow and represents sin, appearing on *capitals and carvings. In the *Labours of the Months, Sagittarius controls the preparations against the approach of winter – gathering logs and fattening pigs on acorns before slaughtering them and salting their carcasses.

Saint From the Latin *sanctus*, 'holy', the name applied initially to all *Christians, but later restricted to men and women of outstanding holiness. The need to define those who were to be thus dignified led to the formalization of processes leading to *canonization, or inclusion in the list of recognized saints. In art, saints are identified by a *halo, *vestments and an *attribute or emblem which refers to some key event in their lives, such as miracles or martyrdom.

Salamander A fire-breathing creature, generally depicted as a small lizard or wingless dragon, but sometimes as a dog or a man-like figure, standing in the midst of flames. So cold that it quenched heat, the salamander was able to live and breed in the hottest fire. The name 'salamander's wool' was given to asbestos. If a fire were kept burning for seven years, a salamander would be born in it. The salamander symbolized the triumph of faith over passion. It also represented Fire, one of the *Four Elements.

Salome Daughter of *Herodias, consort of Philip the Tetrarch, who became the wife of *Herod Antipas. Salome is not named in the NT (Mk 6 : 17-28; Mk 14 : 3-11) but is given a name by *Josephus in his *Antiquities of the Jews* (XVIII. 137). St *John the Baptist incurred the enmity of Herodias because he denounced Herod for his adulterous union with her, as she had been his brother Philip's wife. At a banquet in honour of his birthday, Herod was so excited by Salome's dancing that he promised her whatever she should request, up to half this kingdom. On her mother's advice she asked for the head of St *John the Baptist who was then languishing in prison. Regretting his rash promises and fearful of the consequences, Herod ordered the execution and the head was brought to Salome on a platter. She then presented it to her mother.

Salome the midwife On the way to Bethlehem St *Mary the Virgin was taken by birth pangs in a desert place, and knew that her time was near. St *Joseph found a cave and left her in the care of his sons by his first marriage, and returned with a midwife. After *Jesus was born the midwife met Salome, another of her profession, and told her of the miracle she had just witnessed, a virgin had given birth. Salome refused to believe that this was possible until she had herself made a medical inspection, but when she applied her finger, her arm was paralysed. On the advice of her colleague she prayed, repenting of her unbelief. An angel

Saints, among them SS Francis, Jerome and Sebastian, are grouped around the enthroned Virgin and Child in this **sacra conversazione** by Giovanni Bellini (late 15th century).

Richard Strauss based his opera *Salome* on Oscar Wilde's drama *Salome* (1893). An illustration by Aubrey Beardsley (1894) showing **Salome** gloating over the head of John the Baptist.

appeared to say that her prayers had been heard and that if she touched the child she would be healed. She did so and left the cave rejoicing. This apocryphal legend first appeared in the *Book of *James*. Salome, or both midwives, are sometimes included in depictions of the *Nativity.

Salt Salt is a preservative, so blessed salt is regarded as a protection against evil. It is used in the sacrament of infant *baptism, when a few grains of salt are put in the mouth of the child. In the early Church, *catechumens (adults being prepared for baptism) were handed salted bread as a symbol that they were guests in the house of the Lord, since bread and salt were an ancient sign of hospitality. Jesus called his *disciples the 'salt of the earth' (Mt 5 : 13), implying that if they possessed the qualities indicated in the *Beatitudes they would preserve mankind. He went on to say, 'but if the salt have lost its savour, wherewith shall it be salted', meaning that they would lose the power if they lost faith in him.

Saltire A *cross in the form of the *Greek letter X, *chi*, symbolizing *Christ. Since at least the 14th century it has been the *attribute of St *Andrew who was said to have been crucified on a cross of this design.

Salvator Mundi Latin for '*Saviour of the World', the title of a devotional picture of Christ blessing the world with his right hand and holding in his left an *orb surmounted by a *cross.

Salve Regina Latin for 'Hail, Queen', the opening words of the *antiphon in honour of St *Mary the Virgin, appointed for the season after *Pentecost in the Catholic Church. The hymn certainly dates from the 11th century and has been attributed to various authors. Jacobus de Voragine said in his *Golden Legend* that it was composed by a certain Bishop Peter of Compostela. Another candidate is Herman the Cripple (Herimannus Contractus [1013-54], a monk of Reichenau). It has also been associated with Bishop Aimar of Le Puy, France.

Samson Eponymous strong man, unfortunate lover, one of the *Judges of Israel and hero of the *Israelite struggle against the *Philistines. He was revered by Christians because some of the events in his life were thought to prefigure those of *Jesus Christ. He is represented as a brawny young man with long flowing locks. It was said that his strength resided in his hair. His mother was a pious woman and was childless for many years, until she was told by an angel, perhaps *Gabriel (foreshadowing the *Annunciation), that she would bear a son, consecrated to God. He would be forbidden to cut his hair, eat unclean food or drink wine, and he would deliver the Israelites from the Philistines. On his second appearance, the angel advised Manoah, Samson's father, to sacrifice a kid. He then vanished in the flames which arose from the altar which Manoah had made on a rock (Jg 13 : 2-20). Samson's birth and circumcision (although this is not scripturally

recorded) foretold the *Nativity and *Circumcision of Jesus.

Samson demonstrated his superhuman strength by slaying a young *lion which roared at him (Jg 14 : 5-6). He is depicted forcing open its jaws with his bare hands. This action foreshadowed Christ's *Descent into Hell, when he broke open the gates and released the *Just of the Ancient Law.

Against his parents' wishes, but in accordance with God's plan, Samson had fallen in love with a Philistine girl from Timnath. On his return from a visit to her, finding that bees had made a hive in a dead lion's mouth, he extracted the honeycomb. At his wedding feast Samson wagered thirty young guests that they could not answer the riddle, 'Out of the eater came forth meat and out of the strong came forth sweetness'. They prevailed upon the bride to coax the answer out of her husband. She wept for seven days and finally Samson gave in 'because she lay sore upon him'. When Samson discovered how he had been tricked and that the men of the city knew the answer, he said, 'If ye had not plowed with my heifer, ye had not found out my riddle'. He killed thirty Philistines at Ashkelon and then returned to his parents' home (Jg 14 : 1-4; 8-19).

Overcome by longing for his bride, he went back to her village at the time of the wheat harvest, only to find that her father had given her to another man. Scorning the offer of her younger sister, he avenged himself by tying firebrands to the tails of 300 paired foxes and sending them to burn up the Philistine wheat fields, vineyards and olive groves. In reprisal, the Philistines set fire to the house of the faithless bride and her father and burned them alive. Samson in revenge 'smote the Philistines hip and thigh' and went into hiding on the top of a rock in Judah (Jg 15 : 1-8).

Fearful of their enemies, the men of Judah captured Samson, bound him with two new cords and handed him over to the Philistines, but he snapped his bonds like 'flax that was burnt with fire' and, seizing a new jawbone of an ass, slew 1000 men and hid himself in the wilderness. (*Cain is supposed to have killed Abel with the same instrument.) When he was overcome by thirst, God caused water to gush from a hollow in the barren ground so that he could drink his fill. (A mistranslation of the Hebrew word for 'spring' gave rise to the legend that he drank out of the jawbone of an ass [Jg 15 : 9-18].)

The Philistines later tried to ambush Samson at the city gates of Gaza at dawn when they knew that he would take leave of a harlot with whom he used to spend the night. Samson got up at midnight, wrenched up the gates and the two gate posts and carried them on his shoulders thirty miles to a hilltop near Hebron (Jg 16 : 1-3). This foreshadowed Christ carrying the Cross along the *Via Dolorosa*, and the *Resurrection, when Christ burst out of the tomb. Samson's end came through his fatal love for *Delilah.

Samuel The last of the *Judges of Israel, whose main story is told in the first twelve chapters of the *First Book of Samuel*. His mother vowed to dedicate him to God, and as soon as he was weaned she placed him with the priests at the shrine of Shiloh. She and her husband brought him a little coat each year. Hearing a mysterious voice in the night, Samuel was advised by an aged priest to answer, 'Speak, Lord; for thy servant heareth' (1 Sam 3 : 9). He was told by God, 'Behold, I will do a thing in Israel, at which both the ears of every one that heareth shall tingle'. Samuel was favoured with many revelations and was able to save the *Israelites from their *Philistine enemies because they heeded his exhortations and ceased to worship Canaanite gods. He judged Israel 'all the days of his life' (1 Sam 7 : 15).

When Samuel was very old, the elders of Israel objected to the conduct of his two sons whom he had made judges, saying, 'Behold, thou art old, and thy sons walk not in thy ways: now make us a king to judge us like all the nations' (1 Sam 8 : 5). He was guided by God to *Saul and anointed him king with a vial of oil (1 Sam 9 : 14-27; 10 : 1). Saul's conduct later displeased him and he rebuked him for not keeping the divine commandments. He told the king that God had 'sought him a man after his own heart' to rule the kingdom in his stead (1 Sam 13 : 11-14). The man was *David, whom Samuel found keeping his father's sheep (1 Sam 16 : 1-18). When beset by his enemies before the fatal battle of Gilboa, Saul went to the *Witch of Endor so that she might conjure up the shade of Samuel to advise him (1 Sam 28 : 7-20).

Sanbenito A yellow dress with a red St Andrew's *cross on the front and back, which those condemned by the *Inquisition for heresy were obliged to wear while doing penance. They also had on their heads a conical hat like a dunce's cap. Those who refused to acknowledge their crime wore at their execution a similar garment, only black and with demons and the flames of *Hell depicted on it. The word is derived from the Italian for St *Benedict and is probably so called because it resembled his *scapular.

Sanctam ecclesiam catholicam Latin for 'the Holy *Catholic Church', the phrase which St *Matthew contributed to the *Apostles' Creed and which is inscribed on the scroll which he displays.

Sanctorale A service book used in the Middle Ages, often beautifully illuminated and containing the *Masses or Offices of the *saints of each day.

Sanctuary The east end of a church, containing the *high altar, and reserved for the *clergy. It is separated from the *nave by altar-rails or by a *screen. (In *Orthodox churches an *iconostasis encloses the sanctuary.) In a broader sense, the word was previously applied to the whole of the church and its sacred precincts, which were inviolate and thus provided asylum for anyone fleeing from *persecution or the forces of the law. By entering the church, or even by holding the ring attached to a church door, fugitives used to obtain 'sanctuary' by *Roman Catholic canon law.

A Frankish stone cross with a **saltire** cross at the base (7th century).

Samson forcing open the jaws of a lion, prefiguring Christ's Harrowing of Hell (capital from Vienne, *c*.1152).

Sanctus Latin for 'holy', the Trisagion or thrice holy, a Christian adaptation of the cry of the *seraphim, 'Holy, holy, holy, is the Lord of Hosts' (Is 6 : 3), used after the Preface or introduction to the central section of the *Mass or *Eucharist. A sanctus or sacring bell may be sounded at this point.

Sandals Slippers with embroidered velvet or silk tops, worn as *vestments by *Popes, *bishops and other *prelates at solemn *pontifical services. Also leather sandals worn principally by members of *discalced Orders, but also by some other religious.

Sanhedrin From the Greek *synedrion*, 'council', the highest Jewish court in NT times and persisting until the fall of *Jerusalem in the year 70. Pro-Roman *Sadducees were its members. It met in the *Temple area. Its jurisdiction was limited to Judaea so that it could not take action against Jesus while he was in *Galilee. They arranged for his arrest when he came to Jerusalem. Although they condemned him to death for blasphemy, the sentence could not be carried out without the consent of *Pilate, the Roman procurator. After the *Crucifixion, they persecuted SS *Peter, *John the Apostle and *Stephen (*See* *Trials of Jesus).

Santa Claus 'Claus' is the Germanic abbreviation of Nicholas, but why this name should be preceded by the Romance feminine form for 'saint' is unexplained, unless the 'a' facilitated pronunciation of the hybrid title. It refers to St *Nicholas of Myra, who on the night of his feast (6 December) was believed to leave presents in the shoes of good children. With the growth in popularity of giving gifts at *Christmas, parents began to play the part of St Nicholas on *Christmas Eve instead of his feast day. The assimilation of this ascetic if benevolent saint to the fat, jovial, pagan Father Christmas was achieved in the USA in the 19th century.

Sapphira Wife of *Ananias. She and her husband withheld part of their agreed contribution to the common fund of the first Christians in *Jerusalem. When accused of deceit, Ananias fell dead. Sapphira, on being told what had happened to him, also expired (Ac 5 : 1-5).

Sarah Half-sister and wife of *Abraham. Originally called Sarai, but renamed *Sarah (Hebrew for 'princess') when told that she would bear a son (*Isaac) in her old age (Gen 17 : 15-16). In her youth she was so beautiful that Abraham twice passed her off as his sister, fearful that others might kill him to possess her. First *Pharaoh took her into his harem when they travelled to Egypt, but released her when he and his household were afflicted with plagues (Gen 12 : 10-20). On the second occasion, Abimelech, ruler of Gerar, made her one of his wives but let her go when told in a dream that she was Abrahams (Gen 20 : 1-16).

Sarah, believing that she was barren, gave Abraham her Egyptian slave-girl *Hagar as a concubine, but was so jealous of her when she became pregnant with *Ishmael that the maid fled from her (Gen 16 : 6). An *angel prevailed upon her to return, but she was later forced, by Abraham after Sarah's entreaties to leave the household when she and her son mocked their mistress at Isaac's weaning feast (Gen 21 : 8-14).

Sarcophagus A stone or terracotta coffin, meaning 'flesh-eating'. Pliny the Elder (23 or 24-79), in his *Historia Naturalis* ('Natural History') says they were lined with a stone which devoured corpses. Christians followed the custom of their pagan and Jewish contemporaries in placing their dead in these containers. Those used for rich members of the community were ornamented with elaborately carved biblical scenes, usually having symbolic reference to the resurrection of the body and life after death.

Satan The Hebrew for 'enemy' or *'adversary', used in the OT as a common noun, but personified as Satan (Vg *Satanas*) in the NT as the name of the *Devil, the enemy of God and of mankind. Originally one of the *angels, he led a rebel band against God. They were defeated by St *Michael and expelled from *Heaven before the *Creation (*See* *Lucifer). Satan was permitted by God to test the faith of *Job. He also assailed Jesus (*See* *Temptations in the Wilderness). Other names for Satan are *Beelzebub and *Belial.

Sator The first line of a Latin palindrome found in Pompei and on a Roman wall in Cirencester, England. It is in the form of a square.

```
S A T O R
A R E P O
T E N E T
O P E R A
R O T A S
```

Read as a sequence of words, either across or down, it could be construed as 'The sower Arepo holds carefully the wheels', which makes little sense. It was noted that the letters TENET, read down and across, formed a cross, so the square was thought to have a Christian reference, especially as all the letters could also be rearranged to read *pater noster*, 'our father', in the form of a cross with A-O (*Alpha and *Omega) at each end.

```
        A
        P
        A
        T
        E
        R
A P A T E R N O S T E R O
        O
        S
        T
        E
        R
        O
```

Moreover, the letters may also be rearranged to make the sentence: *Oro Te Pater oro Te Pater sanas*, translatable as 'I pray to you Father, I pray to you, you cure'. The palindrome could be either a pagan or a Christian charm. Some hold, however, that its discovery in Pompeii (destroyed in 79) would suggest too early a date for it to be *Christian, and that the palindrome may be of Jewish origin.

A further complication is that the names *Sator*, *Arepo* and *Teneton* have been found depicted in conjunction with the *Shepherds adoring the *Christ-Child in murals decorating rock-hewn Byzantine churches in Cappadocia.

Saturday The seventh day of the week (Old English *Saeterdaeg*, from the Latin *Saturni dies*, 'Saturn's day'), the equivalent of the Jewish *sabbath. It is dedicated to the memory of St *Mary the Virgin's trust in her son's *Resurrection even while he lay in the tomb on *Holy Saturday.

Satyr There were two kinds of satyrs, one resembling an ape and given to pantomimic movements, the other like a man, but with the legs, horns and the tail of a goat. The latter resembled the pagan god Pan, so it was deduced that satyrs were his companions in the forest. A false derivation of 'satyr' from the Greek *sathi*, 'male organ', led to satyrs being represented with enlarged phalluses. They were addicted to wine and lechery. Because of their cloven hoofs they were thought of as devils, a belief reinforced by the AV mistranslation of 'he-goat' as 'satyr' in Isaiah's prophecy (Is 13 : 21).

Saul The first king of Israel (11th century BC), anointed by *Samuel when the people became tired of being ruled by *Judges. His unhappy history occupies the greater part of the *First Book of Samuel* (1 Sam 9-31). He is known in art and literature because of his interventions in the early career of his renowned successor, King *David.

Samuel was obliged on three occasions to stop Saul disobeying God's commands and offering sacrifices, a function which pertained to a priest, not a king (1 Sam 13 : 8-15). David was therefore revealed to Samuel as the one chosen to replace Saul (1 Sam 16 : 1-13). The young shepherd boy was brought to the court to soothe Saul's patholo-gical melancholy by playing to him (traditionally) on a harp, and he was made the king's armour-bearer. But his victory over *Goliath changed Saul's favour into blind hatred. When David was entertaining him with music, he tried to kill him with his javelin. He cheated David of his promised bride, but allowed him to marry his other daugh-ter Michal, making a marriage settlement which he hoped would result in David's death. David formed a deep friendship with Saul's son *Jonathan, who protected him. He fled from Saul and took refuge in the cave of *Adullam, later sparing the king's life when he came unwittingly upon him. Eventually, Saul was defeated by the *Philistines – as the *Witch of Endor had foretold – and died when he fell upon his own sword.

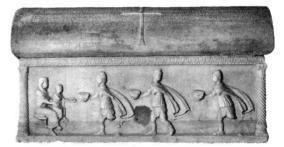

A **sarcophagus** showing the Magi bringing gifts to the Christ-Child (early 5th century).

An elaborate Milanese **sarcophagus** crowded with incident, including Christ teaching, the ascension of Elijah, and Noah receiving the dove in the ark.

Saul grasps the javelin with which he will attempt to kill David, playing the harp to assuage his melancholy (Rembrandt, 1606-69).

Saviour A title of *Jesus who gave his life for the salvation of mankind (See *Salvator Mundi).

Saw An *attribute of St *Joseph, who was a carpenter; also of SS *Jude, *Simon the Zealot and the prophet *Isaiah, all of whom were said to have been sawn in pieces.

Scala Santa The Italian for 'Holy Stair', in Latin Scala Pilati, 'Pilate's stairway'; the name given to twenty-eight marble steps in the Lateran Palace in Rome, which according to tradition were the steps up which Jesus climbed to be judged by *Pilate in his praetorium, or audience chamber. St *Helena brought them to Rome c.326. Plenary *indulgence was granted by Pius X (1835-1914) to those who ascend the stairs on their knees.

Scales *Symbol of judgement and, combined with a sword, of justice. One of the *Four Horsemen of the Apocalypse carried a pair and at the Last *Judgement St *Michael weighs good and bad deeds in them. *Libra, the seventh sign of the *zodiac (associated with September), is represented by scales. They are also carried by the angelic choir of *Thrones, because of the text, 'For thou hast maintained my right and my cause' (Ps 9 : 4).

Scapegoat One of two goats chosen by lot on the *Jewish Day of Atonement. It was driven out into the wilderness, carrying the sins of the people which had been symbolically transferred to it. The other goat was sacrificed.

Scapular From the Latin scapularium, 'cloak worn over the shoulders', an outer garment made of two strips of cloth joined across the shoulders (scapulae). Originating in the working dress of *Benedictines, it is now part of the *habit of *monks and *tertiaries, symbolizing the *yoke of Christ.

Scarlet woman The popular name for the great *Whore of Babylon dressed in scarlet, whom St *John the Divine saw in his vision 'drunken with the blood of the saints' (Rev 17 : 3-6).

Schism, Eastern The 'split' (Greek schisma) which severed the *Roman Catholic Church ('the *West'), from the *Orthodox Church ('the *East'). It began in 857 when Patriarch Photius of Constantinople, excommunicated by Pope St Nicholas I (858-67), replied by challenging the orthodoxy of Rome, particularly with regard to the procession of the *Holy Spirit – the filioque ('and from the Son') clause of the *Nicene Creed. It culminated in 1054 when papal legates excommunicated Patriarch Cerularius of Constantinople (1043-58) for stigmatizing compulsory clerical celibacy and the use of unleavened bread in the *Mass as heretical practices. Despite attempts made to heal the breach at the Second Council of Lyons in 1274 and the Council of Florence in 1439, the final break came in 1472. The schism has persisted up to the present, although attempts are now being made to reach a new understanding.

Schola Cantorum Latin for a group of singers or a *choir who sing church music. It may also mean the place where they are trained. St *Gregory the Great founded one of the earliest of these establishments at Rome.

Scholastica, St Twin sister (b.c.480) of St *Benedict of Nursia, from whom she received the veil and under whose auspices she founded the first community of Benedictine nuns at Plombariola near Monte Cassino. St *Gregory the Great, in his Dialogues (II 34; 35), gave the following account of her last moments. St Benedict and some of his monks visited St Scholastica and were prevented by a violent thunderstorm from returning to their monastery. Brother and sister were thus able to spend the night discoursing on spiritual matters. Three days later, St Benedict had a vision of Scholastica's soul ascending to Heaven as a *dove (her *attribute). He told his monks to escort her body to the monastery because he knew that she was dead. She was buried (547) in the grave which he had prepared for himself and in which he was later interred. Their remains (discovered in 1950 after the destruction of the monastery by bombing during the Second World War) now lie under the *high altar of the church in Monte Cassino.

Sciapod A naked man with one leg, depicted on ancient maps and *misericords. He lives in a cave in a remote region where the sun burns bright. To shade himself from its rays he lies on his back, one hand beneath his head and the other holding up his huge foot which acts as a sunshade.

Scorpio The eighth sign of the *zodiac, represented as a *scorpion. It governs the period from about 24 October to 21 November, and is associated in the *Labours of the Months with treading grapes.

Scorpion A venomous creature, a symbol of jealousy or treachery because its sting inflicts a poisonous wound. As *scorpio, it is the sign of the *zodiac which presides over October, the month of the wine-harvest. King Rehoboam of Judah threatened to chastise his people with scorpions instead of whips (1 Kg 12 : 11). A scorpion may be caught, it is said, if it is surrounded with a ring of fire. It will then sting itself and die.

Scourging of Jesus After the crowd had demanded the release of *Barabbas instead of Jesus, *Pilate 'took Jesus and scourged him' (Jn 19 : 1). This episode of the *Passion (also called the Flagellation) was mentioned briefly in the Gospels, but was depicted with much elaboration from the 15th century onwards. Jesus was shown bound to a column or *pillar (one of the *Instruments of the Passion), recalling Pilate's praetorium or audience chamber. A scourge (another *Instrument of the Passion) lay on the ground. Soldiers may be shown administering the flagellation. The weals from the strokes (five thousand according to a vision of St *Bridget of Sweden) were painted in luridly realistic detail. After the scourging, Jesus was shown lying untethered, exhausted on the ground; or he painfully collected his garments before being subjected to a mock coronation by the Roman soldiers. The *Sibyl Agrippa is shown with a scourge because she foretold the scourging.

Screen A stone or wooden partition dividing the *chancel or *choir from the *nave of a church. Screens were often intricately carved or ornamented with statues or pictures of saints. When surmounted by a cross (the *rood) – usually with St *Mary the Virgin and St *John the Apostle as the *Beloved Disciple standing on either side – they are called *rood screens. The equivalent screen in an *Orthodox church is an *iconostasis.

Scriptorium The room in a *monastery used for writing or copying manuscripts and books.

Scroll A strip of parchment on which the text of ancient books was written. The strips were sewn together and rolled around a stick. In reading the scroll, the loose end would be wound on to another stick. In art, the sticks are usually omitted and the scroll represented as rolled-up parchment. It symbolizes wisdom or knowledge. When held by *Apostles or *Prophets, scrolls may be displayed partly open and inscribed with texts referring to clauses in the *Apostles Creed or to corresponding prophecies.

Seamless robe See *Holy coat.

Sebastian, St A young nobleman of Narbonne, an officer in the Praetorian Guard and a favourite of Emperor Diocletian. He was a secret Christian until he made an outraged declaration following the tortures inflicted on his Christian friends Marcus and Marcellinus. He converted many by his bold example. For this he was condemned to be killed with arrows. He is therefore usually depicted tied to a tree, stake or cross; his body, shown naked from the 15th century onwards, is transfixed with arrows, although he was earlier represented as a knight holding an arrow. After his ordeal he was left for dead, but St Irene mother of one of his other friends, revived him. She dressed his wounds and cared for him in her house until he was again able to proclaim his faith. Diocletian, surprised that he had survived, ordered that he should be beaten to death with clubs and his body thrown into the great sewer of Rome. It was recovered, following a vision, by a pious matron called Lucina and buried c.287 near the relics of SS *Peter and *Paul. The church of San Sebastiano stands at the entrance to the catacomb on the Via Appia.

During the Middle Ages, St Sebastian, together with St *Roch, protected people and cities against a plague which was said to strike with the swiftness of an arrow. He is thus one of the *Fourteen Holy Helpers and patron saint of archers.

Second Adam St *Paul called Jesus Christ the 'last Adam' (1 Cor 15 : 45), because, as sin entered the

William Holman Hunt visited the Holy Land for the accurate setting of this **scapegoat** expiring by the Dead Sea (1854).

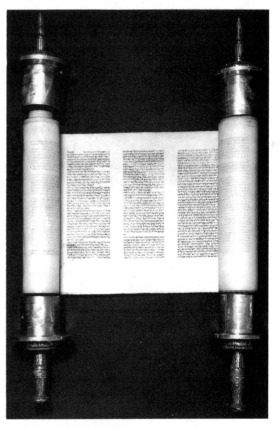

This parchment **scroll** of the Pentateuch, used in Jewish ritual, preserves a form of book well known in biblical times (19th century).

world through *Adam's disobedience, so man was redeemed by the sacrifice of a new Adam.

Second Coming The *parousia (Greek for 'arrival') of Christ, who will return to judge the living and the dead. His appearance will herald the Last *Judgement (See *Signs of the Times).

Sedilia In the *sanctuary there are usually three seats (four or five in large churches) for *priest, *deacon and sub-deacon, or other additional *clergy. On the Continent *sedilia* were usually wooden chairs, but in England in the Middle Ages they were stone seats recessed in the wall of the sanctuary, and often graduated according to the rank of the clergy occupying them.

See The 'seat' (Latin *sedes*), 'chair' or 'throne', on which a *bishop sits in his *cathedral and, by extension, the *diocese where the church is located. The *Holy See is the seat of the *Pope, the bishop of Rome.

Septuagesima The third Sunday before *Lent, the ninth before Easter; from the Latin for 'seventieth day'.

Septuagint The name (represented by the Roman numerals LXX) given to the oldest Greek translation of the Hebrew OT. It is derived from the Latin for 'seventy', because traditionally the translation was undertaken in Alexandria by seventy scholars (one from each nation of the world). Other versions say there were seventy-two scholars (six from each of the *Twelve Tribes). They worked on the orders of Ptolemy II of Egypt (3rd century BC). They were shut up on the island of Pharos in separate cells with manuscripts and writing materials for seventy-two days, and at the end of that time they emerged bearing identical versions. *Simeon, who beheld the *Christ-Child at the *Presentation of Jesus in the Temple, was said to have been one of the translators. He was told that he would not see death until the fulfilment of the prophecy, 'Behold a virgin shall conceive' (Is 7 : 14), which he had refused to credit when he was translating the text, but which came to pass through the *virgin birth of Jesus.

Sequence In the early Middle Ages it was the practice to sing a short *hymn, called a prose or sequence (Latin *sequentia*), after the *gradual at Mass on certain *feast days. Sequences became so numerous and of such varying quality that all except four were abolished by Pope Pius V (1566-72) in 1570, although many survived in the *rites of the Dominican and certain other religious *Orders. The four permitted were: at Easter, *Victimae Paschali*, 'To the Paschal victim', composed by Wipo of Swabia or Burgundy (*d.c.*1050); at *Pentecost (Whitsun), *Veni, sancte Spiritus*, 'Come Holy Ghost'; at *Corpus Christi, *Lauda Sion*, 'Praise to Zion', composed by St *Thomas Aquinas; and for *All Souls' Day, *Dies Irae*. A fifth, *Stabat Mater*, was added in 1727 when the Feast of the Seven *Sorrows of the Virgin was made universal.

Seraphic Order The *Franciscan Order, since its founder, St *Francis of Assisi, was given the title of 'Seraphic Doctor'.

Seraphim (seraphs) The first choir of the first hierarchy of *angels who stand above the throne of God. Their *colour is *red or crimson, indicating burning love. They are depicted in accordance with *Isaiah's vision (Is 6 : 2), each having six wings, two covering the face, two the feet and two for flying. Their bodies and wings often have eyes and they may stand on winged wheels. They carry *scrolls with the words, 'Holy, Holy, Holy is the Lord of Hosts' (Is 6 : 3; Rev 4 : 8), because their function is to sing praises around the throne of God (See *Sanctus). Their leader is *Uriel. The singular of seraphim is seraph.

Sermon on the Mount A lengthy discourse (Mt 5-7) containing the essence of Jesus' teaching which he delivered to his *disciples when he withdrew from the multitudes who followed him 'and went up into a mountain'. (In the *Gospel of Luke* [Lk 6 : 20-49], the sermon was given when he descended from the mountain 'and stood in the plain', surrounded by his disciples and by the crowds who pressed around him hoping to be healed when they touched him.) Part of the Sermon is devoted to the Eight *Beatitudes. The Russian novelist Tolstoy distilled from the teaching five rules (chastity; no oaths; no anger; non-resistance to violence; and love of one's enemies) which, if followed, would bring about the *millennium.

Serpent Because *Eve was tempted by a serpent (assumed to be *Satan in disguise), this reptile stands either for the *Devil or for *sin. At the feet of St *Mary the Virgin it represents the defeat of sin through the *Incarnation. A serpent wound around a cross signifies Christ, because Moses lifted up the serpent in the wilderness to heal the suffering Children of Israel (Num 21 : 8) – the OT type of Christ on the Cross, a parallel made by Jesus himself (Jn 3 : 14). A serpent in a *chalice is one of the *attributes of St *John the Divine. St *Patrick rid Ireland of serpents.

Server One who 'serves' in the sanctuary at the *Mass or *Eucharist. His main duties are to make the responses (or to lead the congregation in saying them); to bring the bread and the wine to the altar; and to wash the *celebrant's hands (See *acolyte). He wears an *alb or *surplice.

Servites Members of the *Order of Servants of the Blessed Virgin Mary, founded in 1233 by seven wealthy Florentines to whom St *Mary the Virgin had appeared on the Feast of the *Assumption, exhorting them to retire from the world and to devote themselves to her service. They followed the *Rule of St Augustine and wore a black *habit, conferred upon them by the Virgin when she again appeared to them in their secluded retreat on Monte Senario. Their Order, recognized in 1259, was finally sanctioned by a bull of Pope

Benedict XI (1303-04) in 1304. By that time an
Order of Servite nuns had come into being. Servite
houses spread rapidly and missionaries were sent
as far as India. Servites have continued to be
contemplative, but are also active in teaching and
missionary work. They promoted especially the
devotion of the Seven *Sorrows of the Virgin.

Servus servorum Dei Latin for 'The servant of the
servants of God', a title used by the *Pope. First
used by Pope St Gregory the Great (590–604), and
in general use since the time of Gregory VII
(1073-85).

Seth Third son of *Adam and *Eve. Eve called
him Seth (Hebrew for 'granted') because he was
given to her in place of the murdered *Abel (Gen
4 : 25). According to legend he journeyed to
Paradise to seek the *olive branch of Mercy for his
dying father, and there saw a child. A cherub told
him that the babe was destined to be born on earth
as the *Redeemer of Mankind. He also placed the
seeds of the tree from which the *Cross was made
under the dying Adam's tongue.

Seven The most frequent of the symbolic
*numbers. As a combination of *four (the earth)
and *three (the heavens or the *Trinity), it
symbolizes the universe. Groups of seven, too
numerous to detail, were discovered everywhere.
Some examples are: the seven days of *Creation;
the seven planets; the seven seas; the seven kine
and the seven ears of corn of *Pharaoh's dreams;
the seven *Sacraments; the seven *Gifts of the
Holy Ghost; the seven last *Words from the Cross;
the seven penitential *psalms; the seven cardinal
*Virtues; the *Seven Deadly Sins; the seven
*Works of Mercy; the seven *Joys of St Mary the
Virgin; and the seven *Sorrows of St Mary the
Virgin.

Seven champions of Christendom The seven
patron saints of Christian nations: SS *George of
England; *Andrew of Scotland; *David of Wales;
*Patrick of Ireland; *James of Compostela, Spain;
*Denis of France; and *Antony of Padua, Italy.
Their legends were related at length by Richard
Johnson (1573-1659?) in his *Famous Historie of the
Seven Champions of Christendom* (c.1597).

Seven cities Cities believed to have been founded
on an island somewhere in the Atlantic by seven
Spanish *bishops when they were forced to leave
Spain after the Moorish invasion in 711.

Seven deadly sins The sins or *Vices for which
punishment is eternal damnation (as distinct from
venial sins for which forgiveness is possible). They
are *pride, *covetousness or *greed, *lust, *envy,
*gluttony, *anger, *accidie (or sloth).

Sexagesima The second Sunday before *Lent, the
eighth before *Easter. From the Latin for 'sixtieth
(day)'.

Sext The part of the *Divine Office appointed to

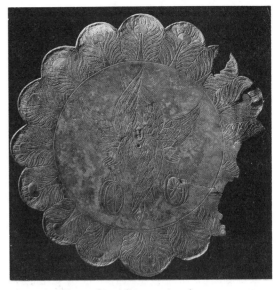

A six-winged **seraph** standing on winged
wheels, as in Isaiah's vision, decorates this
6th-century liturgical fan.

Attacked by the **Seven Deadly Sins,** this man
pleads for forgiveness, knowing that he is
suspended on a cobweb over the well of the
Abyss (from the *Spiritual Exercises* of St Ignatius
of Loyola, 1689).

be said at noon, the sixth hour of the day (See *Hours, canonical).

Sexton Assistant to the *parish clerk. His duties are to toll the bell for services, clean the church and dig graves (See *sacristan; *verger).

Shadrach, Meshach and Abednego The three Jewish youths whom Nebuchadnezzar cast into the *Fiery Furnace (Dan 3 : 19-30).

Shamrock A symbol of the *Trinity, like the *trefoil, because its three leaflets grow from one stem, demonstrating that the three persons of the Trinity are a unity. St *Patrick used it to illustrate dogma when preaching to Laoghaire, the chieftain who came to arrest him for lighting the *Easter fire on the Hill of Slane, which the clans held sacred to their pagan gods. It is thus an Irish emblem.

Shell A symbol of *baptism, possibly because St *John the Baptist is shown pouring water from a shell on Jesus' head at the *Baptism of Christ. A scallop shell or cockleshell is worn by St *James of Compostela and by *pilgrims to his shrine. St *Roch, dressed as a pilgrim, displays a shell.

Shem The eldest son of *Noah (Gen 5 : 32; 6 : 10), one of the eight people saved in the *Ark from the *Flood. When Noah lay drunk, he and his brother Japheth covered their father's nakedness (Gen 9 : 18, 23-7). He was the ancestor of the 'Shemites', the Semitic peoples, according to the ancient division of the *Races of Mankind. The genealogy of Jesus was traced through his descendants (Lk 3 : 36) (See *Jesse).

Sheol The Hebrew for 'chamber', or 'pit', used in the OT for the land of oblivion, the abode of the souls of the dead. In the Greek of the NT it is named as *Hades and in the AV, *Hell. Another synonym is *Gehenna, the place of torments, where sinners are punished (See *Abaddon).

Shepherds, manifestation to the The first of the *Epiphanies or manifestations of the new-born *Christ to his people. It is depicted in two episodes derived from the *Gospel of Luke*. The first is the announcement to the shepherds. When Jesus was born in Bethlehem (See *Nativity) there were shepherds in the nearby fields 'keeping watch over their flocks by night', to protect them from robbers and wild animals. When *Christmas came to be celebrated on 25 December it presented an exegetical problem, as sheep were not usually left in the open at midwinter in Palestine. (Jacobus de Voragine in the *Golden Legend* explained that it was a Palestinian custom for shepherds to be out of doors on the nights of the solstices.) An angel of the Lord, traditionally St *Gabriel, appeared to the shepherds in a blaze of glory and told them that he brought 'good tidings of great joy', because the long-awaited *Saviour had been born. They would recognize him by two signs: he would be wrapped in swaddling clothes and would be lying in a *manger. The heavenly host then joined the angels, singing, 'Glory to God in the highest, and

on earth peace, goodwill toward men'. (The first part of the sentence in Latin, *Gloria in excelsis Deo*, is shown on scrolls in depictions of the scene.) The shepherds left their flocks and hastened to seek out the child (Lk 2 : 8-15).

The second episode is the adoration of the shepherds. They found St *Mary the Virgin, St *Joseph and 'the babe lying in a manger' (Lk 2 : 16-17). This scene was greatly elaborated in religious drama and art. Three shepherds are the central characters, corresponding to the three *Kings, although shepherdesses and a shepherd boy were sometimes added. As in pastoral poetry and drama, they offer symbolic gifts: a musical instrument (because Christ, like *Orpheus, will draw all men to him); a shepherd's crook (because he will be the Good *Shepherd); and a lamb (foretelling his death on the cross as *Agnus Dei*, the sacrificial *Lamb of God). When it was asked how the shepherds, who unlike the three Kings had no star to guide them, knew where to find the *Christ-Child, it was explained that they owned the shelter where the *Holy Family had taken refuge when there was no room for them at the inn.

Shibboleth When the Ephraimites were repulsed after attempting to attack Gilead, *Jephthah cut them off at the Jordan fords. Those who sought to cross back to their land by denying that they were Ephraimites were asked to pronounce 'shibboleth' (which means 'ear of wheat' or 'flowing stream'). Ephraimites revealed their nationality by mispronouncing it 'Sibboleth', and were slain (Jg 12 : 1-6). Thus 'shibboleth' has come to signify a linguistic test, an accent or trick of speech, something which singles out a person as a member of a particular group.

Ship Symbol of the Church in which the faithful find salvation from the storms of life. St *Jude has a ship as his *attribute in East Anglian churches because he was said to be a fisherman. It may also represent his reputed travels to distant lands. SS *Brendan, *Elmo (Erasmus), *Francis Xavier and *Nicolas of Myra may also display a ship.

Shrine From the Latin *scrinium*, a box or chest for papers and books, later used for a *reliquary and then for the place in which a reliquary rested. A shrine is now a hallowed spot, usually a church, chapel or tomb, or a place with a sacred image which is the object of special devotion. Shrines were the goals of *pilgrimages, directed at first to the tombs of *martyrs and later to the burial places of other *saints, or to places where miracles had occurred.

Shroud, Holy A *relic preserved since 1578 in Turin Cathedral, Italy, the first historical reference to which is c.1360 at Lirey in the diocese of Troyes, France. It is said to be the linen cloth in which St *Joseph of Arimathea wrapped the body of Jesus after it had been taken down from the Cross. It bears the faint imprint of a man's features, thought to be the authentic face of Christ.

227

Shrovetide The English name for the *carnival period before the rigours of *Lent, which begins on *Ash Wednesday. The word is derived from the practice of hearing confessions and granting absolution (Old English *shrivan*, 'to shrive', 'absolve') on the Monday of that week, and especially on the Tuesday (*Shrove Tuesday).

Shrove Tuesday The last day of *Shrovetide.

Sibyls Priestesses of Apollo whose prophecies are recorded in the Sibylline Books and were thought to foretell the coming of *Christ. The two most famous Sibyls were the Tiburtine, who told *Augustus of the birth of a mightier emperor than he, and the Cuman, who warned of the Last *Judgement and is mentioned in the *Dies Irae. In the Middle Ages, twelve Sibyls were set alongside the *prophets, were given attributes and identified with prophecies of events in the life of Jesus as follows (although there are variants):
1 Persica holds a *lantern with a faint light, because she foretold the coming of Christ, 'but obscurely'. A *dragon at her feet recalls her prophecy that he would overcome the powers of evil.
2 Libyca has a *candle or a torch, because she said that the Light of the World would shine in the darkness.
3 Erythraea has a *rose or a *lily, because she foretold the *Annunciation.
4 Samia has a cradle or *crib, because she prophesied that a child would be born of a poor maiden and the beasts of the earth would adore him (See *Nativity).
5 Europa's *sword recalls the Massacre of the *Holy Innocents and the *Flight into Egypt, because she said that the Saviour would cross mountains and hills and the streams of Olympus.
6 Cimmeria's horn represents a feeding-bottle, because she said that a virgin would nourish her son with milk (See *Virgin birth of Jesus).
7 Tiburtina's hand refers to the hands which struck Jesus after his arrest. (She also appears with *Augustus.)
8 Agrippa has a scourge, because she foretold the *Scourging of Christ.
9 Delphica has a *crown of thorns, because she prophesied that the Saviour would fall into the hands of wicked men and be crowned with a crown of thorns.
10 Hellespontica has a Cross, because she foretold the *Crucifixion.
11 Cuman's sponge refers to the sponge dipped in vinegar which was offered to Jesus as he hung on the Cross. (When she holds a basin, it may be a reference to the washing of the *Christ-Child, because she was also thought to have prophesied his birth.)
12 Phrygia's cross and banner foretell the *Resurrection.
The original Sibylline oracles were kept in Rome but destroyed in the fire of 82 BC. A new version perished in 405. Hellenistic Jews had their own versions.

Sic transit gloria mundi Latin for 'thus passes the

In the background, on the right, an angel announces the Nativity to the **shepherds,** one of whom arrives on the left, to join Mary and Joseph at the crib (Hugo van der Goes, *c.*1480).

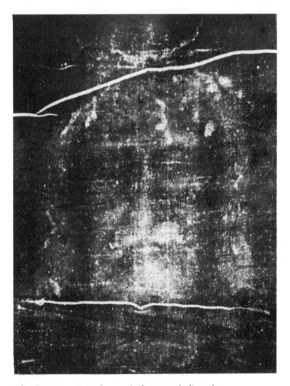

The faint imprint of a man's features, believed to be the face of the crucified Christ, on the **Holy Shroud** of Turin.

glory of the world', words addressed to a new *Pope at his coronation when a symbol of worldly pomp is burned before him.

Sign of the cross A gesture with the right hand, sometimes holding a liturgical object, outlining the shape of a cross. One says: 'In the name of the Father, and of the Son, and of the Holy Ghost. Amen' (In Latin, *In nomine Patri, Filii et Spiritu Sancti'. Amen*).

Signs of the times The signs which Jesus predicted would herald his *Second Coming, or *Parousia: false prophets (*See* *Antichrist), wars and rumours of wars, nation rising against nation, famines, pestilences and earthquakes (Mt 24 : 3-28). These will be followed by the appearance of 'the Sign of the Son of man in Heaven', thought to be his *cross, and the gathering of his elect (Mt 24 : 29-31). This is known as the Little *Apocalypse. It is the source of many of the episodes depicted in representations of the Last *Judgement.

Simeon When the parents of Jesus obeyed Jewish law (Ex 13 : 2) and took him to the *Temple in Jerusalem to present him to God (*See* *Presentation in the Temple), they were met by a devout old priest called Simeon who had been given a divine promise that he would not die before seeing the hoped-for *Messiah. He took the child in his arms, blessed God and said, 'Lord, now lettest thou thy servant depart in peace, according to thy word; for mine eyes have seen thy salvation which thou hast prepared in the presence of all peoples, a light to lighten the Gentiles and for the glory of thy people Israel' (Lk 2 : 29-32). This Song of Simeon, called the *Nunc dimittis* from the Latin for its first two words, forms part of the evening offices of the Church. As he handed Jesus back to his mother, Simeon prophesied, 'Yea, a sword shall pierce through thy own soul also' (Lk 2 : 35), a forecast of the *Sorrows of the Virgin.

Because Simeon had been told that he would not die until he had seen the promised Saviour, the legend grew up that he was one of the 3rd-century BC compilers of the *Septuagint, the Greek translation of the Hebrew Bible. When he laughed at the impossibility of the text, 'Behold, a virgin shall conceive, and bear a son' (Is 7 : 14), he was condemned to live on until he could witness with his own eyes the fulfilment of the prophecy.

Simon Magus Simon 'the Sorcerer', a magician who exercised great power over the people of Samaria. When *Philip the Deacon preached the Gospel there and performed miracles, Simon was so impressed that he was baptized (Ac 8 : 9-13). SS *Peter and *John the Apostle arrived soon afterwards and gave Philip's converts the gift of the *Holy Spirit by the laying-on of hands. Simon offered the Apostles money, hoping to purchase their seemingly magical powers, but Peter rebuked him, saying, 'Thy money perish with thee, because thou hast thought that the gift of God may be purchased with money' (Ac 8 : 20). Simon

repented, but his name survives in 'simony', the buying or selling of ecclesiastical benefices.

Simon of Cyrene A countryman, possibly on his *Passover pilgrimage to *Jerusalem, who was a bystander as Jesus made his way to *Calvary bearing his Cross. When he stumbled, exhausted, Simon was made to carry the Cross for him (Mt 27 : 32; Mk 15 : 21; Lk 23 : 26). He is not mentioned in the *Gospel of John*, but *Mark* records that he was the father of Alexander and Rufus, who must have been known to the Early Christian community. This suggests that Simon's experience made him a follower of the crucified Christ. *Gnostics, who claimed that Jesus only *appeared* to die on the Cross, argued that he stood by laughing as Simon was crucified in his place.

Simon the Leper Simon (also identified as *Simon the Pharisee) probably suffered from a skin disease which was thought to be leprosy. He would have been regarded as unclean, as there is no record of his having been cured by Jesus, although this may be inferred. He was entertaining Jesus to dinner in his house in Bethany when the *Anointing with precious ointment took place (Mk 14 : 3-9; Mt 26 : 6-13).

Simon the Pharisee Simon, equated with *Simon the Leper, although he lived in Galilee and not in Bethany, was one of the *Pharisees who tried to discover who Jesus really was. He invited him to dine in his house and there, according to the *Gospel of Luke*, the *Anointing took place. The woman who made the symbolic act, possibly in this case intended to indicate kingship, was a prostitute. If Jesus were a *prophet, argued the Pharisees, he would know that he had been defiled by being touched by a sinner. Jesus countered by telling Simon the *Parable of the Two Debtors, and contrasting the honour done to him by the woman with the scant courtesy with which Simon had received him. Her many sins were forgiven, 'for she loved much' and her faith had saved her (Lk 7 : 36-50).

Simon the Zealot, St An *Apostle. He is called 'the Cananaean' in the *Gospel of Mark* (Mk 3 : 18) and in the *Gospel of Matthew* (Mt 10 : 4), in Aramaic *kananaiso*, meaning someone who is 'jealous for the *Law (of Moses)'. The Greek equivalent, used in the *Gospel of Luke* (Lk 6 : 15) and in the *Acts of the Apostles* (Ac 1 : 13), is *zelotes*, 'the Zealot'. This may imply that Simon was a member of the *Zealots, the Jewish extremists who opposed the Roman occupation of Palestine. Apart from appearing in lists of the Apostles and being present at *Pentecost, Simon receives scant attention in the NT, but legend links his later exploits with those of St *Jude. According to Craton's *Ten Books* (probably dating from the 4th century) and Abdias' *Apostolic History* (617-21), the two apostles conducted their evangelical missions in Syria, Mesopotamia and Persia. They aroused the wrath of the magicians Zaroes and Arfaxat who opposed them wherever they went. In the city of Suanir they confounded seventy pagan priests by proving that their deities, the sun and the moon, had been created by the one true God of the Christians and by driving out of their temple two hideous and black evil spirits. Nevertheless, the populace rose against them, hurling stones and finally beating them to death with clubs and sticks (which often appear as their *attributes). Another version is that Simon was cut to pieces with a *saw, also his attribute. He exhibits the clause, *remissionem pecatorum*, 'the forgiveness of sins', which he contributed to the *Apostles' Creed.

Simon Stock, St Third Prior-General of the *Carmelite Order, elected *c*.1245. One account names him as Simon Angulus, a Kentish boy of Aylesford (where his relics repose), who earned the appellation 'Stock' because he spent twelve years in the forest living on herbs and sheltering in the hollow of a tree (a stock), worshipping St *Mary the Virgin. He encountered two Carmelite hermits who had come from the *Holy Land to Rochester in the company of an English nobleman and joined their community. Another account states that Simon became a Carmelite after he visited Mount *Carmel while on a *pilgrimage. He spent the next twenty years, until his death at Bordeaux in 1265, supervising the transformation of the Order (which had been confirmed in the *West in 1229 by Pope Gregory IX [1227-41]) from one of *hermits to mendicant *friars. It is said that he was favoured with a vision of St *Mary the Virgin who gave him the brown *scapular which became characteristic of Carmelites, promising that whoever cherished it, and died piously wearing it, would be saved from the torments of *Hell.

Simon Stylites, St There are two saints of this name, both of Antioch. The younger (*c*.521-*c*.592) has not attracted as much attention as his senior (*c*.390-459), although both spent their days living on top of a high pillar (Greek *stylos*). The elder first lived in a disused watertank, but found that his ascetic life attracted too many invalids who wished to be cured by touching him; so in 423 he built a *column out of three blocks of stone (representing the *Trinity) and established himself at the top, although there was room only for him to stand. Over the years he gradually increased the height of the column until it was sixty feet high. It was said that he was able to fly from there like a bird. After his death the column was enshrined in a church, and the monastery of St Simon was built in his honour.

Simony The vice, common in the Middle Ages, of purchasing ecclesiastical offices and benefices, named after *Simon Magus who tried to buy magical powers from St *Peter.

Sin Usually defined by the words of St *Augustine of Hippo, 'Any thought word or deed against the law of God'. Capital sins are those to which man in his fallen state is most inclined. They are called 'capital' or 'cardinal' because other sins are derived from them (*See* *Seven Deadly Sins). Venial sin is

A donor contemplates St Mary Magdalene's symbolic washing of Jesus' feet in the house of **Simon the Leper.** Dieric Bouts sets the scene in a Dutch interior (*c*.1415-75).

In the central register of this illumination to the Golden Gospels of Heinrich III (1039-43), **Simon of Cyrene** is shown carrying Jesus' cross. *Above* is the crowing with thorns; *below*, the Crucifixion between two thieves.

a less serious transgression which does not deprive a soul of sanctifying *grace, and is hence pardonable (Latin *venia*, 'pardon'), whereas mortal (Latin *mortalis*, 'deadly') sin does, because of its grievous nature. The 'sin against the *Holy Ghost' (Mt 12 : 31) is blasphemy, or being deliberately unrepentant for sins against the Seven *Gifts of the Holy Spirit, and remaining impenitent in the hour of death. Mankind fell through *Original Sin. Sins 'crying to Heaven for vengeance' (based on Gen 4 : 10) are murder (*See* *Cain); the sin of *Sodom (homosexuality); oppression of the poor; and not paying fair wages (*See* *Wages of sin).

Siren A mythical woman-like creature, either half bird and with feathers, or, more commonly, half fish and like a mermaid. She had the power to lull men to sleep with her song or with a musical instrument in order to destroy them, so those who fall into sexual sin are punished by death. One legend was that a siren tempted Eve to eat the *Forbidden Fruit. Thus the *serpent is sometimes depicted with the face of a beautiful woman.

Sisera The commander of a Canaanite army who was defeated by the *Israelites. He took refuge with Heber the Kenite, whose wife *Jael pretended to receive him as a guest , but when he was asleep she slew him by driving a tent-peg through his head (Jg 4 : 15-21; 5 : 24-7).

Skull Symbol of death, often with crossed bones beneath. It is shown with penitent saints (SS *Francis of Assisi, *Romuald, *Mary Magdalene and *Jerome). At the foot of the Cross it represents Adam's skull (*See* Legends of the *Cross).

Sleepers of Ephesus, seven Seven young Christian nobleman of Ephesus in the 3rd century who took refuge in a cave during the *persecutions. Emperor Decius (*c*.250) ordered that the cave should be walled up, and the seven fell into a deep sleep which lasted 208 (in some versions 187) years. They were awakened when the stones at the entrance to the cave were being removed by the servants of Adolius, a lawyer, who wanted to build a stable. Unaware that they had slept for so long, the seven sent one of their number to the town to buy bread, but he was arrested and taken before the governor when he tried to pay for the provisions with an ancient coin. Thinking that the money had come from a treasure-trove, the governor went with the bishop to the cave, where he found a sealed chest with documents recounting how the seven had come to be immured. The awakened sleepers then praised God, bowed their heads, and died. Their attribute is a poppy, because poppy-seeds are a drug.

Sloth One of the *Seven Deadly Sins, equated with *accidie and represented by a fat man riding on an ass or a pig.

Snake A reptile which was confused with the *serpent and the *dragon. Like them it symbolizes *sin. When it represents Prudence, it recalls the text, 'be ye therefore wise as serpents, and harmless as doves' (Mt 10 : 16).

Snow, Our Lady of the A title given to St *Mary the Virgin, derived from the legend of the foundation of the church of Santa Maria Maggiore, Rome. Giovanni Patricio (John the Patrician), being without an heir, prayed to the Virgin for guidance as to how best to use his wealth. That night, 5 August 352, she appeared to him, his wife and to Pope Liberius (352-66), and ordered them to build a church in her honour on the spot where, next morning, they would find a patch of snow. They went in procession to the Esquiline hill and there, despite the heat of midsummer, they discovered snow. Liberius outlined the plan of the church with his *crosier and the magnificent *basilica was eventually built on that spot.

Sodom and Gomorrah Two *Cities of the Plain of the River Jordan, notorious for their wickedness and destroyed by God with fire and brimstone. The men of Sodom, where *Lot dwelt, gave their name to the homosexuality they practised (Gen 18 : 16-33; 19 : 1-29).

Solomon The third king of Israel (*c*.971-931 BC), his predecessors being *Saul and his own father *David. His mother *Bathsheba contrived to obtain David's blessing for him as heir to the throne, despite the opposition of the rival claimants, *Absalom and Adonijah, the latter supported by the deposed general *Joab (1 Kg 1 : 11-53). Solomon rode into Jerusalem on his father's mule to be anointed by *Zadok the priest, foretelling Jesus' *Entry into Jerusalem. After David's death, Solomon sat upon his throne. Bathsheba came to petition him to allow Adonijah to marry *Abishag, David's handmaiden, but Solomon refused because it would be a threat to his supreme power. Nevertheless, when Bathsheba entered his throneroom he 'rose up to meet her, and bowed himself unto her, and sat down on his throne, and caused a seat to be set for the king's mother; and she sat on his right hand' (1 Kg 2 : 19). This foreshadowed Christ's reception into Heaven of his mother, St *Mary the Virgin, and her *Coronation.

Solomon gained the reputation of being the wisest man who ever lived. To him was attributed not only the authorship of the *Song of Songs* but also the wise sayings and reflections on life of *The Proverbs*, *Ecclesiastes* and *The Wisdom of Solomon*. He is also thought to have composed at least two Psalms (Ps 72; (71) and 127 (126)). He owed his wisdom to the choice of that attribute when God appeared to him in a dream by night in Gibeon and asked him to name what he would like. Solomon requested 'an understanding heart to judge thy people, that I may discern between good and bad' (1 Kg 3 : 9). The classic example of his use of this gift is the *Judgement of Solomon, when he restored a child to its rightful mother. He is credited in Jewish and Islamic folklore with many similar examples of his powers of discernment. He was believed to have been a sorcerer and to have

recorded esoteric knowledge. Solomon's seal, a six-pointed star or *hexagram formed by two interlaced triangles, is a magical symbol.

Solomon's name in its Hebrew form was interpreted as 'peaceful', and this made him prefigure Jesus who brought peace to the world. His reign was one of peace and prosperity for the Israelites. A skilled trader, he took advantage of the strategic position of his kingdom at the centre of several caravan routes. His people were not seafarers, but an alliance with Hiram of Tyre gave him access to the trade of the Mediterranean (1 Kg 5 : 1-12). Copper and Eastern luxuries were brought to his capital through the Gulf of Aqabah. His wealth thus accumulated, enabled him to build the magnificent *Temple of Jerusalem, a wonder for all ages.

Solomon secured his international position by contracting numerous foreign alliances, including marriage to the daughter of one of the last 21st Dynasty pharaohs of Egypt, and a liaison with the *Queen of Sheba. Towards the end of his life he had a harem of 'seven-hundred wives, princesses, and three hundred concubines' (1 Kg 11 : 3), most of them foreign. They induced him to sacrifice to their gods, and this idolatory was punished by God in the next generation, by the troublesome reign of Solomon's son, Rehoboam (1 Kg 11 : 9-11).

Song of Songs The anglicization of the Hebrew way of expressing a superlative, meaning 'the best of songs'. The Vg title is similarly *Canticum Canticorum*, hence the name *Canticles. The work is traditionally attributed to *Solomon because it contained references to him (Sg 1 : 1; 3 : 7; 8 : 11), so is also entitled the *Song of Solomon*. Primarily an intense and lyrical dialogue of love, it has been interpreted symbolically by Rabbis as well as Church *Fathers. St *Ambrose wrote that the Shulammite maid (*See* *Abishag) mentioned in the poem foreshadowed St *Mary the Virgin. Other commentators, both *Catholic and *Protestant, have found in the rich imagery of the songs the expression of Christ's love for the Church and for the individual soul.

Sophia, St The Greek *Sophía*, 'wisdom', called in Latin *Sancta Sophia*, 'Holy Wisdom' (of God), was mistaken for a female saint. Thus the mosque in Constantinople, formerly a Christian church, is erroneously called St Sophia instead of the church of the Holy Wisdom.

Sorrows of the Virgin, Seven Meditation on the seven sorrowful events in the life of St *Mary the Virgin is encouraged on 15 September, originating in the prophecy of *Simeon, 'Yea, a sword shall pierce through thy own soul also' (Lk 2 : 35). It began with the *Servites in 1668 (who observe it on the third Sunday in September) and was extended to the whole of the *Roman Catholic Church by Pope Pius VII (1800-23) in 1814. Previously the Sorrows were also recalled on *Good Friday, a practice which began in Cologne in 1413 in expiation for the sins of the Hussite

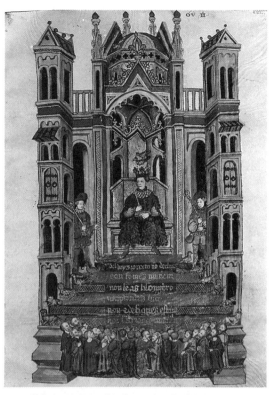

King **Solomon** sits on his throne in a Gothic temple (Spanish, Alba Bible, 15th century).

St **Sophia,** the church of the Holy Wisdom, now a museum, in Istanbul (Constantinople).

heretics. The devotion was made universal by Pope Benedict XIII in 1727, but was discontinued in 1960.

The events included vary, and are frequently depicted separately, or as part of a sequence on an *altar-piece. They were eventually fixed as: **1** *Circumcision of Jesus (or *Presentation of Jesus in the Temple); **2** *Flight into Egypt; **3** Jesus lost in Jerusalem when he disputed with the *Doctors; **4** the meeting with Jesus on his way to *Calvary; **5** St Mary the Virgin at the foot of the Cross at the *Crucifixion *(*Stabat Mater)*; **6** the *Descent from the Cross; **7** the *Entombment.

Soul The spiritual part of each person, which separates from the body at death. In art it is depicted as a newborn baby carried up to *Heaven, or in a cloth (representing *Abraham's bosom). Young babes clutched in a fist or open palm represent the text, 'the righteous, and the wise, and their works, are in the *hand of God' (Eccl 9 : 1). A *butterfly also represents the soul in the art of the *catacombs, an image derived from Classical sources.

Sparrow Symbol of God's care even for the humblest of his creatures. Jesus said, 'Are not two sparrows sold for a farthing? and one of them shall not fall on the ground without your Father' (Mt 10 : 29. *cf* Lk 12 : 6).

Stabat Mater A hymn attributed, among others, to St *Bonaventure and also to Jacopone da Todi, a Franciscan friar (*d*.1306). It begins in Latin, *Stabat mater dolorosa, juxta crucem lacrymosa*, 'the sorrowing mother stood in tears by the Cross', and goes on to describe her grief and to praise her part in the plan for *redemption of mankind. It has been frequently set to music for liturgical use, particularly in conjunction with the Seven *Sorrows of the Virgin and the *Stations of the Cross.

Stag *Attribute of St *Julian the Hospitator and, with a *crucifix between its horns, of SS *Eustace and *Hubert. It may also stand for the *hart, symbol of the soul seeking God (Ps 42 (41) : 1), and for purity, because it retires from the world to the remoteness of the mountain top.

Stalls Seats in the *choir of a church, partly or wholly enclosed at the back and sides. In the Gothic period ornamented with carvings. The *misericords under the seat were often carved with symbolic devices or scenes.

Stanislas Kostka, St A Polish youth (*b*.1550) who was educated in Vienna by the first *Jesuits to establish themselves in that city, and one of the patron saints of Poland. His father opposed his joining the Order but he made the journey to Rome barefoot and was there received by St Francis Borgia at the age of seventeen into the Society of Jesus. His health had never been good and he died (1568) from heart trouble which he had tried to relieve by putting cold compresses on his

breast. He is therefore invoked by those who suffer from palpitation. An angel (or in some accounts St *Barbara and two angels) brought him the *Blessed Sacrament, and he is therefore depicted with an angel beside him and a *lily (emblem of his purity) in his hand. He may also be shown driving out the sinful enemies of his native country. He was canonized in 1726.

Star Symbol of the *Epiphany, recalling the star which guided the three *Kings to *Bethlehem (Mt 2 : 9). Also of *Christ, 'the bright and morning star' (Rev 22 : 16), who is also a 'Star out of Jacob', as foretold by *Balaam (Num 24; 17). A star is the *attribute of St *Mary the Virgin who is *Stella Matutina*, 'Star of the Morning', and *Stella Maris*, 'Star of the Sea', two stars whose brightness never fades. She is also symbolized by twelve stars (*See* *Woman clothed with the Sun). Stars are attributes of SS *Dominic and *Nicolas of Tolentino. *Lucifer, or *Satan, is a star seen to 'fall from heaven unto the earth' (Rev 9 : 1).

Stations of the Cross Pictures, carvings or statues surmounted by a Cross, depicting episodes on the road to *Calvary placed around the inside perimeter of a church, or ranged along a road leading to a church or shrine. At each station, or point along the route (*Via Calvarii*, or *Via Crucis*, 'the *Way of the Cross'), it is customary to pray or to meditate on the event represented. This devotion earns an *indulgence and is popular during *Lent and *Passiontide. It was fostered by the *Franciscans, guardians of the Holy Places in *Jerusalem, as a simulation of the *pilgrimage procession along the *Via Dolorosa, the traditional route taken by Jesus on the way to his *Crucifixion.

The number of stations has varied throughout the centuries, but fourteen are now authorized: **1** Jesus is sentenced by *Pilate; **2** he is given the Cross; **3** he stumbles; **4** he meets his mother; **5** *Simon of Cyrene is ordered to carry the Cross; **6** St *Veronica gives him the napkin; **7** he falls a second time; **8** he tells the women of Jerusalem not to weep for him; **9** he falls a third time; **10** he is stripped of his garments; **11** he is nailed to the Cross; **12** he dies; **13** his body is taken down from the Cross (*See* *Descent from the Cross); **14** he is laid in the tomb (*See* *Entombment).

Stephaton The name given to the bystander at the *Crucifixion who took a *sponge (Greek *spongon*, deformed into a proper name), filled it with vinegar, put it on a reed and gave it to Jesus to drink (Mt 27 : 48; Mk 15 : 36). In the *Gospel of John* the sponge was placed on a *hyssop (Jn 19 : 29), and the name of the man in Byzantine art is therefore Aesop (Greek *husswp*).

Stephen, St One of the seven *deacons and 'a man full of faith and of the Holy Ghost' (Ac 6 : 5), whom the Apostles appointed to look after the day-to-day administration of the first Christian community in Jerusalem while they devoted themselves to prayer and to the ministry of the word.

Stephen, 'his face as it had been the face of an angel', defended himself before the *Sanhedrin, the council of the Jews, against false accusations of blasphemy. His lengthy speech, which was more a prototype sermon, so outraged them that they cast him out of the city and stoned him, making him the first male Christian martyr. The witnesses against him, whose obligation it was to cast the first stones, 'laid down their clothes at a young man's feet'. One of these was St *Paul, who was still known as Saul and was a persecutor of Christians (Ac 6 : 8-7 : 60).

St Stephen is depicted dressed as a deacon, in *alb and *dalmatic, praying for his executioners as the stones rain down upon him. In the sky there may appear the vision with which he concluded his defence, 'Behold, I see the heavens opened, and the Son of man standing on the right hand of God' (Ac 7 : 56). His *attributes are a stone, or stones, and a book (because of his sermon). His feast day is 26 December.

There are two late legends relating to St Stephen. One, dating from the 10th century, said that the *Devil stole the infant Stephen from his cradle and substituted a baby devil in his place. The Devil put him on a ship, and he was abandoned in a strange land where he was nursed by a white doe and was discovered by Julian, a *bishop, who was told by the doe to adopt him. When he reached manhood, Stephen was told by an *angel to preach in Cilicia in Asia Minor. Bishop Julian gave him his blessing and he was able to destroy idols there and convert many people. The angel next directed him to his parents' home, where he found them weeping over the substitute child which would not grow up and was still in his cradle. Stephen proved that it was a devil and had it thrown into a fire.

The other legend states that after the stoning, Stephen's body was rescued by *Gamaliel and buried in the same grave as *Nicodemus (in some versions *Nathanael and Abiba). Four centuries later, a priest called Lucian was told by Gamaliel in a vision where to find the relics, and said he would be able to identify Stephen's body by the red roses which bloomed beside it. The remains of the three saints were then taken from Jerusalem to Constantinople and later to Rome, where those of St Stephen were laid in the *basilican church of San Lorenzo, in the tomb where St *Lawrence had earlier been interred. St Lawrence moved over to provide a place for St Stephen and thus earned for himself the title of 'the courteous Spaniard'. Because their relics repose in the same tomb, the two saints are frequently shown together in art.

Stigmata Purplish patches or blood marks which appear spontaneously on the feet, hands, side, forehead and back, simulating the Five *Wounds inflicted on Jesus. The first person known to have received them was St *Francis of Assisi during an ecstasy on Mount Alvernia on 17 September 1224, and they have been experienced by some hundreds of ecstatics who have meditated fervently on the sufferings of Christ, including SS *Catherine of Genoa and *Catherine of Siena.

Angels transport the **soul** of St Bertin from his monastery at St-Omer, Pas-de-Calais, to Christ on his judgement-seat (Simon Marmion, c.1459-80).

Stole A long narrow strip of silk (Latin *stola*, 'a long garment'), usually with a cross embroidered on it. It is worn by a *deacon as a sash over the left shoulder, and by a *priest or *bishop crossed over the breast, or falling straight down in front from the neck. It was used in the *East as early as the 4th century to denote clerical rank, and in the *West from the 9th century onwards as a mark of clerical calling. It is worn as a *vestment at the *Eucharist when administering the *Sacraments, when preaching, or hearing *confessions. The colour of the stole conforms usually to the liturgical *colour of the season. In the East the equivalent garment for a deacon is an *orarion* and for a priest an *epitrachelion*.

Stone An instrument of *martyrdom. St *Matthew may hold two stones, St *James the Less three, St *Stephen one or more, and St *Matthias three or more. St *Jerome is shown beating his breast with a stone as a penitential act.

Stoup A basin or font containing *Holy Water often near the entrance to a church. It is a pious or *sacramental act, symbolizing purification, to dip the fingers in the water and to make the *sign of the cross when entering or leaving a church.

Sudarium Latin for the 'napkin' or 'sweat cloth' which St *Veronica gave to Jesus to wipe his brow on his way to *Calvary, and on which his features were said to have been imprinted. Also the Holy *Shroud.

Sun Symbol of *Christ, 'the Sun of righteousness' (Mal 4 : 2); of the splendour of God, who is 'a sun and a shield' (Ps 84 : 11); and of his care for all of humanity, because 'he maketh his sun to rise on the evil and on the good' (Mt 5 : 45). Christians are told, 'Let not the sun go down upon your wrath' (Eph 4 : 26). The sun was darkened at the *Crucifixion (Lk 23 : 45). 'A *woman clothed with the sun, and the moon under her feet' (Rev 12 : 1) is thought to refer to St *Mary the Virgin.

Sunday The English equivalent of the Latin *dies solis*, 'the day of the sun', a pre-Christian name for the weekday, but retained by Christians because Christ was the *sol verus*, 'the true sun'. It persists in the Germanic languages (German *sontag*, Dutch *zondag*), but Romance languages use words derived from *(dies) dominica*, the *Lord's Day (French *dimanche*, Spanish *domingo*, Italian *domenica*). This was the Early Christian name for the first day of the week, when the faithful gathered to celebrate the *Eucharist in commemoration of the *Resurrection which happened on the day following the *Sabbath. The assembly, 'to break bread' (Ac 20 : 7), took place at first in the early morning, but after the *Peace of the Church in 313 it became customary to meet at 9 am, the third hour of the day according to Roman reckoning. This meant that Christians missed vital hours of employment. It was Emperor *Constantine's practice to give his soldiers a day's rest on Sundays, and he made this obligatory for all townspeople in 321, although farm labourers were excepted. After the Council of Laodicea (*c*.380), Christians were encouraged to avoid all but essential work on that day and were obliged to attend the Eucharist.

In Latin countries Sunday is traditionally a holiday, and the faithful are expected to go to *Mass in the early part of the day but permitted to use the rest of the time for recreation. Protestant countries, since the late 16th century, have tended to equate Sunday with the Jewish *Sabbath and to make it a day of rest and spiritual refreshment in obedience to the fourth of the *Ten Commandments. *Puritans, *Calvinists and *Evangelicals advocate strict observance and attendance at church, and forbid sport and all but essential work. This *sabbatarianism is at odds with a secular society, and with the view of other more liberally-minded Christians who go to church but who would not wish to prevent others from enjoying the day of rest in their own ways, provided it does not impose a burden of work on others.

Sunflower Because it always turns to face the sun, it represents the soul seeking God.

Superior A person with authority over others, either ecclesiastical (in the *Roman Catholic Church: *Pope, *cardinals, *archbishops and *bishops, in descending order), or religious, one who governs a community, e.g. *abbot, *prior, or, in the case of women, *abbess, mother superior and *prioress.

Surplice A liturgical *vestment – a loose, white garment worn by officiating *clergy. The word is derived from the Latin *superpelliceum*, 'worn over fur', because in cold climates clergy dressed in a fur coat and needed a looser and fuller garment than an *alb to put over it during the *choir office. Surplices seem to have come into use at the beginning of the 11th century.

Sursum corda Latin for 'Lift up your hearts', a request addressed by the *priest to the congregation.

Susanna and the elders Susanna's story is told in the AV *Apocrypha, 'set apart from the beginning of *Daniel* because it is not in the Hebrew', and given the title of *The History of Susanna*. She was the wife of a rich man 'who had a fair garden joining unto his house'. Among the Jews whom he entertained were two elders who had been appointed judges. They were both inflamed with lust when each day they saw Susanna walking in the garden. Having revealed to each other their mutual longings, they concealed themselves, hoping for an opportunity to find her alone. Susanna 'was desirous to wash herself in the garden for it was hot' and told her maids to fetch 'oil and washing balls' and to shut the garden gate. Seizing the opportunity, the elders emerged from their hiding place and threatened Susanna that unless she agreed to lie with them, they would say that they saw her committing adultery under a tree with a young man. Susanna refused, saying that she preferred to die rather than 'to sin in the sight of the Lord'. Like Joseph, who refused to be seduced by *Potiphar's wife, she is thus an example of *chastity.

Susanna was brought weeping before the people and the elders accused her of adultery, two witnesses being sufficient to secure death by stoning for this crime. Susanna 'looked up toward heaven, for her heart trusted in the Lord'. The young *Daniel appeared, sent by God, and asked to examine the witnesses separately. To the question, 'Under what tree sawest thou them companying together?', one elder answered, 'Under a mastick tree', and the other, 'Under an holm tree', thus convicting themselves of false witness. For this they were put to death 'according to the law of Moses', an example of the triumph of justice.

The story concludes, 'Thus the innocent blood was saved the same day'. Susanna therefore became the symbol of salvation for those who trust in God. She is named in the Prayer for the Dying *(Commendatio animae)* and is depicted in the art of the *catacombs as a *lamb between two wolves. Renaissance and Baroque artists used the story as an opportunity to depict the female nude, showing the chaste Susanna preparing for her bath in the garden and the two elderly voyeurs peeping at her from behind the trees.

Outside his cell in the desert St Jerome beats his breast with a **stone** in penance for his sins (Cima, 1459/60–1517/18).

Swallow A symbol of the *Resurrection because it was thought to hibernate in the winter and emerge from hiding in the spring.

Swan *Attribute of St *Hugh of Lincoln whose constant companion was a swan. Also a symbol of deceit because a swan's white wings and plumage cover black flesh. As a swan is said to sing only when it is about to die – its 'swan song' – it also represents the end of life.

Swiss Guard Ceremonial bodyguards of the *Pope, so called because Swiss soldiers were recruited as early as the 14th century for the defence of the *Holy See. They carry halberds and swords, wear breastplates on ceremonial occasions and a uniform, designed by Michelangelo Buonarroti (1475–1564), consisting of a white ruff, tunic, breeches and stockings with wide stripes of blue, red and yellow. Their undress uniform is black beret, blue tunic and breeches.

Lascivious elders spy on **Susanna** at her toilet (Tintoretto, 1518–94).

Swithun, St Bishop of Winchester, appointed in 852 by King Aethelwulf of the West Saxons, who made him his adviser on ecclesiastical affairs. He gained a reputation for his skill in obtaining revenue and for his financial administration of his *diocese. He kept careful records of expenditure and used the money he saved to reconstruct churches which had fallen into decay. He was renowned for the simplicity of his life and for his lack of pomp (he travelled by night to avoid display). A miracle attributed to him in the *Golden Legend* illustrates his understanding of ordinary folk. A poor woman was pushed in a market-day crowd and dropped her basket of eggs. St Swithun blessed the broken shells and the eggs were made whole again. He died in 862 and was buried on the north side of Winchester Cathedral. His fame spread during the following century and a large number of churches were dedicated to him. Because of his saintly renown, his body was removed on 15 July 971 to a shrine within the cathedral. Torrential rain fell and lasted for forty days. This is said to be the origin of the popular belief that if it rains on his feast day (15 July) the bad weather will persist for forty days, but that if it is fine it will be fair for the same period.

Sword An *attribute of saints who were beheaded or who had swords thrust into them, notably SS *Agnes, *Catherine of Alexandria, *Cecilia and *Justina of Padua among the female saints. The males include SS *Boniface, *Cyprian, *Genesius, *James the Great, *Matthias and *Thomas of Canterbury. St *Paul holds a sword with the hilt held upwards, a reference both to his martyrdom and to his preaching for 'the sword of the Spirit, which is the word of God' (Eph 6 : 17). One of the *cherubim, traditionally *Jophiel, held a flaming sword to protect the entrance to the Garden of *Eden (Gen 3 : 24). Seven swords refer to the Seven *Sorrows of St Mary the Virgin. *Justice holds a sword, symbol of authority, and a balance. St *Michael's sword symbolizes his victory over *Lucifer (the *Devil).

Sylvester, St A 4th-century Pope (314-35), depicted with a *tiara, who is believed to have been responsible for the *baptism of Emperor *Constantine and to have obtained from him the *Donation of Constantine, later shown to be a forgery. An old man when he was made Pope, he fled from persecution to a cave near Monte Calvo (or Socrate). The emperor, according to legend, contracted leprosy and his priests and doctors advised that he should bathe in the blood of 3000 children, but when they were assembled he was moved by their parents' lamentations and resolved to die from his disease rather than have them massacred. That night SS *Peter and *Paul appeared to him and told him that Sylvester would show him a pool in which he could bathe and be cured. Sylvester was sent for. He showed the emperor a picture of the two saints, whom Constantine immediately recognized as the persons in his dream. Cured by baptism, the emperor proclaimed the legality of the Christian religion, ordered that the *bishop of Rome should take precedence over all other bishops and that the Church should receive tithes from all Roman lands. He then took a spade and cut the foundations of the *basilica of St John Lateran and escorted Sylvester in triumph into the city. (In fact, Constantine was baptized on his death-bed.) Empress *Helena thought that her son should have recognized the Jewish religion, not the Christian faith, according to the *Golden Legend, and assembled 140 learned rabbis to debate the truth of their religion with Sylvester, but his logic overcame their arguments. A test was then prop-osed to find out who knew the name of the Almighty which no one could hear and live. A magician whispered into the ear of a wild *ox or bull and it fell down dead, but Sylvester, saying the name was that of the *Devil, made the sign of the cross and the animal came to life. A bull is therefore his principal *attribute. He may also be shown with a *dragon at his feet because he bound up the jaws of a dragon which was poisoning 300 men a day with its breath. Another legend tells how he warned Tarquinus, a pagan governor who had demanded the property of a martyred Christian called Timotheus, that he would soon die. That night at dinner the governor was choked by a fishbone that stuck in his throat. (Another version is that Sylvester cured his jailor who had a fishbone stuck in his throat.)

St Sylvester's feast is on 31 December, so the German for New Year's Eve is Silvesterabend.

Symbol From the Greek *simbolon*; originally one of the two broken halves of a ring or some other pledge, which, if fitted together again, proved the authenticity of the persons presenting them. The word came to mean any object, action or graphic sign which points to something beyond what is at first apparent. The true significance is completed when the visible sign and the inner meaning are fitted together. In this sense a symbol differs from a natural sign in that the interpretation of the latter is based on experience, whereas the meaning of a symbol is conventional and is usually derived by analogy. When Robinson Crusoe saw footprints on the beach on his solitary island, his experience told him that this was a sign that a man had been there. In contrast, when the Early Christians used signet-rings with the image of an *anchor, they intended that they would be recognized by their fellow-Christians who had been taught that an anchor was not only a nautical object but also a symbol of the Cross and hence of salvation.

Christians were inheritors of both the Jewish and Classical civilizations in which symbols were freely employed, so they evolved their own symbols of faith. By the Middle Ages they had elaborated a complex symbolic system which pervaded the whole of their existence, influencing their preaching, teaching, literature and art. The key to the understanding of the Christian past (and also the present) is the interpretation of these often arcane symbols (*See* *symbolism).

Symbolism In Christian thought, the whole of the visible universe is a collective *symbol of the divine truth which can be discovered if the diverse phenomena which compose it are interpreted aright. The process of interpretation reached its height in the Middle Ages, by which time almost everything which was part of everyday existence had been given a spiritual significance. Architecture, sculpture, painting and even musical modes were thus endowed with symbolic values. Nothing was introduced inadvisedly. It was there because of its symbolic significance. An *apple is put into the hand of *Eve to recall the *Fall of Mankind. A *goldfinch held by the *Christ-Child is a forecast of his *Passion. These were agreed or conventional symbols, the meaning of which would be apparent to those familiar with an immense body of learning, conveniently summarized in encyclopaedic works like the *Etymologies* of *Isidore of Seville (*d.c.*450) and the works of Vincent of Beauvais (*c.*1190-1264). Explanation of the symbols by clerics helped the laity to understand and recall the mysteries of the faith.

Almost every aspect of the universe was examined to discover symbolic meaning, but the symbols most frequently occurring in art, architecture and literature are derived from *numbers, *geometrical figures, *colours, *fruits, *flowers, stones and gems, *animals, *birds, *fish and insects. These are listed alphabetically in the present work. A distinction is made between symbols of this type and *attributes, the symbols which serve to identify *prophets and *saints.

Synagogue The meeting place of a Jewish community, where *Jews assemble for prayer and the reading of the Scriptures. The word was first applied to a gathering of at least ten persons for worship or study and then to the building where they met. *Jesus frequented the synagogues of *Nazareth (Mt 13 : 54; Lk 4 : 16) and *Capernaum (Mk 1 : 21; Jn 6 : 59). After the destruction of the *Temple of Jerusalem in the year 70, the local synagogue assumed even greater significance as the focus of Jewish religious, educational, benevolent and social activities.

In the Middle Ages, at a time of regrettable persecution of the Jews, allegorical interpretations of biblical texts were used to demonstrate the falsity of the Synagogue as opposed to the Church, although for the Jews the synagogue never had such a symbolic role. Thus the pretended mother in the *Judgement of Solomon, and *Satan who was the antagonist of *Job, are used as types of the Synagogue. A blindfolded or veiled maiden (who has not seen the light of the new *Law) also represents the Synagogue, in contrast to unbandaged eyes of a virgin who stands for the Church.

Synod An assembly (Latin *synodus*, from the Greek *sunodos*, 'meeting'), particularly of *bishops and other ecclesiastics, to discuss doctrine, *liturgy and discipline.

Synoptic Gospels The name given to the *gospels of *Matthew, *Mark and Luke, because they present a 'simultaneous view' (Greek *synopsis*) of the life and teaching of *Jesus of Nazareth. Because 606 out of *Mark*'s 661 verses can be found in similar form in either *Luke* or *Matthew*, it is argued that *Mark* was the earliest gospel to be written, and that Matthew and Luke had it before them when they composed their work. The 200 or so verses which are common to *Matthew* and *Luke* are thought to be derived from a source conveniently designated Q (German *Quelle*, 'source'), but there is no evidence that such a document ever existed. The exact relationship between the three gospels, the dates when they were composed and the sources of their information, whether oral or

The interior of the Cologne **synagogue,** 1861.

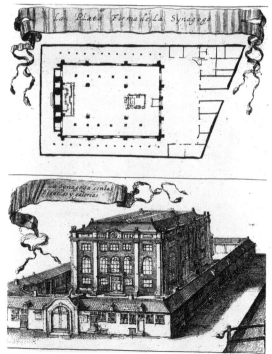

Plan and elevation of the Portuguese **synagogue,** Amsterdam, 1675.

written, constitute the much debated 'synoptic problem'.

T The Greek letter *tau*, representing the *Tau cross, a cross without its upper arm, thought to be the protective mark placed on the doorposts of Israelite dwellings in Egypt on the night of the *Passover, and thus signifying salvation. It was also said to be the form of the staff on which Moses lifted up the *Brazen Serpent in the wilderness, thus foreshadowing the *Crucifixion. SS *Matthew and *Philip were crucified on crosses of this shape and bear a Tau cross as *attribute. *Dismas and *Gestas, the thieves put to death alongside *Christ, are also depicted on Tau-shaped crosses. The Tau cross symbolizes the season of *Advent and eternal life in Christ. T also stands for the Greek *theos*, 'God', and is borne on the left shoulder of St *Antony of Egypt (the Great).

Tabernacle A tent (Latin *tabernaculum*), the portable sanctuary and dwelling of God which the Israelites carried with them in their journey through the wilderness and which was eventually placed in Solomon's *Temple. A veil hanging from golden hooks divided it into two sections: the Holy Place which contained the seven-branched candlestick, a table for the shew-bread and the altar of incense; and the *Holy of Holies in which the *Ark of the Covenant rested.

In Christian usage a tabernacle is a cupboard or other receptacle in which the *Reserved Sacrament for the communion of the sick and dying is kept. (In some *Orthodox churches it takes the form of a dove-shaped vessel suspended before the altar.) The *Council of Trent made it obligatory to place the tabernacle in the middle of the altar in *Roman Catholic churches, but in other churches it may be on the *Gospel side of the *sanctuary.

Tabitha An Aramaic personal name, equated in the *Acts of the Apostles* with the Greek name *Dorcas, 'gazelle'. Tabitha, who had dedicated her life to good works, died at Lydda and was laid out by friends in an upper room. Two men from the Christian community heard that St *Peter was at the nearby town of Joppa and sought his help. Peter found the body being watched over by wailing widows who displayed to him the clothes which Tabitha had made for them. He prayed and then said, 'Tabitha, rise'. She opened her eyes and sat up. The miracle encouraged many converts in Joppa (Ac 9 : 40-2).

Tablets of the Law Hidden in a cloud, God spoke to *Moses on Mount Sinai and gave him two tablets of stone on which were inscribed the *Ten Commandments, the foundation of the *Law of Israel, the OT type of the handing of the law to St *Peter (See *Delivery of the Law). Moses spent forty days and forty nights on the mountain, and then descended, his brow shining with rays of

light. (The Hebrew word for 'light' was mistranslated as 'horns', resulting in the portrayal of Moses with two horns on his forehead.) This episode is the OT type of the *Transfiguration of Christ and the *Descent of the Holy Spirit. Moses returned to the Israelites to find them worshipping the *Golden Calf, and was so outraged by their idolatry that he broke the tablets. He later returned to Mount Sinai where he received new tablets which he placed in the *Ark of the Covenant (Ex 20 : 1-17; Dt 4 : 5-13).

Talents, hidden A *parable (Mt 25 : 14-29) told by Jesus to illustrate the paradox, 'Unto everyone that hath shall be given . . . but from him that hath not shall be taken away'. A man went into a far country and gave to each of his servants according to his ability – five, two and one talents respectively. On his return, the servants who had received five and two talents had doubled them, and each was commended with the words, 'Well done, thou good and faithful servant'. The third, knowing his master to be a hard man, had hidden his talent in the ground instead of investing it. The master ordered the talent to be taken from him and that he be cast into the outer darkness, where 'there shall be weeping and gnashing of teeth'. The details are different in the *Gospel of Luke* (Lk 19 : 12-27) but the essentials are similar.

Tamar The name of two OT women. The first was successively the wife of Judah's elder sons, Er and *Onan, but neither gave her children. When Judah refused to marry her to his third son, Tamar disguised herself as a prostitute and tricked Judah into sleeping with her (Gen 38 : 6-11, 13-30). The second was the beautiful half-sister of King *David's son *Amnon, who fell in love with her, enticed her to his chamber on the pretence that her cakes would cure him of his illness, and then raped her. Afterwards, overcome by loathing, he cast her out. She was avenged by her brother *Absalom (2 Sam 13).

Tau cross A cross in the shape of the letter T (See *T).

Taurus The bull, the second sign of the *zodiac, governing the period from *c*.20 April to *c*.20 May. In the *Labours of the Months this is the time for sowing seeds and scaring birds from the furrows.

Te Deum The opening words, *Te Deum laudamus*, of the ancient Latin hymn of praise and thanksgiving sung at matins on Sundays (except in penitential seasons) and on feast days. In the Anglican *Book of Common Prayer* of 1662 it begins with the words, 'We praise thee, O God'. The hymn has been ascribed, among others, to SS *Ambrose and *Augustine, but its author may have been St Niceta of Remesiana (*d.c*.414).

Temperance One of the four cardinal virtues (the others being *Justice, Prudence and Fortitude). Personified as a modest woman holding a clock (a regulated life); a bridle or bit (to curb lust); a pitcher of water (to put out the fires of sexual desire); or pouring water into a goblet of wine (to temper alcoholic indulgence).

Temple of Jerusalem The first temple was built during King *Solomon's reign, *c.*968 BC, on the spot where an angel had appeared to King *David after he had captured the city of *Jerusalem. Much ingenuity has been expended in vain attempts to discover mystical and prophetical significance in the detailed measurements of this magnificent structure. It was destroyed by *Nebuchadnezzar in 586 BC, but rebuilt after 70 years by Israelites who returned from exile in Babylon and completed the work in 516 BC. The comparative simplicity of this second temple, which contrasted so markedly with the glories of Solomon's original edifice, caused Herod the Great in 19 BC to plan a splendid building to adorn his capital. This was the temple of NT times which Jesus and his disciples frequented in the last days of his life, and where the members of the Jerusalem Church continued to meet after his death. When Titus captured the city in AD 70, he intended to preserve this outstanding structure, completed only seven years previously, but one of his soldiers set fire to the Holy Place which contained the seven-branched candlestick (one of the objects depicted on Titus' Arch being borne back to Rome in triumph) and the whole temple was destroyed, as Jesus had foretold (Mt 24 : 2).

Temptation in the wilderness Immediately after his *baptism in the River Jordan, Jesus spent a period of fasting and prayer in the hill country of Judaea, meditating on the right way to use his special powers to fulfil his divine mission. Either he could cater for the physical needs of his people by seeing that the hungry were fed, or he could pin his faith on military revolution and make himself the temporal ruler of the world. A third possibility was to use his supernatural gifts to impress the crowd by posing as a magician who could overcome nature. These three choices were the subject of the story of the temptations of Jesus by *Satan. The gospels of *Matthew* (Mt 4 : 1-11) and *Luke* (Lk 4 : 1-13) agree as to their nature, but *Luke* changes the order of the second and third temptations. The *Devil first attacked Jesus at the point where a man weakened by hunger would be most susceptible, saying, 'If thou be the Son of God, command that these stones be made bread'. Jesus replied by quoting *Deuteronomy*, 'Man doth not live by bread alone' (Dt 8 : 3). Jesus was then transported to a pinnacle of the *Temple and the *Devil suggested that he should test his supernatural powers by jumping off, citing scripture to his purpose, 'For he shall give his angels charge over thee' (Ps 91 (90) : 11). Again Jesus retorted by quoting *Deuteronomy*, 'Ye shall not tempt the Lord your God' (Dt 6 : 16). His answer to the third temptation, domination over all the kingdoms of the world, came likewise from *Deuteronomy*, 'Thou shalt fear the Lord thy god, and serve him' (Dt 6 : 13). When the Devil left him for a while, angels appeared and waited on Jesus. They are depicted

A 15th-century attempt to reconstruct the **Tabernacle,** depicted as a tent containing a menorah, a sacrificial altar, the Ark of the Covenant, and a high priest within the Holy of Holies (Spanish, Alba Bible, 15th century).

Jesus, at the **Temptation in the wilderness,** repulses the Devil who has offered him dominion over the cities of the world. Angels wait on him (Duccio's Maestà altar-piece, Siena, 1308-11).

bringing him fruit, bread and water. Theological difficulties were presented by the spectacle of the 'one without sin' (Heb 4 : 15) suffering temptations like other mortals, but were explained as the consequence of Jesus' complete humanity.

The Temptation was associated with *Lent, at first a period of varying duration. Later the 'forty days' (probably a phrase meaning 'a long time') which Jesus spent in the wilderness were understood literally, and equated with the period of abstinence before Easter which was adopted by the Latin Church from the 7th century onwards. The narrative of the Temptations was the *Gospel for the first Sunday in Lent, read to remind the faithful of the call to mortification; of the importance of overcoming the lusts of the flesh; and of the need to be on guard against the wiles of the Devil.

The story of the Temptation is represented either in single scenes or combined on one canvas showing the three temptations and the final scene with the angels ministering to Jesus' needs. If the Devil proffers a stone, the artist is following the account in the *Gospel of Luke* ('this stone'); if he points to the stones in the wilderness, the painter is following the *Gospel of Matthew* ('these stones').

Ten A symbolic *number recalling: the *Ten Commandments; the ten *Plagues of Egypt; the ten brothers who maltreated *Joseph the Dreamer; the ten Roman *Persecutions of the Early Church; and the ten *Wise and Foolish Virgins. As ten is a perfect number it also symbolizes order.

Ten Commandments Ten warnings, declaimed by the voice of God from Sinai and heard by the Israelites during their sojourn in the desert (Ex 19 : 16-20). They were written by the finger of God on two *tablets of stone that were given to Moses on the mountain (Ex 31 : 18; 32 : 15-16). Angered by the discovery that the Israelites in his absence had begun to worship the *Golden Calf, Moses shattered the tablets (Ex 32 : 19). After the people had been punished and the idol destroyed, Moses returned to Mount Sinai and received two new tablets which were placed in the *Ark of the Covenant (Ex 25 : 16; 40 : 20).

The Ten Commandments, otherwise called the *Decalogue, are the *Law which Jesus came not to destroy but to fulfil (Rom 5 : 18). They may be declaimed in full during the *liturgy, or replaced by Jesus' summary of the Law, 'Thou shalt love the Lord thy God with all thy heart, and with all thy soul, and with all thy mind . . .' and, 'Thou shalt love they neighbour as thy self' (Mt 23 : 37-40). In some post-Reformation English churches the words of the Decalogue (shortened from the version in the *Book of Common Prayer* of 1662) were displayed on two stone or wooden tablets: 'I am the Lord thy God: I. Thou shalt have none other gods but me; II. Thou shalt not make to thyself any graven image; III. Thou shalt not take the name of the Lord thy God in vain; IV. Remember that thou keep holy the Sabbath day; V. Honour thy father and thy mother; VI. Thou shalt do no murder; VII. Thou shalt not commit adultery; VIII. Thou shalt not steal; IX.

Thou shalt not bear false witness against thy neighbour; X. Thou shalt not covet.'

Ten tribes of Israel The so-called 'lost' ten tribes, held by the British Israelites to be the ancestors of the British nation. They were the ten tribes of the kingdom of Israel who had separated from the *Twelve Tribes and who were conquered by the Assyrians in 721 BC. Many of their members were deported to Assyria where they merged with the inhabitants and thereafter disappear from Hebrew records. One theory was that they migrated to America and were the ancestors of the American Indians (See *Races of Man).

Tenebrae Part of the liturgy of *Holy Week, when passages from the *Lamentations of Jeremiah* are chanted. The name is the Latin for 'darknesses' and is so called because fourteen candles are extinguished one by one at the conclusion of each of the fourteen *psalms sung during the service. A fifteenth is put out at the end of the *Benedictus and is lighted behind the altar and remains lit. It is brought out to symbolize the coming *Resurrection. The service ends with the chanting of the *Miserere. The candles are fixed on a triangular tenebrae candlestick, which, because of its shape, was called a *hearse, or harrow.

Terah A maker of idols, according to legend. His son, *Abraham, having realized that there was only one true God, smashed the images when he was sent to sell them in the marketplace. Terah is reputed to have coined the gold pieces which Caspar, one of the three *Kings, offered to the *Christ-Child.

Terce The office said at the third hour (See *Hours).

Teresa, St A Spanish *Carmelite nun (1515-82) of Ávila, Castile. Sickly until middle age, she suddenly displayed unbounded energy, wrote of her religious experiences, communicated with Philip II and travelled all over Spain to promote her new foundations, the houses of the reformed or *discalced Carmelites, who were dedicated to an austere life. She was canonized in 1622 and declared the patron saint of Spain. Her most famous representation in art is Bernini's sculpture of her vision of the angel who wounded her to the heart with a flaming dart. She is also shown receiving from Christ the *Holy Nails and being given a white cloak by St *Joseph, to whom she dedicated her convents.

Terrebolem (or Terrobuli) Said to be two stones (one male, the other female) which, if they touch, burst into flames. This fiction may be a warning against the fires of *lust or of conflict between man and woman.

Tertiary A member of the *Third Order of certain religious *Orders, notably a *Franciscan, *Dominican or *Carmelite.

Testaments, Old and New The covenants or pacts made between God and mankind. The first, the Old Testament, was made with *Noah and later with *Abraham, and then renewed with *Moses. The record of its operation is contained in the books of the Hebrew Bible, which are therefore given the collective name of the Old Testament. God's final compact, the New Testament, was made through the sacrifice of *Jesus Christ. It is expounded in the *Gospels and *Epistles which collectively, together with the *Book of Revelations*, compose the New Testament (*See* *typology).

Tetragrammaton The four Hebrew consonants which are transliterated as YHWH and vocalized as *Yahweh, the name of the God of Israel, as revealed to *Moses.

Tetramorphs Four figures – a man, a lion, an ox and an eagle – which represent the four *Evangelists. The symbolism is derived from *Ezekiel's vision (Ez 10 : 14).

Thaddaeus In the gospels of *Matthew* (Mt 10 : 3) and *Mark* (Mk 3 : 18), the name given to the *Apostle who is called 'Judas of James' in *Luke* (Lk 6 : 16). He is usually identified with St *Jude, but the historian *Eusebius wrote that he was one of the Seventy *Disciples (Lk 10 : 1) and was sent by Jesus to King *Abgar of Edessa because he himself could not go in person. St *Jerome insisted that he was also called Lebbaeus and was the same person as Judas of James.

Thaïs, St A prostitute of Alexandria who was converted by St *Paphnutius and made an act of penitence by setting fire to her possessions and giving away her jewels and all that she had earned by her profession. She then retired to a narrow cell, which had a door with a small hole through which she received her daily ration of bread and water. After three years, Paphnutius was told in a vision that her sins were forgiven and she was released. She died *c.*348.

Theatines The Order of Clerks Regular of the Divine Providence, a religious *Order founded in Rome in 1524 by St Cajetan (1480-1547). Their popular name arose because one of their first members was Gian Pietro Caraffa (later Pope Paul IV [1555-9]) who was bishop of Chieti (Latin *Theate*).

Theban legion The Christian legion led by *St Maurice, martyred because its members refused to acknowledge the divinity of Emperor Maximian.

Thecla, St A virgin of Iconium, converted to Christianity by St *Paul. Her story is told in the apocryphal *Acts of Paul and Tecla* (*c.*180). Resolved to follow a religious life, she refused to marry her rich young suitor and travelled to Antioch, Myra and Seleucia with St Paul, suffering imprisonment and many tortures with such patience, that although she died peacefully in the cleft of a rock

St **Teresa** in ecstasy as an angel pierces her heart in a vision, with the flaming dart, symbol of the love of God (Bernini, 1645-52, Rome).

Christ in majesty surrounded by the **Tetramorphs,** symbols of the four Evangelists (West front of Chartres Cathedral, *c.*1150).

which opened up to protect her, she is accounted the first Christian woman martyr.

Theotokos The title (from the Greek *theos* 'God', *tikto*, 'to give birth to') bestowed on St *Mary the Virgin, Mother of God, by the Council of Ephesus in 431, because 'she brought forth according to the flesh the Word of God made flesh'. It gave rise to devotional depictions of her seated on a throne and holding the *Christ-Child on her knees.

Thief in the night The *parable told by Jesus (Mt 24 : 43-4; Lk 12 : 39-40) to illustrate the unexpectedness of the *Kingdom of Heaven which comes stealthily, like a thief in the night.

Third Order Associations of *laymen and women (called tertians or *tertiaries) who retain their lay status but are attached to certain religious *Orders whose habit they may wear. They may be either secular and live an ordinary life but maintain the discipline of their Order, or regular and live in a community under vows.

Thirty-nine articles A credal statement made by the *Church of England in 1563 and revised 1571, setting out what was then regarded as the essentials of the faith and the points of divergence from *Roman Catholic dogma.

Thistle Symbol of *sin and of sorrow because of the curse pronounced on *Adam: 'in sorrow shalt thou eat of it [the ground] all the days of thy life; thorns also and thistles shall it bring forth to thee' (Gen 3 : 17-18). As the thistle is a thorny plant, it also recalls Christ's *Crown of Thorns and his *Passion.

Thomas, St One of the twelve *Apostles. His name comes from the Aramaic for 'twin', the Greek equivalent of which is given in the *Gospel of John* as a proper name, Didymus. But it is uncertain whose twin he was. Thomas, although frightened, accompanied Jesus to Bethany when news came that *Lazarus was sick (Jn 11 : 16). At the *Last Supper, when Jesus said to the Twelve, 'I go to prepare a place for you', Thomas retorted, 'Lord, we know not whither thou goest; and how can we know the way?'. Jesus replied, 'I am the way, the truth, and the life' (Jn 14 : 2-6).

Thomas gained his nickname, 'Doubting Thomas', because he would not believe that the other Apostles had seen the risen Christ. He said, 'Except I shall see in his hands the print of the nails, and put my finger into the print of the nails, and thrust my hand into his side, I will not believe'. Jesus reappeared through closed doors and told Thomas to touch his wounds, 'and be not faithless but believing'. Thomas then recognized the truth of the *Resurrection, exclaiming, 'My Lord and my God' (Jn 20 : 26-9). In the same way, he refused to believe in the *Assumption of St Mary the Virgin, and she let her girdle fall to earth to convince him.

Traditions diffused through the apocryphal *Acts of St Thomas* say that he went to India and established Christian communities there, baptizing the three *Kings and making them the first *bishops there. Thomas was an architect (a set-square is one of his *attributes) and the pagan King Gondophorus ordered him to build a magnificent palace. In the king's absence, Thomas spent the money on the poor and told the king that he would find his palace ready for him in *Heaven where his treasure had been laid up. Gondophorus put Thomas in prison, but had a vision of his recently deceased brother who revealed that a palace really awaited him in the next life, and he thereupon became a Christian. There are two versions of Thomas' death. One is that he was speared on the orders of a pagan priest (a spear is one of his attributes); another that while he was praying at the place later renamed São Thomé, peacocks hid him from sight and he was transfixed by the arrow which a hunter intended for the birds. In 1523, Portuguese seamen discovered his relics there and took them back to Portugal.

Thomas Aquinas, St The Angelic Doctor (1226-74), renowned for his immense learning and his theological and philosophical writings, patron saint of booksellers (he holds a book with rays of light issuing from it) and of universities and seats of learning. His mother saw a star in the sky before he was born at Aquinas, Italy, and a star is therefore shown on his breast. According to the *Golden Legend*, his family thought that he was too devoted to study, and his brothers tried to distract him by introducing a young maiden into his chamber. He seized a brand from the fire, drew the *sign of the cross on the chimney-breast and drove her out. Two angels then brought him a girdle of chastity and he was thereafter free from sexual temptation. He joined the *Dominican Order and studied Aristotelian philosophy in Paris. Because of his sullen ways, his fellow-students called him a 'dumb ox', but his teacher, Albertus Magnus, said 'You may call him a dumb ox, but he will give such a bellow in learning that will astonish the whole world'. Thomas once went to St *Bonaventure's cell to ask him how he knew so much about God. The Franciscan saint drew aside a curtain to reveal a crucifix and said that his knowledge came from the contemplation of the passion of Christ. Thomas was taken ill at the Council of Lyons and died at the Cistercian monastery of Fossanova (near Terracina), his head being placed in the nearby cathedral at Piperno before the rest of his remains were removed to Toulouse. He was canonized in 1323 and made a *Doctor of the Church in 1567.

Thomas of Canterbury, St Thomas à Becket (1118-70), a man of outstanding ability who became chancellor of England and a close friend of Henry II (1133-89). In 1162, much against his will, he was made archbishop of Canterbury and so exasperated his royal master by siding with the Church against the Crown in the long quarrel over their respective privileges that he was obliged to seek refuge in France. On his return, Henry's incautious outburst, 'Will no one rid me of this turbulent priest?', caused three (in other versions, four) knights to cut him down with their swords as he knelt before the altar in his cathedral. Angels sang *Laetabitur justus* at his *requiem. He was canonized in 1173, three years after his death. His fame as defender of the Church against the temporal power spread rapidly. Innumerable miracles occurred at his tomb, depictions of his martyrdom appeared in churches throughout Western Europe, and Henry was obliged to do public penance for his murder. Canterbury remained a popular pilgrimage centre until Henry VIII destroyed his shrine, removed his name from the list of saints and surpressed his cult.

Thomas of Villanueva, St Otherwise Thomas the Almoner (1488-1555), a learned Augustinian whom Charles V (Charles I of Spain) made *archbishop of Valencia. He was renowned for his charity, and is represented in episcopal robes, surrounded by beggars to whom he gives alms from an open purse.

Thorns Symbol of grief and sorrow, recalling the *crown of thorns mockingly placed on *Christ's head by Roman soldiers. Also, when associated with saints, the sign of triumphant martyrdom (*See* *goldfinch).

Three One of the most frequent of Christian *number symbols because of the triads found throughout the *Bible. It is primarily the symbol of the *Trinity, but may also refer to the three days which *Jonah spent in the whale's belly, and during which Jesus' body lay in the tomb (counting inclusively). Other references are to the three elements in man (body, soul, spirit); the elements of faith (knowledge, assent, confidence); the elements of repentance (contrition, confession, restitution); notable duties (fasting, almsgiving, prayer); evangelical counsels (poverty, chastity and obedience); and theological virtues (faith, hope and charity). The three *angels who visited *Abraham and *Sarah also represent the Trinity.

Three living and three dead A *memento mori* ('Remember that you must die'), an illustration of the story of three young men out hunting who come across three corpses which either speak to them or exhibit three warnings: 'Thus will ye be, and as ye are, so once were we'; 'Rich must die as well as poor'; and 'None may escape death'.

Throne A chair placed on the *Gospel side of the main *altar in a *cathedral church where a *bishop (or *cardinal) sits when presiding at a service.

Throne of Grace This representation of the *Trinity became widespread after the *Council of Trent. *God the Father, depicted as the *Ancient of Days, sits on a throne and either sustains the body of the crucified Son on his knees, or holds a *crucifix suspended between his hands. The *Holy Spirit, as a dove, hovers above.

Thrones The third choir of the first hierarchy of *angels, so called because they support the throne

St **Thomas** doubting the risen Christ's wounds, in a symbolic depiction, with the patron kneeling to the right (Bertucci, *c*.1495).

St **Thomas of Canterbury** murdered as he kneels before the altar because he sided with the Church against the king (East Anglian psalter, *c*.1300).

St Macarius of Ghent, appearing to **Three living** nobles, exhibits a scroll with the warning that they too will be like the three men who have died of plague (Campo Santo, Pisa, *c*.1350).

of God. They have six wings, sit on golden thrones, or stand on red winged wheels with eyes on them (recalling the vision of *Ezekiel). They sometimes hold towers. They carry *scales because they represent the justice and majesty of God. Their leader is *Japhkiel.

Thurible The vessel which contains *incense for liturgical use. It is carried by a lay *server or a cleric who is called the *thurifer.

Thurifer The cleric or *server who carries the *thurible.

Tiara The triple crown surmounted by a cross worn by the *Pope only on rare occasions, e.g. speaking *ex cathedra, or in solemn processions. Originally in the 8th century it was a white, pointed headdress, but a crown was added to the lower rim c.1130 and two more in the 14th century, as three-fold symbolisms of the *Trinity; the three papal offices of pastor, priest and prophet; and the Pope's threefold spiritual power as teacher, ruler and sanctifier. The tiara is worn in art by SS *Gregory the Great and *Sylvester, to signify that they were Popes.

Tiger An evil *animal, cunning like the *Devil. It attracts its victims by its beautiful coat, as the weak are deceived by outward appearances. But it may itself be tricked by the cunning hunter: he robs the tiger of her cub so that she swiftly pursues him, but he must throw a glass ball or mirror in her path, so that she mistakes her reflection for the cub and lies down to feed it, thus losing both her offspring and her revenge.

Timothy, St A disciple of St *Paul, by whom he was converted and who circumcised him to placate the Jewish Christian party (Ac 16 : 3). He accompanied Paul on his travels and received epistles from him on Church order and the correction of abuses. The historian *Eusebius wrote that he became the first *bishop of Ephesus. An apocryphal *Acts of Timothy* narrates that he was killed with *stones and *clubs at a festival in honour of Diana (or possibly Dionysus) because of his opposition to pagan cults.

Tippet A small black cape with fringed edge or tassels, worn as a vestment by *priests over the *surplice. It replaced the fur cape with ermine tails used in the Middle Ages. *Anglican clergy wear in *choir a tippet in the form of a broad black scarf.

Tithes A 'tenth part' of annual income or produce which, in obedience to the text, 'Thou shalt truly tithe all the increase of thy seed' (Dt 14 : 22), was expected of the *laity for ecclesiastical use. These contributions were used for the payment of the incumbent or his deputy (*rector, *vicar), the upkeep of the church and the relief of the poor.

Titulus Latin for the 'title' or placard which Pilate caused to be put on the cross over Jesus' head at the *Crucifixion. On it was written 'his accusation' –

the reason why he had been condemned. The 'superscription' was in Hebrew (perhaps, in fact, Aramaic), Latin and Greek (Jn 19 : 20). There are four versions in the Gospels: 'The King of the Jews' (Mk 15 : 26); 'This is Jesus the King of the Jews' (Mt 27 : 37); 'This is the King of the Jews' (Lk 23 : 38); and 'Jesus of Nazareth, the King of the Jews' (Jn 19 : 19). In art it is shown as a board or scroll with the Latin words, *Rex Iudaeorum*, 'King of the Jews'.

These words annoyed the chief priests who wanted the *titulus* to read, 'he said, I am King of the Jews'. Pilate refused their request saying, 'What I have written, I have written' (Jn 19 : 21-2) (See *INRI).

Toad A loathsome creature, inhabitant of *Hell and a familiar of witches. In depictions of the tortures of Hell, toads are shown crawling over the pudenda of lustful women and of women who refused their husbands their marital rights.

Tobias Son of the righteous *Jew *Tobit who was a captive in Nineveh. He was sent to Media, with a guide called Azarias and the family dog as a companion, to collect a debt due to his father. When they rested for the night by the River Tigris, Tobias, on Azarias' orders, caught a big fish and kept its gall, heart and liver as medicine. At Ecbatana Tobias lodged in the house of a relative called Raguel and wished to marry his beautiful daughter, Sarah. She had already been married seven times, but on each wedding night the demon *Asmodeus had killed her bridegroom. Azarias told Tobias to burn the heart and liver of the fish in the bridal chamber, and this exorcised the demon. He took his bride back to his father's house and restored Tobit's sight by rubbing the gall of the fish on the white film over his eyes. Azarias then revealed that he was the Archangel *Raphael, who had been sent by God to protect the family.

Tobit A devout and charitable *Jew held captive in Nineveh, Assyria, whose life, together with the adventures of his son *Tobias, are narrated in the book which bears his name. One of his pious acts was to bury the bodies of murdered Jews. This earned him the disfavour of his neighbours and of Sennacherib, the Assyrian ruler. On the Feast of *Pentecost he was jeered at because he retrieved the body of a Jew who had been strangled. The night was hot and he slept in the courtyard of his house. The droppings from sparrows fell on his eyes and he was blinded. He was reduced to poverty, and his wife Anna went to work for a cloth-merchant. When her employer gave her a goat in addition to her wages, Tobit accused her of stealing it. Her reproaches sent him into a fit of despair and he wished to die, but the return of his son *Tobias, whom he had sent to collect a debt from a distant kinsman, revived him. Tobias cured his father's blindness with the gall of a fish, and Tobit lived to an honourable old age, praising God for his mercy.

Tonsure Cutting off or shaving the hair of

candidates for minor ecclesiastical *Orders, indicating acceptance into the clerical state. Secular clergy wear a circular shaved patch at the crown of the head, but members of some religious *Orders have all their hair removed from the top of the head, leaving a circle below, recalling Christ's *Crown of Thorns and, because a circle symbolizes completeness or perfection, his perfect life.

Tower of David One of the titles (Latin, *Turris Davidica*) given to St *Mary the Virgin by Honorius of Autun (*d.c.*1135). *David (the type of *Christ) defended himself from his enemies in a tower (Sg 4 : 4), and Mary is the tower which protected Christ from the *dragon, *Satan.

Tower of ivory A title (Latin, *Turris eburnea*) given to St *Mary the Virgin. It is derived from the *Song of Solomon* (Sg 7 : 4): 'Thy neck rising proudly like a tower but all of ivory'. Honorius of Autun (*d.c.*1135), who first used the term, explained that she was as bright, pure and exquisite as ivory.

Trades, Christ of the A depiction of *Christ (who was reputed to be a carpenter) showing his wounds (incurred through his sacrifice on the wood of the Cross) and surrounded by the tools of various crafts. It symbolizes the sanctity of labour and the dignity of craftsmen, recalling the text, 'All these trust to their hands: and every one is wise in his work' (Eccl 38 : 31).

Transfiguration of Christ Jesus took his disciples SS *Peter, *James, and his brother *John, up a high mountain – Mount Tabor, according to St Cyril of Jerusalem (315-86). There he was transfigured before them, his face shone like the sun, and his garments became white as light. *Moses and *Elijah appeared and talked to him. A bright cloud overshadowed them, from which a voice said, 'This is my beloved son, with whom I am well pleased'. The disciples fell on their faces and were filled with awe. As they descended the mountain Jesus told them not to mention what they had seen. A man came up and knelt before Jesus and begged him to cure his epileptic son (Mt 17 : 1-14, with variants in Mk 9 : 2-13 and Lk 9 : 28-36).

The feast of the Transfiguration, celebrated on 6 August, originated in the *East in the 4th or 5th centuries and was adopted by the *West *c.*850. Pope Callistus III made it a feast of the universal Church in 1456, to commemorate the victory over the Turks at Belgrade in that year. At this festival, the *Pope presses a bunch of grapes into the *chalice and uses new wine at *Mass. In Rome, raisins are blessed on that day.

Transitus See *Falling asleep of St *Mary the Virgin.

Transubstantiation The doctrine that in the *Eucharist the entire substance of the *bread and *wine is converted into the entire substance of the Body and Blood of Christ; only the appearances (or 'accidents') of the bread and wine remain. It

Tobias, escorted by the Archangel Raphael, carries the fish which will enable him to defeat the demon on his wedding night (Florentine, 15th century).

Two Dominican saints witness the **Transfiguration** of Jesus, within an aureole, accompanied by Moses and Elijah, and seen by SS Peter, James and John (Fra Angelico, *c.*1437-45).

was explained in medieval philosophical terms by St *Thomas Aquinas and reaffirmed by the *Council of Trent. It is denied by *Protestants.

Trappists The popular name for *monks of the *abbey of La Trappe who, from 1664 to 1892 when they were absorbed into the *Cistercians of the Strict Observance, followed an austere *rule of perpetual silence, communicating only by sign language, except in cases of extreme necessity. They continue to observe this rule of abstinence from meat, fish and eggs, and of hard manual labour. They are renowned as farmers.

Tree of Knowledge The Tree of the Knowledge of Good and Evil was planted by God in the Garden of *Eden, but man was forbidden to eat its fruit (popularly thought to be an *apple). Disobedience to the divine command resulted in the *Fall of Man and *Expulsion from Paradise (Gen 3 : 1-19). The *Cross was thought to have been made from the miraculously preserved wood of this tree.

Trefoil A *symbol of the *Trinity, because the three leaves of the clover (or *shamrock) are joined to one leaf. St *Patrick used the clover to demonstrate the mystery of the *Trinity to the Irish. It has thus become their national emblem.

Tre Fontane 'Three Springs', the name of a monastery near Rome built on the site where St *Paul was martyred. When his head was cut off it bounced three times, and at each point where it touched the ground a spring of water gushed forth.

Trials of Jesus After his *betrayal and arrest in the Garden of *Gethsemane, Jesus was brought by night before *Annas; then before his son-in-law, the High Priest *Caiaphas; and finally at daybreak before members of the *Sanhedrin. These examinations were interrogations rather than formal trials, designed to provide material for a case to be presented to the Roman governor, *Pilate. Jesus was arraigned on a charge of blasphemy, because he was alleged to have said that he would destroy the *Temple (Mt 26 : 61), and to have claimed that he was the *Christ, the promised *Messiah. It was during his questioning that St *Peter denied his master three times before cock-crow.

All four *Gospels give a detailed account of the events which followed, albeit with some variations and additions (Mk 15 : 1-20; Lk 23 : 1-25; Mt 27 : 11-31; Jn 18 : 28-40; 19 : 1-16). The chief priests would not enter 'the palace' – the *praetorium*, the governor's residence – because they would be defiled; therefore Pilate, who examined Jesus inside, from his judgement seat, had to go out to them whenever he needed to consult them. Pilate failed to understand Jesus. When he asked him, 'Art thou a king then?' (suspecting sedition), Jesus replied, 'My kingdom is not of this world'. When he added, 'Every one that is of the truth heareth my voice', Pilate said, 'What is truth?' (Jn 18 : 33-8).

Hearing that Jesus was a Galilean, Pilate next sent him to *Herod Antipas, tetrarch of Galilee, who had jurisdiction over him. Herod had been told that Jesus was a wonder-worker, and he wanted him to perform a miracle, but Jesus remained silent when questioned. Herod and his soldiers therefore treated him with contempt, dressed him up as a king and sent him back to Pilate (Lk 23 : 6-16) (*See* *Mocking of Jesus).

Pilate could not find any grounds on which Jesus could be condemned to death. To placate the chief priests, he offered to scourge him and set him free. When they cried 'Crucify him!', he tried again, asking whether they would have him release Jesus or *Barabbas. They clamoured for Barrabas. *Procla (or Procula), Pilate's wife, sent word that she had suffered a nightmare and warned him not to condemn a righteous man (Mt 27 : 19). Pilate again tried to reason with the crowd but when they insisted, 'Crucify him', he feared a riot. In a symbolic gesture, he called for water and washed his hands before the multitude, saying, 'I am innocent of the blood of this righteous man'. The people answered, 'His blood be on us, and on our children' (Mt 27 : 24-5). Most scholars think it unlikely that Pilate would be familiar with the Jewish action of handwashing to remit guilt (Dt 21 : 1-7), and that the whole scene is probably an interpolation made at a time when Jewish Christians were in conflict with the *synagogue and when Romans needed to be atracted to the Church. Unfortunately, throughout the ages, these words have been made the excuse for the most horrible pogroms.

Pilate, fearing a revolt, had Jesus scourged (*See* *Scourging of Jesus); his soldiers performed a mock coronation (*See* *Crown of Thorns); and Pilate then showed him to the crowd thus arrayed *(See* *Ecce Homo)* and sent him to *Calvary (*See* *Way of the Cross).

Triangle, equilateral Symbol of the *Trinity because it has three equal sides, yet is one figure (*See* *Delta). An *eye within a triangle (or a circle) symbolizes the all-seeing eye of God. It became a masonic symbol because the Masonic guilds were under the protection of the Holy Trinity.

Tribute money, miracle of the Every male *Jew over twenty was required in OT times to pay a yearly half shekel for the maintenance of the *Temple in Jerusalem. At Capernaum, where Jesus was staying with St *Peter, the collectors asked whether Jesus would pay the tax. Jesus told Peter that his followers, who were subjects of the *Kingdom of Heaven, were exempt, but that rather than offend those who were loyal to the Temple they should pay the tax. He told Peter to cast his line into the lake. In the mouth of the first fish he caught he would find 'a piece of money' (a *stater*, worth a shekel) which would pay for the two of them (Mt 17 : 24-7).

Trinitarians Members of the Order of the Most Holy Trinity, founded in 1198 by St *John of Matha (*d*.1213), so they are also known as

*Mathurins. They are dedicated to an austere interpretation of the Augustinian *Rule, wear a white habit with a cross composed of a red upright and blue crossbar. Their special function was the ransoming of captives, especially those held in Algiers and by the Turks in the 16th and 17th centuries.

Trinity Christians believe that God reveals himself in three persons: *God the Father, *God the Son (Jesus) and God the *Holy Spirit (or *Holy Ghost), but these three persons are one and indivisible. This article of faith, which fundamentally differentiates Christianity from Judaism and Islam, was defined at the Councils of Nicea (325) and Constantinople (381) and is enshrined in the *Nicene and Athanasian creeds. The final separation of the *Orthodox from the *Roman Catholic Church in the 11th century was the result of a prolonged dispute as to the relationship of the Holy Spirit to the other persons of the Trinity. The Greek Church maintained that the Holy Spirit proceeded only from the Father, whereas the Latin Church insisted that the Holy Spirit proceeded from the Father and the Son (the *filioque* clause).

Many English churches are dedicated to the Holy and Undivided Trinity, attesting the long tradition of devotion to the Trinity, a cult which was introduced into England at the time of the Norman Conquest. Other churches with the same dedication were associated with the Order of the Most Holy Trinity (*Trinitarians), founded in 1198 for the purpose of ransoming captives, esecially those in Moslem hands. The Feast of the Holy Trinity, fixed for the first Sunday after Whitsunday (*Pentecost), was offically recognized in the calendar in 1334.

*Symbols of the Trinity are based on the concept of 'three-in-one': the *Greek letters *delta, *omicron and *ipsilon; geometrical devices such as *triangle and *triquetra; the numeral *three and many groups of three things or persons, e.g. three faces, three *fishes, three *angels, and a *trefoil.

The 'Arms of the Holy Trinity' is a heraldic shield with the device:

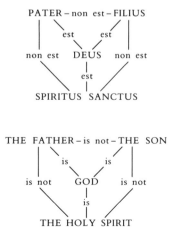

The all-seeing eye of God within a **triangle** appears above the head of Jesus as he blesses bread at the supper at Emmaus (Pontormo, 1528).

The **Trinity** – God the Father as the Ancient of Days, God the Son as the crucified Christ, and the Holy Spirit as a dove – depicted in this Austrian 15th-century painting of the Throne of Mercy.

Trinity Sunday The first Sunday after *Pentecost (Whitsunday), instituted as a universal feast in honour of the Most Holy *Trinity by Pope John XXII (1316-34). A plenary indulgence is gained by those who take *communion on that day.

Triquetra An ornamental device made up of *three interlaced ovals (symbolizing the *Trinity) enclosed in a circle, representing eternity.

Trope The expansion, by the interpolation of additional words, of the sung part of the *Mass.

True Cross, finding of the The *Cross on which Jesus died disappeared after the *Crucifixion but was found again by St *Helena, mother of Emperor *Constantine. Accounts of the discovery are contradictory. It is not mentioned by the Church historian *Eusebius who wrote a *Life of Constantine* early in the 4th century, but is by St Cyril of Jerusalem (c.315-86) in a letter written in 351 to Constantine's son, Constantius II, who says that the wood had been found in Jerusalem. St *John Chrysostom wrote c.387 that three crosses had been excavated. The True Cross, the one on which Jesus was crucified, was distinguishable from those of *Gestas and *Dismas by the super-scription, or *titulus which was still fixed to it.

St *Ambrose in 395 appears to have been the first to attribute the discovery to St Helena. His account was accepted by St *Gregory of Tours, who was able confidently to fix the date when it was found as 3 May 326, a day which was therefore established in the *calendar as the feast of the *Invention (or discovery) of the Holy Cross.

St Gregory's account was influenced by the early 5th-century *Acts of Judas Cyriacus* which, although condemned as apocryphal, supplied many of the colourful details of the story, details which were later incorporated into the *Golden Legend* and depicted in medieval art. After her baptism by St *Sylvester, it was said, St Helena had a vision of the Holy Cross and knew that it was her mission to find it. She travelled to Jerusalem and assembled all the learned Jews of the land to question them as to its whereabouts. At first they refused to give any information, but when threatened with death by burning, they indicated that a certain Judas, one of their number, knew where the Cross could be found. Judas (who claimed to be a nephew of St *Stephen!) at first remained silent, but when he was thrown into a dry well and left there for seven days without food, he relented. He led Helena to a temple, dedicated to Venus, which Emperor Hadrian had erected on *Calvary. They destroyed the temple and then Judas dug down twenty feet below the surface, uncovering three crosses. To discover which of these was the True Cross, he laid each in turn on the coffin of a dead youth. At the touch of the third cross the youth came alive. (Another version, that of Rufinus [c.345-410], records that a dying woman was revived by the True Cross and that Bishop Macarius of Jerusalem assisted in the identification.) St Gregory added that Judas was later baptized and given the name Quiriacus.

St Helena left one piece of the Cross in Jerusalem, where it remained in the Church of the Holy Sepulchre until it was carried off by Persian invaders in 615. (For its return to Jerusalem, *See* *Exaltation of the Holy Cross.) Relics said to have come from the other pieces were to be found in many churches in the Middle Ages.

Tubal-Cain A descendant of *Cain, and the son of *Lamech and his second wife Zillah. He was the 'instructor of every artificer in brass and iron' (Gen 4 : 22) and is thus the first metalworker.

Tunicle An outer garment formerly worn by a subdeacon (*See* *vestments).

Tutivillius The name of the *Devil, popularly called Tittyvally, who haunted churches and collected in a sack the words of those who gossiped or made jokes during the service, and the verbal mistakes of clerics who were slipshod in declaiming the office. These were stored up to be used as evidence against them when they came to *Judgement.

Twelfth Night The Feast of the *Epiphany on 6 January, twelve days after *Christmas. Also the date of the new year in the Alexandrian calendar, where the feast originated. It commemorated *epiphanies, or manifestations of Christ: to the *shepherds; to the wise men from the east; at his baptism; and to the world when he performed the miracle of changing water into wine at *Cana. When the *West adopted the festival in the 4th century, the visitation of the three *Kings predominated over the other epiphanies. Twelfth Night in England became the occasion for games, feasting and merriment.

Twelve A symbolic *number with many references, including the *Twelve Tribes of Israel; the twelve *Prophets; the twelve *Sibyls; the twelve gates of the New *Jerusalem (Rev 21 : 10-14); the twelve stars crowning the *Woman clothed with the Sun; and the twelve baskets full of bread (*See* *Loaves and Fishes). As a multiple of *three (the *Trinity) and *four (the world), twelve represents *Heaven and Earth. There are twelve signs of the *zodiac.

Twelve tribes of Israel A symbolic *number chosen for the descendants of the *twelve sons of *Jacob, who formed separate tribal units, the number of which varied between eleven and thirteen in the OT (*See* *Ten Tribes).

Twins A sign of the *zodiac (*See* *gemini).

Two A symbolic *number representing the two-fold (divine and human) nature of *Christ; the two *First Parents, *Adam and *Eve; two of every kind of creature saved in the *Ark; the *Widow's two mites; *Dismas and *Gestas; and many other pairs in the OT and NT.

Tympanum The semi-circular or pointed space resting on a lintel and enclosed by an arch above the doorway of a *church or *cathedral. Over the west door it usually contains a carved representation of the Last *Judgement. The *Coronation of St Mary the Virgin is also found above porches.

Type, Typology The conviction that the *Bible was a unified account of the divine plan for the salvation of mankind, and that what was hidden in the OT was revealed in the NT, led to the establishment of concordances between the two parts. The event or person in the OT is the type (Greek *tupos*, 'mold'), and the corresponding event or person in the NT is the *antitype (Greek *anti*, 'against'). Thus the *Brazen Serpent is the OT type which prefigures the *Crucifixion, the NT antitype. Great ingenuity was shown by exegetes in the Middle Ages in the allegorical interpretation of biblical texts, in order to create these relationships even in the most unlikely circumstances, e.g. *Joseph the Dreamer riding in Pharaoh's chariot foretells the *Entry into Jerusalem, the link word being 'triumph'. There is also a typology of St *Mary the Virgin *(See *Biblia Pauperum)*.

St Helena, convinced by a miracle that one of three crosses excavated in Jerusalem is the **True Cross** (Piero della Francesca, *c*.1452).

The **Twelve tribes** of Israel draw sustenance from Moses in this 3rd-century wall-painting from the synagogue at Dura Europos.

Ulrich of Augsburg, St Born near Zurich, *c*.890, he became a *monk in the *monastery of Saint-Gall and died at Augsburg in 973, where he had been *bishop for fifty years. He was the first saint whose *canonization (993) was solemnly decreed by a *Pope, in this case John XV (985-96). His fame in the popular mind rests less on the record of his work as a bishop and his defence of the city against the Hungarians, than on the miracle of the *fish (his *attribute). He was having supper on a Thursday with a fellow bishop. They became so deeply engaged in theological discourse that they failed to notice that the night had passed and that it was already Friday. A messenger from the emperor (or in some accounts the duke of Bavaria) saw a goose on the table and threatened to report them for breaking a fast. Ulrich cut off the drumstick and told the messenger that if he wished to inform against them he should take it to the emperor as evidence, but when the informant drew it out of his bag in the presence of the emperor, it had changed into a fish.

Unction, extreme The sacramental *rite of anointing with holy oil (pure olive oil, blessed by a *bishop on *Maundy Thursday) those in a state of *grace who are in danger of death (Latin *in extremis*, hence 'extreme'). It is administered by a bishop or *priest and completes the act of *penance. Since the Second *Vatican Council it is called 'Anointing of the Sick' *(See *viaticum)*.

Uncumber, St The English name for St *Wilgefortis, because she would help wives to get rid of a cumbersome spouse.

Unicorn A *fabulous creature with the head of a stag and the body of a horse (but simplified in art

Christ in majesty, supported by angels, appears here above the Last Supper (**tympanum** at Saint-Julien-de-Jonzy, France, mid-12th century).

to a white horse). On its forehead is a sharp-pointed horn, four feet long, that gave it its name (derived from Latin *unus*, 'one', and *cornus*, 'horn'). It is the enemy of the *elephant, which fears its sharp horn. Hunters cannot approach the unicorn because of its long horn and great strength, but may capture it by a stratagem. They send a beautiful maiden ahead of them, and the unicorn, attracted by her chastity, runs to her, places its head on her lap and goes to sleep. The hunters then bind the beast and lead it to the royal palace.

This pagan description of the fabulous beast, popularized by the *Physiologus*, was turned into a Christian allegory. *Christ, 'who raised up an horn of salvation for us' (Lk 1 : 69), is the spiritual unicorn; laying its head on the Virgin's lap symbolized the *Incarnation, and being led captive to the royal palace, Christ's *betrayal in the Garden of *Gethsemane and his appearances before *Pilate and *Herod. The unicorn's horn, as the 'horn of salvation', also symbolized the *Cross of Jesus. It was an antidote against poison because it was thought to purify anything with which it came into contact.

As an emblem of *chastity, the unicorn is depicted at the feet of St *Justina, the 3rd-century saint of Antioch, who repelled the advances of the pagan magistrate Cyprian (in some versions a magician) and converted him to Christianity by her example. It is also associated with the 4th-century St *Justina of Padua, distinguished from the former saint of the same name by her *attribute, a *sword (which recalls the manner of her death when she was stabbed through the side because she refused to yield her virginity to pagan soldiers).

Unknown God As he walked through the streets of Athens, St *Paul saw an altar with the inscription, 'To the unknown God'. He used this as the text of his sermon before the Areopagus to prove to the Greeks that they had unwittingly worshipped the one true God (Ac 17 : 23).

Upper room The guest chamber, 'a large upper room furnished and prepared' (Mk 14 : 15), where Jesus ate the *Passover at the *Last Supper with his disciples.

Urbi et Orbi Latin blessing, 'to the city [of Rome] and to the world', given by the *Pope from the balcony of St Peter's following his election and on certain special occasions throughout the year.

Uriah the Hittite One of the thirty men chosen to command King *David's armies under *Joab. During his absence at the siege of Rabbah, David seduced Uriah's wife *Bathsheba, but when she discovered she was pregnant he had Uriah brought home so that he would be the putative father. The plan miscarried because Uriah did not visit his wife on his return to Jerusalem, but spent his leave with the palace guard. To conceal his act of adultery, David sent Uriah back to the siege with secret orders to Joab to leave him in the thick of the fight so that he would be killed. When this evil deed was accomplished David married Bathsheba, but was castigated for his sin by the prophet Nathan (2 Sam 11; 12 : 1-14).

Uriel One of the principal *archangels. His name in Hebrew means 'flame of God', or 'God is my light'. He has two wings, wears armour and carries a book or a scroll because his special function is to interpret prophecies. Uriel appeared in a vision to *Esdras to rebuke him for his presumption in questioning the ways of God (2 Esd 4 : 1; 5 : 20). He was thought to have been the messenger of the risen *Christ who appeared to the disciples on the road to *Emmaus and to be the guardian of the *Holy Sepulchre (hence he is depicted with a drawn sword).

Urim and Thummin In the AV (Ex 28 : 30) these are mysterious objects, possibly oracular stones, which were carried in the breastplate of the *High Priest and used to divine the will of God. It is thought that they represented contrasting ideas like 'light' and 'darkness', 'yes' and 'no', 'life' and 'death'. They were shaken, or drawn out of the 'ephod' (possibly the High Priest's pocket). If each showed the same side, the answer was auspicious or inauspicious, according to the designation of each side; if different, no answer was forthcoming.

Ursula and the eleven thousand virgins, St A legend which apparently developed in the 10th century from the discovery in Cologne of a 4th- or 5th-century inscription of the Latin numerals XIMV, recording the restoration by a certain Clematius of a *basilica on the site where eleven holy virgins had earlier been martyred. This was possibly misread as referring to eleven thousand virgins who were said to have died during the *persecutions of Maximian. The story was elaborated, by the chronicler Geoffrey of Monmouth (*c.*1100-54) and in the *Golden Legend*, into the romance of Ursula, Christian daughter of King Theonestus of Brittany (hence she is shown wearing a *crown and a cloak of *ermine with *fleur-de-lys, the arms of Brittany). She was sought in marriage by Conon, pagan son of King Agrippinus of England, who agreed to delay their nuptials for three years so that she could make a *pilgrimage to Rome. Ursula, with ten maidens, each attended by a thousand more, sailed down the Rhine to Basle, piloted by an angel, and crossed the Alps to Rome where Conon, who had arrived the same day by a different route, was baptized by 'Pope' (or some say 'Bishop') Cyriacus and given the new name of Ethereus. Then the *Pope, accompanied by his *cardinals, made the return journey with Ursula, her maidens and the prince. At Cologne they were captured by the Huns who were besieging that city. Ursula refused to marry their chief and was slain with an *arrow (her *attribute); the virgins chose death rather than ravishment and were massacred. In the 12th century, heaps of bones found in a communal burial ground in Cologne were declared to be their relics.

Scenes of the martyrdom of Ursula and her companions, based on the earlier legend but elaborated from the visions of Elizabeth of Schönau, were frequently depicted in the Middle Ages. Ursula is variously shown sheltering the virgins under her cloak; carrying a *pilgrim's staff to recall her journey to Rome; and grasping a banner with a red cross, symbolic of victory over death. The inclusion of a *dove in her picture is a reference to the legend that a dove revealed her burial place to St Cunibert, archbishop of Cologne. A series of eight paintings of episodes in the life of St Ursula was executed by Vittore Carpaccio (active 1490-1523) for the orphanage in Venice, the *Scuola di Sant' Orsola*, because she is the patron saint of orphans. One shows Ursula asleep on her bed in Cologne as an angel enters to tell her of her impending martyrdom.

Ursulines Congregations of sisters – religious women engaged in the education of girls – who have St *Ursula as their patron saint. The oldest one, the first authorized teaching *Order for women, was founded by St Angela Merici in 1537.

Usury Taking interest for a loan, originally forbidden among Jews (Ex 22 : 25; Lv 25 : 35-7), but permitted later in their dealings with Gentiles. Christians for centuries avoided money-lending for interest, and in the Middle Ages depended on Jewish financiers. A distinction is now made whereby charging interest on loans is permissible, but exorbitant interest is usury, therefore morally wrong and a *sin.

Hun bowmen martyr St **Ursula,** Bishop Cyriacus, her fiancé and her virgin companions when their ships arrive at Cologne (Hans Memlinc, 1489).

Valentine's Day, St Two saints called Valentine are commemorated on 14 February. One was a bishop of Terni (whose *attribute is the crow which, after he was beheaded *c*.270 in Rome, indicated to his followers where he was to be buried). The other was a priest or physician (invoked against epilepsy because he cured a youth who suffered from fits) who was martyred *c*.269 under Emperor Claudius (his attributes are the *sword with which he was killed and a sun, because he gave sight to a blind girl, the daughter of his jailor). Neither saint seems to be responsible for the courting convention associated with St Valentine's day. It may be a continuation of the Roman pagan mid-February season of Lupercalia, a festival in honour of the goddess Februata Juno, when boys drew by lot names of unmarried girls. Birds were also said to choose their mates on that day. Youths were once given billets-doux with the names of girls to be courted, their 'Valentines'. St Francis de Sales (1579-1622), in an unsuccessful effort to improve the occasion, suggested that the names of saints to be emulated should be substituted for girls' names.

Vallombrosans A small independent Order of *Benedictine monks founded by St *John Gualber-

St **Valentine,** bishop of Terni, often confused with the physician saint of the same name (Italian, 1662).

to c.1030. They take their name from the mother house at Vallombrosa (Italian for 'shady valley') near Florence. They wear the black *Benedictine habit, live an austere life and are strictly *enclosed.

Vashti Queen of Persia (her name means 'beautiful' in Persian) who was ordered by King *Ahasuerus, her consort, to appear unveiled before him and his guests at a feast so that they might admire her beauty. When she refused, the king divorced her for disobedience and she was later replaced by *Esther (Es 1 : 9-21).

Vatican Since 1377, when the papal court returned from Avignon, the main residence of the *Popes in Rome. The Vatican City was granted extra-territorial status in 1871, and special rights by the Lateran Treaty concluded in 1929 with the Italian government. Its centre is St Peter's basilica.

Vatican councils General (or Oecumenical) councils of the *Roman Catholic Church, held in the *Vatican. The First Vatican Council, which opened on 8 December 1869, defined the doctrine of Papal *Infallibility. This led to the secession of the Old Catholics in Austria and Germany, who could not accept that dogma nor the Primacy of the *Pope which was promulgated at the same time. The Second Vatican Council (1962-5), convoked by Pope John XXIII (1958-63), brought about radical liturgical, disciplinary and other reforms, intended to intensify the relevance of the Church to the contemporary world. The use in worship of national languages in place of Latin was permitted.

Veil A 'covering' (Latin *velum*) for a person or sacred object. Religious women and *nuns wear veils over their heads and shoulders. In the past they had different forms with symbolic significance, widows wearing the veil of continence; *novices the veil of probation (usually white); virgins the veil of consecration. Nuns who had taken their final vows were given the veil of profession. St *Agatha's veil stopped the flow of lava from Etna. A veil is used as a sign of reverence to cover a *ciborium when it contains the *Blessed Sacrament. In some *Anglican and *Roman Catholic churches it is customary to veil crucifixes and pictures during *Lent and *Holy Week.

Veil of the Temple There were two great veils or curtains in the *Temple in Jerusalem, one screening the entrance of the Holy Place and the other covering the *Holy of Holies. In the *Gospel of Luke*'s account of the *Crucifixion, at the sixth hour (3 pm), darkness covered the land, the sun's light failed 'and the veil of the temple was rent in the midst' (Lk 23 : 45). Although not stated, the probability is that the veil over the Holy of Holies was torn, symbolizing the removal of the barrier between man and God, for man was thus enabled 'to enter into the holiest by the blood of Jesus' (Heb 10 : 19). According to legend, St *Mary the Virgin spun the veil of the Temple (See *Education of St Mary the Virgin).

Venerable In *Anglican usage, the mode of addressing an *archdeacon; in *Roman Catholic, the title of a person of exemplary holy life, such as the Venerable *Bede, or a deceased person in the process of *beatification.

Veneration of the Cross A *Good Friday rite, sometimes called Creeping to the Cross. The faithful kneel in turn at the *chancel steps and kiss a *crucifix.

Veni creator spiritus Latin for 'Come, creator spirit', the opening words of a *hymn attributed to the *Benedictine abbot Rabanus Maurus (776-656). It is sung at *vespers at *Pentecost; at the ordination of *priests and *bishops; and at the consecration of churches.

Veni sancte spiritus Latin for 'Come, *Holy Spirit', the opening words of the *hymn sung at *Pentecost (*Whitsunday) invoking the seven *Gifts of the Holy Spirit. It was called the *Golden Sequence* and attributed to Stephen Langton (d.1228), archbishop of Canterbury.

Venite Latin for 'Come', the first word of the 95th *psalm (Vg 94th), familiar in *Anglican morning worship as the Invitatory Psalm, 'O come, let us sing unto the Lord'.

Verger One who carries a 'verge' (a rod or a mace) before a church dignitary, but ordinarily the person who looks after the church building (See *sexton).

Vernicle The Middle English name for the veil (or *sudarium*) held by St *Veronica.

Veronica, St The story is told in a late Latin insertion into the *Gospel of *Nicodemus* how Jesus stumbled under the weight of his cross on the way to his *Crucifixion, and a woman stepped out of the crowd and wiped the sweat from his face. After he had moved on, she found that his features were imprinted on the handkerchief, cloth, or *veil which she had used. This relic (in Italian *Il Sudario*, in Latin*sudarium*) has been in Rome since the 8th century. It is now in a chapel in the crypt of St Peter's and is one of the three sacred relics (the others being St *Longinus' spear and a piece of the *True Cross) which are exhibited on great festivals. As other cities also claimed to possess the *sudarium*, the Roman clergy asserted that the woman who had stepped out of the crowd had become a Christian and had suffered martyrdom in Rome during *Nero's reign. She had given the handkerchief to Pope Clement. This was the *vera icon* (Latin for 'the true image'). Gerald of Wales (1147-c.1223), among others, claimed that this was the reason why the woman was traditionally known as Veronica, but the name is more likely to be the Latinized form of Bernice. Some have thought, on the authority of the original text of the *Gospel of Nicodemus*, that she was the *Woman with the issue of blood, named in that book as Berenike; others have identified her as *Martha, or

as the wife of *Zacchaeus, whom she converted and with whom she was martyred in France. Some claim that it was in order to account for the presence of the relic in Rome that the story of Veronica was interpolated into the Latin translation of the *Gospel of Nicodemus.

In the *Golden Legend there is another version of the story which may account for the presence of the *sudarium* in Rome. Emperor Tiberius, who suffered from a distressing malady, had heard of Jesus and learned that he cured all ills. He sent an officer named Volusianus to *Pilate to ask for Jesus to be transported to Rome. Pilate, terrified because he had crucified the miracle-worker, begged for a short delay. In the meantime Volusianus discovered an old woman named Veronica who told him how the face of Jesus had been imprinted on her linen kerchief. She refused to sell the relic but accompanied Volusianus to Rome. When Tiberius looked on the Holy Face, he was cured.

St Veronica is represented in art as a woman holding the *sudarium* (in Middle English, the *vernicle) which bears the face of Christ. Her compassionate action, the subject of the sixth of the meditations of the *Stations of the Cross, was popularized by the *Franciscans. In France, where she is said to have gone with St *Mary Magdalene, she is known as St Venisse. She brought a phial of the blood of St *John the Baptist (said to be her cousin) to Bazas, and died at Soulac, where angels carried her to *Heaven. The pillar which marked her grave was miraculously discovered after a lapse of eight centuries. She is associated with the sanctuary of Rocamadour because she was said to be the wife of Zacchaeus, who, after his conversion, accompanied the saints Veronica, *Martha and *Mary Magdalene to France where he took the name of Amadour and lived in a cave in the rock called after him.

Versicle From the Latin *versiculus*, 'a little verse', a line (usually from a *psalm) which is said or sung and is answered by a response, a phrase with a similar theme, by *choir or congregation.

Vesica piscis Latin for 'fish bladder' and, presumably because of its oval or almond-like shape, an alternative name for *aureole or *mandorla.

Vespers One of the monastic *hours, so called because the service originally began at the rising of *vesper*, the evening star. It is also the Evening Office of the *Western Church. (*Anglican *Evensong was modelled on it.) Vespers is said or sung with great solemnity and reaches its climax with the chanting of the *Magnificat and the *censing of the altar.

Vessels, sacred At the celebration of *Mass or *Eucharist, a *chalice and *paten, consecrated by a *bishop, are used for the wine and sacred *host respectively. Both are placed on a *corporal made of pure linen. The chalice is covered with a silken chalice-veil, of the liturgical *colour of the day or season. It is dried after use with a pure linen purificator. The *Blessed Sacrament is placed in a

St **Veronica** displays the *sudarium* with the face of Christ miraculously imprinted on it (church of St Lawrence, Cologne, early 15th century).

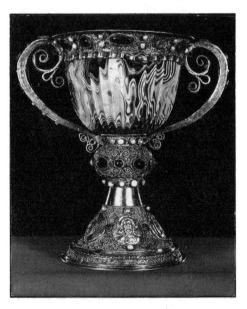

A golden chalice (*c*.1140), the **vessel** used by Abbot Suger at the abbey of Saint-Denis, 1122-51.

*ciborium covered with a silken veil. A *monstrance is used for the exposition of the Blessed Sacrament on devotional occasions.

Vestments Strictly, the special garments worn by *clergy on liturgical occasions: the celebration of *Mass or *Eucharist; the administration of the *Sacraments; when giving blessings; and in solemn processions. They thus differ from clerical *dress, and from the *habit of religious *Orders. The basic vestments were originally the everyday dress of men of the first centuries AD, not the ritual costume of the priesthood of *Aaron, as was once mistakenly supposed. Fashions changed around the 4th century, and again in the 6th century under the influence of the Germanic invaders of the Roman Empire. The toga was shortened and trousers were worn. In contrast, Christian clergy retained the old dress for ceremonial occasions, adding to the original items as the need arose. By the late Middle Ages these additions were numerous and elaborate.

At the time of the *Reformation, *Protestant Churches placed less emphasis on ceremonial and more on preaching, so vestments were abandoned in favour of a plain black Geneva gown derived from academic dress, and a white neckband with two pendant strips.

In the *Church of England the *Book of Common Prayer* of 1559 laid down that the liturgical dress of clergy should be that authorized by Parliament 'in the second year of the reign of King Edward VI', i.e. 1547. This so-called 'Ornaments rubric' gave rise to a variety of conflicting interpretations, according to Low or *High Church predilections and traditions. At one extreme, plain gowns, *tippet and academic *hood; at the other, an elaboration of the garmets of the later Middle Ages. The *Anglo-Catholic movement of the 19th century encouraged a return to pre-Reformation vestments in many *Anglican churches. In the *Roman Catholic Church, as a reaction against Protestantism, vestments were increasingly decorative and elaborately styled. Their form and use was modified following the Second *Vatican Council.

Vestments in *Orthodox Churches resembled in the main those of the *West, but were influenced in design by styles characteristic of the Byzantine imperial court, the *mitre recalling the emperor's crown. Following the Great *Schism of 1378 which divided the Church into the Latin West and the Greek *East, Orthodox Churches retained a modified traditional vesture, without the additions made in the West in later centuries.

Western vestments worn on eucharistic and sacramental occasions may be classified as:
1 basic garments: *alb, *amice, *girdle (or *cincture), *maniple, *stole.
2 over-garments: *cassock, *chasuble, *cope (or *pluviale), *dalmatic (or *tunicle), *stole, *surplice.
3 on the head: *biretta.
4 indications of status: *buskins, *gloves, *mitre, *pallium, *ring.
A vesting prayer, emphasizing the symbolism of

the basic vestments, may be said when each item is put on in the *sacristy before proceeding to the *altar.

At the celebration of Mass, the *celebrant, *deacon and sub-deacon wear the basic vestments, amice, alb, girdle and maniple. In addition, the celebrant wears a chasuble and stole; the deacon a dalmatic and stole; and the sub-deacon a tunicle. A pontificating (i.e. presiding) *bishop wears a chasuble, stole, gloves, buskins, sandals and *mitre. He carries a *crosier. On certain days a Roman Catholic archbishop wears a pallium, a strip of white woollen material with six black crosses.

Vestry The room (also called the *sacristy) where the sacred liturgical *vessels are kept and where the *clergy vest, i.e. put on their *vestments. In England, the parochial church council used to meet in this room to transact the business of the *parish, and thus became known as 'the vestry'.

Vexillum Latin for 'standard', a banner carried in processions or the flag (usually with a red cross on a white ground) held by *Christ or the *Agnus Dei, symbolizing the *Resurrection. The hymn *Vexilla Regis*, 'the banners of the King', by the Latin poet Venantius Fortunatus (c.530–c.610) is sung at *Vespers during *Holy Week.

Via Dolorosa The route (Latin for the 'painful way') in *Jerusalem which Jesus is believed to have followed as he walked from Pilate's judgement hall to his place of *Crucifixion (*See* *Stations of the Cross).

Viaticum From the Latin for 'provisions for a journey' – *Holy Communion given to a person thought to be about to die, to provide him with grace and strength for his voyage to eternity (*See* *Unction, Extreme).

Vicar Literally, one who is a representative or substitute (Latin *vicarius*, 'deputy'). Since the 8th century, the *Pope has been called the Vicar of Christ, as he represents him on earth. In the *Anglican Church, a vicar is an *incumbent of a parish who substitutes for a person or body which receives the appropriated revenue or *tithes.

Vices, Seven The *Seven Deadly Sins, personified in art, and opposed to the Seven *Virtues.

Vigil The evening service, often continuing through the night, before a *feast day. Since 1969 only the Easter vigil is permitted in the *Roman Catholic Church.

Vincent, St A *deacon of Zaragoza, Spain (d.304), whose story is told by the hymn-writer Prudentius (348–c.410). He was tortured by order of the Proconsul Dacian during the Diocletian *persecutions and his body was left for wild beasts to devour, but a *raven (one of his *attributes) drove them off. Dacian then had the body tied to a *millstone and cast into the sea, but it was washed ashore and eventually buried in Valencia Cathedral. In the 8th century, to save the relics from the Moors, Christians transported them by sea and buried them on the promontory in Portugal now known as Cape St Vincent. Ravens continued to protect Vincent's remains until they were finally brought to rest around 1147 in the Cathedral at Lisbon, of which city he is the patron saint.

St Vincent was reputed to be a brother of St *Lawrence (who appropriated one of his attributes, a *gridiron, as both were roasted over a fire). In art he is dressed as a deacon, with an iron hook recalling how he was tortured by having his flesh torn, or with a millstone near him. He may also appear naked, bound to a tree. A bunch of grapes recalls his patronage of vine-dressers and vine-growers, because lack of frost on his feast day is an indication of a good vintage.

Vincent Ferrer, St A *Dominican, born c.1350 of poor parents (his father was English) in Valencia, Spain. He joined the Dominican Order in 1367, and became a missionary and eloquent preacher who terrified his audiences as he described in his booming voice the terrors of *Hell. He travelled all over Europe (including England, at the invitation of King Henry IV) and was everywhere understood because, although a good linguist, he had the miraculous *gift of tongues. He died while on a preaching mission in 1419 at Vannes in Brittany, where his body is preserved in the cathedral. Among his *attributes, a winged *crucifix, or a book with wings, symbolize the speed of his travels; a trumpet, his strident calls to sinners to repent. The sacred monogram *IHS is sometimes shown on his breast. If a child is included among his attributes, it recalls the story that his hostess in a small town in France, in a fit of madness, had chopped up her son and roasted him for dinner. The saint restored the boy to life. He also saved a boy who had fallen from a wall while listening to him preach.

Vincent de Paul, St A *Franciscan, patron of charitable works and societies (hence he is shown with a child in his arms), and founder of the Congregation of Mission Priests (called Lazarist after their Paris church of Saint-Lazare) and of the Sisters of Charity (who may be shown kneeling at his feet). Of peasant stock, born in 1581 in Ranquine, Landes (now renamed in his honour), he was captured by pirates and spent two years in Tunis as a slave. After his escape he devoted his life to succouring the poor, outcasts, and the victims of war. He died in 1660 and was canonized in 1737.

Vine Symbol of Christ who said, 'I am the true vine' (Jn 15 : 1). Its flowering or fruitful branches represent the faithful of the Church of God, because Jesus went on, 'and my Father is the husbandman. Every branch in me that beareth not fruit he taketh away; and every branch that beareth fruit, he purgeth it, that it may bring forth more fruit.'

Vinegar Bible The name given to the AV edition of 1716-17, because of a misprint in a headline whereby 'The Parable of the Vineyard' (Lk 20 : 9-16) reads, 'The Parable of the Vinegar'.

Christ carries his Cross along the **Via Dolorosa:** *(above)* detail of a stone altar-piece at Troyes, France (c.1500) *(below)* El Greco's visionary depiction (late 16th century).

Vineyard *Symbol of the Church, where the faithful (the vines) are nurtured by God (the Keeper); derived from the text, 'For the vineyard of the Lord of hosts is the house of Israel, and the men of Judah his pleasant plant' (Is 5 : 7). In the teaching of *Jesus it also represents the inheritance of Israel and the mission field for his disciples (See *Parables).

Violet A *flower which is the symbol of humility ('the humble violet'), and of the humility of God who became man in *God the Son. The *colour violet indicates suffering or sorrow.

Virgil Roman poet (70-19 BC), who, although a pagan, is revered as a prophet because comments in his Fourth Eclogue were understood to herald the advent of *Messiah.

Virgin A sign of the *zodiac (See *Virgo).

Virgin birth of Jesus It has long been an article of the Christian faith that *Jesus was 'born of the Virgin Mary'. (Liberal theologians now claim that the *Septuagint rendering of the Greek parthenos, 'virgin', in the Messianic prophecy in *Isaiah, 'and a virgin shall conceive' [Is 7 : 14] was a mistranslation of the Hebrew word for a 'young girl' and that this gave rise to the references in the Gospel of Matthew [Mt 1 : 18] and the Gospel of Luke [Lk 1 : 34-5; 3 : 23] to the *Incarnation and Virgin Birth of Jesus.) Mary, it was held by some medieval theologians, conceived through the ear (in some portrayals a ray of light strikes her ear) and thus her virginity was preserved intact. When the *Christ-Child was born there was no rupture and Mary remained a virgin. Testimony to this fact is the legend of *Salome the midwife. The *Fathers also explained the mystery by using the analogy of light passing through glass without breaking it, a symbol introduced into scenes of the Virgin's life by Flemish and other artists. Other symbols of the Virgin Birth are the *Closed Gate (Latin Porta Clausa), the *Enclosed Garden (Hortus Conclusus), the Sealed *Fountain, the *Burning Bush, the sealed *Book, the ostrich *Egg and *Gideon's Fleece.

Virginity of St Mary, perpetual As well as conceiving and giving birth to Jesus without loss of her virginity (See *Virgin Birth), St Mary the Virgin is held to have remained a virgin throughout her life. This dogma, defended by the early *Fathers of the Church, was defined at the Lateran Council of 649 and confirmed by the sixth General Council held at Constantinople in 680. It was accepted that the description of Jesus as Mary's 'first born' (Lk 2 : 7) did not imply that she afterwards bore more children, and that references to the *brethren of the Lord were either to children of St *Joseph by a first marriage, or to Jesus' cousins or kinsmen. After miraculously bearing God, it was argued, it would have been incredible if Mary had then had sexual relations with St *Joseph (who was considered by some of the *Fathers to have been over eighty at the time of

Jesus' birth, and impotent). He accepted his wife's dedicated role and lived with her without consummating their marriage. The *lily is the emblem of her purity, recalling 'the lily of the valleys' of the *Song of Songs (Sg 2 : 1), which is believed to refer to her. Other symbols of her perpetual virginity are the *Fountain, *Porta Clausa and the spotless *Mirror.

Virgo The virgin, the sixth sign of the *zodiac, governing the period from c.23 August to 22 September, and represented as a maiden carrying a sheaf of wheat because of her association with the harvest. In the *Labours of the Months she presides over the threshing of corn.

Virtues The second choir of the second hierarchy of *angels, possessed of supreme courage. They are depicted in human form but with four wings, and either covered with blue feathers or dressed in shining armour, and carrying sceptres, battle-axes, swords, or spears. They hold shields decorated with the *Instruments of the Passion of Christ. Their leader is *Haniel.
Also the Seven Virtues, divided into the Theological Virtues, *Faith, *Hope and *Charity; and the Cardinal Virtues, *Temperance, *Prudence, *Fortitude and *Justice, called 'cardinal' because other moral virtues, such as purity and *patience, are 'derived' from them. In art they are personified as women and are opposed to the Seven *Vices (the *Seven Deadly Sins) with whom they may be shown in combat. *Jacob's ladder was said to have had fifteen rungs, one for each of the cardinal and derived virtues.

Visitandines Nuns of the *Order of the Visitation of the Blessed Virgin Mary, founded in 1610 by St Francis de Sales and St Jane Frances de Chantal. Its most famous member was St *Margaret Mary Alacoque (1647-90), whose visions and revelations led to the devotion to the *Sacred Heart of Jesus.

Visitation of Our Lady After the *Incarnation, St *Mary the Virgin went to a town in the hills of Judaea (identified as Ain Karim, near Jerusalem) to visit her kinswoman St *Elizabeth, who was then over six months pregnant with St *John the Baptist. When Elizabeth heard Mary's greeting, her child leapt in her womb. Elizabeth was filled with the *Holy Spirit and said, 'Blessed art thou among women, and blessed is the fruit of thy womb', a sentence which was incorporated in the *Ave Maria (*Hail Mary). Mary replied with the hymn known as the *Magnificat. She remained with Elizabeth for about three months (Lk 1 : 39-56). The medieval motive of showing the two children in their mothers' wombs, John the Baptist kneeling to acknowledge Jesus, was condemned by the *Council of Trent. Mary and Elizabeth usually greet one another standing, either bowing to each other or embracing. They may also be shown each with a hand on the other's womb. As a result of the development of Marian devotion, Elizabeth is later depicted as kneeling before Mary to show her acceptance of Mary's superiority.

Although not mentioned in the *Gospel of Luke*, the husbands, SS *Joseph and *Zacharias, and the kinswomen, *Mary Cleophas and *Mary Salome, are sometimes introduced into the scene. The Feast of the Visitation was first celebrated by the *Franciscans on 2 July in 1263. Since 1969 it is celebrated on 31 May in the revised *Roman Catholic calendar.

Vitalis, St Two saints of this name were confused in legend. One was a 3rd-century nobleman of Bologna, who was converted to Christianity by the example of his slave Agricola who refused under torture to renounce his faith. Both were martyred. It is now held that he was the titular saint of the renowned *basilica in Ravenna. The other was a Roman soldier, who, with his wife Valeria and his sons *Gervasius and Protasius, was said to have been converted to Christianity by St *Peter. Seeing a tortured Christian, later known as St Urcicinus, waver in his faith, Vitalis encouraged him to remain steadfast and for this act, and for burying the body, was himself martyred in 171 by being stoned and then buried alive on the spot in Ravenna where the famous church of San Vitale was built about 545. One of the mosaics in that church shows this Vitalis receiving his martyr's crown from *Christ. His wife and twin sons fled to Milan where they too were put to death. In 386, St *Ambrose had a vision while praying in which Vitalis and his sons, accompanied by SS Peter and Paul, appeared and told him that he was kneeling on the spot where they were buried. Excavations revealed the bodies, together with a manuscript describing their martyrdom. They were reinterred beneath the high altar of the church of San Ambrogio.

Vitus, St A young Sicilian nobleman who was secretly converted to Christianity by his tutor Modestus and his nurse Crescentia, martyrs who are revered with him. To bring him back to paganism, his father had him scourged and put in prison. Angels came to dance to him (hence he is the patron of dancers and mummers and invoked against St Vitus' dance [Sydenham's *chorea*] and epilepsy). Their light blinded his father, but Vitus restored his sight and then left with Modestus and Crescentia for the mainland. In Rome he drove the *Devil out of Emperor Diocletian's son, but because he refused to abjure his faith he was tortured and thrown to a lion. The beast only licked his feet, so Vitus and his companions were put to death *c*.303 in a cauldron of boiling oil, together with a *cock, one of his *attributes. A wolf guarded their bodies until they were given Christian burial. St Vitus is one of the *Fourteen Holy Helpers and may be invoked by those who find difficulty in getting up in the morning or who cannot get to sleep. He is also to be called upon for protection against the bites of snakes and mad dogs, hence a dog is another of his attributes.

Volto Santo Italian for 'Holy Face', a name applied to several *relics alleged to bear the imprint of Jesus' features, such as the veil or napkin of St

SS Zacharias and Elizabeth greet St Mary the Virgin on her **visitation** to their home in the Judaean hills (Albrecht Altdorfer, 1480-1538).

An angel holds a martyr's crown for St **Vitalis** in this mosaic decoration on the apse of the church of San Vitale, Ravenna (6th century).

*Veronica in St Peter's, Rome; the Holy *Shroud preserved at Turin since 1578; and the miraculous 'Holy Face' which has been in the *Lateran basilica since 754. More particularly the description is applied to the 'Sovereign Lord' of Lucca Cathedral, a cedar-wood *crucifix bearing the body of *Christ, crowned and dressed in a long velvet garment, said to have been carved by *Nicodemus. It may be a 13th-century copy of an 8th-century original, as the presence of a crucifix of this type in Lucca Cathedral was recorded in 797. The cult of the Holy Face was widespread in Europe from the 11th century onwards.

Voluntary A musical interlude or addition to a church service intended to emphasize the spiritual nature of the occasion. Since the 19th century it has usually been provided on his own volition or choice by the organist, hence 'organ voluntary'.

Vows Members of religious communities and *Orders take three vows: poverty, chastity and obedience. By poverty is meant giving up the personal ownership or the independent use of worldly goods. Chastity implies abstinence from sexual gratification and marriage. Obedience requires an oath or promise to obey a *superior, *confessor and spiritual director.

Vox clamantis in deserto Latin for 'the voice [of one] crying in the wilderness' (Mk 1 : 2), written on the scroll carried by St *John the Baptist, or displayed near him, because he quoted *Isaiah's command: 'Prepare ye the way of the Lord, make his paths straight' (Mk 1 : 3).

Vulgate The Latin version of the *Bible is mainly the work of St *Jerome, who at the request of Pope St Damasus I (366-84) in 382, spent fifteen years establishing a definitive text to replace the old Latin manuscripts which contained many variants. For the OT he used for comparison the *Septuagint and Hebrew manuscripts, and for the NT, Greek manuscripts. The Vulgate was first printed in the Gutenberg Bible of 1456, then carefully revised and declared by the *Council of Trent to be the approved text for *Roman Catholic use 'in public readings, disputations, sermons and exposition'. The name 'Vulgate' is derived from the Latin *Vulgata (editio)*, 'popular edition'.

Vulture Because of its voracious appetite, a symbol of greed, *Gula*, one of the *Seven Deadly Sins.

Wafer A thin disc of unleavened bread, the *Host, one of the two elements consecrated in the *Eucharist. An angel carried a wafer to St *Bonaventure who was too humble to approach the altar to receive the *Holy Sacrament.

Wages of sin St *Paul in his letter to the Church in Rome developed the analogy between the freeing of a slave by payment made to his master and the redemption of the sinner through the death of Christ. The slave to *sin becomes the slave to God and his reward is everlasting life, 'for the wages of sin is death; but the gift of God is eternal life' (Rom 6 : 20-3).

Wake Originally applied to the all-night *vigil before holy days or saints' days; later to the merrymaking associated with the day itself, and particularly to jollifications at the fair held in honour of a patron saint. In the Midlands and the North of England it now denotes the summer holiday period. For the Irish it signifies a vigil over a corpse before the day of burial.

Walburga, St (or Waldburg, Walpurgis, Vaubourg, Gauburge) A nun of Wimborne, Dorset, (b.c.710) who assisted her uncle St *Boniface in his mission to the German pagans. She studied medicine, founded convents and became head of the monastic house of *monks and *nuns at Heidenheim, where she died in 779. Her remains were later taken to Eichstätt in Bavaria, later a *pilgrimage centre because of the curative oil which flowed from the rock on which her reliquary rested. She is represented as an *abbess with a *crosier, and wears a *Benedictine habit. She carries a flask of her miraculous Walpurgis oil and has a crown and sceptre at her feet, possibly because she was the daughter of St Richard (d.720), wrongly supposed to be king of Essex (See *Walpurgisnacht).

Walking on the water, Christ After the miracle of the *Loaves and the Fishes, *Jesus went into the hill country to pray, leaving his disciples to row across the Sea of *Galilee. In the early hours he saw them worn out with rowing and in distress in the middle of the lake. He went to their assistance, walking on the water. They thought he was a ghost and cried out, but he reassured them, got into the boat and the winds died down (Mk 6 : 45-56). The rationalist explanation is that the Greek phrase, 'walking on the water', could also be translated, 'walking by the water', and that Jesus waded through the shallows. The story may have been symbolic, an interpretation of an earlier incident, with the disciples in their boat representing the persecuted Church who are rescued by *Christ. In the *Gospel of Matthew*, St Peter attempts to walk on water, sinks, but is rescued by Jesus (Mt 14 : 22-33).

Wallet Also called scrip, a bag hanging from a shoulder or staff, used to contain provisions or the proceeds of begging: the mark of *pilgrims and the *attribute of the Archangel *Raphael and SS *Roch and *James of Compostela.

Walpurgisnacht The night of 1 May, when witches were said to hold their orgies at Blocksberg in the Hartz mountains in Germany. It derived its name from Walpurgis, one of the forms of the name of St *Walburga, who was commemorated on 1 May, the day when her relics

were interred in the church of the Holy Cross at
Eichstätt, in Bavaria. As well as being unwittingly
associated with a diabolical festival, the saint
appears also to have been confused with Waldborg
the pagan fertility goddess, and because of her
acquired role as protector of crops, she has three
ears of corn among her *attributes.

Walsingham, Our Lady of A *shrine dedicated
to St *Mary the Virgin in the medieval St
Katherine's (or Slipper) chapel about a mile from
Walsingham, Norfolk. It was restored in 1931 and
is visited by *Anglican and *Roman Catholic
*pilgrims.

A verse account of the origin of the shrine was
written in 1465. It relates that Richeldis de
Faverches, a pious widow, was told by angels (or
by St Mary the Virgin) in 1061 (but probably a
century later) to build a chapel of the
*Annunciation – a replica of the *Holy House at
Nazareth – on the site they indicated. The structure was enclosed within a *Lady chapel which
was richly adorned with the gold and silver gifts
brought by generations of pilgrims. *Augustinian
canons who served the shrine were accommodated
in an adjoining *priory, built in the 13th century.
England was given the title of 'Our Lady's Dowry'
because of the international fame of the shrine. It
was destroyed by *Protestant mobs in 1538. The
priory seal survived, bearing the image of the
Virgin and Child, and was used as the model for
the statue which was carved for the parish church
at the time of the *Anglo-Catholic revival, being
later removed to the Slipper Chapel (the origin of
that name is unknown).

Wand A slender rod or staff possessing magical
powers. Notable examples of the use of wands or
rods to produce a supernatural effect are *Aaron's
rod, which turned into a serpent before Pharaoh
and swallowed up the serpent-rods of the royal
sorcerers, and *Moses striking the rock with his
wand to bring water to the thirsting Israelites in
the wilderness. The suitors at the *Betrothal of St
Mary the Virgin carry wands which they break to
demonstrate their chagrin when St Joseph's wand
flowers to indicate that he is the chosen spouse.
Grammar, one of the seven *Liberal Arts, holds a
wand with which she chastizes her pupils.

Wandering Jew A *Jew condemned to wander
over the earth until the *Second Coming. As Jesus
left the hall where *Pilate had sentenced him to
death, and was carrying his cross to Calvary, the
Jew struck him on the back and told him not to
linger on the threshold but to go faster. Jesus
retorted that he was indeed going quickly to his
death but that the Jew would tarry until he came
again.

The legend is first mentioned in the *Flores
historiarum* of Roger of Wendover, a monk of St
Albans, England, and was expanded by his successor, Matthew Paris (*d*.1259), in the *Chronica
Majora*. An Armenian archbishop who visited the
monastery of St Albans in 1228 claimed that he had
recently entertained the Wandering Jew, who said

Jesus holds up for. adoration the consecrated
wafer in this symbolic representation of the
institution of the Eucharist at the Last Supper
(Juan de Juanes, *c*.1523-79).

Christ, **Walking on the water,** rescues St Peter
from drowning (Eugène Delacroix, 1789-1863).

that his name was originally Cartaphilus, door-keeper to Pontius Pilate, but that after his encounter with Jesus he had been baptized and had changed his name to Joseph. A similar account, also derived from the archbishop, appeared *c*.1240-50 in the rhymed chronicles of Philippe Mousket, a Fleming, later bishop of Tournai. In an Italian version of the story the Jew's name is given as Giovanni Buttadeo or Bottadio (John Strikegod). Centuries later, a German pamphlet, *A brief description and narration regarding a Jew named Ahasverus*, published in 1602 and translated into many languages, identified the Jew as *Ahasuerus, whom Paulus von Eitzen, Lutheran bishop of Schleswig, was said to have encountered in Hamburg in 1542. Unlike Cartaphilus he had not been converted, and was living out his doom. Since that time the Jew has been seen on various occasions in many countries, his appearance being thought to indicate the approaching *End of the World.

Wanderings in the wilderness The period which the *Children of Israel, led by *Moses and *Aaron, spent in the Sinai and Negev deserts between their *Exodus from Egypt and their sight of Canaan, the *Promised Land. They were sustained by *manna; saved from thirst when Moses struck the *Rock; seduced into worshipping a *Golden Calf; and given the *Ten Commandments and the *Ark of the Covenant as a portable temple. Finally, despite their loss of heart on many occasions and their longing for 'the fleshpots' of Egypt (Ex 16 : 3), their spies brought back news that they were near the land 'flowing with milk and honey' (Ex 3 : 8). Because ten of these spies reported that it was inhabited by giants who made them look like grasshoppers (Num 13 : 33), they refused to invade. In his wrath, God condemned them to spend forty years more wandering in the wilderness of Zin. Moses died as he looked down on *Jericho (Dt 34 : 1), but his successor *Joshua led them against that city and they entered Canaan.

Washing of the disciples' feet This episode (in Latin *pedilavium*) took place during the *Last Supper, and is recounted only in the *Gospel of John* (Jn 13 : 1-17, 34-5). Jesus took off his clothes (although he is never depicted without his garments, presumably because it would be unseemly), tied a towel around his waist, took a basin of water and proceeded to wash his disciples' feet. This act was usually performed by a servant before guests reclined at table, but Jesus interrupted the meal because he intended to make a symbolic gesture, the significance of which had to be impressed upon his disciples. By undressing, he foretold his approaching death, and by putting on his garments again, his *Resurrection. Water represented the cleansing of the disciples through his forthcoming sacrifice on the Cross. The act of washing was a lesson in humility. He, their master, was their servant and they likewise should serve one another, 'for I have given you an example, that ye should do as I have done to you'. Jesus ended his discourse by saying, 'A new commandment I give unto you, that ye love one

another; as I have loved you, that ye also love one another'.

According to the *Meditations on the Life of Christ, Jesus rose from the table in the *Upper Room and went with his disciples to a lower place in the same house to perform the act of ablution. This tradition influenced some early sculptural and manuscript depictions, but the later convention of showing the washing of the feet when Jesus' disciples are seated at supper became common from the Middle Ages onwards. Jesus may be portrayed standing, because it was not thought proper for him to kneel, but mostly the humility of the act was stressed by showing him bending down. St *Peter at first protested against his master washing his feet, but when the symbolic cleansing was explained to him, he exclaimed, 'Lord, not my feet only, but also my hands and my head'. He is therefore shown pointing to his head.

Association of the washing of the disciples' feet with the *baptismal rite is found in many liturgies from the 4th century onwards. The *font was thought of as the basin, and the act of baptism as cleansing from sin. It was formerly customary to wash the feet of a baptized infant and of an adult neophyte. In monasteries, it was regarded as an act of humility and brotherly love to wash the feet of the poor and of travellers seeking shelter. On *Holy Thursday *abbots wash their monks' feet and *bishops wash the feet of twelve poor men. From the first (Latin) word of Jesus' saying, *mandatum (novum)* 'a (new) commandment', is derived the English *Maundy Thursday, when the sovereign gives alms to twelve poor persons, usually in Westminster Abbey or in another specially chosen church.

Water Used symbolically to indicate purification, as in *baptism, or in the ceremony called *asperges, when the congregation is sprinkled with *Holy Water. The penitential significance of the act is derived from David's psalm, 'Wash me thoroughly from mine iniquity' (Ps 51(50) : 2). A few drops of water are added to the *wine, one of the two elements used in the *Eucharist. The water is the people and the wine *Christ, but they are united by his sacrifice of himself. Water moreover represents the human nature and wine the divine nature of Christ who was both man and God. A symbolic reference to the blood and water which flowed from Christ's side at the *Crucifixion is also intended. God is likened to a fountain of living waters (Jr 2 : 13; 17 : 13), and Jesus offered the *Woman of Samaria 'a well of water springing up into everlasting life' (Jn 4 : 14).

Water-carrier A sign of the *zodiac (*See* *Aquarius).

Water into wine The miracle performed by Jesus at the marriage feast at *Cana in Galilee (Jn 2 : 1-11).

Way of the cross The route (also called the *Via Dolorosa) taken by Jesus through the streets of Jerusalem and along the road to *Calvary and his

*Crucifixion. Incidents along the way are commemorated in the *Stations of the Cross.

Weasel An unclean *animal (Lev 11 : 29) said to conceive through the ear and to give birth through the mouth, or vice-versa. It was thought to be skilled in medicine and could revive its young with the herb called rue. As the enemy of the *basilisk it could nevertheless typify *Christ, who overcame *Satan.

Weather vane Symbol of instability, or wavering in religious faith. In contrast the *cock on the vane denotes watchfulness against the snares of the *Devil.

Weighing of souls An episode in the Last *Judgement originating in ancient Egypt, with St *Michael playing the role of the god Thoth. *Souls, shown as tiny men or women, stand by as their good deeds are weighed against their bad ones in a balance or pair of *scales. The *Devil tries to prevent their salvation by putting his thumb on the tray containing their bad deeds, or trying to hold it down with a hook. Sometimes a number of devils hang on the tray.

Wells, holy In many parts of Europe, but especially in Celtic areas, wells and springs which were centres of pagan cults were transformed into Christian *shrines. A *crucifix or an image of St Mary the Virgin was placed by them, and the heathen custom of 'dressing' the well with garlands or flowers (as at Bisley, Gloucestershire) thus became a Christian festival. Miraculous cures said to result from drinking or bathing in the waters caused some wells to be centres of *pilgrimages, as was the case with *Walsingham in Norfolk; Muswell ('mossy well') Hill in London; Shadwell (St Chad's Well) in Yorkshire; and Holywell in Clwyd (See *Winifred, St).

Wenceslaus (or Wenceslas), St Patron saint of Bohemia (modern Czechoslovakia) *b*.907. He lived at a time when that country was only partially Christianized. He wished to rule as a Christian king but was opposed by his brother, Boleslav (or Boleslaus) leader of the pagan party and of the Bohemians, who disapproved of his alliance with the Germans. Wenceslaus' marriage and the birth of a son, put an end to their hopes of supplanting him. Boleslaus therefore decided to kill him. He invited his brother to commemorate with him the feast of SS *Cosmas and Damian. As Wenceslaus went to *Mass he was struck down at the door of the church and died (28 September 929) asking God's mercy for his brother (hence his *attribute is a *dagger). His relics were enshrined in the cathedral church of St *Vitus in Prague. His crown is the symbol of Czech nationalism, and he is said to be sleeping in a cave awaiting a call to save his country.

The familiar English Christmas carol, based on a medieval spring song, *Tempus adest floridum,* was written in the 19th century by J. M. Neale (1818–66), who elaborated a story which was said

The **Wandering Jew,** terrified when his shadow is transformed into the shape of Jesus stumbling beneath his cross (Gustave Doré, 1832–83).

The Devil is defeated by St Michael in this **Weighing of souls.** St Peter welcomes the redeemed soul into Heaven (Catalan, altarfrontal, late 13th century).

to have originated in the writings of the 10th-century monk called Christian, but not found in other lives of the saint. It tells how, one freezing night, the saint carried on his own shoulders a bundle of logs for a poor man's fire. His attendant walked more easily by treading in the imprints made in the snow by the saint's feet.

Werburg (or Werburga), St Daughter of King Wulfhere, of Mercia, she became a nun at Ely and was later active in founding and reforming a number of nunneries at the behest of her uncle, King Aethelred. She was buried *c.*700 at Hanbury, Staffordshire, but in the late 9th or early 10th century her relics were taken to Chester to save them from Danish invaders. Her shrine in the cathedral remained a centre of pilgrimage until the *Reformation. She is represented as an *abbess (she was abbess of Repton), crowned because of her royal lineage, and carrying a model of an *abbey to represent her many foundations. Her *attribute is a goose (or geese) because she is said to have locked away in a stable flocks of geese which were devastating the villagers' crops, releasing them the next day when they said that they were sorry (although her biographer Goscelin [*d.c.*1107] explains that her symbol is a goose because she restored one such dead bird to life).

West, the A convenient phrase for the Western Church, especially the *Roman Catholic Church which was separated from the Eastern *Orthodox Church at the time of the Great *Schism (1054–1492).

Whale The 'great fish' which swallowed *Jonah was thought to be a whale. The *three days which he spent in the whale's belly prefigures the time which Jesus was in the tomb; and his being vomited forth, the *Resurrection of Christ. The story also symbolizes the salvation of the Christian soul. In art and in medieval drama the whale's maw is hell-mouth and its belly *Hell.
According to the *bestiary, a whale would lift its back above the waves and anchor itself in one place so that sailors would mistake it for an island, land and light a fire. Feeling the heat of the fire, the whale would plunge into the depths, dragging ship and sailors down with it. This is a warning to be on guard against the deceits of the *Devil.

Wheat Symbol of the earth's plenty. When shown in conjunction with *wine, it represents the *bread of the *Eucharist.

Wheat and the tares One of the *parables by which Jesus illustrated the mysteries of the *Kingdom of Heaven. A farmer sowed good wheat seed, but his enemy stole up by night, while he and his men were asleep, and sowed tares, or darnel, in the furrows. When the seeds germinated, the farmer's servants wanted to pull up the weeds, but their master forbade them to do so because the roots of the good and the bad plants were entwined and they would lose the wheat. It was better, he said, to leave the crop until the harvest when the tares would be more easily

gathered up in bundles and burnt and the wheat put in his storehouse (Mt 13 : 24–30).
Jesus later interpreted the parable for the benefit of his disciples. He was the farmer who would appear at harvest time, the Last *Judgement, and order the *angels, his men, to gather in the good plants, the people who had accepted his teaching, into his barn, *Heaven. The *Devil was the enemy who had sown the tares, the children of the wicked one. At the end of the world they would be gathered up and cast into a furnace of fire (*Hell), and 'there shall be wailing and gnashing of teeth'. Jesus concluded, 'Who hath ears to hear, let him hear', that is, be warned that evil, which initially appears to triumph, will in the end be defeated (Mt 13 : 36–43).

Wheel Symbol of the dynamic power of *God the Father, derived from *Ezekiel's vision of the Throne of God carried on flaming wheels adorned with eyes and wings (Ezk 1 : 1-28). It is also an attribute of St *Catherine of Alexandria who was tortured on a spiked wheel. When placed near one of the *Patriarchs, *Prophets or *Apostles the wheel may indicate incomplete revelation of the divine message. A wheel with a *butterfly on it indicates *Lust. Wheels with internal divisions may contain the *Seven Deadly Sins or the *Works of Mercy, which respectively carry men either to *Hell or to *Heaven. Five divisions within a wheel symbolize the *Five Senses.

Wheel of fortune Medieval symbol of the instability of human existence, showing men carried up on a wheel to the height of fortune, only to be borne downwards again to poverty and despair as the wheel turns.

Whip An *Instrument of the Passion, sometimes replacing a scourge. Also an *attribute of *Grammar (*See* *Arts, liberal).

White One of the liturgical *colours; also the symbol of purity, 'wash me, and I shall be whiter than snow' (Ps 51 : 7); innocence, holiness, joy, love and St *Mary the Virgin. It may be represented by silver or by a diamond.

White Canons *Canons regular of the *Premonstratensian Order who wear a white *habit.

White Friars The popular name in England for *Carmelite fathers who wore a white *habit.

White Ladies In England, the popular name for *Cistercian nuns, because of the colour of their *habit.

White Monks *Cistercian monks, so called in England because they wore *habits made of undyed wool.

Whitsunday The common name in England for *Pentecost, derived from the Anglo-Saxon *hwita Sunnandaeg*, 'white Sunday'. Why the adjective 'white' is used has not been satisfactorily explained, although it may refer to the white baptismal robe worn when *baptism by total immersion was administered at Pentecost if it had not been possible previously at *Easter.

Whore of Babylon The woman, 'drunken with the blood of the saints', clothed in purple and scarlet, and seated on a scarlet beast with seven heads (the seven hills of Rome) and ten horns, seen in a vision by *St John the Divine. She held a golden cup 'full of abominations and filthiness of her fornication'. She symbolized Rome and was destined for perdition. At the time of the *Reformation, *Protestants saw her as the corrupt papacy, and in their pictorial propaganda depicted her wearing a *tiara (Rev 17 : 1-18).

Widow's cruse In a time of drought and famine, God told *Elijah to go to Zarephath (Vg Sareptha) where a widow would sustain him. She had 'but an handful of meal in a barrel, and a little oil in a cruse [jar]'. Elijah told her that God had promised that there would be meal in the barrel and oil in the cruse until the rains returned (1 Kg 17 : 8-16). The 'widow's cruse' thus stands for a supply of food which is constantly replenished.

Widow's mite As Jesus sat watching people casting their offerings into the *Temple treasury, he saw the rich (depicted as well-dressed men and women) ostentatiously putting in large amounts, but noted that a poor widow gave two mites, two of the smallest coins, all that she possessed, although she could have kept one for her needs. He told his disciples that she had put in more than the wealthy because they had given out of their superfluity, but she, although in want, had given all her money (Mk 12 : 41-4; Lk 21 : 1-4).

Wild man Also called *wodewose, a forest-dweller, resembling a man but unable to speak. His body was covered with shaggy green hair, he carried a club, was lustful, and abducted women and unbaptized children. He appears carved on *misericords and bosses, and is depicted in illuminated manuscripts, where he possibly represents pagan or unregenerate man. SS Abdon and Sennen have power over them.

Wilgefortis, St This saint never actually existed, but was said to be the Christian daughter of a pagan king of Portugal who wanted her to marry the king of Sicily. As she had taken a *vow of virginity, she prayed that she would be made ugly, and soon grew a beard. Thwarted, her father had her crucified. On the cross she prayed that all who sought her aid should be freed (hence her Latin name Liberata, 'liberated') from their troubles. St Thomas More (1478-1535) noted that her name in English was *Uncumber and that women who vowed a peck of oats to her statue believed that they would be freed from a cumbrous husband. It is thought that her legend and her cult originated in Flanders in the 14th century when earlier *crucifixes which bore a clothed and bearded

Angels shatter the **wheel** on which St Catherine is being tortured (Lelio Orsi, 1511-87).

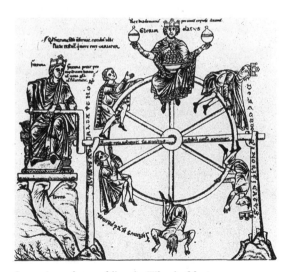

Some rise and some fall as the **Wheel of fortune** is turned inexorably in this 12th-century German illustration to a *Hortus deliciarum*.

Christ were assumed to represent a female saint who had been crucified. The name Wilgefortis was a popularization of the Latin *virgo fortis*, 'steadfast virgin'.

William of Norwich, 'St' A scandalous excuse for anti-Semitism, based on a trumped-up charge of 'ritual murder', like the case of 'little' St *Hugh of Lincoln. William, a twelve-year old skinner's apprentice, was found dead in a wood in 1144. He had been crucified and a crown of thorns placed on his head. Godwin, his uncle, proclaimed that he had been murdered by *Jews. The boy's relics were placed in the Martyrs' Chapel of Norwich Cathedral in 1151. His local cult flourished until at least the middle of the 14th century. To their credit, Innocent IV (1243-54) and the Blessed Gregory X (1272-6), in papal letters of 1247 and 1274 respectively, both rejected the culpability of the Jews.

Willow The weeping willow symbolizes grief and death. It thus appears in paintings of the *Crucifixion. It is also a symbol of the *Gospel because, even if its branches are cut and distributed among the people, it does not perish. So also, the Good News (the Gospel) flourishes however widely its message is spread.

Wimple A woman's headdress, often of fine white linen, covering the head, neck, cheeks and chin, worn in the Middle Ages as protection against the cold. It is a characteristic adornment of women in 14th- and 15th-century Flemish art. In modified form, it survives as part of the *habit of *nuns of some religious *Orders.

Windlass The attribute of St *Elmo (or *Erasmus) who was martyred by having his intestines wound onto a capstan or windlass.

Wine One of the two elements (the other being bread) used in the celebration of the *Eucharist. It recalls the identification by Jesus at the *Last Supper of the wine in the cup which he blessed with the blood of his sacrifice on the Cross. St *Paul advised his follower Timothy to take a little wine for his stomach's sake (1 Tim 5 : 23), but warned also that *bishops and *deacons should not be addicted to wine drinking (1 Tim 3 : 3, 8). One of the allegorical sayings of Jesus, recorded in all three *synoptic Gospels, was an injunction not to put new wine into old bottles for they will burst. Put new wine into new bottles and all will be well (Mt 9 : 17; Mk 2 : 22; Lk 5 : 37-8).

Winepress Symbol of the wrath of God, derived from one of the prophecies of *Isaiah, 'I have trodden the winepress alone; and of the people there was none with me; for I will tread them in mine anger and trample them in my fury' (Is 63 : 3). Christ is also shown being crushed in the winepress, the wine symbolizing his redemptive blood. The winepress also represents the doctrine of the *Real Presence, and is derived from the typological linking of Christ on the Cross with the bunch of *grapes which the Israelite spies brought back on a pole from the *Promised Land (Num 13 : 17-29).

Winifred, St (or Winifrede, Wenefred, Gwenfrewi) A 7th-century Welsh saint, whose *Life* was written after her relics were translated in 1138 from Gwytherin to the *Benedictine abbey in Shrewsbury. She chose death rather than seduction under promise of marriage. Her disappointed suitor, a prince called Caradoc of Hawarden, cut off her head at the entrance to a church to which she had run to escape him. A fountain with curative powers welled up where her head touched the ground. This is supposed to be at Holywell, Clwyd, whose *well became (and still is) a pilgrimage centre. Her head was put back on her body and she was restored to life by St Beuno, a white (or red) mark around her neck being the only sign of her ordeal. She is represented as an *abbess (she died as head of the nunnery at Gwytherin) with a *sword (to commemorate her martyrdom) and, at her feet, a *fountain. The chapel dedicated to her at Holywell was built by Lady Margaret Beaufort, mother of Henry VII, as a thank-offering for the victory of Bosworth Field (1485).

Wisdom. One of the Seven *Gifts of the Holy Spirit, personified as Sapientia, or the Classical goddess Minerva. The Greek word for 'Wisdom', *Sophia* – as in the name of the Byzantine basilica (now a museum) in Constantinople, 'The Church of the Holy Wisdom' (*Sancta Sophia*) – was personified as St *Sophia, who was supposed to be the mother of three virgin saints, Fides (Faith), Spes (Hope) and Caritas (Charity).

Wise and foolish virgins A *parable (Mt 25 : 1-13) by which Jesus emphasized the need to be constantly ready for his *Second Coming. It was based on the custom whereby a bridegroom was escorted in procession to his bride's house and back to his own. Ten virgins were waiting for him. Five were wise and had brought plenty of oil for their lamps (they are depicted with their lamps burning); five were foolish and their supply of oil ran out (so that they are shown with their lamps turned downwards to indicate that the lamps were empty). When the foolish ones went away to buy oil, the bridegroom arrived and on their return they found the door where the marriage was taking place shut against them. The ten are included in representations of the Last *Judgement; the foolish five who were shut out being consigned to *Hell, the wise five being welcomed into *Heaven.

Wise men, three One of the traditional titles of the wise men (or *Magi) who came from the East to do homage to the *Christ-Child (*See* the Three *Kings).

Witch A person subject to the *Devil and capable of actions beyond natural powers. White witches were believed to help, black ones to hurt, and grey ones to be able both to help and hurt. They were usually thought of as ugly old women who had made a compact with the Devil, assigning their bodies and souls to him in parchments signed in blood. In return they received pieces of money, and bore the Devil's mark on their bodies. They were allotted familiars, or imps, usually in the shape of toads or cats. They had the power to fly at night to the witches' sabbath (the assembly, or coven) where, with obscene rites, they worshipped their master who appeared to them in the form of a he-goat.

The biblical injunction, 'Thou shalt not suffer a witch to live' (Ex 22 : 18; Deut 18 : 10) was responsible for brutal persecutions and executions in Western Europe, especially from the late 15th to the 17th centuries. The last witch judicially put to death in Scotland was in 1722, when an old woman was burnt for transforming her daughter into a pony and riding her to a coven. Prosecutions for witchcraft were abolished in the United Kingdom in 1736.

Witch of Endor On the eve of a crucial battle with the *Philistines, *Saul prevailed upon a witch who inhabited a cave in Endor to call up the spirit of the prophet *Samuel who could foretell the outcome of the fight. The shade of Samuel told Saul that neither he nor his three sons would survive the next day. When his children were killed in battle, Saul, sorely wounded, threw himself on his sword and died (1 Sam 28 : 7-25).

Wodewose Another name for a *wild man, *homo silvestris*, sometimes called the Green Man or Jack-in-the-Green, whose face was carved on *misericords.

Wolf An *animal symbolizing avarice, greed, rapicity and *Lust. A she-wolf signifies either a lewd woman or a prostitute because she preys on her lover, or she may represent a depraved woman who would prefer a lusty man to a worthy husband. According to the *bestiary, wolves copulate only on twelve days of the year, and their whelps are born during the first thunderstorm of the month of May. Jesus' injunction, 'Beware of false prophets, which come to you in sheep's clothing, but inwardly they are ravening wolves' (Mt 7 : 15), has led to *heretics, hypocrites, rapacious *clergy and *monks false to their calling being depicted as wolves. The *Devil appears as a wolf wearing a sheep's skin. Wolves also characterize the Devil in that they prey by night, terrorize their victims by magnifying their voices, and are said to spit on their paws so that their footsteps cannot be heard as they approach the sheepfold against the wind, ensuring that the sheep are not repelled by their foul breath. They are also supposed to be unable to turn their heads, and therefore represent the stiff-necked and the proud. The most famous wolf in art is the wolf of Gubbio, who became the companion of St *Francis of Assisi.

Woman According to the first account of the *Creation of the World, woman was formed on

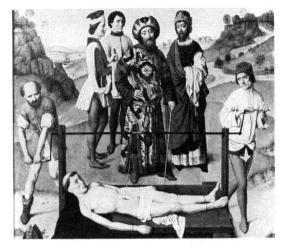

St Elmo's intestines being wound on a **windlass** (Dieric Bouts, c.1415-75).

The **Wise Virgins,** their lamps alight, rebuke the foolish ones who have exhausted their oil (William Blake, c.1826).

the sixth day, at the same time as *Man (Adam) (Gen 1 : 28). In the second account she is created last of all living things (Gen 2 : 21-2). God did not think that it was good that the man should be alone, and decided to make a helpmate for him. But no suitable one could be found among the birds and beasts which had been created. So God caused the man to fall into a deep sleep, took out one of his ribs, put flesh on it and made it into a woman whom he then presented to the man. She is sometimes shown emerging from *Adam's side. The man called her 'woman' (Hebrew *ishah*) because she was taken from man (*ish*). The name *Eve was given to her later by Adam.

This story explains how man and woman in marriage can be said to 'become one body'. It also exemplifies how women, made from a rib, were regarded as subservient to man. In contrast, St *Paul proclaimed the equality of the sexes in Christ (Gal 3 : 28).

Woman bathing Two notable women are shown being spied on in their bath. *Susanna excited the lust of the elders but was saved by *Daniel. *Bathsheba was espied in her bath by King *David and induced to commit adultery with him.

Woman clothed with the sun In one of his visions on the island of Patmos, St *John the Divine saw in the sky 'a woman clothed with the sun, and the moon under her feet, and upon her head a crown of twelve stars'. She was suffering birthpangs and cried to be delivered. A 'great red dragon, having seven heads and ten horns, and seven crowns upon his heads' then appeared 'and his tail drew the third part of the stars of heaven and did cast them to earth'. The *dragon waited to devour the child as soon as it was born, but the man-child which the woman brought forth was 'caught up unto God and to his throne'. St *Michael and his angels then drove the dragon and his angels out of heaven, but the dragon persecuted the woman who had fled to the wilderness. She was given two wings of a great *eagle that she might fly into her place, 'where she is nourished for a time, and times, and half a time, from the face of the serpent'. The dragon then tried to drown the woman with a flood of water from its mouth, but the earth swallowed up the flood (Rev 12 : 1-17).

The complex *symbolism of this vision has been variously explained. Its eschatological significance, and the calculation of 'a time, and times, and half a time', has inspired many prophecies as to the exact date of the *End of the World. The woman is said to represent St *Mary the Virgin, her child is *Jesus, and the dragon is *Satan. Proofs of the doctrines of the *Immaculate Conception and the *Assumption of St Mary the Virgin (because of the wings given to her) have also been deduced from his vision. When the woman is depicted in a blaze of sunlight it denotes Mary's merciful nature, because the sun shines on both the just and the unjust. A crescent moon at her feet may recall St *John the Baptist, but in the years following the Battle of Lepanto (1571) it also signified the victory of the Cross over the Crescent, of Christ-

ianity over the Islamic Turks. The twelve stars are the twelve *Apostles. The woman clothed with the sun appeared in a vision to Emperor *Augustus when he consulted the Tiburtine *Sibyl.

Woman of Samaria When Jesus travelled from Judaea to *Galilee, he had to pass through Samaria, a region inhabited by Samaritans, a people at variance with the *Jews of Jerusalem. Outside the city of Sychar, at noon, exhausted by the journey, he sat down by the spring called *Jacob's Well. A woman, usually depicted as a prostitute (because Jesus revealed to her that he knew she had had five husbands and was living with a sixth man) came to the well with a pitcher to draw water. He asked her for a drink. She was astonished that an apparently pious Rabbi, and conceivably a *Pharisee, should speak to a Samaritan woman. In a long conversation, Jesus told her that he was the expected *Messiah, that he would give her the water of eternal life and that God must be worshipped in spirit and in truth (Jn 4 : 1-30).

Woman taken in adultery When Jesus was teaching in the *Temple in Jerusalem, *Jewish lawyers (or scribes) and *Pharisees tried to trap him by seeking his opinion on a point of law. They brought captive a woman who had been discovered in the very act of adultery, so that there could be no doubt as to her guilt. Would Jesus uphold the Mosaic *law (Lev 20 : 10; Deut 22 : 22-4) which required that she should be stoned to death? It was a trick question. If he did not, then he could be denounced as denying the law of Moses; if he did, then he would be flouting the Romans who alone could administer the death penalty. Jesus did not answer at first, but bent down and wrote with his finger on the ground. When his questioners insisted on a reply, he rose up and said, 'He that is without sin among you, let him first cast a stone at her' (Jewish law required witnesses to take the lead in the execution) and then he stooped down and wrote again on the ground. One by one, beginning with the eldest, 'being convicted by their own conscience', the accusers stole away. Jesus then stood up and asked the woman, 'Did no man condemn thee?'. She answered, 'No man, Lord'. Then Jesus said, 'Neither do I condemn thee: go and sin no more' (Jn 8 : 2-11).

This episode, omitted by the *synoptic Gospels and by other ancient authorities, and neglected by the Eastern *Orthodox Churches, occurs only in the *Gospel of John*. It was accepted by St *Jerome for inclusion in the *Vulgate. It is often adduced as authority for tempering justice with mercy and for dealing understandingly with fallen women. There has been much speculation as to the words which Jesus wrote on the ground. They may have been a text from *Deuteronomy*, or a mischievous imitation of a Roman governor writing a death sentence. According to medieval legend, Jesus wrote down the sins of the accusers. In art either part or the whole of Jesus' words directed to the accusers is given in Latin, *Si quis ex vobis sine peccato est, primus in illam lapidem mittat.*

Woman with the issue of blood As the crowd pressed around Jesus when he was about to enter *Jairus' house in the country of the Gadarenes, a woman (later said to be St *Veronica) who had had an issue of menstrual blood for twelve years and had spent all her money in seeking a cure, touched the hem of his garment from behind. She was ritually impure and could not speak to him. Jesus perceived that some of his power had gone out of him and asked who had touched him. St *Peter protested that it was impossible to single out anyone from the multitude which thronged about him, but the woman came up trembling to confess what she had done. Jesus said, 'Daughter be of good cheer; thy faith hath made thee whole'. In the *Meditations on the Life of Christ the woman is identified as *Martha, sister of Mary Magdalene and Lazarus (Mt 9 : 20-2; Mk 5 : 24-34; Lk 8 : 43-8).

Woodpecker As this *bird destroys a tree by steadily chipping away bits of its trunk, so the *Devil stealthily undermines a man's good nature. In the same way, *heresy attacks and attempts to destroy the Church from within.

Word, the The second person of the *Trinity, *God the Son, in Greek the Logos, which in the *Incarnation 'was made flesh, and dwelt among us' (Jn 1 : 14). The Word of God signifies the Holy Scriptures, the Old and New *Testaments, which were divinely inspired by the *Holy Spirit.

Words from the cross The seven last utterances of Jesus at his *Crucifixion. They are: **1** 'Father forgive them for they know not what they do' (Lk 23 : 34); **2** 'Today shalt thou be with me in paradise' (Lk 23 : 43), said to the *Good Thief; **3** 'Woman, behold thy son!', 'Behold thy mother' (Jn 19 : 26-7), addressed to St *Mary the Virgin and the *Beloved Disciple; **4** *Eli, Eli, lama sabachthani?*, 'My God, my God, why hast thou forsaken me?' (Mt 27 : 46); **5** 'I thirst' (Jn 19 : 28); **6** 'It is finished' (Jn 19 : 30); **7** 'Father, into thy hands I commend my spirit' (Lk 23 : 46).

Work of six days There are two accounts in *Genesis* of the *Creation of the World. In the first (Gen 1 – 2 : 4a) the original state is emptiness, a watery darkness over which God's spirit hovered. In six days God created the heavens and the earth. On the first day he divided light from darkness and day from night. On the second day he caused the firmament, or vault of heaven, to rise and separate the waters into those above and those below. On the third day the waters below became the seas and dry land arose. Plants, trees and other vegetation sprang from the earth. On the fourth day God placed lights in the vault of heaven, the smaller ones being stars and the two great ones the sun and the moon to rule over day and night respectively. On the fifth day were created fish in the seas; birds below the vault of heaven, and animals on earth. On the sixth day he created Mankind. On the seventh day (the *Sabbath) he rested from his labours.

Jesus heals the **Woman with the issue of blood** (4th-century Roman sarcophagus).

Eve is created from the sleeping Adam's side in one of Michelangelo's **Work of six days** (Sistine Chapel, 1508-12).

The second account (Gen 2 : 4b-25) does not mention the time spent in the creation and differs in the order in which events took place. The earth was a dry, barren, waste, but God made waters rise and water the earth. He created Man (*Adam) from the dust, planted a garden in *Eden, in which every kind of tree grew, including the Tree of Life and the *Tree of the Knowledge of Good and Evil, whose fruit Adam was forbidden to eat. Then God created beasts and birds, to each of which Adam gave a name. Then from Adam's rib, while he slept, God made *Woman (*Eve).

These two accounts were conflated in art to make a cycle, illustrating the Work of the Six Days of Creation.

Works of mercy, seven Frequently depicted in art are scenes or stories illustrating the Seven Corporal Works of Mercy: to feed the hungry; give drink to the thirsty; clothe the naked; visit the prisoner; shelter the stranger; visit the sick; and bury the dead. Parallel to them are the Seven Works of Spiritual Mercy: to correct the sinner; teach the ignorant; counsel the doubtful; comfort the sorrowful; bear wrongs patiently; forgive all injuries; and pray for the living and the dead.

World Used as a synonym for the deceits and allurements of human civilization which distract the soul from God; as in 'the World, the Flesh, and the Devil'. *Monks, *nuns and other religious are said to have left the world when they take their final vows.

Worship Adoration and reverence paid only to *God (Ex 20 : 1), called *latria* in Latin, as distinct from *dulia*, honour or veneration given to the *saints. God must be worshipped 'in spirit and in truth' (Jn 4 : 24), the outward expression of which is in the rites and ceremonies of the *liturgy.

Wounds of Christ, five The wounds received by Jesus at his *Crucifixion, one on each hand and foot, and one in his side (which gave rise to devotion to the *Sacred heart of Jesus). There have been cases, the most notable being that of St *Francis of Assisi, where these wounds have been reproduced in the form of blood spots on human bodies (See *stigmata).

Wrath One of the *Seven Deadly Sins, personified as a man shown brandishing a *sword or attacking a defenceless victim.

Wrath of God, day of the The Last *Judgement when God will separate the sheep (the good) from the goats (the bad), and welcome the good into *Heaven and send the wicked to eternal *damnation in *Hell.

Wreath *Angels hold it usually in readiness to be placed on the head of a *saint. If depicted by itself, a wreath's meaning depends on the material from which it is made. If of *laurel, it signifies victory over *persecution, or distinction in writing Christian poetry or literature. If of *oak, it symbolizes

strength; of *yew, immortality; and of *cypress, mourning. An *Advent wreath is made of *holly.

Writing on the wall The mysterious words, *Mene, mene, tekel, upharsin*, which the 'fingers of a man's hand' wrote on the palace wall during *Belshazzar's feast, now a popular expression indicating that the end is near.

Wyvern A *fabulous beast, like a flying serpent or *dragon, with two eagle's legs and a barbed tail coiled into a knot, symbolizing either pestilence or *Satan.

X Symbol of the *saltire cross on which St *Andrew was crucified. Also the first letter of the *Greek word XPICTOC, pronounced 'Christos', *Christ, representing the Second Person of the *Trinity. In the following combinations it forms a Sacred *Monogram:

XC (Greek, Chi-Sigma, since the Greek Ɛ was also written C in the Early Christian centuries.) The first and last letters of XPICTOC, pronounced 'Christos', Christ.

XI (Chi-Iota) The initial letters of the words XPICTOC IHCOYC, pronounced 'Christos Jesous', Christ Jesus. Often superimposed (See figure a).

XP (*Chi-Rho) The first two letters of XPIC-TOC, pronounced 'Christos', Christ. Often superimposed (see figure b). Read backwards, as letters of the Latin alphabet, they make the word *pax*, 'peace', and thus have a double symbolism.

Y The letter Y of the Latin alphabet. It may symbolize the *Trinity because it has three legs joined into one figure, or *free will because of the choice of ways offered at the intersection of the stem with the two arms.

Yahweh The presumed vocalization of the sacred and unutterable name of God, represented by the *Tetragrammaton. It may mean in Hebrew, 'He brings into existence whatever exists'. Biblical scholars now use this form in place of *Jehovah.

Yale A *fabulous animal, black, shaped like a hippopotamus, but with the jaws of a boar and the tail of an elephant. It has two moveable horns, one which projects forward for fighting, the other backwards in reverse, to be brought into action if the front horn is blunted or broken.

Year, Christian The Christian year was based on the Julian Calendar (with 365.25 days in one solar year), called after Julius Cæsar who introduced it in 46 BC. This was replaced in the *Roman Church in 1582 by the Gregorian Calendar, established by Pope Gregory XIII because, by then, the Julian calendar was ten days behind the position of the sun. Following the practice of ancient Rome, New Year's Day was fixed on 1 January. *Protestant Churches gradually conformed between 1700 and 1811, although the adoption of the Gregorian Calendar in England in 1752 led to riots, with crowds shouting 'Give us back our ten days!'. Most of the *Orthodox Churches came into line between 1916 and 1923, although a few still keep the ancient usage and are thus thirteen days behind the others. The designation AD (*Anno Domini*, 'the year of the Lord') for the numbering of years from the *Incarnation of Jesus Christ (AD1 beginning on 25 March) was introduced in 525, based on calculations made in Rome by the Scythian monk Dionysius Exiguus, who was unfortunately between four and seven years out in his computation.

Christians followed the Jewish division of the year into weeks of seven days as set out in the accounts of the creation of the world (See *Work of Six Days). But instead of keeping Saturday as the *Sabbath, the seventh day of rest, they observed *Sunday, the first day of the week, as their principal day of worship, commemorating the *Resurrection of Christ. In 321 Emperor Constantine issued an order forbidding all but essential work on Sunday.

In the *West, the Christian liturgical year begins on the first Sunday in *Advent and follows the medieval practice of recalling in its calendar the events of Christ's earthly life, and of appointing days for the commemoration of the *Saints. Of the principal festivals, the dates of *Christmas and *Epiphany are fixed according to the Roman solar year, but the date of *Easter – and its dependents, *Whitsunday (*Pentecost) and the penitential season of *Lent – varies because of its connection with the Jewish liturgical calendar which is lunar.

The Orthodox year, based on Easter, is divided into three parts: the ten weeks before Easter (*triodion*); the *paschal season (*pentecostarion*); and the rest of the year (*octœchos*).

Yellow A *colour with contradictory connotations: it may represent divinity, the sun, or revealed truth; or, in contrast, it may symbolize jealousy, deceit, or treason. *Judas was supposed to have had yellow (or red) hair and is often shown wearing a yellow robe.

Yew A tree found in British churchyards, often on the south side, symbolizing death and the hope of resurrection into eternal life. In Wales yews were given the names of saints during the Middle Ages, and there was a fine of fifteen pence for cutting them down unlawfully. Yew branches were sometimes carried instead of palms on *Palm Sunday, a festival which was also called Yew Sunday in medieval times.

YHWH The *Tetragrammaton, the transliteration of four Hebrew consonants representing the personal name of the God of *Israel, as revealed to *Moses (See *Yahweh).

The **Work of six days,** a conflation of the two accounts of the Creation (French Bible, 1585).

An angel prepares to crown St Mary the Virgin with a **wreath,** on her bodily Assumption into Heaven (Rubens, 1620).

Yod A letter of the Hebrew alphabet (י). Within a *triangle or rays it represents YHWH, the unutterable personal name of *God the Father. Three yods (י י י) symbolize the *Trinity, three co-equal persons. It is also the initial of *Jesus.

Yoke Symbol of *obedience, especially obedience to *Christ, whose yoke is easy and whose burden is light (Mt 11 : 30) and of *Cain, whose burden of guilt and punishment was more than he could sustain (Gen 4 : 13).

Yule The modern form of the Old English word *geol*, related to the Old Norse *jol*, a heathen and then Christian period of feasting about the time of the winter solstice. It had been revived in popular usage as the equivalent of *Christmas, as in 'yuletide' and 'yule-log'.

Yves, St A Breton, the son of a landowner at Kermatin, near Tréguier, celebrated as an incorruptible lawyer. He is thus the patron *saint of lawyers and an example to them, as expressed in a Latin rhyme:

> *Sanctus Ivo era Brito*
> *advocatus et non latro*
> *res miranda populo*

('St Yves was a Breton, a lawyer and not a thief, which astonished everybody'). A *tertiary, a member of the Third Order of St Francis, he is sometimes depicted in a lawyer's robe with the cord of the *Franciscan habit round his waist. Renowned as 'protector of the poor', he defended widows and orphans without fee and usually appears in art between two poor litigants, his back turned in a gesture of refusal to a rich man holding out a purse of gold, who is either trying to bribe him or to engage his services. An *angel or a *dove may hover approvingly nearby. His name (and the feminine form Yvonne) is given to patriotic Bretons. He is not the saint commemorated in the placename St Ives, which is found in Cornwall and Huntingdon. The Cornish saint was Ia, or Ives, an Irish maid who sailed across the sea on a leaf. St Ives of Huntingdon was a Persian *bishop who came to England and lived as a *hermit at Slepe, later renamed in his honour. This fact was revealed to a peasant in a dream in 1001, when Ives' body, one of four in bishop's dress, was discovered at Slepe. His shrine was a place of *pilgrimage in the Middle Ages because of the curative virtues of a nearby spring.

Zacchaeus A rich man of *Jericho, and one of the chief tax collectors, or publicans – a hated occupation, thought by *Jews to be fit only for sinners. When *Jesus entered that city on his way to the *Passover festival in *Jerusalem, Zacchaeus, having heard of his fame, wanted to see what kind of man he was. Being short of stature, he could not see Jesus over the heads of the crowd thronging around him, so he ran ahead and climbed a sycamore – a kind of fig tree – hoping to get a glimpse of the one who was being acclaimed as *Messiah. When Jesus reached the spot he called to Zacchaeus to come down quickly because he intended to stay at his house. Zacchaeus welcomed him joyfully, but strict Jews complained that Jesus had broken the *Law by accepting the hospitality of a sinner. Zacchaeus offered to make restitution for any wrong that he had done by giving half his property to the poor and paying back fourfold anyone whom he might have cheated. Jesus silenced his critics by reminding them that Zacchaeus was also a son of *Abraham, with a right to salvation. His own mission was to seek out and save the lost sheep of *Israel (Lk 19 : 1-10). According to legend he married St *Veronica and lived in France as St *Amadour.

Zacchaeus was also the name of the Jewish teacher who, according to the apocryphal *infancy gospel of *Thomas* and *Pseudo-Matthew*, offered to teach the child Jesus his letters, but who was astounded by his innate knowledge (*See* *Boyhood of Jesus).

Zacharias, St Father of St *John the Baptist. One of the priestly 'sons of *Aaron' (not the high priest, as stated in the *Book of James*) who served in the *Temple in Jerusalem. He was chosen by lot to enter the *Holy of Holies, the inner sanctuary, alone, to burn incense while the congregation remained outside in prayer. His *attribute is therefore a *censer. The angel *Gabriel appeared and told him that his barren wife *Elizabeth would bear a son who would be called John. When Zacharias protested that he and his wife were old, Gabriel announced that he would be struck dumb until the child was born – hence Zacharias is depicted with his finger laid to his lips. In due course a son was born, and on the eighth day, when Zacharias circumcised him and he was to be given a name, Elizabeth insisted that he should be called John, although their relations wanted him to be named after his father. When appealed to, Zacharias wrote on a tablet, 'His name is John', and immediately his speech returned. He thereupon praised God in a Messianic hymn, the *Benedictus, which is enshrined in the *liturgy (Lk 1 : 5-25, 57-79).

According to the *Book of James*, Zacharias was also the priest who presided over the choice of suitors at the *Betrothal of St Mary the Virgin, and he was later slaughtered on the steps of the altar in the Temple at the time of the massacre of the *Holy Innocents because he would not tell where John was hidden. His blood left indelible traces on the sanctuary stones. A knife is therefore sometimes shown as one of his *attributes. He may also hold a lighted candle or taper because he spoke of the coming of the 'dayspring from on high', to bring light 'to them that sit in darkness' (Lk 1 : 78).

Zadkiel Leader of the *dominions and the angel of God's justice (his name means in Hebrew, 'the righteousness of God'). His *attribute is a knife, because he is said to have stayed the hand of

*Abraham when he was about to carry out the
sacrifice of *Isaac.

Zadok *High priest in the time of King *David,
and father of a priestly line which lasted for eight
centuries. His name is associated with coronations
because he anointed *Solomon king at Gihon (1
Kg 1 : 38-9).

Zealots The 'zealous ones', resistance fighters
who regarded themselves as appointed by God to
rid their land of foreign invaders. In the lifetime of
Jesus they fought against Roman occupation. One
of the twelve *Apostles was called *Simon the
Zealot (Lk 6 : 15), but this may mean no more
than that he was zealous by nature. *Barabbas,
whom the people wished *Pilate to release instead
of Jesus, may possibly have been a Zealot. One
tradition is that *Judas Iscariot was also a Zealot
and that he betrayed Jesus because he refused to
lead an insurrection against the Romans.

Zebedee A prosperous fisherman of *Galilee,
husband of *Mary Salome, and father of St *James
the Great and St *John the Apostle (Mk 1 : 19-20)
(*See* *Calling of the Apostles).

Zechariah (Zacharias) A minor *prophet, active
520-518 BC, who urged the *Jews who had
returned from exile in Babylon to rebuild the
*Temple as the necessary prelude to the inaugura-
tion of the Messianic era (*See* *Messiah). He had
eight apocalyptic visions which are recounted in
the OT book which bears his name: four horsemen
who report that the earth is peaceful (Zech
1 : 7-17); four horns broken by four smiths,
signifying the overthrow of the heathens (Zech
1 : 18-21); a man with a measuring-line (Zech
2 : 1-13); Joshua the High Priest cleansed of his
filthy garments (Zech 3 : 1-10); a seven-branched
candlestick (his *attribute) fed with oil from two
olive trees (Zech 4 : 1-14); a flying roll (Zech
5 : 1-4); a woman named Wickedness carried away
from the Holy Land (Zech 5 : 5-11); and four
chariots drawn by four horses – red, black, white,
and piebald – representing four winds carrying
God's judgement to the ends of the earth (Zech
6 : 1-8). He also saw the stone with seven eyes on
which the sacred name of God will be inscribed
(Zech 3 : 9). Many of his images of the hoped-for
*Messiah were applied in the NT to *Jesus, and
also appear in apocalyptic literature and art. The
reference to thirty pieces of silver to be paid to the
potter (Zech 11 : 12-13) was thought to foretell the
betrayal of Jesus by *Judas, and the words, 'They
shall look upon me whom they have pierced'
(Zech 12 : 10) to presage his *Crucifixion. He also
foretold the *Entry to Jerusalem (Zech 9 : 9) on
*Palm Sunday.

Zeno, St Bishop of Verona from 361 until his
death *c*.372; patron saint of that city and author of a
large number of homilies which give a fascinating
picture of his times. Supposedly of African origin,
he is sometimes represented as dark-skinned.

Zechariah holding the book containing his
apocalyptic visions (Michelangelo's Sistine
Chapel, Rome, 1508-12).

St **Zeno** exorcizes a devil which escapes through
the mouth of his woman victim (from the door
of St Zeno's Cathedral, Verona).

When summoned to *exorcize Emperor Gallienus' daughter, he was discovered fishing in a river (he is thus shown with rod and line). One of the envoys stole a fish from him, but discovered that he could not cook it. When the daughter was cured, the emperor rewarded Zeno with his crown, but the bishop broke it into pieces and gave the fragments to the poor. An ox-cart stopped at a ford in the River Adige, and could not go forward until Zeno exorcized the driver. Pistoia Cathedral is dedicated to Zeno because he saved that city from a devastating flood. The doors of the church of San Zeno Maggiore at Verona have bronze reliefs with scenes from his life and a statue of him fishing. He is sometimes depicted with a fish hanging from his crosier. He is invoked on behalf of children learning to speak and to walk.

Zenobius, St Bishop and patron saint of Florence, shown with the city of Florence behind him and with a Florentine *lily on the *morse of his *cope. Born 334 of a pagan family, he refused the wife who had been chosen for him, had himself baptized, and later converted his family. His miracles, medieval in origin, were frequently depicted by Florentine artists. Those he restored to life included: a child who had been trampled to death by oxen; the son of a French lady who had left her child with him while she completed her *pilgrimage to Rome; and a bearer of *relics whose mule had carried him to his death when it fell over a precipice. When Zenobius died in 424, the people of Florence, trying to touch his body, pushed it against a withered elm which promptly burst into new leaf. His supposed remains lie in the cathedral of that city in a bronze tomb ornamented by Lorenzo Ghiberti (1378-1455).

Zephaniah (Sophonias) A minor *prophet and supposed author of the OT book which bears his name. He warned of the imminent Day of the Lord when all nations would be judged (*See* Last *Judgement). His *attribute is the *lantern with which God would search *Jerusalem (Vg *Sophonias* 1 : 12; AV Zeph 1 : 12 has 'candles'). Part of the text of the *Dies irae* was taken from Vg *Sophonias* 1 : 15-16 (AV Zeph 1 : 15-16).

Zion (Sion) The principal hill of *Jerusalem and later the whole city, called the City of David because King *David captured it, brought the *Ark of the Covenant there and made it his fortress capital (2 Sam 5 : 7). King *Solomon built his *Temple on the adjoining Mount Moriah, often also called Zion. Allegorically, Zion, the holy hill

of God (Ps 2 : 6), is the Heavenly City, the New Jerusalem (Rev 14 : 1). During their *Babylonian Captivity, the Israelites wept when they remembered Zion (*See* *harp).

Zita, St Patron saint of Lucca, Italy, and of domestic servants; *b*.1218 at Monsagrati, Tuscany. For forty years she worked as a maid (one of her *attributes is a *key or bunch of keys) in the house of a wool merchant named Fatinelli in Lucca, dedicating herself to good works, some of which were occasions for miracles. Water in a pitcher (another of her attributes) which she gave to a *pilgrim turned into wine; bread which she was taking without her master's knowledge to a starving household changed into roses when he challenged her; loaves which she had forgotten to bake while at her devotions were supernaturally put into the oven for her; and when she lent her master's coat on *Christmas Eve to a shivering old man, it was returned to him by an angel. At her death in 1272 a bright star shone above her attic window as a sign that her pure spirit had gone to *Heaven. She was venerated in England under the name of Sitha, and her effigy appeared in many churches showing her holding a key, a *rosary and a book of devotions. She was invoked for help in finding lost keys.

Zodiac, signs of the Twelve astrological signs of pagan origin, representing the celestial bodies which controlled sections of the circular heavens into which the sun was supposed to enter at fixed times of the year. These divisions did not correspond exactly to the twelve lunar months, but their signs were used to represent them, especially in depictions of the *Labours of the Months. The signs (equated approximately with the months from January to December) are: *aquarius, the water-carrier; *pisces, the fish; *aries, the ram; *taurus, the bull; *gemini, the twins; *cancer, the crab; *leo, the lion; *virgo, the virgin; *libra, the scales or the balance; *scorpio, the scorpion; *sagittarius, the archer; *capricorn, the goat.

Zophiel *See* *Japhkiel.

Zucchetto A small silk skullcap worn towards the back of their heads by *Roman Catholic clergy to cover the *tonsure. Kept on under a *biretta or a *mitre. Its *colour represents the rank of the wearer: white, the *Pope; red, *cardinals; purple or violet, *bishops; black, *abbots. The word is the diminutive form of the Italian *zucca*, 'head', or 'pate'.

Medallions with three signs of the **zodiac**: capricorn, aquarius, pisces.